A Practical Study of Argument

Second Edition

Trudy Govier
University of Calgary

Wadsworth Publishing Company
Belmont, California
A Division of Wadsworth, Inc.

Philosophy Editor: Kenneth King
Production: Robin Lockwood, Bookman Productions
Designers: Donna Davis, Hal Lockwood
Copy Editor: Ruth Cottrell
Technical Illustrators: Carl Brown, Joan Carol, Marilyn Krieger, Salinda
    Tyson
Compositor: Thompson Type
Cover: Donna Davis, Michael Rogondino

Printed in the United States of America

    1 2 3 4 5 6 7 8 9 10—92 91 90 89 88

ISBN 0-534-08262-9

Library of Congress Cataloging-in-Publication Data
Govier, Trudy.
  A practical study of argument.
  Includes bibliographies and index.
  1. Reasoning. 2. Logic. I. Title.
BC177.G65 1988   160   87-14759
ISBN 0-534-08262-9

Contents

Preface

This book is intended for all those who are interested in arguments and in arguing, and especially for university and college students taking courses designed to improve their ability to understand, construct, and criticize arguments. My goal has been to present enough theory to explain why certain kinds of arguments are or bad and enough examples to make that theory useful in practice.

My interest in the theory and practice of natural argumentation stems from an occasion in 1976 when someone asked me to review a text on informal fallacies. At the time, I was teaching an elementary course in formal logic to a large group of students who had been required to take the course and had little interest in it. The greater practicality of the informal logic fascinated me, and I began to read other texts in the field. From that point my interest grew in a more practical approach to the criticism of natural arguments than can be derived from a purely formal treatment.

Like most texts, this one initially developed from teaching experience and from my reflection on the complaints that I and others had about existing books. I have tried to combine some elementary formal logic with an informal approach to natural argument. This is because I believe that there are some natural arguments that do exemplify logically valid forms, and for these the understanding of basic formal patterns is very useful. I also believe that the basic concept of deductive entailment is important for the correct interpretation of arguments—whether or not they are themselves deductive. The text, then, is basically one in informal logic, but unlike some texts in this area, it allows formal logic to contribute part of the answer to the question of why some arguments are good ones. In taking this stance, I hope to satisfy those who, like myself, believe that formal logic must have some role in the analysis and evaluation of argument, even though its role is not as exhaustive as some formalist philosophers appear to believe.

Another worry expressed by students and teachers of informal fallacies concerns the place of these fallacies in the evaluation of argument. Teachers worry that an approach to argument that is based solely on informal fallacies may be too "negative" and risks turning students into facile and hostile critics. Students reflect on the approach and begin to wonder whether there are any good arguments anywhere! Although the fallacies are interesting and important, there is a growing sense that they cannot tell the whole story about natural argumentation. In an attempt to meet these concerns, I have treated informal fallacies against the background of various standards of good argument.

Analogies receive a more extended treatment in this text than in many others, both because of their frequent occurrence in ordinary argumentation and because of my own intellectual fascination with them. The final two chapters of the book treat social science, with special emphasis on practical skills laypersons can use to evaluate media reports concerning the latest expert "findings" on social relationships.

I culled examples from diverse sources as illustrative material in the text and as a basis for exercises. In response to requests, I have in this edition included some simple exercises at the beginning of each set. About one-fourth of the examples given as exercises are answered in the back of the book. Examples and illustrations in the body of the text are drawn from many sources, including political speeches, letters to the editor, and nonfiction works in various disciplines.

A discussion of definition has been added in this edition. The lengthier treatment has yielded a new third chapter, "Looking at Language." That chapter also includes new exercises on problems of definition and a brief discussion of euphemism. A "Review of Terms

Introduced," previously a feature only of Chapter 1, now appears at the end of every chapter.

The chapter on analogies has been amended to include some more specific guidelines for evaluation. The discussion of conductive arguments has been similarly enlarged, and an exercise set on conductive arguments has been added in response to requests. The treatment of propositional logic, which is now contained in Chapter 9, includes the shorter truth table technique, which was omitted in the first edition. In the discussion of social science, explanatory induction is given a somewhat fuller treatment, and exercises have been added on this topic.

The use of the ARG conditions to articulate a nonclassic sense of soundness perturbed some instructors, who feared that my departure from orthodoxy might confuse students going on to further courses in logic. In the second edition, "cogent" replaces "sound," and the rationale for the ARG conditions is further explained in a short, theoretically oriented appendix. Many topics pertaining to theory may be found in my book, *Problems in Argument Analysis and Evaluation* (Dordrecht, Netherlands: Foris Publications, 1987).

The distinction between argument and explanation has been preserved but qualified and refined. Several additional fallacies are discussed: appeals to ignorance and popularity. The accounts of authority and complex questions have been amended and the final chapter, which some reviewers regarded as redundant, has been eliminated. Throughout the book there are changes in exercises, made with a consideration for currency of topics, greater simplicity, and diminished use of philosophical examples. Of course, this edition also incorporates other changes too minor to mention here. I hope these alterations have resulted in a book which will continue to be useful to those engaged in the important and challenging tasks of teaching and studying argument analysis.

Acknowledgments

I have benefited from studying other texts in informal logic, particularly Michael Scriven's *Reasoning*, Ralph Johnson and Tony Blair's *Logical Self-Defense*, John Hoaglund's *Critical Thinking*, and Stephen Thomas's *Practical Reasoning in Natural Language*. The treatment of analogies owes much to John Wisdom's "Virginia Lectures" on Explanation and Proof. These lectures never appeared in print, and I am grateful to Prof. Wisdom for permitting me to examine them in manuscript. Carl Wellman's *Challenge and Response: Justification in Ethics* is another work that has influenced me greatly. The term "conductive argument" is taken from his work.

Students in Philosophy 105 at Trent University and in adult education courses in Calgary and Vancouver have helped me a great deal—first by expressing their enthusiasm for the study of natural argumentation, and second by asking good questions. I have benefited from discussions of theoretical and pedagogical points with Ralph Johnson, Tony Blair, David Hitchcock, David Gallop, Bernard Hodgson, Sandy McMullen, Jonathan Adler, John Burbidge, Yuen Ting-Lai, Dennis Rohatyn, Charles Caton, and Steve Simon, and from the encouragement and prompting of Wadsworth's Philosophy Editor, Kenneth King. I would also like to thank the publisher's readers for both editions: Malcolm Acock, University of Alabama at Birmingham; John M. Lincourt, University of North Carolina; Andrew Lugg, University of Ottawa; Henry F. Nardone, King's College; Paul Roth, University of Missouri; Anita Silvers, San Francisco State University; G. A. Spangler, California State University at Long Beach; Everett Traverso, Santa Rosa Junior College; and Frank Williams, Eastern Kentucky University.

For any errors remaining in the text, I am solely responsible.

My greatest debt is to my husband, Anton Colijn, who has been involved in the planning and writing of this book at more stages than he might have wished. Without his patient listening, continued enthusiasm for the subject, contribution of examples, and sustained assistance with word processing, this book would not exist.

What Is an Argument? (And What Is Not?)

This is a book about arguments. It is about the nature of arguments—what arguments are and the different structures they have—and about the standards for judging arguments to be good or bad. Many people think that if a question is controversial, then what somebody thinks about it is "just a matter of opinion." This view ignores the fact that even for controversial issues such as capital punishment and nuclear strategy, there is evidence supporting various views. The evidence may be reliable or unreliable, and it may give good or poor support to the position. One opinion is not just as good as another, even though we cannot always prove beyond every doubt that our own position is correct. In this book we hope to convince you that opinions on important controversial matters can and should be defended by rational arguments, and that rational arguments can be analyzed in a careful, logical way. You can do better than saying "that's just a matter of opinion" when someone disagrees with you; you can learn to critically assess the reasons for the view and defend your positions with solid arguments of your own.

What Is an Argument?

An argument is a set of claims that a person puts forward in an attempt to show that some further claim is rationally acceptable. Typically, people present arguments to try to persuade others to accept claims. Sometimes, too, they construct arguments to explore how claims may be justified or as part of a process of intellectual inquiry.

There are many ways of trying to persuade others. When we use arguments in rational persuasion, we try to persuade by citing evidence or reasons to back up our views. The evidence or reasons are called the *premises* of an argument, and the view being defended is called its *conclusion*. A person who argues does not merely state what she thinks; she states what she thinks and gives some reasons intended to back up her view.

Sometimes we use *argument* to mean "dispute or fight," as in the sentence "The parents got into so many arguments over the child's problems that finally they got a divorce." Colloquially, this use of the word *argument* is quite common. But this is not the way we use the word *argument* in this book: in our sense an argument is a reasoned attempt to justify a conclusion. There is some connection between the two different meanings because people who have disputes often use arguments in our sense of the word. They try to persuade each other that they are right, citing reasons for their views. But disputes typically involve much more than this; sometimes people call each other names, make accusations, and even resort to physical violence. It's important to keep the two senses of the word *argument* distinguished from each other.

Here is a simple example of an argument:

> There are three factors which show that a free enterprise ideal does not fit our economic system at this time. First of all, unionization protects labor from vulnerability to market conditions. Secondly, government supports and regulates industry. Thirdly, protective tariffs work selectively to isolate some domestic products from foreign competition.

Here the writer is trying to convince her audience that a particular claim is true: the economic system is not the type described by the free enterprise model. She offers three reasons: it is because of unionization, government policy toward industry, and tariff regulations that the free enterprise model does not fit. By saying these things about the economic system, the author is offering her opinions. However, she is also supporting those opinions with grounds, premises purporting to show that what she claims is true. She puts her audience in a position where it can go beyond mere agreement or disagreement with her opinion. Her audience can look with a critical, rational eye at the support she has offered—the evidence for her conclusion—and it can determine whether that evidence gives rational support for the conclusion. Are the premise statements acceptable? If acceptable, would they show that her conclusion is acceptable? These are the kinds of questions we should ask to determine rationally whether the argument she has offered is a good one.

Let us look at another example. This one is taken from a letter to the editor of a newspaper. It deals with the controversy over teaching evolutionary theory in high schools. The author of the letter is trying to respond to a claim often made by those who are against the teaching of evolution, and he refers to that claim in the opening sentence. He gives reasons—that is, offers an argument—to show that the claim he is opposed to is incorrect.

> *It has been claimed that evolution is taught as dogma, when it is in fact only a theory. This confusion indicates the inadequate nature of scientific training apparently provided to some educational administrators. Evolution is a theory in exactly the same sense that gravity and magnetism are theories. No one has ever seen gravity, for example, but surely we should not stop teaching this "dogma" in our schools. The evidence for evolution is no less convincing, and evolution is called a theory rather than a law simply because the term "law" is no longer scientifically fashionable. Were Newton alive today, he would talk about the theory of gravity exactly the same way Einstein wrote of the theory of relativity and Darwin wrote of the theory of evolution.[1]*

Here the author is trying to show that when the expression "only a theory" is used to downgrade evolutionary theory, it indicates inadequate understanding of the scientific method. He cites a comparison with other areas of science and mentions the fact that the notion of law is no longer popular in the theory of science, in order to show that evolution, as a theory, is no less scientific and no more disputable than current physical theory. Since he gives reasons to back up his difference of opinion with the critics of evolution, he has an argument.

Insofar as people who argue are trying to persuade others that their positions are right, they resemble politicians, advertisers, and other persuaders. Insofar as they are trying to persuade by offering supporting reasons, they may differ from these others because these persuaders and would-be persuaders typically employ nonrational methods. A politician may try to persuade you that he is a competent businessman by wearing a dapper blue suit when he appears on television. A car company may try to persuade you to buy a new car by showing a photograph of the car beside an enticing beach resort—and printing the ad in the bleakest winter months. Here we have attempts at persuasion, but not argument, because the persuasion is not done by setting out premises to back up a conclusion.

A person who tries to persuade you by rational means offers an argument in which he claims that because his premises hold, his conclusion should be accepted. He is saying, in effect,

—— Premise
Premise
Premise
So,
Conclusion

This model is for an argument that has three premises. However, arguments may have any number of premises—from a single premise to a very large number. We have illustrated three only because that was convenient. Here the word *so* indicates that the conclusion is being inferred from the premises supporting it. The word *so* is one of a large number of words that logicians call *indicator words*. These words may indicate the presence of an argument. Some come before the premise or premises; others before the conclusion. Here are some of the many indicator words and phrases that come before the premises in arguments:

since

because

for

follows from

as shown by

as indicated by

may be inferred from

may be derived from

may be deduced from

for the reasons that

Indicator words and phrases that come before the conclusion in an argument include the following:

thus

therefore

hence

accordingly

for all these reasons we can see that

on these grounds it is clear that

consequently

proves that

it follows that

we can conclude that

demonstrates that

The really interesting part of the study of arguments comes when we begin to distinguish good arguments from bad ones and when we look at the logical and philosophical theory that backs up these distinctions. But before we can evaluate arguments, we have to be able to distinguish arguments from other things that are not arguments at all, and we have to develop our skill at identifying the conclusion and the premises. A set of claims certainly can't amount to a bad argument if it is not an argument at all!

What Isn't an Argument?

Even the most rational speakers and writers do not offer arguments all of the time. Sometimes they raise questions, describe events and problems, explain occurrences, tell jokes, and so on. In none of these cases are they trying to justify conclusions as true on the basis of supporting reasons. Consider:

(a) The cause of John's being late for school was that he stopped to pick flowers in the park.

(b) What were the causes of World War I?

(c) It was a crisp and frosty September morning, but so many problems occupied their minds that the beauty of the day went unappreciated.

None of these sentences express arguments. The first sentence gives a brief explanation for John's being late for school. The second sentence raises a question rather than trying to claim anything. The third sentence simply describes a situation, saying how it was on that morning in September. In these passages there is no attempt at rational or nonrational persuasion. Rather, the passages serve other purposes in human life and language. None contain arguments because none put forward premises in order to justify conclusions.

Let us look at several more interesting, longer passages that do not contain arguments and see just why they do not. The following excerpt is taken from a newspaper editorial.

It's not the sort of chatter you hear at cocktail parties, but the muscle fibres of the cockroach are almost human. Really. That's why biologists at Atlanta's Emory University are teaching cockroaches to jog. They attach little weights to the roaches' legs and send them racing along the treadmill.

Frankly, we're leery about doing anything that might give the insects an edge. It's hard enough trying to catch the little sprinters without having to listen to them wheezing behind the walls after a five-metre workout. But we shouldn't carp; there's always a chance the roaches will adopt not only the jogging, but the jogger's healthy lifestyle and scrupulous diet. If they start by keeping decent hours and giving up greasy foods, we'll be satisfied.[2]

This passage does not contain an argument. It first gives a humorous report of some research at Emory University and then expresses, in jocular terms, some possible risks and benefits of the research—to the insects and us! The writer obviously regarded the research as rather silly, and the style and tone of his editorial express that view. But he did not argue for it: no serious reasons are given as to why this kind of research is not worthwhile. (Probably the writer thought the point was too widely agreed-upon to bother arguing about.) Because the writer merely expressed his views in a witty and entertaining way and did not try to persuade us by reasons of the truth of any conclusion, the passage does not contain an argument.

Another example of a passage that contains no argument is taken from a report on the education of young children. The author of this report discussed the use of educational research material by teachers. He said:

What struck me as scandalous is that frequently, to prove a research theory became more important than finding out about children. Believing that education is science rather than art, many researchers tend to ask only those questions which will validate their pet theories and allow for experimental control in the laboratory or the classroom. What they get is no doubt the evidence they seek. How much of it has to do with the real world of children is another story.[3]

The author of this report—a Canadian television personality—expressed his belief that research is not closely tied to what he calls "the world of children." This is a claim for which he could have presented supporting grounds. However, in the passage quoted he does not do this; he merely states that it is "another story" how closely the scientist's world approximates the child's world. He strongly suggests that the scientist's world does not approximate the child's world at all, but he doesn't specify any general facts, or even any examples, that would provide evidence for that implied criticism. He writes as though there is a kind of opposition between doing scientific research on matters concerning children and really understanding children, but he does not give any grounds for believing that that opposition exists. He suggests that he disapproves of what he sees as a lack of proper connection between scientific research and the classroom. (This is suggested by the opening phrase, "it strikes me as scandalous.") He does not even try to give any rational support for any of these claims or attitudes. Hence, although the passage is opinionated, it contains no argument.

Arguments are fascinating, and getting the knack of identifying and criticizing other people's arguments can be entertaining and fun. In fact, it is easy to get so carried away by the feeling of intellectual power that this activity gives you that you start to see arguments everywhere—even where there aren't any! Although arguments are important and they are common in ordinary life and in academic scholarship, we do have to remember that much of what is written and said is not argument at all. Rather it is description, explanation, questioning, storytelling, gentle ridicule, or any of a number of other things. Passages having these other functions can be perfectly respectable, intellectually and rationally, without containing any arguments. You need arguments when views put forward are controversial and persuasion is attempted. The passage about children's education and scientific research could be faulted for not containing any argument because the author dodged some important questions and tried to put across an opinion on a significant topic without citing any evidence. Also, since the passage appeared in a serious report on educational policy, the author was responsible for conveying a carefully developed view to a concerned professional audience. The editorial on cockroaches' jogging had no argument and that was no fault. The author of that work gave us some amusing facts and entertained us. His readers probably do not need to be persuaded that teaching cockroaches to run a treadmill has little utility. Since neither passage contains an argument, it would not be appropriate to try to find premises and conclusion in either one. Nor would it make sense to accuse either author of using a bad argument.

Where and How Do You Find Arguments?

Indicator words can often help you to find arguments, because they show that one claim is being given rational support by others. Consider the following examples:

> (a) There can be no such thing as a just war in modern times, because all modern wars involve weapons and strategies that kill many thousands of innocent people, and no war in which many thousands of innocent people are killed can be a just war.
> (b) Since the meaning of a word must be understood by all the people who use that word, the meaning of a word cannot be a mental image in any one person's head.
> (c) There is probably life somewhere in the universe as well as just here on earth, for it is really unlikely that, in an infinite cosmos, only one place would have the special features needed to make life possible.

In (a), the conclusion is "there can be no such thing as a just war in modern times." The indicator word *because* introduces two premises that support the conclusion. They tell us why the conclusion should be believed. In (b), the word *since* introduces the premise that tells you why the conclusion (that the meaning of a word can't be a mental image) is supposed to hold. In (c), the conclusion is "there is probably life somewhere in the universe as well as just here on earth," and the word *for* introduces the reason offered for this claim. In these simple examples the indicator words make it very easy to see that there are arguments and to see what the premises and conclusion are.

It is not always this easy to find the premises and conclusions of arguments. And, unfortunately, indicator words and arguments do not always go together. For instance, it is possible to argue without inserting any indicator words between the conclusion and premises or before the premises. We can see this by changing example (c) only slightly so that the same argument is presented but there is no indicator word. Changing (c) into (d), we get:

> (d) John: I think the earth is the only place in the universe where life has developed and can flourish.
>
> Mary: I doubt it. After all, the universe is infinite. It is very unlikely that, in an infinite cosmos, only one place would have the special features needed to make life possible. Probably there is life somewhere else in the universe as well as on earth.

In (d), Mary replies to John and asserts all the claims asserted in (c). Even though she does not use the word *for* she is still giving an argument, and her conclusion is still the conclusion of (c). The point is the same. The context of her discussion with John makes it apparent that she is giving reasons for her point, which runs counter to John's suggestion. In this example, as in many others, there is an argument, but there are no indicator words pointing to its presence.

The other complicating factor about arguments and indicator words is that many of the indicator words such as *so, since, because, for, thus*, and even *therefore*, can occur outside arguments. The words *since* and *for* often precede premises and indicate the presence of an argument. However, these words also serve quite different purposes. Here are some examples:

> (e) Since Christmas John has been upset about his mother's illness.
> (f) Jean bought a gift for Mary.

Explanations differ from arguments in subtle ways. Yet in explanations there is reasoning, and we often find such words as *so, since, because, thus*, and *therefore*. Here is an example:

> (g) He was suffering terribly from allergies since he was overtired, and due to wind conditions, the air pollution was just awful.

In this passage, "he was suffering terribly from allergies" is not the conclusion of an argument. It is an accepted fact that is being explained by two factors: fatigue and air pollution. The word *since* does not introduce premises in this example. Instead, it introduces the explaining factors. Even though *since* very often does introduce the premises in an argument, in this case it is used where there is no argument.

You have to develop your sense of context, tone, and natural logical order in order to spot arguments. It is a matter of seeing when people are trying to justify claims rationally and which claims they are trying to justify. Even though arguments as discussed by logicians and philosophers are not just disputes, it is common to find people offering arguments in contexts where there is controversy or disagreement about a subject thought to be of some importance. For instance, union negotiators present arguments based on higher living cost figures in order to try to persuade management negotiators that workers need higher salaries. This is an attempt at rational persuasion. (Nonrational persuasion is attempted if members stop the discussion and go on strike!) A scientist might be called on to account for the fact that his results were not confirmed by a colleague who performed the same series of experiments. If he contended that the other scientist's laboratory was affected in a relevant way by unusual atmospheric conditions, he would be giving an argument to defend his own results as the preferable ones in the controversy.

Argument is a natural, nonviolent way of attempting to resolve controversy. One clue to the identification of arguments in written discourse is the denial of someone's theory or claim. (This was a feature of the argument about whether evolution was only a theory.) For example, if someone writes, "John Jacobs has long insisted that such and such is the case, but actually, such and such is false," it will be natural for the writer to follow up the contention that Jacobs's view is false by offering an argument.

Occasionally we construct arguments when there is little controversy about the conclusion, just to see how we could justify the conclusion if we needed a justification. For instance, many philosophers have constructed very complicated arguments for such conclusions as "there are enduring physical objects outside the mind." Although almost no one believes the opposite, this claim is a fundamental one in our picture of the physical world, and whether we have a good argument to back it up is an important issue in the theory of knowledge. Controversy, then, is not always a feature of the contexts in which arguments are found, though it is very often one.

When we regard a passage or part of a speech as containing an argument, we are regarding it as offered by the writer or speaker for the purpose of rational persuasion or rational justification. Jokes should not be seen in this way. Neither should questions or descriptions. Nor, as we shall see, should explanations because none of these kinds of discourse has the purpose of defending a claim with supporting reasons. If you are trying to determine whether a passage contains an argument, and if you are having some difficulty interpreting it, you can start by asking yourself what the conclusion would be if it were an argument. If you cannot come up with a conclusion, you cannot see the passage as containing an argument. If you think you have found a conclusion, you then look at the rest of the passage to see whether it gives reasons that are intended to support that conclusion. If you can do this, and if there is some good reason to regard the writer or speaker as trying to persuade others that a claim is true, then the passage you are reading contains an argument. Letters to the editor, advertisements, and political speeches are natural homes both for arguments and for non-rational techniques of persuasion. So too are academic meetings where people with differing theories about biology, history, economics, philosophy, and other subjects get together to thrash out issues. Descriptions, jokes, explanations, and questions can all be criticized, but not by the same standards that are applied to arguments. In this book we concentrate on identifying, understanding, constructing, and evaluating arguments. To do this, we obviously need to develop a good sense for what is and what is not an argument.

EXERCISE SET

Exercise One

For each of the following passages, determine whether it does or does not contain an argument, and give reasons for your judgment. If the passage does contain an argument, underline the conclusion. *Answers to exercises marked with an * are provided in the back of the book.*

1. A man who has Dutch citizenship is legally entitled to work in Great Britain because a man who has Dutch citizenship is legally entitled to work anywhere in the European Economic Community, and Great Britain is in the European Economic Community.

*2. The sun was setting on the hillside when she left. The air had a peculiar smoky aroma, the leaves were beginning to fall, and she sensed all around her the faintly melancholy atmosphere that comes when summer and summer romances are about to end.

3. Smith is taller than Jones.

*4. Any diet poses some problems. If the diet does not work, that is a problem. If the diet does work, then the dieter's metabolism is altered. An altered metabolism as a result of dieting means a person will need less food. Needing less food, the person will gain weight more easily. Therefore, after dieting a person will either not have lost weight or will have lost weight but will gain more easily. Either is a problem.

5. The woman who took the lead role in the film was quite beautiful, as everyone noticed right away. She was tall, with red hair and green eyes. The flowing costumes she wore were elegant and creatively styled.

*6. Hockey is an active winter game which is quite popular in northern countries such as the Soviet Union and Canada. The game requires strength, good skating, and terrific eye-hand coordination.

7. Everybody who dreams is asleep. When a person is asleep, he cannot control his mind so as to plan things. Therefore, dreams cannot be controlled by the person who is dreaming.

8. "A simple philosophy guided Charles Cameron's early years: a man must avoid regrets. He must do what he feels he should do, so that he need never face the day when he might ask himself, 'Why didn't I take that plunge a decade ago?'"
(Thomas J. Cottle, "A Single Life, A Single Regret," *Psychology Today*, November 1979.)

9. *Background:* At a conference at Queen's University in Kingston, Canada, Prince Philip of the United Kingdom reflected on the role of universities in solving the problems of contemporary society. The Toronto *Globe and Mail* (July 10, 1978) covered the conference and reported Prince Philip's comments as follows:
    "For Prince Philip, the question facing mankind is not to find solutions to the world's problems, but to find problems that suit the solutions.

"'The world is full of solutions, particularly in universities, but the trouble is you've got to find a problem to fit them,' he told a news conference at the close of the fifth Commonwealth study conference."

As he is quoted here, did Prince Philip offer an argument?

*10. "If all goes well, the reactor and the steam generators in a nuclear power plant of the pressurized-water variety maintain a stable, businesslike relationship such as might obtain between two complementary monopolies. The reactor can be thought of as selling heat to the steam generators."
(Daniel Ford, *Three Mile Island: Three Minutes to Meltdown* [Middlesex, England: Penguin, 1982].)

11. "You not only need to control it [toxic radioactive substances] from the public, you also need to control it from the workers. Because the dose that federal regulations allow workers to get is sufficient to create a genetic hazard to the whole human species. You see, these workers are allowed to procreate, and if you damage their genes by radiation, and they intermarry with the rest of the population, for genetic purposes it's just the same as if you irradiate the population directly."
(Quotation from medical physicist John Gofman, cited in Leslie Freeman, *Nuclear Witnesses* [New York: Norton, 1982].)

12. "An ant is crawling on a patch of sand. As it crawls, it traces a line in the sand. By pure chance the line that it traces curves and recrosses itself in such a way that it ends up looking like a recognizable caricature of Winston Churchill. Has the ant traced a picture of Winston Churchill? A picture that depicts Churchill?
"Most people would say, on a little reflection, that it has not."
(Hilary Putnam, "Brains in a Vat," in *Reason, Truth, and History* [Cambridge, England: Cambridge University Press, 1981].)

13. "Britain is no longer a Christian country and makes no pretence of being one. Churches are being closed throughout the nation. On Sundays in London's West End, the congregations are in the shops, some of which do booming business. There is as little attention paid to God in Britain as in Cuba. We see emerging there the grim paganism of twentieth-century life."
(Patrick O'Flaherty, in "A Growing U.K. Religion: Animal Worship," Toronto *Globe and Mail*, February 10, 1986.)

14. Either the bilingual schools will continue to thrive at a cost to the public system, or the special funding for bilingual schools will be discontinued. There is too much investment for funding to be discontinued, so the public system will continue to suffer.

*15. "When they took my documents away, obviously for a closer look, I almost fainted. As far as I could see, they had not done that to anyone else. But the fright passed when after a time they brought them back and resumed the questioning: 'Anything to declare? The truth! Dollars? Gold?'
"'Absolutely not! Go ahead and search.'
"They did, but cursorily. And then I was through."
(Doan Van Toai, in "Vietnam: How We Deceived Ourselves," *Commentary*, March 1986.)

*16. If a person really stays on the Weight Watcher's diet, he or she is bound to lose some weight. Joe didn't lose any weight, so he can't have kept to the diet.

17. *Background:* In the summer of 1978, Andrew Young was the American ambassador to the United Nations. Mr. Young, a black, made the controversial statement that there are large numbers of political prisoners in the United States. In the public uproar that followed, American black activist Jesse Jackson contended that Mr. Young's statement was quite correct:
"'Some may debate the diplomacy and timing used by Ambassador Young, but the truth and accuracy of his statement is beyond question,' Jackson told the Leavenworth prisoners.
"'Thousands are in jail because they are too poor to pay bail bond,' Jackson said. 'Thousands are in jail because of delayed trials. Thousands are in jail because they were not tried by a jury of their peers. That is political.'"
(Calgary *Herald*, July 17, 1978.)

As he is quoted here, did Jackson offer an argument?

Argument and Explanation: What's the Difference?

We have seen some of the indicator words that may appear in arguments and have noted that these words are also quite common in explanations. Because this is so, it is often difficult to know whether a passage or speech contains an argument or an explanation.

> In an argument, premises are put forward as grounds to justify a conclusion as true.

> In an explanation, claims are offered to make a further claim understandable.

Much has been written about the nature of explanations in science, history, psychology, and ordinary life. In this book, however, we are concentrating on the logic of arguments, so we look at explanation only in a preliminary way.

We have seen that arguments are formed of premises and conclusions, which may naturally be arranged as:

> Premise
> Premise
> Premise
> So,
> Conclusion

What makes it especially difficult to distinguish arguments and explanations is that explanations can also be set out in this way. The very words that are so often used before the conclusion of an argument—words such as *therefore, so*, and *thus*—are also often used before the statement that describes what is explained in an explanation. Consider, for example:

> The window had been shut all summer and the weather was hot and damp.
> So the room smelled awfully musty when he returned.

Here the word *so* introduces the fact that is explained: the mustiness of the room. The passage is not an argument but an explanation. When we say this, we are relying partly on a sense of which sorts of beliefs people are likely to try to justify by arguments. We could imagine a context in which someone would try to demonstrate that a room had smelled musty, but this takes some ingenuity! It seems more natural to think that the *so* in the passage introduces an admitted fact for which the writer is suggesting causes. The window being shut and the hot damp weather *caused* the room to smell musty, according to this passage. The writer is not trying to prove a point, but rather trying to say how it was that a fact came to be as it is. Whether a set of statements expresses an argument or an explanation is often determined by the context in which it appears and our knowledge of what people would be likely to try to prove or justify in that context.

Sometimes, instead of offering reasons for their beliefs, people merely explain that they hold these beliefs. They explain themselves but make no attempt to justify their beliefs as acceptable. You can see this in the following example:

> His parents had been fundamentalist Christians, and his religious education was a strong feature in his character. The church had always emphasized social concern. Thus he accepted the Bible as a basis for action to relieve the suffering of the poor.

In this passage the word *thus*, which usually indicates the conclusion of an argument, precedes the description of a belief that is explained, not justified. Nothing in the passage would indicate that it is true that the Bible is the basis for social action. Rather, the facts that are specified show how this man came to believe that the Bible has that particular role. The explanation of why people hold beliefs is very interesting but does not by itself show that the beliefs are either true or false.

In an *explanation* someone tries to show how something came to be as it is—how the government came to be corrupt, how the roof became warped, how the institution of insurance against bad weather for holidays developed in Holland, and so on. Typically, explanations are given by citing causes of the event or institution to be explained. The explanations may naturally be set out as:

Factor (1)
Factor (2)
Factor (3)
Therefore,
Event (x) came to be.

There need not be only three explanatory factors; there may be one, two, or any number. We have merely selected three factors for the purpose of illustration. Very often the factors cited in an explanation are causal factors; the event (x) is explained by citing causes that produce it. However, not all explanations are causal. Some explanations proceed by fitting the phenomenon into a recognizable pattern or relating it to a human purpose. We may also explain the meaning of words, or the meaning of human behavior, and in these contexts the explanations are not put forward in causal terms. When you begin to use the distinction between explanations and arguments, it may help to think of all explanations as being explanations-by-cause. (Do this just to get started. Actually this is an oversimplification.) You can then contrast explanation and argument by seeing the explanation as an account that specifies the causes of an event that is assumed to have occurred and the argument as putting forward reasons trying to justify a claim as true.

Here is an explanation taken from an article dealing with the politics of pro- and antiabortion movements in the United States in the early 1980s.

> The generation that crusaded for abortion rights that first time around cannot believe that it has to fight for them all over again. The younger generation takes the rights for granted and cannot believe it has to fight for them at all.
>
> To a rather astonishing degree, the feminist movement of the 1970s was carried to its zenith by a particular generation of women which came of age in the late 1960s. It was a time in their lives when freedom from forced reproduction was one of their greatest needs. These women are in their mid to late thirties today and are not as enthusiastic about leading a pro-abortion struggle. Two things stall them. First, by now many have full-time careers—feminism simply does not have the access to the volunteer womanpower that is available to the antichoice forces. Second, although they still depend on having the right to have an abortion, in personal and political terms they are now far more concerned with having children.[4]

In this passage the author offers an explanation of what she takes to be a fact—the fact that women in their thirties are not keen to lead a struggle against prolife forces on the abortion issue. She provides no rational justification for the views of these women, or for the claim that this really is a fact. Rather, she offers an explanation suggesting two causes for their unwillingness to engage in another political struggle over abortion. "Two things stall them," she says. That is, two things are causal factors holding these women back from reentering the fray of the abortion struggle: they have full-time careers, and they are currently more interested in having children. Obviously these factors are not premises the author uses to try to prove the truth of any kind of stance on abortion. She is specifying two causes of the unwillingness of these women to recommence a political battle.

When an explanation is given, it is not in question whether the claim to be explained is true or not. Rather, the purpose of the explanation is to provide understanding as to causes or patterns. Arguments offer justifications; explanations offer understanding. Even though reasoning is used both in arguments and in explanations, and even though the same indicator words may appear in both, they have very different purposes. The principles of criticism that apply to arguments may not necessarily apply to explanations. Also, it is important to notice when someone has not argued for a point but has merely tried to explain something. (The point might need argument that it does not receive.)

We shall look at two imaginary dialogues in order to bring out the different purposes of arguments and explanations. We shall suppose that two businessmen, Smith and Wilson, have a business that offers second mortgages. Wilson takes the business into a town called Slumptown, where people have little money to buy homes and where there is, as a result, a great demand for second mortgages. Wilson and Smith operate profitably in Slumptown for several years, but then the economy of Slumptown worsens, and many people are forced to default on their mortgages. Smith and Wilson lose heavily. We can imagine the following dialogue between them:

Dialogue I

Wilson: Well, it's too bad we lost so much, but you can't win all the time. I just don't understand how it happened.

Smith: Actually, it's perfectly understandable. The causes of our good business in Slumptown were the poverty of the people and the bad job market there. Because people could not quite afford the houses they bought, the market for second mortgages was good. And yet these factors did indicate how vulnerable Slumptown's economy was. When the powerful XYZ company laid off workers, people in Slumptown were worse off than before, and they just couldn't keep up with the payments on their houses. It is easy to see what led to our losses in Slumptown.

There is no argument offered by Smith here. Smith is explaining why he and Wilson lost their money.

Now look at Dialogue II, which does contain an argument and does not explain anything.

Dialogue II

Wilson: We were unlucky in Slumptown. Perhaps we should transfer the firm to Hightown, down the road. In Hightown, there are plenty of jobs, the real estate market is booming, and people are crying out for second mortgages.

Smith: That would be a mistake, I think. Hightown is different from Slumptown in many ways, but it is similar in having a vulnerable economy. All of the economic activity in Hightown depends on one aircraft parts firm, which is expanding at the moment. If the firm loses a contract with Nigeria, it will have to lay off thousands of workers, and Hightown's economy will be very severely affected. In such a situation, Hightown would become another

Slumptown, and we would have the same problem with defaults all over again.

This time Smith does offer an argument. He gives reasons against taking the business to Hightown because he and Wilson do not initially agree on what should be done. In Dialogue I both knew that they had incurred losses and there was no attempt to prove that proposition. In Dialogue II they initially disagree. Smith then tries to persuade Wilson that moving to Hightown would be unwise, and he gives premises—reasons to support that conclusion.

Passages that do not contain arguments may contain explanations, or they may contain descriptions, suggestions, jokes, questions, illustrations, and so on. We have emphasized explanations not because all *nonarguments* are explanations, but rather because explanations most closely resemble arguments and are hardest to distinguish from them.

We have suggested here that a set of claims can be either an argument or an explanation and never both at once. Unfortunately, things are not quite this simple. Two qualifications must be made. The first, which you will soon discover for yourself, is that some passages seem to be classified either as arguments or as explanations, depending on what you assume about them. Here is a simple example:

—— John is the best math student in the class because he is going to a special school for gifted students.

We could interpret this statement as an argument if we assume that the person making it is trying to persuade others that John is the best math student. As an arguer, that person would then be giving as evidence for her conclusion the claim that John goes to a special school. Making this assumption about the context, we would see the argument:

—— Premise: John is going to a special school for gifted students.
Therefore,
Conclusion: John is the best math student in the class.

On the other hand, we could assume that the person making the statement is addressing others who already accept that John is the best math student in the class. Believing this already, they are in a position to hear a proposed explanation for the phenomenon. It goes like this:

—— Proposed explaining fact: John is going to a special school for the gifted.
That is the cause of
Fact to be explained: John is the best math student in the class.

When statements and short passages are taken out of context, it is sometimes quite hard to classify them definitely as argument or as explanation. You have to make some assumption about what is likely to need justification and what is not.

The second problem that arises is more rare. Occasionally, the very same statement or set of statements can serve both as argument and as explanation. This happens because the same premises that constitute evidence will also, by coincidence, serve to explain why the conclusion is true.[5] Because these cases are quite special, we will not describe them in detail here.

In subsequent chapters, we try to avoid these difficult cases. In practical life, you know more of the context than you are given in a logic textbook, and it is thus easier to judge whether an explanation or an argument is being put forward. Here, you have to use your background knowledge and sense of what needs to be rationally justified to try to determine whether an argument is being offered.

EXERCISE SET

Exercise Two

For each of the following passages, state whether it does or does not contain an argument. If you think that the passage does contain an argument, briefly state why you think this, and underline its conclusion. If you think that the passage does not contain an argument, briefly say why.

1. The cause of the traffic jam was an abandoned truck in the center lane of the freeway.

2. It is not essential to be tall in order to be good at basketball. This point is quite easy to prove. Just consider that basketball teams often have players of average height who make contributions to the game through fast running and expert passing.

3. Good health depends on good nutrition. Good nutrition requires a budget adequate to buy some fresh fruits and vegetables. Thus good health requires a budget adequate to buy some fresh fruits and vegetables.

*4. *Background: Time* magazine ran an article describing a television show designed by astronomer and publicizer of science Carl Sagan. The article gave rise to a number of letters, including the following one, which appeared in the November 10, 1980, issue.

   "Perhaps Carl Sagan's strongest message in his efforts to bring science to the people is this: Science is the true language of the present and of the future. Only a small fraction of this planet's populace, however, can speak the language. The most significant question facing us is whether our civilization, as a whole, will learn to utilize science for the benefit of mankind. The answer will surely determine our future course: noble greatness or self-inflicted extinction."

*5. We know that males and females have different hormones. Now scientists have discovered that these hormones affect verbal and spatial abilities that are connected with different sides of the brain. Therefore, probably men's brains are organized slightly differently from women's brains.

6. The natural world is very complicated. A complicated thing could not possibly come into existence just by accident. Therefore, the natural world must have been created by an intelligent designer.

7. The Olympics are a good way to improve relations between opposed countries, such as the United States and the Soviet Union, because they provide occasions where people can meet and come to understand each other as individuals.

8. "Never before in history has a nation so freely shared the treasure of its hard work; never before has a nation provided others with so much security; never before has a nation so responsibly shouldered the burden of world leadership, or combined both the material and human aspirations of man to such a reality.

   "Yes, we have faltered. We've made mistakes. We have not been perfect. But when one weighs the good and bad, there can only be one conclusion: The vision of our founding fathers has become a reality."
   (From "For This We Stand," personal reflections on U.S. foreign policy by William Westmoreland, *Daily Press*, Newport News–Hampton, Virginia, April 13, 1986.)

9. "It is characteristic of Newtonian physics that it has to ascribe independent and real existence to space and time as well as to matter, for in Newton's law of motion the concept of acceleration appears. But in this theory, acceleration can only denote 'acceleration with respect to space.' Newton's space must thus be thought of as 'at rest,' or at least as 'unaccelerated,' in order that one can consider the acceleration, which appears in the law of motion, as being a magnitude with any meaning. Much the same holds with time, which of course likewise enters into the concept of acceleration. Newton himself and his most critical contemporaries felt it to be disturbing that one had to ascribe physical reality both to space itself as well as to its state of motion; but there was at that time no other alternative, if one wished to ascribe to mechanics a clear meaning."
   (Albert Einstein, "Relativity and the Problem of

Space," in *Ideas and Opinions* [New York: Dell, 1973].)

10. The human mind will always be superior to the computer because computers are only the tools of human minds.

11. Only if they are quick and capable readers can students easily master the books required for the English courses here. But many students are poor readers. Therefore they will have problems. Those who call our English curriculum easy are simply wrong.

*12. Because she was an only child, she did not develop the independence necessary to care for herself. Even at seven, she was unable to put on her own skates, for example.

13. "The man who prefers pushpin to poetry may not actually be able to imagine what it would be like to have a developed sensitivity to the nuances of real poetry, and if his intelligence could be raised or his imagination improved, he might be brought to see that he is making a mistake."
(Hilary Putnam, *Reason, Truth, and History* [Cambridge, England: Cambridge University Press, 1981].)

14. "Licensing a nuclear power plant is, in my view, licensing random premeditated murder. First of all, when you license a plant, you know what you're doing—so it's premeditated. You can't say, 'I didn't know.' Second, the evidence on radiation producing cancer is beyond doubt. . . . Radiation produces cancer, and the evidence is good all the way down to the lowest doses.

"The only way you could license nuclear power plants and not have murder is if you could guarantee perfect containment. But they admit they're not going to contain it perfectly."
(John Gofman, quoted in Leslie Freeman, *Nuclear Witnesses* [New York: Norton, 1982].)

15. "Like their prophet, Freud, psychoanalysts think of themselves as experts on sex and as individuals espousing daringly progressive positions on sex. Such a claim has no basis in fact. On the contrary, psychoanalysts have continued to regard unconventional sexual behavior as illness—which they are especially adept at diagnosing and treating."
(Thomas Szasz, *Sex by Prescription* [New York: Anchor Press, 1980].)

*16. If a person knows in advance that his or her actions risk death, then if the person voluntarily takes those actions, he or she accepts a risk of death. These conditions surely apply to mountain climbers, so they have accepted a risk of death.

17. "Mortal battles between males are not common, though they occur. A weaker male does not want to pick a fight he would be likely to lose; nor would a stronger male be selected to risk a wound that would make his victory pointless. A period of symbolic conflicts, of 'showing off,' is therefore adaptive for both parties."
(Fred Hapgood, *Why Males Exist* [New York: Mentor Books, 1979].)

18. "Through his father, moreover, Kim Philby acquired his richest asset as a spy; an effortless familiarity with the quarry. Through his father and the education which his father gave him, he experienced both as a victim and as a practitioner the capacity of the British ruling class for reluctant betrayal and polite self-preservation. Effortlessly he played the parts which the establishment would recognize—for was he not born and trained into the establishment?"
(Bruce Page, David Leitch, and Phillip Knightly, in *Philby: The Spy Who Betrayed a Generation* [London: Sphere Books, 1977].)

Why Are Arguments Important?

In general, arguments are no better or worse than other forms of communication; they are merely different, serving a different purpose. The lack of any argument can be a fault sometimes—but only sometimes. Imagine that you are reading a history of World War II, and the author asserts that Winston Churchill, British prime minister during the war, had latent pro-Nazi sympathies. Suppose that the author offers no evidence for the claim. In this case the lack of any argument would be a major fault in the work since the claim is a serious accusation! It is not the sort of thing a historian should simply assert without backing it up with good reasons. However, many claims don't require argument; they are claims on which people agree anyway or claims for which arguments have been given in other places.

Some people use the word *argument* as a term of praise and say, "He has not given us any argument at all," when what they really mean is that the person has used poor arguments. This usage is quite confusing, and we do not follow it in this book. In our sense of *argument*, a person has offered an argument if he or she has put forward premises intended to justify a conclusion. Even if those premises do not in fact justify the conclusion, it is an argument nevertheless. In our sense of *argument*, arguments may be either good or poor.

In response to a proposal by *Reader's Digest* to condense the Bible, a fundamentalist minister in the United States voiced strong objections. He said that the proposal was "hellish," and he argued that the Bible should not be condensed by anyone because condensing the Bible amounts to censoring God. This line of argument struck many people as pretty unconvincing! But it is an argument, at least. It goes like this:

1. To condense the Bible would be to censor God.
2. God should not be censored.
So,
3. *Reader's Digest* should not condense the Bible.

The minister did argue for his position, even though his argument is not a very good one.

Some nonarguments are perfectly acceptable; some arguments are poor arguments. This leads us to the general question as to why people bother offering and assessing arguments. Why all the fuss about arguments? One answer is that arguments, and arguing, give us a nonviolent way of resolving conflicts in society. People try to persuade others by reasoning with them, instead of beating them up or blowing them up. Careful attention to the arguments of people who disagree with you will help you understand why they think as they do. When you have the ability to criticize these arguments step by step, you will have an important strategy for persuading them to look at your point of view. You will also be far better equipped to understand their point of view and see how they are led from some beliefs to others. In addition, arguments are very significant in contexts in which knowledge is being constructed. We want to know how well justified a theory or claim is, and we can find out by assessing the arguments that are (or can be) offered in defense of the position. A careful understanding of these arguments is extremely important when we are deciding whether to accept a new position. It also helps us to better understand positions we already accept—and can sometimes lead us to revise them.

The question whether emotion, authority, style, or something else is a viable alternative to rational argument has often been raised. Many people believe that sometimes (in religion and love, for instance) arguing is beside the point, and the careful use of reason is inappropriate. We could write profound books on this issue. In fact, people have. At a commonsense level, the answer to the question "Why use reason and argument to resolve issues?" is really very simple. Careful reasoning from acceptable premises to further conclusions is the best method of arriving at decisions and beliefs because this method is the most likely to lead to true beliefs and correct decisions. This is due to the fact that other methods are not based on the need to respect standards of evidence and logical principles. Those relying on emotion, for instance, simply respond with feelings and make no attempt to work from true or plausible claims by safe steps to the most accurate conclusion. Similar things may be said of the other alternatives to reasoned argument.

Our purpose here is to cultivate your ability to construct and evaluate arguments. These are not new activities, of course. You have been doing these things nearly all your life. What is new is that we are going to think reflectively about these natural activities and set out standards we can use to judge arguments as good or poor. Thus we shall be directing our attention explicitly toward things that we normally take for granted, in order to improve skills we already have.

Review of Terms Introduced

Argument: A set of claims put forward as offering support for a further claim. The argument is composed of the supporting claims and the supported claim. A person offers an argument when he or she tries to justify a claim by offering reasons for it.

Premise: A supporting reason in an argument. It is put forward as being acceptable and as providing rational support for a further claim.

Conclusion: In an argument, the claim for which premises are intended as support. It is this claim that the arguer tries to make credible.

Nonargument: A passage or speech that does not contain an argument.

Explanation: An account showing, or attempting to show, how it came to be that a fact or event is the way it is. Frequently explanations are given by specifying the causes of an event. An explanation is one kind of nonargument.

Indicator words: Words such as *for, since, thus, therefore,* and *because,* typically used in arguments to *indicate* that a person is reasoning from premises to a conclusion. However, these words may also occur in explanations and elsewhere. They do not appear *only* in arguments.

NOTES

1. Letter to the Toronto *Globe and Mail,* February 8, 1982.

2. Editorial in the Toronto *Globe and Mail,* October 23, 1980. Reprinted with the permission of the *Globe and Mail.*

3. Laurier LaPierre, *To Herald a Child* (Toronto: Ontario Public School Men Teachers Association, 1981), p. 42.

4. Deirdre English, "The War Against Choice," *Mother Jones,* February/March 1981, pp. 16–24. Reprinted with the permission of *Mother Jones* magazine.

5. I discuss the fact that the same statement can occasionally be both an argument and an explanation in a theoretical paper entitled "Why Arguments and Explanations Are Different," forthcoming in a book on the theory of argument to be published by Foris Publications. Such cases are also discussed by S. N. Thomas in the Teachers' Manual to the second edition of his text, *Practical Reasoning in Natural Language* (Englewood Cliffs, N.J.: Prentice Hall, 1983). Thomas thinks these cases require that we renounce the distinction between argument and explanation altogether. But since it is differing features, simultaneously satisfied, that make a passage constitute a good explanation or a cogent argument, we do not endorse this recommendation.

2

Pinning Down Argument Structure

In most of the examples in the last chapter, it was easy to see which claims were conclusions and which were premises. Most examples were relatively short and worded in a straightforward way so that the line of reasoning used in the argument was easy to follow. However, things are not always quite so simple. We sometimes have to look closely at passages, and listen closely to speeches, in order to see just what the line of reasoning is. In this chapter we look at the problem of identifying the premises and conclusions of arguments and see how important it is to examine carefully the particular language in which arguments are stated.

Standardizing an Argument

In order to understand the exact line of argument that someone is using, it is helpful to set out the premises and conclusion in a simple standard format such as the following:

1. Premise
2. Premise
3. Premise
So,
4. Conclusion

We'll call this standardizing an argument. To standardize an argument is to set out its premises and conclusion in clear, simple statements with the premises preceding the conclusion. By numbering the premises and the conclusion, we can refer to specific statements in an efficient way. We can simply refer to (1) or premise (1) instead of copying out a lot of words. We can say such things as "The author uses statements (1) and (2) to defend statement (3)." Standardizing arguments gives us a clear version of where they are going and forces us to look carefully at what the arguer has said. When we come to the more interesting stage of criticizing arguments, we will find standard-izing extremely helpful, for it allows us to see just which stage of the argument our criticisms affect and which points are really crucial to establishing the author's conclusion. Here is a very simple example:

> (1) All nuclear reactors pose some risk of accident because (2) nuclear reactors are very complex, technological structures, and (3) all complex technological structures are susceptible to breakdown at some point.

In this example, the conclusion is stated first. It is "All nuclear reactors pose some risk of accident. . . ." The indicator word *because* is used, and it precedes two premises offered as support for this conclusion. The premises are "nuclear reactors are very complex technological structures," and "all complex technological structures are susceptible to breakdown at some point." Standardized, the argument looks like this:

> 2. Nuclear reactors are very complex technological structures.
> 3. All complex technological structures are susceptible to breakdown at some point.
> Therefore,
> 1. All nuclear reactors pose some risk of accident.

One important point about arguments that we didn't emphasize in Chapter One is that arguments very often proceed in stages. That is, the premise of an argument may be defended in a subargument, so there are really two arguments in one. A subargument is a subordinate argument inside a main one. A premise in a main argument can be the conclusion of a subargument. Here is a simple example:

> (1) A computer cannot duplicate the creative processes of a human mind because (2) a human mind does not create according to the sorts of rules that are needed to program computers since (3) human creativity is intuitive and original.

The premise supporting the main conclusion, (1), is (2), as indicated by the word *because.* But (2) itself is supported by (3), as indicated by the word *since.* You could call (2) both a premise and a conclusion since it supports another claim but is also supported itself. We'll reserve the term *conclusion* for the main conclusion and consider (2)—and statements having a similar role—to be premises in the main argument. The argument from (3) to (2) in this example is a subargument used along the way to the main conclusion, and in this subargument, statement (2) is the conclusion.

It occasionally happens that the same premise or premises are used to establish two distinct conclusions so that one argument has two conclusions. Here is a simple example:

> (1) Labor is the basis of all property. From this it follows that (2) a man owns what he makes by his own hands and (3) the man who does not labor has no rightful property.

This example is a statement (approximately) of John Locke's theory of the moral basis of a right to private property. It uses (1) as its single premise, and from (1) two distinct conclusions, (2) and (3), are derived. There is no subargument here although there are two conclusions, for (2) is not intended to support (3) in this example, nor is (3) intended to support (2).

From Colloquial Writing to Standardized Form.   To see the greater clarity that results when we standardize an argument, let us look at an example from Christian writer and religious theorist C. S. Lewis.

Creatures are not born with desires unless satisfaction for those desires exists. A baby feels hunger. Well, there is such a thing as food. A duckling wants to swim: well, there is such a thing as water. Men feel sexual desire: well, there is such a thing as sex. If I find in myself a desire which no experience in the world can satisfy, the most probable explanation is that I was made for another world. If none of my earthly pleasures satisfy it, that does not prove that the universe is a fraud.[1]

Here Lewis seems to be offering an argument. What is the point he is trying to establish? He talks about babies and ducklings and sex: this is to indicate that there are creatures on earth who are born with desires that can be satisfied on this earth. The examples seem to be Lewis's basis for saying that we do not have desires unless they can be satisfied. He goes on to consider what would be the case if people were to have desires that could not be satisfied in this world. Most likely, he says, those beings would be made for another world. The last sentence in the passage virtually repeats this point in different words. This seems to be the point Lewis is trying to establish: it is his conclusion. The claims about the desires of babies, ducklings, and humans (sex) are used to back up his general premise about creatures being made with desires that can be satisfied, and it is from that general premise that he seeks to derive his conclusion. We should note that the conclusion is *not* that people are made for another world. (As a Christian, Lewis may very well believe that, but he does not assert it in this passage.) Lewis asserts that *if* people have desires that can't be satisfied in this world, they are *probably* made for another world. ("If I find in myself a desire which no experience in the world can satisfy, the most probable explanation is that I was made for another world.") It's very important to notice that his conclusion is qualified in this way.

In standardized form, Lewis's argument looks like this:

1. The desires of ducklings who want to swim, babies who are hungry, and men who desire sex can be satisfied in this world.
2. Creatures are not born with desires unless satisfaction for those desires exists.
So,
3. If people find in themselves desires that no experience in the world can satisfy, then the most probable explanation for this is that they were made for another world.

It is worth noting what we had to do to Lewis's original paragraph in order to get this clear argument out of it. First, we had to look at the logical flow of the passage and identify the conclusion. Second, we had to decide which parts of the passage were stated as reasons intended to back up that conclusion and put these into the most natural logical order. Third, we had to abbreviate and simplify Lewis's prose, putting it into clear complete statements that could be used as premises. These tasks are not always easy to do. People write and speak in a way that is more disorganized (and more interesting!) than the "(1) and (2), therefore (3)" format that is best for logicians to work with. They word statements in the form of questions and commands, repeat themselves, include background and aside remarks, tell jokes, wander off the topic, and so on. These elements of colloquial writing are eliminated when we put the argument in standardized form.

The following passage contains some background material leading up to an argument. The passage is a letter to the editor in which the writer is replying to another previously published letter. That letter, by Strome Galloway, presented arguments for the belief that women should not have combat roles in the Canadian armed forces.

With reference to Strome Galloway's letter on why women do not belong in combat:

As a woman, I have no desire to be involved in any area of the armed forces. But those women who do want to emulate men and join in their violence mythology should be allowed to, even though they have, as Mr. Galloway so quaintly puts it, "physical problems which men don't have."

I assume he is referring to the menstrual cycle, which can be taken care of very simply physically and which tends to make women—because they must be flexible and adapt to change throughout the month—psychologically stronger than most men.

Ultimately I agree with a button I saw recently saying, "War is menstruation envy." Put that in your kit bag, Mr. Galloway.[2]

Read this passage carefully to see whether it contains an argument. (If it doesn't, we don't have any problem about finding the premises and conclusion!) The letter is slightly disjointed. It has an air of sarcasm about the benefits of armed forces in general. Several comments merely introduce the context and describe or express the desires of the author herself about her own activities. But then she states quite definitely that women who want to join in "violence" with men should be allowed to. Here the author explicitly disagrees with the previous writer. This disagreement could give us a conclusion if there are premises in the letter to back it up. She says that women don't have physical problems that would keep them out of combat; she urges first that menstruation can be taken care of physically and second that menstruation makes women psychologically stronger than men. After that, the writer returns to her personal attitudes about war, referring humorously to a feminist antiwar button.

The actual argument against Galloway is found in those parts of the letter where the writer gives reasons against his view that women are not physically equipped for combat. Basically, it goes like this:

1. Menstrual problems can be taken care of very simply, in a physical way.
2. Due to menstruation women have to be flexible and adapt to change throughout the month.
So,
3. Women are psychologically stronger than most men.
Thus,
4. Menstruation is no obstacle to women participating fully in the armed forces if they wish to do so.

There is a subargument structure here. Premise (3) is supported by premise (2); thus, as well as being a premise in the main argument from (1) and (3) to (4), it is itself the conclusion of a small subargument. (*Note:* By identifying the structure of an argument here, we do not wish to imply that it is a good argument.)

This example about women in armed forces illustrates an important point about standardizing arguments. A passage may contain an argument even though it also contains sentences that are not premises or conclusions in that argument. Background information, or material inserted just for added interest or for humor, is not strictly speaking part of the argument because it is neither a premise nor a conclusion. The reference to a button saying, "War is menstruation envy," adds interest and humor, but since it does not support the conclusion and there is no evidence that the author intended it to support the conclusion, we do not interpret it to be one of the premises.

Often passages require a great deal of shortening and editing before we can represent them as arguments in standard form. It is hard to learn to do this, but it is a very important skill that you will find helpful in many contexts. It forces you to read (or listen) with a view to determining the main point, and it trains you to ask why the author or speaker is saying what he says. What are the reasons offered for his view-point? You may discover there are none at all—but that too is a discovery well worth making, especially if his theme is a controversial one requiring some argument. The following is a repetitive, disorganized example that illustrates the need to standardize and the simplification you can achieve by setting out the central argument in stan-dardized form:

In the letter "Any group could abuse children," in response to Professor Edward Shorter's column referring to the "great child abuse scam," Dr. J. Jacobs suggested: "Would it not be better to disturb the feelings of 99 families in the hope of finding one family who needed help in preventing further child abuse?"

In my "unprofessional" opinion as a mere full-time mother of three, I would say that families have been "disturbed" too much for far too long by far too many profes-sionals and that is why incidents of child abuse have increased by 34 percent in the past year.

The professionals may not want to admit the possibility, but I believe that all the anti-parent, anti-family attitudes that gushed from the International Year of the Child campaign last year probably have a lot to do with that 34 percent increase in incidents of child abuse.

The "professional observers of human nature" don't seem to understand just how much stress and pressure you have injected into North American families, bombard-ing young struggling parents with one shelling of modern philosophy and psychology after another for decades now.

These "professionals" have not only brought stress, but distress into many families. Parents have been told so much that they don't know what to do any more. They have been conned into believing that their parents didn't raise them properly and they can't possibly trust their own instincts or judgments about what is right or wrong for their children.

I say to all the "professionals" who've been minding everybody's business but their own: Let parents return to being intelligent individuals who desire to make their own judgments about what is best for their own children; stop trying to "diagnose and treat" us as though we were one great massive lump; and stop making us feel like criminals for spanking a child—maybe some of them won't feel so frustrated that they end up abusing them.[3]

This is a rather rambling letter. The author does seem to be arguing. As the first paragraph tells us, she has written to oppose a suggestion made by a Dr. Jacobs, and she tries to give some basis for her stance. The conclusion may be found in her opposition to Dr. Jacobs's view: professionals should not risk disturbing 99 families in the hope of finding the one family in 100 that would need help in preventing child abuse. (Check back to the first two paragraphs.) The author contends that profes-sionals disturb parents and that parental disturbance is probably a major cause of child abuse. These points are made in the second, third, and fourth paragraphs of the letter. The fifth and sixth paragraphs try to provide some justification for the claim that professionals have harmed parents. Parents mistrust their own judgment because of extensive professional literature, and they feel like "criminals" when they spank their children because of the attitudes professionals take.

These are the main points. If you look back at the letter, you will see that it is quite repetitive. You don't need to state the same point more than once in the premises. Nor do you need to insert such expressions as "in my unprofessional opinion as a mere mother" and "I say to all the professionals." In these comments the author is adding a kind of editorial commentary to her substantive remarks. She is expressing her reaction rather than stating substantive reasons for her view. Obviously, there will be many deletions before we get a clear model with only the premises and the conclusion. This version seems reasonably accurate and tolerably short:

> 1. Professionals have made parents mistrust themselves and their own judgments about their own children. (fifth paragraph)
> 2. Professionals have brought stress and distress into many families. (fourth and sixth paragraphs)
> Thus,
> 3. Professionals have probably brought about an increase in the incidence of child abuse. (second and third paragraphs)
> So,
> 4. Professionals should not risk disturbing 99 families in the hope of finding the one family in 100 whom they might help in preventing child abuse.

We now have a simple version of the original. Various flaws in it will more easily appear. But it is wise, in a case like this one, to look back at the original when you are about to accuse the author of a major mistake in arguing. We won't make any comment on the merits of this argument now because in this chapter our job is to concentrate on picking out the premises and conclusions. The appraisal of arguments comes later.

General Strategies for Standardizing Arguments

1. Confirm that the passage you are dealing with actually contains an argument. It contains an argument if the author is trying to support a position with claims offered in its defense.

2. Identify the main conclusion or conclusions. Indicator words should help. Often the context is helpful, particularly when one person argues against another. Typically in that case, one person's conclusion will be the denial of the other person's position.

3. Identify those statements in the passage that are put forward as support for the main conclusion.

4. Omit any material that serves purely as background information.

5. Omit material that you have already included. This instruction applies when the same premise or conclusion is stated several times in slightly different words. If this happens when the different wording indicates first a premise and then a conclusion, *do* put the statement twice in your standardized version. (As we will see later, this situation means there is a serious flaw in the argument.) Otherwise, *don't* repeat the statement.

6. Omit such personal phrases as "I have long thought," "in my humble opinion," and so on. These are not part of the content of the argument but are stylistic indicators of the author's direction.

7. Number each premise and conclusion, and write the argument in the standard form with the premises above the conclusion.

8. Check that each premise and conclusion is a self-contained complete statement. This means that premises and conclusions should not include pronouns like *he* and *my.* Instead the appropriate nouns should be used. Also premises and conclusions should be in the form of statements—not questions, commands, or exclamations.

9. Check that no premise or conclusion itself expresses a whole argument. For instance, if one premise says, "John has lied before so he is unreliable," you need to break down this premise further into (1) John has lied before and (2) John is unreliable. In the structure (1) will be shown as supporting (2) in a subargument. The subargument is not shown when you write "John has lied before so he is unreliable" as a single premise.

EXERCISE SET

Exercise One

Examine the following passages to determine whether they contain arguments. For those passages that do contain arguments, represent the argument in a clear, standard form, numbering premises and conclusion(s). Remember, if a passage does not contain an argument, it does not contain premises or a conclusion either.

*1. If a car has reliable brakes, it has brakes that work in wet weather. The brakes on my car don't work very well in wet weather. You can see that my car does not have reliable brakes. Of course I should get them fixed.

2. He is getting fat because he eats too many potato chips, drinks too much beer, and spends too much time watching television.

3. When unemployment among youth goes up, hooliganism and gang violence go up too. So unemployment is probably a major cause of these disruptions.

4. Weapons tend to make people fearful and distrustful. Fear and distrust often lead to hostility. Therefore, building up weapons is a poor way to work for peace.

*5. Every logic book I have ever read was written by a woman. I conclude that all logicians are women.

6. A stitch in time saves nine.

7. Either the butler committed the murder or the judge committed the murder. Since the butler was passionately in love with the victim, it was not he who committed the murder. Therefore the judge committed the murder.

*8. "Swimming bacteria are able to recognize about 30 different attractants and repellents, evolutionarily chosen from the vast array of chemicals to which the species has been exposed. Since the response to each is different, the final behavior must integrate these varied responses. This allows for a sophisticated assessment of the opportunities and dangers in the habitat and provides the cell with the best pathway through them."
(H. J. Morowitz, "Can Bacteria Think?" *Psychology Today*, February 1981.)

*9. "If the Soviet Union's calculation is that it can back Vietnam successfully in the war with China, as it did in Vietnam's war with the United States, it may be mistaken. While it is abundantly true that Vietnam is a defiant nation and is unlikely to capitulate to China, it is also true that China is a more difficult adversary than the United States—it is near at hand, patient, and has the means (one of them being the Chinese inside Vietnam) to keep Hanoi on the boil."
(From Bruce Grant, *The Boat People* [Middlesex, England: Penguin, 1979, p. 199].)

10. What is it that enables ants, bees, and other social insects to coordinate their behavior so closely?

11. The cause of his interest in dinosaurs was a school program he had been involved in at the age of ten. Due to the school's having several scientifically trained teachers, it was able to put on stimulating and challenging programs, and as a result, several prominent scientists were given inspiration and an early start.

12. "Since we are not under an obligation to give aid unless aid is likely to be effective in reducing starvation or malnutrition, we are not under an obligation to give aid to countries that make no effort to reduce the rate of population growth that will lead to catastrophe."
(Peter Singer, "Famine, Affluence, and Morality," in *World Hunger and Moral Obligation*, ed. William Aiken and Hugh LaFollette [Englewood Cliffs, N.J.: Prentice-Hall, 1977].)

13. "The source of much of California's shakiness is, as any school child knows, the San Andreas fault. On a geological map, it isn't hard to find, but in ground truth—as geologists call their legwork—the fault can be elusive. Serpentine and secretive, it lurks just below the surface along six-sevenths of California's length. A 650-mile crack in the earth, it cuts, largely unnoticed and often intentionally ignored, through almost every other geological feature of the state."
(Shannon Brownlee, "Waiting for the Big One," in *Discover*, July 1986, p. 56.)

14. "Famous men testify to having solved difficult problems in their sleep. This can seem a paradox until we understand what it means: namely, that they went to sleep without a solution and woke up with one."
(Norman Malcolm, "Dreaming and Scepticism," in *Meta-Meditations*, A. Sesonske and N. Fleming [Belmont, Calif.: Wadsworth, 1965].)

*15. *Background:* Descartes claimed that a person is made up of a physical body and a mind that has no spatial characteristics or parts. Speaking of Descartes's theory, seventeenth-century philosopher Pierre Gassendi said:
   "If you are wholly without parts, how can you mix, or appear to mix, with its [the brain's] minute subdivisions? For there is no mixture unless each of the things to be mixed has parts that mix with one another."
(Pierre Gassendi, "Remarks," in *Meta-Meditations*, A. Sesonske and N. Fleming [Belmont, Calif.: Wadsworth, 1965].)

*16. "The non-mathematician is seized by a mysterious shuddering when he hears of four-dimensional things, by a feeling not unlike that awakened by thoughts of the occult. And yet there is no more commonplace statement than that the world in which we live is a four-dimensional space–time continuum."
(Albert Einstein, *Relativity: The Special and the General Theory* [London: Methuen, 1954].)

17. "With twenty-two states and the District of Columbia conducting legal lotteries and raising billions of bucks, it will not be long before Congress authorizes a national lottery. Many legislators have long regarded lotteries as a pernicious and addictive form of gambling. But the fact is that a large share of the public likes to gamble and lotteries constitute a most effective revenue-raising device. The California lottery, for example, grossed more than $1 billion in the first four months of its existence, and its popularity rolls on. At least half a dozen national lottery bills—each with a laudable objective—are before Congress, and it appears likely that Uncle Sam eventually will get into the lottery business."
(News item in "Parade," *Daily Press*, Newport News–Hampton, Virginia, April 13, 1986.)

18. The Canadian government has an ongoing problem as to how to make its influence felt with the United States government. In 1985 and 1986, the Canadian government tried to acquire influence in the free trade negotiations by firmly supporting most aspects of U.S. foreign policy and announcing its friendliness to the U.S. and openness to U.S. business. This approach did not serve to counter protectionism in the U.S. nor did it help the negotiations toward freer trade. Nor did it give the Canadian government influence over the U.S. administration in arms-control matters. We can conclude that a tougher, more independent approach is the one the Canadian government should take for success. The U.S. is a big powerful country that is not going to pay attention to its northern neighbor unless compelled to do so.

Finer Points about Conclusions

To put an argument in standardized form, you have to know what its conclusion is. Identifying the conclusion is even more basic than identifying the premises, for your sense of the *point* of the passage will make you decide that certain statements are merely background or "asides" and that others are intended to support the author's point. It would certainly be nice if we had some definite rules about where conclusions had to be stated—if, for instance, speakers and writers always had to state their conclusions last, or if they always had to state them first. Unfortunately there are not any rules like this, and as language works, the conclusion in a passage or a speech can come at any point. It may be first, as in the following:

> *The film* Blue Lagoon *was poor* because its plot was thin and superficial, and it neglected some of the more frightening aspects of life on an isolated island.

Or it may be last, as in the following:

> Humans were said to be the only animals that use tools. Now it has been discovered that other animals use tools as well. For instance, chimpanzees use sticks to dig for termites, which they then eat. Thus we cannot prove that humans are unique from their use of tools.

A conclusion may even be stated right in the middle of a passage, with supporting premises on either side of it. Here is a passage exemplifying that arrangement:

> Rats who are only occasionally rewarded for behavior become frantically anxious to repeat the behavior to obtain a reward. We can see that *inconsistent behavior towards children is likely to lead to their being very demanding,* for it is well established that young children respond to punishment in much the same way animals do.

Unfortunately, then, there is no simple mechanical method for picking out the conclusion of the argument when you are studying speeches or writings. You have to read carefully—or listen carefully, if it is an oral argument—and try to determine what the main claim is. It is a matter of getting the main drift of what is said.

Degree of Certainty.   Another crucial point about conclusions is the degree of certainty, or commitment, with which they are put forward. An author or speaker may state her point quite emphatically, with no qualification whatsoever. On the other hand, she may make the point more tentatively, saying only that it is probably true, or could be true. What is said matters very much for proper understanding. Obviously it will make a difference to our evaluation of the argument. For instance, much better support will be needed for a categorical conclusion, such as "Abortion is always wrong after ten weeks of pregnancy," than for a more tentatively expressed conclusion, such as "Abortion could be wrong in some circumstances."

Here is an example in which it would be especially important to note that the author is putting forward only a very tentative conclusion. We will misunderstand him if we fail to see this.

> *The malaise within English studies, like the university's other complaints, has been described as a temporary crisis in the evolution of a venerable and necessary institution. Yet it should be remembered that both the university and its departments have not always existed, and that during their tenure they have not always served as indispensable channels for the flow of the cultural stream. Less than a hundred years ago, English studies hardly existed. Moreover, when they replaced classical studies, that discipline passed quietly into desuetude while hardly anyone noticed. It is not at all inconceivable, given the history of the humanities, that English studies, though at present the seemingly irreplaceable guardian of the Western cultural tradition, should decline to the current marginal status of the classics.*[4]

The conclusion of this passage comes at the end: "It is not inconceivable . . . that English studies . . . should decline to the current marginal status of the classics." (The author is comparing the role of English to that of classics and suggesting, on the basis of this comparison, that the fate that met classics might possibly befall English studies also.)

It's very important to note that this author has not claimed that English studies *will* decline, or that they ought to decline. He merely says they *might*.

It would be very useful if people always used words like *certainly, probably, possibly,* or *perhaps* in front of their conclusions. If they did this, we would always know just how firmly committed they were to these conclusions on the basis of the evidence they put forward in their premises. But these words aren't always used, so we have to infer from the tone of a passage and the context in which it appears just how firmly the arguer is asserting the conclusion.

Unstated Conclusions.   Another matter about conclusions is that sometimes they are not stated at all! This may strike you as an odd thing for us to say. After all, didn't we define an argument as a set of claims put forward to defend a conclusion? If that's what an argument is, a conclusion is by definition part of every argument. Why, then, are we telling you that in some arguments the conclusions aren't stated? This happens not because such arguments *lack* conclusions but because they have unstated conclusions. The conclusions are suggested by the stated words as they appear in the context.

Obviously you have to be sure that a person intends to argue if you are going to add a conclusion. If we were willing to do this all the time, anything could be turned into an argument! We have to be careful. When the conclusion is not stated, but is strongly suggested by the statements that are made or by the context in which the speech or passage appears, we have a missing conclusion. To standardize the argument in this case, we have to write in the conclusion.

Here is an example:

> *If the Christian churches wish to refuse ordination of gay people to the clergy, they have a right to their decision (however misguided it may be). But when the churches organize public referendums to repeal the civil rights of homosexual citizens, that's another matter. In Dade County, St. Paul, Wichita, and Eugene County, Oregon, the churches openly ran petition drives, distributed the political literature and raised the funds needed to bring out the public vote that revoked the rights of gays in those places. Unfortunately America is currently besieged by an army of religious zealots who see the Government and the ballot box as instruments for enforcing church dogmas. If the trend continues, we'll have Government-enforced religion and the end of a 200-year-old democratic tradition.[5]*

The passage is a letter written to *Time* magazine. The writer wrote to express his opposition to the activities of organized religions against homosexuals. Obviously he is against their efforts, and in his letter he expresses that opposition and gives some reason for it. But he never states, in just so many words, that these activities should cease. He suggests this; it is left unstated. His conclusion is "Organized religions should not campaign against civil rights for homosexuals." But these exact words are not to be found in his letter. We have to supply the conclusion, and we have to look carefully at the letter to see that we have a basis for doing so. The evidence is in the first two sentences and especially in the expression "that's another matter." In the sentence beginning "In Dade County," the writer describes the activities to which he is opposed. This sentence is not part of an argument but gives background information. In the next sentence, beginning with "Unfortunately," the author seems to be expressing his attitude toward the religious activists. His reason for being against their activities is not given until the last sentence. The argument, then, has one explicitly stated premise and an unexpressed (missing) conclusion. In standardized form it would look like this:

> ▬▬ 1. The trend of bringing organized religions into political affairs will lead to Government-enforced religion and the end of a 200-year-old democratic tradition.
> So,
> <u>2</u>. Organized religions should not campaign against civil rights for homosexuals.

The line is put under the number for the missing conclusion, (<u>2</u>), because we supplied those words ourselves; we need to remind ourselves that this conclusion was written in.

A similar example may be found in a short letter written to the popular science magazine *Discover* about evolutionary theory. The author of this letter refers to Carl Sagan, a well-known scientist and supporter of evolutionary theory. Sagan's television series "Cosmos" had occasioned a number of letters.

> *Could evolution ever account for the depth of intellect that Carl Sagan possesses? Not in a billion years.*[6]

The author strongly suggests here that evolutionary theory is inadequate. But he does not state this in just so many words. Rather, he states that there is something evolutionary theory could not account for: Carl Sagan's intellect. The tone of the passage is argumentative. (Could it? No!) The issue is one of public controversy, and the writer is suggesting that the failure of the theory to account for Sagan's intellect marks it as an inadequate theory. Given the implication, the context, and the tone, it seems appropriate to regard the letter as an argument with a missing conclusion. To regard it as an argument, we have to supply a conclusion, because there is no argument without a conclusion. The standardized version of the argument would look like this:

> ▬▬ 1. Evolution could never account for the depth of intellect that Carl Sagan possesses.
> Therefore,
> <u>2</u>. Evolutionary theory is inadequate.

Often the mere act of standardizing an argument will reveal flaws, for these are much more obvious when the argument is set out in a simple clear format. The main reason for standardizing arguments is clarity. But when you add to the original, as we have by inserting the missing conclusions, you should make sure that you can justify your addition with reference to the context and wording of the original.

The Problem of Missing Premises

Sometimes we may have the impression that the author of an argument has left out something important that he must have been implicitly claiming in order to support his case. It seems as though there is an additional premise—or even several additional premises—but these are unstated. Arguments can have missing premises, just as they can have missing conclusions. However, there are some differences, and unfortunately, the matter of missing premises is more complex and controversial than that of missing conclusions.

What makes an argument appear to have a missing premise? It is that, as stated, the argument strikes us as having a kind of hole or gap—a hole that we could fill in quite naturally if we added another premise to those the arguer has already stated. For example, many children argue that dads know more than moms because they are taller than moms. That is, they infer greater knowledge from greater height. This strikes most adults as quite a logical leap. You can fill it in if you realize that these children are relying on a premise that they haven't stated: namely, taller people know more than shorter people. When you hear or read an argument and think that it has one or more missing premises, you are perceiving a kind of logical gap that you would like to fill in.

What makes the problem of missing premises tricky is that we can't go around filling in every gap we perceive in other people's arguments just so that we can build up those arguments into something we find clear. We want to find missing premises when there really are some, but we don't want to rewrite other people's arguments just to suit our own sense of how things should hang together. When we see a gap in an argument, how do we know that the author was omitting exactly the premise that we would want to use to fill in that gap? The difficulty is to balance our own sense of logical direction with due respect for what other arguers actually said and meant.

It is hard to strike just the right balance here, and this makes the problem of missing premises one of the most difficult in the theory of argument. In fact, even trained philosophers and logicians disagree quite vehemently about it. In this book we take a very cautious approach to the problem, and we urge that you add missing premises quite sparingly, paying careful attention to what arguers really said or wrote, and being sure to justify any additions by reference to the material that is present.

The question of whether to add missing premises arises when you see a gap in an argument as stated. You will then see that this gap could be filled in, making the flow of the argument much more natural and clear, if a particular missing premise were written in. When this arises, write down what you think is a missing premise and then look carefully at what the author has actually said. Make sure that you can justify the addition of the premise with reference to the wording and context that are actually there. This will prevent you from wandering too far from the stated text and turning other people's arguments into your own. Of course, you have a different situation if you are listening to someone present an argument and you think that she is relying on unstated premises. This is an easier case because you can simply ask her whether she is using the premises you see as missing as part of her argument. If she is, she can say so; if she is not, you can point out what you think is a logical gap in her argument. In the case of written arguments, even when you think that by adding premises you can improve an argument, you should not do this unless you can justify it with reference to the stated text and any background knowledge you may have about what the author would accept. Our policy amounts to this: *no supplementation without justification*. The reason for this restriction is that we appraise other people's arguments in order to find out how strong their reasons are for their particular conclusions. If we start adding extra premises whenever we don't find the logical flow of an argument natural, we will end up wandering away from the arguments we started with and working on new arguments, which we have invented ourselves. In doing this, we will risk reading our own minds into other people's reasoning and, possibly, failing to understand what those others really have to say.

We will look at several examples so that you can get a sense of how this policy is applied. Here is an argument that can be considerably clarified by the addition of a missing premise. As we shall see, in this case, there is sufficient basis in the stated material for adding that premise.

DON'T TAKE THE ADVICE OF THE NUCLEAR ESTABLISHMENT ON THE ISSUE OF NUCLEAR SAFETY. The people that make and run nuclear power plants have assured us that there will never be a major catastrophe. But manufacturers of nuclear reactors also make toasters, dryers, washers, and television sets, and other household appliances. These simple appliances are not completely reliable and there is much less reason to believe that complex nuclear reactors are completely dependable.

Remember: We're talking about millions of lives and billions of dollars in property damage.[7]

The stated premises and the conclusion are as follows:

1. Manufacturers of nuclear reactors make toasters, dryers, washers, and other simple household appliances.
2. Toasters, dryers, washers, and other simple household appliances made by the manufacturers who also make nuclear reactors are not completely reliable.
So,
3. Complex nuclear reactors are very unlikely to be completely reliable.
4. Unreliable nuclear reactors could cause millions of lives to be lost and billions of dollars to be lost in property damage.
Therefore,
5. We should not take the advice of the nuclear establishment when it assures us that nuclear energy is safe.

You can see that there is a subargument here. (1) and (2) support (3), and then (3) and (4) support (5). In this case we'll concentrate only on the subargument, since that is where the problem of a missing premise arises. In (1) the author deals with appliances like toasters, which he says are "simple." In (2) he states that these simple appliances are unreliable. From these statements, he concludes in (3) that nuclear reactors, which are complex, are less likely to be reliable than the simple appliances made by the same companies. What is missing here is an explicit assertion that complex items are less likely to be reliable than simple items made by the same company. This claim is never overtly made, but it is strongly suggested in the author's wording when he says, "these simple appliances are not completely reliable and there is even less reason to believe that complex nuclear reactors are reliable." "Even less reason," in this context, suggests:

<u>6</u>. Companies are less likely to make complex items that are reliable than they are to make simple items that are reliable.

The subargument may be regarded as having (<u>6</u>) as a missing premise. It moves from (1), (2), and (<u>6</u>) to (3), instead of from (1) and (2) to (3). By adding (<u>6</u>) as a missing premise, we make the structure of the original argument clearer, for we can see just how the fallibility of toasters is supposed to be related to the fallibility of nuclear reactors.

Another example with a missing premise is the following argument put forward by C. S. Lewis:

And immortality makes this other difference, which by the by, has a connection with the difference between totalitarianism and democracy. If individuals live only seventy years, then a state or nation, or a civilization, which may last for a thousand years, is more important than an individual. But if Christianity is true, then the individual is not only more important but incomparably more important, for he is everlasting and the life of the state or a mere civilization, compared with his, is only a moment.[8]

If we used the stated material only, the argument would look like this:

1. If Christianity is true, then the individual is everlasting.
2. States and civilizations are not everlasting.
So,
3. If Christianity is true, the individual is incomparably more important than the state or civilization.

Let us check back to the original passage to see whether this standardized version is accurate. The first sentence of the paragraph introduces the topic, and in it Lewis adds an "aside" ("which by the by"), which is not part of the argument. The second sentence states what Lewis regards as a consequence of non-Christian views: what would follow if individuals lived only seventy years. But Lewis's main concern is with the consequences of the Christian view; the alternative view is included as part of the background and is not really a premise or conclusion. The word *but* indicates a return to his main line of thinking: he spells out the consequence of Christianity for the importance of the individual. This is his main point and his conclusion. He does not state here that Christianity *is* true, but that *if* it is true, the individual is incomparably more important than the state or civilization. The word *for* (an indicator word) in that sentence introduces the reasons for the conclusion: the individual would be everlasting and the state or civilization would not. Our standardization omits the background and the aside, and contains only the premises and conclusion.

In this passage Lewis reasoned from the longer life of an individual, under the Christian hypothesis, to the greater importance of that individual, under that hypothesis. In reasoning this way, he seems to be committed to the belief that longer life makes for greater importance. We can see this commitment because longer life is the only feature of the individual referred to, and it is said to make him or her "incomparably more important" than states or civilizations, which last for less time than all eternity. We might consider adding as a missing premise:

4. Of different entities, the one that lasts for the longest time is the most important.

We have seen that Lewis is committed to (4) by other things he says and by the direction of his argument; adding (4) will make the argument much clearer. It will then look like this:

1. If Christianity is true, then the individual is everlasting.
2. States and civilizations are not everlasting.
4. Of different entities, the one that lasts for the longest time is the more important.
Therefore,
3. If Christianity is true, the individual is incomparably more important than the state or the civilization.

This standardization of the argument will be very helpful when we come to evaluate Lewis's reasoning, for having that missing premise written out clearly will bring it to our attention. (The missing premise seems rather disputable, but here we'll continue to concentrate our energies on standardizing, not on appraisal.) Often missing premises are quite disputable, and when you write them in, you immediately see a basis for criticizing the argument. If you go on to make a criticism disputing a premise you have written in yourself, make sure that you have good reasons for interpreting the argument as you have.

A final example of an argument with a missing premise is the following:

In fact, the ordinary orange is a miniature chemical factory. And the good old potato contains arsenic among its more than 150 ingredients.

This doesn't mean natural foods are dangerous. If they were, they wouldn't be on the market.[9]

This argument was part of an advertisement put out by a food processing company. The overall thrust of the advertisement was that there is no general difference, so far as safety is concerned, between naturally grown and artificially manufactured foods. What we have shown here is a subargument used on the way to establishing that more general conclusion. The advertisement stated (first quoted sentence) that natural foods like oranges and potatoes contain chemicals; this is said in order to associate these foods with processed foods. But many of us now think that foods containing chemicals are dangerous, and the ad wishes to assure us that they are not. This is the conclusion: "This doesn't mean natural foods are dangerous." The reason in support of this conclusion is offered in the final sentence. The first two sentences have to do with the larger argument of the ad; the last two contain the subargument, which we still concentrate on here:

———— 1. If natural foods such as potatoes and oranges were dangerous, they would not be on the market.
So,
2. Natural foods such as potatoes and oranges are not dangerous.

Now if you look at the reasoning from (1) to (2), you will see the ad depends on an obvious fact: such natural foods as potatoes and oranges are on the market. If we were to write in as a missing premise:

———— <u>3</u>. Natural foods such as potatoes and oranges are on the market.

the structure of the reasoning would be very clear indeed. Since (<u>3</u>) is a matter of common knowledge, which the advertiser certainly would have accepted, there is no danger of writing in something that he or she didn't believe. This is a case in which the unstated premise is something so well known both to the arguer and to the intended audience that it does not even seem worth saying. In fact, the obviousness of a given claim is often a reason for not bothering to say it or write it in just so many words. The argument as stated here had (<u>3</u>) as a missing premise, and the supplemented argument will go from premise (1) and premise (<u>3</u>) to the conclusion, (2).

In this example about potatoes and oranges, the missing premise was not exactly suggested by the wording used in the original. It was added on the grounds that it is such an obvious matter of fact that the arguer would have been sure to accept it. It is legitimate to add a missing premise if the wording of the text or speech provides good reasons for doing so or if that premise is required to make the argument fit together and it is something that the arguer would accept.

In some other kinds of examples, we have a choice between seeing a gap in reasoning and adding something that is not specifically suggested by actual wording or a matter of common knowledge. The direction of the reasoning itself will seem to indicate that there is a missing premise. Here is a simple example:

———— 1. John is a short, slim, unathletic man.
So,
2. John probably has an inferiority complex.

If anyone were to argue this way, he would effectively be assuming a connection between being a man's being short, slim, and unathletic and having an inferiority complex. We can make the argument logically clear by spelling out this connection. The arguer would not need to assume that all such men have this problem, for the conclusion includes the word "probably." Because of the direction of the reasoning and because of this qualifying word, we can justifiably add a missing premise to the effect that most short, slim, unathletic men have an inferiority complex. The resulting argument will then be:

1. John is a short, slim, unathletic man.
<u>3</u>. Most short, slim, unathletic men have an inferiority complex.
So,
2. John probably has an inferiority complex.

Criticism of the argument would no doubt be directed to this missing premise, which is not terribly plausible. Even so, the missing premise is somewhat more plausible than another we could have added, which would also have served to link the stated premise with the stated conclusion. Consider:

<u>4</u>. Most short, slim, unathletic people have an inferiority complex.

This statement is less plausible than (<u>3</u>) because it makes a more sweeping claim and, given our background knowledge about the different expectations people still have of men and women, (<u>4</u>) is not nearly so likely to be true as (<u>3</u>). We have to be careful when adding premises not to make the original argument worse than it is. (If we do this, we commit something called the Straw Man Fallacy, which is discussed in Chapter Six.) We should add the most plausible premise that will link the stated premises to the stated conclusion and that we can reasonably insist the arguer would accept or is committed to.

In short, missing premises should be added under the following conditions:

1. There is a logical gap in the argument as stated.

2. This logical gap could be filled by inserting an additional premise.

3. This additional premise is either something that the arguer accepts, or it is something to which he or she is committed. Evidence that an arguer accepts a claim can either be found in the wording of the surrounding text or be based on the fact that the claim is a matter of common knowledge or belief—something that nearly everybody would accept. Or it can be based on the direction of the reasoning, which shows that the arguer is committed to the claim because only by such a commitment can he or she move from the stated premises to the stated conclusion.

4. Statements inserted as missing premises should be as plausible as possible, consistent with the previous conditions.[10]

Concluding Comments

Properly identifying arguments and understanding their structure with subarguments and missing conclusions and premises (if any) are absolutely fundamental steps in argument evaluation and critical thinking. In fact, sometimes it is more work to see this basic structure than it is to determine the merits of the resulting argument. People speak and write in fluid or elliptical or redundant ways. In addition, even when they are arguing, they often include many statements and suggestions that are not strictly part of their argument. Practicing your interpretive skills now will bring valuable returns later.

Review of Terms Introduced

Standardizing an argument: Picking the conclusion and premises of an argument from a passage and setting them up in a standard simple format.

Subargument: A smaller argument within a larger one, in which a premise of a main argument is itself defended.

Unstated conclusion: A conclusion not put into words but suggested by the context, wording, and natural logical order of a passage. *Note:* Unstated conclusions should be added only when there is a clear interpretive justification for doing so.

Missing premise: A premise not stated in just so many words but suggested by the context, wording, and natural logical order of a passage and needed to fill a gap in the reasoning. *Note:* Missing premises should be supplied only when there is a clear interpretive justification for doing so.

EXERCISE SET

Exercise Two

For each of the following examples, decide whether the passage contains an argument and, if it does, represent the argument in a standardized form with premises preceding the conclusion. Check carefully to see whether any passage requires either a missing conclusion or a missing premise. If you add material that is not explicitly stated by the author, give interpretive reasons for doing so.

*1. If you've eaten a banana, you've eaten everything in Nutrasweet.

2. To get your blood pressure down, you have to diet and exercise and lose some weight. High blood pressure is a real health hazard. Therefore, anyone who is overweight should get to work and reduce.

3. Anyone who has the capacity to kill should avoid keeping guns around the house. So no one should keep guns around the house.

*4. The crime rate among teenagers is going up. Can we believe that drug use is declining if teenage theft is on the rise?

5. If people were truly unselfish, they would give as much to worthy charities as they save for their old age. And they do no such thing!

6. Chicken pox is a common childhood disease which can be unpleasant but which never leads to dangerous complications.

*7. Secondhand smoke can cause minor health problems to non-smokers, because some non-smokers suffer from headaches, runny noses, and itchy eyes as a result of exposure to smoke. In addition, it has been shown that secondhand smoke can cause lung cancer even in non-smokers who are regularly exposed to smoke. Thus secondhand smoke can be injurious even to the health of non-smokers.

8. It is only because we are lazy parents that we permit our children to watch television instead of pursuing healthy or creative activities. Such parental laziness has high social costs, which we can expect to feel more acutely as the television generation comes of age.

9. "[T]here seems little chance that a conventional war between nuclear powers could stay limited. And this means that a conventional war between nuclear powers must not even be begun, since it threatens the same holocaust that the limited use of nuclear weapons threatens."
(Jonathan Schell, *The Fate of the Earth* [New York: Alfred A. Knopf, 1982].)

10. "Dr. Joyce Brothers visited Weight Loss Clinic and

went home impressed. It's one thing for us to tell you that we offer a superb weight loss program. But it's even more impressive when Dr. Joyce Brothers does the talking:

"'One of the problems I'm asked about most often is overweight. If I could put together the best possible weight loss program, I'd make sure it was run by trained professionals . . . counsellors and nurses, who were not only dedicated . . . but enthusiastic about helping each individual client achieve success. A program like the one at Weight Loss Clinic.'

"Dr. Joyce Brothers was impressed. There's no reason why you shouldn't be."
(Advertisement, Toronto *Star*, February 25, 1981.)

11. *Background:* In 1978, Russian dissident novelist Alexander Solzhenitsyn made a widely publicized speech criticizing the materialism of western societies. He said:

"If humanism were right in declaring that man is born to be happy, he would not be born to die. Since his body is doomed to die, his task on earth evidently must be of a more spiritual nature. It cannot be unrestrained enjoyment of everyday life. It cannot be the search for the best ways to obtain material goods and then cheerfully get the most out of them. It has to be the fulfillment of a permanent, earnest duty so that one may leave life a better human being than one started it."
(Calgary *Herald*, July 6, 1978.)

12. *Background:* David Hume, an eighteenth-century Scottish philosopher, wrote an essay in which he contended that no testimony could ever reliably establish the occurrence of a miraculous event. (Assume in the following passage that by the word *prodigies*, Hume means "events believed by some people to be miraculous.")

"I may add as a fourth reason which diminishes the authority of prodigies, that there is no testimony for any, even those which have not been expressly detected, that is not opposed by an infinite number of witnesses, so that not only the miracle destroys the credit of the testimony, but the testimony destroys itself. To make this better understood, let us consider that in matters of religions whatever is different is contrary, and that it is impossible that the religions of ancient Rome, of Turkey, of Siam and of China, should all of them be established on any solid foundation. Every miracle, therefore, pretended to have been wrought in any of these religions (and all of them abound in miracles), as its direct scope is to establish the particular system to which it is attributed, so has it the same force—though more indirectly—to overthrow every other system."

(David Hume, "Of Miracles," in *The Empiricists* [New York: Anchor Books, 1974].)

*13. "The mere philosopher is a character which is commonly but little acceptable in the world, as being supposed to contribute nothing either to the advantage or pleasure of society, while he lives remote from communication with mankind and is wrapped up in principles and notions equally remote from their comprehension."
(David Hume, "Of the Different Species of Philosophy," in *The Empiricists* [New York: Anchor Books, 1974].)

14. "The most important feature of the bacterial lifestyle is its boom-and-bust quality. In general bacterial populations either are growing explosively, collapsing catastrophically, or lying completely dormant. They live like Dionysiacs, waking only when they can live orgiastically, gulping food with a technique that wastes far more than it uses, reproducing riotously, and polluting everything about them with their toxins. As soon as they have destroyed the conditions that wake them up, they just slip away again into dormancy. Bacteria are total hedonists, living only for the short run (and the shortest of short runs at that). And it is this lifestyle which makes possible every one of the scrimp-and-save, puritan, accumulating species on earth."
(Fred Hapgood, *Why Males Exist* [New York: Mentor Books, 1979].)

*15. Either the will is free or the will is not free. If the will is free, a person is responsible for his or her actions. If the will is not free, a person is not responsible for his or her actions. But something must be there to produce the actions people perform. So, if the will is not free, something outside people produces actions.

*16. "In the spring of 1930 she was sent as a delegate to the All-China Soviet Congress. Friends afterwards put her in a hospital, and she was operated on for the abscess. During this period she kept the translation of Marxian studies under her pillow, and she once remarked: 'Now I have time to study theory.'

"There are those who will ask, 'Is Shan-fei young and beautiful?'

"Shan-fei is twenty-five years of age. Her skin is dark and her face broad; her cheek bones are high. Her eyes are as black as midnight, but they glisten and seem to see through a darkness that is darker than the midnight in China. She is squarely built like a peasant, and it seems that it would be very difficult to push her off the earth—so elemental is she, so firmly rooted to the earth. Beautiful? I do not know—is the earth beautiful?"

(Agnes Smedley, *Portraits of Chinese Women in Revolution* [Westbury, N.Y.: The Feminist Press, 1976, pp. 160–161].)
(*Hint:* If there is an argument stated or implied here, it will have to have a missing, or unstated, conclusion.)

17. The *Challenger* shuttle explosion could not have been caused by a leaky valve. If the valve had leaked, the instrument panel would have registered it, and the astronauts would have had time to report this malfunction back to the base. Since the only other possibility is an expanded, overheated O-ring, that must have triggered the explosion.

*18. "Dictionaries cannot settle all questions about how words are to be used, nor are they intended to. If they were, then such a heated debate as the current one about abortion could be settled by looking up definitions for 'human being' or 'person.'"
(John Hoaglund, *Critical Thinking* [Newport News, Va.: Vale Press, 1984, pp. 45–46].)

19. "Jesus Christ died for our sins. Trust him."
(Billboard near Salem, Ontario.)

*20. What accounts for Twain's greatness as a novelist? Instead of delivering a sermon or writing a treatise on race relations, he teaches by example, by telling a story and involving the reader in it. The image of Huck and Jim on the raft endures, long after moral principles, statistics on unemployment, crime, and legal discrimination have faded from memory. We cannot change people by rational argument, much less force. But literature can persuade us because it touches the heart. We need more writers, not more laws or guns with which to enforce them.
(Thanks to Dennis Rohatyn of the University of San Diego for this example.)

21. "Everyone who exercises to improve his muscles knows that what is physical can be altered by behavior. The brain is a physical organ; as such, we have every reason to expect that it can be altered by behavior and cultural patterns. Work with retarded infants, in which great strides have been made by the technique of extra stimulation to 'ex-

ercise' the brain, is an illustration of the truth of this claim."
(G. R. G. Kemp, "Sexy? Or Sexist?" Not in print.)

22. "Common sense tells us that men and women are different because they are different. With respect to sexuality, there is a female human nature and a male human nature. Throughout the immensely long hunting-and-gathering phase of human evolutionary history, the sexual desires and dispositions that were adaptive for one sex were a ticket to reproductive oblivion for the other."
(Interview with Donald Symons, author of *The Evolution of Human Sexuality*, in *Psychology Today*, February 1981.)

23. "As a torch sends rays of light out into dark places, so America should send out messages that will, if heeded, eventually improve life in other parts of the world."
(Garret Hardin, "A Lamp, not a Breadbasket," which appeared as an advertisement in *Harper's*, in May 1981.)

*24. *Background:* The following excerpt is written against environmentalist Jeremy Rifkin, who has been active against DNA research on the grounds that changing genes so as to produce new organisms, which are then released into the environment, poses problems. The author calls Rifkin a "fear monger," saying: "As you (*Time* magazine) reported, organisms lose genes through mutations all the time. If removing a gene would unleash a monster on the world, nature would surely have produced it by now."
(Letter to *Time*, May 12, 1986.)

25. *Background:* Actor Bill Cosby, well known for his love of children and successful television comedy based on family life, is quoted regarding his beliefs about bringing up children: "A father must never say 'Get the kids out of here. I'm trying to watch TV.' If he ever does, he is liable to see one of his kids on the 6 o'clock news."
(Quoted in *Time*, May 12, 1986. *Hint:* Assume that Cosby thinks you will see the child on the news because the child has done something wrong.)

NOTES

1. C. S. Lewis, *Mere Christianity* (New York: Macmillan, 1953), p. 106.

2. Toronto *Globe and Mail*, August 7, 1985.

3. Letter to the Toronto *Star*, October 25, 1980.

4. Peter Shaw, "Degenerate Criticism," *Harper's*, October 1979, pp. 93–99.

5. Letter to *Time*, June 1978.

6. Letter to *Discover*, November 1980.

7. *Informal Logic Newsletter*, Examples Supplement for 1980.

8. C. S. Lewis, *Mere Christianity*, p. 100.

9. Advertisement by the Monsanto Chemical company, *Harper's*, October 1980, p. 25.

10. I am grateful to Allan Spangler for suggestions about this discussion of missing premises. The problem is so difficult and yet so basic that it poses real problems for textbooks. It is a challenge to say something that is complex enough to be accurate and yet simple enough to be comprehensible at an early stage in a course. I discuss the problem at length in *Problems of Argument Analysis and Evaluation* (Amsterdam: Foris Publications, 1987). See especially Chapters Five, Six, and Seven.

3

Looking at
Language

For understanding and resolving disputes and for constructing and evaluating arguments, it is very important to determine what is meant by the words people use. Language can help or hinder understanding, and a good sense of the meanings of words used and their role in persuasion is extremely valuable.

Definitions

When we think of clarifying meaning, what first comes to mind, probably, is the matter of definitions. The demand "define your terms" is often heard. Some disputes seem impossible to resolve just because people mean different things by words or cannot agree on meaning. Words like *democracy, justice, freedom, imperial,* and *colonial* have powerful emotional associations and may be defined in very different ways by people of differing political beliefs. In recent decades, advances in medical technology have made it necessary to redefine *death* in terms of absence of brain activity or respiration rather than the cessation of heartbeat or respiration, as was the previous traditional definition. The new definition is very important. Without it, doctors who remove a heart from a traffic victim could be charged with murder!

Though many people feel frustrated at talking about mere words and think this is different from dealing with real problems, language is so important to the way we think and reason that it is an integral part of knowledge and debate. The impatience we may feel should be curbed because words so often have crucial attitudes, assumptions, and interests tied to them. People who differ on how words should be used very often differ in these attitudes, interests, and assumptions. Thus looking at their different definitions and their reasons for holding them is an important step in achieving understanding. The modern definition of *death*, for instance, is the result of more than a mere decision that the word will begin to mean something else ("cessation of brain activity,") rather than "cessation of heartbeat or respiration"). The new definition was made necessary by the technology of life-support systems that can keep some human bodies breathing and operating for a long time when there is too little brain activity for consciousness. It is based on the belief that consciousness is more definitive of human life than are breath and pulse—as well as on an interest in legally and morally obtaining viable organs for transplants.

It is not necessary to define every term, of course. Many words are commonly used in various ways and understood by everybody. Often when words have several meanings, the context of a discussion will make it clear which meaning is the right one.

Trying to define all words would be a hopeless task in any case because we need some words just to define others. We look for a definition when we see a claim or argument that is hard to understand or seems very unreasonable as we would interpret it. Then we may suspect that the person speaking or writing might mean something other than we would.

For instance, suppose a person from England tells you that in England only the children of the upper classes go to public schools. This is an amazing statement from the point of view of North Americans. In North America, *public school* means "school supported by taxpayers and open to all children without special handicaps." In some areas, parents are dissatisfied with public schools and select private schools for which they must pay tuition fees (usually of at least several thousand dollars annually). Such parents are nearly always comparatively wealthy. The statement about England is very surprising against this background; it would surely be odd if only well-off people sent their children to public schools. We may suspect that the expression *public school* is used differently in England. And, indeed, this is true. In England, public schools are "endowed grammar schools—usually boarding schools—preparing students for university." The claim which seemed so peculiar makes perfect sense given this different definition.

When evaluating claims and arguments, we look for a definition when we suspect there may be a misunderstanding. Various kinds of definitions can be given, and it is useful to distinguish the different types.

Reportive Definitions.   A *reportive definition* is one that has the goal of accurately describing how a word is used. Its purpose is to state in a clear way the meaning of the word as people do use it. For example, a reportive definition of the word *chair* as used to refer to furniture is "a piece of furniture that is to seat one person; it typically has a straight back and is raised from the floor by legs." Such a definition is supposed to describe how people use the word *chair* to refer to pieces of furniture. They don't call stools chairs because stools don't have backs. They don't call sofas chairs because sofas seat more than one person. They do call large bags filled with small pellets *bean bag chairs* because they shape into a kind of back and seat and hold one person, even though they are not raised from the floor by legs. As used for a piece of furniture, the word *chair* poses few problems. It seems relatively easy to give a descriptive (reportive) definition.

However, even a simple word like *chair* has other meanings, as in "The chair [person in charge of a meeting] called the meeting to order" and "The college established a chair [professorial position] in Roman history." Usually the context makes clear which of these meanings is intended.

For reportive definitions, a dictionary is a good place to start. A dictionary seeks to describe how a word is actually used and uses other words to sum up that pattern of usage briefly. We must remember, however, that even dictionaries sometimes offer imperfect definitions. Because they have to be quite brief, they may leave out features that are important to understanding normal usage. Also, dictionaries may not reflect variation in use in different places and times.

A reportive definition is open to correction against facts of usage even when it comes from a dictionary. For one thing, the definition may be too broad (implying that the word can apply to more things than it really does) or too narrow (implying that it applies to fewer things than it really does). For instance, the *Abridged Oxford English Dictionary*, Fourth Edition (1951) defines *chair* (in the context of furniture) as "separate seat for one, of various forms." This definition may be criticized as too broad, because it allows stools and piano benches to count as chairs. A reference to a back is needed to make the definition describe common usage more closely. On the other hand, we have too narrow a definition if we define *chair* as "separate seat for one having a back and four legs" because many chairs have only three legs, and bean bag chairs have none.

In addition to being too broad or too narrow, reportive definitions may be inadequate in two other basic ways. They may use terms that are too obscure and, therefore, are not helpful in explaining the meaning of a word. For instance, a definition of *eating* as "successive performance of masticating, humectating, and deglutinating" would be open to this objection! Anyone who needed a definition of a simple English term like *eating* would not understand such complicated words to define it.

Reportive definitions may also be inadequate because the word to be defined occurs again in the definition. For instance, if we define *drug* as "substance commonly used to drug someone," we have a circular definition. The word *drug* is used again in the definition itself, so no progress in explanation can be made. A similar problem arises in proposed definitions such as "poets are literary artists who compose poetic works" or "philosophers are those intellectuals who study problems that are peculiarly philosophical."

To a certain extent, the seriousness of obscurity and circularity in definitions depends on the audience for whom those definitions are intended. The examples of obscurity and circularity just mentioned here are so extreme that virtually anybody who needed such a definition would find that the definition didn't help to explain the meaning of the term. Other examples might be obscure to some audiences but all right for others, or they might be circular in some contexts but legitimate in others. For instance, one dictionary defines *hocus pocus* as "jugglery, deception, or a typical conjuring formula." Though the words used in the definition are quite advanced, to many people they would be better known than the expression *hocus pocus* itself. Thus this definition can probably be helpful for many people. If *scholar* is defined as "one devoting his (or her) life to school and its disciplines," the circularity in the close relationship between *school* and *scholar* may well be harmless—nearly everyone knows what schools are. (This definition is open to other criticisms, however.)

People who know and use a language are in a position to check reportive definitions for themselves. If you can find a case where people would typically not use the word defined, even though the definition would allow it, the definition is too broad. If you can find a case where people would typically use the word although the definition would not allow it, the definition is too narrow. It can even happen that a definition is both too broad and too narrow! For instance, if we offered a reportive definition of *swimming pool* as "enclosed artificially constructed area of water intended for public use," this definition would be both too broad and too narrow. It would be too broad because it allows wading pools with only six inches of water to count as swimming pools. It would be too narrow because it requires that swimming pools be intended for public use. (Many people have private swimming pools.) You can also judge whether proposed definitions are too obscure or circular to be helpful to the people for whom they are intended.

Ostensive Definitions. It can be difficult to accurately describe the use of even quite ordinary words. People do not typically learn words from purely verbal definitions, of course. As children we learn our first language by participating in social life and by copying things others say and do. Often children are taught words by having objects pointed out to them. The technical name for this kind of procedure is *ostensive definition.* We can ostensively define *lime green*, for instance, by pointing to something that color. This direct approach is often very appropriate, and it is satisfying because it helps us tie language to the world we are talking about. However, it does not avoid all possibilities of misunderstanding. The person to whom the definition is given must attend to the features of the thing pointed out that are central to the meaning and use of the word. (If he is shown a swimming pool and mistakenly thinks the cement sides must be features of all swimming pools, he won't go on to use the word correctly even though it has been defined ostensively.)

Stipulative Definitions.　A *stipulative definition* is one in which someone creates or restricts word usage rather than describing it. He stipulates, or lays down, a meaning for a term. This may be done for a special purpose, such as in the context of a technical development of a subject or because we are actually inventing a new term. A stipulative definition does not have the purpose of reporting actual usage so we cannot test it against either dictionaries or the facts of ordinary usage.

An example of a stipulative definition is "For the purposes of this scholarship award, full-time student shall mean any student enrolled in eight or more semester-length courses in a given calendar year"—stated in the context of a description of a scholarship and explaining eligibility conditions. Such an explanation will stipulate how the expression *full-time student* is to be used in the competition for this scholarship. Its purpose is practical—to make applicants and administrators understand who is and who is not eligible for the award. A stipulative definition like this applies only in a limited context. Legal contracts and specific legislation may include stipulative definitions of similar kinds.

Definitions constructed in technical areas may become standard in those fields and may eventually extend to common usage. American mathematician Edward Kasner defined an expression for the number "10 raised to the 100th power." He called it a *googol*. The word is now found in some contemporary dictionaries. Robert E. Kelley of Carnegie-Mellon University coined a term *gold-collar worker*, which he defined as "an employee in a brain-intensive business who regards his or her intellect, experience, and inventiveness as monetary assets to be leveraged with respect to relationships with current or potential employers."[1] The distinction between blue-collar (factory) and white-collar (office) workers is often supplemented by *pink-collar workers*, a term already in some popular use to refer to female workers who occupy secretarial positions with relatively little independent decision-making power. Kelley has coined this further term, presumably because he thinks the creative intellectual worker in a certain business has a distinct economic and social role that makes him or her importantly different from other white-collar workers. Perhaps the term will come into common usage.

We might think that stipulative definitions cannot really be criticized. It seems natural to suppose that if a person is laying down a meaning for a term, that person has the final say on what the term means. This is not quite correct, though. Usually, stipulative definitions are made for some particular purpose, and they can be criticized with reference to that purpose. A scholarship eligibility condition requiring an eligible person to be a full-time student and defining *full-time student* as "student who is enrolled in at least fifteen semester courses in a calendar year and does no nonacademic work for pay" could be criticized as too narrow to be fair. A stipulative definition should serve the interests of those who need it, and it can rightly be criticized when it fails to do so.

In the case of words that have very important social, moral, or emotional content, stipulations that go too far from ordinary usage can be very misleading, and they can be criticized for that reason if the stipulated meaning is intended for public use.[2] For instance, if a university defined *science* as "the quantifiable study of the nonhuman physical world" and then insisted, on the basis of this definition, that psychology and mathematics were not sciences, it would be open to criticism for having made an unreasonably narrow stipulation that would be misleading to students, prospective employers, and the public at large.

People may seek to win arguments merely by stipulating definitions, but this strategy is unfair and misleading. To see this, suppose we stipulate that *resource* means "any valuable substance in the earth owned jointly by all the world's people." We can then argue that since oil is a resource, all the world's people jointly own all the world's oil. But this stipulation only hides the moral and political issue of ownership of the world's materials. Obviously, if anyone believes that separate nations separately own those valuable materials within their own territory, then he will not be willing to call these *resources* in the stipulated sense. Oil is a resource, as the word *resource* is normally used. The proposed stipulation only confuses the issue and seeks to avoid an important substantive question. The conclusion might be correct, but no reasons are given for it when the only premise is based on an implicit stipulative definition.

If a stipulation gains currency, as with *googol*, the word then becomes part of public language, and it is open to changes and variations in use just as other words are. Its original author loses his authority as the only person who can say for certain what the word means. If Kelley's term *gold-collar worker* becomes part of our language, it will not be up to just him to say, for instance, whether computer programmers are or are not gold-collar workers. This decision will depend both on facts about the creativity and ambitions of computer programmers and on how the expression *gold-collar worker* comes to be used by the general public.

Persuasive Definitions.   A fourth type of definition is rather like a stipulative definition, but it is disguised. In a persuasive definition, there is an attempt to alter beliefs and attitudes by redefining a term. Often words like *true, real*, and *genuine* are used in stating these definitions. Suppose we were told that a real democracy is one in which the voice of the people can be heard without interference from the press. The implication would be that the United States, Canada, and other western countries are not real democracies because their people can achieve a wide audience for their views only by working through the mass press or other mass media such as television. Thus this definition would be a disguised redefinition of *democracy* for the purpose of persuasion. Most people have favorable attitudes toward democracy. By imposing a new condition for *real* democracy, a person would be trying to transfer those attitudes to a different kind of state and society.

The concept of persuasive definition was first put forward by philosopher Charles L. Stevenson more than forty years ago. Stevenson developed it in the context of his interest in moral reasoning. He emphasized that some words have a very strong emotional component and that people may wish to preserve the attitudes accompanying them while changing the factual basis for applying the words. Terms like *art, justice, freedom, socialism*, and *security* are particularly common objects of this technique. Stevenson quoted an example from a novel by Aldous Huxley:

> But if you want to be free, you've got to be a prisoner. It's the condition of freedom— true freedom.
>
>   "True freedom!" Anthony repeated in the parody of a clerical voice. "I always love that kind of argument. The contrary of a thing isn't the contrary; oh, dear me, no! It's the thing itself, but as it truly is. Ask any die-hard what conservatism is; he'll tell you it's true socialism. And the brewer's trade papers: they're full of articles about the beauty of true temperance. Ordinary temperance is just gross refusal to drink; but true temperance, true temperance is something much more refined. True temperance is a bottle of claret with each meal and three double whiskies after dinner. . . ."

"What's in a name?" Anthony went on. *"The answer is, practically everything, if the name's a good one. Freedom's a marvellous name. That's why you're so anxious to make use of it. You think that, if you call imprisonment true freedom, people will be attracted to the prison. And the worst of it is, you're quite right."*[3]

The important thing about persuasive definitions is to notice them and not be tricked into transferring favorable or unfavorable attitudes on the basis of someone else's idea of the *real, true,* meaning of a word.

EXERCISE SET

Exercise One

1. Consult a recent dictionary for reportive definitions of the following words. Are the dictionary definitions open to any criticisms such as being too broad, too narrow, circular, or obscure? If so, explain the problem and fix the definition so that it is more accurate.
   a. geography
   b. preacher
   c. swimming
   d. money
   e. shy

2. Construct your own reportive definitions for the following terms and, if possible, have a friend check their accuracy and usefulness.
   a. triangle
   b. judge (as court official)
   c. mercury
   d. allergy
   e. language (*hard*)

3. Assume that the following are put forward as reportive definitions. Test their adequacy as to whether they are too broad, too narrow, circular, or obscure.
   *a. "Money is a medium of exchange."
   b. "A brave man is one who does not run away when the enemy approaches."
   *c. "A liberal is a practical person with no real political principles who is ready to compromise anywhere between socialism and conservatism when the situation demands it."
   d. "A hawk is a bird of prey used in falconry, with rounded wings shorter than a falcon's."
   *e. "To study is to concentrate very hard with the goal of remembering what you are concentrating on."

4. Specify appropriate stipulative definitions for the following situations:
   a. You are making a legal agreement to rent a small building. After discussion, you and the landlord have agreed that you will, on the terms of the lease, be able to use the building either as a private residence or as the site of a small family business. You want to be able to live there with three friends, not related to you, and he agrees to this. Also, you want to conduct either a modest secretarial business, taking in papers to type, or a small daycare center, admitting five to ten children. He agrees to this, but he does not want you to have any business that will bring a lot of traffic or noisy machinery to the neighborhood. Construct suitable stipulative definitions for *private residence* and *small family business* that will serve your purposes and those of the landlord.
   b. Your English teacher has asked you to write an essay comparing the novels of two great twentieth-century English novelists. You wish to write an introduction to your essay, explaining why you have chosen Theodore Dreiser (American) and Margaret Atwood (Canadian). Give a stipulative definition of *great twentieth-century English novelists* that will serve your purposes without deviating too far from standard usage. *Hint:* Concentrate on the terms *great* and *English.*
   *c. You are moderating a panel on terrorism. The other members of the panel are an American–Irish sympathizer of the Irish Republican Army (a violent group active in Northern Ireland and Great Britain) and a spokesperson for the Reagan administration, which has been greatly concerned about violence by anti-Israeli groups to civilians, particularly American citizens on airplanes in Europe and the Middle East. You wish to stipulate a definition of *terrorist* that the other panel members will agree to and that will help the discussion be as reasonable as possible.
   d. You are a civil servant working for the income tax department. Tax credits are allowed for donations to charitable institutions or groups, but there are disputed groups. These groups include antinuclear groups offering films about the dangers of the nuclear arms race for use in schools; "right to life" groups offering counselling to women with unwanted pregnancies and seeking laws to make abortion strictly illegal; the Girl Guides and Boy Scouts of

America; and the United Nations Association, an educational and fund-raising group organizing events intended to further the goals of the United Nations. Suggest a stipulative definition of *charitable institutions or groups* that would help the tax department make efficient and reasonable decisions.

e. You own a small orchard and have been experimenting grafting branches of some trees onto other trees. By clever experimentation, you have produced a fruit that is a cross between an apple and a pear. Coin a word for your new fruit, and stipulate a definition for it.

5. Which of the following are persuasive definitions? How can you tell that the definition is persuasive, and what attitudes is the speaker trying to change?

a. "Reform means having me as your new leader." (Comment by a candidate for the leadership of the Social Credit party in British Columbia, quoted on CBC television, July 7, 1986.)

b. "With our earth shoes and the lowered heel, you can do pure walking." (Adapted from an ad popular in the 70s.)

*c. Tea is a beverage consumed widely in England, particularly in the afternoon.

d. A true intellectual is one who takes nothing on authority and is always willing to explore new problems for himself.

*e. A policeman is a criminal with a special license from the government to assault or even kill people whose activities he disapproves of.

f. A mammal is a kind of animal in which the female of the species supplies milk to its young.

g. A genuine student is one who is working not for grades and not for future income but out of curiosity, dedication, and a love of knowledge.

h. Photography is not an art because art requires artificial reproduction of reality and photography is a natural reproduction that does not select among those aspects of reality to be presented. (*hard*)

i. I shall mean by *total institution* an institution such as an asylum or prison in which there are physical barriers preventing the free departure of inmates and the free entry of visitors. (Adapted from sociologist Erving Goffman.)

j. Consciousness must include self-consciousness. An infant or animal not aware of itself may be believed to feel twinges of pain or fleeting moments of pleasure. But it is not really conscious because real consciousness requires that a being have an idea of itself as a single subject that can extend into past and future. (Adapted from philosopher Immanuel Kant.) (*hard*)

k. An obituary is a brief notice of death including a shortened biography of the deceased person, customarily published in a newspaper.

*l. "Insanity is the product of an accurate mind overtaxed." (Adapted from Oliver Wendall Holmes.)

m. "Objectivity in journalism is an act of advocacy for the status quo."
(Tom Wicker, *The New York Times*.) (*Hint*: A key question here is whether or not you regard this statement as trying to offer a definition.)

Further Features of Language

Ambiguity. A simple example of ambiguity can be seen in the newspaper headline "Home Delivery Sought." As it stands, this headline might refer either to a desire for babies to be born at home rather than in hospitals or to a desire for mail to be delivered to private homes rather than to group mailboxes. In such a case, the ambiguity is easily resolved when we read the accompanying story. Other ambiguities can be more significant and harder to detect. A word may have several meanings, any of which could fit naturally in the context in which it is used. It is important to watch for this; if you miss it, you may not understand what is said. Arguments and claims often gain a spurious plausibility because of hidden ambiguities.

Consider, in this connection, the very common claim that "Evolution is only a theory." The word *theory* has two different meanings:

───── *Meaning (1):* "Theory": A theory is a mere speculation that is not fully supported by any firm facts.

Meaning (2): "Theory": A theory is a body of scientific principles that are intended to explain observed phenomena.

When people insist that evolutionary theory is "only" a theory and go on to criticize the educational system for concentrating on it, they must be using *theory* to express meaning (1). But in this sense of *theory,* it is by no means obviously true that evolutionary theory is a theory. In the second sense of *theory,* it is true that evolutionary theory is a theory, but there is no reason not to teach theories in science classes. The comment gets its force from confusing meaning (1) and meaning (2) of *theory* in "Evolution is only a theory." The first meaning would allow the inference that this view isn't the only one that should be taught; the second makes it obviously true that evolutionary doctrine is theory. By confusing the two meanings, people making this comment can get both acceptance of their view and the social consequence they desire.

We can see, then, that it is very important to try to get meanings clear. If structures or words are ambiguous in the contexts in which they are used, several different meanings could be intended. No analysis of an argument that ignores this factor can hope to be complete or correct. Needless to say, if you are constructing your own argument, you should make your structures and terms as unambiguous as possible. If you use a term, such as *theory,* which has several distinct meanings, you should make it clear which sense of the term you are using.

We haven't said very much yet about standards for evaluating arguments as good or bad, but you can see that being aware of different interpretations is bound to be important. Here is an example in which an argument on an important subject incorporates a very significant ambiguity. The argument was offered by black activist Jesse Jackson in the summer of 1978. At that time Andrew Young was the American ambassador to the United Nations, and Mr. Young had made the very controversial and unpopular statement that there are large numbers of political prisoners in the United States. In the public uproar following this statement, Jackson argued that Young was quite correct. This was his argument, as it was reported in a Canadian newspaper:

> *"Thousands are in jail because they are too poor to pay bail bond," Jackson said. "Thousands are in jails because of delayed trials. Thousands are in jail because they don't have the political clout to be released on personal recognizance. Thousands are in jail because they were not tried by a jury of their peers. That is political."*[4]

Jackson wanted to demonstrate that there are thousands of political prisoners in the United States. Let us look at this intended conclusion and ask ourselves what *political* means in the expression "political prisoner." A political prisoner is one who is imprisoned because of his political beliefs—because of his beliefs about how the government and state should function. Now if we look at Jackson's premises, we see that he is referring to various factors that are causes of some people being in jail: poverty, delayed trials, lack of power, and lack of trial by peers. These factors are undesirable to be sure, and they don't give much justification (as opposed to explanation) for people being in jail. But do these factors indicate, or prove, that the prisoners are political prisoners? They specify causes, and these causes are in some sense political. But in what sense? A delayed trial is political only in the sense that it is a product of the political system and could be different if the political system were changed. The term *political* has this meaning for all the other factors Jackson mentions too. Thus *political,* as used in "that is political," must mean simply "due to the political structures and alterable by alteration of those structures." That is, the term *political* is used very differently in the premises and in the conclusion. The premises really have no bearing on the conclusion, but we could miss that fact due to the ambiguity of the term *political.*

Ambiguity is not the only problem we can find with language. As we have seen, ambiguity occurs when the language, as it is used in the context, could have several quite distinct meanings. We don't know just which one is appropriate. Or, as in the last case, the very same word is used with several distinct meanings in the same context, and these meanings seem not to be distinguished from each other, leading to imprecision and flaws in argument. Another major problem with language is *vagueness*.

Vagueness.   We speak sometimes of words being vague. This way of speaking is slightly misleading, for really vagueness arises from the way a word is used in a particular context. If the context is one requiring that we be able to determine when the word applies to a thing and we cannot determine that due to insufficient precision in the word, that word is used vaguely, and the vagueness in the language will pose a practical problem. However, the very same word might be used in another context in such a way that there is no problem of vagueness. For example, if a buyer tells a real estate agent that he needs a big house for his family, *big* in that context is too vague. The agent needs guidance as to how many bedrooms, bathrooms, and so on, the person has in mind. What one means by *big house* can vary a great deal; if the agent is going to search for houses, he needs more precise guidance than he will get from the unclarified expression "we need a big house." On the other hand, if a woman comments that size 16 is a big size in women's dresses, it is probably not necessary to have further clarification of just what she means by *big*. The point is that the size is bigger than average and bigger than the person would like to wear herself. It is of no great practical importance to attach a precise meaning to "size 16 is a big size" in the context of this familiar lament.

Ambiguity arises when a word, as used, might have several distinct meanings and we are unable to tell which of these it has. Vagueness arises when a word, as used, has a meaning that is insufficiently clear to convey the necessary information in that context of use. To contrast vagueness and ambiguity, you might think of words as being used to mark out boundaries. With a word used vaguely, the boundaries are fuzzy so that we cannot see just which area is marked out. With a word used ambiguously, there are several different bounded areas, and we won't know which of these the word is pointing to.

When you have written down an argument's premises and conclusions, read each one over carefully to make sure you know what is being asserted. Are there any statements that are so vaguely stated that you honestly wouldn't know how to tell whether they are true or false? Sometimes you don't know whether statements are true because you don't know the relevant facts. For instance, we don't know how many people in the Republic of China claim to have at least one Jewish ancestor because we don't know the relevant facts. But sometimes we don't know whether statements are true because the language in which they are worded is just not clear enough. For instance, we don't know whether the Jewish people constitute a distinct race because *race* is too vague. The same problem arises with the question of whether French Canadians constitute a distinct nation within Canada. Unless we specify a clear meaning for *race* or *nation*, the issues have no determinate answer. When terms like this surface in an argument, you should try to specify a more precise meaning appropriate to the context and then check to make sure that that same meaning will be appropriate each time the term is used. If it's just impossible to do this, you may decide that the premise or conclusion in which the vagueness occurs is just too indeterminate to be either accepted or rejected.

Vagueness can be dangerous in legal or administrative contexts because it permits abuse. For instance, if it is illegal to loiter, and if there is no clarification in law or custom as to what *loitering* is, police can charge teenagers with loitering whenever they choose and ignore middle-aged citizens who stand around on street corners. A currently popular term that is vague in a rather dangerous way is *sexual harassment*. This term needs considerable clarification before it can be part of a suitable code of ethics or legal rights. An indication of the wide range of meanings people attach to the term can be found in the following passage, based on a 1981 survey by the women's magazine *Glamour*:

> *How do you define sexual harassment? Fifty percent say that even sexual comments, innuendoes and jokes constitute sexual harassment, while at the other end of the spectrum, 8 percent regard only an explicit sexual invitation as harassment. "My boss harassed me to the point of pulling down his pants and showing me pictures of himself nude. But even a meaningful stare can be harassing."*
>
> *What do you consider sexual harassment? Fifty percent say sexual comments, innuendoes, or jokes; 33 percent say touching, or unnecessary closeness; 6 percent say suggestions for outside meetings; 8 percent say explicit sexual invitation; 2 percent say other.*[5]

Without further agreement about what constitutes sexual harassment, it hardly makes sense to formulate policies to deal with it. Sexual harassment is a serious problem, but reasonable policies to cope with it will have to clarify terms. Clarification of language will have to be the first step here, and then a reasonable policy can be adopted.

Just as arguments can get their persuasiveness from ambiguity, some can trade on vagueness. The arguer may begin with a vague term and proceed through his argument applying the term to anything and everything, getting away with it because the term is so vague that it's not easy to say he's wrong. Here is an example:

> *There are two types of abuse of children. The first is described as extreme and includes such elements as murder, rape and incest, multiple bruises, broken bones, gross neglect, and starvation. In many instances such abuse is fatal. The second form of abuse is more general and more moderate in that while it neither kills nor fatally wounds, it may do considerable psychological harm. Included in this abuse are parental and professional neglect through ignoring parents, inattentive teachers, and incompetent professionals. In addition, hundreds of children are abused because they are unwanted, poor, or are victims of the undue expectations of adults, or are subjected to authoritarianism in the name of religion, tradition and discipline, to physical punishment at home and at school, to name calling, to judgmental comparison, to the achievement syndrome, to pornography and violence, and to unnecessary labelling that proves to be detrimental.*
>
> *Children suffer abuse as well, I think, when budgetary restraints limit daycare or render it of poor quality, deny needed services for the handicapped, close school libraries, and force children to be bussed hundreds of miles a week in unsafe vehicles.*[6]

At the beginning of this passage, the author seems to be using *abuse* as it is normally used in "child abuse": deliberate assault or gross neglect resulting in physical harm. We should be on the alert when he starts to speak of "moderate abuse." As the word *abuse* is usually used, "moderate abuse" would be a contradiction in terms! It turns out that inattentive teachers and insufficiently funded daycare systems also *abuse* children, according to this author. By *abuse* now, he must simply mean "harm"; note that this is a much less precise meaning than he started out with and that it is also a departure from the meaning *abuse* usually has in contexts where people speak of child abuse. The stretching of language is virtually absurd when the author comes to the point of calling the unnecessary labelling of children *abuse*. This may not be a good thing, but to use the same term for it and for gross physical beating is to stretch language too much. This author makes *abuse* so vague that it loses its meaning. (Think about it. Why would he want to do this?)

Emotionally Charged Language.   These questions about the motivations behind vague or ambiguous language lead naturally to another topic: the role of language as a substitute for rational argument and as a disguise for the fact that controversial points have not been argued at all. We have seen that it is important to pay attention to language in interpreting speech or writing, and we noted that some arguments exploit ambiguity or vagueness so that people who are not on the alert for problems of language may be deceived by them. But much more common than these failings is the use of language in such a way that controversial issues are settled by wording, not by argument. Whatever child abuse is, we are bound to be against it, because *abuse* is an emotionally negative term. You can see this better, perhaps, by imagining that a friend tells you his dentist *abuses* him. Most people's dentists hurt them to a degree, at least when the needle goes in. We don't normally call this abuse, however, because the hurting is done for a beneficial purpose, not to bring harm to the patient. By saying his dentist *abuses* him, your friend would be making a very critical remark because *abuse* is an emotionally negative word. Clearly this is why the author of the paragraph about child abuse is stretching the word so much. He is against child pornography, inadequate daycare funding, and all the other things he terms *abuse;* by calling them all cases of child abuse, he can convey the idea that they are bad without having to argue for it.

Good and bad arguments are common in all the academic disciplines and in ordinary life, but the substitution of emotionally loaded, persuasive language for argument is perhaps even more common. It would be unrealistic to insist that all language should be emotionally neutral. It isn't clear that this is possible, and even if it were, it would make writing and speaking terribly boring. What we should be on the watch for is emotionally loaded language that conveys a view on a controversial point where there is just no supporting evidence.

To see how this works, take a look at the following two brief letters, both of which were sent to *Time* magazine shortly after the Reagan election in 1980.

> (a) *Reagan is our clown prince, and we are his foolish subjects. Don't look now, America, but the whole world is laughing. Maybe he deserved an Academy Award for his startling performance, but he certainly didn't deserve to be President.*[7]

> (b) *Laurence Barret's pre-election piece on Candidate Ronald Reagan was a slick hatchet job, and you know it. You ought to be ashamed of yourselves for printing it disguised as an objective look at the man.*[8]

Clearly the author of (a) believed Reagan is not qualified to be president. The author of (b) seems to support Reagan in that he expresses hostility to a critical piece *Time* ran on him, calling it "a slick hatchet job." Neither (a) nor (b) contains any argument or evidence. In (a) the author gives absolutely no basis for thinking Reagan is not qualified to be president; nor does he give any reason for his view that Americans who voted for Reagan in 1980 made a silly mistake. In (b) the author gives no basis for calling the piece slick, cites no errors in it, and gives no reason to back up his judgment that the piece was only disguised as objective. Both passages use loaded language instead of argument (a) in referring to the "clown prince" and his "subjects," and (b) in its use of "slick hatchet job." If these two letter writers were to get together, they would no doubt strongly disagree on political affairs in the United States. But they would never be able to resolve their disagreement if they stuck to the practice of hurling emotionally loaded words into a discussion! They could reach agreement (if ever) only by getting down to the issue of what does or does not make Reagan a person qualified to be a president.

If you look at (a) and (b) carefully, you will see that you cannot find a conclusion in either one; nor can you find supporting premises. In (a) the writer calls Reagan a "clown prince," suggesting that he is rather silly and that he is lording it over the voters. And he refers to the voters as "foolish subjects," suggesting that they don't know what they are doing and that they are powerless (*subject* to this "clown"). He comments that everyone is laughing at Americans and says Reagan did not deserve to be elected president. Here there is no argument, and there is not one bit of support for the judgment he is trying to convey about Reagan's abilities. The language, especially "clown prince" and "foolish subjects," carries the burden.

Similar comments can be made about (b). Look at it again. You cannot find a conclusion or premises, for (b) does not contain any argument. The writer states his case firmly, using strong terms like "slick hatchet job" and "ashamed"; he does not say why *Time*'s coverage was not "objective."

Passages like these do not contain any failings in argument because they don't express arguments at all. You should notice that a controversial viewpoint is expressed with no supporting argument, and note the emotional tone of the language used. You do not want to let the language carry you into the author's viewpoint for no good reason.

Here is another letter illustrating the same thing:

> Indonesia's Mochtar Lubis hit the nail right on the head concerning the so-called free and balanced flow of information. The Third World attempt at news management represents little more than a self-serving exercise in journalism designed for the self-perpetuation of some authoritarian regime. National development is not supposed to be a juggernaut demanding the sacrifice of freedom of speech and justice. What developing countries cannot afford is not the luxury of a critical press, but the white elephant of an inept or corrupt government.[9]

A writer in Taiwan sent this letter to *Discover* after the magazine had run an article about efforts by non-European countries to see that coverage of their affairs was not done solely by European and North American journalists affiliated with large western news networks. (Their complaint had been that lack of linguistic and cultural understanding, and a concern for western interests particularly, had led to distorted coverage of Third World affairs.) In the first sentence the writer agrees with an Indonesian commentator, who had apparently criticized the effort. In the second sentence he expresses his disapproval of the Third World journalistic movement, saying it is little more than a "self-serving exercise" and that it is "designed for the self-perpetuation of some authoritarian regime." There is no argument here; again, we have loaded language as a substitute for argument. No reason is given that such a journalists' movement would have to be self-serving, nor that it would always work to buttress authoritarian regimes. (In fact, given that western countries often back authoritarian regimes in such parts of the world, we might suspect that nonwestern coverage would work against those authoritarian regimes.) The third and fourth sentences of the letter suggest an argument, although they do not clearly state one. A *juggernaut* is a great big useless thing; the writer says that national development shouldn't be a juggernaut pursued by the "sacrifice" of freedom of speech and justice. By saying this, he suggests, but does not quite state, that the Third World press movement is proposing to limit freedom of speech in order to further development in the Third World. No substantiation is made for this accusation. The final sentence states that developing countries can't afford a corrupt or inept government. Surely few would disagree with this point, but the writer helps it along with some more loaded language in "white elephant."

The argument that these last two sentences suggests could be:

1. Developing countries need a critical press.
2. Developing countries do not need an inept or corrupt government.
3. A critical press will help to prevent a government from remaining in power when it is inept or corrupt.
4. New efforts by Third World journalists to manage some of their own news would mean that there would not be a critical press in the Third World. Therefore,
5. New efforts by Third World journalists to manage some of their own news are misguided.

However, we have to do a great deal of tidying up to extract this argument from the letter. We have read in much material that is not stated in order to supply two premises and a conclusion. When this much alteration is required, we cannot plausibly interpret the original passage as containing an argument. Basically, the writer has relied on language to carry his allegations and opinions (in *self-serving, self-perpetuation, authoritarian, juggernaut, sacrifice,* and *white elephant*). In the argument we constructed, which *might* be extracted from the letter, the premises don't have much to do with the conclusion unless we write in (4), stating the premise that these efforts would mean the absence of a critical press. That claim is never argued for; we are to be lured into accepting it by the expression "self-serving exercise . . . for the perpetuation of some authoritarian regime."

Emotionally charged language, then, can work as a substitute for argument—a kind of disguise for the fact that a speaker or writer has no evidence or reasons to back up his controversial views. In addition, it can work within an argument to carry over questionable claims and suggest the author's views. Even when an author or speaker has an argument, he may rely on a premise that really should be defended in a subargument but is not. Stating that premise using words such as *vicious, abuse, splendid reform, sacrifice, white elephant, clown, shining achievement,* and so on, can disguise the fact that it needs defending just as it can hide the complete absence of argument. Here is an example:

1. The church is led by old-fashioned and ill-informed old men who wouldn't have a hope of understanding the oppression of women.
2. People who don't understand a problem are not the proper ones to educate others about that problem.
3. The church should play some role in educating people about social problems.
So,
4. Women within the church should take the lead in educating others about women's oppression.

Here the emotionally charged terms are *old-fashioned, ill-informed, old men,* and *oppression.* The first premise really should be defended in a subargument, but it is carried by loaded language instead. There is no support for the views that the leaders of the church are old men, that they do not know pertinent facts about women, that they are old-fashioned, or that women are oppressed. All these notions would likely be controversial in any context where this argument would be needed. We have emphasized loaded language as a substitute for a whole argument (which it often is), but we see here how it can work within a larger argument as well. Either way, the reader or listener is supposed to go along with the arguer's viewpoint for no reason.

Euphemism.   Euphemism might be seen as the opposite of loaded language. With loaded language, terms are more emotional than appropriate. Euphemism, on the other hand, involves a kind of whitewashing effect of language. Bland, abstract, polite language is used to refer to things which, in a more concrete description, would be found appalling, horrible, or embarrassing. Language can function to dull our awareness of such things.

In 1946 author George Orwell wrote a famous essay called "Politics and the English Language," attacking the use of euphemism in political speech. Orwell pointed out that people are led to condone political horror partly because of the use of euphemism. If thousands of peasants are evicted from their villages and have to flee on foot, there will be great suffering, but when we call such a procedure "the rectifying of the frontier," we are almost sure to forget these human consequences. Comments like "There is extensive fighting in the de-militarized zone" (notorious during the Vietnam War) should cause us to stop and think. If the zone really is de-militarized, there cannot be fighting there. If there is fighting, it is a war zone and should be named appropriately.

When the nuclear reactor at Three Mile Island was close to a dangerous meltdown, many commentators were still following the nuclear industry in calling the crisis an "incident." This expression is euphemistic in functioning to minimize the seriousness of the situation. In the face of criticism of American nuclear policy from the nuclear freeze movement in 1982, President Reagan called the controversial MX missile system the "Peacekeeper." The name discourages us from thinking about the millions of deaths the weapons carried on this missile would cause if it were used, and it encourages us to assume uncritically that it would help prevent a Russian nuclear attack. An even more extreme example, again from military thinking, is the expression "violent peace," used by Pentagon analysts to describe a doctrine of "low-intensity conflict" throughout the Third World as a substitute for direct nuclear confrontation between the United States and the Soviet Union.[10]

The following letter to the editor criticizes a major Canadian newspaper for using euphemisms in an editorial about treatment of institutionalized retarded children.

> *Your editorial on behavior modification is ethically indefensible.*
>
> *Behavior modification procedures—such as aversion therapy, including electro-shock and electric cattle-prod shocks inflicted on institutionalized retarded children—are unethical. They are forms of cruel and unusual punishment, not treatment. They all should be immediately abolished in Ontario and everywhere else in Canada.*
>
> *Yet they are still legal, and Canadian psychiatrists are still inflicting these tortures masquerading as treatment on many mentally ill and retarded children and adults.*
>
> *Incredibly, the* Globe and Mail *believes that such torture is perfectly all right, as long as it's "clearly appropriate and . . . closely monitored." Torture, whether labelled "treatment" or "behavior modification," is never appropriate, as its victims know all too well.[11]*

This writer objects to a euphemistic use of language in which the use of an electric cattle-prod on a retarded child can be called "appropriate treatment" or "behavior modification" or "aversion therapy."

Euphemisms are not always a problem. They are innocent when the aspects of reality blurred over are things that it is not really important for us to think about. For instance, if garbage men are called "sanitary engineers," the euphemism is pretentious but probably harmless. The usage may slightly increase the self-respect of garbage men, and probably does not limit our understanding of what these workers do. Similarly, the custom of saying "I need to use the washroom" instead of "I need to go to the toilet" or (more frankly) "I need to urinate" likely does no harm.

Euphemistic language is dangerous to our understanding when the aspects of reality blurred over are aspects that we need to think about. War, nuclear energy, nuclear weapons policy, and therapy techniques are areas in which immense suffering can be caused or great benefits obtained. These matters are profoundly important. If words like "incident" and "peacekeeper" hide serious harms and risks and discourage us from thinking about them, they are dangerous—just as Orwell maintained.

Concluding Comments

The points we have been making here about language should be applied to your own writing and speaking as well. You can see how frustrating it is when wording is ambiguous or vague and you cannot determine just what is being said. This discussion should provide an incentive to make your writing as unambiguous and precise as the topic permits. You can also see what a cheat it is to substitute loaded language for evidence and reasoning or to hide important suffering and cruelty by using bland euphemistic words. Such words are dishonest ways of getting a point across. Language should neither prejudice our attitudes on matters of controversy nor disguise relevant features of realities that may be ugly.

Review of Terms Introduced

Reportive definition: A definition seeking to describe how a word is actually used.

Ostensive definition: A kind of reportive definition in which the meaning of a word is indicated by pointing at the thing the word applies to.

Stipulative definition: A definition specifying a new or special use for a word.

Persuasive definition: A definition, usually implicit, in which there is an attempt to give a new factual content to a word while preserving its previous emotional associations.

Ambiguity: Language is used ambiguously if, in the context in which a word appears, it could have any one of several distinct meanings.

Vagueness: A word is used vaguely if, in the context in which it appears, we cannot determine what things or what sorts of things the word would apply to.

Emotionally charged, or "loaded" language: Language with strong emotional tone, whether negative or positive.

Euphemism: Bland, polite, usually abstract language used to refer to things that are embarrassing, terrible, or in some other way appalling. Euphemisms disguise these undesirable features.

EXERCISE SET

Exercise Two

Check the following statements and arguments to see whether they contain examples of ambiguity, vagueness, or loaded language. If you find an example of ambiguity, explain which features of the passage give rise to this ambiguity and state what the possible different meanings are. In the case of vagueness, explain where vagueness arises and see whether there is a more precise expression that you can substitute to make the meaning more clear. If you find loaded language, note loaded terms and say whether you think they are functioning to hide the lack of rational argument.

*1. John is tall compared to Peter and he is short compared to Jim. Therefore John is both tall and short!

2. You can't lose weight unless you love yourself, and you can't love yourself unless you lose weight. Loving yourself requires respect for yourself, and no self-respecting person could bear to be fifty pounds overweight.

3. Those who say that education will help to prevent AIDS are nothing but two-bit do-gooders, blind optimists, and knee jerk liberals.

*4. *Background:* Carl Sagan produced a popular science presentation for television, called "Cosmos." *Time* magazine printed an extensive article covering the series. The following letter appeared in the wake of *Time's* story:
"Sagan promotes Sagan and 'Cosmos' promotes Sagan. As he postures before lingering cameras and delivers overdramatic monologues from *Star Wars*, he skillfully blends fact with fiction, leaving viewers perplexed. By adding gimmicks and schmaltz to fascinating scientific subjects, Sagan cheapens them. This type of presentation imbues science with the razzle-dazzle of show biz and reduces it to bubble gum mentality. Fortunately a flick of the TV dial can leave Sagan out in space."
(Letter to the editor, *Time*, November 24, 1980.)

5. People are not all the same. Therefore, they are not equal.

*6. Homosexuality must be natural because it appears in the animal kingdom in a variety of species and under a variety of circumstances. People have said that because homosexuality is unnatural, it's wrong. But this view is just mistaken. Homosexuality is natural and, therefore, it is good.

*7. Putting people in prison without trial is oppression. Making people fearful of the government is oppression. Taxing people is oppression. Making children go to school is oppression. Having parents care for children is oppression. Every human society is based on some or all of these practices. Therefore, every human society is based on oppression.

8. *Background:* Jan Roberts, of Elmira, New York, was mentioned in a *Psychology Today* article and was referred to as a housewife. She wrote to the magazine in December 1980 to object to this form of reference:
"In regard to the mention of me in John Kofend's article as a 'housewife' who is susceptible to trances . . . while I enjoy my house, I don't have any sexual relationship with it; I am not the wife of a house."

9. *Background:* In the fall of 1980 the Ontario government was planning cuts in funding daycare as part of a general austerity program. Daycare workers and parents demonstrated in protest, with young children accompanying them. Asked to comment on the protest, Keith Norton, then provincial minister of Community and Social Services, said:
"I refuse to participate in any demonstration that exploits young children. It is irresponsible in my view to use children as pawns in the political arena."
(Toronto *Globe and Mail*, October 24, 1980.)

10. *Background:* We have seen part of this advertisement already. In this case, concentrate on the use of language, and see whether you think the ad is exploiting ambiguity, vagueness, or loaded language in order to get a point across. The ad appeared in *Harper's* in October 1980:
"*Mother Nature is lucky her products don't need labels.* All foods, even natural ones, are made up of chemicals. But natural foods don't have to list their ingredients. So it's often assumed they're chemical-free. In fact, the ordinary orange is a miniature chemical factory. And the good old potato contains arsenic among its more than 150 ingredients. This doesn't mean natural foods are dangerous. If they were, they wouldn't be on the market. All man-made foods are tested for safety. And they often provide more nutrition, at a lower cost, than natural foods. They even use many of the same chemical ingredients. So you see, there really isn't much

difference between foods made by Mother Nature and those made by man. What's artificial is the line drawn between them."

11. "Art is energy. It is a privileged communication that passes between something and the spirit of a human."
(R. Pannell, "Arts Criticism: How Valid Is It?" Toronto *Globe and Mail*, March 3, 1979.)

12. There is no commonsense wisdom because sense isn't common.

13. "Humility is, however, the first requisite to understanding, and it is comforting to discover economists who are at least privately admitting that they no longer have full confidence in their omniscience. It is a good sign and the beginning of wisdom."
(George W. Ball, "An Overdose of Economists," *Washington Post*, July 4, 1980.)

14. Jones: Pesticides are safe because they have been used for a long time, and there is only a small chance that they will cause cancer or widespread environmental damage.
White: This is an outrageous position you are putting forward! Pesticides cannot be safe. They are chemical agents introduced unnaturally into the environment. There is some risk that they will harm the water, air, plants, fish, animals, and humans. Whenever there is some risk of damage, a product is not safe.
(*Hint:* What does "safe" mean?)

*15. There's no reason for professors and teachers to try to cultivate independent thinking in their students. Independent thinkers would have to start human knowledge again from scratch, and what would be the point of doing that? There's no point. Students should forget about independence and learn from their masters.

16. *Background: Harper's* published an article entitled "Coming to Terms with Vietnam" by Peter Marin. The article developed the theme that Americans have tried to bury, rather than solve, a number of psychological and political problems that arose from the Vietnam War. It occasioned a number of letters, including the following:
"Peter Marin's 'Coming to Terms with Vietnam' comes to terms with nothing. It is full of liberal intellectual horseshit, and its mention of guilt, as it deals exclusively with Vietnam vets, does not deal with the current totalitarian horrors in Vietnam, Laos, and Cambodia that the war was meant to abolish. Jane Fonda and her pro-totalitarian pals are not only without guilt concerning the boat people, the poison-gassed Laotians, and the Cambodian victims of the Khmer Rouge genocide; they are avid apologists for such practices."
(The letter appeared in *Harper's* in January 1981.)

*17. *Background:* On April 15, 1986, the United States bombed the Libyan capital of Tripoli. A number of civilians were killed, including young children. The U.S. government justified the action as a response to terrorism in the Middle East that, it claimed, was sponsored by the Libyan government and was directed against innocent Americans. Some critics of the action claimed that the U.S. was as guilty of terrorism as terrorist agents in the Middle East because it had killed innocent people in an attempt to influence a political situation. (Compare the answer to 4(c) in the preceding set of exercises.) The following letter to *Time* appeared in this context.
"The U.S., aided by Britain, acted to protect all of us from the nightmarish insanity of terrorism. This (the attack on Tripoli) is survival, not terrorism."

NOTES

1. Quoted in the *Atlantic Monthly*, July 1986.

2. Compare this discussion of stipulative definition with the discussion of operational definitions in Chapter 12.

3. Aldous Huxley, *Eyeless in Gaza*, as quoted by C. L. Stevenson in "Persuasive Definitions," *Mind* 1938.

4. Calgary *Herald*, July 17, 1978.

5. "This Is What You Thought about Sexual Harrassment," *Glamour*, January 1981, p. 31.

6. Laurier LaPierre, *To Herald a Child*, (Toronto: Ontario Public School Men Teachers Association, 1981), p. 47.

7. Letter to *Time*, November 24, 1980.

8. Ibid.

9. Letter to *Discover*, November 1980.

10. Described at length in the Calgary *Herald*, October 14, 1986.

11. Toronto *Globe and Mail*, July 7, 1986.

4

When Is an Argument a Good One?

We are now ready to proceed to the stage of evaluating arguments—reaching informed judgments as to how good or poor they are. Of course many different issues bear on the evaluation of arguments. We can't study them all simultaneously. The approach we have chosen in this book is to introduce the basic conditions of good argument first in a fairly simple way, and then move to more fully explain related details later. In this chapter we work at a simple level. As you use the conditions developed here, you will come to appreciate the need for the more detailed and more complete explanations that are given in subsequent chapters.

Two Basic Conditions of Argument Cogency

So far we have spent most of our time helping you to appreciate how arguments differ from explanations and other nonarguments and training you to extract premises and conclusions from prose passages that are worded in confusing ways. We haven't said one thing yet about whether these arguments are cogent or not. A cogent argument is an argument in which the premises give good rational support to the conclusion. Two things must happen for an argument to be cogent:

1. *The premises of the argument must be acceptable.*

2. *The premises of the argument must be properly connected to its conclusion.*

In a cogent argument, *both* these conditions have to be met. You can easily see why this is so. If we have acceptable premises but we fail to connect those premises properly to the conclusion we are trying to support, we won't give that conclusion any real support. The premises are all right, but they don't make the conclusion acceptable unless they are appropriately related to it. On the other hand, if the premises are properly connected to the conclusion but are *not* acceptable, we won't have any genuine support for the conclusion; the conclusion isn't made acceptable by being linked up to premises that aren't acceptable. It is clear, therefore, that in a cogent argument the premises must be *both* acceptable *and* properly connected to the conclusion.[1]

Let us look at some simple examples to clarify these points. Here is an argument in which the premises are completely acceptable but are not properly connected to the conclusion. The argument is not cogent, as you will see, because the proper connection is not there—the conclusion gets no real support from the premises.

1. It often snows in the winter in Minnesota.
2. It often snows in the winter in Manitoba.
3. It often rains in the summer in Ontario.
Therefore,
4. In both the United States and Canada, the majority of citizens have English as their native language.

Here all three premises are clearly acceptable because in each case we can rationally believe the premise, based on our common knowledge and experience. There is no problem so far as granting the basis of this argument is concerned. But there is a problem with the way the premises are connected to the conclusion. They aren't properly connected to it because the premises deal only with the weather and the conclusion makes a statement about language in the two countries. This conclusion could not receive rational support from such premises. The argument is not cogent because the premises, though acceptable, are improperly connected to the conclusion. They have no bearing on its truth; statements about the weather do not tell us anything about what language people speak.

Let us now consider the other type of unsound argument—that is, where the premises are properly connected to the conclusion but are not themselves acceptable. Here again we will look at a simple case in which the failure of the acceptability conditions is very obvious.

1. All women who have ever lived have wanted to be men.
2. What all women who have ever lived want is the best thing in the world.
Therefore,
3. The best thing in the world is to be a man.

Here the premises are very well connected to the conclusion, but they are not acceptable. It would be irrational to accept the first premise because we know from common experience that there are many women who have lived their lives quite content to be women.

Premise (2) is obviously very disputable, for women—even all of them—might want things that aren't so good. Even barring this possibility, there is no reason to label something the best thing in the world just because all women want it. Premise (2) isn't acceptable. Thus this argument has a terrible starting point. You might say it doesn't get off the ground because it has no ground to get off! However, the premises *are* connected properly to the conclusion. *If* all women want to be men, and *if* what all women want is the best thing in the world, then it would follow (as the conclusion says) that being a man is the best thing in the world. The connection is there, but the premises themselves are not acceptable.

To discuss this point further, we can rewrite the argument, removing the positive assertion of the premises and putting the argument into a *conditional* statement. A conditional statement is one with two basic parts: an *antecedent* and a *consequent.* The statement relates the antecedent and the consequent using *if* and *then* or words approximating these in meaning. A conditional statement asserts that if some antecedent holds, then some consequent will hold. For instance, the statement "If Fred eats too much, then he will get fat" is a conditional statement. The antecedent is "Fred eats too much" and the consequent is "he (Fred) will get fat." The conditional statement that if Fred eats too much he will get fat does not assert either that Fred does eat too much or that Fred will get fat. It asserts a connection between these two things: if the one, then the other. Any argument from premises to a conclusion is committed to there being a connection between those premises and that conclusion. Someone who argues that because premise (1) and premise (2), therefore conclusion (3), is committed to saying that if (1) and (2), then (3).

For any argument we can construct a conditional statement that articulates this connection. In the argument about women wanting to be men, we said that the premises are properly connected to the conclusion even though the premises themselves are not acceptable. You can see this when we articulate the conditional statement to which anyone who argued this way would be committed:

> *If* all women want to be men and what all women want is the best thing in the world, *then* being a man is the best thing in the world.

This conditional statement is true even though the clauses that constitute the antecedent express unacceptable premises. The conditional statement is true because it doesn't say either that all women want to be men or that what women want is best; it simply says that *if* these things hold, it will be true that being a man is the best thing in the world. The conditional statement expresses only the connection between the premises and the conclusion; the connection is very strong, and the conditional statement is definitely true. Because it does not assert the disputable clauses that make up the premises of the argument, the conditional statement can be true even though these premises are disputable. However, if we changed the conditional statement to the following:

> *Since* all women want to be men and what all women want is the best thing in the world, the best thing in the world is to be a man.

it would *assert* the premises because of what *since* means. It would state the original argument, so we couldn't say that this statement holds. But the conditional statement that *if* all women want to be men and *if* what all women want is the best thing in the world, *then* the best thing in the world would be to be a man would hold true. This conditional statement does not assert either that all women want to be men and what they want is the best thing in the world or that the best thing in the world is to be a man. It merely asserts that there is a connection between the first two claims and the third. If the first two hold, the third will hold also. The premises are properly connected to the conclusion in this case, even though they are not acceptable.

You can see, then, that there are two issues: whether the premises of an argument are acceptable and whether they are properly connected to the conclusion. In a cogent argument, there are both acceptable premises and a proper connection. Here is an example of a cogent argument:

> 1. If mental states are independent of physical states, then the way in which a person pays attention to a lecture is not affected by lack of sleep.
> 2. The way in which a person pays attention to a lecture clearly is affected by lack of sleep.
> Therefore,
> 3. Mental states are not independent of physical states.

Here the two premises are acceptable, and they are properly connected to the conclusion. Given these premises, the conclusion *follows deductively* from the premises. That means that the truth of the premises logically guarantees the truth of the conclusion; it is absolutely impossible for the conclusion to be false and for the premises to be true. This tight logical relationship is often called *logical entailment* (the premises are said to logically entail, or involve, the conclusion), and it is the tightest connection we can have between premises and conclusions in an argument. It is always a proper connection.

The distinction between evaluating the premises of an argument and evaluating the way in which those premises are related to its conclusion is absolutely basic in logic. Arguments can have:

1. unacceptable premises that are not properly related to the conclusion

2. unacceptable premises that are properly related to the conclusion

3. acceptable premises that are not properly related to the conclusion

4. acceptable premises that are properly related to the conclusion

There are four possibilities. Only one, (4), where premises are acceptable and properly related to the conclusion, gives us a cogent argument.

Another basic aspect of argument appraisal is learning to separate your evaluation of the argument from your prior belief about its conclusion. Some people think that every argument in which they agree with the conclusion is a good argument and that every argument in which they disagree with the conclusion is a poor argument! But just because you happen to agree with the conclusion does not mean that the premises of the argument are acceptable or that they are properly related to the conclusion. For instance, in the case of the argument about Manitoba, Minnesota, and the common native language in the United States and Canada, we probably agree that the conclusion is true. But the argument is still not cogent. The premises aren't properly related to the conclusion and have absolutely no tendency to make it acceptable!

On the other hand, just because you are inclined to disagree with the conclusion, it does not follow that the argument is a bad one. Suppose you are convinced that anyone who helps to manufacture nuclear weapons is effectively planning murder. Then suppose someone comes to you and argues as follows:

1. Murder presupposes intention to kill.
2. Many people who help to make nuclear weapons believe that nuclear weapons prevent war.
So,
3. Many people who help to make nuclear weapons do not intend to kill anyone, nor do they intend that the weapons they make should be used to kill anyone.
Therefore,
4. Many people who help to make nuclear weapons are not effectively planning murder.

Here you may not like the argument. You may want to deny its conclusion. You may be inclined to say, "Well, this has just got to be a bad argument because the conclusion is completely unacceptable. I know these people are really incipient murderers, and nobody can show me otherwise. The conclusion of the argument is unacceptable and, therefore, the argument must be a poor one." This approach just won't do. When you react this way, you are really ignoring the argument and clinging dogmatically to your previous belief. If you don't believe the conclusion, that gives you a *motive* to find something wrong with the argument; it means that you will want to find something wrong with it.

In rare cases you may be absolutely convinced by common experience that the conclusion is false and should not be accepted, and you will be tempted to say that there must be something wrong with the argument. But then your task is to find out what that is.[2] As we have seen, there are two ways of finding out what is wrong. You can find that one or more premises is unacceptable or you can find that the premises are not properly connected to the conclusion. When you do this, you respond rationally to another person's position instead of just rejecting it. If you are sure that an argument has a false conclusion, you will also be sure that there is something wrong with the argument. But what? Your task is to find out.

For thousands of years philosophers have been perplexed by arguments put forward by the Greek philosopher Zeno. Zeno thought he could prove that motion is absolutely impossible and that what we perceive as motion is an illusion. He gave a number of different arguments. One had to do with an imaginary race between Achilles (a Greek hero) and a tortoise. It is imagined that Achilles allows the tortoise a head start—a chivalrous gesture given his obvious advantage. The tortoise moves some distance during these first moments of their race. Achilles sets out and tries to catch up. But it turns out that this is impossible because:

1. To catch up to the tortoise, Achilles has to cover the distance that the tortoise has already covered during the time when he had his head start.
2. By the time Achilles makes it to the point where the tortoise had arrived during his head start, the tortoise will have moved some small distance ahead of that point to a new point.
3. When Achilles reaches this next point, the tortoise will have moved ahead ever so slightly again, and Achilles will have more catching up to do.
4. The problem of not quite catching up will apply every time Achilles proceeds to the point where the tortoise was.
Therefore,
5. Achilles can never catch up to the tortoise.
6. The same points can be made whenever anyone tries to cross any finite distance.
So,
7. Motion is impossible.

Thus the ancient sage argued that motion is impossible. *No one seriously believes this.* But that does not give us a critique of Zeno's argument. Where did Zeno go wrong? If the conclusion is not acceptable, then either he argued from unacceptable premises or his premises don't lead properly to his conclusion. Where is the mistake? Many philosophers now think they can solve Zeno's paradox and show why motion is possible, but there is still not complete agreement on the subject. Philosophers still discuss Zeno's paradoxes of motion thousands of years after he first formulated them. They do not just rest content with denying Zeno's conclusions. Arguments like Zeno's are said to pose a paradox because the conclusion is so contrary to ordinary common-sense beliefs. From such paradoxes important discoveries and theories have been derived. This happens only because people take arguments seriously and aren't content with simply disagreeing with the conclusion. You shouldn't be either!

EXERCISE SET

Exercise One
Part A

Like all arguments, the following short arguments can be classified according to this scheme:

a. Those with acceptable premises that are not properly connected to the conclusion.

b. Those with acceptable premises that are properly connected to the conclusion.

c. Those with unacceptable premises that are not properly connected to the conclusion.

d. Those with unacceptable premises that are properly connected to the conclusion.

For each of the following arguments, say whether it is in type (a), (b), (c), or (d). Specify which group contains cogent arguments.

*1. Either there are people on Mars or there are people on Venus. There are no people on Venus, so there must be people on Mars.

2. Laboratory rats are different from wild rats in various respects, so we can't be sure that the test results we obtain for laboratory rats will be true of wild rats.

3. The sole purpose of going to college is to get a degree, and the sole purpose of getting a degree is to have the best chance of getting a well-paying job. Therefore, the sole purpose of going to college is to maximize the chances of having a good income after college.

4. The only way for countries to disarm is for them all to get rid of all their weapons at the same time. It is impossible for all countries to get rid of all their weapons at the same time. (This statement is obvious because it would even be impossible for all cigarette smokers to get rid of all their cigarettes at the same time, and cigarettes are not fundamental to our ideas of security in the way weapons are.) We can see that total disarmament is impossible. (*Hint:* There is a subargument here, so you actually have to evaluate two arguments, not one.)

5. Whatever is in danger of being abused should not be pursued under any circumstances. Genetic research is in danger of being abused. Therefore, genetic research should not be pursued under any circumstances.

*6. Buy a lottery ticket to win. Of those who win lotteries, 90 percent said before they bought the ticket that they would never win. You too can win even if you think you can't. You have to buy a ticket first, though.
(Argument used by lottery ticket salesman at the Calgary Stampede, summer 1986.)

7. We never thought we could land a man on the moon. But we did it. We never thought we could make a chip less than one-hundredth of an inch in width that would perform thousands of calculations a minute. But we did it. You can see how it goes—for technology, everything is possible.

8. The *Challenger* shuttle failed. Several subsequent attempts to launch U.S. space satellites failed. The nuclear reactor at Chernobyl nearly exploded, and many thousands of people near Kiev in the Soviet Union have been evacuated from their homes as a result. Three Mile Island was the site of a serious nuclear accident in the United States in 1979. What follows from all of this is that complex technology is not reliable.

*9. Individuals in a family are related in intimate and complex ways. For this reason, change in one member of a family usually requires changes in the others.

*10. We have never encountered creatures from other planets. If there were creatures on other planets who are more intelligent than we are, they would have contacted us. We can conclude that there are no such creatures.

Part B

Read the following dialogues. In each one, the *A* character gives an argument and the *B* character responds to it. Find those cases in which *B* responds by following *A*'s argument and criticizing it in a reasonable way, and mark these with *. Find those cases in which *B* responds merely by denying *A*'s conclusion and mark these with **. In each case, explain the basis for your answer by mentioning those aspects of *B*'s remarks that led you to reply as you did.

*1. *A:* Mathematics is the most important subject you can study at a university. First, it is completely precise. There is always just one right answer to every question, and you can prove beyond any doubt that that answer is the right one. Second, by doing proofs in mathematics you learn standards of rigor and exactness. Third, mathematics is the basis of all the sciences—physics, geology, chemistry, engineering, even biology. You can't do these if you don't understand mathematics. It is surely unfortunate that mathematics is so badly taught and that many people don't like it.

B: I hate math and I always will. Boy, my math teacher in elementary school was the crabbiest teacher I ever had. She could never explain anything, and the whole class was lost. I never caught up. Make everyone take math and you'll soon see colleges and universities empty of students.

2. *A:* Animals think and feel. I would defend this conclusion by analogy. We know that other humans think and feel only because of inferences we make from what they do. Well, animals exhibit intelligent behavior and sensitive behavior just as humans do. So animals think and feel too.

B: I disagree. You see, you have assumed that it is by inference from behavior that we know that humans think and feel. The problem is, that is a very controversial theory of knowledge in this area. Many thinkers, such as Wittgenstein and Ryle, contend that we cannot infer such a belief, for we need it before we even reason at all. Also, the premise you use ignores the very important role language plays in our understanding of other people. We can't talk to dogs and lions, so any basis we would have for attributing thoughts to them just has to be less adequate than our evidence for the existence of thoughts in other people.

3. *A:* A broadly based military operation is possible only when a society has an army that genuinely represents the various distinct classes in that society. We need the strength for military operations around the globe. A volunteer army does not represent the population at large because it is chiefly the poor and less educated who volunteer. The middle and upper classes have other opportunities for jobs. Therefore, conscription is the answer. And, furthermore, conscription should not be for men only. Women have to bear their share of the responsibility. I conclude that the draft should be reinstituted, and that it should be for all men and women within the required age range.

B: I'm horrified at the militaristic position you have taken. You are proposing that the whole society should be drained to support the military. This is a simply scandalous suggestion. As a feminist, you should be ashamed of yourself for supporting the militarism that has so long been a central aspect of male power in the world.

4. *A:* When there is government-supported medical insurance, doctors should not be allowed to bill their patients more than the government insurance plan permits. This extra-billing destroys the intended universal coverage of a government insurance plan since poor patients will not be able to afford to see the doctors who extra-bill. The Ontario government was quite right in passing legislation against extra-billing in the summer of 1986. The Canadian government had already put through laws so that for every dollar an Ontario doctor extra-billed his patients, federal legislation took one dollar away from the Ontario government.

B: Banning extra-billing is the first step toward total government control of the health care system. It is socialized medicine, and doctors are right not to tolerate it. The doctors' strike in Ontario in the summer of 1986 was entirely justified and would have been justified even if some of those patients denied emergency service had died.

*5. *A:* In the Soviet Union these days, a major topic of concern is the fact that the Moslem population in central Asia is expanding much more rapidly than the Slavic population in European Russia. This rapid expansion shows us why the Russians went into Afghanistan as they did: they are frightened of Moslem fundamentalism as it is a basic threat to the stability of their own society.

B: It is quite true that the Soviets are concerned about the way in which their population is and is not expanding. But from the fact that this is a major concern, you cannot really infer that it must provide the basis for their excursion into Afghanistan. Other explanations are quite possible. For instance, the Americans' approach to Pakistan and alliance with General Zia probably seemed quite threatening to the Soviets, and this perceived threat may have made them anxious to have a solid basis of control in Afghanistan, Pakistan's neighbor. Your conclusion may be right, but your premise does not fully support it—even though your premise is true.

The ARG Conditions

The basic elements of a cogent argument are as follows:

1. Its premises are all acceptable. That is to say, it is reasonable for those to whom the argument is addressed to believe these premises. There is some good evidence for the premises, even if they are not known for certain. And there is no good evidence known to those to whom the argument is addressed that would indicate either that the premises are false or that they are doubtful.

2. Its premises are properly connected to its conclusion. Traditional logicians have spent most of their time and energy on this condition. The condition may be usefully subdivided into two parts:

a. The premises are genuinely relevant to the conclusion; that is, they give at least some evidence in favor of the conclusion's being true. They specify factors, evidence, or reasons that do count toward the truth of the conclusion. They do not merely describe distracting aspects that lead you away from the real topic with which the argument is supposed to be dealing or that do not tend to support the conclusion.

b. The premises provide sufficient grounds for the conclusion. Another way of putting this is to say that, considered together, the premises give sufficient reason to make it rational to accept the conclusion. This statement means more than that the premises are relevant. Not only do they count as evidence for the conclusion, they provide enough evidence, or enough reasons, taken together, to make it reasonable to accept the conclusion as true or as very probable.

Because we subdivided the second condition, our original two conditions for an argument's cogency have become three conditions. The subdivision is very useful in criticizing arguments. It can happen that a premise is relevant to the truth of a conclusion but not sufficient to show its truth. For example, if a person cites her own two children as evidence for a general claim about all children, as in "My girl is more patient than my boy, so I think girls are more patient than boys," she has given evidence in her premises that is relevant to her conclusion. It does count in a small way toward showing that the conclusion is true. Two children are a small portion of children. Thus in this argument the premise is relevant to the conclusion. But it is obviously not sufficient to show that the conclusion is true. There are many hundreds of millions of boys and girls in the world, and the son and daughter of the person arguing represent just a tiny percentage of them. They may not be typical. We distinguish the relevance of premises from the sufficiency of premises because it is quite possible for a premise to be relevant to the conclusion without being sufficient—as is illustrated in this case.

On the other hand, if the premises provide sufficient evidence or reasons to make it rational to believe the conclusion, they will be relevant as well. Obviously, if they give enough evidence (sufficient grounds) to make the conclusion rationally acceptable, they will clearly at least give some evidence (be relevant) in support of that conclusion. Relevance is a weaker condition than sufficiency of grounds. Any premises that are sufficient are also relevant, but it does not work the other way around. Premises can be relevant without giving sufficient grounds.

If the premises of an argument are not even relevant to its conclusion, they do not offer it any support. They have been put forward to distract us or because the person giving the argument has made an error in logic. The following argument, stated by the

South African ambassador to Canada during a television interview, is an example of irrelevance:

> There is no point in western countries applying economic sanctions to South Africa in an attempt to help the black people there. Sure, sanctions will hurt the economy, but they will hurt everybody. You can see this when you think of killing a zebra. If you shoot him in a white stripe he will die, and if you shoot him in a black stripe he will still die. The whole animal goes down. And so it will be with the South African economy. The whole country will suffer from sanctions—not just the white parts of it.[3]

Information about what happens to zebras when they are shot is irrelevant to the question of whether economic sanctions by western countries will help South African blacks. The premises about the zebra do not give any evidence whatsoever in support of the conclusion.

If premises are relevant and not sufficient, the argument could be turned into a good one by adding more information similar in type. For instance, if the mother arguing that boys are less patient than girls had done a survey of hundreds of children, she might have found more evidence similar to her first bits of evidence, and she might eventually have found sufficient grounds for her conclusion. The evidence about her own children is relevant, but not sufficient. With the zebra and sanctions, however, the premises are not relevant at all. If we were to add more information about more zebras, it wouldn't help!

There is a very convenient way to remember (1) and (2) as they have just been explained. We can write them as follows:

ACCEPTABILITY–(1)
RELEVANCE–(2a)
Adequacy of *GROUNDS*–(2b)

You can keep these basic conditions of argument cogency firmly fixed in your mind by noting that the first letters, when combined, are "ARG"—the first three letters of the word *argument.* Now obviously we will want to know more about what makes premises acceptable in various contexts, what relevance and irrelevance are, and what are different ways in which grounds may be adequate to support a conclusion. But the fundamental idea is quite simple. By using these conditions, you have a basis for a careful, stage-by-stage appraisal of an argument. You first get the argument into a standard form so that you can see exactly what its premises and conclusion are. Then you determine whether the premises are acceptable. Suppose that the audience to whom the argument is addressed is you, and you ask yourself whether you have good reason to accept the premises on which the argument is based. If you do not, the argument cannot possibly provide you with a good basis for accepting its conclusion. An argument moves *from* its premises *to* its conclusion, and you will not get anywhere without a starting point. If the premises are acceptable on the (A) condition, you move on to (R). Ask yourself whether the premises are relevant to the conclusion. How, if at all, do they bear on it? If the premises have nothing to do with the conclusion, they can't be properly connected to it, and (even if acceptable) they can't give you any reason to think that the conclusion is true. An argument with irrelevant premises is a poor argument; it fails on (R) and cannot be cogent. If (A) and (R) are satisfied, you move on to (G). Ask yourself whether the premises, taken together, provide good enough grounds for the conclusion. Premises that are acceptable and relevant may fail to provide sufficient grounds for the conclusion; they may offer an appropriate sort of evidence but fail to give enough of it. If this is a problem, then (G) is not satisfied and the argument is not cogent. A cogent argument passes *all three* conditions of ARG. All its premises must be acceptable; they must be relevant to its conclusion; taken together they must provide adequate grounds for that conclusion.

The same ARG formula may be used when you are constructing arguments of your own. Let us suppose that you are going to appear before a public board to present a brief on some contentious issue. Perhaps, for instance, you are a farmer living in an area where a uranium refinery wishes to buy land and you wish to argue before a public board that the refinery will constitute a danger to public health. You have the task of selecting premises that will be reasonable for this board to believe; some of these premises may have to be defended in subarguments. You have to make sure that these premises are genuinely relevant to your conclusion about the hazardous nature of the refinery, and you have to use premises that provide adequate (full enough) grounds to give reasons for not having the refinery. Thus the ARG conditions are useful both for evaluating other people's arguments and for constructing your own.

Before we go on to look at some real examples of arguments that fail on one or more of the ARG conditions, we should say more about condition (2): the relevance and sufficiency that combine to make for a proper connection between the premises and the conclusion. We have mentioned deductive entailment. This is *one* way in which premises may be properly related to the conclusion. It is *not* the only way. Deductive entailment is a relationship between statements. For simplicity, let us consider only two statements, one of which entails the other. Statement (1) entails statement (2) if it is absolutely impossible for (2) to be false, *given* that (1) is true. The truth of statement (1) logically guarantees the truth of statement (2). Here are some examples: in each of the following pairs, statement (1) entails statement (2).

> *A* (1) John is someone's brother.
>   (2) John is the sibling of someone.
> *B* (1) It is not true that Susan is here.
>   (2) Susan is somewhere away from here.
> *C* (1) Lottery winners are always people who have bought tickets.
>   (2) You won't win a lottery unless you have bought a ticket on it.

In each case, (1) *entails* (2) because it would be impossible for (1) to be true *and* for (2) to be false. This does not say that (1) *is* true in any given case; it says only that *if* (1) is true, then (2) is also true.

Any argument in which the premises, *taken together*, entail the conclusion is a deductively valid argument and satisfies conditions (2a) and (2b). That is, if the *conjunction* of the premises deductively entails the conclusion, the argument satisfies (R) and (G); you only have to worry about (A). A conjunction is one statement connected to another using *and* (or another English word meaning the same thing). Suppose the argument has two premises:

> 1. A true friend puts his friend before his country.
> 2. A true friend does not put his friend before his lover.

The *conjunction* of these is simply: A true friend puts his friend before his country, *and* a true friend does not put his friend before his lover. An argument from these two premises to a further conclusion such as:

> 3. A true friend values a lover more than his country.

will be deductively valid if the conjunction of premise (1) and premise (2) deductively entails the conclusion (3). If it is deductively valid (this one is), the (R) and (G) conditions are satisfied. The argument is sound provided that condition (A) is also satisfied.

Deductive entailment is so tidy and complete a connection that when we have it there is no need to consider separately the relevance of premises and their sufficiency. It is an all or nothing thing; the premises either entail the conclusion or they do not. If they entail it, they give relevant grounds that are also sufficient. If they do not entail it, they are irrelevant from a deductive point of view, so any support they could give would have to be of some other type.

The life of logicians would be simpler if deductive entailment were the *only* way of satisfying the (R) and (G) conditions. But it is not. Statements can be connected in ways other than by logical entailment. There is much controversy about the matter, however. But we could not give a general theory about arguments if we limited ourselves to those in which deductive entailment is the connecting relation that satisfies (R) and (G). The view taken in this book is that there are at least three other ways in which premises may be *properly* connected to a conclusion. These are empirical generalization, analogy, and a cumulation of relevant factors.

1. *Empirical generalization.* Suppose that you have seen 1000 students who have graduated from a particular high school, and every single one has been blind. You infer that the school is a school for the blind. When you make this inference, you *generalize* from past experience to a claim about all the students from the school. You use premises about past experience to get a conclusion about all experience pertaining to the students from the school. Such arguments are usually called *inductive.* The connection between the cases you have observed and other cases is based on the presumption that your experience is likely to be fairly uniform. You also use an inductive argument if you reason that because the 1000 students you have met from the school have been blind, the next one (1001) you meet will be blind also. Life depends on such reasoning even though the connection is not as certain as it is when the premises deductively entail the conclusion. What we mean by saying that the connection is an inductive argument is not as certain as in a deductive one is that the premises could be true and the conclusion false. The possibility cannot be ruled out.

2. *Analogy.* Suppose you want to know whether a once-a-month birth control shot is safe (you have just invented it!), but for moral reasons you cannot test it on people. You get some rats and do an experiment. As things turn out, 50 of your 200 rats develop breast cancers. You conclude that the birth control shot is not safe for humans. Your premises are that it wasn't safe for rats, and humans are similar to rats; you are reasoning from one species to another that is compared with it. Provided that the cases you compare are relevantly similar, the link between premises and conclusion is a proper one. (The example about the zebra and South Africa is an analogy, but the premises are not relevant because a zebra is not similar to the South African economy in any way that would tend to provide any evidence for the conclusion.)

3. *Cumulation of relevant factors.* Suppose you are considering a decision about suitable office space for an activist group. You want to decide what the ideal space would be. You think about the group's needs, which are many and varied, and start listing desirable features: centrality, low cost, acceptable decor, comfort, adequacy of heating and cooling, proximity to related groups, and so on. Then you find a space. To argue that it is suitable, you point out which of the relevant features it has. If it has several, you may wish to conclude that it is a suitable place. In these arguments we often have to deal with pros and cons. Arguments of this type are sometimes called *conductive.*

The (RG) conditions are satisfied in a variety of ways: we may have a deductively valid argument, an inductively strong argument, a good analogy, or an argument that rightly pulls together a number of distinct factors relevant to the conclusion. If you don't feel that you fully understand these four different things right now, don't worry about it. All are treated in more detail in subsequent parts of the book.

Applying the ARG Conditions

Failing on the (A) Condition.   We shall now look at some real examples and see how the ARG conditions can be used to evaluate arguments. First, let us consider this argument, taken from a letter written to *Time* magazine:

> *There can be no meaningful reconciliation of science and religion. Their methods are diametrically opposed. Science admits it has no final answers, while religion claims to have them. Science, despite its excesses, has gone far to liberate the human spirit; religion would stifle it.*[4]

Before evaluating the argument, we have to identify its conclusion and premises. Here the conclusion is the rather controversial claim announced in the first sentence. The second and third sentences are related to each other, since the third sentence gives a reason for the second sentence—that methods are opposed. There is, then, a subargument in these two sentences, both of which deal with the methods of science and religion. The final sentence specifies a quite different contrast between science and religion with regard to their effects (liberation) and intentions (to stifle the human spirit). The writer argued for the conclusion that science and religion are not reconcilable by contrasting them in two ways—with regard to method and to intended effect. His point about method is defended in a subargument. The argument would look like this in standardized form:

1. Science admits to having no final answers while religion claims to have final answers.
So,
2. The methods of science and religion are diametrically opposed.
3. Science has helped to liberate humans, whereas religion seeks to stifle them.
Therefore,
4. There can be no meaningful reconciliation of religion and science.

Given this argument, should we be convinced of the author's conclusion? Has he shown that there can be no meaningful reconciliation between science and religion? This is a sweeping conclusion, asserted categorically with no qualifications, so we are entitled to look for a high standard of argumentation for it. We appraise the argument by working through the ARG conditions. First, consider (A): the acceptability of the premises. Premises (1) and (3) are undefended premises, and they must be acceptable as stated if the argument is to work. There is certainly a problem about (1), which seems to be false as stated. It draws a very sharp contrast between science and religion, a contrast that is not borne out by a careful consideration of various religions and scientific theories. Some scientific theorists (for example, Isaac Newton, author of gravitational theory) have claimed to have the final answers to the questions they asked. And some religious thinkers have not. Many Buddhist thinkers, for instance, see religion as the cultivation of individual peace of mind and harmony with the natural universe. They do not think that religion is a body of doctrines giving definitive answers to a set of specific questions. Thus (1) is not acceptable. For this reason, (2) is not adequately defended since it is supposed to get its support from (1).

Now look at (3). Here the author was at least careful enough to use more qualified terms. He says science "has gone far" to liberate the human spirit and that religion "would stifle" it. But even when these qualifications are considered, the author is overstating the contrast between science and religion. Like (1), (3) is untrue to the facts. There are scientists who seek to use scientific knowledge to control human beings, and there are religious workers who have labored long and hard under the inspiration of religious ideals to improve the dehumanizing material conditions of their fellow human beings. Thus premise (3) is also unacceptable. The argument, then, fails miserably on the (A) condition. All premises are disputable in the face of common knowledge about the role that science and religion have played in human history. The author has overdrawn his contrasts and has been insensitive to the concrete detail that, if recalled, would force dramatic qualification of his claims. The argument is not a cogent argument because it fails on the (A) condition. *All three conditions must be met if the argument is to be cogent.*

Failing on the (R) Condition. We shall now move on to consider an argument that fails in another way—by missing on the (R) condition. The argument was found in a short essay about whether pornographic materials should be subject to regulation by the government.

> *It is assumed that the adult collective majority is a God-fearing, responsible, law-abiding group. Responsibility is the key word here, because without being considered responsible for his physical and intellectual actions, reality for man does not make sense, and it instills in him a feeling of nothingness.*
>
> *For example, civilization has progressed and is progressing because of man's commitment of responsibility to himself, his family and the state; in this sense, then, the idea of the ethical concept of utilitarianism prevails. Moreover, this sense of personal responsibility (or maturity) is why the government does not have a right (morally or paternalistically) to intervene in the adult public's preference for pornography. Consenting, mature adults, therefore, should be able to view pornographic material.[5]*

This piece is stated very loosely. We will concentrate on the second paragraph quoted; the first one is here for background. In the second paragraph, the author tries to prove that mature adults should be able to view pornographic materials. This point is his main conclusion. He states that the government does not have a right to intervene in the adult public's preference for pornography. This is the premise for the main conclusion. This premise is itself defended in a subargument in which the premise is that civilization has progressed because man has a commitment of responsibility to himself, his family, and the state. This statement is, in fact, extremely vague, but we will ignore that problem for the moment.

———— 1. Civilization has progressed and is progressing because man has a commitment of responsibility to himself, his family, and the state.
So,
2. The government has no right to intervene in the adult public's preference for pornography.
Therefore,
3. Consenting mature adults should be able to view pornographic materials.

We cannot accuse the author of irrelevance in the argument from (2) to (3) here. It is the subargument, from (1) to (2), that illustrates the problem. Statement (1) is irrelevant to statement (2) and gives no evidence or reason to endorse (2)—none whatever. The problem with (1) is that it is so very general; it offers a theory of progress in terms of an overall commitment people are said to make. This hypothesis is sweeping and vague, and yet what is inferred from it is something quite particular that governments are not supposed to do. There is no connection—obvious or otherwise—between these things! The premise is irrelevant, and the subargument falls down for this reason.

Failing on the (G) Condition.   We now move to another example—this time one that satisfies (A) and (R) but fails on (G). It goes as follows:

> *We arrived at the park gate at 7:25 p.m. at which time the cashier gleefully took money for admission. Upon entering the zoo and walking across the bridge, the loudspeaker was stating that the zoo buildings were closing at 8:00 p.m. We asked if we would not get a pass for the following day. The answer was no.*
>
> *In summary, it is easy to see that Calgary is anything but a friendly city, but rather out to rake off the tourist for all they can.[6]*

The writer of this letter received shabby treatment at the Calgary zoo and is inferring from this fact that Calgary is an unfriendly city that is out to exploit tourists. His argument is very simply:

1. Some tourists were given unfriendly treatment at the Calgary zoo.
   Therefore,
2. Calgary is an unfriendly city, out to exploit tourists.

Whether the premise is true we cannot know for sure; the writer is describing his personal experiences. But there is no good reason to think that he is either lying or deceiving himself, so we may accept the premise on his word. Thus the (A) condition will be granted. The premise is clearly relevant to the conclusion; if one person (a cashier) in one Calgary institution (the zoo) is unfriendly to tourists, this is *some* evidence for the general conclusion that the whole city is unfriendly. It does count toward establishing that conclusion. Hence the (R) condition is satisfied. But when we come to the (G) condition and ask how good the grounds are for the conclusion, the argument obviously breaks down. The unfriendliness of a single individual in a single institution is not adequate evidence to establish the unfriendliness of a city as a whole! The argument passes on (A) and (R) but fails on (G). It is not a cogent argument.

Satisfying All Three Conditions.   We now move on to look at an argument that is cogent and that passes all three conditions. This example comes from an essay on education written by the British philosopher Bertrand Russell.

> *Freedom, in education as in other things, must be a matter of degree. Some freedoms cannot be tolerated. I met a lady once who maintained that no child should ever be forbidden to do anything, because a child ought to develop its nature from within. "How about if its nature leads it to swallow pins?" I asked; but I regret to say the answer was mere vituperation. And yet every child, left to itself, will sooner or later swallow pins, or drink poison out of medicine bottles, or fall out of an upper window, or otherwise bring itself to a bad end. At a slightly later age, boys, when they have the opportunity, will go unwashed, overeat, smoke till they are sick, catch chills from sitting in wet feet, and so on—let alone the fact that they will amuse themselves by plaguing elderly gentlemen, who may not all have Elisha's powers of repartee. Therefore, one who advocates freedom in education cannot mean the children should do exactly as they please all day long. An element of discipline and authority must exist; the question is as to the amount of it, and the way in which it is to be exercised.[7]*

Russell is arguing that some element of discipline and authority must exist in education. (Another way of stating this point is that freedom must be a matter of degree, rather than being absolute.) He states this point several times in the first two sentences and in the final two sentences. The incident about the woman Russell met is not really a premise; it is a story about someone who held a view that Russell himself disagreed with. He describes the episode as a way of explaining the view he *doesn't* hold and (by contrast) his own view. The vivid and various ways boys can come to harm need not all be mentioned in the standardization of Russell's argument, for his point is simply that they *can* easily come to harm—whether this is by overeating, or catching chills, or whatever won't really matter so far as the fundamental point of the argument is concerned.

The argument can be restated as follows:

1. Both younger and older children, left to themselves, can easily come to physical harm.
2. Older children, left to themselves, often are very annoying to adults.
So,
3. Children simply cannot be left to do as they please all day long.
Therefore,
4. There must be some element of discipline and authority in education.

There is a subargument structure here: the first two premises are intended to support the third one, and that is intended to support the conclusion of the main argument. The undefended premises, then, are (1) and (2). Both are clearly acceptable; these are matters of common knowledge. And they are clearly relevant to (3): that unsupervised children will naturally harm themselves and others are two good reasons for not just leaving them to do as they please all day. Furthermore, the (G) condition is also satisfied in this subargument. These are compelling reasons. The subargument passes all of the ARG conditions and is cogent; thus (3) is acceptable since it is defended by a cogent argument. The final assessment will depend on whether (3) is properly connected to (4). Does it provide relevant and adequate grounds for (4)? To fully explain the relevance of (3) to (4), it helps to recall that children in western European societies (about whom we can presume Russell would have been writing) spend a very substantial portion of their time in the educational system. To have no discipline and authority in education would in effect leave these children to their own devices for a very considerable portion of their time—contrary to what we accepted in (3). Thus (3) is not only acceptable but is properly connected to (4), because it is relevant to it and provides adequate grounds for it. Since the subargument is cogent and the main argument is cogent, the entire argument is cogent.

EXERCISE SET

Exercise Two

Assess the following arguments using the ARG conditions as you are able to understand them at this point. There may be several arguments in combination; if so, specify your comments accordingly, noting each subargument and then pulling together your remarks to appraise the combined structure. The first arguments are prestandardized to make your work easier. In the case of arguments that are not standardized, carefully standardize them before applying ARG. For the purposes of this exercise, do not add missing premises or conclusions.

If you do not have enough background knowledge to determine whether premises are acceptable, omit the (A) condition and concentrate on (R) and (G).

1. *The Sibling Rivalry Case*
   (1) People who have a brother or sister are in a different family situation from those who do not have a brother or sister.
   (2) People who have a brother or sister have to compete with their sibling for the parents' attention, whereas those who are only children do not have to compete with a sibling for this attention.
   (3) Competing for a parent's attention is a phenomenon which can bring out emotions of jealousy, anger, and inadequacy.
   Therefore,
   (4) Jealousy, anger, and inadequacy have a source in the lives of those with brothers and sisters which they do not have in the lives of only children.

2. *The Animal Rights Case*
   (1) Animals are not human beings.
   (2) Animals do not speak the same language as human beings.
   (3) Animals do not have the same advanced cultures and technologies as human beings.
   Therefore,
   (4) Animals are of no moral significance and do not have any moral rights.

3. *The Aggression Case*
   (1) People have given their children war-related toys for many centuries.
   (2) Children have often enjoyed playing cowboys and Indians, and using toy soldiers and related playthings.
   (3) Not every child who plays with war toys becomes a soldier.
   Therefore,
   (4) War toys have no tendency whatsoever to make children less sensitive to violence.

4. *The History Instructor Case*
   (1) The textbooks selected for the history course were very hard to read.
   (2) The assignments for the history course were very difficult to complete.
   (3) Many students do not enjoy studying history.
   Therefore,
   (4) The instructor in the history course was not competent in her subject.

5. *The Obesity Case*
   (1) Obesity is either genetic or environmental.
   (2) Many obese people do not have obese parents.
   Thus,
   (3) It is unlikely that obesity is genetic.
   So,
   (4) Obesity is probably environmental.

6. *The Success of Technology Case*
   (1) People thought an atomic bomb was impossible, even though it turned out to be possible.
   (2) People thought flying machines were impossible, even though airplanes turned out to be possible.
   (3) People thought that landing a man on the moon was impossible, even though that turned out to be possible.
   So,
   (4) Any technological task can be accomplished, if people just try hard enough.

*7. *The Beginning of Time Case*
   (1) Everything that exists has a beginning.
   (2) All beginnings are beginnings in time.
   (3) Time is something that exists.
   So,
   (4) Time has a beginning in time.

8. *A Professor Generalizes about Logic Students*
   (1) Students in my present logic class do not work as hard as students in my logic class last year.
   Therefore,
   (2) Students at the university in general are not working as hard this year as they did last year.
   And,
   (3) Affluence and low standards in the high schools produce poor work habits in students.

9. *Polls on a Doctors' Strike*
   (1) In a poll, 75 percent of the people questioned said that they think people who perform essential services do not have a right to strike.
   (2) Doctors perform essential services.
   So,
   (3) Polls indicate that 75 percent of people think doctors do not have a right to strike.

10. *Canadian Writer Margaret Laurence*
   (1) Laurence's novel *The Diviners* has as its central character a female protagonist who is a successful Canadian writer.
   (2) Laurence's novel *The Stone Angel* has as its central character a female protagonist who is a cantankerous and independent old lady in Manitoba.
   (3) Laurence's novel *A Jest for God* has as its central character a prairie schoolteacher who fervently desires a child of her own.
   (4) Laurence's novel *Fire Dwellers* is about a restless forty-year-old housewife in Vancouver.
   (5) Many of Laurence's short stories deal with the problems of adolescent girls coming to terms with their sexuality and life plans.
   So,
   (6) Female identity questions, set in a Canadian context, dominate Laurence's fiction.
   And,
   (7) Margaret Laurence is a fervently feminist writer.

*11. There are only two kinds of thinkers. There are those who analyze, who like to pull problems apart and reduce them to basic simple units. Then there are those who synthesize, pulling together all sorts of different materials to bring about novel results. Therefore, all thinking is about how wholes result from parts.

*12. In schools in Cuba, girls far outstrip boys in their achievements. Cuba is a socialist state in which equality of the sexes is a matter of law. In Cuba it is even a legal requirement for men to do their share of the housework! Therefore, we can see that under socialism and true equal opportunity, women show up as superior to men.

13. The end of the world is at hand. It has been decreed, and God's intent is everywhere visible. It is God who has brought it about that the new head of the Russian state is the former head of the KGB. It is God who intends that the Israelis should be stirring up trouble in the Middle East. All this was foreseen, and now we are coming to the end. Nuclear weapons are to be God's way of bringing about the final holocaust. Prepare for the end. The end is near!

14. It is unlikely that scientists will ever be fully satisfied with their understanding of matter. Whatever small particle they have most recently discovered, they will seek to understand further, and when they do this, they are very likely eventually to achieve the splitting of such a particle into several smaller ones. This pattern does not show that the explanation for the world is to be found outside science—in theology, art, or mysticism, for instance. But it does indicate that a scientific explanation will not likely regard itself as complete.

15. Children have no rights at all because children are not adults, and all adults have rights.

16. Intelligence tests have often been misused, and several famous psychologists who developed the tests have been widely discredited. For instance, Sir Cyril Burt, an eminent British psychologist who greatly influenced the testing of students in Britain, was found to have used fraudulent data in several of his studies. For these reasons, attempts to measure human intelligence should be completely abandoned.

*17. Competition results in the best system for all. We can easily see why this is the case if we consider how small businesses operate. If a town has only one bakery, the baker can make buns, pies, and muffins just as he wishes and charge the highest price customers will tolerate. But if there are two

or three bakeries, customers can select the best products at the lowest prices. With competition, there is pressure to bring quality up and prices down, which benefits consumers. Thus competitiveness is a force for good and should not be eliminated.

18. The world is a hostile place. People are out there to get you. You have to watch out for yourself and do what you can to remain secure.

19. If Hitler had died at the age of ten, Nazism would not have developed in Germany in the way it did. If Woodrow Wilson had never existed, there would be no League of Nations. And without Mao Tse-Tung, who knows what would have come of the revolutionary movement in China during the thirties and forties? You can see that it is particular individuals who determine world history.

*20. Sexual perversion is sex pursued without respect for one's sexual partner. Respect for one's sexual partner requires attending to the responses of one's partner, and being aware of the partner and aware that that partner is aware of you. When people fantasize during sex, they aren't aware of their partners because they are thinking about being with somebody else. Therefore, sexual relations with fantasy instead of full awareness amount to perverted sex.
(*Hint:* Think about definitions when studying this example.)
(Adapted from Thomas Nagel, "Sexual Perversion," in *Mortal Questions* [Cambridge, England: Cambridge University Press, 1979].)

21. *Background:* The following excerpt is from a letter written to Dr. Joyce Brothers:
   "The problem is that my husband does not want to have children because I underwent therapy before we were married and my husband is afraid that my emotional troubles will be passed on to our child."
   To this inquiry, Brothers responded: "When is society going to come out of the dark ages and recognize that mental or emotional problems should be no more stigmatizing to an individual than a case of German measles or pneumonia? We do not shun those who have suffered and been cured of tuberculosis, polio, or other diseases, do we?" (Cited in the *Informal Logic Newsletter;* Examples Supplement for 1979.)

22. "The killing and eating of animals by man is a recent phenomenon and is related in time to the patriarchal revolution. Greek myth records that it was not until the Bronze Age, almost within human memory, that man defied the matriarch and

learned to eat meat. Lucretius, as well as Plato, tells us that early man lived on roots, berries, acorns, grain, and fruits, and Porphyry that our ancestors sacrificed only fruits and vegetables."
(Elizabeth Gould Davis, *The First Sex* [Middlesex, England: Penguin Books, 1975].)

23. *Background:* In 1980–81, Canada's federal government sought to bring the British North America Act within complete Canadian jurisdiction. It also sought to add to this act a charter of human rights. Concerning these plans, a writer from Willowdale, Ontario, wrote this letter:

"The most glaring fault in the Government's constitutional proposals is the attempt to entrench a charter of human rights. We all want our desires and hopes to be regarded as rights: homosexuals, Portuguese immigrants, native people, short people, females, Christians oppressed by public pornography, Jews oppressed by Christian holidays— the list is inexhaustible. But these are plainly claims, not rights. Yet the constitutional proposals seek to transfer them from the rub of daily life, or from the purview of Parliament, and turn them over to the adjudication of the courts.

"The Americans have tried it. As a result they sue each other daily for preposterous reasons. The courts there have required police departments to hire specific proportions of people hitherto denied their 'rights.' Do we really want the Provincial Court judges telling the Police Commission it must hire some specific number of Serbian females under five-foot-two? Or that the school boards must hire some proportion of homosexuals? What pressures will we face for adding and adding again to the entrenched list of rights?"
(Letter to the editor, Toronto *Globe and Mail*, October 23, 1980.)

24. "The threatened or resentful housewife ought to be told that most working women are housewives too. They also clean bathtubs. They also love and listen to their children. They are working to help keep their families above the poverty line, and their double lives are not meant as a reproach to anyone."
(Michelle Landsberg, "Paying the Price of Mythology," in *Women and Children First* [Toronto: Macmillan, 1982, p. 81].)

Summing Things Up: Arguments and Disagreements

Evaluating an argument, then, is a matter of reaching a carefully grounded appraisal of how cogent the argument is. It is not a matter of simply agreeing or disagreeing with the conclusion. Often, in fact, you may have to admit that an argument is a poor one, even though you happen to agree with the conclusion the arguer is defending. And, of course, you may often find what seem to be cogent arguments in favor of conclusions with which you disagree. When this happens, you have a choice: either change your mind about the conclusion or continue to scrutinize the argument for a flaw. Arguing well and responding well to arguments require the kind of flexibility and reasonableness that allows for the possibility that your previous view was mistaken, and you can be shown good reasons for changing your mind!

It is important to note just what you have shown when you show that an argument is not a cogent one. You have shown that the author of the argument failed to support his or her conclusion with adequate reasons. The conclusion is not justified by the reasoning the author put forward. However, this is *not* to say that the conclusion itself is false or unacceptable. The conclusion might be true, and there might be other evidence showing it to be true, even though the argument you considered did not.

Suppose you were to argue this way:

1. Jones offered a poor argument for the conclusion that English should be a compulsory subject in universities and colleges.
Therefore,

2. There is no good reason for having English as a compulsory subject in universities and colleges.

Your own argument would be very faulty in such a case. It would fail on the (G) condition; the grounds offered are not adequate. If you were to argue in such a way, you would have only the flimsiest of evidence for your conclusion. After all, Jones is only one person among many. The fact that he happened to come up with a poor argument on a topic does *not* show that there are *no* good arguments for the conclusion he sought to reach on that topic. To show that a person's argument is faulty is to show that his conclusion is not well supported by the evidence he has put forward, and that is all. It is important to remember that you have not refuted a claim or a theory by showing that one or more of the supporting arguments for it is faulty. To refute it, you would have to come up with an independent argument in which the conclusion was the denial of the original conclusion. Often this is much harder than simply finding faults in the argument for the original conclusion.

When you decide that someone else has offered a poor argument and you give an appraisal of the argument to show which of the ARG conditions are not satisfied, you are actually offering an argument yourself. The response to an argument is either agreement with the conclusion or—as in this case—another argument, contending that the first argument goes wrong in some way. We emphasize that the critical response to an argument is another argument to emphasize that the ARG conditions must be constructive as well as destructive. You use the conditions destructively, in a sense, when you use them to object to someone else's argument. But at the same time you should use them constructively, for you are putting forward an argument of your own when you give a reasoned basis for objecting to someone else's position. For instance, if you say:

1. The arguer used a false premise.
2. The arguer's second premise is irrelevant to his conclusion.
So,
3. The argument given fails on the (A) condition and on the (R) condition.
Therefore,
4. The argument offered is not a cogent argument.

you are offering an argument yourself. Here you really need to define (1) and (2) in subarguments, for it is up to you to show why the premise is false, or irrelevant. (Presumably the arguer thought his premises were acceptable and relevant; otherwise, it is unlikely that he would have used them.)

The proper response to an argument is a reasoned one: you follow the reasoning, accept it, and accept the author's conclusion; or you offer your own argument designed to show why acceptance of the original argument is inappropriate. When you offer your own argument, you are working constructively, and your own argument, in order to be a good one, will itself have to satisfy the ARG conditions. Make sure that what you say about the argument is acceptable and relevant and that it provides adequate grounds for your judgment that the original argument is not cogent. This practice of reasonableness is not as common as it should be. But it is worth cultivating, both in the interest of truth and in the interest of resolving disputes in a sensible fashion.

A textbook can hardly be based on arguments that students invent because the students who are reading it are not handy when the author is writing it. For this reason, textbooks include many arguments written by other people, and students working through the textbook are asked to analyze these. This process is very useful, but it can lead all of us to forget that there are two sides to critical reasoning skills.

There is the matter of spotting ambiguities or reasoning flaws in other people's arguments, and there is also the matter of becoming good at constructing arguments yourself. The most natural way to construct cogent arguments is to concentrate on the ARG conditions and the other things you work on in a logic course when you are writing or speaking on other subjects. Try to use premises that are acceptable—both to you and to those who will be hearing or reading your argument. Have a keen sense of which conclusions you are trying to defend, and make sure that what you have to say is either relevant to those conclusions or else clearly stands out as a background, or an "aside" comment. Make sure there are enough relevant premises to provide adequate grounds for your conclusions.

You have no doubt noticed that most of the arguments invented here to illustrate various themes in this book are much easier to follow than the real arguments quoted from letters to the editor and from nonfiction works. With the real arguments, sometimes it seems as though most of your work comes in standardizing, rather than in appraisal. You cannot apply the ARG conditions until you have a clear argument to apply them to. If you find this matter really difficult, it might be worthwhile to spend some time reviewing Chapter Two.

The difficulties we may experience in standardizing can teach us something. We must try to make ourselves very clear when we are constructing our own arguments. We need not be so boring as to number our premises and conclusions, but we can introduce important conclusions with useful phrases such as "I wish to argue that" or "What I am trying to prove is," and we can state conclusions clearly either at the beginning or at the end of what we have to say. We can avoid vague and ambiguous terms, or clarify terms that could be misinterpreted by the audience whom we are addressing, and so on. All of this is simply to say that the various things that cause problems of interpretation or weak arguments when they appear in other people's writing also can appear in our own work, and we should try hard to eliminate them. Becoming a competent critic of other people's arguments and gaining the ability to argue clearly yourself are opposite sides of the same coin.

Review of Terms Introduced

Cogent argument: An argument in which the premises are rationally acceptable and also properly connected to the conclusion.

ARG conditions: The conditions of a cogent argument. The premises must (1) be ACCEPTABLE; must (2a) be RELEVANT to the truth of the conclusion and; when considered together, must (2b) provide sufficient GROUNDS for the conclusion. For an argument to be cogent, all ARG conditions must be satisfied.

Conditional statement: A statement of the type, "If *A*, then *B*." As such, it does not assert either the clause labelled *A* or the clause labelled *B*. It asserts only that there is a connection between *A* and *B*; given *A*, *B* must be true as well.

Antecedent of a conditional statement: The clause after the "if" in a conditional statement. In a statement of the type "if *A*, then *B*," *A* represents the antecedent.

Consequent of a conditional statement: The clause after the "then" in a conditional statement. In a statement of the type "if *A*, then *B*," *B* represents the consequent.

Acceptability of premises: Premises of an argument are acceptable provided there is appropriate evidence, or reasons, to believe them.

Relevance of premises: Premises of an argument are relevant to its conclusion provided they give at least some evidence, or reasons, in favor of that conclusion's being true.

Sufficiency of grounds: Adequacy of premise to provide full evidence for the conclusion. Premises offer sufficient grounds if, assuming that they are accepted, it would be reasonable to accept the conclusion. Taken together, the premises present enough evidence to make the conclusion something it would be rational to believe.

Deductive entailment: Most complete relationship of logical support. If one statement entails another, then, given the truth of the first statement, it is impossible that the other should be false. In an argument, the premises deductively entail the conclusion if, given the truth of the conjunction of the premises, it would be logically impossible for the conclusion to be false.

Conjunction: Connection of two or more statements using the English word *and* or another word or symbol equivalent in meaning.

Empirical generalization: When premises are connected to a conclusion on the basis of an empirical generalization, the premises describe observations about some cases, and the conclusion, which is more general, attributes the same features reported in the premises to a broader range of cases.

Analogy: Comparison based on resemblances. When the premises are connected to the conclusion on the basis of an analogy, the premises describe similarities between two things and state or assume that those two things will be similar in further ways not described. The claim is made that one of the things has a further property, and the inference is drawn that the other thing will have the same further property.

Conductive argument: An argument in which premises (nearly always several in number) describe factors that are supposed to count separately in favor of a conclusion because each is relevant to it. Typically, in conductive arguments we deal with matters on which there are pros and cons.

EXERCISE SET

Exercise Three

1. Construct your own arguments in response to one of the following questions after critical examination and reflection:

    (a) Does football encourage harmful aggressive tendencies in players?

    (b) Would gun control mean that only criminals had guns?

    (c) Should a world power such as the United States be willing to abide by judgments of the World Court in The Hague (Holland) as to the legitimacy of its actions?

    (*Background:* The United States did not send lawyers to represent it when the World Court heard Nicaragua's case against U.S. activities, such as the mining of a harbor and the support for Contras, who are in rebellion against the government. The U.S. government's position was that the World Court did not have authority in this area. Nicaragua won the case.)

    (d) Is a college education more than a means to a job?

    (e) Should women keep their maiden names after marriage if they wish to do so?

Strategy for doing this exercise: First, think about the question you have selected to discuss, and think about your tentative response to it. Next, think about your reasons for wanting to answer in this way. Write them down. Now, look at what you have written and organize it into a clear argument. You should not hold your position dogmatically. Think about the question again, and think about how other people might answer it. Think of a response different from your own that strikes you as quite plausible. What reasons could be given for that response? How good an argument could be constructed for it? After developing the alternative response, look back at your original response. Revise your original argument if thinking through an alternative position has led you to change or moderate your first one.

Example: Question: Is nuclear energy necessary?
First response: Nuclear energy is necessary.
Reasons: Nuclear energy would not have been developed unless experts thought it was necessary and, by and large, energy experts know what is likely to be needed; oil, gas, and coal are alternative sources of energy, and they are not going to last forever; growth in manufacturing, which is important to give people jobs, will require more energy; we can get virtually unlimited amounts of energy from small amounts of uranium, so nuclear energy has virtually unlimited potential and can meet these needs.
Alternative response: Nuclear energy may not be necessary under some conditions. *Reasons:* We could change our habits so that we do not consume so much energy (much is wasted); solar and wind energy may be viable alternatives to oil, gas, coal, and nuclear energy; perhaps if we put massive resources into researching solar and

wind energy, we would find vast potential there too; solar and wind energy do not pose the safety hazards nuclear energy does.
Resulting argument:

1. Energy experts used to think nuclear energy was needed and they were probably right in the judgments they made, considering the time at which these were made.
2. Coal, oil, and gas are the major alternatives to nuclear energy, and they will not last forever.
3. Probably solar and wind energy will not have the same potential for expansion as nuclear energy.
4. We need vast amounts of energy to keep economies going and give people jobs.
So, probably,
5. Nuclear energy is necessary unless there is successful research on how to develop solar and wind energy.

Note any subarguments and clearly mark the premises and conclusions in your final argument. Then rewrite your argument in more natural language as though it were a letter to the editor of your local newspaper. (*Note:* This is only an example and does not represent our final position on nuclear energy.)

2. Show that the argument you constructed in response to question (1) satisfies the ARG conditions of argument cogency.

3. Ask a friend in the course to evaluate your argument. Note disputed points, if any, and either revise your position to accommodate these or defend your position with subarguments.

NOTES

1. (For instructors) The term *acceptable* has been used instead of *true* to express a condition of premise adequacy for cogent arguments. We are aware that this shift is very significant. It has been made because we believe that the truth of premises is neither sufficient nor necessary for them to provide a basis for cogent argumentation. Truth is not sufficient because there are many premises that are true but whose truth is not known either to the audience or the arguer. An argument based on such premises would not be epistemically adequate. People would not be in a position to determine the adequacy of the premises; the premises' truth, in such a case, is irrelevant to the issue of the practical or epistemic value of the argument. The truth of premises is not necessary because an argument can lead from acceptance to acceptance and be of immense practical value, and because of

such argument types as the *reductio ad absurdum*. Those who maintain that the truth of premises is a necessary condition for the cogency of arguments are forced into choosing between a rather dogmatic dismissal of skeptical/fallibilist arguments that have not attained the goal of truth and an admission that there are singularly few sound arguments available. Neither alternative is satisfactory.

2. Compare this point with the discussion of *reductio ad absurdum* arguments in Chapter Five. In those arguments, it is so obvious that the conclusion is false (it is either contradictory or absurd) that we reason backwards that there must be something wrong with one or more of the premises. This reasoning is still different from just rejecting the argument, because we have to figure out what is wrong with the premises.

3. Glenn Babb, interviewed on CBC television, July 13, 1986. The same argument was used a week later by President Reagan, who attributed it to a South African official.

4. *Time* magazine, February 26, 1979.

5. Rudleigh B. MacLean, "For Responsible Adults, a Right to Pornography," Toronto *Globe and Mail*, May 3, 1984.

6. Letter to the Calgary *Herald*, July 5, 1978.

7. Bertrand Russell, "Freedom Versus Authority in Education," in *Sceptical Essays* (London: George Allen and Unwin, 1953), p. 184.

5

Premises: What to Accept and Why

An argument starts from premises and uses them to support one or more conclusions. If these premises are known to be false or inconsistent or highly controversial, then even the most elegant reasoning will not render the conclusion acceptable. When appraising an argument, we have to ask ourselves whether there is good reason to accept the premises on which the argument is based. Unfortunately it is very difficult to get an adequate answer to this question. When we say that the premises of an argument are *acceptable,* we mean that it would be reasonable for the person appraising the argument to accept them. If you are appraising the argument, then, for the moment at least, that person is you. Of course, the argument might have been intended originally for an audience that was quite different from you in various ways, and premises that would have been acceptable for that audience may not be acceptable to you. But we'll ignore this complication here and attend to acceptability from the perspective of you, the reader, as the audience for the argument. This is the most practical point of view in any case.

If you could accept—that is, *believe*—the premises of an argument without violating any standard of evidence or certainty, then you find its premises acceptable. The discipline within philosophy called "theory of knowledge" studies standards of adequate evidence in a general and highly theoretical way. Here we only touch the surface of the theory of knowledge, setting forward some standards and giving a brief defense of them that is directed more toward practice than theory.

When Premises Are Acceptable

Defended in a Cogent Subargument.   Clearly, a premise in an argument is acceptable if the arguer has already shown it to be acceptable by a cogent subargument. That means he has supplied evidence or reasons which make it rational to accept that premise. But people cannot always prove all the premises they use in arguments because every argument must start somewhere. Every argument is based on a premise, or a set of premises, and proceeds from those premises to its conclusion. To prove a premise, you would need to construct a further argument. And you could do this. But then, to prove the premises of that further argument, you would need yet another argument, and to prove the premises of this further further argument, yet another. And so it would go on. Obviously the demand that every premise of every argument should be proven in an argument would require an infinite series of arguments. And no one can construct and present an infinite series of arguments. We can see from this situation that the demand that every premise be proven is, ultimately, an impossible and unreasonable demand. If argument and justification are going to proceed at all in human life, people will have to be willing to accept some premises without further proof. This is the background of our search for conditions of acceptability. We will suggest conditions such that the satisfaction of any one of these by a premise will make that premise acceptable. A premise does not have to satisfy all of these conditions to be acceptable. Just one will do.

Necessary Truths. A premise in an argument is acceptable if it is necessarily true. "Necessarily true" means that it would be a complete impossibility for the proposition to be false. The denial of a necessarily true statement would amount to a contradiction. For instance, the statement "sisters are female" is necessarily true because the word *sister* means "female sibling," and it would be a *contradiction* for female siblings not to be female. A contradiction is a statement that asserts and denies the same thing. If female siblings (sisters) were not female, then they would both be female and not be female—a contradiction. No contradiction can be true. When a statement is a necessary truth, its denial is a contradiction; we therefore know that its denial is false and that the statement itself is true. If a premise in an argument is necessarily true, then it cannot possibly be false. If it cannot possibly be false, it will be acceptable.

Here are some examples of necessarily true statements:

a. Anyone who has property is the owner of something.
b. Either the committee will bring forward its report or it will not bring forward its report.
c. All triangles have three sides.
d. Five is an odd number.
e. No false statement is true.
f. Every object that has a shape occupies some space.

In each of the preceding cases you can see that if you were to deny the statement, you would get yourself into a contradiction. In (a), this contradiction would come because of what it means to have property. The words *property* and *owner of* are logically related, so it is a logical impossibility to have property and not be the owner of anything. Because of the logical relations between these words, statement (a) is a necessary truth. Statement (b) is also a necessary truth because of the way *not* and *or* work logically. Bringing forward a report is something the committee will or will not do: there is no third possibility, as a matter of logic. So statement (b) also expresses something that cannot be false: it is a necessary truth. See if you can work out the relations between words and concepts that show why (c), (d), (e), and (f) are necessary truths.

Any premise in an argument is acceptable if it is necessarily true; in that event it could not be false, and you could not possibly go astray by accepting it.

Common Knowledge. A premise in an argument is acceptable if it is a matter of common knowledge. That is, if the premise states something that is known to virtually everyone, it should be allowed as an acceptable premise. Or, if a premise is very widely believed, and there is no widely known evidence against it, it is often appropriate to allow it as acceptable. Society operates on the basis of many things that people know or believe as a common basis for communication and cooperation.

A simple example of a statement that is common knowledge is "Human beings have hearts." Obviously this statement is not a necessary truth. It would not involve a contradiction for the human species to have some other organ to circulate the blood. The statement is, however, true, and virtually all human adults know it to be true. It is a factual proposition that is widely known and that would be acceptable as a premise in an argument, requiring no further supporting evidence.

For those who follow international politics, it is presently common knowledge that Margaret Thatcher is the first female prime minister of Great Britain. As this example suggests, what is common knowledge at one time and in one place may not be common knowledge at another time or in another place. Thirty years from now it will still be true that Mrs. Thatcher was the first woman to become prime minister of Great Britain, but it is unlikely that this will still be common knowledge. At that time, even some who follow international politics carefully may not know the fact that Mrs. Thatcher had no female predecessors. Mrs. Thatcher's personality and policies will be a matter of history, and many women may have been leaders by that time. So common knowledge does vary with time and place and culture.

Nevertheless we cannot realistically dispense with common knowledge as a condition of premise acceptability. Typically people argue back and forth with others with whom they share a culture and a broad background of beliefs and commitments. Arguments go on within this shared context and could not proceed without it. As we have seen, arguments have to start from premises, and not every premise can be defended in a further argument. Looking at the necessary truths, you can see that these alone would be far from sufficient as starting points for argument. They only relate concepts to each other; they do not state facts about the world. In order to engage in argument and discussion, people must understand common issues and problems. They must share many beliefs and assumptions. The "common knowledge" condition for acceptability reflects these basic facts about argument and social context. Many arguments proceed from premises taken as common knowledge and move on to new conclusions. Even though the common knowledge premises are not as obvious and certain as the necessary truths, they should be accepted in virtue of the required social context for arguments.

Here is an example that starts from points of common knowledge and reaches a rather surprising conclusion:

1. There are many trees in Canada.
2. If anyone tried to count all the trees in Canada, it would be a very long time after he started until he reached the last tree.
3. Before he finished his counting task, some trees already counted would have died due to fire or animal destruction and new trees would be sprouting.
4. Having a number of people count these trees would not avoid these problems of destruction and growth.
So,
5. It is practically impossible to determine by counting just exactly how many trees there are in Canada.
Therefore,
6. The question "How many trees are there in Canada?" is a question that has no practically determinable answer.

In this argument, premises (1), (2), and (3) are matters of common knowledge—for current North American audiences at least. To deem the argument inadequate by questioning one of these premises would be quite unreasonable. The fourth premise, however, is a different matter. It is not, as such, a matter of common knowledge and does need further defense. But to insist on proof or further evidence for something like "there are many trees in Canada" is a violation of the social conditions of argument. Someone who takes this kind of stance on the acceptability of premises will soon find that he has no one to argue with and nothing to say.

Testimony.   A premise is acceptable if it concerns a matter for which the testimony of a person is appropriate, and if the author of the argument is someone whose testimony on the matter is credible. Here there are two issues to clarify: when is testimony appropriate, and when does the person giving testimony have credibility? The need to accept things on testimony arises because we cannot be everywhere at every time. We have experience, but so do others. Knowledge is built up by *compounding* human experience. Thus, someone who has never been in Brazil may be given testimony that there was heavy rain in Rio de Janeiro on January 7, 1979. Someone may be given testimony by a friend that her husband has beaten her on several occasions. We may have testimony that Indian railway passengers often sleep huddled together on the floor in railway stations. And there are literally millions of further claims that we would have to accept on the testimony of other people or not at all. With claims like these we are not in the realm of necessary truth or common knowledge. Nor are we dealing with specialized claims on matters where people have technical or scholarly expertise. Rather, we face a situation where we might be inclined to accept claims on the testimony of other people. We can accept these statements based on the testimony of other people about what they have experienced. Or we can refuse to accept them. The alternative to some acceptance of testimony is widescale skepticism.

Sometimes we must accept the testimony of other people. People tell us of experiences we have not had—sights, sounds, places, and personal encounters not within our own experience. Life would be short and knowledge limited if human beings could not extend their knowledge by relying on the experiences of others. However, sometimes it is not rational to accept the testimony of another person. If, for instance, someone is a liar, a biased observer, or a practical joker, it is not reasonable to accept a story about events he claims to have witnessed. But typically people are not liars, biased observers, or practical jokers. (If these things were typical, human life could scarcely go on.) People normally tell of their experiences to communicate information and attitudes to others, and we grant them credibility when they do so. This credibility is relevant to the acceptability of premises in many arguments. Often people argue beginning from their own experience. (They may begin an argument by recounting an anecdote that they wish to use as illustrating or indicating a general claim, for instance.) There are often problems with such arguments. But you cannot refuse to accept premises just because they are based on what other people have experienced. All of our language and life is based on taking many things from others on trust. Unless there is a special reason to doubt, premises based on testimony from people about their own experience should be accepted.

Suppose that one mother claims that boys are always more active than girls, and another mother counters, saying this is not true because her own girl was more active than her own boys. The second mother is trying to refute the first by offering a counterexample to her very general claim. The counterexample is based on the second mother's experience, and there is usually no special reason to discount such experience. A mother is better qualified than virtually anyone else to comment on the activity level of her own children! This is a particular judgment about her own experience; she is not generalizing to a conclusion about other children, merely recounting what she has experienced in her own life. The counterargument shouldn't be rejected for having a premise that isn't acceptable. The premise should be accepted on the basis of the mother's testimony because it is directly within her own experience and there is no special reason to think that she is lying.

Often arguments are based on premises about people's personal experiences. The policy recommended here is that we accept these premises on the testimony of the arguer provided that the arguer is not a person whom we have a special reason to regard as unreliable. If he has lied about matters like this before, is biased, has a vested interest in the matter, or is nearly blind (where the matter concerns what he has seen), then there are special reasons not to regard him as a credible source for testimony. But in the absence of any such special defects, we should accept the testimony of others.

Credibility is something everyone starts out with. It is an aspect of respecting people. You don't systematically doubt every description that is based on someone's own experience of the world. It is true that people can behave in ways that make them lose their credibility. We can all think of politicians who have frequently lied and have now lost all credibility with the public. Sometimes when such a person says something, we think we have reasons for thinking the very opposite must be true! But we must give people initial credibility. Unless there is some special reason not to do so, we take their word for it so far as their own accounts of their experience of the world are concerned.

A simple example that illustrates this point is the argument about the Calgary zoo.

> We arrived at the park gate at 7:25 p.m., at which time the cashier gleefully took money for admission. Upon entering the zoo and walking across the bridge, the loudspeaker was stating that the zoo buildings were closing at 8:00 p.m. We asked if we would not get a pass for the following day. The answer was no.
> In summary it is easy to see that Calgary is anything but a friendly city but rather is out to rake off the tourist for all they can.[1]

Here the author bases an argument on his personal experience. His argument is quite poor because it does not give a sufficient basis for the conclusion. (He wants to generalize about a whole city on the basis of one encounter at the zoo!) But in such an argument, the premise should be accepted on the basis of testimony. We need not go so far as to doubt that these events occurred. He tells us they did and we have no special knowledge that would undermine his credibility.

Proper Authority.   Sometimes arguments are put forward by people who possess specialized knowledge about the subject they are talking about. For instance, an archaeologist may present arguments based upon scholarly claims about pottery at Knossos, or a chemist may present an argument about the presence of carbon in amino acids. When people are experts or authorities in some area of knowledge, they are said to "speak with authority." It may be reasonable for us to accept what they say simply because they have said it. And this can bear on the acceptability of premises. If an archaeologist who is the world expert on Knossos tells us that the colors used in designs at Knossos are unlike colors used in sites in Syria, we may accept this simply because he said so.

Accepting a premise for this reason is like accepting a premise on testimony in the sense that in both cases we are relying on claims because other people have sincerely asserted them. However, there is an important difference between authority and testimony. Authority requires specialized knowledge in a field where there are recognized standards of expertise. Testimony does not require specialized knowledge: we can all testify about our own experience. Whatever undermines testimony (dishonesty, vested interest, suspicion of joking, and so on) would also undermine authority. In addition, further conditions exist for the proper understanding of authority. If we are to accept a premise just because Jones says that it is acceptable, where Jones is an authority, then that premise must be within a field of knowledge. Jones must be recognized within that field as an expert. It cannot be the case that experts in the field disagree about the matter. Also, Jones must have credibility that has not been undermined by his being paid by one side of a dispute, by his having lied in the past about related matters, and so on. Only if all these conditions are met can we reasonably think to ourselves:

1. Jones has asserted premise P.
2. P falls within area of knowledge K.
3. Jones is a recognized expert regarding K.
Therefore,
4. P is acceptable.

If we reason to ourselves as in the preceding, we have, in effect, constructed our own subargument on behalf of a premise used by Jones. We have determined that we should accept the premise because Jones, as an authority, endorsed it.

We grant the legitimacy of such arguments, provided that the following conditions are met:

1. P falls within K, where K is a recognized body of knowledge.
2. The person whose authority is cited is an expert on K.
3. The experts on K agree about P.
4. The person whose authority is cited does not have a vested interest in P's being true, nor has he been dishonest about matters related to P in the past. (This condition concerns the person's credibility.)

We are allowing, then, that some claims can be made acceptable by proper appeals to authority.

We should note, of course, that there are many fallacious appeals to authority as well as some legitimate ones. For instance, often people who are authorities in one area make pronouncements in another area in which they are not authorities, in the hope that their expertise will transfer from one area to another. When this happens, they have as much claim to be taken seriously as anyone else, but *no more*. An authoritative scientist is not, by virtue of his position in the scientific establishment, an authority about the future of mankind or the question of when human life begins or the existence of God. (In these areas there is no related established body of knowledge and there are no authorities.) A doctor may be an authority on some aspects of medicine, including the damage radiation does to human health and the insurmountable medical problems that would be posed by a nuclear war. But as a doctor, she cannot be an authority on nuclear weapons strategy and policy. If she tries to use her authority as a doctor to establish authority on which political policies can best prevent a nuclear war, she is making an illegitimate attempt to transfer credentials from one area of expertise to another. (In fact, this whole issue is so complex and involves theories and facts from so many different disciplines that probably no one can claim to be an authority on it. We are all nonexperts entitled to work out ideas and have them listened to.)

Where there is disagreement in a field, it will not be sufficient to cite one expert and defend a claim as true because that expert said so. In 1982, weapons experts disagreed on whether proposed cruise missiles would present a new problem of verifiability (being easily hidden) or whether they would merely extend an already existing problem. In the face of such disagreement, no one expert can be appealed to as an authority on the matter. Anyone who disagrees with you could just present his own expert, and you would end up saying that you had two good arguments, each justifying a conclusion that contradicted that of the other.

When any of the conditions for proper use of authority are violated, an argument of the type:

1. So-and-so has asserted P.
2. So-and-so is an authority as to P.
Therefore,
3. P is true.

is a fallacious appeal to authority. The claim of authority will not properly support the conclusion because the authority will not be of the appropriate type.

Accepting Premises "for the Sake of Argument." The conditions given so far certainly do not cover all the premises people use in their arguments. Sometimes we may want to entertain premises just tentatively in order to explore their consequences. In such contexts we might grant "for the sake of argument" premises that are not made acceptable under any of the preceding categories. For instance, someone might say, "Now let us suppose that political chaos in Iran will continue for at least another five years. Then oil production will decline by 20 percent in the Middle East and . . ." Here we cannot simply accept his initial premise about Iran. In fact, he may not himself accept this premise. He may merely be putting it forward as a supposition and then reasoning on from there. We can grant the supposition for the sake of argument, reasoning forward on this basis to see what conclusions might emerge. It is important when we do this that we realize that any conclusion we get is *conditional* upon our suppositions. We will not prove a detached conclusion; rather, our conclusion would be that *if* the chaos continues in Iran, *then* such-and-such is likely. In contexts like these the word *if* is very important and should not be forgotten.

A special kind of argument falling into this category is the *reductio ad absurdum.* In this kind of argument we suppose that some premises are true and then show that these premises lead either to a contradiction or to a statement that is obviously false. Because the premises we have started with lead to a false consequence, we know that there is something wrong with those premises. Our original suppositions cannot all be true. One, at least, must be false. Here is a simple example of a *reductio* argument:

Some people say that no one ever makes a mistake. This theory, put forward in the name of tolerance, can easily be shown to be wrong. For if we suppose it true, we can see that it will have the consequence that two people who disagree with each other are both correct. This means that if Jones says that the Battle of Hastings occurred in 1066 and Smith says that it occurred in 1166, both Jones and Smith are correct. There was only one Battle of Hastings and it did not occur twice, in two events separated by a century. Yet this example of a disagreement is just one of very many we could give. People disagree all the time, and when they do, if we suppose that no one ever makes a mistake, we are led into absurdity. You can easily see that the theory that no one ever makes a mistake is false.

In a *reductio* argument, some or all of the premises are never really accepted. They are "supposed" and then rejected on the grounds that they lead to unacceptable consequences. Paradoxically, we might say that such premises are acceptable precisely because they don't have to be accepted at all!

Summary of Acceptability Conditions. A premise in an argument is acceptable if any *one* of the following conditions is satisfied:

1. It is defended in a subargument that is cogent.

2. It is necessarily true.

3. It is a matter of common knowledge.

4. It is a matter of reliable testimony from the person arguing.

5. It is backed up by an appropriate authority.

6. It does not really have to be accepted at all since it is used only as a supposition either to get a conditional conclusion or in a *reductio ad absurdum* argument.

EXERCISE SET

Exercise One
Part A

For each of the following statements, determine whether or not it is necessarily true and explain the basis for your answer.

1. Every rectangle has four straight sides.

2. Every parent is the relative of someone who is younger than himself.

3. There is a great problem with acid rain in the lakes and forests of northeastern North America.

*4. Everyone who is a parent is legally responsible for the well-being of at least one child.

5. Grass is green.

6. A number is an expression of quantity.

*7. Either a person is happy or he is not happy.

8. Animal behavior is a product of instinct and stimulus-response rather than a product of learning or deliberation.

9. There are two, and only two, distinct sexes in human beings.

10. All is fair in love and war.

*11. Any action that is fully caused is the effect of something.

12. Playing with guns is likely to make young children see violence as something natural and approved by adults.

13. If a tribe has members who fight with each other over titles and lands to the point of causing each other severe physical injury, then that tribe is not one where expressions of jealousy and aggression are absent.

*14. Girls brought up by their mothers are brought up by a parent of their own sex.

*15. Obesity is genetically caused.

Part B

For each of the following pairs of statements, (a) and (b), imagine that (a) is used as a premise in an argument that is put forward to establish (b) as the conclusion. Then try to reach a decision as to whether (a) would constitute an acceptable premise in such a case. State why you think it would be acceptable, referring to the conditions of acceptability developed earlier.

*1. (a) Every living creature has some kind of reproductive system.
(b) The fundamental behaviors of living creatures are established by patterns of genetic inheritance.

2. (a) The British legal system makes precedence and the pattern of established cases just as important as codified law.
(b) British law is less based on legal formula than French and American law.

3. (a) No mental desire is in any way a physical thing.
(b) The mind is completely distinct from the body.

*4. (a) The Bible was composed on the authority of God.
(b) God's nature has been revealed to us by prophets whose words and deeds are recorded in the Bible.

5. (a) If exercise leads to a feeling of well-being and a feeling of well-being leads to a greater zest for life, then exercise leads to greater zest for life.
(b) For most people, exercise will bring better physical and mental health.

*6. (a) An event like the Royal Wedding of 1981 recalls the splendor of past times at the cost of a great deal of taxpayers' money.
(b) The Royal Wedding is to the British what the inauguration of a president is to the Americans.

7. (a) Football is more popular in North America than soccer.
(b) North America and Europe differ insofar as their love of soccer is concerned.

8. (a) As the impoverished father of three sons, I can say that it is hard not to buy expensive sports equipment for children whose school virtually requires that they have such eqiupment.
(b) The schools should not pursue sports programs that require children to have expensive sports equipment.

9. (a) As a professional therapist, I would say that the primary cause of divorce today is problems with money.
(b) Credit counselling should be developed by governments if we are to preserve the modern family from total breakdown.

10. (a) Farmers in Crete may still be seen transporting hay and other goods on small donkeys, as we observed during a recent family holiday in Crete.
(b) Crete is a part of Greece ill-suited to the high technology of Common Market farming.

When Premises Are Unacceptable

When considering whether premises are acceptable, we will find some acceptable and others unacceptable. Now that we have described some general conditions that make premises acceptable, we will go on to deal with some of the things that make premises unacceptable. But there is an intermediate range in which we can say neither that premises are acceptable nor that they are unacceptable, and we have to leave you to fend for yourself. Logic is not the source of all knowledge, and it is important to remember that the division between acceptable and unacceptable does not cover every premise. It is like the distinction between white and black. Some things are neither white nor black; and some premises are neither acceptable nor unacceptable—as we have specified these conditions here.

Falsity. The condition of falsity is the simplest of all, obviously. (The only trick is that you have to know it applies!) If you know that a premise is false, then you know that it is not acceptable. This may happen when the premise denies what is common knowledge or because you have access to specialized knowledge that puts you in a position to know that it is false. If a premise is false and you have the basis for showing that it is false, you will not accept it and the argument in which it appears will fall down on the (A) condition of argument adequacy.

Here is an example taken from a discussion of the acceptance of refugees by the United States:

> *A century ago an open-ended invitation may have been safe enough. America was a new country then, unfilled. The supply of possible immigrants wasn't so great. Now the huddled masses of the wretchedly poor amount to 800 million. More than three times the U.S. population. It would be insane to invite them all in. Even one percent would be too many.*

Variety in a nation is good. So also is unity. But when variety (of which we've always had plenty) overwhelms unity, how are we to keep a complex society like ours running? When newcomers arrive too fast, they gather into enclaves and resist learning the national language. Immigrants then become the new isolationists. Tribalism becomes a reality: Goodbye, unity![2]

One premise in this argument against admitting refugees to the United States is the following:

——— When newcomers arrive too fast, they gather into enclaves, resist learning the national language, and become isolationists.

This premise is rather vague since it is not clear how fast "too fast" is. But when refugees have come in large numbers to Canada and the United States in the past, they have not, in fact, refused to learn the language and adapt to a new life. Many Hungarians came to Canada and the United States in the 1950s and learned English, assimilating into the mainstream of life. Many Italians and Germans did the same thing after the Second World War. Unless he has a very strict meaning for "coming too fast," the author has simply asserted a *false* premise. Most Americans and Canadians could, from their own personal experience of their own societies, see that this premise is false. If it is false, and known to be false, it is unacceptable.

Inconsistency.   Sometimes an argument will contain a number of premises, and several of these premises will explicitly or implicitly contradict each other. They explicitly contradict each other if one premise asserts what another premise denies. For example, if one premise asserts, "All women are temperamental" and another premise asserts, "Some women are not temperamental," the argument in which both premises occur has premises explicitly contradicting each other. As you can imagine, this mistake is too obvious to occur very frequently. It is more common for premises to contradict each other implicitly. This means that when we think about what the premises say and make some simple deductive inferences, we can arrive at an explicit contradiction from the premises. If there is either an explicit or an implicit contradiction in the premises of an argument, we know that not all its premises can be true.

Here is an example of an implicit contradiction:

——— 1. Women have taken jobs away from men who need work to support families.
2. Hiring should be by merit only.
3. Until now, hiring has been by merit only.
4. To prefer women to men, or to hire women when men are available, would be a betrayal of the merit system.
So,
5. Women should never be hired for jobs when men are available to take those same jobs.

Looking closely at this argument, you will see an inconsistency among (1), (3), and (4). The author allows, in (1) and (3), that women have taken jobs away from men when hiring has been by merit. And yet, he also insists, in (4), that if women are hired when men are available, the merit system of hiring will be violated. Premises (1) and (3) taken together entail that some women have been more meritorious than men (those men whose jobs they have taken away)—and there are some, according to (1). Premise (4), however, requires that no women are more meritorious than men. It insists that in any case where women were hired and men were available, the merit system of hiring would be violated.

You can see that the author's premises are *inconsistent* because they implicitly contradict each other. Making some very obvious inferences from premises (1), (3), and (4), we can see that the author is committed to claiming *both* that some women are more meritorious than some men *and* that no women are ever more meritorious than any men. The author is, in fact, contradicting himself in his premises. Even without knowing anything about the hiring of women and men, you can know that this argument has faulty premises. The premises are inconsistent and cannot all be true. When premises are explicitly or implicitly contradictory, they are inconsistent and therefore unacceptable.

Contradiction is the opposite of necessary truth. A statement that is necessarily true is one that is made true by the meanings of the words used to express it and by basic logical relationships. A necessarily true statement could not be false. A contradiction, on the other hand, is made false by the meanings of the words used to express it, and it could not possibly be true. In the preceding example, the premises commit us to this contradiction:

> Women are sometimes more meritorious than men, and women are never more meritorious than men.

This statement is false, purely for reasons of logic. No matter what the facts are about women and men, they can't make this statement true. Since the premises commit us to this contradiction, they are unacceptable. At least one premise used in the argument must be false, for no set of true statements can entail a contradiction.

Dependence on Faulty Assumptions. Sometimes problems with false premises are more obvious when we see the assumptions underlying those premises. We may find an argument and suspect that there is something wrong with the premises, but we may see this only when we stop to ask why these premises are stated as they are. When we do this, we can see that what the arguer says makes sense only if we grant her a particular assumption or set of assumptions. Then it is worthwhile to take the time to state the assumptions clearly and see just how the stated premises depend on them. Often background assumptions on which an argument is based are false, or highly questionable. When they are, it is worth finding them and discovering this, for the argument will be faulty as a result. If premises depend on an assumption that is unacceptable, then those premises are themselves unacceptable. If premises depend on an assumption that is highly questionable, then they themselves are highly questionable.

You can see how this business of assumptions works by looking at this advertisement:

> *If you think advertising is a bunch of baloney, why are you reading this ad? You read to learn. Reading brings new ideas and thoughts into your life. It opens up a whole new world. That's what advertising does. It communicates information from one source to another. Advertising gives you the opportunity to make up your own mind by familiarizing you with a product. That's why advertising is a freedom. The freedom to know quality and what is available. You read and listen to advertising to obtain information. Information on just about anything. Including the price of baloney.*[3]

This passage is rather repetitious; its basic point seems to be that advertising is good and useful because advertising gives us knowledge and information. The premises, then, are based on the assumption that advertisements consist largely of true statements. This assumption is clearly necessary because both information and knowledge can be obtained only if the statements made in advertisements are true. Thus the advertisement depends in its premises on the assumption that advertisements are primarily composed of true statements.

Let us set out that assumption and take a close look at it:

———— Advertisements are composed primarily of true statements.

There is much evidence against this assumption. Common knowledge is enough to indicate this! Many advertisements contain no statements at all but consist merely of questions, suggestions, pictures, jokes, and so on. Others contain exaggerated or misleading statements, and some even contain statements that are downright false. If the author had tried to prove, or justify, his underlying assumption, he would have faced an impossible task. Instead the assumption is unstated in the hope that readers won't notice it. It is smuggled in through words like *knowledge, learn, information,* and so on. You have only to spot this assumption to see that the argument breaks down.

If you can see that the premises of an argument depend on an assumption that is either false or highly controversial, then you know that the argument has unacceptable premises. Looking for background assumptions, which you can then criticize, is a very powerful technique for finding flaws in premises. But it should be used with some care. It is easy to "see" assumptions that are not really there! If you think you have spotted a faulty assumption, you should stop to make sure that the premises really do require it. If they do, then they are unacceptable.

Premises Not More Certain Than the Conclusion.   The purpose of an argument is to lead an audience to rational acceptance of a conclusion from the premises. For this purpose to be achieved, the premises of an argument should be more certain than its conclusion. That is, they should be more readily acceptable in themselves than is the conclusion that they are used to support. *Reductio ad absurdum* arguments are, in a sense, an exception to this rule, because in those arguments we do not really have to accept the premises at all. In the context of a particular argument, premises may be unacceptable because they fail to be more certain than the conclusion that they are used to support.

Let us suppose that someone were to argue as follows:

———— 1. The pyramids of ancient Egypt were built with the assistance of creatures from outer space.
Therefore,
2. There has been at least one extraterrestrial civilization that was advanced enough to send some of its members to visit our earth.

This argument should be extremely unconvincing because it is very unlikely that the premise is true. If an argument is based on a premise that goes against the evidence of common experience and established authority, and if that premise is not itself defended by a persuasive subargument, the argument cannot really get off the ground. In this particular example, the premise makes a very bold claim about a very specific problem of history (how were the Egyptian pyramids built?), and it is even less likely to be true than the conclusion it is used to defend. If anyone were to use such an argument, its premise would be unacceptable.

G. E. Moore, a philosopher who taught at Cambridge University during the first half of this century, was famous for attacking the arguments of philosophers on grounds similar to these. He saw that philosophers invented special theories of their own about how the mind acquires knowledge, or what objects are made of, or whatever, and then used their own theories to argue against the beliefs of common sense. Moore maintained that this strategy of argument could not work because the commonsense claims that such philosophers attacked were always more certain than the philosophical theories that they used to dispute them. The philosophical theories, he maintained, did not have enough strength on their own to serve as a basis for undercutting common sense.

The general problem is this: if you use claims (1) and (2) to prove claim (3), then— assuming you give a watertight argument—your audience can accept (1) and (2) and agree with (3). Or it can insist that (3) is unacceptable and say that if (1) and (2) lead to (3), this connection just shows that there must be something wrong with these premises. This method of arguing is called *reversing* the argument. If you use premises that are so uncertain that the denial of your conclusion is more widely believed than your premises, your argument will likely backfire. People will be so much more convinced that your conclusion is false than they are that your premises are true, they will reason in the reverse direction from what you intend. They will say that since your conclusion is so bizarre, there is obviously something the matter with your premises!

Moore was concerned about the special case in which philosophers tried to undercut commonsense beliefs about such things as the existence of hands and pencils by using philosophical theories about the nature of the mind and knowledge. This is just one kind of case where the argument can go wrong because the premises are not more certain than the conclusion.

Another case is the fallacy of begging the question. When this fallacy is committed, it happens in this way. A person is trying to prove some conclusion, C. In trying to prove it, he needs premises. He chooses premises that are so logically close to C that his audience would have had to accept C already in order to accept those premises. For instance, he might use a premise stating, "Being 10 pounds overweight is unhealthy" in trying to establish the conclusion "Being 10 pounds overweight is bad for you." Since the premise would be in doubt if the conclusion were in doubt, the premise *begs the question* in this case. The issue is not fairly faced because virtually anyone who disputed the conclusion in this case would also dispute the premise. Begging the question is a well-known fallacy in argument. It occurs when the premises are not more certain than the conclusion because the relation between them and the conclusion is just too intimate.

Here is another simple example of the fallacy of begging the question:

1. Only English and German are world languages.
Therefore,
2. French is not a world language.

As it stands this argument has an unacceptable premise. The premise is unacceptable because of what the argument is trying to show and because of the intimate way it is related to the conclusion. If anyone is wondering whether French is a world language, he is not going to have his question answered satisfactorily by being told that because English and German are the only world languages, French doesn't qualify. To wonder whether French is a world language is, in effect, to wonder whether English and German are the *only* world languages. The argument *begs the question;* it avoids the question by using a premise that already assumes that the conclusion is granted by the audience.

When you look at very simple examples like this one, it may seem amazing that anyone would ever use or be fooled by a question-begging argument. Yet this often happens. It happens sometimes because people are not looking closely, do not have the concept of argument with its premises and conclusion very clearly in their minds, or are misled by complicated, ponderous language. In fact, it is quite easy to use a question-begging argument yourself without intending to, especially if you are trying to set out reasons for one of your fundamental and most cherished beliefs. Trying to find premises that will support that belief, you may easily—and quite unwittingly—come up with claims that would be acceptable only to those very people who already agree with the conclusion you are trying to prove. If this happens, you will have begged the question.

Sometimes when we are trying to construct arguments for our most basic beliefs, we cannot find any premises that do not already require acceptance of the conclusion. When this happens, it is better to admit that we have no argument to prove our fundamental principles than to use arguments that look rational but beg the question. We can simply admit that we are operating under an assumption that seems reasonable and effective but cannot be fully defended by arguments.

Here is a simple example. Let us suppose that you smoke cigarettes and you are feeling rather defensive about it, given all the objections nonsmokers are making these days about polluted air and the effects of second-hand smoke on the health of non-smokers. You would really like to be able to smoke in public places like stores and airport departure lounges without feeling guilty. You try to prove to a friend of yours that when you smoke, you are doing something entirely legitimate and within your rights. You come up with the following argument:

1. People have a right to smoke in public places.
So,
2. I am perfectly entitled to smoke in public places if I wish to do so.

The trouble with this argument is that you assume in the premise everything you are trying to prove in your conclusion. This problem can be seen when we think about the expressions "have a right to" and "am perfectly entitled to." These expressions mean just the same thing in this context. You have stated as your premise that people in general are entitled to smoke to prove in your conclusion that you personally are entitled to smoke. This argument would work if your friend and others who object to people smoking in public places had already conceded in advance that people do generally have this right. But, of course, it is just this right that they deny. They think people don't have any such right because smoking results in polluted air and in health damage to nonsmokers. You have, in this context, given an argument that begs the question.

A problem that is not exactly that of begging the question but is closely related to it arises when you have a controversial premise used to support a conclusion, which is, in fact, less controversial than that premise. Here you may not have to believe the premise in order to believe the conclusion. But, nevertheless, the premise may be too controversial to be of any use in the context of the argument.

This problem arises in the following argument, which was used in a report on childhood education. The author is considering the issue of whether languages other than French and English should be taught in public schools in Canada. (Both French and English are official languages in Canada, although there are other native and immigrant groups whose mother tongues are different languages: Cree, Ojibway, Greek, Italian, Japanese, Chinese, and so on.) When you read this argument, keep in mind that the author is trying to answer an objection to having third languages taught in public schools:

It will not surprise anyone that I reject these arguments. A child has the inalienable right to his mother tongue and to his cultural heritage, which not only determine who he is, but also who he will be. No school system, therefore, must be allowed to interfere with that right. The opposite is also true; everything must be done to encourage the child's awareness of his heritage and to develop the language skills of his mother tongue. Without these provisions we will merely be paying lip service to the multicultural reality of Canada.[4]

The author's whole case here rests on the premise that:

> A child has the inalienable right to his mother tongue and to his cultural heritage, which not only determines who he is but also who he will be.

If we knew that every child had an inalienable right to his mother tongue and cultural heritage, we would indeed know that schools should teach all mother languages. The problem is that this starting premise is so controversial—more controversial, even, than the question it is used to resolve. Obviously, if all children had an inalienable right to their mother tongue, and a right that had to be supported at all costs, then schools would have the obligation to teach all mother tongues. But perhaps it is not true that all children have such a right; no independent argument was given for this sweeping premise. Obvious reasons against this premise exist in terms of costs and the need to maintain a society with a common culture and efficient communications. As the premise stands, it is unacceptable, and even though the conclusion can be derived from it, it doesn't give the conclusion any real support. To show that from a sweeping and unsubstantiated supposition a conclusion follows is not to prove that conclusion acceptable.

A number of different conditions, then, will show that the premises of an argument are unacceptable. The following list briefly states these conditions.

Summary: *When Premises Are Unacceptable.* The premises of an argument are unacceptable if any *one* of the following conditions applies:

1. One premise or more is known to be false or is believed on the basis of good evidence to be false.

2. Several premises, taken together, produce a contradiction, so that the premises are inconsistent.

3. The premises, or one premise, depend on an assumption that is either false or very controversial.

4. The premises, or one premise, could not be believed by someone who does not already believe the conclusion, so the argument begs the question.

5. The premises are less certain than the conclusion.

EXERCISE SET

Exercise Two
Part A

Inconsistencies. Can you detect an inconsistency in any of the following sets of statements? If so, which ones? Explain your judgment.

1. The people of Samoa value virginity in young women very highly. However, they do not care how many sexual experiences young women have before they are married.

2. Squares are rectangles, but rectangles are not squares.

3. Most boys have a tendency to shoving behavior at age two. Few girls have a tendency to shoving behavior at age two unless they are the regular playmates of pushy little boys. A degree of aggression is

probably innate in the human species, particularly in the male.

*4. The economic situation of blacks in the United States has not improved as much as we might think since the bad old days before the civil rights movement. Even though some blacks are in successful and conspicuous positions in politics, law, and medicine, it is still true that unemployment affects blacks far more than whites.

5. Either the doctor deliberately murdered his own patient, or the doctor made a mistake in his diagnosis. Mistakes in diagnosis are quite common. The doctor might have made a mistake in diagnosis. Deliberate murder is a terrible crime.

6. If a person owns a house, then the house is her property. If it is her property, she is responsible for taking care of it.

*7. All goodness derives from God and would not exist without Him. God is good. God created all the goodness in the world. No act can create value. Of many values, goodness is the primary one.

8. All human beings are carnivorous. Some human beings are vegetarians.

*9. Knowledge requires proof. Proof requires premises. The premises of a proof must be known to provide the basis for that proof.

10. An extraterrestrial civilization that was both technically and morally more advanced than we are would have some reasons to come to earth and other reasons not to come. Presumably such a civilization would wish to exhibit its technological innovations to others, and presumably it would wish to communicate its advanced moral standards to others. But on the other hand, earth is a pretty repellant place from a moral point of view—full of war, torture, murder, greed, robbery, and hypocrisy. A morally advanced civilization might be too disgusted to wish to visit.

11. Babies cannot focus well in the first weeks of life. However, they can see colors. A baby's favorite color is red.

12. Canadian foreign policy is often vacillating and hesitant. Sometimes it is independent of American foreign policy and sometimes it is not.

*13. The value of life is absolute. We can never justify taking a life. However, capital punishment is morally permissible.

Part B

Evaluate the premises of the following arguments for acceptability using the criteria explained in this chapter. If you think that faulty assumptions lie behind the stated premises, state what these assumptions are and show how the stated premises depend on them. Also, say why you think the assumptions are too questionable to underlie a sound argument. If there is any passage that does not express an argument and therefore contains no premises, say so.

1. Anyone who has the capacity to kill should avoid keeping guns around the house. Actually, when you think about it, we all have the capacity to kill. So no one should keep a gun around the house.

2. Nobody should undertake college education without at least some idea of what he or she wants to do and where he or she wants to go in life. But our world is so full of change that we cannot predict which fields will provide job openings in the future. Given this, we can't form any reasonable life plans. So nobody should go to college.

*3. Withholding information is just the same as lying and lying is wrong, so withholding information is wrong.

4. Nuclear energy is as safe as any other kind of energy, so a large-scale disaster as a result of an accident in a nuclear power plant is very unlikely to occur.

5. If a law is so vague that it is difficult to know what counts as a violation of it, and if there is really no distinct and clear harm that that law could prevent, then the law should be abolished. Laws that prohibit obscenity have both of these defects. The conclusion to which we are driven is obvious.

6. Every even number larger than 2 can be divided by 2, with no remainder. No prime number, other than 2, can be divided by 2 with no remainder. Therefore, no even number larger than 2 is a prime number.

7. A great leader is infallible, and can never be wrong. Hitler was clearly a great leader. Yet anyone advocating genocide was clearly wrong, and Hitler did advocate genocide. Therefore, Hitler was not infallible.

*8. Sex is private and intimate, and things that are private and intimate should not be discussed publicly. So sex should not be discussed publicly.

9. Tennis is a much more demanding game than basketball because it is played either singly or in pairs, which means that a person is moving nearly all the time. Basketball is a team sport, and you can sometimes relax and leave things up to the other members. Also, tennis calls for much more arm strength than basketball.

10. Either the western world will have to take over energy production and marketing to bring about gasoline rationing or the Arabs are going to control everything. It would not be good for the Arabs to take over, obviously, so we are going to have to live with state control of energy industries.

*11. *Background:* The following letter was written in response to a newspaper article dealing with problems of addiction among doctors:

"When doctors become addicts it is because of 'pressures' of their job and the 'lack of family life.' Yet when illiterate employables become addicts, it is because society has failed to train them for a job. If the housewife becomes addicted it is because she is not appreciated by her family. Or if it is addicted youth, their problem is lack of parental understanding. That is, no matter what segment of society is addicted, another segment can be blamed, with rationalized plausibility.

"This circular slipping away from personal responsibility is clever, but it is fundamentally unjust. Obviously no one knows why some persons of all strata of society, including the clergy, become addicts. Why cannot the 'experts' admit their problem—the problem of not knowing final causes—instead of producing plausible but innocent scapegoats?"
(Letter to the editor, Toronto *Globe and Mail*, October 8, 1980.)

*12. A hunger strike to try to influence policy is immoral in a democracy because, in a democracy, an individual already has all the means he needs to influence policy. When Canadian Liberal Senator Jacques Hebert went on a hunger strike to try to save a youth employment program (winter, 1986), he exhibited undignified, presumptuous, and morally outrageous conduct.

13. An introduction should convey the importance of the discussion that will follow. As a matter of fact, it is often easier to write a clear introduction after, rather than before, you have finished an essay.

14. *Background:* In their book *The Architecture of Matter*, Stephen Toulmin and June Goodfield describe Voltaire's efforts, two hundred years ago, to weigh fire. They report asking a scientific colleague how

he would have persuaded Voltaire that experiments directed toward that goal of weighing fire were pointless. The man replied lightly that he should have told Voltaire to use his common sense. Of this response, the authors said:

"But the common sense of Voltaire's time was not, and could not have been, identical with the common sense of our own period. For Lavoisier helped to create our contemporary common-sense ideas about matter, just as Newton, earlier, had helped to establish our common-sense picture of the planetary system. If, in retrospect, it seems to us obvious that fire is not a substance, we should regard this 'obviousness' with grave suspicion."
(Stephen Toulmin and June Goodfield, *The Architecture of Matter* [Middlesex, England: Penguin Books, 1965].)

15. *Background:* The following is taken from a United Nations report, which was quoted in the Calgary *Albertan* for July 6, 1979:

"All over the world people are deciding to have fewer babies. The birthrate among the combined populations of Europe, North America, Australia, New Zealand, and Japan is now barely at replacement level. In Africa, Asia, and Latin America, two out of every three people live in countries where the birthrate is falling substantially."

*16. Swimming is the safest form of exercise for the many people who have problems with their joints, such as arthritis, because the water supports the swimmer, and there is no stress on such problem joints as the knee and the ankle.

17. "To feel confident about how to bring up your child, you've got to know what you stand for, what you want for your family and community and for your nation. If you know what you're in the world for and what the world needs, how you raise your child will fall into place. If you haven't any idea of what you're in the world for or what people should be striving for in America at the present time, then it's terribly hard to put into perspective what you should do with your children."
(Benjamin Spock, "Some Things I've Learned," *The Children's Rights Movement*, ed. Beatrice Gross and Ronald Gross [New York: Anchor Press, 1977].)

Part C

For each of the following claims, imagine that you have to construct an argument in defense. Specify for each case one or more premises that would be acceptable and one or more that would not be acceptable for this purpose, according to the conditions developed in this chapter. Say which conditions make your premises acceptable or unacceptable in each case.

1. The only way for the world to be peaceful is for the United States to have an unquestioned superiority as far as nuclear weapons are concerned.

2. Nine is not a prime number.

3. Change is not always the same thing as progress.

4. Canadian defense policy should be worked out independently of American defense policy.

5. The ability to analyze arguments is an important practical skill.

General Summary: Acceptability and Unacceptability of Premises

There are conditions under which the premises of arguments are acceptable, and there are conditions under which they are unacceptable. Referring to these conditions, as explained here, you can often decide whether to accept the premises of various arguments. However, these conditions don't solve all the problems about premise acceptability. We have specified four general conditions that make premises unacceptable (evident falsity, inconsistency, dependence on faulty assumptions, and improper relation to the conclusion regarding certainty); and we have specified six general conditions that make premises acceptable (a cogent subargument, necessary truth, common knowledge, testimony, proper authority, and acceptance only for the sake of argument). That is, we have specified ten different conditions. If one of the four unacceptability conditions is met, a premise is unacceptable. If one of the six acceptability conditions is met, a premise is acceptable.

There is no guarantee whatever that every premise you look at is going to satisfy at least one of the ten conditions. We could not offer such a guarantee. After all, arguments are presented on all topics, and premises are extremely varied and supportable in a great variety of ways. Some premises just fall into what we might call "a debatable zone." They are neither clearly acceptable nor clearly unacceptable. If you are examining an argument and you find the premises to be in the debatable zone, you simply have to admit that they might be acceptable, for all you know, and go on to appraise other aspects of the argument. It may turn out that the premises are irrelevant to the conclusion, in which case the argument will be without force, even if they are acceptable. The same can be said about sufficiency of grounds. If the premises would not be sufficient to establish the conclusion as acceptable, then even if they are acceptable, the argument will not provide cogent justification for the conclusion.

Because it is not possible to offer full and general conditions about the acceptability of premises, many works on the nature of argument do not discuss conditions of premise acceptability. We can understand this decision, since it is unsatisfying to have to end a rather complex discussion with the admission that some problems have not been covered. Also, some principles used here, with respect to testimony and authority, would be questioned by some people who study the theory of knowledge. Nevertheless, it seems unwise to omit all considerations of premises. Premises provide the starting point of arguments. To omit all considerations about how adequate the premises are would be to leave the rest of our theory of argument with no toehold on reality! And this would be very misleading so far as the real-life evaluation of arguments is concerned. When we are listening to politicians, reading newspapers, and studying academic texts, we do have to decide whether to accept the premises of arguments we encounter. Thus we think that it is worthwhile to make at least a start on understanding some general conditions of acceptability and unacceptability. We can't give a complete answer to the question "When are the premises of any argument acceptable?" We can only make a beginning. You will sometimes find that you have to leave premises in the debatable zone, and when this happens, we can only advise that you turn to the aspects of argument evaluation and work from there.

Review of Terms Introduced

> *Necessary truth:* A statement that is necessarily true because its denial would amount to a contradiction.

> *Common knowledge:* A statement that is acceptable on the basis of common knowledge because it is known by most people to be true, or it is widely believed by most people to be true and there is no known evidence counting against it. What is a matter of common knowledge will vary with time and place.

> *Testimony:* Typically, statements based on personal experience or personal knowledge. A statement is acceptable on the basis of a person's testimony if his or her telling of the statement and certifying it as acceptable is the basis for us to believe it. To accept a claim on someone's testimony, we must be willing to believe that he or she is reliable, can perceive and remember things accurately, and is not lying.

> *Authority:* One who has specialized knowledge of a subject and is recognized to be an expert on that subject. Appeals to authority are arguments of the type "So-and-so asserts; So-and-so is an authority as to P; therefore, P is correct." Appeals to authority are legitimate provided experts in the subject agree, provided the expert cited does not have vested interests in the matter, provided the person maintains credibility, and provided the person is cited on a matter within his or her area of expertise. Otherwise, they are not legitimate and amount to a fallacy in argument.

> *Reductio ad absurdum:* A kind of argument in which the premises are tentatively assumed to be true for the sake of argument; and are then shown to lead logically to a conclusion that is either a contradiction or is obviously false. The argument is then used to show that one or more of the premises assumed is false.

> *Inconsistency:* When one statement asserts just what the other one denies, the statements are inconsistent. Putting them together, we would then have a contradiction—a statement of the type "P and not-P." Explicit inconsistency occurs when the contradiction is apparent right on the surface, in the way the statements are worded. Implicit inconsistency occurs when the meaning of the statements allows us to infer, by valid deduction, a further statement that is a contradiction. In practice, a single statement is rarely explicitly inconsistent, but it may be implicitly inconsistent.

> *Assumption:* A claim that is taken for granted and, typically, not reflectively examined. A premise in an argument depends on an assumption if the denial of that assumption would mean that the premise was pointless or

could not possibly be true. The assumption is a background belief, usually more fundamental and general than the premise itself.

Begging the question: A fallacy that occurs when one or more premises are so logically close to the conclusion that they would not be accepted by the audience to whom an argument is addressed—not unless the audience had already accepted the conclusion. Arguments that beg the question are also sometimes called *circular arguments.*

NOTES

1. Letter to the Calgary *Herald,* July 5, 1979.

2. Garret Hardin, "A Lamp Not a Breadbasket," *Harper's,* May 1981, p. 85.

3. *The Peterborough Examiner,* April 16, 1981. Reprinted with permission of the *Examiner.*

4. Laurier LaPierre, *To Herald a Child.* LaPierre is considering the argument that students would not have time, in Canadian schools, to learn languages other than Canada's two official languages: French and English. (Toronto: Ontario Public School Men Teachers Association, 1981, p. 36).

6

Working on Relevance

We now proceed to discuss the second condition of an argument's adequacy: *relevance*. The concept of relevance is so basic to thought and the development of knowledge that it is difficult to define and explain. But no matter how adequate the premises of an argument are, they cannot possibly support its conclusion unless they are relevant to it. Thus we have to try to improve our grasp of this fundamental, but elusive, concept.

General Remarks about Relevance

Suppose that we consider—in the abstract—two distinct statements. Let us call them A and B. The statement A will be relevant to the statement B if A either counts toward establishing B as true or counts against establishing B as true. If the truth or falsity of A has absolutely nothing to do with the truth or falsity of B, then A is not relevant to B. In such a case, whether or not A is true is irrelevant so far as the truth of B is concerned. For example, suppose that B is the statement that plump people are as healthy as thin people. Now let A be the statement that most plump people's hearts are as healthy as the hearts of thin people. With these specifications for A and B, we can see that A is relevant to B; A counts in favor of B's being true. That plump people's hearts are as healthy as thin people's hearts would be an indication at least that the plump are as healthy as the thin. It is relevant because it is evidence for the claim, even though it is not sufficient evidence to establish it as true.

Contrast this situation with another one in which we consider another statement, C, instead of statement A. Let us suppose that C is the statement that plump people have a greater incidence of diabetes than thin people do. If C is true, that would indicate that B is not true. Again it would not be complete proof. But C is negatively relevant to B—in contrast to A, which is positively relevant to it. Whereas A counts in favor of B being true, C counts against B being true. A third considered statement, Z, might have nothing at all to do with B. Let's suppose, for instance, that Z is the statement that Ottawa is the capital of Canada. Z, in this case, makes no difference at all to the truth or falsity of B. As far as B is concerned, Z is irrelevant.

We can summarize these central distinctions as follows:

1. A statement is positively relevant to another statement if its truth counts in favor of the truth of that statement. That is, if it is true, that gives us some reason to think the other statement is true.

2. A statement is negatively relevant to another statement if its truth counts against the truth of that other statement. That is, if it is true, that gives us some reason to think the other statement is false.

3. A statement is irrelevant to another statement if its truth or falsity has no bearing at all on the truth or falsity of that other statement. It gives us neither a reason to think that the statement is true nor a reason to think that it is false.[1]

Let us look at some simple examples of positive relevance. In each of the following cases, the first statement is positively relevant to the second:

(a) 1. Jones has appendicitis, gout, and cancer of the bladder.
    2. Jones is not healthy enough to run the 26-mile Boston Marathon.
(b) 1. Basketball is a game in which height is a great advantage.
    2. Basketball is a game for which physical characteristics of players, as distinct from their acquired skills, make more substantial difference for their competitive position in the game than they do in other games such as tennis and baseball.
(c) 1. In May 1981, the interest rate in the United States was more than 18 percent.
    2. Banks in the United States in May 1981 were earning a good return on the money they loaned.

In each pair the first statement, if true, would provide some reason to suppose that the second statement is true. In each case, saying that (1) is positively relevant to (2) simply means that if (1) were true, it would constitute evidence in favor of (2). This claim does not say that (1) is true; nor does it say that (1) is complete proof of (2). It merely says that *if* true, it is *some* evidence, at least.

Now let's examine some simple examples of *irrelevance*. A statement is irrelevant to the truth of another statement if it has no bearing on that further statement. That is to say, whether it is true or false makes no difference at all as far as our beliefs about the second statement are concerned:

(d) 1. Smith is old and fat.
    2. Smith's views on Chinese politics are false.
(e) 1. Women, on the average, are not as tall as men.
    2. Women are morally inferior to men.
(f) 1. Many things are beyond human control.
    2. No need exists to control such human responses as discrimination, cruelty, and hatred.

In all these cases, the first claim provides no evidence either for or against the second one: it is completely irrelevant to it. In the flow of natural arguments, irrelevance can easily escape our attention. In (f), the first statement is quite clearly irrelevant to the second. That we cannot control everything does not show that we have no need to control some things. If all of the premises of an argument are irrelevant to its conclusion, the argument will be completely without merit, for no evidence pertinent to establishing the conclusion has been given.

Some Ways of Being Relevant

Relevance can take many forms, as should be obvious from the very general way in which we have had to define it. Premises are positively relevant to the conclusion when, if true, they constitute some reason to believe the conclusion is true. Negative relevance has no bearing on argument adequacy; clearly premises have to be positively relevant to support the conclusion. The problem is that "constitute some reason" is awfully vague. There are many ways in which the truth of one statement can provide us with reason to believe another. (And there are many ways in which it can *fail* to do so.) For these reasons, the notion of relevance is difficult to pin down.

Deductive Entailment.   Obviously if the premises of an argument deductively entail the conclusion, they are relevant to the conclusion. In such a case, as we have seen already, the premises when taken together give full logical support to the conclusion. If true, they logically guarantee that the conclusion is true also. If true, they prove the conclusion, and therefore they obviously provide reason to believe the conclusion. Deductive entailment, then, is one sure way of getting relevance. Here is an example in which the premises are relevant to the conclusion because the conjunction of them deductively entails it:

> *Unilateral disarmament would not work unless all grievances, or hostile emotions, of the neighbors of the unilateral disarmer were zero. Since this is not the case, unilateral disarmament will not work.*[2]

The conclusion here is "unilateral disarmament will not work." The reasons given are that for unilateral disarmament to work, there must be no grievances in neighboring countries and this just doesn't happen.

The argument is very clear as stated, but it can be clarified further if we set it out in standard form as the following:

1. Unilateral disarmament will not work unless the unilateral disarmer has no neighbors with grievances or hostile emotions.
2. Countries for which unilateral disarmament might be proposed do have neighbors with grievances and hostile emotions.
Therefore,
3. Unilateral disarmament will not work.

Since (1) and (2), taken together, deductively entail (3), they provide conclusive reasons for believing (3). Since that is so, they obviously provide *some* reason to believe (3). They are relevant—and also provide full grounds, in this case.

The premises are not only relevant, but in this example they are also sufficient. By providing at least some evidence for the conclusion, they are relevant to it and, in this case, since they also provide sufficient grounds, they go beyond relevance. That means that the adequacy of the argument will depend on the (A) condition. If the premises are acceptable, the argument is cogent.

Analogy.   Deductive entailment is not the only way in which the relevance condition can be met. There are many different ways in which statements can support each other. Another is by an *analogy* between things described in the statements. The basis of arguments by analogy is that when two things are similar in a number of respects, we have some basis for thinking that they may well be similar in further respects also. For instance, if rats and human beings were shown to have similar enzymes and hormones, this would give some reason to suspect a further similarity as to the way the two species digest sugar. We would be arguing on the basis of an analogy between rats and humans if we experimented with doses of sugar on rats and drew a conclusion about the effects of similar doses on humans. No argument by analogy can conclusively prove its conclusion, but when an analogy holds, information about one case is *relevant* to another. Analogies may be used for many different reasons; usually a prime reason is that one case is better known and more familiar than another. In the case of rats and people, often experiments done on rats would be quite immoral if done on people. (In fact, many critics argue they are even immoral when done on rats, but that's another problem.) Relevance can be established by virtue of a basic comparison between one area of experience and another or between one case and another. When we argue on the basis of analogy, the similarities between the two things compared make points about one relevant to our consideration of the other. These basic similarities establish relevance. Arguments based on analogies are not as logically tight as deductive arguments, but their premises are often genuinely relevant to their conclusions because of the close similarities between the things compared.

Inductive Reasoning.   There is also a kind of reasoning in which a hypothesis is confirmed by extrapolation from previous experience of similar events. Events that have been experienced are described, and an inference is drawn that future, or yet-to-be-experienced, events will be similar to those already encountered. Such reasoning, from experienced cases to further cases, is commonly called *inductive*. In inductive arguments of this type, relevance comes from the basic assumption that regularities that have been encountered already will persist; on this assumption, past cases are relevant to future ones. Like analogies and unlike deductively valid arguments, inductive arguments cannot absolutely prove their conclusions to be true. But they make them likely or probable—at least in the case of good inductive arguments. The experienced events are relevant to those not experienced, for the inductive assumption is basically sound. (Without it, we could not function in the world at all.) Here is an example of an inductive argument:

> Nearly every arms race that has occurred in human history has led to a war between the countries that were involved in that arms race. The nuclear arms race is, after all, an arms race, and we cannot be so sure that it will be different from the rest. In fact, all we can go on is the past, and if the past is a guide, a nuclear arms race will be followed by a war in which nuclear weapons are used.

A person who used such an argument would be reasoning as follows:

> 1. Most previous arms races have led to wars.
> So, probably,
> 2. The nuclear arms race will lead to a war.

This argument is inductive. The data about past arms races is relevant to the conclusion about the nuclear arms race because it is basically reasonable to assume that various arms races throughout human history are similar. We expect many aspects of experience to persist over time. The inductive assumption that is behind such arguments makes the data in the premise relevant to the conclusion, though the premise is about past experience and the conclusion is about the future. Of course, in such a case, relevance will not amount to full proof. What has happened in most past arms races gives us reason to think that the present arms race will lead to war, but we can always hope that the present and future will differ from the past in this regard.

Normative Relevance.   Many arguments in this book have *normative* conclusions. By *normative* we mean "having to do with values and bearing on what should be done." A normative conclusion is about what is good or bad, or what should or should not be done. The following letter to the editor was written to defend a normative conclusion. When reading it, ask yourself whether—and how—the information given bears on that normative conclusion:

> *As a person who, in the past, enjoyed many concerts in the Eaton Auditorium, I am deeply concerned that this fine concert hall may be destroyed. Apart from the historical significance is a need for a hall of its size and fine acoustical properties. It is also in a central location with public transportation available. This is often forgotten when locating cultural and recreation facilities but will become an increasingly important factor. Toronto has become a city of ever-increasing cultural activity and facilities are needed for these diverse interests. Many of us who are concerned sincerely trust that this much-needed facility will be retained.*[3]

The author of this letter to the editor wrote to urge that the hall should be preserved. She offered a number of separately relevant premises to support her view: (1) the hall is historically significant; (2) the hall is of a suitable size and has good acoustic properties; (3) the hall has a convenient location; and (4) there is a need for cultural facilities of its type in Toronto, where the hall is located. Each of these four factors is relevant to the author's conclusion because each specifies a feature of the hall that would make it serve the purposes a concert hall should serve. The author points to these features to establish the value of the hall as a concert hall and her conclusion that Eaton Auditorium should be preserved. Her premises are relevant to her conclusion because her conclusion is about something we should do, and her premises each give some reason why we should do it. Each premise states a reason relevant to establishing that the hall deserves to be preserved. In this example, unlike the others we have looked at, each premise is separately relevant to the conclusion. In the other examples, premises have to be linked together to be relevant to the conclusion.

We have explained relevance by looking more closely at some of the ways in which premises can be relevant to a conclusion: by deductive entailment, by analogy, by inductive relationships, and through specifying values, in the context where the conclusion is normative. Usually it is easy to tell in which of these ways relevant premises bear on the conclusion. But even if you cannot tell, the most important thing is to make sure that the premises are relevant somehow. To do this, you have to ask yourself what difference it would make to the truth of the conclusion whether the premises were true or not. If it would make no difference, then the premises are irrelevant, and the argument is not cogent. As we shall see, irrelevance is a fatal—and surprisingly common—flaw in an argument.

Irrelevance: Some General Comments

If a premise used in an argument is irrelevant to its conclusion, it does not matter one bit whether that premise is true or acceptable; it cannot provide any basis for the conclusion. Obviously, in this case, it cannot possibly provide good grounds for the conclusion. Thus an argument that fails on the (R) condition will necessarily fail on (G), and whether it passes on (A) won't matter. From this you can see that irrelevance is a fatal flaw in an argument. If you can show that someone else's argument is based on irrelevant premises, you have given a conclusive refutation of it. An argument in which the premise or premises are irrelevant is often called a *non sequitur*. The Latin words *non sequitur* mean "it does not follow"; the premises won't lead you to the conclusion.

It might seem amazing that *non sequiturs* exist. Yet they are relatively common, and unwary audiences are often deceived by them. Just why this should happen is not fully understood, but one explanation may have to do with the character of the irrelevant premises. Often they are clearly true, and they may be among few points of clear agreement between an arguer and the audience. In contexts of controversy, such agreement can seem so important that an audience may forget to ask just how the uncontroversial points are really related to the topic at hand. Another fact is that irrelevant premises may be very interesting in themselves, or they may be easier or more pleasant to think about than the actual problem. But for our purposes it does not matter so very much what causes people to use or accept arguments containing irrelevance. Rather, our main interest is in understanding what irrelevance is and in learning to recognize some of the common fallacies of relevance.

Logicians have special names for kinds of irrelevance that are especially common and interesting. In this chapter we shall study a number of these, but we shall not try to learn all of them. This itself can become an irrelevant distraction if the basic goal is to learn to understand and evaluate various types of arguments! It is fun to be able to use some of the fallacy labels, such as *ad hominem* and "straw man." Understanding what these common types of irrelevance are is useful because studying them makes you better able to spot them. However, our main goal is to recognize irrelevance when we see it. Provided that you spot irrelevance, it does not matter so very much whether you can give it a label or not. The basic technique, which you can use even before we discuss any specific fallacies, is to find the premises and conclusion and ask yourself just exactly how the premises bear on the conclusion. If you can see that they would provide evidence for the conclusion, they are relevant; if not, they are irrelevant.

Criticizing an argument on grounds of relevance is a strong line of criticism. But you have to back up your criticism by saying why you think the premises used are irrelevant to the conclusion. Presumably the person who used the argument thought her premises were relevant. If you just say, "that's irrelevant," it does not put debate on a very high level! You should explain why you believe that the truth or falsity of these premises will make no real difference to the conclusion. It is not enough to merely say, "that's *ad hominem*," or whatever, because you are just applying a label instead of giving a reasoned response. Your audience might not understand the label. Even if it does, you still have to show how and why this label applies to the argument you are talking about. All of this serves to emphasize a point we have previously made: criticizing an argument requires that you yourself argue. This point is as true for analyses of relevance as it is for any other aspect of argument evaluation.

EXERCISE SET

Exercise One
Part A

For each of the following pairs of statements, comment as to whether the first statement is relevant to the second. If you think it is irrelevant, briefly state why.

*1. (a) Elephants have been known to cover the corpses of other dead elephants with leaves and branches.
  (b) Elephants have a concept of death.

*2. (a) More whites than blacks have taken up jogging.
  (b) More blacks than whites are good artists.

3. (a) There are tribes in which it is normal and economically useful for two brothers to be married to the same woman.
  (b) Marriage as we know it is not a universal human custom.

4. (a) When prices go up, people have to pay more for food, housing, and clothing.
  (b) When prices go up, poor people have more financial problems than they had before the increase.

5. (a) The chemical names of some ingredients of children's snack foods are completely impossible to pronounce.

(b) Some children's snack foods contain dangerous artificial chemicals.

*6. (a) Some French historians dispute whether large numbers of Jews were killed in the Second World War.
(b) The large number of Jews killed in the Second World War would have been larger still had it not been for the protective activities of some outstandingly courageous citizens in Holland, France, and Sweden.

7. (a) Girls are of the same sex as their mother, whereas boys are not.
(b) Boys, in growing up, have to separate more from their mother than girls do.

8. (a) Swimming uses more muscles of the body than nearly any other sport.
(b) Swimming can provide a good form of balanced physical exercise.

*9. (a) Agriculture is a key to the well-being of a country.
(b) The shaky agricultural system of the Soviet Union is an important obstacle to efforts to raise the standard of living there.

10. (a) Children who have a long bus ride to school often arrive at school rather tired and restless.
(b) We may expect that children who have a long bus ride to school will achieve lower grades than children who are able to walk to a neighborhood school.

Part B

For each of the following passages, do you find any cases where an irrelevant premise is used in an attempt to support a conclusion? Determine the conclusion (if any) in each passage, and then underline any premise that you consider irrelevant to the support of that conclusion. State why you think the premise is irrelevant, if you do.

*1. A number of different religious denominations are represented within the public school system. It is for this reason that the system must be secular, not religious.

2. *Background:* In 1984, the former prime minister of Jamaica, Michael Manley, published an essay on poverty and underdevelopment in *Harper's* magazine. Manley claimed that poverty in the Third World was a result of imperialism in the colonizing of many countries during the nineteenth century. Thomas Sowell, of the Hoover Institution, wrote objecting to Manley's theory. He said:

"The notion that either the capital or the standard of living in the West depends upon the Third World will not stand the slightest contact with evidence. When the British Empire was at its zenith (peak), around the First World War, more British capital was invested in the United States than in all of Africa or all of Asia outside Australia. The French had more trade with little Belgium than with all its farflung African empire. Germany's trade with its colonies was less than 1 percent of its exports."
(Quoted in "Just What Was Said," Toronto *Globe and Mail*, January 7, 1984.)

*3. *Background:* In 1978, Russian dissident novelist Alexander Solzhenitsyn made a widely publicized speech criticizing the materialism of western societies. He said:

"If humanism were right in declaring that man is born to be happy, he would not be born to die. Since his body is doomed to die, his task on earth evidently must be of a more spiritual nature. It cannot be unrestrained enjoyment of everyday life. It cannot be the search for the best ways to obtain material goods and then cheerfully get the most out of them."
(Calgary *Herald*, July 6, 1978.)
(Assume that the conclusion is "Man is not born to be happy.")

4. Children are unique and sensitive creatures. They are very imaginative, and they are different from adults. Therefore, every child has an absolute right to state-supported education.

5. Nations such as the United States, Canada, and the United Kingdom support systems of nuclear weapons. Such systems imply a threat to use terrible violence against enemies. Therefore, it is all right for blacks in South Africa to resort to violence in order to change the government of that country.

6. *Background:* In 1983, a scandal emerged in Southern Alberta when it became known that a high school social studies teacher, James Keegstra, was teaching that the murder of six million Jews during the Second World War did not occur. Keegstra lost his position as teacher. The following was a contribution to the controversy:

"I recall one Sunday afternoon I was visiting my uncle, who lived on the outskirts of the city (Udine, Italy). My cousin noticed a train that was not moving, so we decided to investigate. When we got to within 50 metres, we were told to halt by a German soldier. We were close enough to realize what it was.

It was a train (boxcars only) loaded with Jews on their way into Austria, 90 kilometres to the north. The screaming that was coming from these cars was unbelievable. Babies were being held on the upper ventilation openings, perhaps for fresh air. How many died before reaching their destination in concentration camps?

"How do I know they were Jews? Almost all of the cars had in bold letters written on the side, JUDEN. These were Italian Jews going to their final destination.

"Does Keegstra think I can ever forget? Why did I talk to my children about my youth? Because I don't want it to happen again."
(Vic Gomirato, Calgary *Herald*, October 3, 1983.)

*7. Multicolored fish are more restricted to particular territories than fish of less dramatic coloration. The bright colors serve to warn other fish that they are there. The sense of territory has an important survival function for these fish, and it is indicated by the colors that have evolved. We can see that a sense of territory is basic in the evolution and nature of higher primates such as humans.
(Adapted from Konrad Lorenz's work on aggression in humans and animals.)

Fallacies Involving Irrelevance

A fallacy is a common mistake in arguing. It is a mistake in the reasoning that underlies an argument. The mistake can be quite deceptive by seeming to many people to be just like correct reasoning. Fallacies of relevance are mistakes in reasoning and argument that involve irrelevance. There are many different ways of being irrelevant. The specific fallacies of relevance discussed here have been given special names because they are quite common and can be very deceptive.

Not all fallacies involve irrelevance. Some have to do with the acceptability of premises of certain types or with the sufficiency of the premises to establish the conclusion. In this chapter, however, we are concentrating particularly on relevance and irrelevance, so we shall discuss only fallacies in which the mistake in reasoning is due to mistaking an irrelevant point for a relevant one.

The Straw Man Fallacy.   In Chapter Two we discussed the interpretation of passages—whether they contain arguments or nonarguments, how you identify the premises and conclusions, and how to decide whether to add missing premises or conclusions. You were advised not to read in extra premises or conclusions without good evidence that the author of the argument would have accepted them. If you read in something that is not there, you mistake an author's position. If you criticize a position that an author did not really hold and infer from your criticism that his real position is flawed, you have committed the *straw man fallacy.* This fallacy is committed whenever someone distorts a position, criticizes the distorted version, and then takes his criticism to count against the real position. If someone claims that *X* is true, and you represent him as having claimed *Y* and then attack *Y* and believe yourself to have refuted *X*, you have committed the straw man fallacy. Instead of refuting a real man, you have refuted a "man of straw":

───   *The Straw Man Fallacy*
The straw man fallacy is committed when a person misrepresents an argument, theory, or claim, and then, on the basis of that misrepresentation, claims to have refuted the position that he has misrepresented.

To avoid the straw man fallacy, then, you have to interpret other people's arguments and positions accurately and fairly. You have to base your criticisms on the position someone actually holds, not on some other position that (in your mind) is somehow related to it. The best way to avoid the straw man fallacy is to make sure that you direct your comments and criticisms to the actual position held. The actual position held may be identified by the exact words in which a person who holds the position expressed it. In addition, people are committed to anything that is deductively entailed by what they seriously say or write, and also to claims that are strongly suggested by what they say or write. Obviously it is easiest to go wrong when you are working with what is strongly suggested. You have to make sure that the suggestions are not just in your own mind but are interpretations people would typically make, in the context in which the argument or position was stated.

These remarks will be more clear if we see how they apply to a specific example. In an issue of the *Nation* that appeared in the fall of 1982, Sidney Lens, a labor organizer and writer, made the following statement:

It is a mere cliché to say we cannot trust the Russians.[4]

This comment was the theme for a short essay in which Lens went on to argue that no government should be trusted, and that disarmament and foreign policy arrangements had to be made in such a way that international verification agreements and a strong basis in national interests would supplement trust as the grounds for lasting agreements. But the comment is just the sort of thing that could easily be misinterpreted in a hot debate on capitalism, communism, the Cold War, and defense policy. Obviously, if you wished to discuss it, one way to avoid the straw man fallacy would be to quote Lens directly and state his view of trusting the Russians in his own words. A direct quote is sometimes inconvenient, but it would be perfectly feasible in the case of a short remark like this. You might wish to reword the comment; if so, you would have to make sure that what you attribute to Lens is deductively entailed by what he actually said. Suppose, for instance, you attributed to Lens view (i):

— (i) It is a mere common saying that the Russians are not trustworthy.

This rephrasing would be quite all right, for (i) is merely a verbal variation on the original claim; you get (i) by replacing "cliché" with "common saying" and replacing "We cannot trust the Russians" with "The Russians are not trustworthy." The original claim deductively entails (i); in saying it, Lens clearly meant (i). Putting the view as (i) rather than as the original statement would be proper interpretation. You wouldn't commit the straw man fallacy by doing that!

We would venture further in interpretation if we said that Lens had asserted (ii):

— (ii) It is false to say that the Russians are not trustworthy.

This remark, (ii), is not deductively entailed by Lens's original comment. It is perhaps suggested by his expression "mere cliché." A statement that is merely a cliché is one that is only a cliché; that is, it is nothing more than a cliché. One way of interpreting this would be to say that the statement is not true. (Being true could be *one way* of being something more than a cliché.) Whether Lens meant to assert (ii) is a debatable point if you have only this single comment to go by. However, if you read the entire essay, it becomes clear that he did not mean to assert (ii); he goes on to say that indeed the Russians cannot be fully trusted and neither can western governments.

If we represented Lens as having asserted (iii), we would clearly be misinterpreting his comment:

— (iii) The Russians are just as reliable as the British.

No such comparison as this was stated, entailed, or even suggested by the original remark about trusting the Russians.

It is easiest to avoid misrepresenting a theory or position when you have a specific version of it to deal with—as in our example here. You then simply check to see that your interpretation has a firm basis in what was actually said. You do not add premises or conclusions inappropriately, and you proceed with great care in reading into the position anything that is not either explicitly said or deductively entailed by what is said. By taking care in this way, you can avoid committing the straw man fallacy yourself. On those occasions when you are able to compare the author's representation of another position with the original statement of that position, this strategy will help you spot instances of the straw man fallacy.

Let us consider a specific passage and see how natural and easy it can be to commit this fallacy. The following passage is taken from an article in which noted historian and writer Barbara Tuchman discussed an alternative to the nuclear arms race. She said:

> One [suggestion] would be a more massive, more purposeful effort than may now be conducted to promote anti-nuclear sentiment and fear of their own policies among the people of the Soviet Union and satellite countries. We are always blaming the Russians for agitating the peace movement in Western Europe. Why should we not do the same behind the Iron Curtain? We could also try what might be called the stuffed goose option—that is, providing them with all the grain and consumer goods they need in such quantities that they become dependent on us and could not risk the domestic turbulence that would follow if they cut off the sources of supply by war.[5]

Against the background of Cold War attitudes and the prevailing assumption that the best way to counter a rival power is by military strength, Tuchman's suggestions may seem strange. Suppose we represent her as having said:

1. The United States could win a propaganda war, if it took the time to fight one, against the Soviet Union and its satellites.

and

2. The United States should take on the responsibility of feeding and clothing all the people in the Soviet Union and its satellites so as to make them dependent.

These suggestions are, in fact, quite absurd. If Tuchman had been recommending (1) and (2), there would be no reason to take her seriously. However, if we look closely at the quoted passage, we will see that these claims were not made. Instead of (1), Tuchman proposed that the United States try to agitate the peace movement behind the Iron Curtain. Instead of (2), she suggested that the United States could try providing consumer goods in such quantities as to cultivate economic dependence, so that the Soviets would not want to risk a cutoff. This position is a far cry from meeting all needs for food and clothing in the Soviet Union and satellite countries. (That interpretation is, perhaps, suggested by the phrasing "providing all the grain and consumer goods they need," but we can see that this is to be qualified by the immediately following phrase "in such quantities that they become dependent on us.") If we took Tuchman to be claiming (1) and (2), we would seriously misrepresent her position. If we refuted that version of her position and then believed ourselves to have refuted what she actually said in the quoted passage, we would commit the straw man fallacy. The claims attributed to Tuchman are not what she said, not entailed by what she said, and not even strongly suggested by what she said, when her words are carefully interpreted.

The straw man fallacy is more difficult to detect when the views being criticized are not quoted explicitly. This error often occurs even when a specific person's opinions and arguments are discussed. It is extremely common when the positions discussed are general ones, not identified with the stated ideas of any single specific person, such as the environmentalist position on DNA research; feminism; evolutionary theory; the belief in free will; and so on. In these contexts, you have to depend on your own background knowledge to determine the real content of the position. This case makes straw man less clear-cut than it was in the previous example. But often distortions are quite blatant, and you can spot them even in the absence of explicit quotations.

Consider, for instance, an example of an advertisement written to criticize the "soft energy" option. Soft energy advocates urge that solar and wind power be developed as alternatives to nuclear power and oil and gas:

> *Wrong for many. That's the reality of "soft energy"—massive, often unsightly projects. But the dream is appealing partly because it seems small-scale and spread out, like another fantasy of the back-to-nature movement—do-it-yourself farming for everybody. Yet to give every American family of four a 40 acre farm would take more land— including deserts and mountains—than there is in all of the lower 48 mainland states. And such a program would surely mean good-bye wilderness. Besides, what about people who like cities, or suburbs—rather than . . . the "constant ruralism" in between? There may be a lot of good in soft energy to supplement conventional power. But we're uneasy with people who insist it will do the whole job and who then insist on foisting their dreams on the rest of us. Especially when their dreams can't stand up to reality.*[6]

To detect straw man here, you merely ask yourself just what it is that advocates of soft energy are recommending. Their position is that energy sources like the sun and wind are better, environmentally and politically, than nuclear power or oil and gas. Whether their position is correct is a biological and policy issue about the quantities, costs, and production effects of these various sources of energy. Soft energy advocates have a position about how energy should be produced. Their position on energy is not a position about farming or lifestyle. The possibility that there is not enough land on the U.S. mainland states for all families of four to have their own farms is completely irrelevant to the merits of the various sources of energy! The advertisement misrepresents the soft energy advocates, changing their position from one about the economics and biology of energy to one about farms and getting back to nature. The position, as misrepresented, then becomes vulnerable to attack. As far as the real soft energy position is concerned, the comments in the advertisement are completely irrelevant.

In summary, the way to avoid committing straw man yourself is to make sure that you do not misrepresent another person's position. The way to detect straw man in other people's arguments is to check to see that positions criticized are properly represented and that criticism focuses on the points central to, and actually contained in, the position that is being criticized. In these ways you can avoid the kind of irrelevance that results from the straw man fallacy.

The *Ad Hominem* Fallacy.   Another kind of irrelevance deserving special attention is the *ad hominem* fallacy, or argument "against the man." The words *ad hominem* mean "against the man" in Latin. In *ad hominem* reasoning, people try to prove a point by attacking a person who holds the opposite view. Or they criticize a person's personality and background, and from that they infer that his position is faulty. These debating tactics are almost always mistaken as far as logic is concerned. Yet they are often practically and rhetorically very effective. Many a proposal has been defeated because the person putting it forward was not the "right" age, sex, race, or social class. The logically appropriate way to assess a person's theory or argument is to give arguments against it or to show that there are problems with the position. But these approaches require work and careful thought. All too often people substitute personal attacks and name calling.

For instance, someone attacked Susan Sontag's theory about cancer by pointing out that Sontag herself was a cancer victim. In a book entitled *Illness as Metaphor*, Sontag contended that the belief in a cancer-prone personality would disappear when the medical research uncovered the physical causes of cancer, and she supported her case by an extended historical comparison between cancer and tuberculosis. To respond to such a theory by maintaining that:

1. Sontag suffers from cancer.
Thus,
2. Contrary to what Sontag contends, the theory of the cancer-prone personality is an acceptable theory.

is to commit the *ad hominem* fallacy. The premise is irrelevant to the conclusion. The premise is about Sontag's personal state of health and the conclusion is about the concept of a cancer-prone personality. The person who used this argument has just taken the lazy way out. He has pointed out one of Sontag's personal traits, rather than pinpointing any difficulty in the theory she developed. Most of the time considerations about the personality and background of a theorist or arguer are irrelevant to the issue of whether his or her theory is true or his or her argument sound.

Implicitly we reason *ad hominem* when we reject a presentation because the person making it does not look presentable and middle class, or when we are skeptical of a view simply because all those who support it are young and haven't held responsible jobs. Far too often we connect the merits of theories with the personal qualities of the people who support those theories.

In print, *ad hominem* arguments can be hard to spot. It is easy to see that a substantive issue has been sidetracked into a discussion of personalities. But it may be hard to see that there is an explicit argument with premises containing personal information and a conclusion about some substantive point. For instance, seldom would you find in print an argument so blatant as this one:

1. The men who support liberal abortion laws are cowards intimidated by feminists.
So,
2. Liberal abortion laws are faulty laws.

Here, the *ad hominem* element is just so blatant that the argument would not convince anyone. The premise is too obviously irrelevant to the conclusion.

It is more common for *ad hominem* remarks to be inserted more subtly. One tactic is to leave the conclusion unstated. The writer or speaker inserts the personal charges and suggests that the position held by the "disreputable" people is false. How this works can be seen from the following example, which appeared in a Canadian magazine article dealing with abortion:

Women's Lib is chic and news, and the men who praise it become chic and newsworthy. To this group belong the sycophant, the male camp-follower, the half-sexed male who allows his woman to have him gelded and then hits the media trail to brag about it. They are the male counterparts of women who allow their lovers to force them onto the Pill or into an abortion, or who wrote idiot books about male supremacy or sexual surrender.[7]

The article, entitled "On Killing Inconvenient People," took a position strongly opposed to abortion under any circumstances. The question arises as to how these very negative comments about the men who support a liberal position on abortion are related to the author's opposition to liberal abortion laws. The passage is a strong attack on these men: notice the very loaded language in such terms as "half-sexed," "gelded," and "brag." Obviously the author thought that these men were pretty terrible characters. But we should ask ourselves just what the negative characteristics of these people (if they really have them) have to do with the moral correctness of liberal abortion laws. They are irrelevant to issues about the morality and legality of abortion. If male feminists were all saints, it would not make abortions morally good; and if they were all devils, that would not make abortion morally evil! The author was not straightforward enough to reason directly from these insults to her moral stance on abortion law. If she had, the irrelevance of the comments would have been all to obvious. It does seem, however, that she was trying to get support for her antiabortion position from the hostile remarks she makes about men who favor liberal laws.

In view of this, we could read in a conclusion and then we would be seeing the negative comments as part of an argument. If there is an argument, it is certainly an example of the *ad hominem* fallacy. It would go like this:

1. The men who support Women's Lib are weak attention-seekers.
2. The men who support Women's Lib are less than fully male.
3. The men who support Women's Lib are intimidated by the fact that feminism is fashionable.
4. The men who support Women's Lib support a liberal policy on abortion. Therefore,
<u>5</u>. A liberal policy on abortion is wrong.

You may not know whether it is appropriate to read a passage as having a missing conclusion. However, it is certainly important to note that discussions of personalities typically do not contribute to discussions of substance. If you did not regard the passage about half-gelded men as part of an argument, you would still have to note that this discussion is irrelevant to the abortion issue. Either the author uses an argument (with a missing conclusion) and her argument is a fallacious *ad hominem* one, or she has included some insulting remarks that are not relevant to the abortion issue. In neither case can we get substantive support for a view on abortion from the insults addressed to men who support feminism. Whether or not the allegations were intended to support the conclusion, they simply don't.

We have said that "typically" premises about personalities do not lend support to conclusions about matters of substance. Now it is time to explain why we have used the word *typically.* By using this word, we suggest that there are some cases in which personality and character considerations really are relevant to the logical assessment of theories, positions, and arguments.

First, sometimes an argument or stance is actually about a person. For instance, a man may contend that he is a suitable candidate to be mayor. Here he is the issue: so, obviously, someone who brings aspects of the candidate's character into the debate is not committing any fallacy of relevance. If someone were to argue the following:

1. Jones was convicted on a charge of embezzling funds. Therefore,
2. Jones is not a suitable candidate for mayor.

he would not be arguing *ad hominem. Ad hominem* is a fallacy occurring when premises about personal characteristics are brought to bear on matters of substance to which they are not relevant. Here the conclusion is also about Jones himself; the premise is relevant to it; there is no fallacy.

The second category of exception is rather more complicated. Think back to our discussions of authority and testimony in Chapter Four. There, we saw that there are contexts in which a person has to accept a claim on someone else's testimony or else just suspend judgment about it entirely. Suppose, for instance, that you personally were not in Phoenix, Arizona, on December 25, 1981. Now consider the following statement:

> It was sunny in Phoenix, Arizona, on December 25, 1981.

If you are going to accept or reject this claim, it will have to be on the basis of someone else's testimony. The issue may seem trivial, but it could figure in a murder trial! And, as we have seen, many contexts exist in which your acceptance of claims will depend on whether or not to take other people as authorities. For example, statistics regarding low-level radiation and cancer rates are not widely circulated, nor are they easy to interpret. If someone like Rosalie Berthell, a biostatistician, affirms—on the basis of her statistical findings—that there is no safe level of radiation, then you can either accept the claim on her authority or remain agnostic for the time being.

All of this we have seen before in Chapter Five. But now we have to bring these points to bear on the *ad hominem* fallacy. *Ad hominem* and authority are logically related: *ad hominem* has to do with the improper and proper use of personal traits to *criticize* views, and authority has to do with the proper and improper use of personal traits to *support* views. To get back to the example of Rosalie Berthell and the claim about low-level radiation, if you decide whether to accept the claim on her authority, then of course some aspects of her background and character will be relevant to this decision. Some of these aspects are relevant to the question of whether she is an authority, and whether this question is one we should be willing to accept on authority. As a matter of fact, there is considerable disagreement among biostatisticians and biophysicists as to how the data on low-level radiation effects should be interpreted. Thus this question is not one in which we can properly appeal to authority.

If we were to argue as follows:

> 1. Berthell is a figure whose findings have been disputed by other people in her field.
> So,
> 2. We cannot simply accept Berthell as an expert in this field.
> Thus,
> 3. Claims about the effects of low-level radiation are not to be accepted solely on Berthell's authority.

we would not be arguing *ad hominem*. Why not? It is because the information in (1) is relevant to (2), which in turn is relevant to (3). The personal information bears directly on the issue of whether appeal to authority is appropriate in this case. Also, the conclusion is not exactly about low-level radiation. It is about whether such claims can be accepted on the authority of one biostatistician. Reasoning from character and background never establishes points of substance about other topics, but it may be relevant to our decision about how seriously a person's testimony or evidence should be taken. It would be *ad hominem* and fallacious to argue as follows:

> 1. Berthell has never been married.
> Therefore,
> 2. Berthell is not an authority on low-level radiation effects.

Marital status really is irrelevant to expertise on this topic!

The same points can be made for testimony. Suppose you must depend on personal testimony in order to accept a claim. In this case you won't be committing a fallacy if you reason that because the person testifying has lied in the past, he is unreliable and should not be believed in this case without further corroborating evidence. Here information about character (past lying) is relevant to your decision to accept testimony or suspend judgment. Such reasoning is used frequently in courts of law.

We can sum up these exceptions and our account of the *ad hominem* fallacy as follows:

The Ad Hominem Fallacy
A premise about the background, personality, or character of a person is *irrelevant* to the merits of his theories and arguments, except in the very special case in which those theories and arguments happen to be about himself.

Specific points about a person's background may bear on the reliability of his testimony or the legitimacy of his authority. That means that they are relevant to our decision whether to accept his claims on his testimony, even though they are not directly relevant to the question of whether these claims are true or false.

To reason from premises about the backgrounds, personalities, or characters of people to substantive conclusions about their arguments or theories is to commit the *ad hominem* fallacy unless the premises are relevant to the conclusion in one of the ways described earlier.

It would be nice if we could make this summary simpler, but we cannot do that without being inaccurate. Generally, points about personality and character are irrelevant to the substance of a case. Only in quite special circumstances are they more than rhetorical distractions from the main point.

The Fallacy of Guilt by Association. We have seen that in the *ad hominem* fallacy, an argument or theory is attacked through attacks on the person who holds it. The fallacy of guilt by association is rather similar, except that in this case even the attack on the person is indirect. In this fallacy, comments are made linking a person with a group or movement that is commonly believed to be bad. The implication is that the person himself is also in some sense bad and—usually—that his opinions are incorrect. Very frequently references to Hitler and the Nazis are used in fallacies of guilt by association—probably because the Nazi movement is one that nearly everyone agrees was terrible. For instance, many who argue against legalizing voluntary euthanasia (merciful early death) contend that it is morally evil because it was practiced in Hitler's Germany. This is a guilt-by-association criticism. The fact that something once happened in a terrible context does not show that the thing itself is bad or that it would be bad in all other contexts. To associate advocates of voluntary euthanasia with the Nazis is slander pure and simple; here guilt by association has become vicious.

In the example of defenders of voluntary euthanasia and Hitler's Germany, the connection alleged is wholly fictitious; these people are not fascists and never supported Hitler. But sometimes, even when a connection is a real one, it does not give a basis for any criticism. When discussing the *ad hominem* fallacy, we saw that it is only in rare cases that personal characteristics are relevant to the substantive issues under discussion. What we have in guilt-by-association fallacies is a charge against the person on the basis of an association, real or imagined, with a group or movement thought to be disreputable. Such associations are irrelevant to the merits of people's arguments or opinions. Even if someone really is a member of a group that really is disreputable, it is still likely that he has some opinions not held by the group as a whole—and also that the group as a whole has some correct opinions. Given these possibilities, you obviously cannot get very far by arguing from his associated "guilt" to the conclusion that his opinion or argument is wrong. Frequently the association is purely imagined anyway.

Here is a case of guilt by association, found in a report describing the responses of Canadian doctors to a study of medical insurance. The study was done by Emmett Hall. Canada has state-supported universal medical insurance, but many doctors are dissatisfied with the level of payment they receive from the scheme. They have begun to practice something called extra-billing, charging patients more than the state-supported scheme would pay, and having patients make up the difference between the two amounts. Mr. Hall's report on medical insurance recommended that extra-billing be disallowed for doctors receiving payment from the scheme: doctors would have to bill entirely within the scheme or opt out of it altogether. To this suggestion, the following response was made:

> Of Mr. Hall's fear that extra-billing will destroy the health care systems and discriminate between rich and poor, Dr. Mandeville said that this is "a socialist concept that comes through in a socialist report. Hospitals treat people equally more than any other segment of society. Just look at the hospital. We have the low class people who aren't taking care of themselves."[8]

If Dr. Mandeville is correctly quoted here, then he certainly seems to have committed the fallacy of guilt by association. It comes when he terms the resistance to extra-billing "a socialist concept" and says it is part of "a socialist report." For free enterprise-type doctors, socialism appears to be a rather terrible thing, and many of the public in North America have been encouraged to link socialism with communism—and communism with prison camps and secret police. (This link is also guilt by association.) Since it is commonly believed in North America that socialism is pretty awful, Dr. Mandeville tried to dispute Hall's view by linking it with socialism. Linking two things is the classic device of guilt by association. The argument implied would be a fallacy because the connection with socialism—real or imagined—does not show that Hall's view was incorrect. It is irrelevant to that issue. Socialism concerns the ownership and control of resources and the distribution of income, whereas Hall was concerned about equality of access to health care. (We might make a number of criticisms of Dr. Mandeville's argument, but we concentrate here solely on his appeal to the "evils" of socialism, which amounts to the guilt-by-association fallacy.) It's a mistake because there is no real connection between Hall's proposal and socialism. If there were a real connection, it would not show that there is anything wrong with Hall's proposal anyway.

To sum up, we can define the fallacy of guilt by association as follows:

—— *Guilt by Association*
The fallacy of guilt by association is committed when a person or his views are criticized on the basis of a supposed link between that person and a group or movement believed to be disreputable. The poor reputation of any group is irrelevant to the substantive correctness of its own views, or of the views of any member of the group, or of the views held by people or groups that may be loosely connected with it.

Guilt by association is not usually real guilt or real association. Even when the association is real and the guilt of the associated group is real, it does not transfer logically to every opinion held by the associated person.

Fallacious Appeals to Ignorance. There are many things people do not know, or have not been able to prove. Sometimes fallacious arguments are based on this ignorance. If we do not know something, then that point is often an important one to observe. The problem comes with attempts to infer, the truth or falsehood of claims, from the fact that we do not know them. An argument of the type:

1. We do not know that statement S is true.
Therefore,
2. Statement S is false.

is a fallacious argument. The premise is irrelevant to the conclusion because the premise is about what we do not presently know regarding S and the conclusion is about S itself. Similarly, to argue:

1. We do not know that statement S is false.
Therefore,
2. Statement S is true.

would also be a fallacy. If there are discoveries we have not been able to make, this fact shows something only about our present knowledge. It does not show how things in the world are, distinct from our knowledge of them.

Many phenomena exist where it is hard to get compelling evidence either way. Think, for instance, of the existence of ghosts, life on other planets, and UFOs, or of the reality of telepathic communication. Because of the nature of these things, it is very hard to prove either that they exist or that they do not exist. With ghosts, for instance, people seem to see and hear them, and some events that people want to explain by hypothesizing ghosts as the cause have occurred. However, we cannot get conclusive evidence that ghosts are present on any given occasion, no matter how fervent people may be in their testimony. A ghost is supposed to be an immaterial spirit, representing the soul of someone who has died. Representations such as voices and apparitions that have no known natural cause are often thought to be ghosts. But the problem is that you cannot be sure that they are. (Here itself we often have an argument from ignorance. People too easily infer that because we do not know the natural cause of a voice or an apparition, it must have a supernatural cause.)

If arguing from ignorance were a sound way to argue, we could both prove and disprove the existence of ghosts! First, we could argue that since we have not been able to prove that ghosts do exist, ghosts do not exist. Then, we could turn around and argue that since we have not been able to prove that ghosts don't exist, they do exist! That is, we could argue from ignorance in two directions and thus arrive at inconsistent conclusions. Obviously something has gone wrong. The mistake is in thinking that from our inability to definitely confirm or definitely disconfirm the existence of ghosts, we can reach a conclusion about their existence or nonexistence. From our ignorance, we can only infer our own lack of knowledge—nothing more.

Many appeals to ignorance are more subtle than this one. Because of the way they are worded and the context in which they appear, they may escape our attention. Consider, for instance, the following example, taken from a book about bringing up children. The author, A. S. Neill, is trying to show that punishment should never be used:

> *To say that punishment does not always cause psychic damage is to evade the issue, for we do not know what reaction the punishment will cause in the individual in later years.*[9]

Neill suggests that punishment may cause psychic damage in children. His reason is that we do not know what their reaction to punishment received now will be in later years. This appeal is to ignorance. It is fallacious. Neill does at least qualify his conclusion, admitting that he knows that our ignorance does not *prove* that there may be damage. His argument is of the type:

1. We do not know that not-S.
Therefore,
2. S may be true.

If all that is meant here is that for all we know, S may be true, that conclusion does follow. But if what is meant is that there is a significant likelihood of S being true (a probability worth paying attention to in practical decision-making), that conclusion would not follow. Since Neill is giving a practical argument about how children should be treated, he clearly needs a likelihood that has some practical significance.

Another example of a faulty appeal to ignorance is the following:

We do not know what causes AIDS. Thus AIDS may be caused by something airborne, and people who have AIDS should be isolated from the population at large.

The problem here is just the same as it is in the previous argument. There might be *some* possibility that AIDS is caused by something airborne in the sense that, given our ignorance as to what does cause AIDS, that claim is logically consistent with what we know so far. However, the practical recommendation made in the argument requires that any such logical possibility be regarded as something significantly probable, and this significant probability cannot be inferred from our ignorance regarding AIDS.

Sometimes it is extremely important to point out ignorance, even though we have to be careful just what we go on to infer from it. Consider, for instance, the following passage written by scientist R. L. Sinsheimer about research into new life forms:

Can we predict the consequences? (of having new life forms) Except in the most general terms we are ignorant of the broad principles of evolution, of the factors that govern its rate and direction. We have no general theorems to account for the spectrum of organisms that we see and the gaps between. . . . We simply do not know.

We are ignorant of the relative importance of the various factors we currently perceive to participate in the evolutionary process. . . .

We are ignorant of any absolute measure of adaptation. We are ignorant of the depth of security of our own environmental . . . niche. We do not know.[10]

If Sinsheimer were to infer that there are great risks in experimentation simply from this ignorance, he would have committed the fallacy of appealing to ignorance. However, the gaps he notes in biological theory may nevertheless have other important consequences for the direction of genetic research.

To spot fallacious appeals to ignorance, look for premises with phrases like "we do not know," "no one has been able to prove," "is not yet confirmed," "has never been discovered," and "has not been shown." Then check the conclusion to make sure that it does not assert that the statement not known is false or that it is true or that it is quite probable or that it is quite improbable. If you find ignorance used to prove the truth, falsity, probability, or improbability of a statement, you have a fallacious appeal to ignorance.

A good question to ask when looking for this fallacy is whether similar premises could be used to generate the opposite conclusion. If we are ignorant as to whether S is true, we are also ignorant as to whether not-S is true. We may try to use our ignorance of S to infer not-S; but, on the other hand, we could equally well try to use our ignorance of not-S to infer S. When ignorance about a matter would equally well support two conclusions that are inconsistent with each other, we can see that it is irrelevant to establish which of the statements S and not-S we should accept. (Presumably, given this ignorance, we should neither accept S nor accept not-S. We should wait until we have more evidence.)

To sum up, the fallacy of appealing to ignorance may be described as follows:

Appeals to Ignorance
An appeal to ignorance amounts to a fallacy if the premises describe ignorance, lack of confirmation, lack of proof, or uncertainty regarding a statement S and if the conclusion states or assumes that S is false, that S is true, that S is improbable, or that S is probable, simply on the basis of this ignorance. From ignorance we can infer only lack of knowledge. We cannot infer truth or falsity or objective probability or improbability.

Jumping on the Bandwagon.   Many arguments are based on popularity. Someone tries to show that a product is good because many people select it or that a belief is correct because many people hold it. Such arguments are extremely flawed because the merits of something are one matter and its popularity another. The problem is that things can be popular for many reasons, and only one of these is their good quality. It would be different if people selected products for only one reason—quality—and if they held their beliefs as a result of only one kind of cause—careful, deliberate evaluation of pertinent evidence. In an ideally rational world, perhaps these factors might determine human choice and belief. In our world, however, they do not.

People may choose products because those products are cheap, because they have been well advertised, because they are for sale at a convenient store, because their friends have bought them (another appeal to popularity), or for many other reasons having nothing to do with the quality of the product. Similarly, they may believe things that are attributed to a product because they have heard them somewhere, read them in the paper, or picked them up during childhood. A claim may be widely believed only because it is a common prejudice. Thus the fact that it is widely believed is irrelevant to its truth.[11]

Bandwagon arguments are those in which the premises describe the popularity of a thing ("everybody's doing it"; "everybody's buying it"; "everybody believes it"), and the conclusion asserts that the thing is good or sensible. The arguments are fallacious because the popularity of a product or a belief is in itself irrelevant to the question of its real merits. Here is an example of a bandwagon appeal:

The perfume of the eighties. Women of the eighties choose a subtle feminine fragrance. Carfoor is the most popular choice of today's new woman. Career women say, "It's feminine, but discreet enough for the office and for business lunches." Today's woman can work and be a real woman. Today's woman chooses Carfoor.

Such an ad contains a number of appeals in emotionally charged language ("subtle," "feminine," "discreet") and a persuasive definition (*real* women are "feminine" enough to wear perfume). Its basic point, though, is an appeal to popularity. Potential consumers are urged to jump on the bandwagon, do what other *real* women are doing, and buy Carfoor. The point is that this perfume is one a woman should buy; the reason she should buy it is that other women are buying it. Another implicit appeal to popularity exists in the idea that "today's woman" works (presumably outside the home) and is yet aware of the need to be feminine. An unwritten message underlying the ad is that this lifestyle is the one women should choose because it is the most popular today. (Working outside the home is what today's woman does.)

Another example, this time referring to a belief rather than a product, is the following:

> *A majority of the American people now (1974) believe that the American participation in the Vietnam War was wrong. All Americans who resisted such participation were therefore patriotic and serving the American government, and all those who cooperated were unpatriotic and disserving the American government.*[12]

The writer of this letter clearly wishes to infer from the fact that a majority of people believed (in 1974) that participation in the Vietnam War was wrong that such participation was in fact wrong. This implicit conclusion follows from his first statement. There are two explicit conclusions derived from this intermediate step: resistance was patriotic and cooperation was not. The crucial step is the claim about the wrongness of participating in the war. There is only one piece of evidence for this claim, and it is the statement that a majority of the American people believe it. That belief, however, does not show that participation was wrong. However popular it might be, it could still be in error. In fact, years later, there seems to be no consensus among Americans on this matter. If we use popularity as a guide to truth, we shall have to change our minds whenever public opinion shifts.

The bandwagon or popularity appeal is a fallacy that occurs when people seek to infer merit or truth from popularity:

Jumping on the Bandwagon
The premise or premises of such an argument indicate that a product or belief is popular. It is endorsed by most people or by almost everybody. The conclusion of the argument is that you should get the product or that you should accept the belief because it is popular. Bandwagon appeals, or appeals to popularity, are fallacious because the popularity of a thing is irrelevant to its real merits. Too many reasons for selecting products or beliefs exist for the fact of their selection to count as good evidence of quality, truth, or rational acceptability.

Other Fallacies Involving Relevance.   Whenever a type of argument that is normally all right is *grossly* distorted, the results get so bad that the premises have no bearing on the conclusion. They are then *irrelevant* to the conclusion. Thus essentially correct types of argument have counterparts (degenerate versions) that contain irrelevant premises. Since this is the case, some types of irrelevance are covered in other parts of this book. In any case, as we have noted already, it would be futile to try to describe every possible kind of irrelevance. There are just too many: it is a little like the number of ways of getting lost in a forest!

Analogies can, when seriously flawed, contain premises that are irrelevant to their conclusion(s). In fact, we saw an example of such irrelevance earlier (in Chapter Four) in the argument about the zebra and the South African economy. The author was trying to reason by analogy, but the two things he compared are so completely different that his premises were irrelevant to his conclusion.

The same kind of point can be made with *appeals to authority*. As we noted in Chapter Four, appealing to the proper kind of authority, in the proper circumstances, can be a good defense of a claim. But often entirely inappropriate authorities are cited.

Often a person will try to defend a claim by appealing to someone who is an authority in some area entirely unrelated to the matter. For instance, advertisements may use praise from champion skiers to sell chocolate bars, or scientists may be appealed to for comments about international politics or ethical matters. In such cases, appeals to authority are totally flawed, for the expertise of the authorities is in areas that are irrelevant to the question at hand. It is interesting to know the beliefs of famous people, and their opinions are certainly worth listening to. However, an argument of this form:

1. *X* said that statement S is true.

So,

2. The statement S is true.

gives no support for S for the case when the authority *X* has is in some field that is irrelevant to knowledge about S. In such cases, appeals to authority amount to fallacies involving *ir*relevance. (Most of the time when appeals to authority go wrong, the fault is not so fundamental; it is rather that the statement of one expert is—for various reasons—not sufficient evidence for the claim in question to be true. That is, many appeals to authority fail on (G). Some seriously flawed ones fail on (R). Others are cogent and really back up the conclusion.)

EXERCISE SET

Exercise Two

For the following examples, determine whether the passage contains an argument. If it does, assess whether the premises are relevant to the conclusion. If you find any premises to be irrelevant, say why you think they are irrelevant and—if appropriate—label the argument as containing Straw Man, *Ad Hominem*, Guilt by Association, Appeal to Ignorance, Bandwagon, Improper Analogy, or Misuse of Authority. *Note: Not all arguments cited contain mistakes.*

*1. *Background:* In a letter to a Toronto paper, a writer commented on a favorable review of a feminist book. She took the occasion to give her own reasons for rejecting the feminist view of relations between the sexes, saying:

"I will not subscribe to a philosophy that purports to represent some sort of vague liberation from alleged wrongs while at the same time advocating to destroy traditions and democracy. . . . Let me just say that I vigorously oppose any ideology that arrogantly proposes to reduce my husband, my children, and myself (a traditional family) to superfluity simply because we don't fit into some sort of elitist, sexist new order."
(Letter to the editor, Toronto *Globe and Mail*, March 6, 1976.)

2. *Background:* A museum has just fired four people from its board of directors. Jones criticizes the firing, whereas Smith defends it.

Jones: You know, the board of directors has behaved quite badly in firing four new directors. The people who were fired were all conscientious individuals who could have done a good job of administering the museum if they had been given a chance.

Smith: Really, you should not be so sentimental and emotional. Jobs come and go, and people in a competitive field have to be prepared to take some risks. You only reveal your own lack of understanding of the real problems of museum management when you pretend to criticize a public administrative body like the museum board.

*3. *Background:* Smith and Jones are discussing moral vegetarianism. Moral vegetarianism is the theory and practice of not eating meat for the moral reason that the killing of animals is considered wrong, much in the way we consider the killing of people wrong. Jones defends the idea; Smith attacks it:

Jones: People should not kill animals for food. Animals can feel and sense just as humans can. Those being raised for food are often raised in inhumane conditions before they are killed. And, more often than not, they are killed in brutal ways and feel a lot of pain. Besides, people do not need meat in order to maintain their health. Vegetable proteins, such as the ones in peas, beans, and lentils, will do just as well.

Smith: This idea is ridiculous. Carnivorous animals kill other animals for food. Humans are more than carnivorous; they are omnivorous. It is natural for them to eat both plant and animal foods. We do not know what animal consciousness is like, so we must assume that they do not feel pain. Anyway, since animals kill each other, there is nothing wrong with us killing them.

4. These pamphlets that we have for sale contain juicy and fresh public debates. They cost only two dollars. Two dollars is about the cost of a juicy fresh hamburger. Therefore, you should buy our pamphlets.

5. Nature looks fantastic without clothes. Nobody thinks that seals, penguins, elephants, and birds should be covered in the latest fashion. So why should people wear clothing? Nudity is great!

*6. *Background:* Journalist Peter Marin wrote an article in *Harper's* magazine (1981) in which he claimed that Americans had not yet come to terms with the moral questions arising from their participation in the Vietnam War, and that veterans of that war were suffering from their incommunicable questions and feelings of guilt. A critic wrote to say that the article did not discuss any failings of anti-Vietnam spokespersons, such as actress Jane Fonda:

"Jane Fonda and her pro-totalitarian pals are not only without guilt concerning the boat people, the poison-gassed Laotians, and the Cambodian victims of the Khmer Rouge genocide, they are avid apologists for such practices."

7. Science makes theoretical discoveries. Technology works out applications for those discoveries. Thus science and technology are distinct human pursuits.

*8. *Background:* In January 1984, an outspoken critic of pornography, Maude Barlow, published an essay against free distribution of pornography in Canada. She claimed that Playboy bunnies teach us that women have no proper place next to men. An objection to Barlow's views follows:

"Why is it that Maude Barlow and others of her ilk feel compelled to argue their point by portraying the male half of society as a slobbering congregation of dimwits whose poorly formed collective intelligence lies putty-like waiting to be molded by Hugh Hefner and Bob Guccione? This attitude not only constitutes an insult to all men, but, ironically,

betrays tremendous contempt for the real (not fantasy) women who actually shape our view of the world.

"Inasmuch as Maude Barlow, like Mr. Hefner and Mr. Guccione, resorts to stereotypes to sell her product, she should be classed with these other purveyors of drivel, and universally ignored."
(Letter to the Toronto *Globe and Mail,* January 27, 1984.)

9. *Background:* Garrett Hardin wrote the following in 1970 in defense of compulsory sterilization of women as a solution to the world population problem:

"The 'right to breed' implies ownership of children. This concept is no longer tenable. Society pays an ever larger share of the cost of raising children. And on a biological level, the idea of the ownership of children has not been defensible for almost a century. Biologically, all that I give 'my' children is a set of chromosomes which have been sequestered in the germinal area long before my birth and have lived a life of their own beyond my control. Mutation has altered them. In reproduction my germ plasm is assembled in a new combination and mixed with another assortment of a similar history. 'My' child's germ plasm is not mine. It is really only part of the community's store: I was merely the temporary custodian of it."
(Garrett Hardin, "Parenthood: Right or Privilege?" *Science,* July 1970.)
(Assume that the *main* conclusion is that people do not have a right to breed.)

10. "More than 250,000 hairdressers the world over believe in what L'Oreal Hair Colouring can do for you. What more can we say?"
(Ad cited by R. H. Johnson and J. A. Blair in *Logical Self-Defense* [Toronto: McGraw-Hill-Ryerson, 1983], p. 160.)

11. "As a child I accepted evolution until I saw the illogic of it.

"If life originated from non-life, how come our present superscientists can't even define it, let alone reproduce it? Where is the so-called missing link between animal and man? There is just no such thing. Certainly there is no evidence the animal pelvis rotated 90 degrees to produce the upright man, nor can any animal reason or think."
(Letter to the Calgary *Herald,* January 3, 1983.)

12. If evolutionary developments occurred on other planets, they would not terminate in the same species we have on earth today. For conditions on other planets are very different from the conditions that prevail on earth, and also, particular accidents have greatly affected the course of evolution here on earth. These particular accidents are unique to this historical sequence on earth; they would not happen in the same way elsewhere. So there might be other intelligent beings in the universe, but there won't be human beings, apart from earth.

13. *Background:* A proposal was made to eliminate a tax deduction for a spouse who is financially dependent on a wage earner. The Canadian cabinet minister suggesting this elimination was Judy Erola:

"Judy Erola's intent to deprive the family of spousal income tax deduction benefits is a clear indication to me of Socialist–Communist trends. Erola relegates women to the status of a brood sow. Let women produce and the state will take care of the offspring. It puts human reproduction ahead of the sanctity of the home and the quality of family life.

"If a married woman wishes to make her home her castle, and the rearing of their children the most important goal of that period of her life, Erola should not intervene."
(Letter to the Calgary *Herald,* January 3, 1983.)
(*Suggestion:* You should find more than one fallacy in this passage.)

*14. An art college should be administered by a professor or instructor of art, for only someone who knows art can understand art students, art standards, and the special problems an art college has.

15. *Background:* The following appeared as an advertisement in the Canadian magazine *Miss Chatelaine* in February 1976. The advertisement was accompanied by a large photograph of Wolfman Jack, a popular rock disc jockey:

"When those pimples pop up, you should break out the Clearasil Ointment. Listen—if you use a cleanser, that's fine. But I know how you feel when those pimples pop up. So lay out some acne medication on those pimples. Break out the Clearasil Ointment. Clearasil goes right after those acne pimples. Dries 'em up, helps heal 'em up, and that's just for starters.

"Clearasil hangs right in there . . . for hours . . . just soppin' up that extra oil you usually get with pimples. It's Canada's number-one selling acne medication.

"Take it from the Wolfman. Pimples . . . I've been there. I know."

16. *Background:* A judge in New Brunswick, Canada, stated that the herbicides 2,4-D and 2,4,5-T were safe when he issued a judgment in favor of a corporation and against property owners who sought

to prevent spraying near their homes. In the wake of this judgment, the following letter to the Toronto *Globe and Mail* appeared on October 31, 1983:

"It is obvious that most reporters and editorial and letter writers either have not read Judge Merlin Nunn's decision or their reading comprehension scores are abysmally low. . . . He was unequivocal in clearly stating the herbicides 2,4-D and 2,4,5-T were safe for proper use. This legal case exposed the views of many well-known people and scientists testifying for both parties, and the decision was clearly in accord with independent, open scientific reviews held in many countries over the past 15 years. . . . We should all be pleased that one perceived problem has been proved false, so we can concentrate on solving Canada's real ones."

17. "A *Reader's Digest* article entitled 'Was Darwin Wrong?' discloses that biologists are abandoning Darwin's version of evolution. They refuse to question evolution itself, however, simply because creationism would be the only alternative.

"Early scientists sought an explanation of origins which was completely naturalistic, that is, without reference to anything supernatural. Many believed in spontaneous generation. Bacteria were seriously thought to have spontaneously formed in mud. Rats materialized out of rags. Then Louis Pasteur disproved their theory and a few years later Darwin published his theory of evolution.

"People desire a naturalistic theory, but not for scientific reasons. If there is no God, at least not one who intervenes in the universe, man is morally accountable to no one but himself. Evolution will 'win' as long as society desires the illusion of moral 'freedom'."
(Letter to the Calgary *Herald,* February 8, 1983.)
(*Hint:* What motives does the writer assume people have when they endorse evolution and reject creationism?)

*18. *Background:* Joe Clark, a prominent Canadian politician who was briefly prime minister of Canada (1979–80) and later Canadian minister for external affairs, is married to Maureen McTeer, a prominent and outspoken lawyer who has maintained her maiden name after marriage. When the following letter was written, Clark was the leader of the Conservative Party, but his leadership was being challenged:

"Some of my best friends are Conservatives . . . all either holding or yearning for the traditional dominant (male) role in their own households.

"They concede that Joe Clark's capable and attractive wife, Maureen McTeer, is supportive on the platform and brave in her husband's adversity. Yet they do not really believe that any political messiah would permit a wife to retain her maiden name. Even those on the distaff (female) side, some clearly head and shoulders above their spouses, subscribe meekly to this sexist bias. Like it or not, this outdated attitude possibly accounts for the present predicament of the former prime minister."

(Letter to the Toronto *Globe and Mail*, February 12, 1983.)

(*Question:* If people were reasoning as this author suggests, did they have a relevant reason for rejecting Clark as leader of Canada's Conservative Party?)

Some Concluding Comments

Criticizing an argument on grounds of relevance is a strong line of criticism, as we have seen. But you have to back up your criticism by saying why you think the premises are irrelevant to the conclusion. If you just say, "That's irrelevant," it does not put debate on a very high level. You should explain why you believe that premises are irrelevant. It is not enough, either, to just say, "that's *ad hominem*," or "you're using a straw man argument." The person whose argument you are criticizing may not understand these labels. Even if she does, you have to show why they apply to the particular case you are looking at.

In fact, logicians themselves disagree about relevance, but along somewhat different lines. Some claim that when arguments appear to have irrelevant premises, the problem is really that the arguments have missing premises. When these missing premises are added, they will link together with the stated premises, and the stated premises will then become relevant to the conclusion after all. This approach to irrelevance can make even the most blatant cases of irrelevance turn into something else.

For instance, consider our early example of irrelevance:

1. Smith is old and fat.
So,
2. Smith's views on Chinese politics are false.

We claim that in this argument the premise was completely irrelevant to the conclusion. But some logicians would claim that it is quite relevant to that conclusion, *once the appropriate missing premises are written in*. They find a basis for this approach by claiming that the arguer must have thought there was some kind of connection between being old and fat, and having incorrect opinions about Chinese politics, so we should insert premises that will state the arguer's beliefs. Here is one possible account:

1. Smith is old and fat.
<u>3</u>. People who are old tend to become senile and careless about the assessment of evidence.
<u>4</u>. People who are fat are often fat because they are emotionally disturbed, and being emotionally disturbed makes them unreliable interpreters of social affairs.
So,
2. Smith's views on Chinese politics are false.

Let us call this a *reconstructed* argument. Logicians who use the missing premises approach to relevance and irrelevance would claim that this reconstructed argument is a better one than the original, for it contains no flaw of relevance. It is true, indeed, that the reconstructed argument contains no flaw of relevance. But whether it is a better argument is a very debatable point, for the premises we added to avoid irrelevance are not acceptable. Also, the revised argument has the word *tend* in the premises; even if acceptable, the premises would not necessarily include *Smith*, as an individual, who shares these flaws. For that reason, it may be claimed that the revised argument fails on the (G) condition, unless the conclusion is moderated by adding a word such as *likely* or *probably*. What we have done is move the flaw in the original argument from one place (relevance) to others (acceptability of premises and adequacy of grounds for the stated conclusion).

This problem is not the only one. We have changed the original quite a lot by these additions. How did we know that (3) and (4) were the right premises to add? There are always a number of different possibilities as far as adding premises is concerned. For instance, here are two other quite different reconstructions of the argument about Smith and Chinese politics:

Alternative Reconstruction (a)
1. Smith is old and fat.
6. All views on politics held by people who are old and fat are false.
7. Whatever views Smith holds on Chinese politics, these are views held by someone who is old and fat.
So,
2. Smith's views on Chinese politics are false.

Alternative Reconstruction (b)
1. Smith is old and fat.
8. The Chinese flatter the old and fat.
9. A person cannot adequately appraise the society of a country in which he and his kind are flattered.
So,
2. Smith's views on Chinese politics are false.

One difficulty with reconstructing arguments with the very generous addition of missing premises is that there are always a number of different, equally plausible, reconstructions that you can make up. Also, this approach to analyzing arguments is very long and cumbersome. It requires the critic to do so much writing in that it almost seems as though she has been given the responsibility of writing the argument herself! And reconstruction can take you very far from the original in such cases as this one. If an argument has a flaw of relevance, the extra premises that you would add in order to reconstruct it without irrelevance will be unacceptable in any case. For practical purposes, our approach and the reconstructing approach do not give such very different results. They are, however, very different from a theoretical perspective.

Review of Terms Introduced

Positive relevance: A statement is positively relevant to the truth of another statement if its truth would give some evidence or reason to support the truth of that other statement. That is, if the first statement were true, that would count in favor of the second one being true.

Negative relevance: A statement is negatively relevant to the truth of another statement if its truth would give some reason or evidence for the falsity of that other statement. That is, if the first statement were true, that would count in favor of the second one being false.

Irrelevance: A statement is irrelevant to the truth of another statement if its truth or falsity neither counts in favor of the truth of that other statement nor counts toward that other statement's being false. If the truth of one statement is irrelevant to the truth of another, it is neither positively relevant to it nor negatively relevant to it.

Normative conclusion: One having to do with values and bearing on what people should do.

Normative relevance: Positive or negative relevance to a conclusion that is normative. Typically, positively or negatively relevant statements are factual statements put forward as pertinent to establishing or refuting value judgments.

Fallacy: A mistake in argument that has its source in incorrect reasoning underlying the argument. Typically, fallacies do not appear on the surface to be mistakes. They may be quite convincing.

Straw man fallacy: A fallacy committed when a person misrepresents an argument, theory, or claim, and then, on the basis of that misrepresentation, claims to have refuted the position he has misrepresented.

Ad hominem fallacy: A fallacy committed when an irrelevant premise about the background, personality, or character of a person is given in an attempt to show that his theories or arguments are false or unacceptable. Such premises about personality and background are relevant only if the person himself is the issue in question (as in an election) or if the reliability of his testimony or authority is at stake.

Guilt-by-association fallacy: A fallacy committed when a person or his views are criticized on the basis of a supposed link between them and a person or movement believed to be disreputable. This criticism is one of relevance.

Fallacious appeals to ignorance: Arguments in which there is either an appeal to our ignorance about S in an attempt to show that not-S is true or probable, or an appeal to our ignorance about not-S in an attempt to show that S is true or probable.

Bandwagon fallacy: A fallacy in which one reasons from the popularity of a product or belief to a conclusion about its actual merits. Also called the popularity fallacy.

Reconstructed argument: An argument in which the inferences (or steps) have been made more orderly, logical, and sensible by the addition of extra premises. Where the unreconstructed, or original, argument had a fallacy of relevance, the reconstructed argument will not. Typically, however, premises added to produce the reconstruction are unacceptable.

NOTES

1. (For instructors.) Relevance here is defined using the notion of truth. There is no contradiction be-tween this definition and the replacement of truth by acceptability in the ARG conditions. To say that acceptability is to replace truth in conditions of an argument's cogency is not to say that truth is to be eliminated as a central epistemic and logical concept.

2. Adapted from a letter to the Toronto *Globe and Mail*, February 8, 1982.

3. Letter to the Toronto *Star*, April 8, 1981.

4. Sidney Lens, "The Most Dangerous Cliché," *Nation*, September 11, 1982, p. 210.

5. Barbara Tuchman, "The Alternative to Arms Control," *The New York Times Magazine*, April 11, 1982, pp. 44–45.

6. Advertisement cited by *Harrowsmith*, September 1980.

7. Anne Roche, "On Killing Inconvenient People," *Saturday Night*, September 1973, pp. 29–31.

8. Toronto *Globe and Mail*, September 4, 1980, p. 1.

9. A. S. Neill, cited by Richard Robinson in "Arguing from Ignorance," *Philosophical Quarterly*, Vol. 21, No. 83, pp. 97–107. See p. 97.

10. Quoted in Carl Cohen, "Restriction of Research with Recombinant DNA: The Dangers of Inquiry and the Burden of Proof," *Southern California Law Review*, Vol. 51, No. 6, pp. 1081–1113. See p. 1099.

11. Appeals to the popularity of beliefs should not be confused with the notion of common knowledge developed in Chapter Five. The difference is that the belief whose popularity is appealed to is not universal in a culture, nor is it basic and elementary. Typically, its content is somewhat controversial, speculative, or normative, but it is claimed to be popular.

12. Cited by R. H. Johnson and J. A. Blair in *Logical Self-Defense* (Toronto: McGraw-Hill-Ryerson, 1983), p. 167.

7

Fitting Things Together: A Diagramming Technique

When we were discussing relevance, we came to see that whether a premise is relevant to a conclusion may, in many cases, depend on whether other premises are present in the argument—either stated explicitly or as missing premises. A premise that, on its own, appears quite irrelevant to the intended conclusion may be relevant when it is asserted along with another premise, so that the premises link together to support the conclusion. This shift from irrelevance to relevance is a good illustration of the importance of understanding the overall structure of an argument. We have seen that quite frequently arguments include subarguments in which one or more premises are defended. We have also noted that occasionally the very same premises are used to support several quite distinct conclusions. Noting such aspects of structure is important as far as the appraisal of arguments is concerned, because it may very well happen that one conclusion is well supported whereas another is not. Diagrams can be constructed to represent these and other aspects of an argument's structure, and such diagrams are often very helpful in understanding and appraising arguments. In this chapter we will develop and discuss a diagramming technique.

Single Support

Let us first consider a very simple case. Suppose that we have an argument with a single premise and one conclusion. The conclusion, obviously, is supposed to receive its full support from this one premise. If we represent the premise with (1) and the conclusion with (2), we could diagram the argument this way:

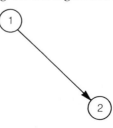

The arrowhead indicates that support is supposed to flow from the premise to the conclusion. Probably you have heard of Descartes's famous argument, "I think, therefore I exist." It can be diagrammed this way. The argument is:

———— 1. I think.
Therefore,
2. I exist.

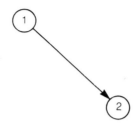

Another case illustrating this simple single support pattern is the following:

———— No single experiment can establish a general scientific result, because *every experiment in science requires replication before it can be known to be reliable.*

1. Every experiment in science requires replication before it can be known to be reliable.
Therefore,
2. No single experiment can establish a general scientific result.

This again is a single support argument. A single premise is used to back up the conclusion, and the argument may be diagrammed as:

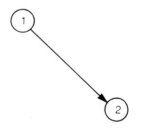

Linked Support

Most often conclusions are drawn from more than one premise. In many cases the premises work *interdependently* to support the conclusion, which means that in their support for the conclusion, the premises depend on each other. One premise could not lend the conclusion any support without the others. In these arguments, premises *link* to support the conclusion. When the support is linked, it is important to consider premises together to determine whether a premise is relevant to the conclusion. As a simple example of an argument in which the premises are linked to support the conclusion, consider the following:

Obesity must be environmental, for we know that it is either inherited or environmental, and it is not inherited.
1. Obesity is either environmental or inherited.
2. Obesity is not inherited.
Therefore,
3. Obesity is environmental.

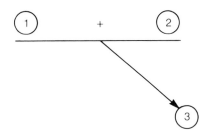

Here we need (1) and (2) working together to lend support to (3). The premises work interdependently in the sense that if one were not there, the other would lend no support at all to the conclusion. (It would, in fact, be irrelevant to it.) For instance, that obesity is not inherited has nothing to do with the conclusion that obesity is environmentally acquired, unless we are willing to suppose that it is either inherited or environmentally acquired. Similarly, the first premise alone could not support the conclusion without the second. Premises work together when support is of the linked type. We indicate the link by the plus sign (+) and by the lines used to relate linked premises to each other in the diagram.

Here is another linked argument—one that forms the basis of that familiar expression "ship of state":

A state in these troubled times is like a ship sailing through a storm, and a ship certainly does need a knowledgeable and reliable captain who is trusted by the crew. We can see, then, that the modern state needs a strong leader in whom its people can have confidence.
1. A state in these troubled times is like a ship sailing through a storm.
2. A ship sailing through a storm needs a knowledgeable, reliable captain who is trusted by the crew.
Therefore,
3. A modern state needs a leader in whom its people can have confidence.

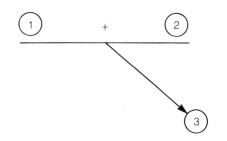

We can see that the two premises link together to support the conclusion. Their interdependency is very important for our appraisal of the argument. If either premise is false or unacceptable, the whole argument will be flawed, since each premise needs the other to support the conclusion. Also, when asking ourselves whether the premises are relevant to the conclusion and provide good reasons for it, we have to consider the premises as they work together, not as they appear separately.

Let us now look at a more natural and longer argument in which the premises work in a linked way. Here is one written by T. M. Penelhum in his book *Religion and Rationality*. Penelhum is considering the idea that religious experience can demonstrate the existence of a Christian God.[1] He argues to reject this idea. (Here, as in all extracts in this chapter, we have added numbers for statements that serve either as premises or as conclusions in the argument.)

> *Even if we were to accept that the occurrence of a given religious experience implied the existence of some supernatural being who produced it, (1) the argument would only allow us to conclude that there existed a being capable of producing that particular experience. Since (2) no developed concept of God could allow us to regard a given phenomenon that we ascribed to him as representing the limit of his creative power, it is obvious that (3) no given religious experience could possibly entail the existence of the Christian God.*

1. If an experience implied the existence of some supernatural being, it would only prove a being capable of producing that particular experience.
2. No developed concept of God would be one in which God's power to produce one phenomenon was ascribed to Him as representing the limit of His creative power.
Therefore,
3. No given religious experience could entail the existence of the Christian God.

Premises (2) and (1) link and are intended to support (3). Penelhum contends that a particular religious experience that would support only a limited god would not entail the existence of the Christian God. Clearly this line of reasoning commits him to the view that the Christian God is a god who is not limited. The argument will become more clear if we write this background belief about the limitlessness of the Christian God into the argument as a missing premise. (Since the claim that God is not finite is absolutely standard in Christian theology, there is no risk of distorting the case by doing this.)

4. An undeveloped and limited concept of God would be inadequate to describe the Christian God.

Including this extra premise, we now represent the argument as:

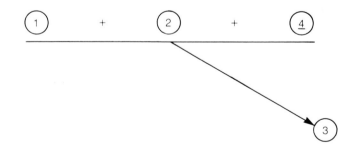

Again the pattern of support is of the linked type. The first premise is conditional—that is, if we had such a proof, it would show only such-and-such. The second premise and the supplementary premise state that the such-and-such that would be proven would not support the existence of the Christian God; the conclusion is inferred from the conjunction of these three premises.

Before we move on to the next pattern of support, here's one further case. This example is taken from *Justice Not Charity* by Douglas Roche.[2] Speaking of schemes for developing the economies and social systems of severely impoverished countries, Roche says:

> *(1) No system of development today is without serious defects. (2) The capitalist countries are strong on production and political liberties but permit too great extremes in economic benefits; (3) the socialist countries limit the economic gap but at the expense of both production and political liberties.*

Given our knowledge of contemporary politics, which this author shares, and the fact that he reaches a universal conclusion from a consideration of just two possibilities, we can see that Roche is relying on an unexpressed additional premise:

<u>4</u>. Capitalist systems and socialist systems are the only systems of development today.

The premises, (2) and (3), linked with the additional premise (<u>4</u>), support (1), which is the conclusion:

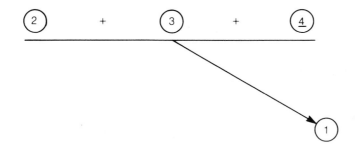

The claim about capitalist countries, taken alone, would not support the conclusion, and neither would the claim about socialist countries. Obviously, the missing premise alone would be irrelevant to the conclusion. But, linked together, the three premises support the conclusion.

Convergent Support

When premises support a conclusion in the linked way, their support is interdependent, as we have seen. By contrast, premises operate separately when support is of the convergent type. That is, in arguments with convergent support, each premise is quite separately relevant to the conclusion and would count as a reason in support of the conclusion, even if the other converging premises were false. A simple example is the following:

(1) The practice of setting aside apartments for adults only is morally wrong because (2) it discriminates against people with children and also (3), it encourages single adults in their pursuit of an overly luxurious lifestyle.

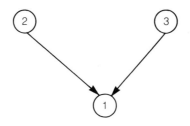

Here (2) and (3) are premises used to support the conclusion, (1). In this argument the premises do not link to support the conclusion. They operate convergently because they support the conclusion quite independently. (Remember, we said that linked premises support the conclusion interdependently.) If premise (2) were false, (3) would still provide a reason for thinking (1) is true; and if (3) were false, (2) would still provide a reason for thinking (1) to be true. Two quite separate points are made in this argument. Each premise lends to the conclusion a separate strand of support.

Here is another simple argument of the same type:

(1) Psychological tests should not be a basis for hiring because (2) these tests are rather unreliable and (3) they are discriminatory. Also, (4) psychological tests constitute an invasion of personal privacy.

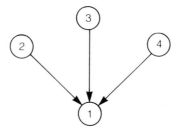

Again the premises deal with quite distinct facts that bear independently on the conclusion. If it should turn out, for instance, that these tests are not discriminatory, the other two factors cited would still be relevant to the conclusion and would still provide reasons in its favor. For instance, whether psychological tests are discriminatory or not, it would remain a reason against the use of such tests that they are unreliable, or constitute an invasion of privacy.

Let us now turn to a more complex example. The following is taken from John Kenneth Galbraith's "Consumption and the Concept of the Household."[3]

(1) Beyond a certain point the possession and consumption of goods becomes burdensome unless the tasks associated therewith can be delegated. . . . (2) the consumption of increasingly elaborate or exotic food is only rewarding if there is someone to prepare it. (3) Otherwise, for all but the eccentric, the time so required soon outweighs whatever pleasure is derived from eating it. (4) Increasingly spacious and elaborate housing requires increasingly burdensome maintenance and administration. . . . So also with (5) dress, (6) vehicles, (7) the lawn, (8) sporting facilities, and (9) other consumer artifacts.

Galbraith supports a generalization by citing a number of distinct areas of life in which it holds. The support lent to his claim is of the convergent type. One easy way to see this is to imagine that Galbraith should turn out to be wrong about several of the various phenomena he cites. For instance, suppose that it turned out, as a matter of human psychology, that the very people who enjoy dressing elaborately also enjoy fussing over their attire—or that the very people who enjoy golf also enjoy mowing the lawn on the golf course. If these suppositions were true, it still would not affect the support given the conclusion by (2) and (3), which are about food. These would remain support for the conclusion, even without the others. The same point can be made for any combination of the stated premises. For this reason we say the pattern of support is *convergent*. The premises converge to support the conclusion: they are separately relevant to it. They do not link to support the conclusion but are independently relevant to it.

A Quick Summary

1. The single support pattern. One premise supports the conclusion.

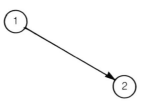

2. The linked support pattern. Several premises support the conclusion, and they do this interdependently. That is, they require each other in order to support the conclusion. If premises are linked, and one is false, then the others do not support the conclusion at all.

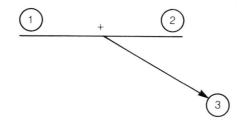

There is no upper limit on the number of linked premises an argument can have.

3. The convergent support pattern. Several premises support the conclusion. They do this independently of each other. Each is separately relevant to the conclusion and would count in its favor even if the other premise(s) were false.

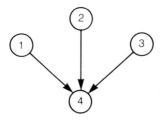

There is no upper limit on the number of convergent premises.

A Minor Complication

As we have seen already, sometimes arguments have several conclusions. When this happens, it may be that one conclusion is reached as a means to reaching a second further conclusion. In that case we have a subargument within an argument. (This is an important sort of structure, which we will soon explore in more detail.) However, sometimes an argument is used to support several distinct conclusions that are reached from the very same premise or premises. Consider, for instance, the following brief argument from the American philosopher C. S. Peirce. It is about the purpose of reasoning, and it appears in a famous paper Peirce wrote entitled "The Fixation of Belief."[4]

> (1) The object of reasoning is to find out, from the consideration of what we already know, something else which we do not know. Consequently, (2) reasoning is good if it be such as to give a true conclusion from true premises and (3) not otherwise.

This argument is based on a single premise, the first statement. Thus the support is of the first type we considered, the single support pattern. However, this time there are two conclusions, numbered (2) and (3). Conclusion (3), which is compressed by Peirce, is a shorthand way of saying:

(3) Reasoning is not good if it is not such as to give a true conclusion from true premises.

Conclusions (2) and (3) make different claims about reasoning. One of these claims could be true while the other one is false. But both claims are inferred by Peirce from the single premise, (1). There is no indication either that (2) supports (3) or that (3) supports (2). The way to diagram this argument is as follows:

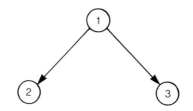

We do not put a plus sign between (2) and (3) because our plus sign does not mean exactly the same thing as the word *and*. It indicates a linked support pattern: interdependency in the way the premises work to support the conclusion. Since there is only one premise here, and since the conclusions are not working interdependently to support any further point, the plus sign would be inappropriate.

Linked arguments may also have two quite distinct conclusions, or, in rare cases, even more. Consider, for instance:

(1) It now seems to be established that chimpanzees are capable of learning a human language.
(2) It is by language that man has sought to differentiate himself from the other animals.
So,
(3) The old basis for differentiation is no longer appropriate, and (4) the possibility of communicating with another species is a real one for contemporary mankind.

Here (3) and (4) are both inferred as conclusions from (1) and (2). These premises, (1) and (2), link to support the two distinct conclusions. Neither conclusion is inferred from the other; both are supported by the two premises. Thus the argument would be diagrammed as:

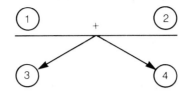

More rarely, a convergent argument may have several distinct conclusions. Here the diagram would look something like this:

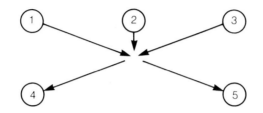

When you can identify several distinct conclusions in an argument, the first thing to do is to ask yourself whether one of them depends, logically, on the other—or whether the author intended that it be supported by the other. If either of these things is the case, then you have a subargument. One conclusion is an intermediate conclusion or, as we described it earlier, a premise that is itself defended by other premises in a subargument. But if the conclusions are based on the very same premises and neither is inferred from the other, they should be diagrammed as in the last example: flowing out from the same premises, not connected by a plus sign or by lines in the diagram. There may even be more than two distinct conclusions in a given argument, flowing from the same premises. However, this structure is quite rare.

EXERCISE SET

Exercise One

Diagram each of the following arguments, indicating whether the pattern of support is of the single, linked, or convergent type, and how many conclusions are drawn in each case. Fill in missing premises and conclusions wherever necessary.

1. In Canada medical insurance is state-sponsored. In the United States medical insurance is private. Thus we can see that the basis of medical insurance is very different in these two countries.

*2. Every teacher is bound to encounter some student who is more intelligent than he or she is. For not even the most intelligent teacher is sharper in every regard than every single one of the thousands of students he or she will encounter in a lifetime of teaching.

3. An international court has no international police to back it up. Without international police, judgments of the court cannot be fully enforced. Therefore, judgments of an international court cannot be fully enforced.

4. Josie must be in love with Fred. She frequently talks about him. She gets very excited when he is about to visit. She blushes when you ask her about him. And she has given up several dates just on the chance she might have an opportunity to see him.

*5. Canada is an extremely spread-out country that depends on road and air transport to a far greater extent than do European countries. In European countries rail service can be more efficiently and economically run than it can in Canada. Without an effective rail system, more shipping is done by air and road, and air and road are more expensive than rail. Therefore, we cannot say that Canadians are wasteful of oil simply on the grounds that they use more oil per person than the Europeans.

6. "Science, since people must do it, is a socially embedded activity."
(Stephen Jay Gould, *The Mismeasure of Man* [New York: Norton, 1981].)

7. "It is not mere hubris to argue that *Homo sapiens* is special in some sense—for every species is unique in its own way. Shall we judge among the dance of the bees, the song of the humpback whale, and human intelligence?"
(Gould, *The Mismeasure of Man.*)

8. "They laughed at Galileo. They laughed at Newton. They laughed at the Wright brothers. And now they are laughing at me. So I must be right."
(Used by a television comedian in Toronto.)

9. "Since dreams can be remembered, they must be conscious experiences."
(Yost and Kalish, "Miss Macdonald on Sleeping and Waking," *Philosophical Quarterly,* 1955.)

10. *Background:* In February 1983, the Canadian Conference of Catholic Bishops delivered an "economic sermon" on the state of Canada's economy, warning about the inhumanity of the increasing gap between rich and poor. Some members of Parliament (MPs) criticized the bishops for issuing their report, saying that they were offending against the principle of the separation of church and state. Commenting on this criticism, an editorial writer said:

"The MPs are wrong to suggest the bishops had no license to criticize the Liberal Government's economic recovery program or suggest alternatives. The bishops have this right as certainly as the MPs have the right to challenge their views."
(Toronto *Globe and Mail*, February 8, 1983.)

11. If we perceived only sense impressions rather than objects, the world would look like a kaleidoscope. But the world does not look like a kaleidoscope. Thus it is apparent that, whatever the explanation of perception may be, we do not perceive only sense impressions.

12. "China's formidable, if underdeveloped, military machine complicates Soviet defense, tying down at least a quarter of the Soviet Union's military strength that could otherwise be shifted elsewhere. China's role in the anti-Soviet guerrilla war in Afghanistan and the anti-Vietnamese war in Cambodia serves Western government interests. China has played a stabilizing role in the Korean peninsula, applying a steadying hand on North Korean adventurism and balancing Soviet influence there. China has also acquiesced in the resurgence of U.S. military power in the Pacific and encourages a moderate strengthening of Japan's defenses. It is therefore in Western interests that China's security position not be eroded or made less credible."
(Toronto *Globe and Mail*, July 23, 1985.)

*13. "Virtue generally, in all sorts of subjects, is somewhat that is valued for eminence; and consisteth in comparison. For if all things were equally in all men, nothing would be prized."
(Thomas Hobbes, *Leviathan*, ed. C. B. MacPherson [Middlesex, England: Penguin Books, 1961].)

14. Individuals are not reliable in their judgments. Groups are made up of individuals. Therefore, groups are not likely to be reliable in their judgments.

Arguments Building on Each Other

We have described the simple ways in which a single premise or several premises can work to support a conclusion. These patterns are also used occasionally to support several conclusions that are independent of each other. However, as we have already noticed frequently in the preceding chapters, it is common for the premises used to support a main conclusion to be supported themselves in subarguments. This fact makes a lot of sense when you think about it. If an argument is about a controversial topic, it is quite likely that any premises strong enough to support the main conclusion will themselves need support. On occasion, the premises used to support these premises may be defended in a sub-subargument. This whole process obviously has to stop somewhere. One of the major benefits of diagramming an argument is that we are able to represent the structure of arguments, subsidiary arguments, and any further supporting structures. The three patterns of support may be used in extended arguments in any combination. If the single support pattern is repeated several times, we get a longer argument that looks like this:

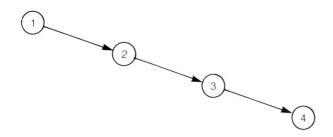

If the linked pattern is repeated, the resulting argument would perhaps look like this:

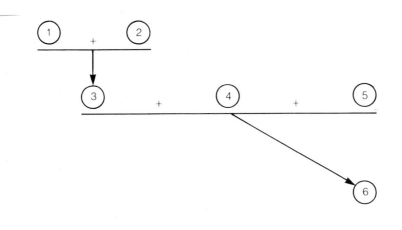

or like this:

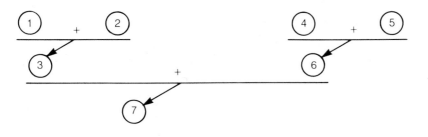

Many combinations are possible. The same may be said of convergent arguments. If, for instance, we had a convergently patterned argument in which several premises were themselves based on premises defended by convergently patterned premises, the diagram for the whole argument would look something like this:

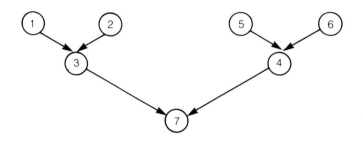

A more common situation, however, is that in which we have several of these distinct patterns of support used in one argument. For instance, an argument might have three converging premises, one of which is in turn defended by a single support-ing subpremise. The pattern of support would be essentially convergent, but one in which one premise is given a defense in the single support pattern.

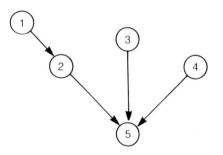

Often a main conclusion will be defended by some premises that are linked with each other *and* by others that do not link but converge. You can see that many combinations are possible.

Examples of Extended Structures.   Let us take a look at some arguments that do use extended structures of these kinds and see how they may be represented in these diagrams. We'll begin with an argument about the issue of whether experimenting on animals is morally justified. This argument is from an essay entitled "Why Knowledge Matters" by Mary Midgley.[5]

> And most of us would agree that (1) it is wrong to cause suffering for an entirely trivial issue. (For instance, in the case of the U.S. cancer programme, it seems pretty uncon-troversial that it is wrong to commission the performing of experiments on animals when you care so little about the results that you scarcely bother to look at them. . . .) (2) Justification must therefore rest on importance. (3) But an important issue is by definition a pervasive one. It is not an isolated matter, it is something far-reaching which crops up in many contexts and has many widely varied effects. If this is so, (4) it

can be tested in many ways. So (5) it is impossible that tests which involve inflicting suffering on animals are the only ones, and (6) unlikely that they are the best ones, by which an important issue can be settled.

It is worth setting this argument out in standardized form as it is rather complex. Several points are stated several times in different words, and when this happens, only one number is used. The argument goes like this:

1. It is wrong to cause suffering for an entirely trivial issue.
So,
2. The justification of the infliction of suffering on animals during scientific experimentation must rest on the importance of the issue being studied.
3. An important issue is one that crops up in many contexts and has varied effects.
Thus,
4. An important issue can be tested in many ways.
Therefore,
5. It is impossible that tests involving animal suffering should be the only tests for hypotheses on any important issue.
And,
6. It is unlikely that tests involving animal suffering should be the best tests for hypotheses on any important issue.

We can see already that Mary Midgley's argument has a rather complex structure. There are two distinct main conclusions, (5) and (6). But statements (2) and (4) are also defended along the way—and indicators have been used in the standardized version to show this. Statement (2) is supported by (1) alone, so clearly this part of the diagram will be the single support pattern. Statement (4) is supported by (3). Once (4) is established, two conclusions are inferred from (4) and (2). These conclusions are distinct. Putting the whole thing together, we arrive at the following representation:

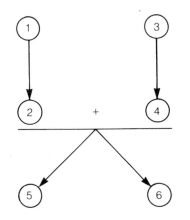

Let us work through this process again, using another example. This time we look at a short excerpt from Sissela Bok's book *Lying*. In that book a major theme was that even "small" lies tend to undermine the human trust that is necessary as the basis for any smoothly running human society. In a chapter dealing with white lies, Bok discussed the giving of placebos (pseudo-medicines) by doctors.[6] She argued against this rather common medical practice as follows:

> When we look more closely at practices such as placebo-giving, it becomes clear that (1) all lies defended as "white" cannot be so easily dismissed. In the first place, (2) the harmlessness of lies is notoriously disputable. (3) What the liar perceives as harmless or even beneficial may not be so in the eyes of the deceived. Second, (4) the failure to look at an entire practice rather than at their own isolated case often blinds liars to cumulative harm and expanding deceptive activities. (5) Those who begin with white lies can come to resort to more frequent and more serious ones. Where some tell a few white lies, others may tell more. Because (6) lines are so hard to draw, (7) the indiscriminate use of such lies can lead to other deceptive practices. (8) the aggregate harm from a large number of marginally harmful instances may, therefore, be highly undesirable in the end—for liars, those deceived, and honesty and trust more generally.

The main conclusion is in the first sentence: lies defended as "white" are not so innocent as they are often thought to be. We have numbered the statements that offer support to this conclusion. A rather confusing thing, perhaps, is that the author herself included a "first" and "second," and these do not coincide with our numbers. Her numbers do indicate something important: support for the conclusion comes from two quite separate lines of thought. One line, developed in our numbers (3) and (2), has to do with the fact that people disagree about how harmful lies are. The other, developed by the other premises, is that the practice of telling lies tends to expand. The basic pattern of support, then, is convergent. The theme of whether people disagree about the harmfulness of lies and the issue of how trust is undermined by expanding truthlessness are two quite independent ideas. For both these fundamental points, there are subarguments within the overall argument. Statement (3) supports (2) in the single support pattern. And statements (4), (5), and (7) link to support (8). These premises link to show that aggregate harm from lies can be quite undesirable in the end. Putting the whole argument together, we see the following pattern:

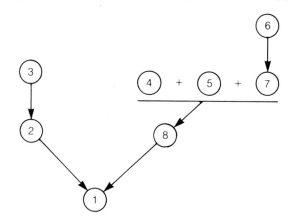

Since this argument is primarily convergent, any appraisal of it would have to proceed in two stages. We might decide that part of the argument works and part does not. An understanding of these structures is useful for the appraisal of arguments because of the independence of premises when there is a convergent pattern of support and because of their interdependence when there is a linked pattern of support.

When premises link to support a conclusion, any flaws in one premise will affect others. If a premise is linked to others and it begs the question or is known to be false, then the whole argument will fall down. Thus faults in premises *transfer* when the pattern of support is linked. And, as we have noted, if the premises link to support the conclusion, you have to look at them together when you are raising questions about their relevance to the conclusion. But when the support is convergent, these matters are quite different. Flaws in one premise do not affect the others. If one premise begs the question, or is false, other premises may be acceptable and give some support to the conclusion. Flaws do not transfer through a convergent pattern as they do in a linked one. The diagrams are useful to make this basic distinction, to represent subarguments, and to see how many distinct conclusions are defended. The diagrams can be used along with the ARG conditions, and they will help you to determine the significance of various flaws you find.

Disjointed Structures.   We'll illustrate this point by working through an example—first getting the structure straight and then applying the ARG conditions. The example comes from an essay about reason and religious belief.[7]

> *(1) If theology were part of reasonable inquiry, there would be no objection to an atheist's being a professor of theology. (2) That a man's being an atheist is an absolute bar to his occupying a chair proves that (3) theology is not an open-minded and reasonable inquiry. Someone may object that a professor of theology should be interested in theology. But (4) a man who maintains that there is no god must think it a sensible and interesting question to ask whether there is a god; and in fact (5) we find that many atheists are interested in theology. Professor H. D. Lewis tells* (Philosophy, 1952) *that an old lady asked him what philosophy is, and when he had given an answer, she said "O, I see, theology." She was nearly right, for (6) theology and philosophy have the same subject-matter. The difference is that (7) in philosophy you are allowed to come out with whatever answer seems to you the more likely.*

This passage seems rather disjointed on first reading, and when we look more closely at the structure, we will understand that there is a good basis for this impression. The passage actually contains three distinct arguments with no definite linkage or relation between them. First there is the linked argument from (1) and (2) to (3). Then the author refers to a view opposed to his own, as indicated in the expression "someone may object that a professor should. . . ." (His own view is that if theology were rational, atheists would be able to be professors of theology.) He tries to refute the opposing view, using (4) and (5) as his premises. These statements are used to support a missing conclusion—the denial of the opposed view. We'll give this missing conclusion a number:

> ─── (8) That a professor of theology should be interested in theology is no justification for barring atheists from being professors of theology.

The premises (4) and (5) support this conclusion, (8), convergently; even if (4) were false, (5) would still be relevant to (8), and conversely. The next theme in the passage is a new one: the relation and difference between theology and philosophy. Here statements (6) and (7) are used to support the view that the lady "was nearly right." Again we need to supply a missing conclusion to the effect that the opinion referred to by H. D. Lewis was nearly correct. We add the following:

> ─── (9): To say that philosophy and theology have the same subject matter is not far from the truth.

Statements (6) and (7) link to support (9).

The passage, then, contains three quite distinct arguments. They look like this:

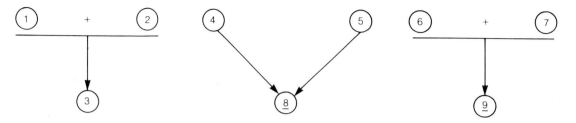

We can see why the passage seemed rather disjointed and difficult to understand. Although the three conclusions, (3), (8), and (9), are in a general sense about the same subject, they are not connected in any logical way; they do not link, or converge, to substantiate any further point. Moreover, the fact that two conclusions were unstated, and only alluded to by references to other people's views, no doubt contributed to making the passage rather hard to follow. (This is a good example of how *not* to make yourself clear!)

When we now begin to use ARG on these arguments, we will rapidly discover that all three are flawed. First, let us look at the argument from (1) and (2) to (3); here the support is linked. But the premises are not acceptable. Premise (1) states that in any reasonable inquiry dissenters must be allowed to hold professorships. That seems too strong a condition: most people would count history as a reasonable inquiry, and those who claim that the world might have been created only five minutes ago are not typically allowed to be history professors. The first premise, as stated, can be known to be false. Since the support is linked, the second premise alone cannot support the conclusion; hence the argument fails completely. In the next argument, where support is convergent, both premises are separately relevant to the conclusion. If both were true, or acceptable, the conclusion would be adequately supported by them. Also, one premise, (5), is a matter of common knowledge: many atheists are interested in the issues and problems of theology. However, (4) is a very controversial premise; as stated, with no qualification, it is just false. Premise (4) states that anyone who maintains there is no god must think it is a sensible and interesting question to ask whether there is a god. But many atheists have long ago dismissed the very possibility that a god exists, turning their attention to other matters. At best it would be true that an atheist must, at one time or another, have been interested in the question as to whether a god exists. Some atheists think that the very concept of a god is ridiculous, and others regard the question of whether a god exists as completely meaningless. Thus we can see that premise (4) is not acceptable, but (5) can give some support to (8). It remains relevant, but it is not by itself adequate grounds for (8).

Moving on to the third small argument expressed in the passage, we find another case of linked support. Here the (R) and (G) conditions are clearly satisfied. If theology and philosophy did indeed have the same subject matter, and if the only difference between them were that in philosophy you can come up with whatever answer seems to you most likely whereas in theology you do not have this freedom, then indeed it would follow that these two are virtually the same subject. It is certainly true that philosophers disagree about most things. Theologians disagree too, even though the range of disagreement is smaller. However, philosophy and theology do not have the same subject matter. There are many topics in philosophy—such as the nature of mental images, the status of logical principles, the definition of causation, and others—that are not topics in theology. We have a linked argument in which one premise is false; hence the argument falls down and is inadequate. The second of the arguments in the passage lent some support to its conclusion; the other two arguments turned out to be not cogent; and the three arguments were quite disconnected. Thus it seems fair to say that the passage is virtually devoid of well-supported conclusions. The only thing the author succeeded in doing was to give a partial reply (in the second argument) to someone else's point of view.

Here is another example, a letter to a newspaper concerning the seal hunt in the Canadian province of Newfoundland. People concerned about animal welfare have been strenuously protesting the killing of harp seal pups for a number of years, and activists and Newfoundland sealers have actually been involved in violent confrontations over the issue. The following letter was written to a Toronto paper on the subject:[8]

> I am a Newfoundlander, and I cannot help but feel some animosity toward (1) those people who approach the seal hunt issue from a purely emotional stance. Surely (3) this is not the way they look in their butcher's freezer, when they are looking for pork chops. Yet (4) the slaughtering method approved by the Department of Health officials for swine is hideous, and (5) nowhere near as humane as the dispatching of a young seal.
>
> (6) Young seals have skulls as soft as egg shells, and a sealer kills the animal instantly. To say it feels no pain would be an exaggeration, but to say (7) that the pain is absolutely minimal would be, I feel, very true. I suggest (8) that they not watch so much Walt Disney. The degree of anthropomorphism displayed by some of your letter writers is appalling.

A major theme of the passage is that those who oppose the seal hunt are doing so on emotional grounds. This point, numbered (1), is the major conclusion. It is suggested as well that the seal hunt is a permissible practice; however, this conclusion is not stated. (It is a moot point whether we should read this conclusion into the argument. We do so, but perhaps you will want to disagree with our interpretation here.) A second conclusion in our interpretation is as follows:

—— (2) The seal hunt is a morally acceptable practice.

We see the argument as directed toward establishing (1) and then hoping to establish (2) as flowing from (1). The author reasons that the opposition is purely emotional and then infers from this—as suggested by the tone and context of the letter—that the seal hunt is morally acceptable, contrary to the claims of the opposition. The stated premises are all intended to support (1), which could in turn be read as intended to support (2).

To diagram the argument, we first ask ourselves whether any of the premises (3)–(8) support each other. It turns out that they do. Premise (5) is supported in a subargument by (6), (7), and (4), which link to give it support. So one part of the argument will look like this:

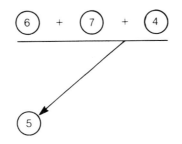

We now have to ask how (3) and (8) fit into the argument. The author's point seems to be that opponents of the seal hunt, who eat pork chops, are inconsistent in their attitudes toward the killing of animals. (Notice that he assumes that opponents of the seal hunt are *not* moral vegetarians who oppose the killing of animals for meat. For most such opponents this point will hold.) The point in this section of the argument is that the killing of pigs is less humane than the killing of seals; therefore, people who implicitly condone the "hideous" killing of swine while opposing the seal hunt are emotional. Thus (3) will link with (5) to support (1).

Now the question remains as to how we should fit (8) into the argument. We might say that (8) just contains a "dig" at opponents of the seal hunt and should not even be a premise. However, it does appear that the author wanted (8) to contribute to his idea that opponents of the hunt are purely emotional; being anthropomorphic means attributing human emotions to animals, and this presumably is one aspect of being emotional about animals and about the seal hunt. It seems then that (8) belongs in the argument as support for (1), even though it is not linked to (3) and (5) in any way. Putting everything together, the whole structure will look like this:

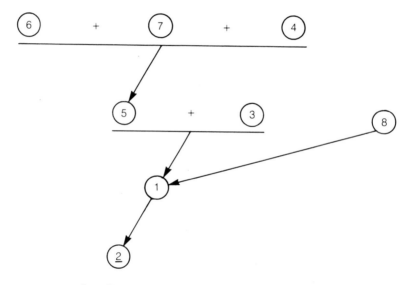

Now we can use this diagram to assess the argument. We can see that (8) is quite separate from the main argument. It amounts to an unsubstantiated "dig" at seal hunt opponents and, even if true, would lend only slight support to (1). However, any flaw regarding (8) will not affect the rest of the argument. Premise (5) is a crucial premise, which is defended in a subargument. In this argument the premises are clearly relevant and would, if acceptable, be sufficient grounds for the conclusion. The author speaks as though he has special knowledge regarding the killing of seals and of swine. We shall grant (5) as established: the killing of swine is less humane than the killing of seals. And, in virtue of the fact that most people in our society are not moral vegetarians, let us also grant (3), for the moment. The question now is whether (3) and (5) can establish (1). The matter is rather curious, for it does not seem that these premises are even relevant to (1). The premises show that opponents of the seal hunt who eat pork chops are inconsistent if they condone the hideous killing of swine while protesting the killing of seal pups. This inconsistency does not show that their opposition to the killing of seal pups is purely emotional. In fact, it is not even relevant to that conclusion.

The opposition to seal pup killing might be based on valid reasons, that should also be applied to the killing of swine. Perhaps the opponents of the seal hunt are right about that hunt and wrong about the killing of swine! The extra conclusion, (2), is certainly not established by the argument. It would not follow from (1) since (1) is only about the characteristics of the opponents of the hunt. (In fact, it would be *ad hominem* to infer (2) from (1).) Whether the seal hunt is or is not acceptable does not depend on the emotions or beliefs of those who oppose it.

These examples have been worked through at some length so that you can see how a clearer grasp of the overall structure of an argument lets you supply the ARG conditions more accurately. The task of diagramming arguments may still seem difficult. The following set of procedures should make the job easier.

Strategies Useful in Diagramming Arguments

1. Identify premises and conclusions, and give each a number. If the argument is worded in a relatively simple and straightforward way, you need not write it out in standardized form. However, if the original wording contains a number of rhetorical questions and commands, or if it includes extensive illustrative or background material, or if it requires the separation of existing statements into several components, you will do best to first write out a version in standardized form and then make a diagram based on that version. In the standardized form each distinct premise and conclusion should have a distinct number. Any missing premises or conclusions should be supplied. Underline their numbers to indicate that these were missing in the original and were added by you.

2. Identify the main conclusion or conclusions. If there are several conclusions, determine whether one is the conclusion of a subargument or whether they are simply distinct conclusions drawn from the same premises.

3. Look at the premises. Ask yourself whether any premises function to support other premises. If some do, there is a subargument in the main argument. For any subarguments, regard the premise defended and those serving to defend it as a group. Use a bracket or other device to indicate this group.

4. For each argument or subargument identified, look at the number of supporting premises. If there is only one premise, the pattern of support is the single support pattern.

5. Now look at all cases in which several premises are used to defend a conclusion, whether this is in the main argument or in subarguments. Ask yourself whether the premises work interdependently to support the conclusion (linked pattern) or whether they work separately to support it (convergent pattern). The way to determine the pattern is to imagine all premises except one in this group to be false, and to ask whether the remaining premise would still give any support to the conclusion in this case. When you have decided whether the jointly supporting premises work convergently or in a linked way, diagram that part of the argument.

6. Repeat procedures (4) and (5) until all subarguments for the premise of the main argument have been diagrammed. Then check your diagram to see whether it makes sense. If there seems to be something amiss, reread the original statement

of the argument to make sure that your diagram does not misinterpret what the arguer had to say.

7. Appraise the argument using the ARG conditions. The diagram will help you to distinguish between significant and insignificant flaws as far as acceptability and relevance are concerned.

EXERCISE SET

Exercise Two

Diagram the following arguments and offer an appraisal of each one, using the ARG conditions and relating them to the diagram to assess the significance of any flaws. If the passage does not contain an argument, simply explain why it does not, and proceed to the next example.

1. "Of the varied forms of crime, bank robbery is the most satisfactory to both the individual and society. The individual of course gets a lot of money, that goes without saying, and he benefits society by putting large amounts of cash back into circulation. The economy is stimulated, small businessmen prosper; people read about the crime with great interest, and the police have a chance to exercise their skills. Good for all."
(Harry Harrison, *The Stainless Steel Rat Saves the World* [Lindhurst, N.J.: Putnam Press, 1972].)

*2. A good team player is someone who can work with other people. Someone who wants all the glory for himself cannot work with other people. Thus a very competitive person is not going to be a good team player. We can see, then, that the quality of team sports will not be improved if we emphasize competitiveness in individuals.

3. Every human activity involves some risks. We can see this by considering such activities as building houses, driving cars, and playing football. In all these cases, innocent people can get hurt. Thus the fact that innocent people can be executed under a system of capital punishment is just something that we have to accept.

4. In the United States, people have rights that are established under the Constitution. In the United States, there are many law suits by people trying to protect these rights. We can see from this situation that a legal system emphasizing rights can be costly and inefficient in terms of law suits. Therefore, Canada should not implement a Bill of Rights, establishing strong individual rights.

5. "The peculiar evil of silencing the expression of an opinion is that it is robbing the human race: posterity as well as the existing generation: those who dissent from the opinion still more than those who hold it. If the opinion is right, they are deprived of the opportunity of exchanging error for truth; if wrong, they lose, what is almost as great a benefit, the clearer perception and livelier impression of truth, produced by its collision with error."
(John Stuart Mill, "On Liberty," in *The Utilitarians* [New York: Doubleday, 1960], p. 491.)

*6. "It should be easy to limit a woman's reproduction by sterilizing her at the birth of her nth child. Is this a shocking idea? If so, try this thought experiment: let $n = 20$. Since this is not shocking, let n diminish until population control is achievable."
(Garrett Hardin, "Parenthood: Right or Privilege?" *Science*, July 1970.)

7. The black hole is a key scientific concept that is virtually impossible for nonexperts to comprehend. The notion of antimatter, required to account for what happens in nuclear explosions, is a real metaphysical paradox. And there is no clear understanding of what "causation" means when we come to the context of elementary physical particles. Thus we can see that modern physics is a mysterious discipline indeed.

8. There must be a devil, because there is so much evil in the world.

9. *Background:* In his book *Escape from Childhood,* author John Holt states the theory that contemporary North Americans tend to regard childhood as a separate romantic stage of life. Holt maintains that this attitude toward childhood has undesirable effects upon both children and adults. He says:
"'A child's world.' 'The experience of childhood.' 'To be allowed to be a child.' Such words seem to say that childhood is a time and an experience very different from the rest of life and that it is, or ought to be, the best part of our lives. It is not

and no one knows it better than children. Children want to grow up. While they are growing up, they want, some of the time, to be around the kind of adults who like being grown-up and who think of growing up as an exploration and adventure, not the process of being chased out of some garden of Eden. They do not want to hear older people say, 'These are the best years of your life; we are going to save them for you and keep the wicked world from spoiling them.' What could be more discouraging? For they are going to grow up, whether they want to or not. They would like to think that this is something to look forward to. What they want to hear from the older people is that it gets better later.''
(John Holt, *Escape from Childhood* [New York: Ballantine Books, 1974].)

*10. "If women can sell sex and men can't, then sex must be less readily available, on the average, to men than to women. Of course, this is well known because women are socially conditioned to believe they don't need sex, while men are conditioned to actively pursue sex. As a result of this, women seeking sex at any one time can usually secure a sexual partner whenever they want one, so they really don't have any need to pursue sex.''
(Roy M. Schenk, "Why Do Rapes Occur?" *The Humanist*, March/April 1979.)

11. *Background:* In his *Republic*, Plato discussed the motives that just and honorable men might have for entering into positions of political authority and power. He offered the following comments:

"Good men are unwilling to rule either for money's sake or for honor. They have no wish to be called mercenary for demanding to be paid, or thieves for making a secret profit out of their office; nor yet will honors tempt them, for they are not ambitious. So they must be forced to consent under threat of penalty; that may be why a readiness to accept power under no such constraint is thought discreditable. And the heaviest penalty for declining to rule is to be ruled by someone inferior to yourself. That is the fear, I believe, that makes decent people accept; and when they do so, they face the prospect of authority with no idea that they are coming into the enjoyment of a comfortable berth; it is forced upon them because they can find no one better than themselves, or even as good, to be entrusted with power."

12. *Background:* In her book *Sexual Politics*, feminist author Kate Millett considers the common belief that early forms of social organization were along the lines of patriarchal families—men, women, and their children, with the women and children subordinate to the power and authority of the men.

In this view the weakness of females while pregnant and the needs of a hunting culture ultimately explain the subordination of women. Against this theory, Millett said:

"There are several weaknesses in this theory making its hypotheses insufficient to constitute necessary cause; social and political institutions are rarely based on physical strength, but are generally upheld by value systems in cooperation with other forms of social and technical force. Hunting culture was generally succeeded by agricultural society which brought different environmental circumstances and needs. Pregnancy and childbirth may be socially construed or socially arranged so that they are very far from debilitating events, or the cause of physical inferiority, particularly if child care is communal and fertility is reverenced or desired. Finally, since patriarchy is a social and political form, it is well here, as with other human institutions, to look outside nature for its origins.''
(Kate Millett, *Sexual Politics* [New York: Avon Books, 1969].)

13. *Background:* In the fall of 1980 the popular science magazine *Discover* published an article on the activities and theories of creationists who are trying to have a creationist theory of human origins taught in public schools alongside evolutionary theory. The article brought many letters in response, including the following, which appeared in the November 1980 issue:

"I hold a bachelor of science degree in electrical engineering from Georgia Tech and a master of science degree in electrical engineering from M.I.T. I find that the belief in a divine creator and the facts of science, as far as we have discovered the material world, do not contradict but complement each other.

"To my mind, it takes much more so-called blind faith to believe that things like gravitation, magnetism, electromagnetic waves, etc., just came by blind chance than to believe that there had to be a great Creator and Designer. Moreover, it would seem extremely unscientific to believe that the higher forms of life—the human brain, the intangibles of personality, the mystery of memory, came without any direction.

"The very least the scientific community, which wants to be known as liberal, could do, would be to allow the teaching of what they might call the 'theory of creationism' along with the theory of evolution. For evolution has certainly never been proved. It is still only a theory with many, many gaps and holes and missing links.''

*14. Teachers of mathematics can approach it as a practical subject or they can approach it as a theoretical subject. If they approach it as a practical subject, they risk losing some of the precise simplicity and beauty of mathematics. If they approach it as a theoretical subject, they risk completely boring students who may find the approach too abstract. Thus teaching mathematics in an interesting and comprehensive way is very difficult indeed.

15. "A pregnant woman who says she was accused of hiding a basketball under her dress has filed a $600,000 suit against the store that alleged she was shoplifting.

"...A cashier had told her supervisor Ms. Nelson had stolen a basketball and put it under her dress, said Stephen McCarron, Ms. Nelson's lawyer. The lawsuit says Ms. Nelson was given the option of opening her dress or going to the police station. 'I had to disrobe in front of six male security guards and police officers in the store,' Ms. Nelson told the *Washington Post*. She went into labor shortly after the incident and gave birth the next day to a healthy baby boy, Darius."
(Incident in Falls Church, Virginia; reported in the Toronto *Globe and Mail*, July 20, 1985.)
(*Hint:* Does this report contain an argument?)

Problems That May Arise

Although useful, diagramming arguments can be quite difficult. Some of the difficulties with diagramming are the same ones we faced earlier when learning how to standardize arguments. A person who presents an argument often adds nonargumentative material, repeats ideas, or writes rhetorically. It can be difficult to spot premises and conclusions and set them out accurately in clear, straightforward sentences. If this aspect of argument analysis is posing problems for you, you might review previous work on standardizing at this point.

However, extracting premises and conclusions is not the only source of problems. Sometimes it is difficult to determine just how an arguer's premises and conclusions fit together. When this happens, we may not be certain, for instance, whether we should diagram in a convergent or linked pattern. Or we may not see clearly whether two premises are simply both asserted or whether the first is intended to offer support for the second in a subargument. Sometimes we get the impression that a single argument could be diagrammed in several different ways, and we might not have any definite way of knowing which of the possible diagrams is right. Probably you have already experienced these problems in working through the exercises. It is not always easy to get one and only one clear diagram for a stated argument.

What do such difficulties indicate? It is possible that some arise only because you are not yet adept at diagramming arguments. When you become more accustomed to looking for these basic structures, any difficulties that are due only to your own inexperience will disappear. Skeptics might suggest that the difficulties arise because the diagramming technique itself is imperfect and could be remedied by a more rigorous definition of such key terms as *convergent* and *linked.* We have to admit there may be something in this suggestion: perhaps further academic studies in informal logic will improve the matter. However, something else is at work here. Faults are not just in the student or the system of diagramming; rather, naturally worded arguments are simply very often *capable of more than one interpretation.* When this happens, you have problems diagramming because the language an arguer uses can quite properly be interpreted in several different ways. The argument has a kind of *structural ambiguity,* and trying to diagram it reveals that this ambiguity is there. In such cases arguers themselves sometimes cannot identify the structure of the argument. They have said or written things without considering all the logical relations between the claims they made.

Let's look at a case in which this kind of problem arises. We will choose an argument in the second set of exercises, in the expectation that it has already presented you with some problems. Look again at John Stuart Mill's famous argument in defense of freedom of speech:[9]

> *(1) The peculiar evil of silencing the expression of an opinion is that it is robbing the human race; (2) posterity as well as the existing generation; (3) those who dissent from the opinion still more than those who hold it. (4) If the opinion is right, they are deprived of the opportunity of exchanging error for truth. (5) If wrong, they lose, what is almost as great a benefit, the clearer perception and livelier impression of truth, produced by its collison with error.*

There are a number of different diagrams that might be proposed as models for this argument—as you have no doubt already discovered. Here are three:

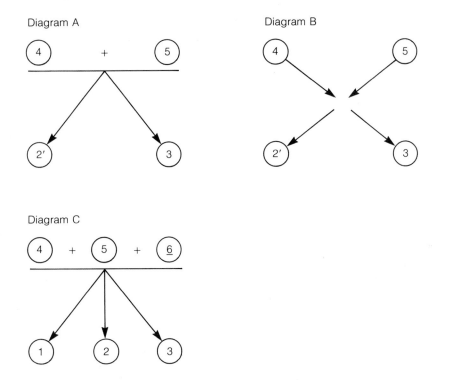

Diagram A

Diagram B

Diagram C

Why have we represented (2′) in Diagrams A and B? This representation indicates a reluctance to separate (1) and (2) into two distinct conclusions. Let us look back at Mill's exact words. He said that to limit freedom of speech would be "robbing the human race, posterity as well as the existing generation." Now we might take this as making *one* claim about robbing the existing generation of humans and *another* claim about robbing posterity (future generations of humans). To use two numbers as we did in Diagram C is to imply this interpretation. Diagram A uses (2′), a statement that includes both (1) and (2). If you interpret Mill as making basically the same point about "robbery" when he refers to posterity as when he refers to the existing generation, you will not wish to use two separate numbers to refer to that single statement. Statement (2′) just says that to silence the expression of an opinion is to rob the human race; it doesn't distinguish between present and future members of the human race. To us this interpretation seems best since "human race" is implicitly general and has no restriction to the present time. However, we could not prove that this interpretation is right and the other one wrong. Mill's way of writing does allow either one as a possibility. Thus the argument can be represented either as having three distinct conclusions or as having two. This problem does not arise because we are stupid about diagramming; nor does it arise because the diagramming technique is imperfect. It arises because the words Mill wrote can genuinely be interpreted in several different ways.

Another source of difficulty with Mill's argument is that the supporting premises (4) and (5) may be regarded either as working in a linked way or as working in a convergent way. If you start by thinking of them as linked, that will make sense of the argument; but then, if you start by thinking of them as convergent, *that* will make sense of the argument. What has gone wrong?

Suppose that (4) is true and (5) is false. To see whether the argument is of the convergent or linked type, we ask ourselves whether (4) could lend any support to (1) and (3) without (5). The answer to this question is not entirely clear. Since the claim in the conclusion is that any suppression of opinion is harmful, clearly Mill has a much stronger case asserting both (5) and (4) than he does asserting only one. Yet it does seem that either premise alone would give some support to the conclusion. There is, then, a basis for either a convergent or a linked interpretation. Just to compound the matter, we could add a premise that would make a linked interpretation very natural and clear. This is the following:

—— (6): Every opinion is either right (correct) or wrong (incorrect).

This extra premise is, in fact, necessarily true, so there is no danger of misinterpreting Mill's argument when we read it in. Diagram C incorporates this decision: the argument has a missing premise, and that premise, when added, links to (5) and (4) to support the conclusion. This model seems to us to be the clearest and the best so far as the relationship between the premises is concerned. But can we insist that the alternatives are just plain wrong? The actual wording of the passage is not clear enough to justify such a dogmatic stance.

It has to be admitted, therefore, that some passages can legitimately be represented by several different diagrams. When this happens, the difficulties we experience don't arise because we are incompetent or because our diagramming technique is inadequate. They simply indicate that the structures of argument and subargument are not always completely clear from the natural wording of arguments. Sometimes the passage or speech we are trying to analyze is simply ambiguous. When this happens, diagramming—or trying to diagram!—is still useful because it reveals ambiguities that are there in the natural argument but that might easily escape our attention if we did not attempt to analyze its structure.

If people always told you exactly what their premises and conclusions were, and if they warned you when they were and when they were not trying to prove things by argument, making remarks like "well, now I am going to use three linked premises to try to support two distinct conclusions," then we would not have these problems. But obviously people do not speak and write in such a boring (though clear) way. They use language more naturally and include in their arguments questions, wit, explanations, illustrations, jokes, and background comments. This makes life more interesting and prose more elegant than they would be if we spoke in standardized arguments! But it also means that we may face problems of ambiguity and indefiniteness when we try to understand precisely how someone's argument fits together. If you are working on an argument, trying to construct a diagram, and you find that several distinct models are plausible, it is worth cross-checking with the original to see whether you have missed something. But it is also a real possibility that both models are in some sense "right" interpretations, even though they differ from each other in some respects. In this situation you should work with the diagram that seems to fit the passage best, while noting that your interpretation of the argument's structure is not the only plausible one.

Representing Counterconsiderations

Often in arguments we may find authors acknowledging points that count against their own conclusions. These may be termed *counterconsiderations*. They are relevant to the conclusion, but they count against it, rather than for it. (That is, they are negatively relevant, rather than positively relevant.) An author may acknowledge counterconsiderations to show her audience that she has not simply ignored or been unaware of these points, but rather has taken them into consideration and believes them to be "outweighed" by other factors. We may puzzle over how to fit this recognition of counterconsiderations into the structure of an argument. Counterconsiderations obviously are relevant to the conclusion, and they also tell us something about the way in which the author is supporting that conclusion. But they do not themselves lend support to the conclusion, of course. Being negatively relevant to it, they cannot count as premises in the argument.

We can easily adapt our diagramming technique so that counterconsiderations can be represented. The method is simple: you give the acknowledged counterconsiderations numbers just as though they were premises. Then you put them on the diagram, as in the convergent pattern. But you connect them to the conclusion with a wavy line instead of the straight line you would otherwise use. The wavy line indicates that these points count against the conclusion, rather than for it. It is important to understand this, because if you don't, you may mistakenly accuse an author of inconsistency simply because she is honest enough to admit that there are some points that count against her point of view.

Such words as *even though, although, despite the fact that, notwithstanding the fact that,* and *while* often serve to introduce counterconsiderations. The words *but* and *yet* are often used to indicate a return to the author's own line of thought after the counterconsideration has been acknowledged. You can see how this works by looking at these simple short cases:

▬▬ (a) Although (1) he is fat, (2) he is still a very agile dancer.

The word *although* indicates that we should expect a contrast between (1) and (2), or that (1) tends to count against (2). And *still* (return to main line of thought) (2) is true. If this sentence were included in a larger argument, the counterconsideration would be represented as:

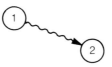

▬▬ (b) Notwithstanding the fact that (1) we think of science as impersonal, it is (2) ultimately motivated by the deep personal curiosity and concern for truth.

Here the words *notwithstanding the fact* indicate that (1) is a counterconsideration, some evidence against the author's main statement, which is (2). That we think of science as being impersonal is acknowledged, *but* he says this view is undercut by the fact that personal instincts and concerns drive science ahead.

Acknowledging counterconsiderations is very important. It makes explicit the fact that there are pros and cons to questions and that the arguer is an honest person who will admit this fact. It shows clearly that he takes his "pro" factors to outweigh the "cons" in significance and makes obvious to the audience the fact that this judgment is required if his conclusion is to be accepted. To acknowledge counterexamples is not a sign of weakness or inconsistency. It is a sign of fair judgment and honesty.

For a sense of how counterconsiderations may be recognized within the context of an actual argument, consider the following example:

> It is true that (1) the Soviet government is a totalitarian one, and we may find this deplorable. And it is true, also, that (2) the Soviet government behaves badly toward the Polish people and toward its own dissident citizens, by our standards. Nevertheless, (3) there is no good evidence that the Soviet Union has aggressive intentions toward Western Europe. After all, (4) it needs trade with Western Europe and (5) would be quite incapable of governing Western Europe even if it desired to do so. In point of fact, (6) the Soviet Union has been the follower rather than the leader in the nuclear arms race since its beginnings in the late nineteen forties. Remember, at that time (7) the United States had nuclear weapons and had used them, whereas the Soviet Union was struggling to become a nuclear power. (8) The role of the Soviet threat in the momentum of the arms race is more propaganda than truth, and (9) it is the United States which bears primary responsibility for the beginning of the race and for its technological innovations.

Here the author acknowledges points (1) and (2), which are claims made by those who see the Soviet Union as an evil power threatening the world and necessitating a nuclear arms race. He lets us know that he is not denying these points. They count, in a sense, against his conclusion that the United States, rather than the Soviet Union, is primarily responsible for the arms race. By acknowledging the counterconsiderations, the author lets us know that he is not a supporter of the Soviet government in all its actions, and that he is aware of those arguments opposed to his own. He then goes on to argue in favor of his own conclusions.

The whole argument, including the counterconsiderations, can be diagrammed as follows:

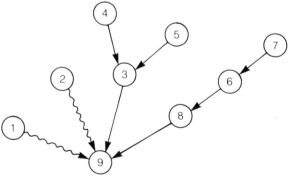

You can see that the counterconsiderations do not really weaken the case. They make the standpoint of the arguer more clear, and help us to see how he judges the significance of various different aspects that bear on the subject he is telling us about.

Further Explanatory Comments

It is important to understand which aspects of argument structure are revealed by these diagrams and which are not. The diagrams show a kind of medium level of structure. They show how the distinct premises and conclusions of an argument are related to each other. By looking at one of these diagrams, you can see whether a conclusion is supported by these premises working convergently, by one single premise, or by two premises that are linked, and so on. If there are two premises, the diagram will represent whether one supports the other in a small subargument or whether they stand separately. If there are two conclusions, the diagram will indicate whether the duality of conclusions is due to the support of several distinct claims with the very same premises or due to the presence of subarguments. These are all very important matters to understand. Nevertheless, they are not the only structural aspects of argumentation that we might want to consider.

One easy way to understand this point is to remember that each number on the diagram stands for a distinct statement. Each statement may have internal structure, but this structure would not appear on the diagrams we are working with in this chapter. For instance, the first premise will appear simply as (1), whether it is a conditional statement, a statement connecting two others with *and*, or whatever. As we shall see, all conditional statements (if so-and-so, then such-and-such) have a common structure, and this structure is very important in some arguments. But it will not appear on the diagrams we draw here, for these represent the way premises and conclusions are arranged in supporting patterns and do not represent internal structures of premises or of conclusions. We might say, then, that our diagrams do not represent the *microstructure* of the argument.

You might understand this point better by thinking of a map. Given a map of England and Scotland, you would be able to see where London is with respect to Edinburgh (south, north, east, etc.), and you would be able to see whether roads connect the two cities. But such a map would not show you internal details of either city. It would not show you the location of the Parliament buildings with reference to St. Paul's Cathedral, and so on. Only some elements of structure are depicted, and so it is with our diagrams too.

A larger dimension would also be left off our map. We can use our analogy with the map of England and Scotland to explain this. As well as omitting small details within cities, a map of England and Scotland would typically omit information about how these places are located with regard to other countries on other continents. It would not, for instance, show where Argentina is in reference to London and Edinburgh. Similarly, our diagrams omit certain "large-scale" information. They do not show, for instance, whether acknowledged counterconsiderations represent statements by someone against whom the arguer is stating his position, or whether the argument is put to people who have previously indicated they accept the premises. They do not show whether the arguer is only stating a conclusion that everyone believes already or whether he is a radical social critic whose views are at odds with almost everyone's. That is, there are many aspects of *personal interchange* that could be important when we are constructing or appraising an argument but that are not represented on these diagrams. Just as for some purposes knowing about Argentina is relevant to knowing about Britain, for some purposes knowing these broader interpersonal aspects will be relevant to our assessment of arguments. (Knowing about the broader context is especially important when you are evaluating the acceptability of the premises.) However, no map can show everything; no diagram of an argument can show everything either. Our diagrams represent a kind of "middle level" of structure.

Practicing with these diagrams is very useful and important for developing your understanding of how arguments fit together. Nevertheless making a diagram for every single argument you encounter is not realistic. We have seen that in some cases, no single diagram is clearly the single correct representation of the argument. Even if it were, the diagram itself would not tell you whether the argument is cogent or not. It would be very convenient if we could say that all arguments in which two premises link to support one conclusion are cogent, whereas all those in which three premises converge to support two conclusions are weak. But obviously we cannot do so. It would not be correct. The diagramming technique, for all its merit, does not answer any of the ARG questions for you. It merely shows you more precisely where and how to ask these questions. That is clearly a very important step in answering them.

We do not urge that you make a complete diagram for every argument you encounter. We do urge, however, that you use the skills you have acquired in working through this chapter to gain a better appreciation of how an argument fits together. If you regard a premise as unacceptable, check to see how essential that premise is to the rest of the argument. See also whether the arguer supported it in a subargument that you may have neglected. If you regard a premise as irrelevant, make sure that you have not neglected some other premise that would link with it in such a way as to make it relevant after all. Are there several distinct conclusions in the argument you are considering? If so, one may be well supported while the other is not, and you will wish to note this.

You can see how and why the level of structure used here is basic and essential for understanding arguments. There are smaller and larger levels of structure. But this one is well worth grasping, and working on diagrams is a good way to do it.

Review of Terms Introduced

Single support pattern: An argument in which one premise alone supports the conclusion exemplifies the single support pattern.

Linked support pattern: An argument in which two or more premises work together, interdependently, to support the conclusion exemplifies the linked support pattern. If premises are linked and one is known to be false or is unacceptable, then the others cannot by themselves support the conclusion.

Convergent support pattern: An argument in which the premises work independently to support the conclusion exemplifies the convergent support pattern. Premises are put forward as separately relevant to the conclusion. If one premise is known to be false or is unacceptable, it is still possible for the others to count in favor of the conclusion.

Structural ambiguity: An argument worded so that there are several possible interpretations of how premises support the conclusion or several possible interpretations of what the premises and conclusion (or conclusions) are.

Counterconsideration: A claim that may be acknowledged by an arguer but that runs counter to his intended conclusion. In acknowledging its truth and negative relevance, the arguer is committed to the belief that the counterconsideration is outweighed in significance by other considerations that count in favor of his conclusion. Counter-considerations are often acknowledged in the context of arguments where the pattern of support is convergent.

EXERCISE SET

Exercise Three
Part A

Diagram the following arguments, including counter-considerations. Choose any five and apply the ARG conditions to assess the cogency of the argument. If any passage does not contain an argument, say so and briefly explain why.

1. Professions that have highly qualified people are professions in which good salaries are available. In most regions of the United States, good salaries are not available for teachers. Thus, even though many people do not want to pay higher education taxes, salaries for teachers should be increased.

2. Language is necessary for communication, and communication is necessary for advancement. Therefore, language is necessary for advancement. For this reason, any attempt to censor language could restrict advancement. You can see why censorship of books is always wrong.

*3. Thought without language is impossible. People deny this statement and talk on about thoughts that they cannot fully express, but the problem is that we just cannot verify that any such thoughts exist. In fact, skepticism about ideas that can be communicated to no one else is definitely the best policy. Of course, you have to realize that "language" is a very general term. It includes gestures and picture symbols as well as the words that are most familiar to us. When we understand language in its broadest sense, we see that life itself would be impossible without language. And obviously if life itself—for human beings, that is—is impossible without language, then thought is impossible without language.

4. "Single men have another way of getting the rest of society, however reluctantly and unconsciously, to take part in their problems. That way is crime.

   "It is by now well known that about half of all violent crime is committed by and against blacks. But the central facts about crime are not racial: they are sexual. Groups of sociologists venturing into urban streets after their seminars on violence in America do not rush to their taxis fearing attack by marauding bands of feminists, covens of single women, or angry packs of welfare mothers. Despite all the movies of the Bonnie and Clyde genre and the exploits of the Symbionese Liberation Army, one need have little fear of any group that so much as contains women—or, if the truth be known, of any group that contains men who are married to women. Crime, like poverty, correlates better with sex and singleness than it does with race. Although single men number 13 percent of the population over age fourteen, they comprise 60 percent of the criminals and commit about 90 percent of the major and violent crimes." (George Gilder, "In Defense of Monogamy," *Commentary*, November 1974.)

*5. *Background:* This piece is taken from George Orwell's famous essay, "Politics and the English Language." Orwell argued that abstract and pompous terms often serve to disguise ugly realities from lazy minds:

   "The present political chaos is connected with the decay of language, and one can probably bring about some improvement by starting at the verbal end. If you simplify your English, you are freed from the worst follies of orthodoxy. You cannot speak any of the necessary dialects, and when you make a stupid remark, its stupidity will be obvious, even to yourself. Political language—and with variations, this is true of all political parties, from Conservatives to Anarchists—is designed to make lies sound truthful and murder respectable, and to give an appearance of solidity to pure wind. One cannot change this all in a moment, but one can at least change one's own habits, and from time to time one can even—if one jeers loudly enough—send some worn-out and useless phrase—some 'jackboot,' 'Achilles' heel,' 'hotbed,' 'melting pot,' 'acid test,' 'veritable inferno,' or other lump of verbal refuse—into the dustbin where it belongs."
   (George Orwell, "Politics and the English Language," in *Collected Essays*, 2nd ed. [London: Secker and Warburg, 1961].)

6. The motions of the stars proceed in a fixed order. The succession of the seasons also proceeds according to fixed laws. The change from day to night

takes place without variation. We can see from these facts that nothing is better organized than the universe. A household governed by a plan is better organized than a household without a predetermined plan. The same point holds for a ship. So the same point holds too for the universe as a whole. Since the universe as a whole is the best organized thing of all, we can conclude that it is governed according to a predetermined plan.
(Adapted from the Roman writer, Cicero, in *De Inventione;* cited in V. H. van Eemeren, R. Grootendorst, and T. Kruiger, *The Study of Argumentation* [New York: Irvington Publishers, 1984], p. 76.)

7. "There are two methods of fighting, the one by law, the other by force. The first method is that of men, the second of beasts; but as the first method is often insufficient, one must have recourse to the second."
(Niccolò Machiavelli, *The Prince*, Chapter 18, quoted in John Hoaglund, *Critical Thinking* [Newport News, Va.: Vale Press, 1984], p. 126.)

*8. "No one has a right to use a relatively unreliable procedure in order to decide whether to punish another. Using such a system, he is in no position to know that the other deserves punishment; hence he has no right to punish him."
(Robert Nozick, *Anarchy, State, and Utopia* [New York: Basic Books, 1974], p. 106.)

9. "Women are no more mysterious, unpredictable, capricious, or baffling than men. Mythic woman is a thing of the past.

"Or is she? Have the notions of woman as earth mother, seductress, and paragon of virtue really disappeared? Not entirely. For these images persist—and seem to be shared by both men *and* women. They are reflected in the lingering double standard about sexuality, in the popular view of rape, and in the tendency to condone wife beating. They are expressed—albeit in modified form—in the current stereotypes of femininity and masculinity. In fact, modern versions of these myths are reflected in almost every area of our lives."
(Joanne Rohrbaugh, *Women: Psychology's Puzzle.*)

10. "Religion promised us a certain place. Science put us in our real place.

"In Darwin's context, we are part of nature and natural law. People who do not rule nature have to learn to live within it. In that sense, our children could do worse than remember that we are animals.

"But the creationists don't want them to know our heritage. It seems to me that there is no intrinsic conflict between faith and science, believing and knowing. The theory of change doesn't begin to explain the ultimate mystery; the origin of the origin of the species. The beginning of the beginning is a subject for philosophers and theologians and the scientists in their ranks.

"To suggest that we give Genesis equal time with evolution is like giving Pope Urban's math equal time with Galileo's. The creationists are people for whom the Bible is the only textbook. They would leave a chill wind for our children to inherit."
(Ellen Goodman, "The New Creationists," *Washington Post*, April 15, 1980.)

*11. *Background:* In the period 1979–1982, Nestle, a multinational corporation manufacturing chocolate, cocoa, coffee, and infant formula, was accused of overly aggressive advertising of infant formula in developing countries. Critics charged that because mothers in these countries were vulnerable to pressure to copy a western way of life, they were encouraged to switch unnecessarily to infant formula. Due to unsanitary conditions, use of such formula frequently caused the illness or even death of their children:

"No one questions that marketing of infant formula in the Third World can pose serious problems. Everyone, including the infant-formula industry, agrees that breast-feeding provides the best and cheapest nutrition for babies. Because mothers who are lactating are less likely to conceive, breast-feeding also helps to space out births. Therefore, marketing practices should not induce mothers who otherwise would be willing and able to breast-feed to switch to the bottle."
(Herman Nickel, "The Corporation Haters," reprinted in Eleanor MacLean, *Between the Lines* [Montreal: Black Rose Books, 1981], p. 91.)

12. "It is hard to be a good citizen of the world in any great sense, but if we render no interest or increase to mankind out of that talent God gave us, we can at least preserve the principle unimpaired. One would like to be making large dividends to society out of that deposit capital in us, but he does well for the most part if he proves a secure investment only without adding to the stock."
(Henry David Thoreau, in *Thoreau on Man and Nature*, comp. Arthur G. Volkman [Mount Vernon, N.Y.: Peter Pauper Press, 1960].)

13. No one can have a private language because in every language there must be rules. If a word could mean just anything, or could be used in any old way, there would in fact be no meaning at all. To have a rule, we have to have more than one person following a rule because a *single person* could make anything he wanted be right, and his so-called rule would not really be a rule at all. Thus, private language is impossible. All language is necessarily public. It follows from these conclusions that words do not mean whatever individuals want them to mean.

*14. "One of little faith looks for his rewards and punishments to the next world and despairing of this world, behaves accordingly in it; another thinks the present a worthy occasion and arena, sacrifices to it, and expects to hear sympathizing voices. The man who believes in another world and not in this is wont to put me off with Christianity. The present world in which we talk is of a little less value to him than the next world. So we are said to hope in proportion as we do not realize. It is all hope deferred. But one grain of realization, of instant life, on which we stand, is equivalent to acres of hope hammered out to gild our prospect."
(Henry David Thoreau, in *Thoreau on Man and Nature*.)

15. Is it better to be red than dead? This is a false question because these are not the only alternatives. The question is not only false, but dangerous. It presupposes that slackening the dangerous nuclear arms race would make it likely that communists would take over the world. And there is no reason whatever to believe that they would. The communists have no desire to dominate the world militarily, and even if they did, they do not have the personnel or expertise to occupy Western Europe and United States and Canada. In fact the famous question "Is it better to be red than dead?" is a classic example of how political slogans can first distort reality and then help to alter that reality by making people think stupidly about important issues.

Part B

Invent arguments having the following structures, as specified. Try to make these arguments reasonable and plausible; do not just construct anything that will fit the pattern described. Put each argument on a separate sheet of paper and do not number your answers. When you are finished, exchange papers with a classmate and try to diagram each other's arguments. Discuss the results.

1. A linked argument with three premises and two distinct conclusions.

2. An argument that has four convergent premises and one conclusion.

3. An argument in which two premises link to support one conclusion and in which each of these premises is, in turn, supported by a subargument in which the support is of the single support type.

4. A set of connected arguments in which there are, in all, three subarguments and one main conclusion. In each subargument the support is of the linked type, but in the major argument, the support is convergent.

5. An argument in which the support is linked, but in which the entire argument will fall down due to the presence of one false premise. (Make the rest of the argument as plausible as you can.)

6. An argument in which one single premise supports two distinct conclusions.

7. An argument of whatever structure you choose, provided that it contains both subarguments and sub-subarguments.

NOTES

1. T. M. Penelhum, *Religion and Rationality* (New York: Random House, 1971), p. 166.

2. Douglas Roche, *Justice Not Charity* (Toronto: McClelland and Stewart, 1976), p. 49.

3. John Kenneth Galbraith, *Economics and the Public Purpose* (New York: New American Library, 1973), p. 29.

4. C. S. Peirce, "The Fixation of Belief," in J. Buchler, *Philosophical Writings of Peirce* (New York: Dover Publications, 1955), p. 7.

5. Mary Midgley, "Why Knowledge Matters," in D. Sperlinger, *Animals in Research* (New York: Wiley, 1981), p. 325.

6. Sissela Bok, *Lying* (New York: Pantheon Books, 1978), p. 60.

7. R. Robinson, "Reason and Faith," in J. R. Burr and M. Goldinger, *Philosophy and Contemporary Issues* (New York: Macmillan, 1976), pp. 136–7.

8. Letter to the Toronto *Globe and Mail*, January 3, 1979.

9. John Stuart Mill, "On Liberty," in *The Utilitarians* (New York: Doubleday, 1960), p. 491.

8

Those Tidy Deductions: Categorical Logic

We have now discussed two of the conditions of an argument's adequacy: acceptability and relevance. And we have worked on diagramming to get a better idea of how arguments fit together in cumulating patterns. We now move on to the (G) condition to see various ways in which premises may work together to provide good and sufficient grounds for the conclusion. In this chapter and the next one, our project is to become more clear about deductively valid arguments by learning about some simple forms of arguments in which the premises deductively entail the conclusion.

Deductive Relations: Some General Comments

One statement deductively entails another if it is impossible for the second one to be false, given that the first one is true. That is, the state of affairs in which statement (1) is true and statement (2) is false is logically impossible. That a person is a mother deductively entails that she is female, for it is a logical impossibility for a person to be a mother and not be female. A logical impossibility is a state of affairs that just could not exist. Statement (1) entails statement (2) if a state of affairs where (1) is true and (2) is false is logically impossible.

When an argument is deductively valid, a state of affairs in which all the premises are true and the conclusion is false is logically impossible. An argument like this is entirely adequate as far as the (R) and (G) conditions are concerned, so any question about its cogency must have to do with the acceptability of the premises.

Many arguments that are deductively valid owe their validity to their logical form. The validity of such arguments comes from a general structural property they have, and all other arguments sharing that property are also deductively valid. Here are several simple examples of formally valid arguments.

▬▬▬ *Example One*
This example is deductively valid by virtue of its *categorical* form. That is, the deductive connection depends on the way in which the categories of things are related to each other in the premises and in the conclusion.

1. All consistent opponents of killing are opponents of capital punishment.
2. No opponents of capital punishment are orthodox traditional Catholics.
So,
3. No consistent opponents of killing are orthodox traditional Catholics.

Leaving out some words, we could rewrite this argument as:

All . . . are . . .
No . . . are . . .
Therefore,
No . . . are . . .

Now we will replace the words that have been left out with letters. Let C = consistent opponents of killing; let O = opponents of capital punishment; let T = orthodox traditional Catholics. Then the argument can be written as follows:

All C are O.
No O are T.
Therefore,
No C are T.

The connection between the premises and the conclusion depends on the way *all* and *no* and the categories are related. It does not depend on any special feature about the Catholics, killing, and so on. Any argument with the same pattern of letters and the same basic logical terms (those we did *not* replace with letters) would be deductively valid as well. Consider the following:

1. All politicians are lovers of power.
2. No lovers of power are entirely trustworthy people.
Therefore,
3. No politicians are entirely trustworthy people.

This second argument has the same *logical form* as the original example and is also deductively valid:

─────
Example Two
This example is a deductively valid argument that is valid in virtue of its *propositional form*.

1. Either interest rates will fall or unemployment rates will rise.
2. Interest rates will not fall.
So,
3. Unemployment rates will rise.

Leaving out the simple sentences "interest rates will fall" and "unemployment rates will rise," we can rewrite this argument as follows:

. . . or . . .
Not . . .
So, . . .

The dots appear where there were simple statements. Now if we let I = interest rates will fall and U = unemployment rates will rise, the argument then appears as follows:

I or U.
Not I.
So,
U.

The connection between the premises and the conclusion depends only on the remaining logical terms, not on which particular statements or abbreviating letters appear. Thus the argument is deductively valid by virtue of its form, and any argument with the same form will also be deductively valid, even though its content may be very different. For instance:

> Either racism will persist or there will be sweeping changes in the school system.
> There will not be sweeping changes in the school system.
> So,
> Racism will persist.

is also a deductively valid argument, by virtue of its propositional form. This argument and the one about interest rates differ in content, but they have the same form, and both are deductively valid in virtue of this form.

You may have been puzzled to read that the arguments in Examples One and Two were deductively valid when you were perhaps skeptical about whether their premises were acceptable. Deductive validity has to do with the (R) and (G) conditions, *not* with the (A) condition. If an argument is deductively valid, then its premises, *if* true, prove its conclusion true also, which does not say that the premises are acceptable.

It is important, then, not to confuse the matter of deductive validity with the issue of how acceptable the premises are. These are quite distinct issues. Just to emphasize the point, take a look at the following argument. The premises are demonstrably false, but the argument *is* deductively valid:

> 1. All politicians are warm-hearted mothers.
> 2. No warm-hearted mothers are people who would do anything to increase the likelihood of war.
> Therefore,
> 3. No politicians are people who would do anything to increase the likelihood of war.

In this example, both premises are known to be false. The conclusion is also known to be false. However, the argument is deductively valid by virtue of its form. It has the same form, in fact, as Example One earlier. If both premises were true, the conclusion would be true. The premises are connected to the conclusion because of the connections between the categories of things referred to. A deductively valid argument with false or unacceptable premises gives no real support to its conclusion, even though such an argument has a certain logical elegance and very cleanly and neatly satisfies the (R) and (G) conditions:

> The formal validity of an argument is distinct from the truth, or acceptability, of its premises.
> A cogent argument must satisfy all three of the ARG conditions. Deductively valid arguments satisfy (R) and (G) but *may* fail to satisfy (A).

One further thing to note is that it is not always by virtue of logical form that deductive relations hold. Sometimes one statement deductively entails another by virtue of its meaning. For instance, the statement "Joan is a mother" entails "Joan is female" because of what it means to be a mother. It is logically impossible for anyone to be a mother and not be female. The meanings of the terms *mother* and *female* are what make the inference from the first statement to the second a deductively valid inference.

Simple deductive relationships based on form and meaning are essential in our understanding of written and spoken language. Indeed we have been presupposing these relationships all along in this text—just as we presuppose them everywhere. Whenever we scrutinize a passage to see whether it contains an argument, or ask how to best represent its premises and conclusions in clear simple language, we are—in effect—asking what is and what is not deductively entailed by what was said.

Probably you can intuitively grasp the fact that:

1. All *S* are *M*.
2. No *M* are *P*.
Therefore,
3. No *S* are *P*.

is a form representing a deductively valid argument. If most people could not, in some sense, understand this fact, formal systems would not have developed at all! Nonetheless, the logical intuitions people have can be usefully systematized, explained, and developed by the articulation of *formal systems* in logic. These systems take us beyond the point where we have to understand (or not understand!) deductive relationships. When arguments depend on their form for deductive validity, we can represent them in a symbolic way that will reveal that form without representing the specific content of the argument. Then, using rules dealing only with formal relationships, we can determine the deductive validity of the symbolized arguments. In some cases this technique can be very helpful and enlightening because the content of an argument may distract us from formal relationships.

Formal logic is a highly developed and intricate subject, and there are many excellent texts in the field. Our book, however, will not go into formal logic in great detail. We cover a broader area and aim to provide a general strategy for appraising real arguments. (Formal techniques are often hard to apply to real arguments, and sometimes they cannot be appropriately applied.) In our brief treatment of formal logic, we concentrate on those aspects of the subject most pertinent to ordinary speech and writing, and we emphasize the *application* of formal tools. Our treatment of formal logic will cover two areas: categorical logic (this chapter) and propositional logic (Chapter Nine).

Four Categorical Forms

Categorical logic uses *all*, *some*, *are*, and *not* as its basic formal terms. These terms are used to connect categories of things. Categorical logic is the oldest branch of formal logic. It was first systematized by Aristotle and was for many centuries thought to comprise all of formal logic. (As we shall see later, this belief is no longer held: it is now known that categorical logic is an important *part* of formal logic.)

In our simple example we considered the following argument:

1. All consistent opponents of killing are opponents of capital punishment.
2. No opponents of capital punishment are orthodox traditional Catholics.
So,
3. No consistent opponents of killing are orthodox traditional Catholics.

In this argument both premises and conclusion are in *categorical form*. That is, they are statements in which a subject category is connected to a predicate category. The first statement makes a universal affirmation, whereas the second two state universal negations:

—— Universal Affirmation: All *S* are *P*.
Universal Negation: No *S* are *P*.

For convenient reference, logicians call the universal affirmation an "*A* statement" and the universal negation an "*E* statement." The letters *S* and *P* stand for categories of things.

Not all statements in categorical form are universal. There are two further categorical forms:

—— Particular Affirmation: Some *S* are *P*.
Particular Negation: Some *S* are not *P*.

The particular affirmative is referred to as the "*I* statement" and the particular negation as the "*O* statement." These shorthand ways of referring to the categorical forms come from two Latin words: *affirmo* and *nego*. *Affirmo* means "I affirm" and *nego* means "I deny."

The four categorical forms are arranged in a square called the *Square of Opposition*. It looks like this:

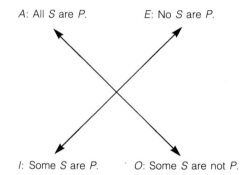

The opposition comes in when we look at the diagonals on the square. Each proposition is the *contradictory* of the one diagonally opposed to it: if all *S* are *P*, then it must be false that some *S* are not *P*; and if no *S* are *P*, then it must be false that some *S* are *P*.

The *A* and *E* statements are fully universal. They are true only under the condition that every single member of the subject class is included in the predicate class (*A*) or excluded from the predicate class (*E*). That is, an *A* statement states that everything in the subject category is included in the predicate category, and an *E* statement states that everything in the subject category is excluded from the predicate category. A technical way of putting this is to say that in both *A* and *E*, the subject term is *distributed* because something is said about every single thing in that category.

The *I* and *O* statements do not include or exclude the whole subject category, only part of it. But *part* is rather vague. The word *some* is taken to mean "at least one" for the purposes of categorical logic. Thus, the *I* statement that some men are fathers is true if at least one man is a father. In the *I* and *O* statements, the subject term (*S*) is not distributed because the statements are not about all the items within the subject category. However, in the *O* statement, the predicate term *is* distributed, because the subject items are, in effect, excluded from the entire predicate category.

Natural Language and Categorical Form

A number of useful formal rules of inference can be applied to statements in categorical form. These rules can be extremely helpful in getting deductive relationships straight. But in order to use them, we have to be working with statements that really are in categorical form. The rules don't necessarily apply to other statements. Few statements in English or other natural languages, however, are spoken or written in perfect categorical form. Many statements in natural languages are basically of the subject-predicate type, and these statements can be put into categorical form. Because our purpose in this text is practical, we shall emphasize the relation between natural wording and categorical form.

The Universal Affirmative: *A*. The *A* statement in categorical form begins with the word *all*. *All* is followed by a noun or noun phrase specifying a category of things; the category is followed by the word *are*, which in turn is followed by another noun or noun phrase specifying a category of things. Strictly speaking, the sentence "All mothers are human" is not in categorical form, because the predicate is only an adjective. To put that sentence in categorical form, we would have to rewrite it as "All mothers are human beings." In a somewhat similar way, many sentences in English can be put into the form of *A* statements with slight linguistic alterations. (You must be careful, however, that the statement as reworded has the same meaning as the original one.)

Consider, for instance, these statements:

Any *S* is *P*.
Every single *S* is *P*.
The *S*s are all *P*s.
Whatever *S* you look at, it is bound to be a *P*.
Each *S* is a *P*.

All can be translated into *A* statements as "All *S* are *P*."

Very often statements are made in such a way that it is not explicitly said whether the statement is universal or particular. Look at these statements, for instance:

A monkey has a tail.
A bachelor is an unmarried man.
A bank is in a good position when interest rates are high.
A woman came to the door trying to raise funds for Greenpeace.
Wars lead to pillage and rape.
Politicians are overworked.

All these sentences are of the subject-predicate type. But as they stand, none are in categorical form. To put them in categorical form, we would have to determine whether the intent is to make a universal or particular statement, and we would have to make sure we have two categories of things—not just an adjective in the predicate. The results for these statements would look like this:

All monkeys are creatures with tails.
All bachelors are unmarried men.
All banks are things that are in a good position when interest rates are high.
Some women are persons who came to the door trying to raise funds for Greenpeace.
All(?) wars are things that lead to pillage and rape.
All(?) politicians are overworked people.

Sometimes, as in the last two cases here, merely asking whether the statement is universal or particular can be an important critical step. Often people make unqualified statements without making it clear whether they really wish to make an assertion about *all* of the category or part of it. The ambiguity as to how many entities are being discussed can be exploited: a statement about *all* is more interesting, but a statement about *some* is more likely to be true.

You can be led into accepting stereotypes by an uncritical response to unqualified statements. For instance, if you hear that welfare mothers are too irresponsible to care properly for their children, you may naturally accept the statement because it is consistent with stories you have heard about extreme cases. Taken as an *I* statement that *some* welfare mothers are too irresponsible to give proper care, the statement may be true. But taken as an *A* statement, it is certainly false. We know that many welfare mothers are on welfare precisely because they cannot both work outside the home and provide good care, at a reasonable cost, for their young children. The distinction between "all" and "some" is extremely important in cases like this.

Statements in which the word *only* is used are implicitly universal. Consider this example:

> Only students fluent in English are permitted to enroll in the University of California.

Let us allow *F* to represent "students fluent in English" and *U* to represent "people allowed to enroll in the University of California." The statement may be written in simpler form as:

> Only *F* are *U*.

We have to rewrite this as an *A* statement because the four categorical forms do not let us use the word *only*. The right way to do it is as follows:

> Only *F* are *U* = All *U* are *F*.

That is, if only students fluent in English are allowed to enroll, then we know that all students allowed to enroll will be fluent in English.

Think about this example carefully. Statements like this can easily confuse people. They may want to interpret them as saying:

> Only *F* are *U* = (?) All *F* are *U* (Wrong!)

Reading this over, you can see how absurd it is. It says that everyone fluent in English can enroll! Clearly this is not what the original statement asserted. Rather, it asserted that all admitted will be fluent, since the others will have been disqualified.

The Universal Negative: *E*.   There are also many different ways of expressing *E* statements in English. Consider the following:

> Not a single man can give birth to a living baby.
> Men can never give birth to living babies.
> None of the beings who are male can give birth to living babies.
> There never was a man who could give birth to a living baby.
> No man can give birth to a living baby.
> Men are not able to give birth to living babies.

All of these sentences are variations of the following:

> No men are persons who can give birth to living babies.

This statement is in proper categorical form; it has two categories of things plus *no* and *are*.

There are some other cases that people occasionally find tricky. For instance:

Not all doctors are rich. (not an *E* statement)

Here, *not all* does not mean "none." The statement that not all doctors are rich is the denial of an *A* statement (all doctors are rich); as such it is the assertion of the *I* statement, not *E*. The words *not all* before the subject should *not* be translated as "none."

A type of statement that is easy to confuse with the "not all" statement is "All so-and-so are not such-and-such." Statements of this type are quite ambiguous and can be very confusing in some contexts. Consider the following:

All women are not aggressive.

This statement could be read as being of the *A* type and would then appear in categorical form with the *not* taken as part of the predicate: "All women are nonaggressive." With this reading, the statement attributes a property to all women, and the property just happens to be a negative one—negatively defined, that is. However, it can also be read as an *O* statement. With this reading, *not* really applies to the whole sentence, which is equivalent to "Not all women are aggressive," which is to say that (*O*) some women are not aggressive. Given such ambiguity, you should avoid statements written this way when you are writing yourself. If you come across them, you have to do your best to decide whether an *A* statement, with a negated predicate, or an *O* statement, with the original predicate, is being asserted.

The Particular Affirmative: *I*.   The real trick with *I* and *O* statements is to get a good grasp of what they do *not* say. Often, when we use statements of these forms, we suggest more than we actually assert. For instance, imagine a student who remarks to his professor that some professors are competent. He may easily be taken as suggesting that some other professors are *not* competent! But this is not what he says, nor is it deductively entailed by what he says. He says only that there is at least one competent professor, according to strict categorical logic.

When an indefinite article such as *a* or *an* precedes the subject, the statement made can be either universal or particular. We already saw some examples in which there is a universal intent, as in "*A* monkey has a tail." In contexts in which the statement clearly refers to some one indefinitely specified individual, as in:

A woman came to the door canvassing for Greenpeace.

the sentence should be put into categorical form as *I*:

Some women are persons who came to the door trying to raise funds for Greenpeace.

Categorical logic allows us to speak of all, some, or none of the items in a category. It does not allow us to speak of individuals as such. Notice how tense is handled in this example. The categorical forms cannot handle tense except by inserting it into the specification of the predicate category: here it appears as "persons who *came* to the door...."

The Particular Negative: *O*.   We have seen that *not all* before the subject is a way of denying the universal affirmation, and thus a way of asserting the particular negation: *O*. Thus:

—— Not all mammals live on land.

goes into categorical form as:

—— Some mammals are not creatures that live on land.

Just as *I* often suggests *O*, but does not assert it, *O* may suggest—but not assert—*I*. A person who says, for instance, that some patrons of health food stores are not fanatics may be taken to say that some of their patrons are fanatics. This, however, is only suggested by his comment: it is not said and not deductively entailed. (In deductive logic, we do not take what is suggested to be part of the content of people's remarks.)

In *O* statements, the word *not* must perform the function of excluding some items in the subject category from the predicate category. The word *not* should not be replaced by a negative particle within the predicate category. The statement:

—— Some teachers are persons who are not happy with their work.

is *not* a statement of the *O* form. It is an *I* statement that happens to have a predicate category (persons who are not happy with their work) with a negative particle in it.

EXERCISE SET

Exercise One

Translate the following sentences into categorical form and state which of the four forms—*A, E, I, O*— you have used. Be prepared to defend your answer.

1. Every nuclear installation is at risk of being attacked by terrorists.

*2. A student came to the office asking to be excused from the final examination.

3. Every dog has its day.

4. The early bird gets the worm.

*5. Only the rich can afford to stay at London's prestigious hotels.

6. I love you.

7. Spare the rod and spoil the child.

8. At least one winning athlete was from Peterborough, Ontario.

9. A planet is a heavenly body that circles the sun.

*10. Not all textbooks are boring.

11. Some politicians are not impressed with environmental lobbyists.

12. Mathematicians love abstraction.

13. A dinner was held in honor of the successful authors.

14. A place for everything, and everything in its place. (*Hard. Hint:* Use two statements.)

*15. A woman with a job outside the home and no assistance with household work is burdened with at least two jobs.

16. Any friend of yours is a friend of mine.

17. To become a lawyer, you must pass the bar exams.

18. A stitch in time saves nine.

19. Not all human beings are purely selfish.

20. An invasion of the Falkland Islands took the British government entirely by surprise.

Rules of Immediate Inference

We are now in a position to see some of the formal rules of categorical logic. First, we will look at rules for immediate inference. If you have two statements, and the first deductively entails the second, then you can immediately (that is, without intermediate steps) infer the second from the first. There are a number of operations involving the *A*, *E*, *I*, and *O* statements. These are common and important, and some will give us valid immediate inferences.

Conversion. To convert a statement in categorical form, you simply reverse its subject and predicate. Thus:

Statement	*Converse of Statement*
A: All *S* are *P.*	All *P* are *S.*
E: No *S* are *P.*	No *P* are *S.*
I: Some *S* are *P.*	Some *P* are *S.*
O: Some *S* are not *P.*	Some *P* are not *S.*

For the *E* and *I* statements, the original statement and its converse are logically equivalent. This means that each deductively entails the other. When two statements are logically equivalent, either they are both true or they are both false. It is impossible for one to be false given that the other is true. You can see that the converse is logically equivalent here, in all likelihood, but in any case the logical facts can be represented neatly on Venn diagrams. The shading on the diagrams indicates that nothing is in the shaded areas. The "*x*" indicates that there is something in the area. The *E* statement and its converse look like this:

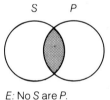

E: No *S* are *P.*   *Converse of E:* No *P* are *S.*

The *I* statement and its converse look like this:

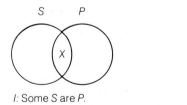

I: Some *S* are *P.*   *Converse of I:* Some *P* are *S.*

(Venn diagrams are named after John Venn, the nineteenth-century logician who invented them. They use circles to represent a category and are drawn to overlap so you can represent which relations of exclusion or inclusion hold between the categories that the circles represent. When an area is shaded on a Venn diagram, the shading indicates that there are no things falling within that area.)

The conversion of *A* and *O* statements does not result in statements logically equivalent to the originals. By looking at these diagrams, you will be able to see why.

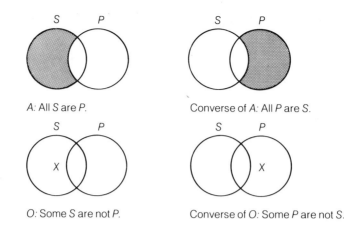

A: All S are P.

Converse of A: All P are S.

O: Some S are not P.

Converse of O: Some P are not S.

Many people mistakenly believe that there is a valid deductive relation between an *A* statement and its converse. This is a common source of errors in reasoning. Consider the *A* statement "All communists are socialists." This is a true statement. But the converse, "All socialists are communists," is not true, and it does not follow from the statement "All communists are socialists." Political history in Canada and the United States would be quite different if the confusion between this statement and its converse were less common!

Contraposition. To contrapose a statement in categorical form, you first convert it and then attach a *non* to each category. It works like this:

Statement	*Contrapositive of Statement*
A: All *S* are *P*.	All non-*P* are non-*S*.
E: No *S* are *P*.	No non-*P* are non-*S*.
I: Some *S* are *P*.	Some non-*P* are non-*S*.
O: Some *S* are not *P*.	Some non-*P* are not non-*S*.

For *A* and *O* statements the original and the contrapositive are logically equivalent. An *A* statement says that all *S* are *P*. Its contrapositive says that all non-*P* are non-*S*. Given the *A* statement, the contrapositive must be true because if it were not true, there would be a non-*P* that was an *S*, which would be contrary to what the *A* statement asserts.

Similarly, if an *O* statement is true, its contrapositive is true. The *O* statement says that some *S* are not *P*. Its contrapositive says that some non-*P* are not non-*S*. Suppose that this contrapositive were false. Then all the non-*P* would be non-*S*. There would be no non-*P* that were *S*—and yet that is what the *O* statement asserts. If the *O* statement is true, its contrapositive must also be true.

The contrapositives of *E* and *I* statements are not logically equivalent to these statements. The *E* statement, no *S* are *P*, has as its contrapositive, no non-*P* are non-*S*. These statements say quite different things. The first says that the two categories *S* and *P* do not intersect at all; there are no items in both at once. The second says that what is outside the *S* category does not intersect at all with what is outside the *P* category—a quite different thing. (Compare "no cats are dogs" with "no non-dogs are non-cats." The first is obviously true and the second is obviously false. They can't be logically equivalent to each other!)

The *I* statement, some *S* are *P*, has as its contrapositive the statement that some non-*P* are non-*S*. These statements are not logically equivalent. The *I* statement asserts that there is at least one thing that is in both the *S* and *P* categories. Its contrapositive, on the other hand, asserts that there is at least one thing that is outside both categories. (Compare the *I* statement "some cats are fluffy creatures" with its contrapositive "some non-fluffy creatures are non-cats." In this instance, both happen to be true, but they assert quite different things and are not logically equivalent.)

Obversion.   Obversion is an operation that can be performed on all four kinds of categorical statements to produce a logically equivalent statement. To obvert a statement in categorical form, you do two things: first you add a *non* to the predicate category; then you change the statement from negative to affirmative, or vice versa. This means you change the quality of the statement (whether it is negative or affirmative). The obverse of "All fathers are men" is "No fathers are non-men":

Statement	Obverse of Statement
A: All *S* are *P*.	No *S* are non-*P*.
E: No *S* are *P*.	All *S* are non-*P*.
I: Some *S* are *P*.	Some *S* are not non-*P*.
O: Some *S* are not *P*.	Some *S* are non-*P*.

Contradictories.   You will have noticed, perhaps, that *A* and *O* work in the same way: conversion does not produce a logically equivalent statement, whereas contraposition does. Also, *E* and *I* work in the same way: conversion does produce a logically equivalent statement, whereas contraposition does not. These relations exist because the *O* statement is the denial of the *A* statement, and the *I* statement is the denial of the *E* statement. *A* and *O* are contradictory to each other; so are *E* and *I*, which means that the truth of one deductively entails the falsehood of the other. If it is true that all swans are white, it must be false that some swans are not white. And if it is true that no bankers are rapists, it must be false that some bankers are rapists.

These relationships of contradiction are extremely important and useful. The *A* and *E* statements, being universal, are open to *refutation by counterexample*, which works through the logical relation of contradiction. Often you find people making unguarded and cavalier generalizations, such as "No men are good listeners." To refute such a statement, you have only to find one man—just one—who is a good listener. If you do, the *I* statement "Some men are good listeners" is true, and the *E* statement "No men are good listeners"—which is its contradictory—is false. People who categorically assert *A* and *E* statements make themselves very vulnerable to refutation. More qualified statements, such as "Few men are good listeners," are not so vulnerable. But then, they aren't so exciting either.

Summary of Rules of Immediate Inference

1. *Conversion.* All *E* and *I* statements are logically equivalent to their converse. No *A* or *O* statements are logically equivalent to their converse.

2. *Contraposition.* All *A* and *O* statements are logically equivalent to their contrapositive. No *E* or *I* statements are logically equivalent to their contrapositive.

3. *Obversion.* All statements in categorical form are logically equivalent to their obverse.

4. *Contradiction.* If *A* is true, then *O* is false, and *vice versa*. If *E* is true, then *I* is false, and *vice versa*.

Exercise Two
Part A

For each of the following statements, put it into proper categorical form and then form the obverse.

*1. The pilgrims who came to Massachusetts left England of their own free will.

2. "A robot would behave like a robot." (Paul Ziff, "The Feelings of Robots," in *Minds and Machines*, ed. Alan R. Anderson [Englewood Cliffs, N.J.: Prentice-Hall, 1964]1.)

*3. Some technological innovations are not needed.

4. Historians are well-educated people.

5. Not all professors are impractical.

6. Any practical skill is developed to obtain a definite result.

7. Art is the pursuit of beauty and truth.

*8. "Nationalism is an extreme example of fervent belief concerning doubtful matters." (Bertrand Russell, *Sceptical Essays*, [London: Unwin Books, 1935], p. 12.)
(*Hint:* You need not try to represent "is an extreme example of" in categorical form.)

Part B

Put each of the following statements into categorical form. Then form the converse and the contrapositive. State whether the converse and the contrapositive are logically equivalent to the original in each case. (Use the *A, E, I, O* labels, and use letters for the formal representation of categories. For instance, "All men have backbones" would be "All *M* are *B*," where *M* represents the category of men and *B* represents the category of creatures with backbones. The converse would be "All creatures with backbones are men"—a statement of the *A*

form. The contrapositive would be "All noncreatures with backbones are nonmen"—also of the *A* form. The converse is not logically equivalent to the original statement, but the contrapositive is logically equivalent to it.)

*1. Only experts understand the new technology.

2. All lonely people are unhappy people.

3. Some advisors think the policy should be changed.

*4. Whales are in danger of extinction.

5. Spring is the season of rains.

*6. Some court procedures are so complicated as to be very inefficient.

7. Some students are not competitive.

*8. No one who has read Russian dissident novelists could doubt that opponents of the current regime are vulnerable to severe penalties in the Soviet Union.

9. Every dog has its day.

10. The ozone layer about the earth could be damaged by frequent uses of aerosol spray cans.

Part C

For each of the following statements, put the statement into categorical form and then form the contradictory.

*1. The advice given to young parents by so-called experts is unreliable.

2. No breaker of the law is a friend of the state.

*3. Some crops are best grown on land that has been left fallow for one season.

4. Raccoons are a danger in urban areas.

*5. The only productive and innovative scientist is the one who enjoys freedom of thought and is not afraid to risk pursuing a new idea.

Contrary and Contradictory Predicates and False Dichotomies

The results of obversion often sound very unnatural to the sensitive English ear because the *non* attached to the predicate category is not so very common in natural English. No doubt you noticed this when working through Part A of the preceding exercise. Because *non* so often has an unnatural ring, people are often inclined to alter it and substitute ordinary words that seem to be equivalent to it in meaning.

For instance, given:

—— (1) All bankrupt persons are non-happy persons.

they would be inclined to substitute:

—— (2) All bankrupt persons are unhappy persons.

However, statements (1) and (2) here are *not* logically equivalent, and (2) is not a version of (1). The reason they are not logically equivalent is that the category of unhappy things is a narrower one than the category of non-happy things. The non-happy include all who just fail to be happy—whether they are in a bland (neither happy nor unhappy) state, or whether they are the kinds of things that just couldn't be either happy or unhappy (carrots, for instance). But the unhappy are those who are miserable (The bland would be excluded). A carrot could not be unhappy, though it could be non-happy. Thus, *non-happy* and *unhappy* do not mean the same thing.

For any predicate, *P*, we can construct a corresponding predicate, non-*P*, such that these two predicates are the basis of contradictory statements. Two statements are contradictory if the truth of one entails the falsity of the other. For contradictory statements one of the two must be true. For example, let the predicate be *fat*. We can construct the predicate *non-fat*, and this is the contradictory of the first predicate in the sense that any item in the universe must necessarily be either fat or non-fat, and no item in the universe can be both at once. For every entity, then, it will be true that it is either fat or non-fat. But notice that *non-fat* does not mean the same as *thin* now. It is not true that every item in the uiverse is either fat or thin. Some items aren't even appropriately classified this way (numbers for instance); others are intermediate—people with a normal weight for their height. Whereas *fat* and *non-fat* are contradictory predicates, *fat* and *thin* are not. They are merely contraries. A thing can't be *both* fat and thin, but it can be neither.

The reason that obversion will always give you a logically equivalent statement is that you are always forming a contradictory predicate by using *non*. You will rarely get a contradictory predicate if you substitute more colloquial terms, such as *unhappy* for *non-happy*, or *thin* for *non-fat*. Mistaking contraries for contradictories is the source of many mistakes. Compare the following lists to see how such mistakes can arise:

Contradictory Predicates, P *and* non-P	*Contrary Predicates*, P *and* P'
happy, non-happy	happy, unhappy
pleasant, non-pleasant	pleasant, unpleasant
healthy, non-healthy	healthy, unhealthy
friend, non-friend	friend, enemy
beautiful, non-beautiful	beautiful, ugly
good, non-good	good, evil
white, non-white	white, black

It is a logical mistake to treat a contrary predicate as though it were a contradictory one.

One common result of not being clear about contraries and contradictories is the belief in *false dichotomies*. People who assume false dichotomies practice a version of black-or-white thinking—believing that every item in the universe has to be either black or white, and that there are no items in gray or other colors. What makes such thinking tempting is its simplicity. But also, it is a necessary truth of logic that everything in the universe is either white or non-white. If we confuse non-white (the contradictory) with black (the contrary), the dichotomy "white or black" will be the result. Thinking that everything is either black or white is a false dichotomy because it falsely divides the world, ignoring the rest of the color spectrum. Similarly, everything in the world is either good or non-good; but it would be a false dichotomy to think that everything is either good or evil. *Evil* and *non-good* are not the same. A person who believes that everyone is either his friend or his non-friend would be believing in a logically necessary truth. But one who believes (as some do!) that everyone is either his friend or his enemy is on the verge of paranoid thinking.

Categorical Logic: Some Philosophical Background

Categorical logic was first discovered by Aristotle more than two thousand years ago. Seeing the formal relationships between the Greek equivalents of *all, none, some are,* and *some are not,* Aristotle formulated rules of inference for simple arguments in which the premises and conclusions were all in categorical form. So impressive was his achievement that for a very long time most logicians believed that categorical logic was the whole of logic. An important aspect of this theory was the belief that all statements—whatever their surface grammatical features—were really of the subject-predicate form and that all deductively valid relationships depended on the aspects of logical form that the *A, E, I,* and *O* statements express. At the end of the eighteenth century, the famous German philosopher Immanuel Kant still clung to this belief in the Aristotelian tradition of logic. In fact, it persisted until nearly the end of the nineteenth century. However, most modern logicians do not subscribe to this theory: they see categorical relations as *some* of the important logical relations, not *all* of them.

Such statements as "If inflation continues, strikes will increase" and "Either it will be cloudy or it will rain" are *not* basically subject-predicate statements. They cannot at all naturally be expressed in categorical form. (Try it for yourself, and see. You have to do a lot of fiddling, and the results are not very close to the original in meaning.) There are more useful logical symbolisms to represent these statements, and these form part of modern systems of *propositional* logic, which are introduced in Chapter Nine.

In our discussion of categorical form we did not consider any statements about particular individuals. These statements can be put in categorical form, but only in a rather unnatural way. Consider the following:

▬ Philosopher Bertrand Russell was a prominent pacifist in World War I.

This statement is not about a category of things: it is about an individual. To put it into categorical form, we have to regard that individual as a member of a group—that is, make him one of a kind. Thus:

▬ All things identical with the philosopher Bertrand Russell are things that were prominent pacifists during World War I.

To many ancient philosophers, this kind of adaptation of the particular into the universal seemed quite natural; they valued universal knowledge above all else, and they regarded individuals as such as comparatively uninteresting. But to most modern philosophers, such recasting seems unnatural and unsatisfactory. In modern systems of logic, statements about individuals can be symbolized using letters that represent one individual—not a group.

These points illustrate the fact that modern logicians do not regard categorical form as the "be-all-and-end-all" of logical form. They would agree with the ancient philosophers, and with the treatment so far in this book, that many statements can be cast into categorical form. But categorical form is not the only way to appreciate logical form, nor is it always appropriate. Categorical form is a natural representation for some English structures, but not for all.

An interesting dispute between ancient and modern theorists of logic concerns the problem of making statements about things that do not exist. Like other Greek philosophers of his time, Aristotle found the very idea of speaking and reasoning about nonexistent things irrational and paradoxical. He developed categorical logic on the assumption that the subjects always deal with things that exist. Aristotle believed that we make assertions only about those things that are real. This view of categorical logic is called the *existential* view. Modern logicians (most of them, anyway) do not share this existential view. They point out that we often make statements about things that might or might not exist, and we want our rules of logical inference to apply to these statements, just as they apply to others. Scientists reasoned about genes, electrons, and black holes before they were sure that such things exist. A scientist who said, "Black holes are invisible" before he knew for sure that there is such a thing as a black hole, meant in effect "If anything is a black hole, then that thing is invisible." The *if* makes the statement hypothetical; the scientist did not commit himself to the claim that there are black holes. Whereas ancient logicians always interpreted *A* and *E* statements as entailing the existence of things in the subject and predicate categories, modern logicians prefer a *hypothetical* interpretation in which the nonexistence of things in those categories is left open as a possibility. For the ancient logicians "All humans are mortal" entails that humans exist. (This is the existential interpretation.) For modern logicians, "All humans are mortal" entails only that *if* anyone is a human, that person is mortal. (This is the hypothetical interpretation.)

In modern logic, the hypothetical viewpoint is taken to be the basic one, which means that *A* and *E* statements can be true, even when there are no members of the subject category. We can make statements about electrons, late students, angels, mermaids, or black holes without committing ourselves to the assumption that these things exist. That is, we can do this *provided* the statements are universal. Modern and ancient logic share the view that the particular statements assert existence. To say that some black holes are invisible is to say that there is at least one black hole that is invisible, and this, of course, commits you to the existence of at least one black hole.

Who is right in this dispute between ancient and modern logicians? Can we speak and reason about what does not exist? Do we need to? These are large metaphysical questions that we cannot try to answer here. By and large we follow the modern view, since this is one you are likely to encounter in courses on mathematics and formal logic elsewhere. In some practical contexts, the modern view yields strange results. One thing it does, which seems very odd, is to prevent us from deductively inferring that some (that is, at least one) lawyers are rich (*I*) from the claim that all lawyers are rich (*A*). Surely, you would think, if all lawyers are rich, then some are! But on the hypothetical interpretation of the *A* statement, we cannot validly infer the *I* statement from it because the *A* statement is interpreted hypothetically as saying that *if* anyone is a lawyer, she or he is rich. And the *I* statement says *there is* at least one lawyer. We cannot validly deduce the actual from the hypothetical, so in the modern view there will be no valid immediate inference of *I* from *A*. The same point holds with *E* and *O*. But in the case of rich lawyers the results seem simply bizarre! Aren't some lawyers rich if all are? The reason the results seem bizarre is that in ordinary life we usually restrict ourselves just as Aristotle did; we talk about things that exist. Everyone knows there are lawyers, and when we talk about lawyers, we aren't speculating about mythical entities!

The solution to this problem is to step back and ask yourself whether the existence of the subject class should be assumed in the context you are dealing with. If it should, you write that assumption into the universal statement. In the case of the lawyers, you would then understand "All lawyers are rich" just as Aristotle would have: you would interpret it as saying that there are lawyers, and all of them are rich. On this understanding of the *A* statement, you can validly infer the *I* statement from it. In contexts like these, where it is a matter of common knowledge that the subject category is a category of existing things, we recommend reading in an existence assumption and reverting—in a sense—to the ancient view of things. But on the whole, we will work with the hypothetical interpretation, since it is the standard one among modern logicians.

The Syllogism

A *syllogism* is an argument with two premises and a conclusion, in which the premises and the conclusion are statements in categorical form, and there are three different categories of things involved in the argument. Each of the categories will be mentioned in two different statements. The example used early in this chapter to exemplify categorical form is a valid syllogism. Here it is again:

1. All consistent opponents of killing are opponents of capital punishment.
2. No opponents of capital punishment are orthodox traditional Catholics.
Therefore,
3. No consistent opponents of killing are orthodox traditional Catholics.

If *C* represents the category of consistent opponents of killing, and *T* represents the category of orthodox traditional Catholics, and *O* represents the category of opponents of capital punishment, then the argument may be formally represented as:

1. All *C* are *O*.
2. No *O* are *T*.
Therefore,
3. No *C* are *T*.

Here *T* is the *major term*; a major term is the one that is the predicate in the conclusion. *C* is the *minor term*; it is the subject in the conclusion. And *O*, which appears in both premises but not in the conclusion, is the *middle term:*

Major Term: the predicate in the conclusion
Minor Term: the subject in the conclusion
Middle Term: in both premises, but not in the conclusion

This example is a valid syllogism because the premises, taken together, deductively entail the conclusion. We can see this by representing the content of these premises on a Venn diagram. To do this, we shall use three circles to represent the three categories.

The premises may be drawn as:

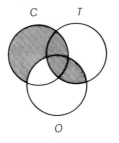

All C are O, and no O are T.

And the conclusion would be represented as:

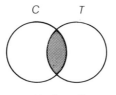

No C are T.

This model shades out all the *C* that are not *O* because of the information in the first premise, and all the *O* that are *T* because of the information in the second premise. To determine whether the syllogism is valid, we represent the premises Venn diagrams and then look to see whether the information we have pictured includes what is expressed in the conclusion. Here the conclusion states that there should be nothing in the area that is both *C* and *T*. If the conclusion were entailed by the premises, then the model of the premises would shade out the entire *C–T* overlap. It does. Thus the Venn diagram reveals that the argument is a deductively valid syllogism.

Venn diagrams vividly illustrate something that philosophers and logicians love to say about deductively valid arguments. In a deductively valid argument, the conclusion is "already contained" in the premises. An argument is deductively valid whenever the premises assert everything needed for the conclusion to be true. In this way the truth of the premises makes it impossible for the conclusion to be false. The Venn diagram for a valid syllogism shows just how this happens. For a valid syllogism, once you have drawn the premises, you need no more drawing to represent the conclusion: it will already be pictured on your circles.

Let's look at another syllogism:

—— 1. Some socialists are communists.
2. Some communists are docile puppets of totalitarian regimes.
Therefore,
3. Some socialists are docile puppets of totalitarian regimes.

Here the major term, *D*, represents the category of docile puppets of totalitarian regimes; the minor term, *R*, represents the category of socialists, and the middle term, *C*, represents the category of communists. Formalized, the argument is:

—— 1. Some *R* are *C*.
2. Some *C* are *D*.
Therefore,
3. Some *R* are *D*.

To test the validity of this syllogism using Venn diagrams, we first diagram the premises. Both premises here are of the *I* form, and this makes our diagram more complicated than before.

Some *R* are *C* and some *C* are *D*.

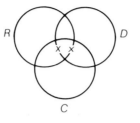

Some *C* are *D*. (The area that is the overlap between *C* and *D* is subdivided into those *CD*s that are also *R* and those that are not *R*.)

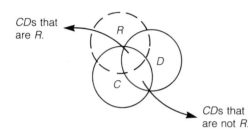

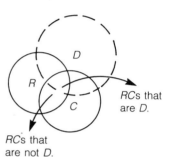

Some *R* are *C*. (The area that is the overlap between *R* and *C* is subdivided into those *RC*s that are also inside *D*, and those *RC*s that are outside *D*.)

To use Venn diagrams effectively, you have to be very careful not to represent on your diagram more information than the premises state. In this example the premises do not indicate whether those *R*s that are *C* are also *D*; thus the *x* that designates that there is something in the area appears *on the line*. A similar technique must be used for the second premise. The diagram of these two *I* statements taken together reflects some *ambiguities*, which the information in the two premises does not resolve. The premises do not say whether those socialists who are communists are, or are not, among those of the communists who are docile puppets of totalitarian regimes. They assert that some communists are docile puppets, but they make no commitment as to whether these are the very same communists who are also socialists. By placing the *x* on the line in these cases, we indicate that there is something in either one of the areas that the line separates, but we do not know which.

To see whether this syllogism about the communists and socialists is valid, we look at our diagram to see whether the premises provide the information in the conclusion. The conclusion was "Some *R* are *D*." We look, then, at the *R–D* intersection in the diagram representing both premises. We check whether the diagram guarantees that there will be something in this area. *It does not.* There is no guarantee that an *x* will be in this area, because the *x*s are on lines, and might both land up in the adjoining areas. Thus the argument is *not* deductively valid.

To check an argument for validity using these Venn diagrams, you first make sure that it is a syllogism. Then you draw three overlapping circles to represent the three categories on which the argument depends. You model the two premises onto the diagram. Then you check to see whether that diagram expresses the information stated in the conclusion. If it does, the argument is deductively valid. The premises contain enough information to guarantee the conclusion logically. If it does not, the argument is not deductively valid. The conclusion has information that goes beyond what is stated in the conclusion. Be especially careful when representing *I* and *O* statements; you will need to represent *x*s on lines.

We'll do one more example:

—————— 1. No lawyers are illiterate.
      2. All lawyers are educated.
      So,
      3. Some educated persons are not illiterate.

Diagramming both premises, we get:

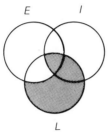

(*I* represents the category of illiterate persons; *E* represents the category of educated persons; *L* represents the category of lawyers.) But the conclusion would have to contain an *x* in the intersection area of the *E* that is outside the *I*; the conclusion says there is at least one person who is in *E* and not in *I*. The premises don't guarantee this, obviously, for there is no *x* in the model of the premises.

What we have run into here is the consequence of the hypothetical interpretation of the *E* and *A* statements. These were drawn as modern logicians do—they do not show any information about the existence of lawyers or illiterate or educated people. If we were to correct for this, on the grounds that it is common knowledge that things exist in all these categories, the premises would then contain more knowledge, as:

—————— 1. No *L* are *I* (and there are *L*).
      2. All *L* are *E* (and there are *L*).
      Therefore,
      3. Some *E* are not *I*.

With these existential assumptions added, there is more information to be represented on our Venn diagram, which will now look like this:

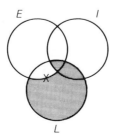

The argument is valid on the existential interpretation. The x is on a line, indicating that it is in either one of the areas that border on that line. However, one of these areas is shaded, indicating that nothing is in that area. Thus there must be something in the other, which is what the conclusion requires in order to be true.

EXERCISE SET

Exercise Three

For each of the following arguments, put the premises and conclusion into categorical form. Check to see whether the argument is a syllogism. (Remember, in a syllogism, there are two premises and one conclusion. All are in categorical form, and there are exactly three categories in the statements.) Test all syllogisms for validity using the Venn diagram technique. Adopt the hypothetical interpretation. Does this give you paradoxical results in any case? Discuss.

1. Herpes is a viral infection. Antibiotics are an effective drug only against nonviral infections. Therefore, antibiotics are not effective against herpes.

*2. I don't know why it is, but some mothers find small children extremely irritating. And some people who find small children extremely irritating just cannot control themselves and suppress their rage. For these reasons, some mothers cannot control themselves and suppress their rage.

3. Some anarchists are pacifists. But no consistent anarchist is a pacifist. The inevitable conclusion is that some anarchists are not consistent anarchists.

4. All foods that can be kept on the shelf for several weeks without rotting are foods containing additives. But all foods that contain additives are hazardous to health. Thus, foods with a shelf-life of several weeks are hazardous to health.

5. Men without money are men without power. Men without power are men without self-esteem. Therefore, men without self-esteem are men without money.

6. Some children are hyperactive because all hyperactive persons are difficult to handle, and all children are difficult to handle.

*7. Because all well-educated persons can read and all persons who can read have heard of Hitler, there are some well-educated persons who have heard of Hitler.

8. All zoos keep animals in captivity for display to curious humans, and no place in which animals just exist to be displayed can be a humane environment. Thus no zoo is a humane environment.

*9. No vacation is complete without a tropical beach. All tropical beaches come with some risk of sunburn. Thus no vacation is complete without some risk of sunburn.

10. Any test of character or ability that can be affected by subjects' learning to control their responses to the test is unreliable. Lie detector tests can be affected by subjects focusing on low-stress events, and that is something they can be taught to do. So you see that lie detector tests are not reliable.

11. Only children who have at least one blue-eyed parent can have blue eyes. Joan has blue eyes. Therefore, Joan has at least one blue-eyed parent.

*12. Some doctors are unhappy. Unhappy persons are unreliable. Therefore, some doctors are unreliable.

13. Only children who have at least one blue-eyed parent can have blue eyes. Bob has brown eyes, not blue eyes. Thus Bob does not have at least one blue-eyed parent.

14. There are several replies to the suggestion that Canada should test Cruise missiles because she depends, in the final analysis, on the American defense arsenal. One is that the Americans are compelled by geography to defend Canada and that since this is a situation nobody chose, it gives rise to no obligation. Another is that Canada does have some obligations to the United States, but that these are to the American people in general, not to a specific administration, particularly not to one that many Americans themselves are questioning as far as defense strategy and defense expenditures are concerned.

15. The skeptic is not afraid to admit his own ignorance. He knows that full knowledge is impossible, and all of us who know that complete knowledge is impossible can certainly admit to our own ignorance without shame.

16. All drying machines consume energy, but some drying machines consume less energy than others.

You should try to save energy, so when you set out to buy a dryer, you should look for an energy-efficient one.

17. A cogent argument, like a true friend, will never fail you.

18. Any position in local government that involves power and influence should be allotted on the basis of a municipal election. The position of spouse of the mayor involves power and influence, so it should be allotted on the basis of municipal election.

(Used by a critic of a mayor who had said that his spouse was an important person to the local government and that for this reason she deserved to use city paid cars to do her shopping.)

(*Question:* Presuming that the mayor sought to avoid this conclusion, which premise of the syllogism should he seek to dispute if he wishes to remain consistent? Or is he compelled, by categorical logic, to admit that his spouse should be selected for him by the voters?)

*19. Some religious people believe that morality depends on religion. All people who believe that morality depends on religion have a false view of morality. Therefore, some religious people have a false view of morality.

The Rules of the Syllogism

Modeling syllogisms on Venn diagrams gives you a system for checking their deductive validity. However, some people find this technique clumsy and awkward—especially when it comes to representing *I* and *O* statements. Another way of checking the validity of syllogisms involves the use of rules. There are five rules, and if none are broken, the syllogism is a valid deductive argument.

In order to use the rules for the syllogism, you need a good understanding of two technical terms that we have introduced previously. These are *distributed* and *middle term*. Whether a term in a categorical statement is distributed or not depends on whether that statement makes a comment about every item in the category specified by that term:

Distribution of Terms

A: All *S* are *P*. The subject term, *S*, is distributed, and the predicate term, *P*, is not.

E: No *S* are *P*. Both the subject term, *S*, and the predicate term, *P*, are distributed.

I: Some *S* are *P*. Neither the subject term, *S*, nor the predicate term, *P*, is distributed.

O: Some *S* are not *P*. The subject term, *S*, is not distributed. However, the predicate term, *P*, is distributed.

The reason that the predicate term is distributed in *O* statements is that the subject category is excluded from the whole predicate category; to say that some men are not fathers, for example, is to say of the whole category of fathers that some men are not in it.

As for the middle term, this is the term that occurs in both premises of a syllogism, but not in its conclusion. It is the middle term that enables us to link the premises together to logically deduce the conclusion. Thus the middle term must be distributed in at least one premise for the syllogism to be valid. If the middle term is not distributed in either premise, then both premises give information about only some of this category. This means that the predicate term and the subject term cannot be securely related to each other. Consider the following example:

1. All barbers are businessmen.
2. Some businessmen are people in debt.
So,
3. Some barbers are people in debt.

We cannot validly connect being a barber with being in debt because the middle term "businessmen" is not distributed in this argument. The first premise is only about some businessmen, and so is the second premise. There is no guarantee that the businessmen referred to are the same ones in each case. Thus, even though the conclusion is only about some barbers, it cannot logically be derived from the premises. The businessmen who are barbers may have no connection at all with the businessmen who are in debt, so it could happen that the premises are true and yet the conclusion is false. This is just to say that the argument is not valid.

The middle term is crucial in any syllogism. The "fallacy of the undistributed middle" is famous in the history of logic. The preceding argument about barbers and businessmen illustrates this fallacy. It is committed whenever a syllogistic argument is used and the middle term is not distributed in at least one premise.

Given an understanding of what distribution is, and what the middle term is, it is very easy to understand the rules of the syllogism:

Rules of the Syllogism
1. For a syllogism to be valid, the middle term must be distributed in at least one premise.
2. For a syllogism to be valid, no term is distributed in the conclusion unless it is also distributed in at least one premise.
3. For a syllogism to be valid, at least one premise is affirmative; that is, a valid syllogism cannot have two negative premises.
4. For a syllogism to be valid, if it has a negative conclusion, it must also have a negative premise. And if it has one negative premise, it must also have a negative conclusion.
*5. If a syllogism has two universal premises, it cannot have a particular conclusion and be valid.

It should be obvious why the fifth rule is marked with an asterisk. This rule makes explicit the hypothetical interpretation of universal statements. If you are going to read existence assumptions into these statements, then you must drop the fifth rule. To be deductively valid arguments, syllogisms must pass all the rules. If even one is broken, the syllogism is not valid. Those who prefer language to diagrams may wish to check syllogisms by using the rules instead of Venn diagrams.

Applying Categorical Logic

If an argument is deductively valid, then the (RG) conditions of argument cogency are perfectly and entirely satisfied; no doubt can be raised on these. It makes no sense to grant that an argument is deductively valid and then go on to complain that the premises are irrelevant to the conclusion or are not adequate to support the conclusion. If anything is wrong with a deductively valid argument, then it must be in the premises themselves. The syllogism provides a context in which we can improve our appreciation of just what "deductive validity" means.

Many of the immediate inferences we study in this chapter are important for the correct interpretation of statements and claims. For instance, a proper understanding of obversion helps us to see why a person saying that some children are not happy may not mean that these children are unhappy. Understanding conversion prevents us inferring that all who support disarmament are communists from the quite different claim that all who are communists support disarmament.

If you read newspapers and magazines, it is not likely that you will be struck by the enormous number of syllogisms you find. Syllogisms worded as straightforwardly as those we have studied so far in this chapter are comparatively rare in natural discourse. Nevertheless, there are *some* clear syllogisms around, and there are also some arguments that are implicitly syllogistic, though their syllogistic form does not stand out as clearly as you might wish. In such arguments, Venn diagram techniques and rules for the syllogism will tell you whether the argument is deductively valid. But you may have to do some careful interpreting in order to apply these techniques. Remember that all the rules in this chapter apply only to those statements that are in proper categorical form. A syllogism must have two premises and a conclusion, all in categorical form, and it must involve three distinct categories of things.

To see what may be involved in the application of syllogistic rules to ordinary prose, we shall work through an example. This is an argument that the philosopher John Locke used in his defense of religious toleration:

> *Speculative opinions and articles of faith which are required only to be believed cannot be imposed on any church by the law of the land. For it is absurd that things should be enjoined by laws which are not in men's power to perform. And to believe this or that to be true does not depend upon our will.*[1]

This argument is a valid syllogism, but we have to do some recasting before we can demonstrate this fact.

Locke's conclusion is in the first sentence: "<u>Speculative opinions and articles of faith</u> are <u>things which should not be imposed by law</u>." The premises are in the next two sentences: "<u>things enjoined by law</u> should be <u>things which it is in men's power to perform</u>" and "<u>beliefs</u> are not <u>things which depend upon our will</u>." Here, as indicated by underlining, we have six categories. Unless we can regard some of these categories as reducible to others, we cannot regard Locke's argument as a syllogism. A syllogism, by definition, is based on exactly three distinct categories of things. We have to look at the differences in wording to see whether we really have the same category described in different words. This does happen in the argument. In this context, "speculative opinions and articles of faith" and "beliefs" mean the same thing. Also, "things which it is in men's power to perform" and "things which depend upon our will" are the same. Now the only remaining problem concerns the *should* in the first premise. Statements in categorical form must use *are*; therefore, *should* will have to be moved from the linking position to the internal specification of a category.

Once we grasp the necessary variations in wording, the argument may be represented as follows:

1. All things which should be imposed by law are things which depend upon our will.
2. No beliefs are things which depend upon our will.
So,
3. No beliefs are things which should be imposed by law.

Allowing *B* to stand for beliefs, *I* to stand for things that should be imposed by law, and *W* to stand for things that depend upon our will, the argument becomes:

—— 1. All *I* are *W*.
2. No *B* are *W*.
So,
3. No *B* are *I*.

As you can see, this argument is a valid syllogism. But it is quite difficult to get Locke's original passage into this form. The passage illustrates some of the problems that arise when we try to transpose the clear, straightforward rules of a part of deductive logic onto natural speaking and writing in English. We have to look for verbally different ways of specifying the same category and rewrite to represent statements in categorical form. If we succeed in doing so, we may produce a model that says the same thing as the original, but says it much more clearly. Our reworded argument is less eloquent than Locke's original, but it is much easier to understand. We can show that the argument is deductively valid, and we therefore know that any problem with its cogency must concern the premises themselves. The only difficult aspect of all this is the *encoding* of the original language into the symbolism.

Another matter that often arises when you try to spot syllogistic reasoning in ordinary speech and writing is the problem of *elliptical syllogisms.* Elliptical syllogisms are implicitly syllogistic arguments in which either one premise or the conclusion is not explicitly stated by the arguer. Here is an example that may have a familiar ring to it:

> *The bigger the burger, the better the burger.*
> *The burgers are bigger at Burger King.*

The point of this advertisement is obviously to convince you that the burgers are better at Burger King. This claim is entailed by the two stated claims. The ad is really a syllogism with a missing conclusion:

—— 1. All bigger burgers are better burgers.
2. All burgers at Burger King are bigger burgers.
So,
3. All burgers at Burger King are better burgers.

Now if *K* represents the category of burgers at Burger King, and *B* represents the category of burgers that are better, and *I* represents the category of burgers that are bigger, we get the following:

—— 1. All *I* are *B*.
2. All *K* are *I*.
So,
3. All *K* are *B*.

This is a valid syllogism. The question of when you should supply a missing conclusion is not different for syllogisms than it is for other arguments. You have to have reason to believe that the author meant to assert the claim you add. If that claim is, in fact, deductively entailed by what is stated, the author of the argument was clearly logically committed to it, and you are not misinterpreting him or her by adding the conclusion.

Even more common than the missing conclusion in a syllogism is the missing premise. Consider the following case:

> *A hundred years from now, should mankind survive that long, Doug Casey may well be remembered as one of the great prophets of our time, for he has displayed in* Crisis Investing *a keen insight into the workings of government and human nature.*[2]

Here the conclusion is that Doug Casey may be remembered as a great prophet a hundred years from now. The premise is that he has displayed a keen insight into the workings of government and human nature. Both these claims can be put into categorical form as follows:

1. All things that are Doug Casey are things that have displayed a keen insight into the workings of government and human nature.
So,
Conclusion: All things that are Doug Casey are things that may be remembered as great prophets a hundred years from now.

Now if we let C stand for the category of things that are Casey and R stand for the category of things that may be remembered in a hundred years, and W represents the category of things that have displayed keen insight into the workings of government, we get a stated premise and conclusion as follows:

1. All C are W.
So,
3. All C are R.

What is missing to make the argument deductively valid is a statement "All W are R"; we need a premise linking a middle term to the predicate of the conclusion. If we were to add this as a missing premise, the argument would be a valid syllogism:

1. All C are W.
2. All W are R.
So,
3. All C are R.

This addition seems appropriate for the original argument does seem to proceed by relations of category inclusion. The arguer has asserted that Casey may be remembered because he understood government. But if this is what will make Casey one who may be remembered, and there are no qualifying comments made or suggested, it would appear that the arguer is using the claim that all who understand government may be remembered. (All M are P.) When we write this in, the argument can be represented as a valid syllogism.

It is not appropriate to regard an argument as an elliptical syllogism unless the premise you are going to add is one that will make the argument valid; the very things that make you justified in reading it in will relate it to stated material in a valid pattern. Also, not all elliptical arguments are elliptical *syllogisms*. To represent an argument as a syllogism, and not some other type, you should have a sense that the argument depends on category inclusion or exclusion in order to relate the premises to the conclusion.

Review of Terms Introduced

Categorical logic: A branch of formal logic in which the basic logical terms are "all," "some," "are," and "not." Categorical logic was first systematized by Aristotle.

Universal affirmative (A): Statement of the form "all S are P."

Universal negative (E): Statement of the form "no S are P."

Particular affirmative (I): Statement of the form "some *S* are *P*."

Particular negative (O): Statement of the form "some *S* are not *P*."

Contradictory statement: That statement that must always be opposite to the original statement in truth value. If the statement is *X*, its contradictory statement is not-*X*. When *X* is true, not-*X* is false, and *vice versa*. For example, the contradictory statement of "all *S* are *P*" is "some *S* are not *P*."

Contrary of a statement: A logically related statement that can never be true when that statement is true, although it can be false when the statement is false. For example, "all *S* are *P*" and "no *S* are *P*" are contraries. They cannot both be true, but they can both be false.

Immediate inference: Inference of one statement directly from another, with no intermediate logical steps.

Logical equivalence: Logical relation between two statements which must necessarily have the same truth value. For instance, "not all *S* are *P*" and "some *S* are not *P*" are logically equivalent.

Conversion: A logical operation on a statement in categorical form. The order of the terms is reversed. Example: The converse of "all *S* are *P*" is "all *P* are *S*." For *E* and *I* statements, conversion produces logically equivalent statements. For *A* and *O* statements, it does not.

Contraposition: A logical operation on a statement in categorical form. The statement is converted, and then "non-" is attached to each category. Example: The contrapositive of "no *S* are *P*" is "no non-*P* are non-*S*." For *A* and *O* statements, contraposition produces a logically equivalent statement. For *E* and *I* statements, it does not.

Obversion: A logical operation on a statement in categorical form. The prefix "non-" is added to the predicate. Then, if the original statement was affirmative, it is made negative. If the original statement was negative, it is made affirmative. Obversion always produces a statement that is logically equivalent to the original one.

Contradictory predicates: Predicates logically related so that it is a matter of logical necessity that a thing possess one or another. For instance, "happy" and "non-happy" are contradictory predicates. By necessity, if a thing is not happy, it is non-happy.

Contrary predicates: Predicates logically related so that nothing can possess both, though things may possess neither. For example, "happy" and "unhappy" are contrary predicates. It is not possible for a thing to be both happy and unhappy, but it is possible for it to be neither happy nor unhappy.

Syllogism: Argument with two premises and a conclusion, in which the premises and the conclusion are statements in categorical form and there are three different categories of things involved in the argument.

Major term: Term that appears in the predicate position in the conclusion of a syllogism.

Minor term: Term that appears in the subject position in the conclusion of a syllogism.

Middle term: Term that occurs in both premises of a syllogism but not in the conclusion.

Venn diagram: Diagram in which circles are used to represent categorical relationships.

Distribution: When the categorical statement in which the term appears is about all the things within the category that term designates. The subject (*S*) term is distributed in *A* and *E* statements. The predicate (*P*) term is distributed in *E* and *O* statements.

Fallacy of the undistributed middle: Fallacy committed when a syllogism is put forward and it is invalid because the middle term is not distributed in either one of the premises.

EXERCISE SET

Exercise Four

For the following arguments, identify the premises and conclusions and, *if possible*, recast the argument as a syllogism. If necessary, supply a missing premise or missing conclusion. Then test the arguments for validity using either Venn diagrams or the rules of the syllogism. If there are any arguments that cannot be expressed as syllogisms, try to explain why not.

1. Some problems experienced by human beings are the result of climate. No problem that is the result of climate is the result of abuses of human rights. Therefore, some problems experienced by humans are not the result of abuses of human rights.

2. "Other men die. I am not another. Therefore I shall not die."
(V. Nabokov, *Pale Fire* [New York: Putnam, 1962].)

3. A completely unprejudiced observation is an observation that is made with no goal in mind. But no observation is made with no goal in mind. Therefore, no observation is completely unprejudiced.

4. Some sports are fiercely competitive and no activity which is fiercely competitive is unaggressive. Therefore, no sports are unaggressive.

5. "Mrs. Ladd Franklin tells the story of a little girl, aged four, whose nurse objected to her table manners. 'Emily,' said the nurse, 'nobody eats soup with a fork.' 'But,' replied Emily, 'I do, and I am somebody.'

"We are not told how the nurse responded to the situation created by Emily's recognition that an indisputable fact contradicted her nurse's statement."
(Susan Stebbing, *Thinking to Some Purpose* [Middlesex, England: Penguin Books, 1939], pp. 29–30.)
(Represent Emily's argument as a syllogism.)

*6. "Among the vowels there are no double letters; but one of the double letters (*w*) is compounded of two vowels. Hence a letter compounded of two vowels is not necessarily itself a vowel."
(C. S. Peirce, "Some Consequences of Four Incapacities," in *Philosophical Writings of C. S. Peirce*, ed. Justus Buchler [New York: Dover Publications, 1955].)

7. "The central pillars of a recovery programme for Africa are stronger economic growth in the industrialized world and a programme of new money and debt write-offs for the affected countries. This is not charity, but enlightened self-interest. It will be to the future benefit of the developed world if Africa can be put on to its economic feet, able to increase trade with the rest of the world."
("Helping Africa Isn't Charity," *The Guardian Weekly*, June 8, 1986.)
(Find the syllogism implicit in this passage. For the purpose of this exercise, ignore any subarguments. *Hint:* What did the writer assume about the relationship between charity and self-interest?)

*8. "Because the nuclear peril, like the scientific knowledge that gave rise to it, is everlasting, our solution must at least aim at being global and everlasting. And the only kind of solution that holds out this promise is a global political one."
(Jonathan Schell, *The Fate of the Earth* [New York: Knopf, 1983].) Schell, having described the horrors of nuclear war, is discussing the role of national sovereignty in preventing lasting solutions to the dangerous nuclear arms race.

9. "The leaders of our country have not told us, the citizens, where they want to lead us. This must mean that they are totally confused themselves."
(Duff Cornbush in the *Canadian*, quoted by Douglas Roche in *Justice Not Charity* [Toronto: McLelland and Stewart, 1970].)

10. "If a much praised government dam was worth the trouble of building, someone would have been able to build it for a profit. Since it's unprofitable, it must be financed at least in part by taxes."
(From Doug Casey, *Crisis Investing* [New York: Stratford Press, 1980].)

11. Despite what industry spokespersons may say, no advertising is entirely honest. Since no advertising is entirely honest and every entirely honest practice is worth emulating, it must follow that some advertising is not worth emulating.

*12. "There is something fundamentally wrong about a theory that defines the best people only in terms of IQ. For one thing, no one really knows how to measure intelligence. And if we did, we might discover that the ability to juggle numbers and concepts is neither the only, nor in some cases, the most desirable, kind of mental sharpness."
(*Detroit Free Press*, March 1980.)

13. "Every well-founded inference to an infinite cause is based upon the observation of an infinite effect. But no inference to God's existence from the design in nature is based upon the observation of an infinite effect. Thus, no inference to God's existence from the design in nature is a well-founded inference."
(Adapted from David Hume, *Dialogues Concerning Natural Religion*, in *The Empiricists* [New York: Anchor Press, 1974].)

14. Any good buy is a real bargain these days, you can be sure of that. Now I checked this morning, and the local store has some real bargains. Go there, and you can pick up some good buys.

*15. Only men from expensive private schools will make it to the top of public life in Britain, for only those schools provide the sort of education that is essential for such a role.

*16. *Background:* This passage is part of a letter written to oppose the censorship of pornography in Canada:
"A nation that permits, night after night, year in and year out, the showing on TV and in cinemas of murders by the hundreds and thousands, and yet can't show one love-making scene without having it labelled obscenity—that nation is guilty of practicing gross obscenity and hypocrisy, and is consequently without redeeming social value."
(Toronto *Globe and Mail*, April 21, 1984.)
(You can find two syllogisms here if you add two extra premises—one for each of them.)

NOTES

1. John Locke, *A Letter Concerning Toleration.* Quoted in S. F. Barker, *The Elements of Logic.* 3rd ed. (New York: McGraw-Hill, 1980).

2. Robert J. Ringer, Preface to Doug Casey, *Crisis Investing* (New York: Stratford Press, 1980).

Those Tidy Deductions: Propositional Logic

Although categorical logic is the oldest developed logic in the western philosophical tradition, it is not now believed to be the most basic part of logic. That role is reserved for propositional logic, which deals with the relationships holding between simple propositions or statements and their compounds. In propositional logic the basic logical terms are *not, or, and,* and *if then.* These terms are used to relate statements and their compounds. The following is a simple example of an argument that is easily formalized in propositional logic:

 1. If inflation continues, social discontent will increase.
 2. Inflation will continue.
 Therefore,
 3. Social discontent will increase.

This argument is deductively valid, but not by virtue of any relations between subjects and predicates. Rather, it is the *conditional* relationship and the assertion of the antecedent of the conditional in the second premise that make the argument deductively valid. In propositional logic we use letters to represent simple statements. Symbols represent the basic logical connecting words: *not, and, or,* and *if then.* Allowing I to represent "inflation continues" and S to represent "social discontent will increase," the preceding argument can be represented in propositional logic as:

 $I \supset S$
 I
 Therefore,
 S

Provided that an argument can be accurately formalized in the sumbols of propositional logic, we can test its deductive validity by a device called a *truth table.*

Definition of the Basic Symbols Used in Propositional Logic

In Chapter Eight we noted that in a system of formal logic, we may have to define terms more precisely than we would in ordinary natural language. For instance, by *some* in categorical logic we mean "at least one." The formal system expresses a kind of core, or residue, of the meaning a term has in a more flexible natural language. This factor must be remembered when we are working with propositional logic. The symbols $-$, $\cdot$, $\vee$, and $\vee$ stand for *not, and, or,* and *if then.* But they do not coincide perfectly with all the shades of meaning that these English words have in all contexts. Rather they represent a logical core that can be put on a truth table. We shall explain what this logical core is and do some work with truth tables before exploring in more detail just where and why the logical symbols fail to express various nuances of meaning.

Let us start with *not.* Suppose that the letter *W* is used to represent a simple statement, such as "A war was being fought in Europe in 1915." This statement may be either *asserted* or *denied.* A person who asserts it affirms that it is true, whereas a person who denies it claims that it is false. Denying the statement that a war was being fought in Europe in 1915 amounts to asserting its contradictory—namely, "A war was *not* being fought in Europe in 1915." When a statement is represented by single letter (in this case, *W*), its contradictory is symbolized by a hyphen preceding that letter, as in $-W$. When *W* is true, $-W$ is false; when $-W$ is true, *W* is false. (You read $-W$ as "not *W*.")

We can represent the simple relationship between any statement and its denial on a truth table, as follows:

P	$-P$
T	F
F	T

This is a simple truth table that defines the operator for *not.* *P* represents any statement that has two possible truth values. *P* can be either true or false, as shown in the column on the left. Its denial, $-P$, also has two possible truth values. The truth of *P* and that of $-P$ are related, as we can see by reading across the rows. When *P* is true, $-P$ is false, and *vice versa.*

Now we move on to *and.* Frequently the word *and* is used to join together two statements, as in the sentence, "A war was being fought in Europe in 1915, and Britain was a major protagonist in that war." Logicians call a combination of statements based on *and* a *conjunction.* A conjunction of two statements is true if and only if both these statements (called conjuncts) are true. That is, our statement about Europe in 1915 will be true if and only if it is true that there was a war then and it is also true that Britain was a major protagonist in that war. If either one of these conjuncts is false, the whole conjunction will be false, for the conjunction asserts both of them. Conjunction is represented in propositional logic by "$\cdot$". This symbol is defined by the following truth table:

P	Q	$P \cdot Q$
T	T	T
T	F	F
F	T	F
F	F	F

This truth table is larger than the truth table for " − " because we are now working with two different statements, *P* and *Q*. Each may have two truth values, so there are four possible combinations of truth values (2 times 2). The truth table must represent all the possible combinations: *P* and *Q* both true; *P* and *Q* both false; *P* true and *Q* false; *Q* true and *P* false. That is why it has four rows.

We now move on to *or*. With *and* we conjoin statements. With *or* we *disjoin* them. That is, we relate them as alternatives: one or the other is true. In a statement like "Either obesity is inherited or obesity is environmentally caused," two simpler statements are disjoined, and the resulting compound statement is called a *disjunction*. The symbol used in propositional logic for the *or* of disjunction is "∨", and "∨" is defined by this truth table:

P	Q	P∨Q
T	T	T
T	F	T
F	T	T
F	F	F

The disjunction, "*P* ∨ *Q*," is true when either one of the disjuncts (*P*, *Q*) is true. It is also true when both are true. The only case in which the disjunction is false is when both disjuncts are false. You can see this by looking at the bottom row. *P* is false, *Q* is false, and *P* ∨ *Q* is false. In all other rows the disjunction is true.

Now for the conditional. We have already discussed conditionals in this book, and we have seen that a conditional asserts neither its antecedent nor its consequent. Rather, it expresses a link between the two. For instance, the conditional statement "If Joe eats too much, he will get fat" says neither that Joe eats too much nor that he'll get fat. It says only that these two things are connected: *if* he eats too much, *then* he'll get fat. It asserts a conditional relationship between eating and getting fat; the second will follow on the first. We have already noted that an understanding of conditionals is very important in logic. But, unfortunately, the conditional relationship is more difficult to define precisely than denial, conjunction, and disjunction.

In propositional logic a symbol called the *horseshoe* (⊃) is used to express a minimal, but basic, meaning common to all conditionals. As we shall see later, the horseshoe does not coincide in all respects in meaning with the English *if then*, and for this reason people sometimes find it hard to understand. It is probably easiest, for the moment at least, to regard the horseshoe as a technical symbol invented by logicians for reasons of their own and simply learn it by learning the truth table. When we come to discuss the relation between English meanings and the propositional symbols in more detail, we'll explain why it is that the horseshoe is different from *if then* and related terms in some ways and nevertheless can be successfully used to symbolize many arguments in which such terms play a crucial role. It is most accurate to think of the horseshoe as a technical symbol that receives its meaning from the following truth table:

P	Q	P⊃Q
T	T	T
T	F	F
F	T	T
F	F	T

Be sure to learn this truth table. Since the horseshoe does not correspond too well to most people's logical instincts, you may not be able to figure this one out as you probably could the others.

Using the logical symbols just defined and using capital letters to represent simple statements, we can represent many arguments in an elegant and compact way. Here is an example:

Argument in English

Either the interest rates will fall or the unemployment rate will rise. If the interest rates fall, the value of the dollar will increase. If the unemployment rate rises, there will probably be a change of government at the next election. So either the value of the dollar will increase or there will probably be a change of government at the next election.

Formalization of Argument

Let I represent "The interest rates fall." Let U represent "The unemployment rate will rise." Let V represent "The value of the dollar will increase." Let G represent "There will probably be a change of government at the next election." The statements in the English argument can now all be represented using these letters and the symbols of propositional logic. The symbolized argument will be:

$I \vee U$
$I \supset V$
$U \supset G$
Therefore,
$V \vee G$

This is a very compact version of the original argument. Once the argument is formalized in this way, we can use a technique involving truth tables to test its deductive validity.

Another important matter pertaining to formalization is the matter of brackets. You are familiar with this, no doubt, from algebra and arithmetic. There is a great difference between the quantity $(30 + 42) \div 3$, and $(30) + (42 \div 3)$. Brackets make an important difference in symbolic logic too. They function much the way punctuation marks do in English—serving to indicate how things are grouped together. Suppose we wish to express in propositional logic the idea that a person may have either jello or ice cream, but not both, for dessert. We need to use the symbol for "not" so that it applies to the *conjunction*. We can do this as follows:

"You may have jello or ice cream, and not both" is rewritten as "You may have jello or you may have ice cream, and it is not the case both that you may have jello and that you may have ice cream," and that is symbolized as $(J \vee I) \cdot - (J \cdot I)$.

Look at the second set of brackets in this example. The symbol for "not" is placed outside the bracket because this symbol has the *scope* of applying to the entire expression within the brackets. If we had simply written:

WRONG: $(J \vee I) \cdot - J \cdot I$

the symbol "$-$" would deny only that we can have jello. What we wish to deny is that we can have both these delights at once. We need the brackets to indicate the scope of the negation. Similarly, we need brackets around the disjunction to indicate that the disjunction is simply between J and I, not between J and a longer formula.

Here are some further examples where bracketing is necessary:

> (a) If she is rich or intelligent, she has a good chance of getting the Liberal nomination in the electoral district.
> $(R \lor I) \supset G$
> The antecedent of the condition is the entire disjunction.

> (b) If the Republicans are anxious and the Democrats lack funds, then no one is ready for the next election.
> $(R \cdot L) \supset -S$
> (Here S represents "Somebody is ready for the next election.") The antecedent of the conditional is the entire conjunction.

Bracketing serves to group things just the way punctuation marks do in English. It is very important to get brackets right. Look at the English sentence to see the scope of negations and other relationships. An obvious, but handy, rule about brackets is that if you have used them properly, you will have an *even* number. Count your brackets: something has gone wrong if the total number turns out to be odd.

Testing for Validity by the Truth Table Technique

Let's begin by looking at a slightly fishy argument. It goes like this:

> If defense spending is cut, social service spending will increase. Defense spending is not going to be cut, so social service spending is not going to increase.

This argument is formally represented as:

> $D \supset S$
> $-D$
> Therefore,
> $-S$

In the symbolized version, D represents "Defense spending is going to be cut" and S represents "Social service spending will increase." The argument does seem a little strange. Is it deductively valid or not? Our logical intuition does not always tell us these things as clearly as we might like! We can represent the argument on a truth table and use a truth table technique to show conclusively that it is not a valid argument in propositional logic.

The argument contains two distinct statement letters, and so our truth table will have to have four rows. We represent the premises and the conclusion on our table. We calculate truth values for these for all the possible combinations of truth values in the component statements, D and S. Then we can check the argument for deductive validity. We have to make sure that in every row in the truth table in which all the premises come out as true, the conclusion comes out as true also. If there is any case where the premises are all true and the conclusion is false, the argument is not deductively valid in propositional logic. If we find just one case where the conclusion comes out false and the premises are all true, the argument is invalid in propositional logic.

Here is what the truth table looks like:[1]

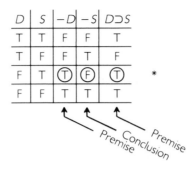

The premises are represented in the rightmost column and in the third column from the left. The conclusion is represented in the fourth column from the left. We check to see where the conclusion turns out to be false. This happens in the first row and in the third row. In the first row one of the premises is false, so the fact that the conclusion is false does not show that the argument is invalid. But in the third row, the conclusion is false and both premises (circled) are true. Thus there is a case in which the premises are true and the conclusion is false. *The argument is not deductively valid.*

The truth table test for deductive validity works for any argument that can correctly be expressed in the symbols of simple propositional logic. If you can do this, you construct a truth table showing all the premises and the conclusion. You then check to see whether there is any row in the truth table where all the premises are true and the conclusion is false. If there is, the argument is not valid. If there isn't, the argument is valid.

There are some convenient rules for constructing these truth tables. First, you need to know how many rows to have. If *n* represents the number of distinct statement letters in the argument, then you need 2 to the *n*th power rows. For two distinct statements, you need 2 times 2 rows; for three distinct statements you need 2 times 2 times 2 rows; for four distinct statements you need 2 times 2 times 2 times 2 rows, and so on. You do not consider a statement and its denial to be distinct statements for the purposes of this calculation because the denial is, technically speaking, a compound statement formed from the original statement. What matters are distinct statement letters. Second, in order for the truth table technique to work properly, you must represent on it all the possible combinations of truth values for the statements you are working with. The Ts and Fs in your columns have to be systematically set out in such a way that this requirement is met. Start in the leftmost column and fill half the rows with Ts. (That is, if the truth table has eight rows, fill the first four with Ts.) Then fill the other half with Fs. Then, in the next column, fill one-quarter of the rows with Ts, followed by one-quarter Fs, and repeat. In the third column (if there is one) it will be one-eighth Ts, Fs, Ts, and so on. This procedure is a standard one, which ensures that the truth tables will represent all the possibilities and that they will be set up in a standard way. (This procedure makes them easier to read and mark than random variations!)

To illustrate the construction of truth tables, suppose that you are setting up a truth table to represent an argument in which the premises and conclusion require four distinct statement letters: *S, C, H* and *G.* The first four columns of your truth table would look like this:

S	C	H	G
T	T	T	T
T	T	T	F
T	T	F	T
T	T	F	F
T	F	T	T
T	F	T	F
T	F	F	T
T	F	F	F
F	T	T	T
F	T	T	F
F	T	F	T
F	T	F	F
F	F	T	T
F	F	T	F
F	F	F	T
F	F	F	F

The next matter is how many columns your truth table needs. It needs at least one for each distinct statement letter, one for each premise, and one for the conclusion. In many cases inserting additional columns is helpful—for clarity and to avoid mistakes. For instance, if you have a premise of the form "$(P \cdot Q) \supset R$," you should have a separate column for "$P \cdot Q$," even if this is neither a premise nor a conclusion in the argument. The reason is that it is a significant component (antecedent of a conditional), and if you enter it separately in its own column, you are less likely to go wrong calculating the truth value of that conditional.

Here is a more complex example so that we can study the truth table technique further:

▬ Argument in English
The Iranian revolution will continue as a fundamentalist movement if there is not a surge of protest from the educated middle classes in Iran. If there is a surge of protest from the middle classes, then the security of the mullahs will be threatened and turbulence in Iran may grow to unprecedented extremes. We don't really expect further turbulence in Iran so it's reasonable to conclude that there will be no strong expression of discontent from the middle classes, and the fundamentalist governing faction will remain secure.

Formal Representation of the Argument
Let *S* represent "There is a surge of protest from the educated middle classes in Iran"; let *C* represent "The Iranian revolution will continue as a fundamentalist Muslim movement"; let *H* represent "The security of the

mullahs will be threatened"; let G represent "The turbulence in Iran may grow to unprecedented extremes." The argument may then be formally represented as:

$$-S \supset C$$
$$S \supset (H \cdot G)$$
$$-G$$
Therefore,
$$-S \cdot C$$

The number of distinct statement letters here is four. Thus we will need 2^4, or 16, rows in the truth table. We have to represent each premise and the conclusion. To avoid calculating errors, we will add columns for $(H \cdot G)$ and $-S$, which are components of premises.

The resulting truth table will look like this:

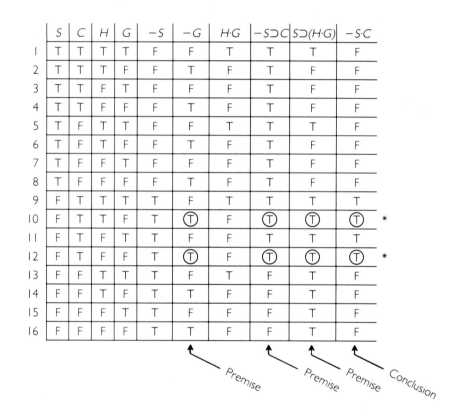

	S	C	H	G	−S	−G	H·G	−S⊃C	S⊃(H·G)	−S·C	
1	T	T	T	T	F	F	T	T	T	F	
2	T	T	T	F	F	T	F	T	F	F	
3	T	T	F	T	F	F	F	T	F	F	
4	T	T	F	F	F	T	F	T	F	F	
5	T	F	T	T	F	F	T	T	T	F	
6	T	F	T	F	F	T	F	T	F	F	
7	T	F	F	T	F	F	F	T	F	F	
8	T	F	F	F	F	T	F	T	F	F	
9	F	T	T	T	T	F	T	T	T	T	
10	F	T	T	F	T	Ⓣ	F	Ⓣ	Ⓣ	Ⓣ	*
11	F	T	F	T	T	F	F	T	T	T	
12	F	T	F	F	T	Ⓣ	F	Ⓣ	Ⓣ	Ⓣ	*
13	F	F	T	T	T	F	T	F	T	F	
14	F	F	T	F	T	T	F	F	T	F	
15	F	F	F	T	T	F	F	F	T	F	
16	F	F	F	F	T	T	F	F	T	F	

Premise   Premise   Premise   Conclusion

The columns for the premises and the conclusion are marked with arrows. There are twelve different rows in which the conclusion is false, but in *none* of these rows are all the premises true. This means that there is no case in which the premises are all true and the conclusion is false. In fact, the only rows in which all the premises are true are the twelfth and tenth rows. There the conclusion is true. The truth table shows that it is not possible for the premises to come out true and the conclusion false; that is, the argument is deductively valid. Whether the argument is cogent will depend, then, solely on the acceptability of these premises.

The truth table technique can be quite cumbersome for arguments with more than three distinct statement letters. But it is completely effective: it shows you reliably which arguments are deductively valid in simple propositional logic and which are not.

The Shorter Truth Table Technique

Because the truth table technique can be so clumsy when there are more than two or three distinct statement letters, it is convenient to have a shorthand version. The shorter technique is based on the fact that in order to discover by a truth table that an argument is invalid, we have to find a row on which the conclusion of the argument is false while all the premises are true. If we cannot find such a row, the argument is valid. To use the shorter technique, we set values of the component statements in such a way as to guarantee that the conclusion will be false. We then see whether we can consistently set values of the premise statements so that the premises turn out to be true. If so, the argument is invalid. If not, it is valid.

Suppose, for example, that we have the following representation of an argument:

$A \vee B$
$B \supset C$
C
Therefore,
$- A$

The conclusion is $-A$. For this conclusion to be false, A will have to be true. If A is true, the first premise, $A \vee B$, is true regardless of the truth value of B. The second premise can be made true by making B false and C true. Making C true makes the third premise true. All these stipulations are consistent with each other. They show that the conclusion could be false while all the premises are true. Hence the argument is invalid.

Here is another example:

$B \supset D$
$D \supset E$
$B \cdot A$
Therefore,
$D \cdot E$

For the conclusion to be false, at least one of D and E will have to be false. Let us suppose that D is false and E is true. Then, for the first premise to be true, B has to be false. The second premise will be true given that E is true and D false. The third premise, however, cannot be true, because we have already stipulated that B is false. So this possibility is ruled out. Another way of making the conclusion false is to make D true and E false, but to do so will immediately make the second premise false, so it does not give us a way of finding the conclusion false while all the premises are true. Alternately, we might stipulate both D and E to be false. But if we do so, we again find that B has to be false for the first premise to be true, and then B cannot be true for the third premise to be true. There is no possible way of making the conclusion false and the premises true. Hence, this argument is valid.

The shorter truth table technique can be very useful. You have to make sure that you check all of the ways in which the conclusion can be false, as we did in the last example. Also, it is of course necessary to assign truth values accurately and consistently to all the component statements for the technique to work as it should.

EXERCISE SET

Exercise One
Part A

Symbolize each of the following passages, using statement letters and the symbols "·", "−", "∨", and "⊃". Be sure to state which letters represent which English sentences. Example: "Joe skates and Susan swims" is symbolized as "$J \cdot S$", where J represents "Joe skates" and S represents "Susan swims."

1. Either Fred will make the basketball team or Joe will make the basketball team.

2. Joan is worried and Fred is upset.

3. If you have no appetite, your basic health is poor.

*4. Either Fred will come or Susan will come. If Fred comes, the outing will be a success, and if Susan comes, at least Joe will enjoy himself.

5. It is not true that human rights are widely respected in El Salvador.

6. If the president is not reelected, the national policy on hospital care may change.

*7. Dieting during pregnancy is not a good idea, and eating well at that time is particularly important.

*8. Both these things are true: extensive public relations efforts are being made on behalf of the nuclear industry, and these efforts are not convincing the public.

9. If the teacher is ill and her substitute is also ill, then school will be cancelled.

*10. If it is not the case that species are in danger of extinction, then wildlife foundations are not telling us the truth.

Part B

Symbolize each of the following simple arguments and test them for deductive validity using the truth table technique. Be sure to stipulate what your statement letters represent.

1. Either the behaviorists are right or the liberal humanists are right. Since it's been conclusively demonstrated that the behaviorists aren't right, it is the liberal humanists who must be right.

*2. Provided that you master calculus, you will have no difficulty with the mathematical aspects of first-year university physics. But really, you know, you have mastered calculus successfully. Thus the mathematical part of the physics course should go smoothly for you.

3. If the mind is entirely distinct from the body, there is no lessening of concentration due to fatigue. And yet fatigue does lessen concentration. We can infer from this fact that the mind is not entirely distinct from the body.

4. If oil prices increase, the western provinces will improve their economic situation, and if the western provinces improve their economic situation, easterners will move west for better jobs. Thus if oil prices increase, easterners will move west for better jobs.

5. An owl is reputed to be wise. If an owl is reputed to be wise, this belief shows that people use the word *wise* in a nonliteral way. Therefore, people use the word *wise* in a nonliteral way.

6. Either the murder was voluntarily committed or it was a compulsive action. If the murder was voluntarily committed, the murderer should be sent to jail. If the murder was a compulsive action, the murderer should be sent to a psychiatric institution. So the murderer should either be sent to jail or be sent to a psychiatric institution.

7. Either Canada is a superpower or it is a minor power or it is a middle power. Canada is not a superpower and it is not a minor power either. We can conclude that Canada is a middle power.

*8. If you are a suitable student of philosophy of science, you know either philosophy or science. You do not know philosophy and you do not know science. Therefore, you are not a suitable student of philosophy of science.

*9. If Trudeau exercises, he is in good shape. Trudeau is in good shape. So Trudeau exercises.

10. Either the disarmament meetings will be successful or the world will continue in peril of nuclear war. The world will continue in peril of a nuclear war, so the disarmament meetings will not be successful.

Part C

Represent the following arguments in letters and propositional symbols and test them for validity using the shorter truth table technique.

*1. If the United States subsidizes grain sales to the Soviet Union, then Canadian farmers will receive less for their grain. If Canadian farmers receive less for their grain, then some Canadian farmers will go bankrupt, and if some go bankrupt, Canadian taxpayers will be called upon to help support farmers. The United States is going to subsidize grain sales to the Soviet Union. So we can expect that Canadian taxpayers will be called upon to help support Canadian farmers.

2. Well-educated people should either know science or know literature. Since well-educated people should know science, they should not know literature.

*3. Both these things cannot be true: that nuclear weapons free zones are meaningless symbolic gestures and that nuclear weapons free zones hinder important alliances such as NATO. Therefore, either these zones are meaningful or they do not hinder alliances.

4. If the zoo is well administered, the animals are well cared for. If the animals are well cared for, some animals will reproduce in captivity. If some animals reproduce in captivity, we can expect that there will be baby animals at the zoo. There are some baby animals at the zoo. Therefore, the zoo is well administered.

*5. Either the murderer used a kitchen knife or the murderer carried an unusually large pocket knife. If the murderer carried an unusually large pocket knife, then either he was wearing loose clothing or he would have been noticed by the neighboring observers. The murderer was not noticed by the neighboring observers. If he was wearing loose clothing, either he was very thin or he was not wearing the clothing that was found at the scene of the crime. We know that the murderer was not wearing loose clothing and that he did not use a kitchen knife. Therefore, he was not wearing the clothing that was found at the scene of the crime.

Translating from English into Propositional Logic

So far we have used examples that are easy to put into symbols. But just as with categorical logic, where you sometimes have to do considerable manipulating to express statements correctly in categorical form, there are sometimes difficulties in expressing English statements in the symbols of propositional logic. We'll work through some of the common problems that arise in connection with the basic connecting symbols.

Not.   Let us suppose that you have decided to represent a particular English statement in an argument with the letter *P*. If you represent another English statement in that same argument as $-P$, the second statement must be the *contradictory* of the first. That is, it must always have the opposite truth value. It cannot merely be the contrary of the first statement. If a statement is true, its contrary must be false. However, it is possible for *both* a statement and its contrary to be false. A statement and its contrary would have the same truth value in this case: both would be false. Thus a contrary is quite different from a contradictory, which must have the opposite value. For instance, if *P* represents "Joe is fat," then $-P$ cannot be used to represent "Joe is thin." "Joe is fat" and "Joe is thin" are not contradictory statements. They need not have opposite truth values; they can both be false in the case that Joe is a person of normal build. Propositional logic is based on the idea that a statement and its contradictory must have opposite truth values. One or the other must be true. The symbol for *not* must serve to make a contradictory statement, not merely a contrary one.

And.   As it is represented and defined on the truth table, the symbol "·" carries no implication that the two statements that it conjoins have any real relationship to each other. That is, if *C* is "Colds frequently occur in winter" and *W* is "The Falklands War was very expensive," there is nothing wrong with "*C* · *W*" from a formal point of view.

The conjunction just asserts both the separate statements and is not supposed to suggest that there is any kind of connection between them. But in natural speech and writing we do not usually conjoin entirely unrelated statements. Usually we assert two statements, *P* and *Q*, together when we believe that they are related in some way. It is important to understand that this aspect of ordinary language is not reflected in propositional logic. Fortunately few arguments turn on this particular feature of *and* in English.

Occasionally in English and other natural languages the order of the components in a conjunction has significance. One conjunct will be stated first to imply a sequence in time. In such contexts, the word *and* is used in English to suggest "and then." For instance, if we say "They declared war and sent out the fleet," this way of speaking suggests that war was declared *first*. To say "They sent out the fleet and declared war" suggests that the fleet was sent out first. In diplomatic contexts, the difference between these two ways of expressing the conjunctions could be extremely important. Similarly "The doctor operated and she recovered" suggests that the operation came before the recovery and led to it, whereas, "She recovered and the doctor operated" suggests grounds for a malpractice suit! But these differences would not show up at all on a truth table. Both statements would be represented as the very same conjunction of facts, and they would come out as true and as false in all the same circumstances. We have to recognize, then, that "·" and the English *and* differ. The former *never* states a temporal relationship, and the latter sometimes strongly suggests one. In any argument or context where the suggested time sequence is important, "·" would not accurately represent *and.*

Another point to be noted is that "·" must be used to conjoin two statements. In English, the word *and* is often used this way. But it may also appear between two subjects and between two predicates, as in these examples:

1. Joe and Fred passed the final examination in university algebra.
2. Mary mowed the lawn and weeded the garden.

To symbolize these statements, you have to move *and* out of the subject or predicate and construct two simple statements, which you can then link with "·". Thus:

1. Joe passed the final examination in university algebra and Fred passed the final examination in university algebra. ($J \cdot F$)
2. Mary mowed the lawn and Mary weeded the garden. ($M \cdot W$)

Sometimes this simple strategy is not appropriate because it may be an important part of the meaning of the statement, in its context, that the subjects performed the activity *together*. For instance, when we assert that May and Fred got married, we are not simply asserting that May got married and Fred got married; we are asserting that they married *each other*. This fact will not be represented if we let *M* represent "May got married," and *F* represent "Fred got married," and then use "$M \cdot F$" to represent "May and Fred got married." There are other contexts, too, where the togetherness implied by *and* in English will be important to the force of an argument and cannot properly be omitted in the symbolization.

Here is a simple example:

3. I know that Joe and Fred are good friends. Last week they went swimming, played tennis, and worked on Fred's father's garden.

To establish that these two are friends, it will be relevant not just that they both did these things, but that they did them together. Thus we cannot appropriately represent the argument by conjoining simple propositions in which the subjects have been separated. We would have to do it like this:

> 3. I know that Joe and Fred are good friends. Joe and Fred went swimming. Joe and Fred played tennis. Joe and Fred worked on Fred's father's garden. Let S represent "Joe and Fred went swimming"; let L represent "Joe and Fred played tennis"; let G represent "Joe and Fred worked on Fred's father's garden." We have to keep the subjects together because the togetherness suggested by *and* in this context is important to the argument. The statements are represented as $S \cdot L \cdot G$.

Suppose you try to translate into the symbols of propositional logic a statement that uses *but* or *although*. We have seen that these words are frequently used to introduce counterconsiderations in an argument. In a statement like:

> 4. No Canadian peace group has ever advocated unilateral disarmament although peace groups are constantly criticized for advocating unilateral disarmament.

there is a conjunction asserted, but more is suggested as well. The conjunction that is asserted is as follows:

> 4. No Canadian peace group has ever advocated unilateral disarmament, and peace groups are constantly criticized for advocating unilateral disarmament. $-C \cdot A$ (where C represents "A Canadian peace group has advocated unilateral disarmament" and A represents "Peace groups are constantly criticized for advocating unilateral disarmament").

But the original statement, which uses *although* instead of *and*, says that there is a *contrast* between the two facts, $-C$ and A. It says that the first is surprising in view of the second; the second would run contrary to the first, in terms of our expectations, though they are in fact both true.

This element of *contrast* or *counterconsideration* is not represented by the "$\cdot$" of the truth table. The same point can be made about *even though, but, despite, yet,* and a number of other terms that commonly suggest contrast and introduce counterconsiderations. The truth table and the conjunction symbol in propositional logic represent only conjunction—pure and simple. Any emotional element of contrast or surprise is omitted. This omission means that in any context where the element is crucial to establishing a point, the symbols of propositional logic will not be fully adequate to express the point.

Or. The notable thing about "$\lor$" defined in the truth table is that it specifies what logicians call *inclusive disjunction*. An inclusive disjunction is one that is true when both disjuncts are true, as well as when either one of them is true. If you look at the truth table for "$\lor$", you will notice that on the first row, where P and Q are both true, the compound "$P \lor Q$" is also true. In this inclusive sense of *or*, a statement like:

> 5. Either the disarmament meetings will be successful or the world will continue in peril of nuclear war.

is true when *both* disjuncts are true. Suppose that the meetings are successful, but that the peril of nuclear war continues because the meetings involved only superpowers, whereas smaller countries getting nuclear weapons were not included. Statement (5) would be regarded as *true* in such a case. That is why Example 10 in the first exercise turned out to be an invalid argument, tested by a truth table technique. The inclusive *or* is standard in propositional logic. But in English and other natural languages, it is quite common to use and understand *or* and related words in an *exclusive* sense. We might easily take statement (5) as follows:

> Either the disarmament meetings will be successful or the world will continue in peril of a nuclear war. (not both)

The exclusive use of *or* implies that one and only one of the alternatives will hold. The inclusive *or* implies merely that at least one will hold. A restaurant menu telling you that:

> 6. Jello or ice cream is provided as a free dessert with your meal.

is not telling you that you are allowed to have both. Here *or* is used exclusively—as we know from our background knowledge about the frugality of restaurants! You couldn't draw up a truth table and insist on having both items for dessert!

You can express exclusive disjunction perfectly well using the symbols of propositional logic. Let's see how this works for the jello and ice cream case:

> Let *J* represent "You may have jello for dessert."
> Let *I* represent "You may have ice cream for dessert." The menu is stating:
> $(J \lor I) \cdot - (J \cdot I)$
>
> That is, it allows one or the other, *not both*.

The inclusive disjunction defined on the truth table for "∨" is standard in propositional logic. When you are symbolizing sentences in which *or* is the connective, use "∨"—that is, inclusive disjunction—unless you are sure that an exclusive disjunction is implied. In that case, you have to add *and not both* to capture the meaning.

The other point about "∨" is rather like our point about subjects and predicates linked by *and*. In ordinary speech and writing you often find *or* between subjects or predicates, as in the following:

> 7. John or Sue will help with the gardening.

and

> 8. Sue will either work in the garden or swim.

But just as "·" must link statements in propositional logic, so must "∨". Thus we have to rearrange the preceding examples, as:

> 7. John will help with the gardening or Sue will help with the gardening.
> $J \lor S$

> 8. Sue will work in the garden or Sue will swim.
> $G \lor W$

If Then. With regard to the relation between English and symbols, the *if then* symbol is the really difficult one. To get a fuller understanding of it, let us look again at the truth table that defines the horseshoe connective.

P	Q	P⊃Q
T	T	T
T	F	F
F	T	T
F	F	T

We said that "⊃", as defined on this truth table, was a *minimal conditional*. To see what this means, the first step is to recall that the *P* and *Q* on the truth table can represent any two statements at all. Let us stipulate that *P* represents "Argentina invaded the Falkland Islands in 1982" and *Q* represents "Stephen Jay Gould is the author of a book entitled *The Mismeasure of Man*." These two statements are both *true*. Obviously they are quite unconnected; each is quite irrelevant to the truth of the other. But using the horseshoe to connect *P* and *Q*, we will get the surprising result that the compound statement "*P* ⊃ *Q*" is *true*. If this is hard to believe, just look back at the truth table. On the row where *P* is true and *Q* is also true, *P* ⊃ *Q* is true; this is just how "⊃" is defined. It would be very peculiar to assert:

9. If Argentina invaded the Falkland Islands in 1982, then Stephen Jay Gould is the author of a book entitled *The Mismeasure of Man*.

Statement (9) here hardly makes sense; yet in symbolic logic the statement "*P* ⊃ *Q*" comes out to be true, when *P* and *Q* represent those statements that are components of (9). How can this be?

The answer is that the horseshoe and *if then* do not mean quite the same thing. The horseshoe is based on the core conditionality connection between *P* and *Q*: provided *P* is true, *Q* is not false. This conditionality can hold between any two statements, *P* and *Q*. Because it is so general, it does not require that *P* and *Q* have any further relationship to each other. In ordinary life, we are usually concerned with conditionals where there are further relationships between the statements. Because the horseshoe abstracts from these features, it can mislead us. We have to remember that it is the basic conditionality that the horseshoe represents—not anything more. (It may not reflect any causal dependence, for instance.) The horseshoe is very important in propositional reasoning because it mirrors a core of conditionality that can be very precisely defined on a truth table and related to the other propositional connectives.

To see puzzling aspects of the horseshoe, look at the two rows of the truth table where *P* is false. Remember again that *P* and *Q* can represent any two statements. This time let's allow *P* to represent "Argentina invaded Russia in 1981" and *Q* to represent "Santa Claus exists." Since both statements are in fact *false*, the combination "*P* ⊃ *Q*" turns out to be true. (Check the last row of the truth table to see that this occurs.) But we would never believe that:

10. If Argentina invaded Russia in 1981, then Santa Claus exists.

is true! It is entirely contrary to common sense. Whatever else is wrong with the Argentinian military, it has nothing to do with Santa Claus. There is just no connection. In fact, however, if you look at your truth table, you will see that just because of the way the horseshoe is defined, a statement of the form "*P* ⊃ *Q*" will be true whenever the Proposition *P* represents is false. The reason is that a statement of the form

"$P \supset Q$" is true when the statement Q represents is true and also true when the statement Q represents is false, which just means that it doesn't matter what statement Q represents and it doesn't matter what truth value that statement has; any false statement, P, will always give you "$P \supset Q$" as true.

There is a special technical term for conditional statements in which the antecedent is false. They are called *counterfactuals*. (The antecedent, being false, is contrary-to-fact.) Counterfactuals are, in fact, extremely important both in science and in ordinary life. It is often important to make claims about what would have happened or what would happen if conditions were different from what they are. The problem is that in science and in ordinary life we usually distinguish between counterfactuals, thinking that some are true or plausible and others are false or implausible. We don't regard all counterfactuals as equally true. Consider:

11. If Hitler had died in childhood, the Jewish population of Poland would be larger today than it is.

12. If Hitler had died in childhood, the theory of relativity would not be believed today.

We know, of course, that Hitler did not die in childhood. Both (11) and (12) are counterfactuals. But most of us would find (11) to be quite plausible, given Hitler's central role in the anti-Semitic campaigns of the 1930s and in the extermination of Jews. Most of us would also find (12) entirely implausible. This reaction indicates that we cannot represent the statements using the horseshoe. To do so, we would have to sacrifice our commonsense distinction between plausible and implausible counterfactuals, and this is too great a cost. In fact, logicians have been working on the problem of symbolizing counterfactuals for decades. Some have devised complex and original ways of expressing counterfactuals, but none of these are easy to master and none are agreed to be adequate by all students of the subject. The problem of counterfactuals is a very difficult one. We mention it here only to indicate why we have said that the horseshoe differs from *if then* and to show that counterfactuals should not be symbolically represented using the horseshoe.

The core of conditionality represented by the horseshoe can best be understood by looking back at the truth table for "$\supset$" and focusing your attention on the second line. This line says that for any two propositions P and Q, when P is true and Q is false, the horseshoe conditional "$P \supset Q$" is false. This relationship *does* always hold for conditionals in natural language. For instance, suppose someone tells you, "If you go on the Scarsdale diet for a week, you will lose five pounds." Suppose that you do go on the diet, and you don't lose five pounds. That will show that his conditional assertion was false, which is just what would be indicated if you represent it on the truth table. The second line of the truth table, specifying the conditions under which the horseshoe conditional is false, is absolutely essential. This aspect of the horseshoe lets us say that it represents a minimal element common to all conditionals. A conditional statement at least asserts that it won't turn out that the consequent is false while the antecedent is true.

It is just this minimal element of conditionals that is most basic for arguments because if we put the horseshoe between the premises and conclusion of an argument—as in "Premise and Premise $\supset$ Conclusion"—we will not be able to move from true premises to a false conclusion. This is what we are trying to avoid when we argue and infer—we don't want to proceed from truth to falsehood. Many arguments in which *if then* and related terms play the crucial role are set up in such a way that only this minimal core of the conditional is required for the argument to proceed. In these cases you can use "⊃" to represent *if then,* and it will give you the right results when you test the argument for deductive validity. However, this result will not usually be given for counterfactuals. Do not represent counterfactuals using the horseshoe.

EXERCISE SET

Exercise Two

Using "·", "⊃", "∨", and " − " and using capital letters to represent component statements, represent the following arguments in the terms of propositional logic. Where possible, test arguments for validity using the truth table technique or the shorter truth table technique, as you prefer.

1. If French philosophy continues to flourish in Canadian universities, there will be a pull away from formal logic and philosophy of science among Canadian graduate students in philosophy. If there is such a pull, traditional teaching patterns will be upset. And yet, you know, it is quite likely that the attraction that French philosophy has will persist. I conclude that we've got to expect some disturbance in traditional teaching patterns.

2. My brother is not a bald man, so my brother is a hairy man.

*3. The operation was not painful. Either the operation was painful or it was pleasant. So it must have been pleasant.

4. If July is rainy, there is really no summer. This year July was rainy, so there was no summer worth mentioning.

5. If science is entirely objective, then the emotions and ambitions of scientists have nothing to do with their pursuit of research. But the emotions and ambitions of scientists do have something to do with their pursuit of research. Therefore, science is not entirely objective.

6. If Joe makes the team, Fred will make the team. And if Fred makes the team, the team is sure to win. So if Joe makes the team, the team is sure to win.

7. Either it will snow or it will rain. If it snows, the roads will be slippery, and if it rains the roads will still be slippery. So whatever happens, the roads are going to be slippery.

*8. International politics is either a difficult academic subject or it is such a mishmash that nobody can understand it at all. If respected academics study international politics, then it is not just a mishmash no one understands. Respected academics do study international politics. So it is not a mishmash. It is a difficult academic subject.

9. The textbook is either accurate and boring or inaccurate and interesting. If the textbook is accurate, it will be widely used. And if it is interesting, it will be widely used. Thus, however things turn out, the textbook is bound to be widely used.

10. If women are drafted, wars will have to provide maternity leaves. If wars have to provide maternity leaves, war will become impossible. Therefore, if women are drafted, war will become impossible.

11. Either the United Nations will continue to function as it presently does, with its present financial and political problems, or the United States will agree to virtually subsidize the United Nations, despite having limited control over U.N. activities, or there will have to be a renegotiated basis for funding the United Nations. The United States will not agree to virtually subsidize the United Nations. The United Nations cannot just go on with the financial and political problems that presently exist. Thus there will have to be a renegotiated basis for U.N. funding.

12. If sex education is successful, children learn a lot about sex. If sex education is not successful, children don't learn much of anything. Since it's not good for children to learn a lot about sex, and it's also not good for them to learn nothing, sex education should be abolished.

13. If morality is entirely relative, torture is as virtuous as charity. But torture is not as virtuous as charity. Therefore, morality is not entirely relative.

14. If learning language is recognized as important, students will work hard to learn French, Spanish, and Chinese. Students are working hard to learn French, Spanish, and Chinese. Thus learning language is of recognized importance.

*15. If Socrates influenced Plato, and if Plato influenced Aristotle, then it would be true to say that at least indirectly, Socrates influenced Aristotle. Because Socrates did influence Plato and Plato obviously influenced Aristotle as well, we can see that there was at least an indirect influence of Socrates upon Aristotle.

16. If women are equal to men, then women are as strong as men. But women are not as strong as men. Therefore, women are not equal to men. If women are not equal to men, they have no proper claim to receive salaries as high as men's. But women should receive salaries as high as men's. So women must be equal to men. I conclude that women are both equal and not equal to men.

*17. If Iran wins its war against Iraq, the balance of power in the Persian Gulf area will be upset. If the balance of power in the Persian Gulf area is upset, then the United States will be progressively more tempted to accelerate the development of its Rapid Deployment Force. But if the development of the Rapid Deployment Force proceeds at an even faster pace than presently, world tensions will be aggravated. Thus, if Iran wins its war against Iraq, world tensions will be aggravated.

18. If the superpowers are going to bargain successfully about arms limitations, negotiators will have to communicate in a straightforward fashion. If negotiators take every statement as a political gesture, they do not communicate in a straightforward fashion. Thus if negotiators take every statement as a political gesture, the superpowers will not bargain successfully about arms limitations.

*19. If you go on a diet for more than two months, your metabolism will slow down. If your metabolism slows down, you will need less food than you do now. If you need less food than you do now, you will gain weight on what you eat now. Therefore, if you go on a diet for more than two months, eventually the result will be that you will gain weight on what you eat now. If dieting has the result of making you gain weight, dieting is futile. Thus, dieting is futile.

20. Either the economy will improve or there will be millions of unemployed young people. The economy will not improve, so there will be millions of unemployed young people. If there are millions of unemployed young people, there is bound to be social unrest. So if the economy does not improve, we can expect social unrest.

Further Points about Translation

Let's take another look at the first example from this second exercise:

> If French philosophy continues to flourish in Canadian universities, there will be a pull away from formal logic and philosophy of science among Canadian graduate students in philosophy. If there is such a pull, traditional teaching patterns will be upset. And yet, you know, it is quite likely that the attraction that French philosophy has will persist. I conclude that we've got to expect some disturbance in traditional teaching patterns.

This argument is a simple deductively valid one, and it can be shown valid on a truth table. But to represent the argument in the symbols of propositional logic in such a way that its deductive validity is apparent, we need to gloss over certain verbal and stylistic aspects. The correct representation of this argument in the symbols of propositional logic is:

> $C \supset A$
> $A \supset D$
> C
> Therefore,
> D

Here *C* represents "French philosophy will continue to flourish in Canadian universities," *A* represents "There will be a pull away from logic and philosophy of science among Canadian graduate students in philosophy," and *D* represents "There will be some disturbance in traditional teaching patterns." Notice that *C* is expressed in slightly different ways in the antecedent of the first and second sentences. Also, *D* is expressed in slightly different ways in the conclusion and in the consequent of the conditional in the second sentence. In formalizing this argument we have made decisions that slightly different English words are equivalent in meaning in this context.

This example illustrates the fact that when you are formalizing, you make *decisions* about what you think English sentences mean. You use the same letter to represent two verbally different expressions only when you think that these expressions are functioning to say the same thing. Determining whether these expressions are or are not equivalent can be difficult. But even learning to raise the question is an important step in getting meanings clear. You have to develop your sense for the nuances of language. Also, if your formalization results in some slurring over of slight differences in meaning, you should check back to see that the omitted aspects do not affect the merits of the argument you are dealing with.

Two common expressions that can be represented with the horseshoe seem tricky to many people. These are *only if* and *unless*. We shall explore these two expressions and then move away from this complex topic of translating from English into propositional symbols.

Only If.   Consider a sentence like this:

—— (1) Peter is eligible for medical school only if he has studied biology.

Let us allow *S* to represent "Peter is eligible for medical school" and *B* to represent "Peter has studied biology." Then the sentence as a whole can be represented, using the horseshoe, as follows:

—— $S \supset B$

Many people want to turn examples like this around (*B* $\supset$ *S: WRONG*). This turnaround is wrong because the original sentence states that studying biology is necessary for Peter to be eligible. This sentence means that given that he is eligible, it will be true that he has studied biology; otherwise, he would not be eligible. The turnaround representation, which is wrong, makes a necessary condition of eligibility into a sufficient one. It says that given that he has studied biology, he'll be eligible, which isn't right. The original statement said only that to be eligible he had to (at least) study biology; it didn't say that studying biology was enough for eligibility. (If you think about how hard it is to get into medical school, this point will probably be very obvious!)

A necessary condition is one that is needed or required. A sufficient condition is one that is enough to ensure a result. For instance, having oxygen is a necessary condition for human life, but it is not sufficient. On the other hand, having 3000 calories per day is a sufficient condition for adequate human nutrition, but it is not a necessary condition. (Less will suffice.)

Necessary condition.   We often find claims about conditions that are necessary for various states of affairs. Consider, for instance:

—— (i) For human beings, having oxygen is a necessary condition of being alive.

This claim can be symbolized using the horseshoe. Let H represent "Human beings are alive" and O represent "Human beings have oxygen." Then the relationship of necessary condition can be represented as:

───── $H \supset O$

To say that having oxygen is a necessary condition of being alive is to say that human beings are alive only if they have oxygen. Life requires oxygen. Thus, from the fact that humans are alive, we can infer they have oxygen. (If H and $H \supset O$, then O.)

Sufficient Condition.   Sufficient conditions are not the same as necessary conditions. Sufficient conditions for a state of affairs will, when they obtain, guarantee that that state of affairs exists. For example:

───── (ii) Striking a match in a room full of gasoline is a sufficient condition for igniting a fire.

Let S represent "Someone strikes a match in a room full of gasoline" and let L represent "A fire is ignited in a room full of gasoline." To say that S is a sufficient condition for L is to say that if S, then L, which, of course, is represented as:

───── $S \supset L$

in propositional logic. Given that the match is lit, conditions are sufficient for a fire, and there will be a fire. We should note that sufficient conditions may not be necessary. Lighting a match in a room full of gasoline is not a necessary condition for having a fire in that room, because we could get a fire in other ways—by leaving a lighted candle near a newspaper, for instance.

Necessary and sufficient conditions.   Some conditions are both necessary and sufficient for a given result. For instance, being a male parent is a necessary condition for being a father, and it is also a sufficient condition for being a father. Consider:

───── (iii) Joe's being a male parent is both necessary and sufficient for his being a father.

If we let J represent "Joe is a male parent" and B represent "Joe is a father," then we can represent this relationship as:

───── $(B \supset J) \cdot (J \supset B)$

Necessary and sufficient conditions are represented in a conjunction, as this example illustrates.

Unless.   Consider the statement "We will go on a picnic unless it rains." Clearly this statement is a compound one in which two simpler statements are connected. However, there is no symbol for *unless* in propositional logic. If we are to represent *unless* statements in propositional logic, we must use other symbols for *unless*. It turns out that *unless* can be represented perfectly well by combining symbols for *if then* and for *not*. The simplest way to do this is to rewrite the sentence in English, substituting the words *if not* for *unless*. Thus for:

───── (i) We will go on a picnic unless it rains.

we write:

───── (i') We will go on a picnic if it does not rain.

And we can represent (i′) using the horseshoe, as:

$$- R \supset G$$

where *R* represents "It rains" and *G* represents "We will go on a picnic."

The standard way of representing *unless* in propositional logic, then, is to replace it with *if not* and then use the horseshoe. The antecedent of the resulting conditional statement will be the denial of the statement that came after *unless* in the first place. Let us use this technique on another example:

(ii) You will not pass the course unless you work very hard and attend all classes regularly.

(ii′) You will not pass the course if you do not work very hard and attend all classes regularly.

Let *W* represent "You will pass the course"; *V* represent "You will work very hard"; and *A* represent "You will attend all classes regularly." What comes after *unless* in (ii) is a conjunction, and this whole conjunction has to be negated in (ii′). The resulting symbolization is as follows:

$$- (V \cdot A) \supset - W$$

This system for understanding *unless* in the symbols of propositional logic can be mastered quite easily. Usually this method is adequate. A statement written "*P* unless *Q*" *always* asserts at least that if not − *Q*, then *P*. But *sometimes* "unless" statements appear to assert more than this. This aspect of an extra meaning, which seems to appear in some contexts, is one of the things that makes *unless* very confusing. Here is an actual example, with some background to fill out the context. A scientist wrote to a Toronto newspaper mentioning that in 1816 in North America there was scarcely any summer. This statement was in the context of an ongoing discussion of global trends in climate: is the world getting warmer or colder? Another scientist wrote back, giving more specific information on snowfall patterns and temperatures in 1816. He added the statement that:

(iii) 1816 was not a bad year in North America unless you were a farmer.

According to the standard scheme for *unless*, we would represent this as follows:

(iii′) 1816 was not a bad year in North America if you were not a farmer.

Let *N* represent "You were a farmer in North America in 1816" and let *B* represent "It was a bad year in North America in 1816." Then the statement is formalized as follows:

$$- N \supset - B$$

However, this formalization may strike you as puzzling, for now the statement says merely that if you weren't a farmer in 1816, it wasn't such a bad year. And it would seem, intuitively, that the scientist must have been asserting something about what the year was like if you *were* a farmer. "It wasn't bad unless you were a farmer" would seem to mean that if you were a farmer, it was bad, and if you weren't a farmer, it wasn't bad. Only the second part of this meaning is represented in our formal version, which we completed using the rule for representing *unless*. The added implication, which does *seem* to be genuinely there, would be represented as follows:

$$N \supset B$$

If you are convinced that the scientist *was* making a claim that the year was bad for farmers, as well as saying that it wasn't bad for nonfarmers, you will want to represent (iii) as a *double conditional*, as follows:

$$(-N \supset -B) \cdot (N \supset B)$$

The question is: did the scientist *assert* that for farmers 1816 was a bad year? Or did he merely strongly suggest this by what he did assert—namely, that for nonfarmers it wasn't a bad year?

In deductive logic we formalize only those aspects of meaning that are *clearly asserted.* We omit aspects that are suggested. Our aim is to see what is and what is not deductively entailed by what is asserted. The word *unless* is one of many that can be puzzling in this connection, though, because it is hard to draw an absolutely firm line between what is *asserted* and what is *suggested.* Not surprisingly, this is one of those things philosophers and logicians sometimes dispute.

We have mentioned this problem about *unless* because in our experience many people sense this additional suggested (or asserted?) meaning and this causes them to make mistakes. For a rule of thumb, we suggest that the original way of representing *unless*, using *if not* will *always* give you the core meaning of *unless*. If, in a given context, you are absolutely convinced that the additional meaning is there as well, you can represent *unless* using the double conditional.

EXERCISE SET

Exercise Three

Represent the following passages in the formal apparatus of propositional logic and test arguments using the longer or shorter truth table technique.

*1. Elephants have been known to bury their dead. But elephants bury their dead only if they have a concept of their own species and understand what death means. If elephants understand what death means, they have a substantial capacity for abstraction. Therefore elephants have a substantial capacity for abstraction.

2. Swimming is an excellent form of exercise. If swimming is an excellent form of exercise, then swimming regularly will improve a person's general health. We can conclude that swimming will improve health.

*3. If Joe becomes more fit, Joe will become more physically attractive to women. Actually, Joe has become not more fit, but less fit. Therefore, Joe has become less physically attractive to women.

4. Peter cannot graduate in psychology unless he takes either developmental psychology or experimental design. If he does not take a course in experimental design, Peter will take developmental psychology. So if he does not graduate, Peter will take neither developmental psychology nor a course in experimental design.

*5. Unless there is real snow, the Winter Olympics in Calgary will not be a success. If there is no real snow, artificial snow will be produced. But if there is artificial snow, athletes will not be performing in good conditions. Therefore if there is no real snow, athletes will not be performing in good conditions.

6. Either there is no greenhouse effect problem, or, if there is a greenhouse effect problem, it is too late to solve the problem. If there is no greenhouse effect problem, there is no point in worrying about that problem. And if it is too late to solve the greenhouse effect problem, there is also no point in worrying about it. Thus there is no point in worrying about the greenhouse effect problem.

*7. Unless workers agree not to strike within the next decade, prospects for the recovery of the plant are dim. But unless management agrees to forego special parking and washroom privileges, workers will not agree not to strike. So there can be a recovery in the plant only if management does its part.

8. The French Canadian folk dance tradition includes many elements of traditional Irish dancing. If a tradition includes Irish elements, then either it will include a significant role for the jig step or it will include a great deal of solo dancing. French Canadian folk dancing does not have much solo dancing. So it must have considerable use of the jig step.

9. Only if there is a good real estate market can Smith hope to sell his house at a reasonable price. If he gets no suitable deal on the house, Smith will either rent it at some loss or declare personal bankruptcy. Declaring bankruptcy is pretty unacceptable for someone in Smith's position: Smith won't do it. The real estate market is terrible. Thus we can infer that Smith will rent his house at some loss.

10. Children will not be interested in reading unless schools supply them with interesting books. The books supplied in our schools are deplorably boring and simple-minded. They are not interesting. We can expect that our children will not be interested in reading.

11. Unless he is a saint, the preacher cannot spend all his time tending to the affairs of others. Unless he is a hypocrite, he cannot both advise others to devote themselves to the affairs of other people and fail to do this himself. The preacher is not a saint, but he does tell others that they should consume their entire lives in devotion to other people. Therefore, the preacher is a hypocrite.

*12. Morality has a basis only if there is a god. There is a god only if the world makes sense and is ordered. The world is ordered, so there is a basis for morality.

13. Either television programs will improve in quality and appeal or the large networks will lose their markets to videos. Since significant improvements are impossible, we can expect the large networks to experience losses.

14. The German Green Party must either broaden its platform or sacrifice voter appeal. If the party is to maintain its environmental orientation, it cannot broaden its platform. But if it sacrifices voter appeal by failing to broaden its platform, it will lose some of its influence in German politics. The choice, then, is between some relinquishing of the environmental orientation of the party and some loss of influence in German politics.

15. They say that if children learn to read before the first grade in school, they will not enjoy the first grade. But children who learn to read before the first grade often enjoy the first grade nevertheless. Therefore, the common theory that early learning will rob them of enjoyment is simply false.

16. If the problems in the North American economy are due to the demands of workers, then Japanese firms operating in North America will not be able to run profitably. But Japanese firms operating in North America do run profitably. Therefore, the problems are not due to the demands of workers. Problems of firms must be due either to workers or to management. So it is the fault of management.

17. The Nuclear Freeze movement must either radicalize its demands or risk being co-opted by the establishment. If the movement wishes to retain its wide appeal, it will not radicalize its demands. It does wish to retain its wide appeal, so it will risk being co-opted by the establishment.

18. If education is good, children will grow up retaining their love of learning. But education is not good as things presently stand, so children will not retain their love of learning.

Simple Valid Argument Forms

Working out validity in propositional logic does not have to be done by truth tables—long or short. You can learn to recognize some basic simple valid argument forms, and you can then show that the arguments that you have formalized are valid or invalid by referring to particular forms. Here are some of the simple valid argument forms with their standard names:

P; therefore, $-(-P)$.   Double negation

$P \supset Q$; P; therefore, Q.   *Modus ponens*

$P \supset Q$; $-Q$; therefore, $-P$.   *Modus tollens*

$P \supset Q; Q \supset R;$ therefore, $P \supset R.$　　Hypothetical syllogism

$P \lor Q; -P;$ therefore, $Q.$　　Disjunctive syllogism

$P \supset Q; R \supset S; P \lor R;$ therefore, $Q \lor S.$　　Constructive dilemma

$P \supset Q; R \supset S; -Q \lor -S;$ therefore, $-P \lor -R.$　　Destructive dilemma

$-(P \lor Q);$ therefore, $-P \cdot -Q.$　　De Morgan's rule (a)

$-(P \cdot Q);$ therefore, $-P \lor -Q.$　　De Morgan's rule (b)

It will be well worth your while to learn these simple valid argument forms. An easy way to begin is to test each one for validity by the truth table technique. This way you can prove to yourself that they are valid. In addition, you can amuse yourself by inventing arguments that exemplify each form. By learning the valid forms, you avoid the need to construct truth tables all the time. You can simply recognize many ordinary arguments as deductively valid because they are instances of *modus ponens, modus tollens*, disjunctive syllogism, or whatever the case may be.

Sometimes we find deductively valid arguments that proceed by making several valid moves in sequence. We can see that they are valid by seeing that, for example, if we first do *modus ponens* and then disjunctive syllogism, using the premises, we will arrive at the conclusion. This shows us that the conclusion can be validly derived from the premises by a series of steps, each of which is individually valid. This strategy is the basis of proof techniques in more advanced formal logic. To get an idea of how it works, consider the following example:

Either he will complete his new play or he will achieve success as a political activist. But there is just no way that he can accomplish both. If he completes his play, it will surely be produced, and if he achieves success as a political activist, he will be known across the country. Since the production of the play will also bring fame, he is bound to be known across the country.

C = He completes his new play.
W = He will achieve success as a political activist.
R = His play will be produced.
K = He will be known across the country.
(We assume that "The production of a play also brings fame" may be represented as "$R \supset K$" in this context.)

The argument may be formally represented as:

1. $(C \lor W) \cdot -(C \cdot W)$
2. $C \supset R$
3. $W \supset K$
4. $R \supset K$
Therefore,
K

The argument is deductively valid, and this may be shown without a truth table. We show how we can get to the conclusion from the premises, using deductively valid moves:

5. $C \supset K$. From (2) and (4) by Hypothetical syllogism.

6. $K \lor K$. From (3) and (1) and (5) by Constructive dilemma.

But line (6) really just asserts our intended conclusion, *K*. In order for it to be true, either *K* is true or *K* is true. That is to say, *K* is true.

    7. *K*. From (6), as explained.

Thus we see how an argument can be shown to be deductively valid by proving the conclusion from the premises in a series of steps. At each step we appeal to a deductively valid argument form. This procedure is more satisfying intellectually and more efficient—in terms of amount of writing—than using truth tables. But it does have one deficiency, theoretically speaking. You don't know the argument is invalid just because you fail to derive the conclusion. You could fail either because you lack sufficient ingenuity or because the argument is invalid. For simple propositional arguments, a truth table test for validity will always show you whether the argument is valid or invalid. It is very important to note the difference between proving an argument valid and failing to do so. If you succeed in constructing a proof in which the conclusion is derived by a series of individually valid steps, then the argument is deductively valid. This proof means that there can be only one thing wrong with it: the premises might be unacceptable. An argument you can prove valid is valid, and the premises lead deductively to the conclusion. *But if you can't find a proof, this doesn't mean the argument is invalid.* It might be invalid. But also you simply may not have found the right proof strategy yet.

The truth table technique does have the advantage that it will always show you whether the argument is valid or not. The only problem is that it can be rather cumbersome and involved.

An important valid argument form not mentioned on our original list is the *reductio ad absurdum*. The name is taken from the Latin and means "reduction to absurdity." In this kind of argument the premises are "reduced to absurdity" because it is shown that they lead to a contradiction. They entail some proposition of the form of "$P \cdot -P$," and no such proposition can be true. (If you don't believe this, construct a truth table for yourself, and you'll see how it works out.) If the conjunction of the premises of an argument entails a contradiction, then those premises contain an inconsistency. One or more of the premises must be false. You can use a *reductio ad absurdum* argument to prove a proposition if you start by denying that proposition and then manage to show that its denial leads to a contradiction. Such an argument would go something like this:

    1. Suppose that $-P$.
    2. Show that $-P \supset (Q \cdot -Q)$.
    3. But $-(Q \cdot -Q)$. (Because that proposition is a contradiction)
    4. $--P$. From (3) and (2) by *modus tollens*
    5. *P*. From (4) by double negation

Sometimes people use the term *reductio* in a looser sense to describe arguments in which a supposition is refuted when it is shown that the supposition implies something false or absurd. This sense was described, in fact, in Chapter Five, when the acceptability of premises was discussed. In the strict formal logic sense, however, the *reductio ad absurdum* form requires that the premises are shown to lead to an explicit inconsistency.

We have noted *modus tollens* and *modus ponens* as two valid argument forms in propositional logic. Both are very basic in human thinking. There are two *invalid* kinds of arguments that are relatively common and are deceptive because they are so easily confused with *modus ponens* and *modus tollens*. These are:

——— (1) Invalid move: Affirming the consequent:
$P \supset Q; Q$
Therefore,
P.

(2) Invalid move: Denying the antecedent:
$P \supset Q; -P$
Therefore,
$-Q$.

Actually, in previous exercises, you have already tested examples that had these forms. Both formal fallacies are relatively common: it is worth learning the names and checking these out for yourself on a truth table so that you see that they are, indeed, invalid argument forms. Other invalid moves have no special names, probably because they are not quite so common as these two.

EXERCISE SET

Exercise Four

Represent each of the following arguments in the symbols of propositional logic if appropriate. In any example where you believe that the propositional symbols would not capture aspects of meaning crucial to the way the argument works, say why not, and proceed no further. Test symbolized arguments for deductive validity, using either valid inference patterns and a simple proof procedure or the longer or shorter truth table technique. For those arguments that turn out to be deductively valid, discuss whether the premises used are acceptable. (Remember: deductive validity is not *sufficient* for cogency of argument.)

1. If complex technology leads to occasional bizarre accidents, then complex technology sometimes has unpredictable effects. Complex technology does lead sometimes to bizarre accidents. Therefore, it sometimes has unpredictable effects.

2. Mankind could not understand the natural world unless human beings were equipped with an efficient set of categories in the brain. Mankind does understand the natural world. So it must be true that we are equipped with an efficient set of categories in the brain.

*3. "George Santayana's statement that 'to be happy you must be wise' makes a lot of sense. But one doesn't need to be a formal logician to see the fallacy in Richard J. Needham's conclusion that if you're no happier now than you were ten years ago, this means you're no wiser.

"Santayana doesn't claim that wisdom is the only condition required for happiness, and in fact it often causes just the reverse. Has Mr. Needham never had an experience that left him 'sadder but wiser'?"
(Letter to the editor, Toronto *Globe and Mail*, January 18, 1982.)
Can you formalize Santayana's original claim? Can you formally represent the claim that columnist Needham inferred from it? The writer is implying that Needham made a faulty deductive inference. Test to see whether he is correct.

4. Understanding is impossible if words refer only to private sensations in the minds of speakers. Since we clearly do understand each other, words are not just references to private sensations.

5. If a man has a son, that man is a father. John is a father, so he must have a son.

6. If the world food crisis is solved then either rich nations will voluntarily share their food with poor nations or poor nations will force the world economy to provide them with more. Rich nations will not voluntarily share their food with poor nations. Thus, if the world food crisis is solved, the poor nations will force the world economy to provide them with more.

7. If people could reason only after someone taught them the logic of the syllogism, then there would have been nobody reasoning before Aristotle discovered the logic of the syllogism. There were people reasoning before Aristotle discovered syllo-

gistic logic. Therefore, it is not the case that people can reason only after someone has taught them syllogistic logic.
(Adapted from John Locke's "Essay Concerning the Human Understanding" (New York: Meridian, 1964).)

8. "I do know that this pencil exists, but I could not know this if Hume's principles were true. Therefore Hume's principles are false." (G. E. Moore, "Hume's Theory Examined," in *Some Main Problems of Philosophy* [New York: Collier Books, 1953].)

9. If perfect ideal communism exists anywhere, then there is complete equality of resources among persons in that society. There is no such thing as perfect ideal communism. Therefore there is no complete equality of resources among persons in a society.

*10. *Background:* Some sentences in the following passage have been slightly shortened to make your task easier:

"Either human actions are entirely governed by causal laws or they are not. If they are, then they are necessary. That is, given our heredity and environment we could not act otherwise than as we do. If they are not, then they must occur by chance. If they occur by chance, they are not necessary. But equally we have no control over them. In neither case can we help ourselves."
(A. J. Ayer, "Fatalism," in *The Concept of a Person* [London: Macmillan, 1963].)

*11. "(T)he arrival of nuclear weapons in the world had at a strike opened a fissure down the center of human life, placing whole realms of human existence at odds with one another. The traditional demands of man's international political existence, rooted in sovereignty and pursued through the use of force, were suddenly at variance with the demands of man's existence pure and simple."
(Jonathan Schell, *The Abolition* [New York: Avon Books, 1984], p. 47.)

12. Although people are commonly held responsible for being overweight and although discriminating against people on the grounds that they are fat and unattractive is about the only form of discrimination still thought to be morally respectable in North America, there is increasing evidence that, in fact, many fat people simply cannot help being fat.

13. If astral projection is possible, then people can project themselves up to a book on a very high shelf and read the title. If astral projection is reliably verified, then people can project themselves up to read in this way and have the event verified by a friend. But people cannot read titles in this way with friends there to verify the event. Therefore astral projection is not possible.

*14. The group will be successful and fun only if all members participate willingly. Members will participate willingly only if they have a say in top-level decision-making. Members do have a say in top-level decision-making, so the group will be a success.

15. If children are well trained before the age of five, they seldom lapse into delinquency after the age of five. If women work outside the home, then children will be well trained before the age of five only if daycare centers and kindergartens are extremely well run. Women do work outside the home. Thus either we have extremely well-run childcare facilities or we risk delinquency in our children.

16. If the Liberals gain in Alberta's provincial politics, either the Conservatives will lose or the New Democrats will lose. If the Liberals gain, it will not be the Conservatives who will lose, because people who might vote Liberal are not those who would typically vote Conservative. Therefore, a Liberal gain in Alberta would mean a New Democrat loss.
(*Hint:* Four distinct statement variables are necessary.)

17. Either Peter will attend Harvard or Peter will attend Stanford. If Peter attends a university of high reputation, his prospects in later life will be good if he works very hard to do well. Both Harvard and Stanford are universities of high reputation. Peter is bound to work hard, so his prospects in later life will be good.

18. If the artificial intelligence program is feasible, the human mind is nothing but a very complex machine. However, the artificial intelligence program is not feasible—not at all. Therefore, the human mind is not merely a very complex machine. It is something much more.

Concluding Comments

Formal logic is a highly developed technical discipline that we barely introduced in this book. Because our emphasis is on developing practical skills, we stressed issues of translation and application at the same time as we developed simple formal techniques.

As we noted a number of times, the *deductive validity* of an argument says nothing about the truth or acceptability of its premises. If an argument is deductively valid, then the (RG) conditions of argument adequacy are fully met. But the (A) condition may or may not be satisfied. It's useful to remember this simple point, because a clearly worded deductively valid argument has a kind of logical flow to it that makes it very convincing and sometimes distracts our attention from the fact that the charming reasoning used is based on false or dubious premises. For mental exercise and in the course of speculation, it is often very interesting to see that from P and Q we can deductively derive a further consequence, R. But usually this relationship is of little interest in establishing the conclusion unless P and Q are premises we are willing to accept.

The flaw of a dubious premise, serving as the basis for impeccably accurate deductive reasoning, seems to be particularly prevalent in dilemma arguments. These arguments (which, as you will recall, open with a disjunctive premise) are common in debate and in ordinary life. They often appear irrefutable. But the valid form of a dilemma too often serves only to mask the fact that the disjunctive premise on which it is based is false or unacceptable.

Here is an example of a deductively valid dilemma, which is nevertheless not a sound argument because of a flawed premise:

> Either the interest rates will come down or there will be a world disaster. In either case I won't have to worry about selling my house. If there is a world disaster, the social fiber of life will be destroyed and selling the house will be no problem. And if there is a fall in interest rates it will be easier for people to buy houses, and selling my house won't be a problem. Although the house isn't selling at the moment, I really have nothing to worry about.

The argument begins with a premise that states a false dichotomy. A false dichotomy is a disjunction between two things that are falsely thought to exhaust the possibilities. For instance, "A man is handsome or he is ugly" is a false dichotomy since there are other alternatives—looking moderately attractive, slightly unattractive, and so on. For the disjunctive premise of the argument to be true, there would have to be only two possible courses for world history: that in which there is a world disaster and that in which interest rates come down. If there is even one other possibility, the premise cannot be rationally accepted. (Check back to the truth table for disjunction if you don't understand why.) If you bear this in mind and look closely at the premise, you will see that it is very questionable. No one could be in a position to know that interest rates coming down and there being a world disaster are the *only* two possible futures for our world!

Criticizing dilemma arguments in this way is such a common move that it has a special name. The critic is said to have "escaped through the horns of a dilemma." She does this by showing a third alternative—by showing that the opening disjunction was not exhaustive, so that the argument was based on a false dichotomy. This sort of problem, which frequently arises with dilemmas, is a nice illustration of the general point that arguments that are "perfectly logical" in the formal sense may nevertheless be flawed because they have unacceptable premises.

A further basic point about propositional logic is that it is not *always* the appropriate tool to use in appraising an argument. It is the appropriate tool only when the connection between the premises and conclusion depends on the way in which statements are combined using the basic propositional terms: *or, and, not,* and *if then.* If the force of an argument depends on deductive relations between other terms, or on an analogy, or on empirical evidence for a broader empirical hypothesis, then the argument cannot be properly evaluated by applying the tools of propositional logic. When you represent such arguments in propositional logic, you will no doubt find that they are not valid. However, since your symbolization in such cases will not properly reflect the meaning and direction of the original natural argument, this discovery will be of little importance. Propositional and categorical logic are very basic and important parts of deductive logic. But they do not apply to all arguments. Hopefully you will have discovered this fact already in some of the exercises for this chapter.

The real usefulness of the basic formal tools we have learned comes when we do find arguments to be valid according to the rules of categorical or propositional logic. If they are valid, then there can be no question as to the adequacy of grounds and their relevance to the conclusion. Any question about the merits of the arguments must concern the premises themselves. This is a discovery well worth making.

Review of Terms Introduced

> *Propositional logic:* That part of logic which deals with the relationships holding between simple propositions or statements and their compounds. In propositional logic, the basic logical terms are *not, or, and,* and *if then.*

> *Denial of a statement:* A statement's contradictory or negation. It must have the opposite truth value to the statement. The denial of a statement S is symbolized as $-S$ (not S).

> *Conjunction of statements:* A compound statement in which all the statements are asserted, linked by *and* or an equivalent term. For the conjunction to be true, each component statement or conjunct must be true. The conjunction of statements P and Q is written as $P \cdot Q$.

> *Disjunction of statements:* A compound statement in which the statements are asserted as alternatives. For the disjunction to be true, at least one of the disjoined statements must be true. The disjunction of statements P and Q is written as $P \vee Q$.

> *Inclusive disjunction:* A disjunction that is true if one or both of the disjoined statements is true. The symbol "$\vee$" in propositional logic is used to represent inclusive disjunction.

> *Exclusive disjunction:* A disjunction that is true if one of the disjuncts is true but false if both are true. An exclusive disjunction of statements P and Q is represented "$(P \vee Q) \cdot -(P \cdot Q)$."

> *False dichotomy:* A disjunctive statement, with two disjuncts, that can be known to be false because we can see that the disjuncts do not exhaust the possibilities and are not the only alternatives.

> *Conditional statement:* A statement of the form "if P, then Q." As such it does not assert either P or Q. Rather, it asserts a connection between them in the

sense that provided *P* is the case, *Q* will be the case also. Example: "If Joe eats too much, he will get fat" is a conditional statement asserting a relationship between Joe's eating too much and Joe's getting fat. It does not assert either that he does eat too much or that he will get fat, only that if the one happens, so will the other.

Horseshoe: A connective written as "⊃", used in propositional logic to represent basic conditional relationships. A statement of the form "*P*⊃*Q*" is defined as false if *P* is true and *Q* false, and true otherwise.

Counterfactual: A conditional statement in which the antecedent is known to be false. Example: If Hitler had been murdered when he was twenty, the Second World War would not have occurred.

Necessary condition: A condition that is required for another statement to be true. Using the horseshoe, if *Q* is a necessary condition of *P*, we symbolize as "*P* ⊂ *Q*". To say that *Q* is a necessary condition of *P* is to say that *P* will be true only if *Q* is true.

Sufficient condition: A condition that is enough to establish a further statement as true. Using the horseshoe, if *Q* is a sufficient condition for *P*, we would symbolize it as "*Q*⊃*P*." To say that *Q* is sufficient for *P* is to say that, given *Q*, *P* will be true as well.

Modus ponens: A valid argument form, in which from "*P*⊃*Q*" and *P*, we may infer *Q*.

Modus tollens: A valid argument form, in which from "*P*⊃*Q*" and − *Q*, we may infer − *P*.

Affirming the consequent: An invalid form of inference of the type "*P*⊃*Q*; *Q*; therefore, *P*."

Denying the antecedent: An invalid form of inference of the type "*P*⊃*Q*; − *P*; therefore, − *Q*."

NOTES

1. Strictly speaking, letters that represent particular statements should not appear at the top of columns on truth tables because the truth table allows for two different truth values for every statement letter. To avoid two levels of symbolization, this matter is ignored here, as it is in many other texts.

10

Analogies: Reasoning from Case to Case

In this chapter we shall study various ways in which analogies are used in arguments and in the more general pursuit of knowledge. Also we offer some strategies for grasping the basic structure of an analogy and arriving at a sound critical assessment. Some logicians regard all analogies as merely rhetorical devices—a technique you can use to interest or arouse your audience, but a technique with no logical value or importance. This view is not the one taken in this book. We try to present analogies to emphasize the important role they often play in the administration and development of human policies, and in the grounding of beliefs about phenomena that cannot be studied directly. Nevertheless, it is true that there are many very loose analogies, and these provide only the shakiest base for arguments. Perhaps by concentrating on these faulty analogies, some logicians have been led to dismiss all analogies as logically useless. Here we work on understanding two different kinds of sound analogies, and then we go on to examine some bad arguments based on misusing analogies in one way or another.

The Nature and Functions of Analogy

As we have seen earlier (Chapters Four and Six), arguments by analogy draw a conclusion about one thing by comparing it closely with another. It is convenient to call the central topic—the one dealt with in the conclusion—the *primary subject*, and the case with which it is compared, the *analogue*. In the following unforgettable analogy by C. S. Lewis, the primary subject is the striptease, as it exists in our culture, and the analogue is the unveiling of a mutton chop, as this might exist in an imagined alternative culture:

> *You can get a large audience together for a strip-tease act—that is, to watch a girl undress on the stage. Now suppose you came to a country where you could fill a theatre simply by bringing a covered plate onto the stage and then slowly lifting the cover so as to let everyone see, just before the lights went out, that it contained a mutton chop or a bit of bacon, would you not think that in that country something had gone wrong with the appetite for food?*[1]

Lewis uses our reaction to the analogue to develop a reaction to the primary subject. In the analogous case, we would certainly think that the natural human desire for food had been warped in some way. By drawing an analogy between this case and the case of striptease, which actually exists, he urges us to conclude that our sexual desires in this culture are somehow warped. The argument by analogy uses one case (usually agreed-upon, and familiar to the audience) to illuminate another (usually less familiar). The basis for drawing the conclusion is the relevant similarity between the cases.

In this book we concentrate on analogy as a device in argument, but analogies have many other functions as well. They are of great use in teaching—an analogue may be familiar whereas the primary subject is unfamiliar. Or an analogue may be concrete, whereas the primary subject is abstract. Analogies are a common and important device in explanations; they may also be used to illustrate points, or even simply to make a speech or an essay more interesting. Albert Einstein used an analogy to *explain* how the energy in mass, which is so enormous, could have gone undetected by physicists until the twentieth century. He said:

> It is as though a man who is fabulously rich should never spend or give away a cent; no one could tell how rich he was.[2]

Here the primary subject is the energy within matter, and the analogue is the unspent money of the rich man. Einstein is not trying to demonstrate any conclusion about the energy in matter by this analogy; he is trying, rather, to make the notion of trapped energy intelligible to people who are not familiar with it but would certainly understand the analogue. Einstein's analogy, then, was explanatory, not argumentative.

Many of the claims we shall make about criticizing analogies apply to explanatory and illustrative analogies just as well as they do to the argumentative analogies. For instance, if there is a relevant difference between *A* and *B*, so that an argument using *B* as an analogue would be poor basis for a conclusion about *A* as a primary subject, then the same difference would also mean that an explanation of *A* based on the same comparison would be a poor explanation. Also, in the circumstances, an illustration of *A* based on *B* would be a misleading illustration. Thus, even though we concentrate here on analogies as they appear in arguments, the themes do have a broader application.

Analogy and Consistency

Treating similar cases similarly is a fundamental aspect of rationality. It is by drawing analogies—seeing important similarities and differences—that we determine which are similar cases and which are not. Any application of a general principle or rule—whether in logic, morality, law, or administration—requires that we determine which cases are *relevantly similar* and merit similar treatment. This is one way we can see just how fundamental reasoning with analogies is.

In propositional logic we can prove that a contradiction, a statement of the type "*P* and not–*P*," is never true. If you represent a statement of this type on a truth table, you will see that its column is composed entirely of Fs. One way of being consistent is to avoid asserting or believing statements that are contradictions or that entail contradictions. But this is not the only kind of consistency essential to the rational life. You can be inconsistent by treating similar cases differently—that is, by criticizing in one person behavior you approve in someone else, or by demanding a stiff sentence for one first-time offender while urging probation for another in similar circumstances. If there is agreement that a particular case merits a particular treatment, then consistency demands that relevantly similar cases receive the same treatment. Often agreed-upon cases are used as the basis for arguments to conclusions about disputed cases. The agreed-upon cases serve as the analogues, and on the basis of similarities, one can defend conclusions about the disputed cases. Such arguments depend on the force of consistency—similar cases should be treated similarly.

In fact, this form of argument is common in logic itself. Occasions may arise when we wish to evaluate an argument and we are not certain what to say about it. One technique that may be used is to find a relevantly similar argument on which the verdict is clear and reason from the clear case to the disputed case. The technique of refutation by logical analogy is based on this procedure.

Refutation by Logical Analogy.   You can sometimes show an argument to be a poor one by comparing it with another argument that is obviously poor. If the two arguments can be shown to be relevantly similar, then the logical analogy between them will show that both are poor. If you can do this, you have refuted the first argument using a *logical analogy* or, as it is sometimes called, a *parallel case*. To see how this works, consider this simple example:

First Argument
1. If Jane Fonda exercises, she is fit.
2. Jane Fonda is fit.
So,
3. Jane Fonda exercises.

We can formalize this particular argument, as a matter of fact, and we could easily show it invalid by using the truth table technique. But a nonformal technique may be used if we develop a logical analogy such as:

Parallel to First Argument
1. If Mother Theresa is the richest woman in the world, then Mother Theresa is a woman.
2. Mother Theresa is a woman.
So,
3. Mother Theresa is the richest woman in the world.

We know that this parallel argument is invalid because both its premises are true and its conclusion is false. We can use this fact to show that the first argument is invalid, arguing as follows:

1. The first argument is like the parallel argument in the basic structure that connects its premises to its conclusion.
2. The parallel argument has true premises and a false conclusion.
3. The parallel argument is an invalid argument.
Therefore,
4. The first argument is an invalid argument.

Provided that we have correctly identified the common structure shared by the arguments, this reasoning about the two arguments conclusively shows that the first argument is invalid. As far as structure is concerned, the first argument is just like another argument that is invalid; therefore, it is invalid.

If we know propositional logic, we do not need the logical parallel technique to find out whether the argument about Jane Fonda is valid. It is an example of affirming the consequent, and we could easily prove it invalid by using the truth table technique. But the parallel case technique is extremely valuable in other cases. Many arguments do not depend on basic logical terms such as *and, or, not,* and *if then* in order to draw the connection between premises and conclusion. They may depend on other terms that do not appear in formal systems, such as *cause, property, important, parent, deter,* and so on.

Here is an example in which this technique was used to good effect by a newspaper columnist. The columnist was criticizing a comment by Alberta's energy minister, who had said that since Alberta possessed valuable hydrocarbon resources, it would be silly for the province to develop solar or wind energy. The columnist imagined an ancient character objecting to the development of oil and gas resources in 1914:

> *Puffing reflectively on his pipe, he said, "Mark my words. No good will come of this." He said it quite a lot, leaning back in a chair on the front porch of his livery stable.*
>
> *Of course, anyone who paused to listen stayed to mock, but Max stuck to his guns. "Oil?" he'd say. "What for? We'd look pretty stupid if we came up with anything that reduced the value of our horse resources."*
>
> *"Alberta is the horse capital of Canada," he'd continue. "Are we supposed to dig up gasoline for the Easterners so they can tell us what we can do with our horses? They'd like that, all right, but why should we oblige them?"*[3]

Here the parallel focuses our attention on the basic structure of the minister's argument. The minister was saying, in effect, that if something is useful and profitable now, and if some other prospective development could replace that thing, then the prospective development should be abandoned. The columnist's entertaining parallel points out just how silly the original argument is by showing that it is essentially the same argument as one that could have been used to prevent the development of the very hydrocarbon resources the minister was trying to protect.

Many people who have never studied logic have the ability to construct parallel arguments revealing the logical flaw in a primary argument. This technique of logical analogy brings out the basic connection of the primary argument and shows that, in the analogue argument, the connection does not hold. Refutation of an argument by this method is based on the insistence that we proceed consistently, treating similar cases similarly. If two arguments are fundamentally similar and one is silly, then the other is silly also.

The connection on which an argument is based must hold up for all parallel cases if that argument is to be a good one. If there is a parallel case in which the connection does not work, then it is not a reliable connection, and the original argument fails. The whole trick here, though, is to get the parallel just right. If the two arguments are relevantly similar, and the second is poor, the first is poor. The real question is just when they are relevantly similar and when they are not. To construct a refutation by logical analogy, we need to distinguish between those features of an argument that are incidental to its working and those that are crucial. This is something many people— including even small children—can do quite naturally. But it is not a skill that can be mechanically developed the way formal procedures in logic can be.

Ethics, Law, and Treating Similar Cases Similarly.   The demand for consistency is the basis of many forceful and important moral arguments. These arguments work by bringing an undisputed case to bear on a disputed or problematic case. The claim is made that the cases are relevantly similar and, for example, that since the analogue is known to be evil, the primary subject is evil also. This way of reasoning from one case to another is often important in reasoning about values. Jesus used the technique, implicitly, when he said that a man who lusts after a woman has "already committed adultery with her in his heart." Jesus was drawing an analogy between lustful desire and actual adultery in an attempt to get his followers to extend the disapproval they already felt for adultery to lustful thoughts as well. If you are convinced that the lustful desire and the adulterous behavior are relevantly similar, you will apply the valuation you already make of adulterous behavior to lustful thoughts.

This technique was used by Dr. Joyce Brothers when she replied to an anxious reader who said, "My problem is that my husband doesn't want to have children because I underwent therapy before we were married and my husband is afraid that my emotional troubles will be passed on to my child." Brothers replied with an analogy:

> When is society going to come out of the dark ages and recognize that mental or emotional problems should be no more stigmatizing to an individual than a case of German measles or pneumonia? We do not shun those who have suffered and been cured of tuberculosis, polio, or other diseases, do we?[4]

Brothers is contending that emotional problems are relevantly similar to physical diseases and should be treated in the same way. She relies on our acceptance of the belief that people should not be shunned after they have been cured of physical diseases. She draws an (undeveloped) analogy between emotional and mental problems and these physical diseases and urges that we "come out of the dark ages" to make our attitudes consistent.

The analogy on which the argument depends may be set out as follows:

Analogue
People with such physical problems as German measles or polio
  suffer
  can recover
  are not shunned by others after they recover
Primary Subject
People with emotional or mental problems
  suffer
  can recover
  should not be shunned by others after they recover
Conclusion
People with emotional or mental problems should not be shunned by others after they recover.

Is Brothers's argument a good one? The assessment will depend on the closeness of her analogy; how similar are physical and emotional diseases with respect to extent of recovery after treatment and possible transferred effects on children? The technique Brothers uses, appealing to consistency of treatment between similar cases, leaves her audience with a choice. You can: (1) change your attitude to the primary subject; (2) find a relevant difference between the primary subject and the analogue; (3) change your attitude to the analogue; or (4) admit that you are inconsistent in your treatment of the analogue and the primary subject. Brothers is counting on you not to opt for (3) or (4) and not to be able to do (2). She presumes that you are committed to rationality so far as being consistent in the treatment of cases is concerned.

In law the obligation to treat similar cases similarly is the essence of formal justice. Suppose two people in two separate cases are charged with the same crime. Let us say, for instance, that Jones robbed a bank on Monday and Smith robbed another bank on Tuesday. Suppose that Jones is convicted and Smith is not. If there is not some relevant difference between the two cases, this is an example of formal injustice. *Regardless of the contents of a law, it should be applied consistently.* No two accused people are identical; nor will their circumstances be identical. But if they are relevantly similar, they should be treated similarly. If they are not treated similarly, the judge(s) should specify the relevant differences between them. Such reasoning is the basis of the precedence system of law: to preserve formal justice, cases must be resolved as similar cases have been resolved in the past, or a differentiating point must be specified. You can see, then, that picking out central similarities and differences is an extremely important aspect of legal reasoning. Much of legal reasoning is, in effect, reasoning by analogy. The case under discussion is the primary subject, which is resolved by reference to past cases (analogues, or legal *precedents*).

The same kind of point applies in administrative contexts. Here the context is seldom as structured as requirements for formal justice. Nevertheless, anyone administering a policy seeks to avoid unfairness and the criticism and confusion that will follow if the policy is applied inconsistently. Administrators will seek to treat similar cases similarly and will sometimes argue against a specific decision on the grounds that it will set a bad precedent. (As we shall see toward the end of this chapter, this kind of appeal to precedent is open to subtle abuses that lead to fallacious argument.)

Case-by-Case Reasoning and Issues of Classification.   Are the economies of western nations currently in a recession or in a depression? The most straightforward way of resolving this issue of classification is to see how similar and how different our current situation is to that of the 1930s—a classic economic case of a depression. Is a virus an animal? Is a six-week human embryo a person? Is a car that is equipped with sleeping bag and Coleman stove a private dwelling place? Are Polynesians a distinct race? All these questions have moral, legal, political, or scientific significance, and they call for correct decisions about the application of important concepts ("depression," "person," "distinct race," and so on). Some people regard such questions as purely semantic, thinking that they have to do only with words and nothing more, and that they cannot be resolved in any reasonable way. (You just decide to call a thing this or that, and that is all there is to it.) However, this common reaction is superficial and wrong. Classifications may be of very considerable legal, moral, political, or scientific significance, and reasons can be given on behalf of decisions that are made.

If we ask whether a questionable act counts as an act of negligence, for instance, we are raising a *conceptual* issue, but the conceptual issue is one that often has considerable legal or moral significance. (It might make the difference of several years in jail, or thousands of dollars in fines, for some individual. One way of resolving such an issue is to compare the act with another that is agreed to be a case of negligence. We then ask how like, and how unlike, the standard case our problem case is. To use this technique is to approach conceptual issues by reasoning from analogies.

Consider a dispute that actually arose regarding some books written about the extermination of Jews during the Second World War. Some French historians wrote works alleging that six million Jews had not been killed in Nazi death camps and that there had been a conspiracy to fabricate evidence on this matter. Jewish students at the University of Toronto, understandably enraged at the allegation, urged library officials to *reclassify* the French historians' books, terming them fiction instead of nonfiction. They believed that the historical claims made in the works were so outrageous that they did not properly qualify as nonfiction. B'nai B'rith officials defended the students' request but were very anxious that their position not be identified as one of advocating censorship. They insisted that reclassifying books was not the same thing as having them unavailable, and therefore it was not censorship.[5]

Here both the Jewish students and the League officials raised questions that were, in effect, about the application of concepts. The Jewish students raised the question of whether books that are about such world events as the Second World War but that make outlandish claims about them are to be regarded as nonfiction (history in this case) or as fiction. What makes a book count as nonfiction? Is it solely the intent of the author to describe the world as it was or is? Or is a certain minimum level of accuracy required? This question could be resolved by looking at clear cases of fiction and nonfiction and reasoning by analogy, or by looking at other borderline cases that have been resolved and using them as precedents, again reasoning by analogy. (The library didn't do this, apparently; it simply refused to consider the matter, saying too much public pressure could result.) B'nai B'rith officials were concerned to defend what the Jewish students were proposing, but they did not want to allow that it would be censorship. They asserted that reclassification would not be censorship or book banning; they were against the latter, but in favor of the former. There does seem, in fact, to be a clear difference between banning a book altogether, and putting it on the library shelf in one classification rather than another. In the latter case, the book is still available to readers, and it is this availability that censors wish to prevent.

This event reveals problems of conceptualization that illustrate the opportunity to use argument from agreed-upon cases, even though it does not contain explicit reasoning from cases. The pattern of such reasoning, for conceptual issues, is something like this:

1. The analogue has features a, b, and c.
2. The primary subject has features a, b, and c.
3. It is by virtue of features a, b, and c that the analogue is properly classified as a W.
So,
4. The primary subject ought to be classified as a W.

Sometimes the comparison of cases omits any specification of the similar features, and merely sets the cases side by side—the idea being that similarities will be obvious. Thus:

1. The analogue is a clear case of W.
2. The primary subject is similar to the analogue.
So,
3. The primary subject is a case of W.

A philosophical argument combining conceptual issues with moral ones was offered by Robert Nozick. He was trying to persuade readers that they are far too complacent in accepting the government's policy of redistributing wealth by income taxation. Nozick put his point very provocatively by using the following analogy:

> *Taxation of earnings from labor is on a par with forced labor. Some persons find this claim obviously true; taking the earnings of n hours of labor is like taking n hours from the person; it is like forcing the person to work n hours for another's purpose. Others find the claim absurd. But even these, if they object to forced labor, would oppose forcing unemployed hippies to work for the benefit of the needy.*
> *. . . The man who chooses to work longer to gain an income more than sufficient for his basic needs prefers some extra goods or services to the leisure and activities he could perform during the possible nonworking hours; whereas the man who chooses not to work the extra time prefers the leisure activities to the extra goods or services he could acquire by working more. Given this, if it would be illegitimate for a tax system to seize some of a man's leisure (forced labor) for the purpose of serving the needy, how can it be legitimate for a tax system to seize some of a man's goods for that purpose?*[6]

Nozick's analogy can be set out as follows:

▬▬▬ *Analogue*
The government might force a person to work for some number of hours in order to support the needy.
Point (1): In such a case a person would labor for some number of hours.
Point (2): The laboring person would not receive the payment for those hours of work; he would receive nothing for himself.
Point (3): The laboring person would be forced by the government to spend his time laboring for others.
Point (4): It would obviously be wrong for the government to put people into forced labor to serve the needy, and the wrongness of this act would be, and is, acknowledged by everybody.

Primary Subject
The government takes the earnings from some number of hours of work to support the needy.
Point (1): A person labors for some number of hours.
Point (2): The laboring person does not receive the payment for those hours of work.
Point (3): ? (How does the analogy hold up here?)
Point (4): To take the payment for those hours of labor is wrong.
Conclusion
Taxing earned income to support the needy is morally wrong.

This argument of Nozick's may strike you as shocking. After all, we typically *accept* income tax, which is used (in part) to support such social programs as welfare and medical assistance, and we typically *oppose* forced labor, which we are likely to associate with the concentration camps of totalitarian regimes. Are we being inconsistent in these common attitudes? Nozick is maintaining that we are—that, in fact, labor for which one is not paid due to income tax is just like forced labor and deserves the same bad moral reputation. This is certainly a provocative analogy! To resist it, we must find a relevant dissimilarity between forced labor as in concentration camps and labor that is 100 percent taxed and thus, in effect, unpaid.

Look at the third point in the structures set out here for a clue. People do largely *choose* to work at those jobs for which they are taxed, so their actual labor is not forced in the same sense that concentration camp labor is forced. This difference between the primary subject and the analogue does seem quite significant; it undermines the similarity you need to say that taxed labor is *forced* labor. Also, people who work at paid jobs in our society very frequently receive benefits from these jobs other than the cash income they earn: satisfaction, status, social company, and so on. The analogy is undermined by these differences: since working at your job during hours when you do not receive pay is something you (typically) choose to do and may enjoy for various reasons, it is not strictly comparable to forced labor. Thus Nozick's analogy is not fully convincing: we are not inconsistent if we approve of income tax used for redistributive purposes but disapprove of forced labor.

Some arguments make a rather implicit appeal for consistent treatment of cases. Here we often find such phrases as *by the same reasoning* or *according to those standards.* The following letter to the editor provides an example. The writer is implying that self-declared Christians who think that secular toys are violent and believe that toys based on religion could be more positive have failed to see the violence in the Christian religious tradition itself:

My children read with interest your article "Bible-Based Dolls Set to Oppose Evil-lyn and Ilk," and agree with their marketer, a self-declared Christian, who feels that secular toys are violent and want to "create an atmosphere of positive thought and action."

The younger boy was much taken with the picture of David and Goliath and has been out in the back lane practicing killing other kids with his slingshot. The older boy prefers the story of Jael, and wants a model of her nailing Sisera's head to the floor. For obvious reasons, I am reluctant to tell them about Cain and Abel dolls.

My daughter wants a Samsie'doll, with variable length hair and detachable eyeballs (how cute). Come to think of it, the muscular Samson would look much like He-man, while Delilah (a nasty bit of work) would look like Evil-lyn. As optional extras we could have for $5 a dead lion, and for $35 a temple to be destroyed by Samson in his last agonies. This could be a collapsible Castle Greyskull.

A great idea which should encourage much Bible-reading by little children. How can I get shares in the company?[7]

Exploring the comparison between secular toys and possible religion-based toys, this author points out that a consistent quest for nonviolent toys could require restrictions of religious toys as well as secular toys.

Some Points of Method and Critical Strategy.   We have now considered a number of examples of analogies in which a decision about one case is rejected or defended on the basis of consistency considerations. The analogy may be between two real cases or between a real case and a purely hypothetical case. The examples of people being shunned for physical diseases and of unemployed hippies being forced to work for the needy are hypothetical examples; these things never need to have happened, and yet the analogy can work anyway. It does not matter for such arguments whether the analogue describes any set of events that ever happened. This aspect of case-by-case reasoning sometimes confuses and frustrates people, because they cannot understand why imaginary and sometimes weird examples should be of any importance in rational decision-making. But the answer to their puzzlement is not so hard to find. The analogue must above all be a case toward which our attitude is *clear:* an obviously invalid argument, a clearly wrong action, a clearly illegal action, and so on. We can make no progress by comparing one confusing case with another. The analogue must really be like the primary subject in those ways that are relevant to the conclusion being defended. Provided these conditions are met, we are pushed by consistency into taking the same stance on the primary subject as we do toward the analogue.

Our attitudes and our moral and logical beliefs are about a whole range of actions, events, and arguments—not just about those that have actually occurred, or existed up to the present moment of time. For instance, we do not know whether in fact any mother ever killed her newborn baby by boiling it to death in hot lead, but we do know that our attitude toward such an action should be one of extreme repugnance. Any action that can be shown to be relatively similar to this hypothetical one is also to be condemned.

Because the analogue in this kind of consistency reasoning need not be something that actually happened, the analogy used is sometimes called an *a priori* analogy. The words *a priori* mean "from the first" and are used by philosophers to refer to concepts and beliefs that are independent of sense experience. The analogies examined so far have been *a priori* analogies in the sense that it does not matter whether or not the analogue describes any real experienced events. The point of classifying these analogies as *a priori* will become more obvious when we go on to look at inductive analogies, in which comparisons must be with actual cases. Inductive analogies, which are often used in history and science, form the basis for prediction, rather than decision.

To evaluate an argument from analogy, you can use the ARG conditions as you do for any argument. Suppose that the argument is based on an *a priori* analogy. The conclusion is about one case—the primary subject—and it is reached by comparing that case with another one—the analogue—that need not be real. The premises will describe the analogue and the primary subject. As in any argument, the premises are to be judged for their acceptability. When the analogy is *a priori*, the analogue may be something invented. Thus you cannot question the description of the analogue except on the grounds that that description is inconsistent. You can check to see that the primary subject—the case in question—is accurately and fairly described. If the premises assert that similarities exist between the two cases, then you must reflect to determine whether those similarities are genuine.

If you cannot fault the argument by analogy as far as the acceptability of its premises is concerned, you proceed to the question of relevance: are the premises relevant to the conclusion? You focus more closely on the parallel that is being implicitly or explicitly drawn between the analogue and the primary subject. Look at what the conclusion asserts about the primary subject, based on the analogy, and reflect on the similarities that hold between the primary subject and the analogue. Ask yourself whether the features of the primary subject that are highlighted by the analogy are relevant to the point asserted in the conclusion. Do those features give reasons or evidence suggesting the conclusion should hold true of the primary subject?

If you think that they do have at least some tendency to support the conclusion, move on to the G condition, where you ask whether the acceptable and relevant premises provide good enough (sufficient) grounds for the conclusion. A very useful device here is to depart from the line of thought of the argument and ask yourself about differences that might exist between the analogue and the primary subject. An argument from analogy encourages you to think of two cases as similar and to reason from one to the other. To criticize such an argument, you should ask what differences there might be between the two cases. Of course, there are always some differences. You cannot refute an argument from analogy merely by pointing out that the analogue and the primary subject are different in some respect or other. That point is too trivial. Any two things differ in some respect or other. You have to find differences that are negatively relevant to the conclusion—that is, to find differences that show or at least suggest that the conclusion is false. If you can find decisively relevant differences that upset the analogy in this way, then you can show that the argument fails on the G condition. The difference or differences will reveal that the similarities highlighted in the analogy are not sufficient to give good grounds for the conclusion. Your own reasoning, if this is the line of criticism, will be along the following lines: "The analogue and the primary subject both have features 1, 2, and 3, but the analogue is x and the primary subject is not-x. The reason is that the primary subject has feature 4, which the analogue lacks, and feature 4 is just the one that makes the primary subject not-x."

EXERCISE SET

Exercise One
Part A

Appraise the following refutations by logical analogy. Find the primary subject and the analogue, and check the refutation by logical analogy using the ARG conditions as they apply to *a priori* analogies.

*1. It is said that Japanese corporations are more fairly run than American corporations, just because in Japanese corporations decisions are typically reached by teams of managers, and not just by one top manager, as is typically the case in American corporations. But this is a silly reason for attributing fairness to Japanese corporations. The South African judicial system would not become fair to blacks just because single judges were replaced by teams of judges. Fairness is a matter of the distribution of advantages and disadvantages. It doesn't just depend on how many people are involved in making decisions.

2. In the early 1970s, some people claimed that using marijuana caused heroin addiction. They made this claim on the grounds that most people who use heroin first used marijuana. But isn't this a very incomplete argument? We could just as well argue that using milk causes a person to use cocaine. After all, most people who use cocaine began in life by using milk.

(Adapted from an exchange between Norman Podhoretz and several philosophers in *Commentary* in the late 1960s.)

3. My neighbor says that boys are more difficult to bring up than girls because her own two boys are always in trouble, whereas her girls are no problem for her. Now this argument is a very weak one because a person who happens to have two nice boys and two troublesome girls could equally well use her own experience to prove that boys are easier to bring up than girls. If you can prove a general conclusion from just personal experience in the one case, surely you can equally well prove it in the other case. But the result of putting both arguments together is absurd.

*4. They say that if God had meant us to love persons of the same sex, then He would not have created two different sexes in the first place. But by the same token, if God had meant us to wear clothes, we wouldn't have been born naked. The argument from what God might have intended is ridiculous in this context.

*5. Some have proposed a referendum on the question of worldwide disarmament. An argument often given against having such a referendum is that almost everyone would vote the same way: everyone would favor worldwide disarmament. But if this argument is a reason against such a referendum on disarmament, there would equally well be a reason against an election for mayor if the candidate were likely to win by a very large majority. Nobody would accept that conclusion! Similarly, we should not oppose a referendum just because we expect that almost everyone would respond to it in the same way.

6. In the fall of 1986, a Canadian cabinet minister, John Crosbie, said that people in Canada's Atlantic provinces should not complain about the high level of unemployment in their region. After all, he said, they were well off compared to people in Third World countries. Crosbie said that people in these areas should compare themselves, not with Canadians in central and western Canada, but rather with citizens in poorer parts of Asia and Africa. Calgary *Herald* columnist Alan Connery satirized Crosbie's comments by saying it was as if someone defended the performance of Canadian Prime Minister Brian Mulroney by pointing out that he was better than Hitler and Idi Amin. (Amin was a former Ugandan ruler responsible for thousands of tortures and murders.) (*Question:* Does Connery's satire effectively constitute a refutation, by logical analogy, of Crosbie's original argument?)

Part B

Of the following passages, identify those that contain arguments based on analogy. Then assess the arguments. Identify the analogue and the primary subject. Check the argument according to the ARG conditions. See whether the primary subject is accurately described and is really similar to the analogue in the ways the arguer asserts or implies. See whether the analogue is consistently described. Determine whether similarities are relevant to the conclusion. Use the technique of checking for relevant differences to see whether any relevant differences that provide evidence against the conclusion exist. *Note:* You do not have to write out all of these stages in your final answer; these instructions are intended as a guide to clear thought. (If the passage does not contain any argument, or if it contains an argument that is not based on analogy, simply say so, and proceed no further.)

1. *Background:* This passage deals with the issue of whether old people should be cared for by families or housed in institutions:

"But, we say, old folks get difficult and senile. Children get difficult and act as if they were senile, but no one has sanctioned an institution we can send our children to when we no longer wish to be responsible for them and they are not yet adults. Turn them out and you will be charged by the legal system."

(*Informal Logic Newsletter,* June, 1979.)

2. "In 'Children and Other Political Naifs,' Joseph Adelson says, 'I'm against the feminist movement, not against women.' Feminism is a part of so many women today that I don't think the two can easily be separated. It's like saying 'I'm against the civil rights movement, not against blacks.'"

(Letter to the editor, *Psychology Today,* February 1981.)

*3. *Background:* In December 1982, Pierre Trudeau was prime minister of Canada. His government was subjected to extensive criticism, especially because the Canadian economy was quite weak and unemployment was high. Some urged that Trudeau should resign so that his Liberal Party could select a new leader. Others said an election should be called. Trudeau replied:

"People don't change doctors just because they're sick. Particularly if the other doctor down the street is, you know, dropping his pills and breaking his thermometer and he doesn't know what to do."

(Reported in the Toronto *Globe and Mail*, December 21, 1982.)

(Assume that Trudeau's conclusion was that the people should not change the prime minister just because the economy was poor.)

4. *Background:* The following passage is taken from David Hume's *Dialogues Concerning Natural Religion*. In these dialogues many different analogies are explored as alternative devices for reasoning about gods and the supernatural realm:

"The Brahmins assert that the world arose from an infinite spider, who spun this whole complicated mass from his bowels, and annihilates afterwards the whole or any part of it, by absorbing it again and resolving it into his own essence. Here is a species of cosmogony which appears to us ridiculous because a spider is a little contemptible animal whose operations we are never likely to take for a model of the whole universe. But still, here is a new species of analogy, even in our globe. And were there a planet wholly inhabited by spiders (which is very possible), this inference would there appear as natural and irrefragable as that which in our planet ascribes the origin of all things to design an orderly system and intelligence, as explained by Cleanthes. [Cleanthes is a character in the dialogue.] Why an orderly system may not be spun from the belly as well as from the brain, it will be difficult for him to give a satisfactory reason."

(David Hume, "Dialogues Concerning Natural Religion," in *The Empiricists* [New York: Anchor Press, 1974].)

5. *Background:* In February 1982, the Canadian defense minister, Mr. Gilles Lamontagne, sought a basis for strengthening Canada's commitment to NATO, claiming that NATO had kept the peace for thirty years. His remarks were questioned by a writer from a peace research institute, who said:

"Mr Lamontagne claims that 'it is a well-known fact that, for the last 30-odd years, NATO has been the most efficient peace-keeping movement in the world,' but he cannot prove that to be true. Because A happens before B does not mean that A causes B. Snapping one's fingers to keep the elephants out of Ottawa appears to work because there are no elephants there; but the absence of elephants is no proof that snapping one's fingers is the cause of their absence."

(Letter to the editor, Toronto *Globe and Mail*, February 8, 1982.)

*6. "Voracious toads the size of dinner plates are hitchhiking across northern Australia gobbling up wildlife, and officials are appealing to motorists not to give them lifts. The Queensland cane toad, which locals say eats almost anything, even lighted cigarets, is moving west rapidly. Some have been found travelling on vegetable trucks.

"Northern Territory Conservation Minister Steve Hatton is sending 'wanted' posters to garages, motels, and pubs, depicting the ugly amphibian and warning drivers to check their vehicles for stowaways.

"'It's very worrying,' local conservationist William Freeland said. 'Toads have appeared up to 90 kilometres ahead of the main toad frontier. The bloody things eat some sorts of native wildlife into extinction.'

"The toad, introduced into Queensland early this century to combat a sugar cane parasite, has become a major pest, protected from predators by its poisonous skin."

(Reported in the Toronto *Globe and Mail*, July 6, 1985.)

*7. *Background:* In the spring of 1985, a controversy arose about placing an anti-Jewish book in the collection of the University of Calgary Library. The book, titled *The Hoax of the Twentieth Century*, claimed that the murder of six million Jews in World War II did not occur. The university administration claimed that even though the book contained a false view of history, it was important for the library to have it on file. A letter to an alumni magazine expressed a dissenting opinion:

"The director of the University Library defended placing *The Hoax of the Twentieth Century* in the stacks with this comment: 'Why not both sides of this issue as well?'

"The Holocaust is NOT an issue and there are NOT two sides. We have physical evidence, eyewitness accounts from guards, prisoners and liberators, and film evidence from both German and underground sources. This is more than we have for more historical facts and certainly more than we have for criminal trials. While a university library should present all points of view, this does NOT apply to a tract based neither on evidence nor on logical thought. If a student wishes to know what was of interest during a particular time, does the library offer an equal choice between microfilm of the *Times* of London and bound copies of the

National Enquirer? For geography, is there a choice between a globe and the clever drawings put out by the Flat Earth Society?"
(Letter by A.T., *Calgary Alumni Magazine,* summer 1985.)
(*Hint:* There are, in fact, two analogues here.)

8. *Background:* A young philosopher contended that job security for professors, which results in no job opportunities for younger people, is unjust as an institution. A senior professor of philosophy wrote to object to the view saying:

"But consider this 'injustice' as well. My home was purchased only a decade ago, at less than half what it would bring on the market now, and throughout that period interest charges on the mortgage have averaged a single-digit percentage. A much younger person would find it difficult, if not impossible, to purchase a comparable dwelling now. Yet no one would suggest that, because of this, I should give up ownership and compete with homeless individuals for the three or five year leasing of it. Had that ever been a foreseeable eventuality, I would obviously not have 'bought' it in the first place. And one can multiply examples of similar 'injustice.'"
(Bulletin of the Canadian Association of University Teachers, March 1982.)

9. "It is observed by arithmeticians that the products of 9 compose always either 9 or some lesser product of 9, if you add together all the characters of which any of the former products is composed. Thus, of 18, 27, 36, which are products of 9, you make 9 by adding 1 to 8; 2 to 7; 3 to 6. Thus, 369 is a product also of 9; and if you add 3, 6, and 9, you make 18, a lesser product of 9. To a superficial observer, so wonderful a regularity may be admired as the effect either of change or of design; but a skillful algebraist immediately concludes it to be the work of necessity, and demonstrates that it must forever result from the nature of these numbers. Is it not probable, I ask, that the whole economy of the universe is conducted by a like necessity, though no human algebra can furnish a key which solves the difficulty? And instead of admiring the order of natural being, may it not happen that, could we penetrate into the intimate nature of bodies, we should clearly see why it was absolutely impossible they could ever admit of any other disposition? So dangerous is it to introduce this idea of necessity into the present question! And so naturally does it afford an inference directly opposite to the religious hypothesis."
(David Hume, *Dialogues Concerning Natural Religion,* in *The Empiricists* [New York: Anchor Press, 1974].)

10. *Background:* This analogy was used by one of several panelists in a university discussion on arms control and disarmament:

"The difference between arms control and disarmament is that the arms control approach is a much more gradual one. You can think of it in this way. You can imagine all the nuclear weapons in the world as being a huge chunk of granite. The arms controllers are, in effect, trying to make the chunk smaller by chiseling away at it. But the disarmament advocates, on the other hand, want to get rid of the entire block at once. Rather than using the slow chisel approach, they would prefer to blast the whole thing away with dynamite."

*11. "It is a common myth that each person is a unity, a kind of unitary organization with a will of its own. Quite the contrary, a person is an amalgamation of many sub-persons, all with a will of their own. The 'sub-persons' are considerably less complex than the overall person, and consequently they have much less of a problem with internal discipline. If they are themselves split, probably their component parts are so simple that they are of a single mind—and if not, you can continue down the line. This hierarchical organization of personality is something that does not much please our sense of dignity, but there is much evidence for it."
(Douglas Hofstadter, "Reflections," in *The Mind's I,* ed. D. Hofstadter and D. C. Dennett [New York: Basic Books, 1981].)

12. "But economic activity is by no means the only area of human life in which a complex and sophisticated structure arises as an unintended consequence of a large number of individuals co-operating while each pursues his own interests. Consider, for example, language. It is a complex structure that is continually changing and developing. It has a well-defined order, yet no central body planned it. . . .

"How did language develop? In much the same way as an economic order develops through the market—out of the voluntary interaction of individuals, in this case seeking to trade ideas or information or gossip with one another. At no point is there any coercion, though in more recent times government school systems have played an important role in standardizing usage."
(Milton and Rose Friedman, *Free to Choose: A Personal Statement* [New York: Harcourt Brace Jovanovich, 1979].)

13. Responding to violence with more violence is like trying to put out a fire by adding matches. Matches can set off a fire, and when added to a fire, they will only make it burn more intensely. To put out a fire,

we need to smother it or pour water on it. That is, we need something different from what's making the fire burn in the first place. And in just the same way, we can't stop violence by replying with more violence. Thus the way to stop terrorism is not to launch attacks on countries such as Libya and Lebanon, but rather to inject a genuinely new element into the situation. That element is a real desire to work out the underlying political problems that keep terrorism alive.

*14. *Background:* In the winter of 1986, Ferdinand Marcos was unseated as leader in the Philippines and replaced by Corazon Aquino. The new government displayed the lavish riches of the Marcos regime, including thousands of pairs of shoes previously owned by Marcos's wife, Imelda. One commentator said:

"Compared to Imelda, Marie Antoinette was a bag lady."
(U.S. Congressman Stephen J. Solarz, quoted in the Toronto *Globe and Mail*, March 10, 1986.)

15. The human mind has different parts or aspects. Some of these are superior to others. For instance, we have biological drives for food, water, sleep, and sex. We have emotions of fear, anger, hatred, and love. And we have an intellect that can reason. It is the intellect that should dominate in the mind, for this is the superior part of humankind. And similarly, there are different sorts of people in a society. Just as a mind will be disturbed if it is ruled by biological drives, or by emotions unguided by intellect, so society will suffer if it is not controlled by its superior people.

*16. *Background:* Representative Paul Simon of Illinois had this to say about the dangers of the nuclear arms race and the proposal for a bilateral freeze on the development and deployment of nuclear weapons:

"The United States and the Soviet Union are like two powerful automobiles coming from opposite directions, destined for a spectacular head-on crash that will eliminate both, as well as all the spectators. In this debate, some of us are saying: 'As a first effort, let's agree to have both cars put on the brakes.' But our opponents in this debate argue that we should not put on the brakes; we should put the cars into reverse. All of us share that hope, but for cars headed toward each other at breakneck speed, putting on the brakes is an urgently needed first step and must precede going in reverse.

"'But look at all the power in the other car,' some say. They see the fancy gadgets, most of which are meaningless, as well as the horsepower that is meaningful. That horsepower includes about 8800 Soviet strategic warheads, compared to our car's 9500; greater accuracy on our car but more megatonnage on theirs. So the argument that we should ask these two cars to apply their brakes as a first step toward sanity holds true, no matter who has the 8800 and no matter who has the 9500.

"It's infinitely easier to put both cars into reverse once they have come to a stop. And every minute that we argue and do not act those two cars come closer to a collision. I hope the driver of our car, President Reagan, understands the desperate folly of the present course."
(*The New York Times*, April 25, 1983.)

Inductive Analogies

We have now examined a number of *a priori* analogies and arguments based on them. Such arguments support a decision to classify a case in one way or another, or treat an action or argument as good or as poor. But analogies are used as a basis for predictions as well as for decisions. The *a priori* analogy is a technique used to urge a decision to treat cases in the same way—logically, morally, legally, or administratively. The inductive analogy is a basis for prediction: we know that the analogue has certain characteristics, and because the primary subject resembles it in these aspects, we estimate or predict that the primary subject will resemble it in a further respect as well.

The analogue in an *a priori* analogy is often merely imagined. It need not be a real case. However, in an inductive analogy, the analogue must be something that now exists or previously did exist, and its factual properties are important to the way the analogy works.

We often need to make estimations about things that we are not in a position to observe—because they are in the future or in the past, or because there are moral or practical reasons against examining them directly. In such contexts, inductive analogies are important and useful: if we cannot examine *A*, but we can examine *B*, and if *A* is like *B* in many respects, then, given that *B* has characteristic *x*, we estimate that *A* will have characteristic *x*. This is reasoning by inductive analogy.

Inductive analogies would not be necessary if we had general laws covering the unknown phenomena in the primary subject. Suppose, for instance, that we need to know whether human beings are adversely affected by urea formaldehyde foam, a substance sometimes used to insulate homes. If we knew that all mammals are adversely affected by the substance, our problem would be easily solved by a syllogism:

1. All mammals are adversely affected by urea formaldehyde foam.
2. All humans are mammals.
Therefore,
3. All humans are adversely affected by urea formaldehyde foam.

But we do *not* know the first premise in this argument to be true. Nor can we (ethically) experiment directly on humans to see how they react to living in houses insulated with this material. The standard approach in such cases is to reason by analogy: inductive analogy. We study the effects of the material on nonhuman animals, and then predict what it will be in the case of humans. We will then argue like this:

1. Rats (or some other nonhuman animals) are like humans in respects 1, 2, 3, ...
2. Rats suffer effects *x, y, z,* when exposed to doses at such-and-such levels of urea formaldehyde.
3. A dose at so-and-so level in humans is equivalent to a dose at such-and-such levels in rats.
Therefore,
4. Humans will suffer effects *x, y,* and *z* when exposed to a dose at so-and-so level of urea formaldehyde foam.

In this analogy the primary subject is human beings and the analogue is rats. The two are being compared with respect to their reactions to doses of urea formaldehyde. This inductive analogy differs from *a priori* analogies in a very significant respect: the analogue must describe an actual thing and give factual information about it. The inductive analogy is based on information gained from human experience. The conclusion in an inductive analogy cannot be known with complete certainty, but as a basis for prediction, close comparison with a similar case is much better than no information at all.

Inductive analogies are very important and they are a common way of reasoning about human affairs. Often a past event comes to be a kind of model for a present or future one. In 1982, for instance, many people opposed U.S. government policy in El Salvador on the grounds of similarities between what was happening there and what happened in Vietnam in the early 1960s. For the Americans considering this analogy, the Vietnam saga was over and—in most people's opinion—American intervention in Vietnam had been a disastrous failure. By pointing out what they regarded as crucial similarities between the Vietnam situation and circumstances in El Salvador, critics predicted failure for the U.S. efforts there also, under the slogan "not another Vietnam." The events of Vietnam were known; those of El Salvador yet to come. Hence the need to use the analogy. Disputes about U.S. policy in El Salvador in 1982–84 were, to a surprising extent, disputes about the merits of this analogy.

We assess inductive analogies in basically the same way we assess other analogies—that is, by looking for relevant differences between the primary subject and the analogue. However, some aspects of inductive analogies make them different from *a priori* ones. The most obvious of these is that in the inductive analogy, the analogue must describe something real, and the facts cited must be accurate and true. Imaginary examples are fine for *a priori* analogies but not for inductive ones. The similarities on which inductive analogies are based are between empirical aspects of the primary subject and the analogue. Also, similarities cumulate in an important way. In an *a priori* analogy, what is important is that the similarities relevant to the conclusion hold. If they do, it does not matter whether there are many further similarities or none at all. But in the inductive analogy, the sheer *number* of similarities does matter. The closer the two cases are, in detail, the more likely it is that the inferred conclusion will be true, which means that the evaluation of inductive analogies depends more on factual background knowledge than does the evaluation of *a priori* analogies. If you don't know the background facts about Vietnam and El Salvador, for instance, you will have to do background research before you can properly estimate the strength of the analogy.

Inductive analogies are used by medical researchers in reasoning from one species to another, in drug testing, and by psychologists who study rats, chimpanzees, and other animals' behavior and learning development in the belief these studies have some bearing on humans. They are used by historians and economists who try to predict future events by comparing present circumstances with closely similar ones in the past, and by doctors who make inferences about fetal competence on the basis of their knowledge of what newborn infants can do. When Freud reasoned about the unconscious mind, he did so by analogy with the conscious mind. Even theologians try to use inductive analogy when they reason to conclusions about the supernatural realm on the basis of premises about the experienced natural world. Obviously, not all inductive analogies in these subjects will be reliable. However, they sometimes provide a reasonable basis for predictions.

To evaluate arguments based on inductive analogy, we first identify the primary subject and the analogue, just as we did for *a priori* analogies. Then, again as before, we apply the ARG conditions. At this stage, the difference between *a priori* analogy and inductive analogy becomes significant for our evaluation of arguments. In an inductive analogy, the analogue is a real thing—not a case simply imagined or hypothesized by the arguer. Thus, when we check the premises for acceptability, it is very important to see whether the analogue is accurately described. For example, if someone is using information about a teacher's performance in one course to reason to a conclusion about his likely performance in another course, it is important that the facts about what he did in the first course are correct. Also, it is important to check that information about the later course is also correct, and that any similarities between the two courses that are assumed in the reasoning really do exist.

To determine the relevance of the similarities that exist between the primary subject and the analogue, we have to look closely at the conclusion asserted and reflect on how the features that are similar are related to that conclusion. For instance, suppose a student reasons by inductive analogy that because Smith was a good instructor in a junior philosophy course, he will also be a good instructor in a senior interdisciplinary course. A full evaluation of the relevance of the analogy will require critical thought that goes beyond what is explicitly stated in the premises because you have to ask yourself the following questions. In what respects is the primary subject (the instructor's performance in the senior interdisciplinary course) similar to the analogue (his performance in the junior philosophy course)? How relevant are those respects to the conclusion? Perhaps both courses are small, containing fewer than twenty students, and the instructor is good at conducting student discussions. The similar size would allow a good prediction from the first course to the second, provided there are no relevant features differentiating the two.

If the similarities are at least relevant to the point asserted in the conclusion, we still need to see whether they are sufficient to provide good grounds for that conclusion. To determine whether they are sufficient, you have to reflect on differences that may exist between the primary subject and the analogue. As with *a priori* analogy, there are bound to be some differences. The issue is whether the differences that do exist are negatively relevant to the conclusion. The argument as stated will typically not mention differences because, like all analogies, it is urging you to see similarities and to think in terms of them. You have to find differences for yourself. With inductive analogies, finding the differences requires background knowledge. A senior interdisciplinary course is different from a junior philosophy course in that the former will require both a greater breadth of knowledge and a greater ability to respond to complex questions. These differences between the primary subject and the analogue are negatively relevant to the conclusion in this case. They tend to undermine the force of the analogy.

When we make such judgments, it is important to note the degree of certainty with which the conclusion is asserted. A student who concluded "Smith is sure to be good in Interdisciplinary Studies 400 because he was terrific in Philosophy 100" has a different argument from one who asserts "There is reason to think Smith will lecture well in I.S. 400 because he lectured well in Phil. 100." The second student has a much more qualified conclusion. Since his argument is already sensitive to the limitations of the inductive analogy, it does not succumb to criticism as easily.

EXERCISE SET

Exercise Two

Some of the following passages contain arguments based on inductive analogies. Identify these arguments, and specify the primary subject, the analogue, and the similarities on which the analogy is based. Then assess the strength of the inductive analogy as a basis for the conclusion. If the passage does not contain an inductive analogy, comment briefly as to what sort of passage it is. Does it contain no argument at all? Or another kind of argument? Or an *a priori* analogy?

1. Studying French without ever speaking the language does not result in a good command of French. Latin is a language too, so studying Latin without ever speaking it will not result in a good command of Latin.

2. In the civil service, people are spending other people's money. Civil servants do not have to earn the money they spend; it is given to them by government, which raises it from tax dollars. That makes civil servants careless about their expenditures.

Universities are like the civil service. Their administrations do not have to earn the money spent. It comes from the government. Therefore, we can expect university administrators to spend money carelessly.

3. A watch could not assemble itself. The complex arrangements of parts into a working watch is possible only because there is a craftsman who designs and constructs the watch. In just the same way, the complicated parts of the world could not arrange themselves into the natural order. So there must be a designer of the world, and that is God.

4. Hannibal is well-known for having arranged to get elephants across the Alps when he was fighting against the Romans. That was an unbelievable feat. Hannibal's arrival in Italy, with an army and equipment carried by elephants, must have been a great surprise to the Romans.

*5. "A majority taken collectively is only an individual whose opinions, and frequently whose interests,

are opposed to those of another individual, who is styled a minority. If it be admitted that a man possessing absolute power may misuse that power by wronging his adversaries, why should not a majority be liable to the same reproach? Men do not change their characters by uniting with each other; nor does their patience in the presence of obstacles increase with their strength. For my own part, I cannot believe it; the power to do everything, which I should refuse to one of my equals, I will never grant to any number of them."
(Alexis de Tocqueville, *Democracy in America*, quoted in S. F. Barker, *The Elements of Logic*, 3rd ed. [New York: McGraw-Hill, 1980].)

6. Simple appliances like toasters and washing machines break down. They are not completely reliable. The same companies that make these appliances make nuclear reactors, which are much more complicated. It is very likely, then, that nuclear reactors will also be susceptible to breakdowns.

7. Critics say that the Star Wars program will never work. But they are quite likely to be wrong. These people are being skeptical about what human ingenuity, expressed in science and technology, can accomplish. Skeptics have been wrong before, haven't they? After all, even Einstein said it would be impossible to produce an atomic bomb. And he was wrong. In just the same way, skeptics about the feasibility of Star Wars defense are probably wrong today.

*8. *Background:* This example from Arthur Schopenhauer's *The Art of Literature*, advocates independent thinking.

"Everyone who really thinks for himself is like a monarch. His position is undelegated and supreme. His judgments, like royal decrees, spring from his own sovereign power and proceed directly from himself. He acknowledges authority as little as a monarch admits a command. He subscribes to nothing but what he has himself authorized. The multitude of common minds, laboring under all sorts of current opinions, authorities, prejudices, is like the people, which silently obeys the law and accepts orders from above."
(Arthur Schopenhauer, *The Art of Literature*, trans. T. Bailey Saunders [Ann Arbor, Mich.: University of Michigan Press, 1960].)

9. *Background:* The nineteenth-century philosopher Jeremy Bentham wrote primarily about ethics and politics. However, he also wrote a work called *Handbook of Political Fallacies*, in which he set out a number of arguments common in political life

and maintained they were fallacious. This passage is taken from that work:

"In producing a local or temporary debility in the action of the powers of the natural body, in many cases, the honest and skillful physician beholds the only means of curing it; and it would be as reasonable to infer a wish to see the patient perish, from the act of the physician in prescribing a drug, as to infer a wish to see the whole frame of government destroyed or rendered worse, from the act of a statesman who lowers the reputation of an official whom he regards as unfit."
(J. Bentham, *Handbook of Political Fallacies*, rev. and ed. Harold Larrabee [New York: Thomas Y. Crowell, 1971].) (Bentham is dealing with the argument—common in his day, apparently—that those who criticize dishonesty in a particular government are seeking to undermine government in general.)

10. "We know that surprising phenomena sometimes occur just by chance and for no other reason. For example, a person might deal himself a straight in poker; ordinarily, we attribute this happy event to the vagaries of providence, not to the dishonesty of the dealer. In much the same way, we might wonder whether the death dip and death rise (before and after birthdays and other significant occasions) might have arisen by chance and for no other reason.

"Now suppose our poker player were to deal himself not just one straight, but four straights in a row, in the four times he deals while playing with us. This could have happened by chance, but it is so unlikely that we would prefer some other explanation. The less likely an event is to occur by chance, the more we prefer some other explanation. Similarly, if we find a death dip and death rise in, say, four samples and not just one, there is a small possibility that these phenomena could have occurred by chance, but another explanation might be more plausible."
(David P. Phillips, "Deathday and Birthday," *Statistics: A Guide to the Unknown*, ed. Judith Taner [San Francisco, Calif.: Holden-Day, 1972].)

*11. "The thought was three days and three nights growing. During the days he carried it like a ripening peach in his head. During the nights he let it take flesh and sustenance, hung out on the silent air, colored by the country moon and country stars. He walked around and around the thought in the silence before dawn. On the fourth morning he reached up an invisible hand, picked it, and swallowed it whole."
(Ray Bradbury, "The Time of Going Away," *The Day It Rained Forever* [Middlesex, England: Penguin Books, 1963].)

12. "The moment the slave resolves that he will no longer be a slave, his fetters fall. He frees himself and shows the way to others. Freedom and slavery are mental states. Therefore, the first thing is to say to yourself: 'I shall no longer accept the role of a slave. I shall not obey orders as such but shall disobey them when they are in conflict with my conscience.' The so-called master may lash you and try to force you to serve him. You will say: 'No, I will not serve you for your money or under a threat.' This may mean suffering. Your readiness to suffer will light the torch of freedom which can never be put out."

(Mohandas K. Gandhi, 1946, as quoted by Gene Sharp, in *Gandhi as a Political Strategist* [Boston: Porter Sargent Publishers, 1979], p. 55.)

(*Hard. Hint:* Is the argument here based on an analogy?)

Further Critical Strategies

An interesting critical strategy that can be applied both to *a priori* analogies and to inductive analogies is that of working out a different analogy that suggests a conclusion contrary to the one in the argument you are examining. When an analogy is drawn, you start to think of the primary subject in a specific way, using the analogue as a model. You transfer concepts and beliefs from the analogue to the primary subject. This analogue will almost always be one of a number of different possible analogues. Adopting an alternative and setting out to conceive the primary subject in terms of that alternative will almost always bring fresh insights and new conclusions. If the conclusions are incompatible with those implied by the original analogy and yet the new analogy is just as good, you have undermined the original analogy with a counteranalogy.

This technique of rival analogies was used to great effect by the philosopher David Hume in his famous *Dialogues Concerning Natural Religon*. The *Dialogues* offer a prolonged critical appraisal of the argument that because the world is made of organized interconnected parts like a machine, it must—like a machine—have been created by an intelligent mind. Hume pointed out that the model of the world as a machine is only one of a great number of possible models, and that other models suggest radically different theological conclusions. Here is a passage in which he employed the technique of counteranalogy:

> *Now if we survey the universe, so far as it falls under our knowledge, it bears a great resemblance to an animal or organized body, and seems actuated with a like principle of life and motion. A continual circulation of matter in it produces no disorder; a continual waste in every part is incessantly repaired; the closest sympathy is perceived throughout the entire system; and each part or member, in performing its proper offices, operates both to its own preservation and to that of the whole. The world, therefore, I infer, is an animal, and the Deity is the soul of the world, actuating it, and actuated by it.*[8]

Hume is criticizing the machine analogy by pointing out that an animal analogy seems equally appropriate, and the animal analogy does not yield the conclusion that the world was created by an intelligent mind. Actually he is using the technique of refutation by logical analogy, but the primary subject (argument he seeks to criticize) is itself an analogy. His argument is, essentially, as follows:

Analogue Argument

The world is like an animal and must have a soul like an animal. Therefore, there is a Deity who is the soul of the world.

—is a possible way of thinking of the world

—leads to a conclusion nobody takes seriously

Primary Subject Argument

The world is like a machine and must have an inventor like a machine. Therefore, there is a Deity who is the inventor (creator) of the world.

—is a possible way of thinking of the world

—leads to a conclusion nobody should take seriously

Conclusion

The argument that because the world is like a machine it must have an intelligent inventor or creator has a conclusion that nobody should take seriously.

By showing that there are many different analogies that seem equally plausible when we try to think of the world as a whole, Hume was pointing out that our experience of the world is not sufficiently determinate to make just one of these analogies appropriate. If we think of the world only as a machine, then, because machines have intelligent creators, we will think that the world must have had an intelligent creator. On the other hand, if we think of the world as an organism, we will reach a different conclusion.

An analogy might be thought of as a special sort of screen or filter. (This statement itself is an analogy!) Using an analogy, whether in an argument or an explanation, or merely as a literary device, encourages you to focus on certain aspects of the primary subject—those that are similar to the analogue. An analogy is often said to highlight these aspects. Analogies can be very helpful in creative and critical thought when they highlight important features that we might not have attended to before. However, they can also be misleading, in that features not highlighted may also be very significant. Using different analogies emphasizes different features. Thinking of alternatives can be a liberating and creative experience, especially when language and thought are dominated by one particular analogy.

Thought and language are often dominated by models that we take for granted to the extent that we do not even realize they are models. We adapt a language from one sort of thing and use it to think and talk about another. In doing so, we may export beliefs and assumptions from one area of knowledge to another, often in an uncritical way. Using a new model may reveal that these assumptions need to be questioned. A new model will sometimes suggest fresh ideas and insights.

Thus new analogies can be more than counteranalogies. They may suggest original ways of thinking and talking and new projects and strategies for research. As a matter of fact, it has been pointed out that our culture and language employ a kind of deep metaphor or analogy that is about argument itself. Argument is assimilated in much of our language to battle or even war. Just as people may defend territory in a war, they are said to defend positions in an argument. They may ward off attacks, have opponents, stake out positions, make counterattacks, achieve victories, retreat from positions when attacked, win debates, and so on. Perhaps we would have a very different understanding of argument if we thought of an alternative deep metaphor, or model. It is hard even to imagine what this metaphor would be because the terminology of attack, defense, and so on is very deeply ingrained in our language. But no doubt there are other models. We might think of persons arguing as negotiators trying to work out a compromise, or even as dancers forming a pleasing pattern. If such alternative analogies were explored seriously, new questions about arguments would no doubt arise, and some things like winning an argument might cease to seem as important as they now do.

Loose and Misleading Analogies

As mentioned earlier, we have developed our treatment of analogy in such a way as to emphasize its serious cognitive uses. On the whole, the arguments from analogy considered so far have been sound ones. But this should not be taken as a proof that all arguments by analogy are good arguments. Many are quite dreadful, and analogies can be seriously misleading. We'll explore some common misuses of analogy now that we have seen how *a priori* and inductive analogies can be important, cogent, and useful.

The Fallacy of Faulty Analogy.   Certainly many arguments by analogy are very poor. In fact, sometimes the analogies on which arguments are based are so loose and farfetched that it is impossible even to classify them as *a priori* or inductive. It seems as though a gross image of a primary subject is given by the analogue and the unwary audience is supposed to be lulled into a conclusion. Such loose uses of analogy are often discussed as instances of the *fallacy of faulty analogy*. They involve an appeal to similarities that are highly superficial and give no real support to the conclusion sought.

Here is an example of a grossly flawed argument by analogy. It is taken from a letter to the editor in which the writer urged that the city of Calgary not develop a new subdivision that was proposed in order to provide housing for 50,000 people:

> *Once a pleasant and friendly lady of the foothills, Calgary has become an obese, 200 pound dame and naturally suffers from all the diseases inherent to the distended community: smog breath, body odors, high traffic blood pressure, glandular dollarities, and skin blemishes such as high rises, towers, skyscrapers, and malls. . . . It would be well to consider if this continual expansion of Alberta cities is really needed or just a competitive show-off.*[9]

Here the writer uses the analogue of an obese dame to dispute the wisdom of extending the city. He draws out the image in some detail. But it would be hard to take it seriously, either as an *a priori* analogy or as an inductive one. There is no serious demand for consistency between our attitudes toward obesity in people and size in cities! There is no norm of healthy size for cities anyway. Nor is there any inductive basis for predicting that the poor health a person is likely to experience as a result of gross obesity will somehow emerge in parallel for a city that undergoes expansion. The notion of "health problems" would be quite problematic in its application to a city. The analogy thus provides no support for the author's stance on the proposed subdivision. It gives him an entertaining and vivid way of *stating* his point but provides no rational support for it. As far as careful reasoning about the subdivision is concerned, the analogy is simply a distraction.

Loose analogies can be particularly deceptive when the analogue is something toward which people have very strong or very settled attitudes. These attitudes carry over too easily to the primary subject, even though there is no significant similarity between it and the analogue. You can see this transfer happening in the following argument, which was put forward in the seventeenth century by essayist Francis Bacon:

Nobody can be healthy without exercise, neither natural body nor politic; and certainly to a kingdom or estate, a just and honourable war is true exercise. A civil war, indeed, is like the heat of a fever, but a fever of war is like the heat of exercise, and serveth to keep the body in health; for in slothful peace, both courage will effeminate and manners corrupt.[10]

How is the analogue similar to the primary subject? What, precisely, do they have in common? Do these common features have anything to do with the conclusion reached about the primary subject? Do they give sufficient grounds to support that conclusion? Many analogies such as this one between the body and the state are so loose that they cannot support specific conclusions.

It is obvious and well known that the healthy human body requires exercise. Bacon exploits this common knowledge to try to show that the political organism also needs exercise, and he then contends that war constitutes this "exercise." However, there is at best a loose similarity between the primary subject and the analogue in this case; again there is no clear standard of health for the primary subject, the state. Furthermore, even if we were to grant that a state or "kingdom" does need exercise, it is surely not clear that war would be the only form such exercise could take. Internal campaigns to eliminate poverty or pollution might be just as energetic and unslothful as war! These critical remarks are really very obvious, but the danger is that due to the familiarity of the fact that human bodies do need exercise, and the difficulty of thinking about the state or kingdom as a whole, it would be all too easy to believe that Bacon has really established his point. *Asking how the similarity alleged would function to establish the conclusion can expose the superficiality of the resemblance.*

In addition to this kind of suggestive and loose use of analogy—which has no doubt given all analogies the shady reputation they have in some circles—there are several more specific fallacies of reasoning that involve the misuse of analogy.

The Fallacy of Two Wrongs Make a Right.   We have seen that there is a legitimate way of using analogies to push for consistency between relevantly similar cases. But a rather common type of argument, easily confused with legitimate consistency arguments, amounts to a fallacy of reasoning. This is the fallacy of thinking that two wrongs make a right. It is committed when a person tries to defend one thing that is allegedly wrong by pointing out that another thing that really is wrong has been done or has been accepted. In doing so, he is in effect reasoning that since we have allowed some wrong, we should (to be consistent) permit more.

The following example shows this kind of misuse of analogy. The context is a discussion of a rock concert. A reviewer had criticized the performers for using the language of sex and drugs and for encouraging fantasies of sex and drug use in the audience. A young rock fan, writing to defend the concert, said:

There's not a thing wrong with what Roth did in front of 15,000 people. After all, don't millions of people see worse stuff in front of the television every day?[11]

The arguer is drawing an analogy between Roth's performance at the rock show and things that are shown on television. She is trying to reply to the suggestion that the performance is immoral by saying that it is not worse than something else that is tolerated.

This is a *two-wrongs-make-a-right* argument, and it is a fallacy. It is rather like the use of analogy in consistency arguments, but it differs from them in a subtle, but crucial, way. The writer grants that on television there is "worse stuff," hence granting that some material on television is bad. If Roth's performance is similar to it, as she says it is, the correct conclusion to draw would be that Roth's performance is also bad. Yet this conclusion is just the contrary of the conclusion drawn.

Two-wrongs arguments are common in areas where abuses are spread across many institutions, countries, persons, and contexts. If someone attacks one instance of the abuse, claiming it is wrong and that reform is necessary, he is often criticized by those who use two-wrongs arguments. For instance, when Greenpeace campaigned against the killing of baby seals for pelts, many people pointed out that the killing of baby seals is by no means the only instance when humans treat animals cruelly. Animals raised and slaughtered for food are often very cruelly treated, and this cruelty is tolerated. Critics in effect demanded consistency from Greenpeace, asking, "If you tolerate slaughter for food, why criticize killing animals for their pelts?" This demand for consistency is fair enough. But it is a mistake to infer from the social toleration of killing animals for food (which, it is implied, is wrong) that killing animals for pelts (which is similar) should not be criticized. If the one thing is wrong and the other is similar to it, a correct appeal to consistency will imply that the other is wrong too. Two wrongs make two wrongs; they do not make a right. There is no point in multiplying wrongs in the name of consistency.

Consider two proposed actions: (a) and (b). If both are wrong, and similarly wrong, then the best thing would be to prevent both from occurring. Ideally, then, such groups as Greenpeace would work against the slaughter of animals for meat *and* against the seal hunt. But for reasons of time, available volunteers, money, and other factors, this is not possible. One of the two wrongs, therefore, must be selected as the target of action. Now when this selection happens, critics may allege that the choice of targets is inappropriate; for instance, they may want to accuse the group of unduly emphasizing a problem that is not as important as some others. This criticism is fair enough. But it is not appropriate to argue that because there is more than one wrong, nothing should be done about that wrong. After all, reform has to start somewhere, and it cannot usually start everywhere at once. Following through on two-wrongs thinking would commit us to perpetuating evil in the name of consistency.

The two-wrongs fallacy is common when there is a set of attitudes or beliefs that are connected and that are *all* open to criticism. (Examples include sexism in many areas of life, abuses of human rights in many parts of the world, human behavior toward nonhuman animals in many aspects of our culture, and arms buildups in many countries.) In such cases, would-be reformers who attack any *single* manifestation of the evil may be asked, quite legitimately, why that one is the appropriate one to be worried about. (Why do feminists worry about the use of *he* as a generic word when women's conditions in prisons are so awful? Why do people criticize American attitudes toward human rights in El Salvador when there are so many abuses of rights in Poland and Iran? And so on.) But the target may be selected because it is close to home, because it is one for which we are directly responsible, or because it is relatively easy to change. It is fallacious to infer that a single wrong should be condoned because there are other similar ones in existence. The existence of these other wrongs is no reason to accept another one, however similar it may be.

The Fallacy of Slippery Assimilation.   Perhaps you have heard of the proof that no one is bald. It goes like this: consider a person with 50,000 hairs on his head. If you take away one of these hairs, that will not make him into a bald person. Now suppose you keep pulling out hairs, one at a time. Suppose you get the poor fellow down to the point where he has only 200 hairs left. He won't look very hairy at this point. But is he bald? How can he be? All you do is pull out one hair at a time, and no *one* hair will make the difference between being hairy and being bald. If the first hair doesn't make the difference, neither does the second, nor the third, nor the fourth. Each hair is just like the one before it, and it would surely be arbitrary to say that the 40,004th hair could make the difference when the first or the tenth could not. This proof seems to be a proof that no one can be bald. Very consoling to older men, perhaps, but paradoxical for logicians.

In fact logicians have been puzzled about this kind of argument for several thousand years, and they have given the paradox a special name: *sorites*. The word means "heap." An early form of the paradox was that you could never get a heap of grain from an accumulation of individual grains, because no one grain would make the difference between having just a few separate grains and having a heap.

Let's take a more abstract look at this puzzling line of reasoning:

1. Case (a) differs from case (b) only by amount x.
2. Amount x is a trivial amount.
3. Case (b) differs from case (c) only by amount x.
4. Case (c) differs from case (d) only by amount x.
5. There is a whole series of cases (d) to (z).
6. Within the series (d) to (z), each member differs from those preceding and following it only by amount x.
7. Case (a) is a clear case of W.
Therefore,
8. All the other cases in the series, from (b) to (z), are also clear cases of W.

For baldness, the series would be much longer, and each member would have one less hair than the one before; the conclusion would be that all are hairy. (The absurdity of the argument can also be pointed out by the fact that you could use it in reverse to prove that everybody is bald. Start with Yul Brynner and add one hair at a time. There will be no one hair that makes the difference between being bald and being nonbald. Hence, no matter how many more hairs a person has than the bald man, he will turn out to be bald.)

The argument forces us to *assimilate* all the members in the conceptual series to the first member. The grounds for the assimilation is, essentially, that the difference between a member and its successor is very slight. The argument ignores the fact that differences that are *separately* insignificant can (and often do) *cumulate* to be significant. One hair at a time is not significant, but the cumulative effect of pulling out 40,000 will be! Gaining an ounce won't affect your appearance, but if you gain an ounce a day for 1000 days, the *cumulative* effect (more than sixty pounds) will certainly be noticeable! Even if you were slim at the beginning of this process, by the end of it you would be fat. There is a difference between being hairy and being bald, and a difference between being slim and being fat, even though it may be hard to specify exactly the one hair or the one ounce that will make the difference.

Often slippery assimilation arguments are suggested by the rhetorical question, "But where do you draw the line?" The implication behind this question is usually that since you can't specify the one precise point where a line should be drawn, such distinctions as bald/hairy or slim/fat should not be drawn at all. But something has clearly gone wrong here.

Probably you have heard such arguments in debates about abortion. The strategy is to insist that fetal development is gradual and that each stage of development differs only slightly from those preceding and succeeding it. Thus to select any *one* time in the nine months of development and say that that moment marks the difference between the fetus and human person will look arbitrary. Many antiabortionists infer from these facts that the fetus is a human person from the moment of conception;

since we cannot draw a line, all stages represent a person. (You could equally well infer that all represent a nonperson, since the change into a person occurs at no one point. But this inference is less common.) However, both inferences are mistaken: both involve the fallacy of slippery assimilation. The mistake is that of ignoring the fact that differences that are separately trivial can cumulate to be significant. The argument from slippery assimilation does show that it will be debatable where distinctions are made, and it shows that there will be borderline cases: people who are neither clearly hairy nor clearly bald, neither clearly slim nor clearly fat, and so on. But it does not show that all the items in a conceptual series must be classified in the same way due to considerations of consistency.

The Fallacy of Slippery Precedent. A related abuse of consistency reasoning comes when a specific case is considered in relation to a whole series of further cases, some of which are morally very different from the original one. It is sometimes allowed that a particular action would, when considered by itself, be a good one to perform. However, this good action would, nevertheless, set a dangerous precedent, since it might commit us to allowing further actions that do not share the moral value of the original one. On such grounds it is often urged that even though the action in question is admitted to be good, it should not be taken because it is too closely related to further problematic actions. We shall call this type of argument the argument from *slippery precedent*. Like the slippery assimilation argument, it has some resemblance to the legitimate uses of an *a priori* analogy. Again, like that argument, it relies on a series of cases, using the existence of a related series to justify a conclusion about a member in the series.

Here is an example of this slippery use of precedent:

> As a student whose parents are undergoing divorce, and who has suffered from mononucleosis this term, you clearly would deserve an extension on your deadline. However, even though it would be fine for me to allow you this extension, if I did that, I would be bound to give an extension to every student who asked for one. I would wind up giving extensions to students who were just disorganized or who had been out drinking at parties, and soon my deadline would be completely meaningless.

We can easily imagine the familiar scene in which a professor uses this argument to reply to a student's plea for an extension. It pays the compliment of granting the student that her own request, considered by itself, is legitimate and would merit the extension. But it then insists that this legitimate extension would set a bad precedent, because it would provide a basis for further illegitimate extensions, which, in consistency, would have to be allowed. See if you can detect the same kind of reasoning in this next example, which moves up one level in the university hierarchy. (This one was used by a dean commenting on an action taken by a professor in his faculty.)

> A faculty member has launched an appeal concerning his salary. He says that he did not, in the past, receive all the special merit increments to which he was entitled. In fact, this professor is disliked by the chairman of his department, and that chairman has admitted that in the past not all deserved increments were given to the man. If you consider his appeal just by itself, you have to admit that he deserves to win it. But the problem is, if he can appeal his salary, all the other professors can do that too. To grant his appeal will set the precedent that faculty members can squeal and protest whenever they don't get just what they want from the salary levels committee, and if that

precedent is set, we'll be granting every appeal, and the very point of having such a committee will be defeated. The system would be completely unworkable. Therefore, even though this single appeal is well founded, it should not be granted because of the precedent it sets.

In these arguments, a case that is admitted to be legitimate is assimilated to further cases that are similar in *some* respects but obviously *not* legitimate. The initial case is then set in the context of these others, and the arguer insists that it would set a precedent for them. Since these further cases are not to be allowed, it is inferred that the initial case should not be allowed either on the grounds that *it would set a bad precedent.*

When you reflect on such arguments, you realize that something must be wrong with them. The problem is that the premises are implicitly inconsistent, and therefore they cannot all be acceptable. If case (a) is legitimate and cases (b), (c), and (d) are not legitimate, then *necessarily* these cases cannot all be relevantly similar to each other. There must be something about the first that relevantly differentiates it from the others as far as the decisions to be taken are concerned. Given this relevant difference, the first case *cannot* be a precedent for the others. Let's look back at the example of the student and her deadline. If she has serious family problems and has been ill during the term, her case differs significantly from another one in which a student is pressed for time just because he was disorganized. That she has been seriously handicapped by factors outside her control makes her deserving of special consideration; that line of reasoning does not apply to the other students whose cases are mentioned. To allow an extension in a hardship case is *not* a precedent for allowing it in every case, *provided we get clear why the extension is being allowed.*

Similar points can be made for our second example. A professor who, by general admission, was mistreated in the past is in a different position from others who just happen to want a higher salary. Precedent reasoning is quite legitimate in general, but it is misapplied in these arguments. The reason is very simple: cases that are straightforwardly deserving cannot be relevantly similar to other cases that are straightforwardly undeserving. The former cannot set a genuine precedent for the latter. That is the reason we call these arguments slippery; in them there is a slide from one kind of case to another. Whenever someone urges that a *good* decision would set a *bad* precedent, you can be sure that something has gone wrong. Somewhere along the line, a relevant difference has been ignored.

There are more subtle appeals to precedent that do not involve appealing to premises that are implicitly inconsistent. These more complex arguments play tricks in another way with our sense of what is fair. They admit that the further cases to which the initial case is compared are also deserving, but then they go on to add that for various reasons (costs, administrative overload, or whatever), not *all* deserving cases can be fully recognized as such. It is then argued that because all the cases cannot be treated in the same way and because all are equally deserving and relevantly similar from an administrative point of view, *none* should be allowed. Here again we have a series of cases related by analogy and an inference made, based on consistency reasoning, about the series as a whole. An example would be the following:

It is good for people to know languages other than their native language. It would be good to teach German, Chinese, French, Spanish, and Russian in public schools, if we could. Each one of these languages is important in the world, and each is allied to a culture with a valuable literature and history so that knowing it is a big intellectual advantage. But schools clearly cannot teach all these foreign languages for they just don't have the time or money.

Now we have this request, from the German community in Milwaukee, to put German in public schools as a foreign language. Doing so would be a good thing in itself, but the problem is that so would the teaching of all these other foreign languages. We just cannot fit them all in. We will have to do too much if we accept German as a precedent for foreign language teaching in public schools. We cannot teach them all, so we had better not teach any. After all, you have to draw the line somewhere, and no place is clearer than the very beginning.

The theme here is that too much of a good thing is unbearable, so we'll have to settle for none of it! The problem with this argument is different from the problem in our other slippery precedent cases. Here, since it is admitted that all the cases compared are morally similar (good), there is no inconsistency in the premises. The problem in this case is that the premises, taken together, fail to provide adequate ground for the conclusion. In effect, the argument is asking us to infer that we should allow *none* from premises that show that we cannot allow *all*. This is a hasty inference because it ignores the possibility of allowing *some*. Surely, if we cannot do every good thing, it would be better to select some good things and do them rather than do none at all out of a spurious sense of consistency. In fact, in this argument irrationality seems to be masquerading as consistency. If a number of things are equally good and advantageous, and if for practical or other reasons it is impossible to achieve all of them, we should adopt some decision procedure and select *some*. One might pursue those that are cheapest, closest to home, most closely related to existing goals already endorsed, or whatever. Some process can be used to select cases. Since the appeal to precedent in our example ignores this possibility, it is a hasty argument. Beware of administrative appeals to precedent!

We are not saying, of course, that appeals to precedent always involve mistakes. Quite the contrary: as we urged earlier, these appeals are basic in law, morality, administration, and even in logic itself. It is always important to see how relevantly similar cases would be resolved, or have been resolved in the past, when we are trying to deal with a problem. The slippery appeals to precedent that we have discussed here are abuses of what is basically a sound and important procedure. Cases should be settled in a way that is consistent with the *proper resolution* of *relevantly similar* cases. When an argument admits that a case under consideration is legitimate, but urges that this legitimate case would set a bad or unmanageable precedent, something has gone wrong. Look closely at the reasoning used. You will find that relevant differences have been ignored or that compromise solutions have gone unconsidered. A case is not properly a precedent for another unless they are similar in all features relevant to the handling of the issue.

Summary

There are, then, both legitimate and illegitimate uses of analogy. *A priori* and *inductive* analogies are fundamental in the construction of human knowledge. A refutation by logical analogy can constitute a conclusive refutation of an argument, and reasoning case-by-case is indispensable in achieving the consistent application of terms and of moral and legal principles. Inductive analogies are indispensable in enabling us to bring known cases to bear on the unknown, giving us a basis for estimates that cannot be gleaned from universal or general statements.

Nevertheless, analogies can easily be misused. Some arguments are based on analogies so loose and remote that it is hard even to classify them as either *a priori* or inductive. Others, such as the two-wrongs fallacy and the slippery uses of assimilation and precedent, are subtle abuses of the inherently legitimate case-by-case technique. Our purpose has been to give you a basic understanding of analogy in these different contexts and to develop your ability to spot the primary subject and the analogue and find relevant differences, where these exist.

Review of Terms Introduced

Analogy: A parallel or close comparison between two cases. Analogies may be used as the basis for arguments when people reason from one case to a conclusion about another deemed to be similar to the first. In addition, they may be used in explanations, as illustrations, or purely for literary style and interest.

Primary subject: In an argument by analogy, the thing that the conclusion is about.

Analogue: In an argument by analogy, the thing to which the primary subject is compared and on the basis of which the arguer reasons to the conclusion about the primary subject.

Appeals to consistency: Arguments relying on analogy and urging that similar cases be treated similarly. If A is relevantly similar to B, and if B has been treated as x, then, as a matter of consistency, A should also be treated as x. Appeals to consistency are especially common in logic, law, ethics, and administration.

Refutation by logical analogy: The refutation of one argument by the construction of another that is parallel to it in reasoning and clearly flawed.

Precedent: A relevantly similar case that has already been resolved. Reasoning by precedent is particularly common and important in law.

Conceptual issue: An issue in which the question at stake is how a concept should be applied or how it should be articulated.

A priori analogy: An argument by analogy in which the primary thrust is an appeal to consistency and in which the analogue may be entirely hypothetical or fictitious without undermining the logical force of the argument.

Inductive analogy: An argument by analogy in which the conclusion is predicted on the basis of experience with the analogue. The analogue must be a real case, and the factual features of the analogue and the primary subject are essential for determining the strength of the argument.

Counteranalogy: An analogy different from the one on which an argument is based, and leading plausibly to a conclusion different from, or contrary to, that of the original argument. If the counteranalogy is as well founded as the original one, and if it leads to a different conclusion, its construction constitutes a powerful criticism of the original argument.

Faulty analogy: Name for a fallacious argument in which the analogy is so loose and remote that there is virtually no support for the conclusion.

The two-wrongs-make-a-right fallacy: Mistake of inferring that because two wrong things are similar and one is tolerated, the other should be tolerated as well. This inference is a misuse of the appeal to consistency.

The fallacy of slippery assimilation: Argument based on the logical error of assuming that because cases can be arranged in a series, where the difference between successive members of the series is small, the cases should all be assimilated. This is a mistaken appeal to consistency. It ignores the fact that small differences can accumulate to be significant.

The fallacy of slippery precedent: Argument based on claiming that an action, though good, should not be permitted because it will set a precedent for further similar actions that are bad. Such arguments are flawed in that they use implicitly inconsistent premises. A good action cannot be relevantly similar to a bad action; there must be some relevant difference between them.

EXERCISE SET

Exercise Three

Of the following passages, first identify those that contain arguments by analogy. For each argument by analogy, identify the primary subject and the analogue and comment on the merits of the argument. If any passage contains fallacies such as two-wrongs, slippery assimilation, or slippery precedent, point this out and explain just how the fallacy is committed in that particular case.

1. People say that because nuclear weapons have not been used since 1945, they are safe and will never be used. They think that we can accumulate these weapons and get a balance of nuclear power with the Soviets and still remain safe and secure. But with 50,000 nuclear weapons in the world, we aren't very secure at all. Thinking that because it's been all right so far it will be all right later on is like a chap falling off the Empire State Building. He comes falling down, and by the time he has passed one hundred stories, he's still all right. So he calls out, "Hey folks, look. I'm ok. No need to worry."

2. The altos and tenors in a choir are like the filling in a sandwich. When you first see a sandwich you notice the bread. And, of course, the taste of a sandwich depends very much on the taste of the bread. But what would a sandwich be without a filling of delicious roast beef, cheese, or peanut butter? Just nothing at all. And in the same way, the altos and tenors make a choir's music meaningful. Maybe you don't notice these middle parts as much as you notice the sopranos and bass, but without them, the performance would be empty.

*3. "It is of course quite true that the majority of women are kind to children and prefer their own to other people's. But exactly the same thing is true of the majority of men, who nevertheless do not consider that their proper sphere is the nursery. The case may be illustrated more grotesquely by the fact that the majority of women who have dogs are kind to them and prefer their own dogs to other people's. Yet it is not proposed that women should restrict their activities to the rearing of puppies."
(G. B. Shaw, "The Womanly Woman," in *Masculine/Feminine*, ed. Betty Roszak and Theodore Roszak [New York: Harper and Row, 1969].)

4. Obviously, very small organisms such as algae, do not think. From algae, we progress by small degrees to small sea creatures, insects, birds, reptiles, mammals, and human beings. The behavior of all these creatures exhibits changes only by degrees. Therefore, if we deny mind to algae, we must deny it also to human beings. And if we grant mind to human beings, we must grant it also to algae.

5. There were some armaments limitations agreements before World War I. These agreements did not prevent World War I from occurring. Therefore, arms limitations agreements in the current decade cannot prevent World War III.

6. "Handgun control doesn't necessarily mean taking the guns away from everybody. It can mean simply to license these weapons, making it unlawful to own one without proper registration.

   "After all, what's the big deal? You need a license to get married. You need a license for your dog. You need one for your vehicle and your business. You need permits for nearly everything. Nobody seems to suffer too much. Drivers must meet certain standards in order to obtain a permit to drive. As a result, thousands of lives are saved every year.

"So why not similarly license handguns? It'll cost a little, be a little inconvenient, and maybe it'll save a few lives. It really is the least we can do."
(Letter to the editor, *Los Angeles Times*, January 23, 1981, which was cited in the *Informal Logic Newsletter*, Examples Supplement, November 1981.)

7. *Background:* In 1986, the Ontario government banned the sale of South African wines because of the repressive policies of the white government towards blacks:

"So the Ontario Government is going to stop selling South African wines and spirits. We'll show them we mean business: we'll convey to South Africa by monetary means that they must change their internal policies? No doubt all the left-wingers in the province are applauding with glee. Meanwhile we continue to import Lada cars, caviar, and many more products of Russia and its allies. Are we presumed not to care about the oppression of many times the South African population inside the communist countries?"
(Letter to the Toronto *Globe and Mail*, August 24, 1986.)

8. "If we have come to think that the nursery and the kitchen are the natural sphere of a woman we have done so exactly as the English children come to think that a cage is the natural sphere of a parrot—because they have never seen one anywhere else. I am convinced that there are rationalist parrots who can demonstrate that it would be a cruel kindness to let a parrot out to fall a prey to cats, or to forget its accomplishments and coarsen its naturally delicate fibres in an unprotected struggle for existence. Still, the only parrot a free-souled person can sympathize with is the one that insists on being let out as the first condition of its making itself agreeable. A selfish bird, you may say; one that puts its own gratification before that of the family which is so fond of it; one that, in aping the independent spirit of a man, has unparrotted itself and become a creature that has neither home-loving nature nor the strength and enterprise of a mastiff. All the same, you respect that parrot in spite of your conclusive reasoning; and if it persists, you will have either to let it out or kill it."
(G. B. Shaw, "The Womanly Woman.")

*9. *Background:* Here is a piece of advice from the Trent University Philosophy Department on the matter of footnotes:

"Footnotes, like other conventions of academic writing, have no essential connection with philosophical thinking. They are helpful for making written work easy on the eye and for showing that the writer has, so to speak, funds to support the cheques issued in the main text."

*10. "A man's time, when well husbanded, is like a cultivated field of which a few acres produce more of what is useful to life than extensive provinces, even the richest soil, when overrun with weeds and brambles."
(David Hume, "Enquiry Concerning the Principles of Morals," as quoted by Ronald Munson in *The Way of Words* [Boston: Houghton Mifflin, 1976], p. 202.)

*11. *Background:* Here is a piece on the subject of the moral status of animals. It was written by Lewis Carroll, the author of *Alice in Wonderland.* Carroll was also a logician of very considerable accomplishments. This passage is taken from his essay, "Some Popular Fallacies about Vivisection":

"In discussing the 'rights of animals,' I think I may pass by, as needing to remark, the so-called right of a race of animals to be perpetuated and the still more shadowy right of a non-existent animal to come into existence. The only question worth consideration is whether the killing of an animal is a real infringement of a right. Once grant this, and a *reductio ad absurdum* is imminent, unless we are illogical enough to assign rights to animals in proportion to their size. Never may we destroy, for our convenience, some of a litter of puppies, or open a score of oysters when nineteen would have sufficed, or light a candle in a summer evening for mere pleasure, less some hapless moth should rush to an untimely end! Nay, we must not even take a walk, with the certainty of crushing many an insect in our path, unless for really important business! Surely all this is childish. In the absolute hopelessness of drawing a line anywhere, I conclude (and I believe that many, on considering the point, will agree with me) that man has an absolute right to inflict death on animals, without assigning any reason provided that it be a painless death. But any infliction of pain needs its special justification."
(Lewis Carroll, "Some Popular Fallacies about Vivisection," *The Complete Works of Lewis Carroll* [New York: Random House, 1957].)

12. *Background:* Author Edward DeBono is discussing whether thinking can be taught:

"If thinking is indeed a skill, how is it that we do not acquire this skill in the normal course of events? We develop skill in walking by practice. . . . We develop skill in talking by communicating. . . .

Surely we must develop skill in thinking by coping with the world around us? The answer is that we do. But we must distinguish between a 'full' skill and a two-finger skill.

"Many people who teach themselves to type early in life learn to type with two fingers. This is because they do not set out to learn typing as such but to use typing in their work. With two fingers they can more quickly acquire a more tolerable level of competence than if they tried to develop skill with all ten fingers ... They learn a two-finger skill. Yet a girl who trains to be a typist can, within a few weeks, develop a much higher degree of touch-typing skill, or what we call a 'full' skill. The two-finger journalist has acquired skill in the course of dealing with a limited situation and his skill is only just sufficient to cope with that situation.

"... Similarly the academic idiom taught at schools and refined in universities is a sort of two-finger skill. It is excellent at coping with closed situations where all the information is supplied, but it is very inefficient in dealing with open-ended situations where only part of the information is given, yet a decision still has to be made."
(Edward DeBono, *Teaching Thinking* [Harmondsworth, England: Penguin Books, 1984], p. 47.)

13. Dreams among thoughts are like eagles among birds. They soar to the heights and cannot be controlled.

14. *Background:* Author Donald Griffin is discussing whether animals are conscious and what sorts of thoughts they might have, if they are:

"The content of much human consciousness does not conform to objective reality. Fear of ghosts and monsters is very basic and widespread in our species. Demons, spirits, miracles, and voices of departed ancestors are real and important to many people, as are religious beliefs.

"... Yet when we speculate about animal thoughts, we usually assume that they would necessarily involve practical down-to-earth matters, such as how to get food or escape predators.... But there is really no reason to assume that animal thoughts are rigoristically realistic. Apes and porpoises often seem playful, mischievous, and fickle, and anything but businesslike, practical, and objective. Insofar as animals do think and feel, they may fear imaginary predators, imagine unrealistically delicious foods, or think about objects and events that do not actually occur in the real world around them."
(Donald Griffin, *Animal Thinking* [Cambridge, Mass.: Harvard University Press, 1984], pp. 202–3.)

15. If a ten-year-old can get away with writing on a school fence, then an eleven-year-old can get away with breaking windows, a twelve-year-old can pull off an unpunished mugging, and a thirteen-year-old can get away with murder. Casual vandalism must be punished.

16. Certainly the United States has supported some regimes that have not had full respect for human rights, such as the Shah's regime in Iran, the government in the Philippines, and the current regime in El Salvador. But what about what the Soviets are doing? None of their own people have any civil rights that mean anything, and they are busily fighting an indigenous Moslem movement in Afghanistan and keeping down the Solidarity movement in Poland! This is the real problem, and people shouldn't harp on the errors of American foreign policy.

*17. "In a multitude of situations throughout the world, people have used and will continue to use the technique of nonviolent action for certain limited objectives. As they do so, they will not limit themselves to the same nonviolent means in all other current situations. Nor will they in advance reject the option of violence in all conceivable future situations. There are many people, particularly doctrinal and religious pacifists, who deprecate most strongly this adoption of the nonviolent technique without the nonviolent creed or philosophy or doctrine as well. This response is based on a totally misleading understanding of the situation and the possible choices before the people."
(Gene Sharp, *Gandhi as Political Strategist* [Boston: Porter Sargent Publishers, 1979], p. 124.)

18. *Background:* Here is an excerpt from a letter on the abortion issue, taken from the Calgary *Herald*, January 25, 1983:

"... that single cell is not a baby; it is simply a cell, which, if conditions permit, may become a baby. In other words, it is a 'potential baby' and it is the destruction of this potential baby that Ross calls infanticide. But as he himself puts it, there can be no 'cut off' point in the development of a baby, so why not go one step further and consider the unfertilized ovum? The ovum is half a human cell which, if conditions permit, may become a baby—it too is a potential baby. Following Ross's own logic, the destruction of an ovum would entail infanticide. Does he then denounce the birth control pill (which interferes with the release of the ovum) as infanticide?"
(Ross was a writer who had contended that a fetus achieves personhood at the moment of conception.)

19. "If you had a husband and wife who'd been quarrelling, and they were collecting crockery to throw at each other—more and more plates, bowls, heavy pottery, mugs—one subject would be crockery control. Let's limit the weight of the mugs; let's substitute plastic dishes for the heavy plates, and that would be crockery control. And on that I would welcome the advice of ceramic engineers as to how to design plates adequate without making them dangerous. But anyone realizes that the true problem is: what we need is family counselling. We need to deal with the differences that are bound to come up between husband and wife, or between neighbours, or between us and the Soviets—how to deal with those differences in such a way that nobody will reach for the crockery. And, on that subject, don't ask for a ceramic engineer or a pottery manufacturer. You don't ask for a military man to give us expert advice on how to deal with our differences. That's a subject for every human being who has kids with whom they quarrel, parents, neighbours, boss and secretary; we know more about how to deal with differences than a nuclear physicist who does nothing but study nuclear particles. The more he narrows his mind down to the hardware, the less he understands the problem."
(Roger Fisher, quoted in *Nuclear Peace* [Toronto: CBC Transcripts, 1982].)

*20. *Background:* Representative James G. Martin of North Carolina had this to say about the proposal that the United States and the Soviet Union should agree to a bilateral freeze on the development and production of nuclear weapons:

"Now, let us suppose we had a U.S. team and a Soviet team, and the U.S. team was 28 years old in average age. Many of our 28-year-old players would be superior to the youthful players on the Soviet side; ours would have been around the base paths more, they would have seen pick-off plays that the others have not seen yet, and they would have seen more curve balls across the plate and could better judge those that would just miss the plate.

"Yet, on the other hand, the younger Soviet fellows would have sharper eyesight, they would be a bit faster, and their hand-to-eye coordination would be superior. Their energy and enthusiasm would be higher. So it would be a good competition between relative youth and relative age, and each team would win some games.

"But now, suppose, in the interest of maintaining security of the national pastime, we decided to freeze the rosters so that neither team could replace its players. Well, for a year or two, our older players would still be able to compete. But what about 10 years after that? Then we would have 40-year-old players trying to compete with their 30-year-old players. The will may be there but the capability would not. We would have reached a period of obsolescence on that baseball team."
(Representative Martin was quoted in *The New York Times*, April 25, 1983.)

NOTES

1. C. S. Lewis, *Mere Christianity* (New York: Macmillan, 1952), p. 75.

2. Albert Einstein, as quoted by Jonathan Schell in *The Fate of the Earth* (New York: Knopf, 1982), p. 10.

3. Alan Connery, Calgary *Herald*, July 6, 1979. Reprinted with permission of the Calgary *Herald*.

4. Brothers's advice was reprinted in the *Informal Logic Newsletter* in the examples supplement for 1979.

5. Toronto *Globe and Mail*, February 8, 1982.

6. Robert Nozick, *Anarchy State and Utopia* (New York: Basic Books, 1974), pp. 169–70.

7. Toronto *Globe and Mail*, November 22, 1986.

8. David Hume, *Dialogues Concerning Natural Religion* in *The Empiricists* (New York: Anchor Press, 1974), p. 467.

9. Letter to the Calgary *Herald*, March 12, 1976.

10. Francis Bacon, *The True Greatness of Kingdoms*, quoted by Susan Stebbing in *Thinking to Some Purpose* (London: Pelican Books, 1938), p. 123.

11. Letter to the Calgary *Herald*, May 7, 1984.

CHAPTER

11

Philosophical Connections

We have now looked at the nature of argument, conditions of accept-ability and relevance, a diagramming method for representing argument structure, and several distinct ways in which premises may provide adequate grounds for a conclusion. We have discussed some common forms of formal deductive validity, and we have seen that arguments may be deductively valid by virtue of meaning as well as form. Also, we have examined various kinds of argument by analogy. Now we look at two other ways in which premises provide grounds for conclusions, and we pause to take an overview, bringing in some of the issues that philosophers and logicians have debated regarding the classification and analysis of different kinds of arguments.

Conductive Arguments

Think back to the convergent support pattern that we defined in Chapter Seven. In most deductively valid arguments and in analogies, the support provided by premises is linked, not convergent. There are a few exceptions, as when a person offers two separate premises, both of which deductively entail the conclusion. This example is redundant in a way, and it rarely happens, but it is not unheard of. In an argument in which support is convergent, premises count separately in favor of the conclusion, and if one premise turns out to be unacceptable, the others are not affected as they would be in a linked argument. There are arguments in which support is convergent and the only relation operating is that of relevance, usually conceptual or normative relevance. These arguments we call *conductive arguments*.

Here is a simple example:

(1) She never takes her eyes off him in a crowd, and (2) she is continually restless when he is out of town. (3) At any opportunity, she will introduce his name in a conversation. (4) And no other man has ever occupied her attention for so long. I don't care what she says about it, you can tell (5) she is in love with him.

The issue here is the interpretation of human behavior. The person arguing has offered several pieces of evidence to support his hypothesis. Even if one piece were faulty, the others would still count in support of his conclusion. Each piece of information is relevant, and separately relevant, to establishing that conclusion. This argument proceeds by specifying a number of relevant factors and then by weighing these factors to provide a basis for the conclusion.

All conductive arguments employ the convergent support pattern as this one does. This argument works as follows:

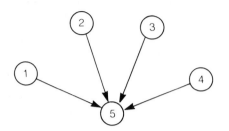

However, it does not follow that all convergent support arguments are conductive arguments. Some of them are the result of combining other types of arguments; several premises might establish an analogy, for instance, while another actually entails the conclusion by itself. All conductive arguments are convergent, but not all convergent arguments are conductive.

Some philosophers have referred to these arguments based on separately relevant factors as *good reasons arguments.* The relevant factors provide *reasons* for the conclusion, though they do not deductively entail it. But one problem with the good reasons label is that it suggests that all these arguments are good ones. And they are not. Some may specify, as relevant, factors that are really irrelevant—as when straw man, *ad hominem,* and guilt-by-association fallacies are used. Others may provide premises that are genuinely relevant but do not add up to give enough support for the conclusion. To avoid the suggestion that all conductive arguments are good ones, we have avoided calling them *good reasons arguments.*

Conductive arguments are common in reasoning about conceptual and normative issues—how phenomena are to be classified or what should be done. Also, they are common when there are disputes about interpretation. Arguments about the correct interpretation of actions are often used in social theory and in history; these are frequently arguments in which independently relevant factors are drawn together, for it will usually be the case that there are several quite distinct pieces of evidence that count for or against one interpretation or the other. The recognition of counterconsiderations is, in fact, especially common and natural when conductive arguments are being used. As you will remember from Chapter Seven, counterconsiderations can be represented on diagrams the way a separately relevant premise can be. But wavy lines are used to indicate that the point counts *against* the conclusion rather than for it. Obviously, when people admit the existence of counterconsiderations and still wish to support their conclusion, they are committed to saying that the supporting relevant factors *outweigh* the countervailing ones.

It is rather difficult to give any general guidelines about appraising conductive arguments. Our previous discussion of relevance will bear on this, and it will help us to sift through premises that are put forward as relevant but are really irrelevant. Fundamentally, the issue depends on how the reasons stated in the premises weigh up against counterconsiderations. Determining their strength requires background knowledge and judgment. Thus rules that apply across a variety of topics will give only rather general guidelines for appraisal. Perhaps it is for this reason that logicians have paid relatively lttle attention to conductive arguments. Counterconsiderations usually bear on the conclusion even though they are not explicitly acknowledged by the arguer. It is, then, a creative task of evaluation to think what these counterconsiderations are and to determine how much they count against the conclusion and whether their import can be overcome by the evidence or reasons put forward in the premises.

We'll illustrate this point by considering an example:

(1) Voluntary euthanasia, where a terminally ill patient consciously chooses to die, should be made legal. (2) The right to life, which is commonly accepted, is the right to live if one chooses. Also (3), voluntary euthanasia would save many patients from unbearable pain. (4) It would cut social costs. (5) It would save relatives the agony of watching people they love die an intolerable and undignified death. Even though (6) there is some danger of abuse, and even though (7) we do not know for certain that a cure for the patient's disease will not be found, (1) voluntary euthanasia should be a legal option for the terminally ill patient.

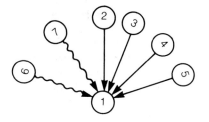

In this argument four factors are cited as support for the normative conclusion that voluntary euthanasia should be legalized. The last statement acknowledges two counterconsiderations. To accept the conclusion on the basis of the supporting premises, we must judge that they outweigh the stated counterconsiderations and any other counterconsiderations that are not stated in the argument. Clearly, a person who put forward the preceding argument would believe that the alleviation of pain and the recognition of the right to life are more important, on balance, than the risk that voluntary euthanasia might lead to abuses and the chance that a cure might be found so that the patient would not have had to die. To appraise the argument, we have to reflect on whether we agree with this judgment—given the acceptability of the premises and their relevance to the conclusion. There is no simple logical formula for such judgments of the balance of considerations. Also, there are counterconsiderations other than those acknowledged by the arguer. For instance, many religious groups oppose voluntary euthanasia, and that may be a reason against legalizing it. (Laws that fail to have significant public support can lead to many problems.) Also, many people believe that patients undergoing severe pain are not capable of making rational decisions about their lives, so that voluntary euthanasia would not really be voluntary after all. Other objections to the conclusion may be raised.

Obviously, evaluating this argument is very difficult. We can set out a logical structure for raising questions about such arguments as this, and the structure is a useful guide for thought. Answers, however, especially for issues as profound as that of euthanasia, will emerge from individual judgment about the significance of the various factors.

The logical scheme for appraising conductive arguments is as follows:

1. Determine whether the premises offered to support the conclusion are acceptable.

2. Determine whether the premises offered to support the conclusion are positively relevant to it.

3. Determine whether any counterconsiderations acknowledged by the arguer are negatively relevant to the conclusion.

4. Think what additional counterconsiderations, not acknowledged by the arguer, there might be that are negatively relevant to the conclusion.

5. Reflect on whether the premises, taken together, outweigh the counterconsiderations, taken together, and make a judgment. Try to articulate good reasons for that judgment.

6. If you judge that the premises do outweigh the counterconsiderations, you have judged that the (G) condition is satisfied. Provided that (A) and (R) are also satisfied, you deem the argument cogent. Otherwise, you deem it not to be cogent.

As with other cases of argument evaluation, following this procedure does not quite take you to the stage of determining whether the conclusion is true, or whether you have good reasons to accept it. It takes you only to the stage of determining whether the stated premises provide good reasons for accepting the conclusion. If you think the argument as stated is cogent, then you do think there are good reasons to accept the conclusion, so presumably you will accept it on the basis of the argument. But if you think the argument is not cogent, you may wish to proceed further to see whether the conclusion could be supported by other evidence or reasons not stated in the original argument. To proceed, you have to reflect on whether there are further considerations, not stated in the argument, that would count in favor of the conclusion and would outweigh any counterconsiderations. Doing so takes you beyond appraising the stated argument and moves you ahead to a stage where you are amending or reconstructing that argument by adding more premises of your own. It is an important stage, of course, when your real interest is in whether you should accept the conclusion and not merely in whether the conclusion is well supported by the particular argument you are evaluating.

To say that the pro factors outweigh con factors is to speak metaphorically, of course. The image brought to mind is that of an old-fashioned scale in which weights are placed on each side to balance the scale or to achieve a state of equilibrium. To say that we weigh the pros and cons, or see how the premises can provide grounds in the face of counterconsiderations, is to think of evidence and reasons as having significance that can be measured. This concept may sound obscure and difficult, but there is a sense in which people use it all the time, and they often seem to achieve reasonably reliable results.

To see that they do, consider some simple examples. Like the example of euthanasia, these examples involve normative conclusions; unlike that one, the issue of significance is clearcut. Suppose a mother is trying to decide which of two babysitters to hire. Jane lives five minutes closer by car than Sue. But Jane has been convicted of theft, whereas Sue, whom the mother has personally known for some years, appears to be very reliable. Clearly the comparative closeness of Jane counts in favor of hiring her, whereas her unreliability counts against it and in favor of hiring Sue instead. A judgment of significance is very easy to make here; reliability outweighs the rather trivial factor of five extra minutes driving time and a little more gas where a babysitter is concerned. We could offer reasons for this judgment of significance in terms of the risk to children and property if an unreliable babysitter were hired. In fact, the weighting of factors here seems so obviously right that few people would question it or bother to support it with reasons.

Weighing pros and cons is nearly always a feature of practical decision-making, and sometimes it is quite simple, as this example illustrates. The fact that evaluating conductive arguments depends on our making such judgments of significance does not mean that the evaluation is an impossible task or that agreement will never be achieved.

As we mentioned earlier, conductive arguments appear in many contexts. Moral reasoning is an especially important one, but we also find conductive arguments in history, science, literature, philosophy, and psychology. In fact, they are likely to occur anywhere we may have distinct factors that count in favor of a conclusion and other distinct factors that count against it. As with moral reasoning, making judgments about how these supporting and countervailing factors weigh up can be either quite difficult or relatively easy.

Suppose that a scientist had five experiments that tended to confirm a hypothesis and three that tended to disconfirm it. Suppose that he needed to make a practical decision as to whether he should continue to investigate this hypothesis, or whether, on the other hand, he should consider the three negative experiments sufficient to disconfirm it. He would almost certainly engage in conductive reasoning—trying to weigh the significance of the positive experiments against the significance of the negative ones, and trying to weigh all of this against the importance of the hypothesis for other scientific work and for human life in general. Judgments would be required. In some cases, reasons could be given for allowing some points to outweigh others. For instance, if the negative experiments were done in a lab in which the machinery had broken down shortly afterwards, then the machinery's possible unreliability when the experiments were done would give the scientist a reason for not letting these negative experiments count very much—for letting the positive experiments outweigh them in significance.

EXERCISE SET

Exercise One

Evaluate the following conductive arguments. State any counterconsiderations on which your evaluation depends. If you believe that you lack the background knowledge necessary to evaluate the argument, state what sort of knowledge you would need and, if feasible, how you could go about finding it if there were a practical need to do so.

1. Susan must be angry with John because she persistently refuses to talk to him and she goes out of her way to avoid him. Even though she used to be his best friend, and even though she still spends a lot of time with his mother, I think she is really annoyed with him right now.

*2. There is no point in giving money to charity. The charitable organizations often waste it. Besides, when people are really needy, governments should support them and not rely on charity to do it. In addition, the advertisements put out by some of these charities are so emotional that they are positively manipulative.

3. You should return books to the library on time. When borrowing them, you in effect contract to do so. Also, other people may need them, and you can avoid expensive fines.

4. Interdisciplinary courses are not worth taking. They are hard for professors to teach. They are hard for students to understand. They demand so much extra research, for essays, that students do not have a hope of getting a good mark. Besides, many interdisciplinary courses try to combine so many different things that they wind up being a mishmash of unrelated theories and ideas.

*5. In 1986 the Soviet Union seemed genuinely anxious for peace and arms control. It has three times committed itself to a ban on testing nuclear weapons. It has proposed a plan to eliminate all nuclear weapons by the year 2000. It has released a number of Jewish dissidents, most notably Anatoly Scharansky, whose imprisonment had been a prime obstacle to improving relations with the United States. It has even approached the Chinese government about improving relations and resolving border disputes. Despite its continued manufacture and deployment of nuclear systems allowed by previous arms agreements, and despite its continued interest in the latest U.S. military technology—an interest the Soviet Union is willing to improve even through spying—the preponderance of evidence indicates that the Soviet Union wants peace and arms control.

6. There is no free will. For the will to be free, it would have to be not caused by anything, and this is almost surely impossible. Besides, we all know people sometimes act out of control and can't fully choose what they do. Look at alcoholics, for instance. Religious people say God made us with free will. But there may not even be a god. And if there is, He would control the whole world and would control human actions so there wouldn't be any free will anyhow.

*7. The American Revolution was not a typical revolution. For one thing, the people in revolt were mainly middle class or upper class—not peasants. For another, the object of attack was something far away—a government in England—and not the close structure of the society in which the war occurred. In addition, the internal workings of the society did not change so very much after the revolution. Despite the fact that it is called a revolution, and despite its great importance for the history of the world, the American Revolution should not be thought of as a model for other revolutions. If we think this way, we will underestimate the importance of poor classes in the revolutionary process and we will fail to see the real potential for lasting violence after a revolution.

8. *Background:* The author is discussing the problems of rape and the question of whether rape is due to natural psychological impulses:

"Another canon in the apologetics of rape is that, if it were not for learned social controls, all men would rape. Rape is held to be natural behavior, and not to rape must be learned. But in truth, rape is not universal to the human species. Moreover, studies of rape in our culture reveal that, far from being impulsive behavior, most rape is planned. Professor Amir's study reveals that in cases of group rape (the 'gangbang' of masculine slang), 90 percent of the rapes were planned; in pair rapes, 83 percent were planned; and in single rapes, 58 percent were planned. These figures should significantly discredit the image of the rapist as a man who is suddenly overcome by sexual needs society does not allow him to fulfill."
(Susan Griffin, "Rape: The All-American Crime," in M. Vetterling-Braggin, F. Elliston, and J. English, eds., *Feminism and Philosophy* [Totowa, N.J.: Littlefield Adams, 1977], p. 315.)
(*Hint:* There is a subargument here.)

9. There are many reasons to doubt whether teachers should be subjected to tests of competence after they have been teaching for some years. After all, teachers were tested at colleges and universities before they became teachers. Furthermore, other professions are not tested in midstream. Some teachers have been given legal and moral guarantees of continued positions, and the tests jeopardize them. In addition, tests for teachers are unreliable. Another problem is that if teachers fail, poor salary conditions may mean that the new teachers hired to replace them are just as ill-qualified as the fired ones.
(Adapted from "When Testing Teachers May be Hoax," by Albert Shanker, *The New York Times,* July 21, 1984.) (Shanker wrote about a teacher test given in Arkansas. Of 28,000 teachers given a three-part test in reading, writing, and math, 10 percent failed.)

10. *Background:* The issue here is whether a particular vaccine should be used against foot-and-mouth disease, a serious and highly contagious disease that sometimes occurs among cattle. The author writes about the problem in Great Britain:

". . . in deciding whether to use vaccine there are several points to be considered which you were unable to detail in your article:

"–It is impossible to forecast which of the 60 known sub-types of virus will be the one to attack British cattle in the next outbreak. The cost of the vaccine rises steeply as each new sub-type is added to give the appropriate 'cocktail' of vaccine.

"–The price quoted is that of the manufacturer. It does not include the massive costs of administering a dose to each of the 5 million cloven-hoofed animals in Britain.

"–Immunity is short-lived, especially in younger stock, so that the vaccine would have to be given twice every year to ensure a good degree of immunity.

"–Pigs do not immunize well, and can become a source of virus for other species on the farm. This has been noted in Italy.

"–Strains of virus attenuated and made safe for one species of livestock may still be dangerous for other species.

"–Vaccinated cattle which happen to come into contact with field strains of virus may become symptomless carriers of the disease. Our livestock trade would vanish if such were the case, as no country will knowingly import this catastrophic disease.

". . . I am certain that if and when there is a safe, efficient, and cheap vaccine for this disease, we shall adopt it; nobody likes the thought of slaughtering herds as we have to do at present. The controversy about 'stamping out' versus vaccination is one which has gone on for years and certainly a vaccination programme would bring rich rewards to the manufacturers. . . . But I doubt whether such a policy would be a scientific or an economic good for Britain."
(Letter by B. H., *The Economist*, April 11–17, 1981.)

*11. The Bible is among the most trustworthy of ancient documents. We can see that this statement is true for a number of reasons. First, the New Testament was written only 20 to 70 years after the events it records. Second, the oldest manuscript of the New Testament is a copy of originals that were made about 250 years after these originals were written. It is closer to the time of the original than other ancient manuscripts, such as those of Aristotle's *Metaphysics*, for instance. Third, there are more than 13,000 surviving copies of various portions of the New Testament, which date from ancient and medieval times. This fact means that it is highly probable that the original documents are well represented. As far as the Old Testament is concerned, the recently discovered *Dead Sea Scrolls* are 700–1000 years closer in time to the original events than earlier manuscripts we used to rely on and yet their wording is very close to that of these other manuscripts. This is strong evidence that the text is accurately transmitted. In addition to all of these reasons, one of the world's outstanding archaeological experts says that archaeology confirms that the events described in the Old Testament did occur. Thus the Bible is among the most trustworthy of ancient documents.
(Based on a leaflet distributed by the Inter-Varsity Christian Fellowship.)

Inductive Arguments

Hume's Account of Inductive Argument. We have referred to inductive analogies but not to a general category of inductive arguments. Some of you may have wondered about this omission, since the concept of inductive reasoning is a familiar and common one. Within philosophy, induction was made famous by Hume, who posed some skeptical problems about it. Consider this very simple argument:

1. Every day in known human history the sun has risen.
Therefore,
2. Tomorrow the sun will rise.

Hume pointed out that although we depend in ordinary life on this inference and thousands more just like it, the argument given does not fully demonstrate its conclusion. (By *fully demonstrate*, Hume seems to have meant "prove by a deductively valid argument.") It is possible, Hume insisted, that the premise of this argument is true and its conclusion false. For all we know, tomorrow could be different in this basic way from all the days humanity has known. The behavior of the sun is not guaranteed by the laws of deductive logic!

We might try to rectify this problem by adding another premise to Hume's argument, thus altering it to read:

—— 1. Every day in known human history the sun has risen.
Added Premise: The future will resemble the past.
Therefore,
2. Tomorrow the sun will rise.

Now the argument appears deductively valid. The premises, if true, logically guarantee the truth of the conclusion. But now the problem is that *we do not know whether the added premise is true*. For one thing, it is terribly vague. In what ways would the future have to resemble the past for this premise to be true? We know that past futures have resembled past pasts in some aspects, though not in others. The added premise is so vague that we would not know how to determine whether it is acceptable, for it does not specify in how many respects and in what sorts of respects the future is supposed to resemble the past. However, apart from vagueness, the added premise poses another problem. It seems simply to assert the very connection that Hume was worried about in the first place. Obviously, *if* we knew that the future would fully resemble the past, then, since we know the sun has risen in the past, we could deduce that it will rise in the future. *But we do not know this.* Within past experience there have been considerable changes in the world, and we cannot rule out future erratic behavior by the sun! To use the added premise in this context is just question-begging.

The problem of induction has puzzled logicians and philosophers ever since Hume posed it in the eighteenth century. Philosophers approach the problem in different ways. Some have argued that Hume's account proves the truth of a kind of skepticism about the everyday world. Even such basic beliefs as the one that the next page of this book will have print on it are founded on induction and cannot be proven to be true. Others accept Hume's account as a challenging problem and try to improve on inductive arguments like the one about the sun. Sometimes they hunt for more acceptable supplementary premises—premises that will strengthen the argument without being question-begging. Other philosophers reject Hume's account as one generating a false and unreal problem. They contend that Hume quite unwittingly assumed a false theory of argument when he developed the problem of induction. He assumed that only deductively valid arguments are rationally respectable, and this assumption is just not true. In this view, Hume's problem of induction simply goes away when we recognize that there are a number of different types of argument, and nondeductive arguments do not count as poor arguments simply because they fail to be deductively valid.

Weaker and Stronger Inductive Arguments. We have some inclination to support this last approach. But the problem is a very large one that will not be fully discussed here. Instead let's take another look at the argument that Hume's philosophy has made so famous and see just which of its features make it an *inductive* argument:

—— 1. Every day in known human history the sun has risen.
Therefore,
2. The sun will rise tomorrow.

In this argument both the premise and the conclusion are *empirical*. That is, they are not necessary truths and they are not normative propositions. They are propositions describing the way the world has been, or will be, experienced. The premise describes a great number of instances within human history; the conclusion makes a statement about one instance that has not been experienced yet. In the *induction* some examined cases are cited, and the inference is made that an unexamined case(s) will be like them. Such arguments are often called *enumerative inductions* since the inference is based on a number of cases enumerated in the premises.

Another famous enumerative induction is as follows:

1. All the swans ever seen in the northern hemisphere before the year 1900 were white.
Therefore,
2. All swans, in all times and places, are white.

In this case, though the premise *is* true, the conclusion turns out to be false. Black swans are found in Australia.

Sometimes enumerative inductions include statistics and more exact numbers, as in the following:

1. Fifty-one percent of the population of Cincinnati is female.
Therefore,
2. Fifty-one percent of the total population of the United States is female.

In these inductive arguments an inference is made from an empirical premise to an empirical conclusion, and the assumption behind the inference seems to be (roughly) that the world we experience is uniform and regular enough so that the *unexamined* cases referred to in the conclusion will resemble the *examined* cases described in the premises. The arguments do seem to provide grounds for the conclusion. But just as Hume wondered whether tomorrow would be like other days, we can wonder whether Cincinnati is a typical American city with respect to the distribution of the two sexes. It is possible that it is not, and therefore it is possible that the premises of the inductive argument should be true and the conclusion nevertheless be false.

All inductive arguments apply a method of inference that depends upon an assumption of continuities within nature and our experience of nature. If we start to doubt that these continuities exist, then these arguments will seem shaky. Indeed, if we start to doubt these continuities, language itself may seem shaky, for the regular use of words presupposes that objects we talk about remain more or less stable. This whole matter has occupied such philosophers as Hume, Kant, Wittgenstein, and Russell, who tried in various ways to demonstrate that the natural world is reliable. No doubt this fundamental assumption behind inductive reasoning is something you will wish to explore further if you study other areas of philosophy.

Hume's question was:

Concerning all inductive arguments, what, if anything, gives them any rational force?

As we have seen, this is a deep philosophical problem. Another problem about inductive arguments, however, can be given a more practical focus:

Within the category of inductive arguments, what makes some such arguments better or stronger than others?

This second practical question is distinct from Hume's question about induction. Hume asked a basic question *about a whole category* of arguments. The second question asks about a distinction *within that category:* the distinction between stronger and weaker inductive arguments. Certainly this is a distinction we make in common life and common reasoning. Contrast, for instance:

Argument (1)
1. I visited the zoo once and people were unfriendly to me.
So,
2. The city in which the zoo is located is an unfriendly place.

Argument (2)
1. Of 400 first-year students tested, 300 passed the reading skills test.
So,
2. Of the entire first-year class of 2000 students, three-quarters would be able to pass the reading skills test if they took it.

Both these arguments are inductive. In fact, both are enumerative inductions. The first is obviously a weak argument, for the inference about a whole city is based on a single experience. Social scientists call such arguments *anecdotal*, for they use a personal encounter or anecdote to make a generalization that is too broad to be fully supported on the strength of limited personal experience. The second example is like the first in being inductive, but obviously it is a stronger argument because the evidence on which the conclusion is based is so much more extensive. The second argument is not based purely on anecdotal evidence, but rather on the test results of 400 students.

It seems, then, that within the category of inductive arguments we can distinguish between stronger and weaker arguments. It is this aspect of inductive argumentation that we shall study in Chapters Twelve and Thirteen. Actually, even Hume acknowledged that in practice we do, and must, distinguish between stronger and weaker inductive arguments. Without doing so we literally could not survive. That most babies have thrived on milk is good reason to believe a particular baby will thrive on milk, whereas a friend's being late once is not a good reason to believe he will be late in the future. In such everyday contexts and in more complex scientific ones as well, inductive reasoning is essential, and strong inductive arguments are—and should be—taken more seriously than weak ones.

Assessing Inductive Reasoning.   If you think about the contrast between argument (1) and argument (2) in the preceding section, one idea that naturally comes to mind is that the distinction between weak and strong inductive arguments depends on *quantity*. When you have more examined cases in the premises, you have a stronger argument, and when you have fewer examined cases, you have a weaker argument. Comparing these two examples could lead you to think that whenever more cases are enumerated, the inductive argument is stronger. This quantitative approach to inductive reasoning has appealed to many students of the subject. Unfortunately, though, it doesn't quite work.

Background Knowledge.   There are two reasons that a quantitative approach to induction is not sufficient to make the distinction between better and worse inductive reasoning. First, a *purely* quantitative approach ignores the role played by background knowledge in induction. We'll use an illustration to show why this background knowledge has to enter the picture. Let's say you are examining robins' eggs for size. Suppose you examine six eggs and you find them all to be between one inch and one and one-quarter inches in diameter. Given what you already know about bird species in general and robins in particular, even this small sample of robins' eggs would be sufficient to give you a strong inductive basis for the conclusion that all robins' eggs are between three-quarters inch and one and one-half inches in diameter. We have good evidence that robins themselves fall within a fairly narrow size range and that eggs will have to be small enough for the robins to lay, and so on. Thus, in this case, an enumerative induction based on only six examined cases would be a fairly strong argument.

But now think of a different enumerative induction based on evidence about six cases. Suppose that we were to go to France to examine six lakes. Suppose that all six turned out to be slightly contaminated with mercury and, on the basis of this evidence, we wanted to infer that all the lakes in France are slightly contaminated with mercury. This would be a very weak inductive inference. Lakes in France just aren't uniform enough! The problem is they are not as similar to each other as are robins, and we do not have background knowledge that bears on their containing or not containing mercury in the same way that the size of robins bears on the size of robins' eggs. The strength of inductive arguments that move from examined cases to unexamined cases depends on *how likely the examined cases are to represent the unexamined ones,* and *this likelihood varies enormously depending on what sorts of things you are talking about.* An argument reaching a conclusion about all birds of a species from a sample of six of them is a much stronger inductive argument than one reaching a conclusion about all the lakes in a country from a sample of six because of what we know independently about the relative uniformity of robins on the one hand and lakes on the other.

Background knowledge shows us how representative the examined cases are likely to be. We cannot get along without this knowledge in inductive reasoning, and we need to appeal to it to back up judgments about stronger and weaker inductive arguments. Because background knowledge is necessary in this way, a purely quantitative approach to inductive reasoning is not possible.

Inferences-to-Explanations.   The other reason that a quantitative approach to inductive reasoning is not adequate is that not all inductive arguments are enumerative inductions. Since enumerative inductions are comparatively simple and since they have been very significant in the history of philosophy, we have concentrated on them first. But there are other inductive arguments too. An inductive argument is one in which a broader empirical hypothesis is inferred from empirical evidence on the underlying assumption that regularities observed in nature will persist. In enumerative inductions, this broader hypothesis makes the claim that some or all unexamined cases will resemble the cases examined already. But other inductive arguments are more complex in that they make an inference to a kind of explanation. A phenomenon, or set of phenomena, is observed, and it is inferred that some hypothesis is true on the grounds that the hypothesis would explain these things. The most common type of inference-to-an-explanation is that in which the conclusion is a statement of *causal relationship.* Some such arguments have enumerative inductive inferences within them.

Here is one example:

1. Every time I have swum in chlorinated water I have come down with a rash.
2. Every time I have swum in lake or ocean water, I have not come down with a rash.
3. Whenever I swim in chlorinated water I will get a rash.
And,
4. Whenever I swim in lake or ocean water I will not get a rash.
So,
5. Chlorine is the significant difference between chlorinated water, and lake or ocean water, with reference to getting a rash.
So,
6. Chlorine causes me to get a rash.
So,
7. I am allergic to chlorine.

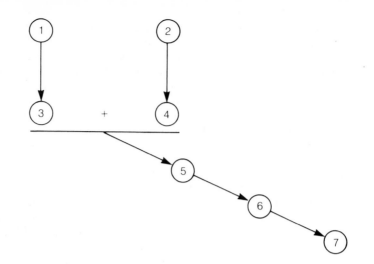

The inferences from (1) to (3) and from (2) to (4) involve enumerative inductions. The arguer goes further than this, though, when she reaches conclusions (6) and (7). She infers from the *correlation* between swimming in chlorinated water and getting a rash that swimming in the water is the *cause* of her getting a rash. The further inductive inference is an inference-to-an-explanation of this causal relationship; the conclusion is that the causal relationship itself may be explained by reference to allergy. In the argument as a whole, then, there are two inductive inferences that are enumerative and two further inductive inferences that are inferences-to-an-explanations.

An inference-to-an-explanation has the following basic form:

1. *P* is true.
2. If *Q* were true, it would be a good (or the best) explanation for the fact that *P* is true.
Therefore, probably,
3. *Q* is true.

You can see how this form is illustrated in the argument about swimming and getting a rash. At one stage we have the following:

1. A correlation between getting a rash and swimming in chlorinated water exists.
2. A good explanation of this correlation would be that swimming in chlorinated water causes me to get a rash.
Therefore, probably,
3. Swimming in chlorinated water causes me to get a rash.

Immediately afterward in a repetition of the same kind of inference, we have the following:

1. Swimming in chlorinated water causes me to get a rash.
2. A good explanation for this causal relationship would be that I am allergic to chlorine.
Therefore, probably,
3. I am allergic to chlorine.

Whatever we need to assess explanatory inductions, it will quite obviously be something other than the mere *numbers* of examined cases described in the premises. Explanatory inductions do not depend solely on quantitative considerations, for a crucial aspect of the assessment will be the acceptability of the premise asserting that *Q* would be a good explanation of *P*. The appraisal of the argument will hinge largely on this matter, which, again, will bring in background knowledge and judgments as to how well different proposed explanations satisfy our criteria of a "good explanation."

All these complications have made some philosophers despair of ever being able to formulate general logical rules that people could use to evaluate the strength of inductive arguments. There are formal systems of inductive logic, but none are widely accepted in the way that formal systems of deductive logic are.

In this book we do not try to put forward a completely general formal set of rules that you can use to distinguish strong from weak inductive arguments. We believe that background knowledge is extremely important in the evaluation of inductive arguments. Relevant background knowledge varies a great deal from one example to another. That was the point of the illustration about robins and lakes. We cannot easily detach any "form" of these arguments from their content. In this respect inductive arguments seem to resemble conductive arguments and analogies.

Our approach to induction will be essentially practical and critical. For cultural reasons we have decided to concentrate on a particular context and a particular type of inductive reasoning. The context is that of short reports in newspapers and magazines and the type of inductive reasoning is that used in scientific studies of people and their problems. Social science enjoys wide public attention and has great political influence through educational systems, psychological testing, and government policy formation in many areas. For these reasons it is important that we gain some tools that we can use to evaluate the reasoning used in social science. In this book we have organized two chapters around a variety of themes selected because they are very useful in enabling you to understand and evaluate those brief reports of "results" that you so often see in the media and that are often cited in documents of public policy. We have organized our study around these reports because this is the form in which most of us consume social science. Our hope is to make you more critical, competent consumers of social science and to make you less likely to take "results" as totally authoritative simply because the work of researchers has been described and some precise-looking statistics have been thrown in. Our approach to induction covers only a part of the subject, but that part we have selected is interesting and socially important. We hope that some of you have had your curiosity aroused by the difficulties of appraising inductive reasoning and that you will go on to study induction further in courses on probability theory and the philosophy of science.

Different Senses of *Inductive*

Before closing this discussion we should deal with one further complication. You may have heard somewhere that "all arguments are either deductive or inductive." In our sense of *inductive*, this statement is not true. *A priori* analogies and conductive arguments are not inductive in our sense, and they are not deductive either. People who say that all arguments are either inductive or deductive use the word *inductive* in a broader meaning than we use it here.

The most typical broader sense of *inductive* is that in which it simply means "nondeductive." Obviously, if inductive arguments are by definition nondeductive, then, since all arguments must necessarily be either deductive or nondeductive, all arguments must necessarily be either deductive or inductive. (Since *deductive* and *nondeductive* express contradictory predicates, these terms will exhaust the possibilities.)

In this book we are giving *inductive* its own definition, which is not formulated by contrast with *deductive*. In our sense, *inductive* and *deductive* will be contrary predicates, not contradictory ones. We have made this choice because we find the definition of *inductive* as "nondeductive" simply too broad to be useful. According to that definition, every argument that is not deductively valid can turn out to be an inductive argument. This situation would put conductive arguments, *ad hominem* arguments, *a priori* analogies, enumerative inductions, cases of guilt by association, explanatory inductions, and many other arguments in the same category. These various arguments are quite different from each other in a number of ways, as you no doubt realize by now. Such a broad definition of *inductive* means that one can scarcely say anything useful about the category.

Historically, induction has been closely associated with empirical science. Influenced by this association, some modern theorists who have used the very broad sense of *inductive* have then gone on to identify inductive arguments with those used in empirical science. The combination of the broad definition of *inductive* as "nondeductive" and a sensitivity to history has led them to forget the very existence of other arguments commonly used in law, history, ethics, and other fields. Thus the broad classification can be quite misleading. We believe that we have excellent reasons not to adopt that system in this book. We do wish to explain it, however, as you will quite likely encounter it in other contexts.

In this book, then, *inductive* does not mean "nondeductive." There are deductive arguments, inductive arguments, and other arguments—conductive arguments and *a priori* analogies—that fit in neither category. In our sense, inductive arguments are arguments in which the premises and conclusion are all empirical propositions; the conclusion is not deductively entailed by the premises; the reasoning used to infer the conclusion from the premises is based on the assumption that the regularities described in the premises will persist; and the inference is either that unexamined cases will resemble examined ones or that a hypothesis is probably true because it has explanatory value. Given this narrower sense of *inductive*, the "inductive-deductive" split does *not* exhaust the possibilities for arguments. Many arguments in everyday life and in empirical science are inductive in our sense, and we do our best to give you some helpful strategies for appraising them.

Review of Terms Introduced

Conductive arguments: Arguments in which the pattern of support is convergent and premises are put forward as separately relevant to the conclusion. Counterconsiderations may be acknowledged.

Inductive arguments: Arguments in which the premises and the conclusion are empirical—having to do with observation and experience—and in which the inference to the conclusion is based on an assumption that observed regularities will persist.

Enumerative inductive arguments: Inductive arguments in which the premises describe a number of observed cases, or a statistical percentage of cases. These cases are implicitly enumerated in the premises.

Explanatory inductive arguments: Inductive arguments in which the conclusion states an explanatory hypothesis and the premises describe evidence that would be explained by that hypothesis. Arguments giving evidence for a causal relationship may be regarded as explanatory inductive arguments.

Anecdotal evidence: Evidence that is about only a single episode, usually something within the personal experience of the arguer. Such evidence is too slight to be the basis for a strong inductive argument. (The (G) condition is not satisfied when evidence for a generalization is purely anecdotal.)

12

The Facts and Figures of Social Science

Newspapers and popular magazines are full of reports of studies by scientists and social scientists. These reports often cite statistics, refer to academic researchers, and state exciting results in an authoritative way. It is a strange fact of modern life that many people who are very skeptical about the powers of rational argument in other contexts are inclined to accept such reports at face value. Understanding the scientific procedures that underlie many such studies and the simplification and exaggeration that can be part of reporting them is important. It will curb any natural tendency you may have to take debatable and sloppily reported results as though they were authoritatively true, simply because they were "established" by researchers who—we are encouraged to suppose—are experts.

In this chapter we try to give you a rational basis for skepticism and caution about the results of some such studies. We set out concepts and analytical tools you can use to evaluate these studies. This evaluation is useful even when you are reading through newspapers and magazines. But it is also useful in contexts in which you are checking out research findings, particularly in the social sciences. These findings are frequently cited as a basis for significant decisions affecting us all—decisions in medicine, education, law, and management. People know that so-called experts often disagree and have made many mistakes in the past. But despite these facts, they are intimidated by specialists. Institutional and political forces encourage people to think that others have to do their thinking for them, and that they cannot investigate significant human questions for themselves. In some very complicated contexts, this is largely true. But often those expert studies that are supposed to be authoritative break down in the light of simple logical analysis.

A study of the way in which social science works and a look at some of the standard devices such as operationalization, sampling, questionnaires, and interviews will make you feel more secure about appraising scientific studies for yourself. Thus the purpose of these chapters on language, statistics, and methods in social science is political as well as logical. We are making a modest move toward taking some of the power away from the experts and giving it back to informed and careful nonspecialists.

Science Is Not All Hard Facts

Sometimes we think of scientific data as being composed of a number of hard facts that are simply uncontroversial and cannot be disputed. In this view, a fact of science is something that simply exists: it is sitting there, as it were, and there is nothing anyone can do but accept it. Historians, literary critics, theologians, and philosophers may deal with fuzzy matters on which many sides need to be considered, but science starts with cold hard facts.

This standard view is seriously wrong. Scientists themselves no longer accept it. But still it retains a powerful hold on the popular imagination. The hard facts idea of science is seriously oversimplified because scientists have to *select* aspects of the world that they are going to pay attention to. Like everyone else, they look at the world with some particular attitude and questions in mind. They observe those facts that seem to them to have *significance.* What is significant is a matter of judgment, not a matter for pure observation to resolve.

Consider, for instance, a scientist who decides to study the formation of attitudes toward gender and job suitability in young children. He will observe many things about these children concerning their play and their relations with parents and teachers. But in all likelihood he will not bother to note what hair color they have because there is simply no reason to believe that hair color has any effect on the attitudes he is interested in. On the other hand, whether the mothers of these children work outside the home as well as inside the home may very well have such an effect. The facts of the case will *include* facts about employment.

Scientists don't collect facts just for the sake of knowing them. They seek to observe and record *significant* facts. Whether some fact is or is not significant is a matter for judgment, and that judgment will depend on many aspects of the situation, including:

> the problem the scientist is studying
>
> the hypothesis, or hypotheses, the scientist is trying to confirm or disconfirm
>
> the tools the scientist has available and can use (financial and ethical matters may pose restrictions here)
>
> the scientist's own background beliefs; what he takes to be common knowledge; what other scientific beliefs he regards as well confirmed; what related scientific hypotheses he regards as plausible
>
> social values, especially those held by funding agencies or institutions by which the scientist is employed
>
> personal values held by the scientist, especially those pertaining to the problems he is investigating

If one or more of these factors were to be varied, the facts emerging from the investigation would be likely to vary also.

Studies of the effects of low-level radiation provide a graphic and appalling example. A number of researchers were unable to continue their investigations when they reached the conclusion that low-level radiation was a causal factor in leukemia and in increased rates of infant death. Their findings were in conflict with the high value that funding agencies and governments put on the unfettered development of nuclear power and nuclear weapons, and funding for their research was cut off. Because of this social situation, facts that might have been discovered were not revealed. On the other hand, it was no doubt the high value these researchers placed on human life that led them to persist in their work as far as they were able.

Actually, though, it is basically not a criticism of science that we are making when we point out that what emerges as scientific data are not simple, hard, unquestionable facts. It is a criticism of an unrealistic and overly dogmatic interpretation of science. Few scientists today would seriously hold this interpretation, for they are aware of the complex theoretical background behind scientific data. Ordinary citizens, however, often do have an overly simplistic view of science. This view can lead them to the false belief that results that are scientific are absolutely authoritative and cannot be questioned by nonscientists. But in science as it exists in our social world, there are more possibilities, more questions, and more distinct interpretations than most people think.

Different Words: Same Thing?   Facts as such do not appear in science at all, really. What appear are descriptions of the facts. It is especially important to realize that the same fact or event may be described in many different ways without any one of these different descriptions necessarily being wrong. Different descriptions may lend different flavor or emphasis to an event. To see how this works, suppose that a young woman enters a drugstore and, after inquiring of the pharmacist which of a number of medicines is a safe sedative, purchases a nonprescription drug. On the face of it, this is a simple social event. But we could describe it in a number of different ways, and our different descriptions make it seem like a different event—or at least, like an event with different effects and implications.

The event might be described in any one of the following ways:

> a. A young woman purchased a mild sedative on the advice of a pharmacist.
> b. An inexperienced woman was advised by a pharmacist to buy a mild sedative drug.
> c. A pharmacist increased his sales by advising an inexperienced young woman to buy a sedative from him.
> d. A rich pharmacist increased his market by persuading an inexperienced young woman that she should spend her hard-earned money on a widely advertised sedative drug.

As we progress from (a) to (d) in these descriptions, the event acquires a rather sinister tone. Yet, given the original information, there is nothing to say that the information added in (b), (c), and (d) need be false. Granted that the woman is inexperienced and the pharmacist is rich, and the sale does increase his profits slightly, there remains the further question of whether these aspects of the event should be mentioned in its description. Thus, the case illustrates some important points about facts in social science. (In fact, these points apply to science generally, but here we concentrate on social science.) Facts in social science appear in language, and different descriptions (with very different implications) are possible for the same event. The event we chose to illustrate the point is a simple everyday one, but the same kind of point can be made for any event. In human affairs it is especially easy to alter implications because so much of language relates to human values and interests.

We might summarize the point of this discussion as follows:

> The same event or fact can be described in a number of different ways, even when none of the available descriptions give false information. Alternative descriptions can vary significantly simply by our specifying various aspects of the truth.

One and the same event or fact can seem to have quite different implications, depending on the description under which it is considered.

This fundamental point already takes much of the hardness out of those hard scientific facts.

If you are wondering about the application of this point to real social science, you might consider the following interchange in which Donald Symons, an anthropologist who wrote a book on the evolution of human sexuality, is being interviewed and questioned about the language in which he chose to describe human sexuality. The interviewer, Sam Keen of *Psychology Today*, asked Symons why he had chosen to describe human sexuality in the language of capitalism. (In Symons's account, males are seen as competing with each other for females, who are regarded as scarce resources. Each male seeks to maximize his advantage by cornering the market in female futures.)

> *Keen: The language you use throughout your analysis troubles me. . . . In your analysis the language of capitalism reigns supreme. . . .*
>
> *Symons: Well, I am naturally inclined to think that the perception is first and that language is used because it is the most accurate available language. It may be economic and capitalist language, but it may nevertheless be right. Michael Ghiselin's book,* The Economy of Nature and the Evolution of Sex, *applies economic analogies in great detail to animal mating strategies. My book may be overly cynical, but I believe in the utility of cynicism: that people act in terms of self-interest.*[1]

The language Keen questioned was that of economic markets. Symons looked at the phenomena of human behavior and saw males choosing females with a view to their (the males') reproductive success from an investment of sperm and time. Keen points out that the model Symons uses describes the phenomena of human sexuality in the language of the economic marketplace, taking as the primary point of view that of the *self-interested male agent.* A very different description would surely result if we assumed that humans are basically sympathetic and sociable, instead of assuming that they are primarily self-interested. Thus there are very large assumptions behind Symons's choice of language. The individual male is primary; the individual male is regarded as acting to maximize his own interest; the individual male interest is in having the maximum number of descendents.

Clearly, it is possible to describe the phenomena of human sexuality as Symons does. Some aspects will be highlighted; others will be omitted. The same can be said of alternative linguistic frameworks that might be adopted. The point is that the model Symons has chosen is just one of many alternatives. Asked to defend it, he does not do very well: he replies only by saying that another author did the same, and commenting, with no supporting evidence, that probably people do act in self-interest. (Even if they do, is their interest their genetic "interest," as Symons's account requires? People might see their interest as having the most pleasure in life, or earning the most money, even if they were self-interested.) We will surely overrate the neutrality of Symons's work if we forget that he has *chosen* an economic, self-interest-based model, and he has *chosen* economic categories of description. This is one way of describing things, but not the only one. The economic model of human sexuality will indicate some questions and problems for scientific research; another model would indicate others.

The choice of language is a *choice.* It is a choice that can make quite a difference as far as the presentation of scientific facts and the foundations of further scientific problems and questions are concerned. Again we see why scientific facts are not the hard, simple things that many consumers of popular science take them to be.

The Operationalization of Terms.   Another way in which decisions about language enter into scientific work is through the operationalization of key terms. The word *operationalization* refers to the way in which a researcher uses procedures to determine whether a term is going to apply in a given instance or not. The most familiar case of operationalization is that of the term *intelligence*. If we were to try to give a precise definition of *intelligence* and spell it out in terms of behavior that someone could measure, doing so would be very difficult. For, as it is ordinarily understood, intelligence can manifest itself in many different ways. (In one situation the intelligent thing to do might be to come up with a devastating counterexample to a false claim; in another it might be to remain completely silent and let the falsehood slip by.) In very general terms, to say that someone is intelligent is to say that he or she can learn to do a broad range of things, and he or she can learn quickly and well. Thus, as a term, *intelligence* carries a reference to human values and standards. (The things learned have to be worth learning, and they have to be learned well.) Yet social scientists have tried to measure intelligence quantitatively. For some purposes, no doubt, this attempt is worthwhile.

As almost everyone knows, social scientists attempt to measure intelligence using IQ tests. Tests are devised, and in virtue of people's performance on these tests, they are said to have quite precise IQs—122, or 98, or 105, for instance. The number 100 is supposed to represent the average level of intelligence.

There are many scientific, social, and political issues about IQ tests. Here we concentrate on only one such issue: the operationalization of our concept of intelligence by IQ tests. The preoperationalized concept of intelligence is a difficult one to pin down; it implies value judgments about activities and skills, and it allows for people to be quite intelligent in some respects (conducting their personal relationships, for instance) and quite unintelligent in others (doing higher mathematics, for instance). The term *intelligent* in ordinary English allows flexibility and uncertainty. As it is normally used, it does not permit precise numerical measurement. (Although Smith may have an IQ of 130 and Jones an IQ of 100, it hardly makes sense to say that Smith is exactly 30 percent more intelligent than Jones! It does make sense to say that Smith's IQ score is 30 percent higher than Jones's IQ score.) The ordinary concept of intelligence is very inconvenient as far as scientific research is concerned. If a researcher wishes to study the effect of intelligence on economic success in middle life, he will have to have some way in which he can measure intelligence; he will have to have some *general test* for intelligence that he can apply to all his subjects. Typically, he uses an IQ test.

IQ tests operationalize the concept of intelligence, replacing a flexible, uncertain, and evaluative concept with a quantitative concept. A researcher who operationalizes intelligence into scores on IQ tests has replaced the ordinary concept by a technical one, and has achieved the reduction of intelligence into something quantifiable. He will speak of IQ instead of intelligence. But nevertheless, it remains intelligence that he is really interested in. The original project was to investigate the effects of intelligence on midlife success. No one would have any interest in IQ tests were it not believed that scores on them tell us something about intelligence. This case is typical of operationalization: an evaluative and somewhat indeterminate concept has been replaced by a quantitative and very precise measurement.

Operationalization is a scientifically necessary procedure for many purposes. It poses, however, some problems of understanding, especially for nonscientists. The *interest* and *applicability* of research work usually depend on the preoperationalized sense of such crucial terms as *intelligence*. No one would have any interest in the relation between IQ tests and economic success unless he or she believed that IQ tests were closely related to intelligence. It is intelligence rather than IQ that people are really interested in. During the process of scientific investigation, the evaluative, indeterminate, and nonquantitative aspects of intelligence are beneath the surface. Researchers can forget about them and work simply with numerical IQ scores. Nevertheless, these nonquantitative aspects of intelligence will surface again in the interpretation and application of the results.

The concept of intelligence has been used here because issues about the measurement of intelligence are relatively familiar. IQ has often been a political issue in our culture, and most people have heard debates about whether IQ really measures intelligence, whether it measures something that is fixed independently of environment, and so on. But the same issues that arise for intelligence arise in many other cases too. The matter of operationalization is fundamental and common in research in the social sciences. Being aware that operationalization has been necessary can contribute to your understanding of empirical studies done in this area. Here is a list of some terms that would have to be at least implicitly operationalized in social scientific research:

persistence

attention span

femininity

masculinity

introspectiveness

impulsiveness

creativity

efficiency

anxiety

belief

bilingual

The terms in the preceding list are:

1. *Mentalistic.* They involve a reference to human consciousness in the way that they are understood in ordinary language. Human consciousness is approached by science only insofar as it is reflected in *behavior,* in *language,* or in *physical states* of the subject.

or

2. *Evaluative.* They involve references, tacitly, to values and to standards of excellence in one or another areas.

or

3. *Both mentalistic and evaluative.*

These terms and many others describing human traits and abilities have to be operationalized before they can be used conveniently in scientific research. Whenever you see a term having any of these features, in a scientific study or report of a study, you should be aware that in some sense the researchers have operationalized it. The operationalization may be through a formally set test, as with intelligence. Or it may be less formal; researchers will simply have agreed on what sorts of behaviors they will *call* "persistent" or "aggressive," or whatever. Even a fairly good operationalization will capture only parts of the ordinary meaning of a term. The significance and applicability of a study can be very much undermined by the parts that are *not* captured.

The points at stake here should become clearer when we look at some examples. This passage deals with a controversy about the effects on children in preschool age groups of watching fast-paced television shows:

> At the University of Massachusetts, Daniel Anderson, Stephen Leven, and Elizabeth Lorch compared the reactions of 72 four-year-olds to rapidly paced and slowly paced segments of Sesame Street. The research team observed the children watching differently paced versions, tested them after viewing to measure their impulsive behavior and the persistence in completing a puzzle, and then observed them during a 10-minute play period. They concluded that there was no evidence whatever that rapid television pacing has a negative impact on pre-school children's behavior and that they could find no reduction in sustained effort and no increase in aggression or in unfocused hyperactivity.[2]

Here the emphasized terms are terms that the researchers have loosely operationalized. They have decided which childish behaviors count as "impulsive" and which do not, and what counts as "persistence" with a puzzle and what does not; what behaviors are and are not to be called "aggressive," and so on.

Let us stop and concentrate on these terms for a moment:

persistent

aggressive

impulsive

hyperactive

sustained effort

unfocused hyperactivity

Now think about the way young children act. You have to ask yourself how a researcher would decide which actions count as exhibiting persistence, aggression, and so on. You can be assured that she has some standard, but of course you don't know what it is just by reading a report of the study, and you might not find out by reading the study itself. The operationalization of all these terms will involve interpretive judgments that could have been made differently, as well as evaluations of childish behavior. Suppose that a child refused to work on a puzzle as directed by the researchers. Would she show less persistence than another child—or just more independence? Suppose a child wants to get attention from a researcher who happens to be busy showing a puzzle to another child. Suppose he pulls the researcher's dress, trying to get her attention. Is this persistence? Or aggressiveness? Or unfocused hyperactivity? Or sustained effort? Or none of these? You can see that the significance of the results here is going to depend very much on how well these key terms have been operationalized. Given the flexibility and evaluative nature of ordinary language, and the fluidity of young children's behavior, many contentious judgments have to be made before a result is determined.

It is worth watching out for operationalization. Without some grasp of how researchers have determined the applicability of mentalistic or evaluative terms to human behavior, you have only a slight understanding of the conclusions they come to. When central terms are evaluative and require judgments about human behavior, operationalization does not escape these aspects. It puts them out of the way for a time, but they inevitably resurface.

It is easy to miss the fact that operationalization has taken place when you are reading about a research study in an informal source such as a newspaper or popular magazine. If you are reading the study itself, the fact will be obvious. Typically, researchers state what operationalizations they have used—whether formal tests were applied, or which behaviors were taken as constituting the phenomenon under observation. But even in these more rigorous contexts, it is well worth reflecting on the operationalization and asking yourself how well the tests correspond to the ordinary sense of the terms. Sometimes researchers use agreement among several different observers as a basis for resolving questions as to what counts as "imaginative," or "aggressive," or "creative." This agreement does eliminate arbitrary judgments of a purely personal kind. However, often scientists working in the same area have been carefully trained in a way that makes them share the same values and assumptions. These values may be very different from those of the ordinary public. What behavioral scientists think is "aggressive," you might regard as "imaginative." Since the words *aggressive* and *imaginative* have quite distinct evaluative implications, such differences can be very important.

We get a peculiar combination of precision and imprecision when terms that have been operationalized are then incorporated into statistical judgments, such as "32 percent of children observed showed aggressive behavior." The number, 32, is *precise*, and the percentage makes it sound as though some very definite results were obtained. But the term *aggressive* is hard to operationalize; the term is implicitly evaluative, and children's behavior is chaotic enough that there are many tough decisions as to whether to call particular behavior aggressive or not. When we hear such claims as "32 percent of the children observed showed aggressive behavior," we are often impressed by the precision of the *numbers*. But this precision is apparent, not real, in the context. The difficulties about *aggressive* have to be taken into account. In such contexts numbers can mislead people. We are inclined to trust statistics more than evaluative judgments about people's behavior. And yet, so often, the evaluations are there implicitly—tucked beneath the surface in the choice of operational definitions. A claim such as "32 percent of children observed showed aggressive behavior" is not precise. Rather, it is *pseudoprecise*, exploiting our tendency to be impressed by numbers.

Data from Questionnaires, Polls, and Interviews.   A common tool in social science is the questionnaire. Here the data of science depend on social relations between people, especially on the relationship of trust. In a questionnaire or poll, people are asked to reply to questions, and the researcher sets out to determine a conclusion about their attitudes, beliefs, or actions on the basis of their responses. Obviously, there is little to prevent subjects from lying, deliberate frivolity, or deliberate inconsistency in their responses; that is why we say that here research depends on trust.

A recent book on Margaret Mead's famous study of adolescent girls in Samoa offers a fascinating example. Derek Freeman points out that when Margaret Mead studied the sexual attitudes and habits of adolescent girls in Samoa, she was an inexperienced graduate student of twenty-three. She had not acquired very much background knowledge of the Samoan people, either through reading current research or through direct experience. Mead lived with a white family while conducting her research. Her informants told her of free love during adolescence, of no stigma attached to loss of virginity, and of no hang-ups about sex. These themes affected generations of anthropology students and scholars through Mead's subsequent well-known book, *Coming of Age in Samoa.* In that book Mead argued, on the basis of her study of twenty-five adolescent girls in 1925, that the Samoans had a culture in which adolescents experienced little stress with sexual development. From this premise she derived the broader conclusion that adolescent stress was a product, not of human biology (for this is universal), but of cultural circumstances and expectations.

Freeman points out that the Samoans had a culture that prized virginity highly, and that delinquency, violence, and even suicide were known to occur among Samoan adolescents at least as frequently as among western teenagers. Before Freeman's book made the issue public in 1983, educated Samoans had long questioned Mead's description of their culture. Freeman does not argue that Mead was dishonest. Rather, after a detailed analysis of conflicting evidence, he eventually concludes that her subjects deceived her. Due to a combination of inexperience and a desire to find an untainted human culture showing human nature at its best, Mead believed them. Other studies had indicated that Samoan girls were shy about discussing sex—a hypothesis that is surely very plausible from a commonsense point of view. Freeman suggests that when Margaret Mead "persisted in this unprecedented probing of a highly embarrassing topic, it is likely that these girls resorted ... to regaling their inquisitor with counterfeit tales of love under the palm trees."[3]

This controversy illustrates the importance of being able to trust the people being studied and to believe they are replying honestly to questions. It offers a warning, too, in its illustration of how a questionable study, based on a small sample and done by an inexperienced researcher, can dominate years of thought and research if it happens to be taken seriously by the right people at the right time.

On questionnaires, techniques may be used to try to weed out dishonest responses. A questionnaire on ethics included the following statement, which respondents were supposed to mark either as true or as false:

───── I have never deliberately made a remark intended to hurt someone else's feelings.

Here anyone who said true would provide researchers with very good evidence that he was not being honest. The word *never* makes the statement so strong that hardly anyone would be able to assert it truthfully. But given that researchers could detect dishonesty in this case, they face a decision about their data. Do they disregard the entire set of responses from this subject? (If so, they might effectively bias their sample toward the honest by omitting the dishonest. If you are studying people's beliefs and actions with regard to ethics, this omission is very significant.) Do they preserve the results and try to allow for a degree of dishonesty? The dilemma here reveals again that decisions have to be made regarding what constitutes data: data are not hard facts that are entirely remote from human policies and decisions.

We have been emphasizing issues of language and the role that conceptual and evaluative issues play in the description of scientific facts. In a poll or questionnaire questions should be carefully formulated. They should not be vague or ambiguous, and they should not pose questions in a prejudicial or loaded way. Some questions may be asked in a way that virtually coerces the respondent into an answer that might not accurately reflect his or her beliefs and attitudes. To see how this might happen, suppose that you are arrested on a murder charge and you are innocent. If a police officer asks, "Did you purchase the murder weapon here in town or elsewhere?" he is asking you an improper question. You will feel forced to accept one of his alternatives when both are wrong. The right response is to reject the question, but this response takes a presence of mind that you might lack in such circumstances!

Questions on polls, questionnaires, and so-called objective (short-answer) tests may be prejudicial in various ways. They may strongly suggest an answer that is inappropriate either due to form (as in the preceding example) or due to special features of wording. We have already seen in Chapter Three how language can be slanted to convey a specific emotional effect or how it can embody questionable assumptions. For an illustration of a question that is prejudicial due to emotional loading, consider the following:

(i) Do you favor raiding dead bodies for organs to benefit the rich?

(ii) Do you favor authorizing doctors to remove organs for transplantation, even in the absence of consent from relatives, in cases where those relatives may not be available for consultation?

It would be hard for anyone to reply affirmatively to the first question because *raiding dead bodies* is such an unattractive idea! Besides, the question assumes an erroneous intent of transplantation—that it is to benefit the rich. The second question is not prejudicial in this way. Results on a poll on organ donorship would almost certainly differ very much if question (i) were used rather than question (ii).

In fact, logicians have a special name for some of these suggestive and falsely coercive questions. They call them *complex questions* and say that those who pose them commit a fallacy—the fallacy of the complex question.

The classic logicians' example is:

Have you stopped beating your wife?

If a person is not a confessed wife-beater and he is asked this question, there is a strong practical implication that he should answer yes or no. The problem is that either answer suggests that he did once beat his wife. If he didn't and does not want to say that he did, he has a problem that can only be solved by rejecting the question.

The fallacy of the complex question occurs when a question is formed in such a way that it tends to coerce a respondent into the position of accepting an unwelcome or even false claim, for no reason other than the posing of the question. Some prejudicial questions can be regarded as committing the fallacy of the complex question because their form suggests emotions, attitudes, and beliefs we may well not accept but which are subtly forced upon us due to assumptions or suggested structuring of information in the question itself.

Polls are often criticized on the grounds that questions can be asked so as to prejudice responses or so as to make the results of the poll difficult to interpret. This can happen either because of the fallacy of the complex question or through a choice of language, so that the question is emotionally loaded in one direction or the other. A significant case of a poll involving the fallacy of the complex question occurred in the United States in the late 1940s. People had been arrested as atomic spies, and the Canadian government had received from Soviet defector Igor Gouzenko evidence of extensive Soviet activity in Canada, Britain, and the United States. Against such a background, American citizens were polled to see whether they were in favor of divulging atomic secrets to the Russians. The question, which was as follows:

Are you in favor of divulging atomic secrets to the Russians?

looks straightforward enough. People simply say yes or no, and then the results are tabulated. (Eighty-five percent were against.) However, the question and, indeed, the whole concept of *atomic* spying, was based on a *false assumption*—the assumption that there were atomic secrets that could be learned through spying. In point of fact, the relevant scientific knowledge was in publicly accessible sources and the only real secret about the U.S. atomic program was that the government and its agencies were making energetic attempts to corner the world supply of uranium.[4] We see here a tragic case of a poll founded on an inappropriate question. The results of the poll were taken as pertinent to public policy. But the results had no real significance, for the question posed was one that simply did not arise.

Canadians in the province of Quebec were faced with an absurdly complex question in their 1980 referendum on separatism. After decades of nationalistic feeling in Quebec, a government that had expressed its own belief that Quebec would be better off as a separate state with loose association with the rest of Canada put the "question" to a referendum. Quebecers had to vote *oui* or *non* to the following:

> The Government of Quebec has made public its proposal to negotiate a new agreement with the rest of Canada, based on the equality of nations; this agreement would enable Quebec to acquire the exclusive power to make its laws, administer its taxes, and establish relations abroad—in other words, sovereignty—and at the same time, to maintain with Canada an economic association including a common currency; any change in political status resulting from these negotiations will be submitted to the people through a referendum; on these terms, do you agree to give the Government of Quebec the mandate to negotiate the proposed agreement between Quebec and Canada?[5]

If anything is a complex question, this is! Many problems arise. One is that the desired aim of sovereignty-association was a policy that other Canadian provinces were not willing to go along with. The question is of the type, "Given *a*, and *b*, and *c*, should we try to negotiate *x*?" If *a* or *b* or *c* does not hold, we have an improper question. The results on this referendum were negative—more votes against separatism. But how to interpret those results is not completely obvious.

Good questionnaires do not have questions like this one. They avoid the fallacy of the complex question, avoid ambiguity and vagueness, and avoid loaded language. They ask questions that can be understood easily and answered simply. If these conditions are not met, then the data generated by questionnaires are simply not significant. Improperly formulated questions make it impossible for a questionnaire to reveal people's real beliefs and attitudes. No matter how many questionnaires are filled out and tabulated, the results are of *no* significance if questions are improperly formulated. It is easy to forget this fact if someone shows you reams of data from a survey of many thousands, but it is true.

Tests for attitudes and character traits can be seriously flawed if the constituent questions are carelessly worded. There is a particularly glaring example of this problem in a scale that was once devised to assess the character trait commonly called "Machiavellianism." (Machiavelli was an Italian political theorist, renowned for his recommendation that political people indulge in manipulative and cynical behavior. You might sum up his ethical view as, "If it will help you do what you want, go ahead and do it, and don't pay any attention to the preachers or your own conscience.") A scale to determine people's degree of Machiavellianism, then, will mark the degree to which they indicate a willingness to manipulate others and to violate moral principles to achieve their own selfish ends.

One such scale included the following items; to each, respondents were to indicate "agree" or "disagree":

   1. The well-being of the individual is the goal that should be worked for before anything else.
   2. The best way to handle people is to tell them what they want to hear.
   3. A person's job is the best single guide to the sort of person he is.
   4. It is wise to flatter people.
   5. All in all, it is better to be humble and honest than to be important and dishonest.
   6. It is hard to get ahead without cutting corners here and there.
   7. Anyone who completely trusts anyone else is asking for trouble.

All these items contain flaws of wording so serious that an indication "agree" or "disagree" is meaningless. Because of these flaws the scale does not measure anything. Let us see why these test items are as flawed as they are.

1. "The well-being of the individual is the goal that should be worked for before anything else" is *ambiguous*. It could mean either that each person should work for his own personal welfare before anything else—a Machiavellian view—or it could mean that each person should work for the welfare of *individuals* before anything else. The problem comes in "the individual"; is this universal or particular? Does it refer only to oneself, or to other individuals also? The second meaning would not indicate Machiavellianism at all. If you agree with the statement interpreting it this way, your agreement indicates the very opposite from what it would if you interpreted the statement the first way.

2. "The best way to handle people is to tell them what they want to hear" is also *ambiguous*. Here the problem is with the word *best*. It could mean either most effective or morally most correct. On the first meaning, agreeing would not indicate Machiavellianism, for one is simply agreeing that flattery is, in fact, effective; one is not agreeing that it should be used. But on the second meaning, agreeing would indicate Machiavellianism, for to agree would be to condone insincere flattery as morally right.

3. "A person's job is the best single guide to the sort of person he is" is too *vague* to be useful on the scale. The problem lies in the expression "the sort of person he is." This could mean any number of different things: the sort of personality he has, how trustworthy he is, how intelligent he is, what sort of moral character he has, and so on. You can't know *what* you are agreeing with here; so your agreement or disagreement indicates nothing about your Machiavellianism or anything else.

4. "It is wise to flatter people" is undermined by an *ambiguity* in the word *wise*. This word could mean smart, as in "it was wise to sell the stocks while they were high." Or it could mean "sound, on the basis of moral criteria," as in "he was wise not to accept a gift from a corrupt client." If *wise* is taken in the second way, then indicating agreement implies Machiavellianism. But if it is taken in the first way, it does not.

5. "All in all, it is better to be humble and honest than to be important and dishonest" is *ambiguous* in that *better* might mean morally better or it might mean more conducive to personal success. Disagreeing with the statement according to the first meaning indicates Machiavellianism, but disagreeing according to the second meaning does not.

6. "It is hard to get ahead without cutting corners here and there" is hopelessly *vague*. The fault lies in the expression "cutting corners here and there." This phrase might refer to immoral acts, illegal acts, or simply the omission of inefficient and unnecessary activities. (In the latter sense, you cut corners when you don't iron your drip-dry shirts, but thinking *this* is all right scarcely indicates a Machiavellian character!) The expression "getting ahead" is also rather *vague*. It is most natural to take it as indicating financial success, but that meaning is not the only possible one.

7. "Anyone who completely trusts anyone else is asking for trouble" is hard to disagree with, due to the word *completely*. If you take this word literally, you would almost *have to agree* with the statement. And yet agreeing is supposed to indicate Machiavellianism.

We have worked through this example in some detail because it illustrates so well what can go wrong with wording on questionnaires or polls. People are asked to make a quick decision on a statement, and their response is supposed to indicate an attitude or belief on a topic of some significance. An accurate response can be given only when questions are simple, unambiguous, and properly related to the subject under investigation. (That matter gets us back to operationalization.)

The same kind of problems can also arise in interviews if questions are not carefully selected. In this case, subjects can ask to have questions clarified, so that problems have a chance of being solved. But interviewing can pose other problems. An interview is a human situation in which people interact, and the interaction between them can affect the results. A very sympathetic interviewer may receive many more significant confessions than another. Thus the personality of the person doing the interview becomes a component of the study, and its effects may be hard to calculate. (If a sympathetic and warm-hearted interviewer finds more evidence of marital troubles than another interviewer, it is not always clear whether there are more troubles or whether it is simply that her personality has led to the admission of more problems by her subjects.) Scientific results are most secure when they can be duplicated by a number of different researchers. But since different people have different personalities that may affect their interviewing techniques, this duplication can be difficult in the case of interviews. Questionnaires, which are less personal, are sometimes regarded as preferable to interviews for this reason. Of course, an advantage of the interview is that ambiguities or other flaws in questions can be cleared up.

Another problem with interviewing is that people have a tendency to tell others what they think these others would like to hear. Thus, if interviewed by a journalist and asked how frequently they read the newspaper, people are inclined to overestimate their reading so they won't disappoint someone who writes for a living. Also, people are often shy about admitting on a face-to-face basis affiliations with political or religious groups that are unpopular. They may be embarrassed to admit things that they would be able to state on a written questionnaire when anonymity is guaranteed. On sensitive topics, then, a questionnaire might give very different data from those that would be revealed in interviews.

Thus many conceptual and personal factors can affect the data that social scientists are able to obtain from polls, questionnaires, or interviews. It is not that their data mean nothing. Rather, the significance will derive in part from the sensitivity to language that is behind the formulation of questions, and from the care that is taken to account for personal factors that could bias data in one way or another. To be told that the average person has a Machiavellianism index of .7 is quite meaningless unless we have confidence in the test used. Even then, the combination of a number (.7) with a concept so hard to operationalize gives a result that can be accused of pseudoprecision. The results of a poll, too, can be no better than the question asked in the poll.

The data of social science are not hard facts. We have to choose the questions on the basis of which data are collected. We have to choose the language in which we work, and this choice will select attitudes and aspects of the world as significant or insignificant. We have to choose whether to use questionnaires, interviews, or direct observation of behavior as the means of finding out what people think and do and what their abilities are. Tricky concepts, involving judgments of value and judgments about human consciousness, have to be operationalized. Human trust is involved. Decisions have to be made as to which parts of the data are in some way biased and need to be eliminated, or discounted. In all these ways, choices, values, and policies enter into the construction of data. Failure to understand such things has given many people a dogmatic and overly simple understanding of what social science is all about.

EXERCISE SET

Exercise One
Part A

Examine the following sets of descriptions. Comment, in each case, on the slightly different implications of the various descriptions within each set. Then invent two similar sets of your own and explain to a friend or classmate what the significance of your variation is.

1. *Weight Descriptions*
   a. Many people weigh 15–30 pounds more than would be healthy for their age, sex, and height.
   b. Many people are obese.
   c. Many people neglect to keep their weight within healthy limits.
   d. Many people weigh at least 15 pounds more than is statistically average for their height and age.
   e. Many people weigh 15–30 pounds more than is normal for their age and height.

*2. *Learning Language Descriptions*
   a. A child looked at a page where the English word *oh* was printed and then uttered, "oh."
   b. A child tried to read the English word *oh* on a page and succeeded.
   c. A child read the English word *oh*, which was printed on a page.
   d. A child looked at a book that appeared to be written in English and had the letters *oh* on a page, and she made a noise that sounded like the English word *oh*.

*3. *Examinations for Children*
   a. Examinations tend to inhibit originality in some children.
   b. Examinations are a countercreative institution.
   c. Fewer children who take examinations than children who do not take examinations go on to do genuinely originally artistic or scientific work.
   d. By resorting to examinations for our children, we sacrifice creativity, originality, and even genius, to the false gods of fact and competition.

4. *Smokers and Nonsmokers*
   a. There is a controversy between smokers and nonsmokers as to whether smoking should be permitted in the school staff room.
   b. Smokers are seeking to protect their right to smoke in the staff room against threats from nonsmokers who seek to curb their freedom of action on a pretense of a so-called right to free air.
   c. Nonsmokers are seeking to protect their health and comfort by defending their right to clean air against the harmful actions of smokers, who presently insist on smoking in the staff room.
   d. There is an irresolvable controversy about smoking in the school staff room because there is no way to balance accurately the frustration of smokers who might want to smoke and be restricted against the discomfort and possible ill health of nonsmokers who cannot avoid air contaminated by cigarette smoke.

5. *The Only Child*

    a. Bob Jones and Enid Jones have one child, a girl.

    b. The Joneses have only a daughter.

    c. The Joneses have an only child, who is a girl.

    d. Bob Jones, as head of the household including his wife and his only daughter, is the head of a nuclear family with three family members.

Part B

In the following examples, comment on the implicit operationalization. Or, if there is no clue as to what means of operationalization would be used, comment on which terms would have been operationalized. If numbers are used, comment as to whether precision or pseudoprecision is achieved.

*1. Suppose that a study is done on the formation of friendships, and researchers seek to discover whether the common belief that it is easier to form friendships in small towns than in big cities is correct. To determine whether this belief is true, they study groups of young people who have moved. One group has moved to a small town and the other group has moved to a big city. The following results are reported:

    Initially, the small-town group reported having nearly double the number of friends. They reported an average of 6.2 friends, as compared to 3.0 for the urban subjects. But six months later, the numbers were 5.4 and 5.2. There was no difference in the frequency with which subjects reported visiting their friends: in both groups, this frequency was about once a week.

2. An advertisement for special programs in listening skills reads as follows: "Research studies show that on the average we listen at a 25% level of efficiency. This is terribly costly. When executives don't listen effectively, communication breaks down. Ideas and information get distorted as much as 80% as they travel down an organization."
(Toronto *Globe and Mail*, February 23, 1980)

3. A newspaper reported a speech about the effect of various forms of therapy. According to the report, "delinquents who went to psychotherapists had a much better success, showing a 78% improvement. But the fly in the ointment is that those who didn't see anyone had a 72% improvement rate."
(Toronto *Globe and Mail*, September 13, 1980.)

*4. *Background:* The use of lie detectors is somewhat controversial. Actually, the lie detector may be regarded as a device that operationalizes truth-telling and lying. A person is lying, according to the device, if his pulse goes up and his palms become moist. He is not lying, but telling the truth, when these responses do not occur. Some critics of the lie detector, notably David Lykken, who has written extensively on the subject, object to its use. Lykken maintains that one can falsify the results by deliberately contemplating upsetting activities when telling the truth. What would you make of the following reply to the criticism:

    "Lying just means having moist palms and a high pulse. Whether someone is saying what he believes is not scientifically testable unless it is operationalized. Lying is operationalized through the lie detector, and thus if the lie detector shows a person to be lying, he necessarily is lying."

5. A report in the Toronto *Globe and Mail* for December 20, 1982, described a study of 98 couples who were divorced, had children, and had to deal with each other in a continuing way because of their children. Among the claims reported were the following:

    "The stereotype that a divorced couple's relationship is disagreeable and conflicting fits about a third of the couples in the study. However, relationships that were generally caring, respectful and friendly were reported by 30 percent of couples who had joint custody, and 20 percent of the couples where the mother had custody.

    "About 65 percent of the former spouses in the second group reported having conversations once a month and one-third reported weekly interactions."

*6. *Background:* An American Roman Catholic organization called Applied Research in the Apostolate is sponsoring a poll of people across the world to determine their values, attitudes, and sources of satisfaction in life. On February 4, 1983, the Calgary *Herald* reported that of 1200 Canadians polled, a surprisingly large percentage claimed to be very happy:

    "We're a happy lot down deep, believe it or not. The evidence of that is an extensive, on-going opinion poll conducted in about 20 countries so far which shows that we Canadians are among the happiest people in the world. In fact the survey conducted by the Gallup organization has 95 percent of us saying we are very happy or quite happy. It sort of gives you a glow just knowing that we're happier than people in the United States and Europe. We even find more pleasure in our lives than the Japanese. Happiness isn't just a matter of selling prodigious numbers of cars and electronic gear."

7. From the same source as the preceding example comes this one:

    "The Canadian profile wasn't totally complimentary. It suggested for example that we have a tendency to be smug. What other interpretation can be put on findings that 87 percent of us profess to obey the commandment against stealing while at the same time believing that only 30 percent of our neighbors obey it?"

Part C

Examine the following questions. Imagine they are to be used on a questionnaire or opinion poll. Would you criticize any on grounds of (1) the fallacy of complex question; (b) loaded language to bias the answer in one direction or the other; (c) ambiguity; or, (d) vagueness? If so, explain your criticisms. Then check the questions you thought were acceptable by asking a friend for a response.

1. Have you ever experienced sexual harassment on the job?

2. Which of your children requires special education programs from the Board of Education? (Assume the question is given to all taxpayers.)

3. Have you ever knowingly paid less tax than you were required, by law, to pay?

*4. On the average, how many alcoholic drinks do you have per day? (Less than 2; between 2 and 4; more than 4.) Pick one answer.

5. Given that every school must have computers, is it preferable to buy small computers, with one for every ten students, or to buy larger computers, with one for every twenty students?

6. Should pornography be illegal?

7. Do you presently weigh more than 10 percent above what would be normal for your height and age?

*8. Do you favor the preservation of human life and the protection of human safety through seat belt legislation?

*9. Should the United States respond to the communist threat in Nicaragua by supporting local rebels, by funding American and other mercenary troops, or by intervention with U.S. troops?

*10. Is your life adversely affected by stress?

11. How many times have you deliberately lied during the past week? On how many of these occasions did you sincerely believe that lying was justified?

12. How many bathtubs are there in your place of residence?

Part D

Construct a set of ten questions to be the basis of an interview. Check your questions carefully to make sure they are appropriately related to whatever topic you have chosen to investigate. Have several friends check them with you. Then interview someone and tabulate the results. Have a classmate, preferably someone whose personality is quite different from your own, do the same interview several days later and tabulate the results. Compare the results. What do you conclude—if anything—about interviewing on the basis of this comparison? Suggested topics for interviews:

(a) Attitudes about the world population problem and whether compulsory sterilization, compulsory abortions, or financial incentives for birth control would be acceptable solutions to this problem under any circumstances.
(b) Attitudes to peace and war; whether nuclear weapons can be maintained with only a very low risk of nuclear war; whether the existence of nuclear weapons makes war obsolete as a method of achieving national goals; how disarmament or multilateral arms reductions could be achieved.
(c) Beliefs about whether living together before marriage is desirable, or whether marriage is a good institution at all.
(d) Beliefs in God or some other supernatural force.

Sampling: The Basis of Enumerative Induction

We have seen that the simplest type of induction is the enumerative induction, in which a generalization about a range of cases, including some unexamined ones, is inferred from premises about cases that have been examined. The examined cases constitute the *sample,* and the whole range of cases covered in the generalization is the *population.* Recall the following simple argument:

1. 300 out of 400 first-year students tested passed the writing skills test. Therefore,
2. Three-quarters of the total first-year class of students would be capable of passing the writing skills test.

Here the *sample* is the 400 students tested and the *population* is all first-year students. (Presumably all first-year students in that college, not all first-year students everywhere. As we shall see, it is really important to be clear about the population being discussed.) The first-year class might be very large, and it might be difficult to test all students; thus a generalization about *all* is based on a sample of 400 of them. The reliability of this generalization will depend on how well this selected sample represents the *population*.

When you read the results of polls or studies, you are often not informed about the sample or even about the population. These omissions make it virtually impossible to assess the reliability of inductive generalizations. Here is an example:

In a recent poll conducted by the National Opinion Research Center, 58 percent of those surveyed said that they believed they had had one or more telepathic experiences.

Usually surveys like this one are taken so that we can make discoveries about a population broader than just those people surveyed; nobody is interested in what exactly these people polled have to say, except insofar as their responses indicate wider attitudes. To have any idea of the evidential support a claim like the preceding one would have, we have to know both the sample and the intended population. It is impossible to get any idea as to how well the sample represents the population unless we have this knowledge. It is very common for people to take surveys as representative of the broader population of adults; without further information as to how many people were surveyed and who they were, we will be making a very hasty generalization if we make this assumption.

In fact, the failure to identify the *population* properly can lead to very significant errors. One common error is to fail to distinguish "adult North Americans" from "adult human beings." Often researchers speak as though they are describing human beings in general, when their sample includes only North American adults. It has been suggested that this logical error may even have something to do with the failure of North American business analysts to anticipate the astounding Japanese success in some areas of advanced manufacturing. Japanese performance certainly caught American managers by surprise. Students of administration, management, and business practice had studied management in the context of North American society and institutions, and they had then generalized, implicitly, to the whole human race. They failed to see that because their samples represented only North American companies and workers, the "laws" of management they had inferred might not apply in a very different culture.[6]

In many reported studies, the intended population is not mentioned. The most charitable and plausible interpretation to make in such cases is that the intended population is that of all adult members of the society or culture in which the study was made—or all children, if it is about children.

Another common error about populations and samples has to do with sexism, and it has its source in the two different meanings that may be given to the words *men* and *man.* These words can mean either "human beings in general" or "male human beings." The ambiguity generates many errors, for people often begin with the generic sense of *man* (humans), and then move, unwittingly, to its specific sense (male humans). We often find generalizations about all people based on data about male human beings. This generalization amounts to an error in sampling. A sample composed entirely of men cannot represent a human population in which half the individuals are women!

Just in case you don't believe this error ever really occurs, we suggest that you examine the following case. In an article on incomes of French and English Canadians in the province of Quebec, columnist William Johnson began his column by saying that the myth that English Canadians earn more than French Canadians was debunked by a study done by Quebec economist Jacques-Andre Boulet. He cited a number of facts and figures from this column and ended on a firm note: the myth of English economic superiority in Quebec has been refuted. The myth was about people in general in Quebec; thus it covered men and women. However, all the data in Boulet's study were about *men*:

> *Mr. Boulet compares* male *income in Montreal at three periods: 1960–61, from specially run off tables of the 1961 census tables; 1970–71, again by running off census tables; and for 1977 by analyzing the data collected in 1978 by two University of Montreal sociologists, Paul Bernard and Jean Renaud. Here are some of his conclusions:*
>
> *English-speaking men earned on the average 51 percent more than French-speaking men in 1960; 32 percent more in 1970, and only 15 percent more in 1977. Mr. Boulet projected that the narrowing gap between anglophones and francophones would be wiped out by 1982 if the trend continues.*
>
> *Male francophones earned more on the average than those whose mother tongue was neither French nor English in 1960, 1970, and 1977.*[7]

This study seems to have been an excellent and interesting one about male incomes, but we cannot reach a conclusion about French incomes overall versus English incomes overall in Quebec on the basis of this work for the elementary reason that workers are of two sexes, not one!

Unwittingly, people may assume that their own culture represents all human cultures; their own time, all human history; or their own sex, both human sexes. Such assumptions can lead to serious errors in inductive generalization. To evaluate an inductive generalization, we have to know whether the sample is large enough, and representative enough, to be a guide to the population. Obviously, if what the sample is and what the intended population is are not clear, we cannot determine this.

Sample Representativeness.   A sample is representative of a population if its members are typical of the members of the population. We can illustrate this statement more precisely with an example. Suppose that you are dealing with a population of 1000 people, and that you sample that population by studying 100 of them. Now suppose that in your sample 30 people have blue eyes. This finding means that 30 percent of the sample have blue eyes. If it is also the case that 30 percent of the population have blue eyes, then your sample is perfectly representative of your population with respect to eye color. We can define representativeness in a little mathematical formula, as follows:

A sample, S, is perfectly representative of a population, P, with respect to a characteristic, x, if the percentage of S that are x is exactly equal to the percentage of P that are x.

In practical terms, this definition is not terribly useful because typically we do not know the percentage of the population that are x. (If we did know this, we would probably not have to take a sample in the first place!) The definition just tells us what *representativeness* means: it does not tell us how to get a sample that is representative when we are still in the position where we do not know all about the population. This is the practical problem of sampling.

It is often thought that the practical problem of sampling is a matter of mathematical statistics. Within statistics, you can prove that a generalization based on a certain number of cases (1000 to 2000) will, with extremely high probability, give reliable information about a population of many millions, *provided the sample is taken randomly.* A sample is taken randomly if every member of the population has an equal chance of getting into that sample.

The problem is that in most real situations in which studies are done on human populations, this strict technical sense of randomness is just about impossible to achieve. If you are a sociologist living in Philadelphia, and you look for 100 children to study, you just cannot honestly say that every child in North America has an equal chance of getting into your study. The chances that the child of a sociology student in Philadelphia will be a subject very greatly exceed the chances that a child from Alaska or Quebec will be a subject! The results of mathematical statistics telling us how many we need in a sample apply only when the sample selected is random. In practice it seldom is, which is unfortunate as far as the progress of social scientific research is concerned. But it is something that should give the nonspecialist a little confidence. How well a given sample can represent a given population in practice is not just a matter of mathematics. We have to use our background knowledge to assess whether a given sample is likely to be typical of a population, and this assessment will vary depending on what characteristic is being examined.

A sample of children from Philadelphia might be representative of American children with reference to the characteristic of knee strength, but it would not be representative with respect to the different characteristics of exposure to crime. We make this statement because the special aspects of living in Philadelphia as opposed to all the other places one might live does not seem likely to affect knees. But it would be likely to affect exposure to crime (probably less than in Chicago; more than in Medicine Hat, Alberta, or a small town in the American Midwest). As far as exposure to crime is concerned, a sample would have to include children from some rural areas, some small towns, some middle-sized cities, and a variety of large cities, to fully represent the population of North American children. When we assert this fact, we are relying on our background knowledge and beliefs about what factors do, or are likely to, affect exposure to crime. We make the sample as representative as we can by taking these factors into account in selecting it. This procedure does not mean that we have a fully random sample. The sample will be only as reliable as the background knowledge that we have used to construct it.

Sometimes the technique of *stratified* sampling is used. This technique also depends on background knowledge. Suppose that we have a large population, P, and we want to determine how many of this population are likely to do x. We may be able to divide P into relevant subgroups: A, B, and C. Now suppose that the composition of P is 10 percent As, 30 percent Bs, and 60 percent Cs. We can then construct our sample so that it has this same composition. This will be a *stratified sample.* The stratified sample is more likely to represent the population because it perfectly reflects these significant subgroups within the population. The word *significant* indicates that we use background knowledge to construct the stratified sample: we have to determine which subgroups are significant with respect to the characteristic we are studying. Age, religion, and sex are known to be significant in voting patterns. But we would not expect religion to be significant, for instance, with regard to exercise habits. So which subgroups we look at depends on what we already know about the significance of possible subgroups—their relevance to the topic we are studying. If the beliefs we rely on to identify relevant subgroups are out-of-date or otherwise flawed, then stratified sampling can produce inaccurate results.

Stratified samples are used by polling centers such as the Gallup organization, and because these organizations have been studying such matters as voting habits for a very long time, they can get reasonably accurate results for populations of many millions from samples of 1000 to 2000 people. The stratification is based on past correlations: more southerners tend to vote Democratic, more blacks tend to vote Democratic, more older people tend to vote Republican, more women than men tend to oppose militaristic attitudes, and so on. But unfortunately this sort of background knowledge is very often just not available in the areas in which social scientific research is done. When it is not available, we are not able to use stratified sampling in a rigorous way to ensure sample representativeness. (We might be said to use it *informally*, as in our example about children's exposure to crime.)

Bearing all these points about sampling in mind, take a look at this report from a study on attitudes toward sex and competence:

When a Man Talks, You Listen

When you want people to listen, it's what you say and how you say it that counts, right? Not always, report researchers Kenneth Gruber and Jacquelyn Gaebelein. When men and women give identical speeches, the men seem to have a significant edge in capturing an audience's attention.

These findings come from a study involving undergraduates at the University of North Carolina at Greensboro. Gruber, a graduate student, and Gaebelein, a psychologist, prepared videotaped speeches by two men and two women whom a panel of judges had selected for their speaking ability. Each speaker read from an identical script on chess (a topic that previous studies have shown people think of as masculine), interior decorating (thought of as feminine), and skiing (neutral).

Each of 60 student subjects viewed either a man or a woman speaking on one of the topics. Afterward, students' ratings of how informative the speech they heard had been were nearly identical, regardless of the speaker's sex or topic. But both men and women who had seen male speakers recalled more information than those who had seen female speakers.

The researchers think the equal ratings of informativeness may be a by-product of the women's movement: students may have felt reluctant, consciously or unconsciously, to admit any bias against women. But previous studies have shown that whether their attitudes on the proper roles for men and women are "liberated" or not, people still expect men to be more competent, intelligent, and knowledgeable than women. If the subjects expected the male speakers to know more, the researchers say, they may well have paid them more careful attention.[8]

In the opening sentences, this report reads as though the findings were universal—about men and women generally. However, since it is obvious that people's attitudes toward competence and sex are likely to vary from one culture to another, we shall take it that the intended population is that of North American adults. This assumption adds some precision to the original. Obviously, this population is one of many millions of people. The sample, on the other hand, is quite small. It contains sixty people. If we knew that the population was uniform with respect to attitudes on sex roles and competence, this size of sample *might* be adequate. But we do not know that it is uniform; nor would the researchers, or anyone else, have the background knowledge needed to construct a stratified sample for this problem. If the researchers had built up a sample using so many Chinese Americans, so many blacks, so many older and younger people, and so on, their sample would have been better than a group of sixty college students. But it would not be as firmly based as the polls that the Gallup organization and others use for voting predictions, for we do not know which subgroups within the larger population are significant as far as attitudes about sex roles are concerned.

In fact, the sample is seriously nonrepresentative. Undergraduates are typically young, educated, inexperienced in life, childless, and of a relatively high income bracket. These features differentiate them from other adults in North America, and it seems entirely likely that some or all of these features would be relevant to attitudes about sexual roles and male and female competence. The sample in this reported study is, in fact, so poor that the enumerative induction at the basis of this study is an extremely weak argument. The argument underlying the study as reported seems to have gone like this:

1. Of sixty undergraduates at the University of North Carolina (Greensboro), men and women recalled more information from male speakers than from female speakers.
So,
2. Adult men and women in North America will recall more information from male speakers than they do from female speakers.
3. A good explanation of adult men and women recalling more from male speakers than from female speakers would be that they expect male speakers to be more competent and listen to them more attentively.
Therefore,
4. In North America, men and women expect male speakers to be more competent than female speakers and listen more attentively to male speakers than to female speakers.

The structure of the argument is like this:

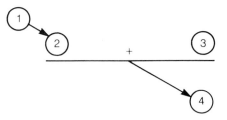

The move from (1) to (2) is an enumerative induction, and it is a very weak argument because the sample is nonrepresentative. From (2) and (3), there is an explanatory inductive argument to (4). But since (2) has such poor support, it is not clear that there is any phenomenon needing explanation. The whole study is undermined by the sampling error.

We may think that the conclusion is plausible anyway, but because of the sampling error, the study cannot support that conclusion. If we do believe the conclusion, it will be on the basis of our own experience or common sense and not because of any evidence these researchers have provided.

How well sixty undergraduates can represent the entire population of North American adults is not an issue of either mathematical statistics or psychology. The sample is entirely inadequate, and any careful nonspecialist is quite competent to reach that conclusion. We don't know on the basis of this study that men are listened to more seriously than women.

It is worth reflecting on this example, for it is relatively common for research studies in the social sciences to be based on samples of undergraduate students. It is quite obvious, however, with respect to most social attitudes and capabilities that undergraduate students constitute a poor sample of the broader population. Serious researchers would not deny this. But a number of practical factors make undergraduates convenient subjects. Hard-pressed researchers are usually also college teachers, and they often have inadequate funds for research. Rather than going to the beer hall, the unemployment office, the hospital, or the daycare center to obtain a more representative group of adult subjects, they can make class announcements or post notices at a university and obtain subjects with a minimum investment of time, effort, and money. Then mathematical statistics can be used to show that a sample of sixty subjects is sufficient to give a reliable indication about a trait in a population of many millions. The problem is that the application of mathematical statistics is, strictly speaking, appropriate only when the sample has been randomly selected. In cases where undergraduates are used to represent the general adult population, it is entirely clear that the sample has not been randomly selected. (The chances that a transient from the streets of Manhattan or a trapper from Alaska will be in the sample group are virtually zero, whereas the chance that a first-year psychology student in Greensboro, North Carolina, will be in it may be as high as 1 in 5.) No amount of mathematical juggling can solve the problem.

More subtle problems may arise in connection with getting representative samples. Social scientists have to restrict their work to subjects whose cooperation they can obtain. If they send out a questionnaire, their sample will be of those who return the questionnaire, which will give the sample a certain bias in favor of people who are relatively well-organized and well-disposed to social science—and rich enough to afford a postage stamp. Similar points may be made for studies in which volunteers are used. People who volunteer for studies will have more time available, and be more favorably disposed to social science, than others who do not volunteer. If these traits turn out to be significantly related to the aspect being studied, the very fact of volunteers being used can work against the representativeness of the sample.

The Biased Sample. As we have seen, there are often reasons to doubt whether samples are fully representative of the population they are supposed to reflect. Occasionally the problem will be even worse than simple nonrepresentativeness. The sample may be selected in such a way that it demonstrably *misrepresents* the population. This is the *biased* sample; the sample is selected in such a way that it is bound either to underemphasize or to overemphasize the characteristic being studied. A simple example would be a sample composed entirely of students of literature, where the purpose was to study reading habits in the broad student population. The sample in such a case would be biased because literature students are a self-selected group as far as love of reading is concerned. The sample would be biased in favor of enthusiastic readers. Sometimes the bias in such a sample is a result of deliberate deception—as when advertisers test group after group of toothpaste users until they finally find one in which ten out of ten people have no cavities. But it may happen too that biased samples emerge from honest mistakes.

An amusing instance of a biased sample occurred in an advertisement for Merit cigarettes. Advertisements are not based on serious scientific research, but they are often written so they borrow the "authority" of such research. ("Science" still functions as a kind of glamour word, and many advertisements seek to exploit it.) The Merit advertisement went like this:

"Best tasting low tar I've tried," report Merit smokers in latest survey.
Taste Quest Ends. Latest research provides solid evidence that Merit is a satisfying long-term taste alternative to high tar cigarettes.
Proof: The overwhelming majority of Merit smokers polled feel they didn't sacrifice taste in switching from high tar cigarettes. Proof: 9 out of 10 Merit smokers reported they continue to enjoy smoking, are glad they switched, and report Merit is the best-tasting low tar they've ever tried. Merit is the proven alternative to high tar smoking. And you can taste it.[9]

The intended population here is smokers. The sample is smokers of Merit cigarettes. We are not told how many were "surveyed." We are supposed to make an enumerative induction, as follows:

1. Merit smokers enjoy Merit cigarettes and find them to be the best low-tar cigarettes.
Therefore,
2. Smokers in general will enjoy Merit cigarettes and find them to be the best low-tar cigarettes.

Here the sample is *biased.* It is not representative of the population, and the inductive argument is therefore a very weak one. With respect to their attitudes toward Merit cigarettes, smokers of Merit are a self-selected group. Obviously they would not smoke these cigarettes if they didn't like them. The reference to proofs and surveys is supposed to make you think that the merits of Merits have been scientifically demonstrated. But since the sample was as biased as it could possibly be, nothing at all has been demonstrated.

It has recently come to light that an extremely influential study of moral reasoning was based on a biased sample. Educational psychologist Lawrence Kohlberg has long been famous for his studies of moral reasoning, from which he concluded that there is a natural progression in all human beings from self-centered concerns to appeals to universal standards of justice. Kohlberg identified six such stages. His work has been the basis for much theorizing in developmental psychology and for many programs of moral education for children. Carol Gilligan has brought to light the amazing fact that the studies on which Kohlberg's theories were based were of 84 boys. Despite this sampling bias, he and many researchers who followed him were willing to say that the theory applied to girls and women; they even commented that many mature women were inferior in moral development because they did not go through these stages in the right way. Kohlberg's sample was clearly biased in leaving out girls. Also—a fact not emphasized by Gilligan—it failed to represent different cultural, language, and racial groups.[10]

Sample Size. We have been emphasizing sample representativeness and flaws in inductive arguments that may come from failings in this area. However, inductive arguments can also be flawed by the small size of the sample. The two facets are connected, of course. Because two people could not be a representative sample for a population of many millions, a sample of two is too small to establish a generalization about millions. Suppose a doctor reported that jogging can cause infertility in young women because he had observed *two* young women in their early twenties whose menstrual periods had stopped while they were regular joggers and resumed when they stopped jogging. He would not have an adequate sample on which to base a generalization!

As we have seen, it is difficult to specify in completely general terms just how big a sample has to be in order to be adequate. We cannot simply stipulate a percentage like

5 percent and say that the sample will be big enough if 5 percent of the population are included in it. For a very large and relatively uniform population, where we have the relevant background knowledge, 5 percent will be far more than we need. As we have already noted, polls of 1000 to 2000 people can accurately reflect a voting population of 80 million or so. This number is only 1/400 of 1 percent, and yet it is enough for reliable inductive generalizations about voting behavior. But in a completely different context, 5 percent might be too small. If we were dealing with a total population of 200 people, and we were studying a variable trait on which there was little reliable background knowledge, sampling 5 percent (only 10) of these people would not give any useful information. Unfortunately, then, it is not really possible to state completely general rules as to how big samples have to be.

These points can easily be missed, and one source of the error seems to be a certain ambiguity in the word *random*. In mathematical statistics, this word means that each member of the population has an equal chance of getting into the sample. The condition of randomness is rarely satisfied. But we have a looser, more everyday, sense of *random* in which something is random if it isn't systematic: it is not thoroughly understood, it seems to appear without pattern, its cause is not known, and so on. In this everyday sense of *random*, a researcher interviewing people in a mall might talk to shoppers at random. That is to say, he would not employ any *system* for selecting the shoppers to whom he spoke. But this haphazard style does not guarantee that his sample of shoppers in the mall is random in the mathematical sense. Far from it. (Where does he stand in the mall: near the liquor store, the children's books, or the cheese shop? What sorts of people does he feel comfortable talking to? What sorts of people are likely to be willing to talk to him?) One problem is that we too easily infer mathematical randomness from randomness in the everyday sense. This inference is a mistake.

When you are trying to determine whether a sample is large enough to be representative of the population, it will sometimes be very helpful to do some elementary arithmetic. If you are told, for instance, that there are thirty male subjects, and that of these, 10 percent had such-and-such interest, stop and calculate 10 percent of thirty. It works out to three.

This simple strategy for criticism yields devastating results when applied to the following report, which describes a study in which 300 residents of Pasadena, California, were asked about their attitudes toward capital punishment:

> *Overall about 75 percent of the respondents in this conservative community favored capital punishment in some form. About half as many men as women were opposed to the death penalty under any circumstances.*
>
> *Among women who had undergone an abortion, only 6 percent were unqualifiedly against the death penalty; 11 percent thought it should be used more frequently; and the rest favored it for some crimes. Twenty-six percent of the women who had not had an abortion were against execution under any circumstances; 20 percent favored more frequent use; and the rest wanted it for heinous crimes. It was suggested that "two factors combine to produce this difference. Women who regard human life less highly are more apt to have abortions and endorse capital punishment; and the abortion itself led them to depreciate the value of life in general as a way of vindicating the abortion to themselves."[11]*

Let us do some arithmetic and then analyze the argument. The researcher surveyed 300 people in Pasadena, California. He does not specify how many were female—not in this summary at least. Let us assume that 150 were female. He wishes to contrast the attitudes of female subjects who have had abortions with those of female subjects who have not had abortions. However, we are not told in the report just *how many* of these (presumably) 150 subjects have had abortions, though we are told that of *these* only 6 percent were unqualifiedly against the death penalty. Six percent of what! Abortion has been legal for only just over a decade, and numbers of abortions were probably somewhat less before it was legal. Presumably some women in the sample would have been in their childbearing years during a period when abortion was less common than it is now. Let us assume that 30 women out of 150 would have had abortions. This is probably a very high estimate. Now 6 percent of 30 is 1.8 or 2 women; 11 percent of 30 is 3.3 (3 women); the remaining 83% is 25 women. These are really small numbers on which to base any generalization that women who regard human life less highly are more likely to have abortions and endorse capital punishment. The sample is just too small, but you would miss this fact if you did not do the arithmetic.

Another questionable aspect of this study, by the way, concerns operationalization. It appears that "valuing life" has been operationalized as "indicating that you are opposed to capital punishment." This operationalization is a poor one because some people favor capital punishment in the belief that it deters people from murder. They favor capital punishment, rightly or wrongly, because of the way they value life. The cognitive value of this little piece of research is simply nothing. We have not learned anything about attitudes and experiences of abortion and how these are related to attitudes regarding the value of life.

One way in which researchers can improve sample adequacy is by combining results of several different studies. It might happen, for instance, that the same hypothesis had been confirmed in several different studies on different subjects. If the results are put together, the total sample is, of course, larger and more varied than the sample in any single study. As a consumer of social science, you are rarely in a position to make these combinations, but the possibility is important as far as the inductive basis of social science is concerned. For this cumulation of several studies to be feasible, it is important that the *same hypothesis* be addressed, and that, in methods used, there be no significant differences that could lead to misleading comparisons.

Concluding Comments

By discussing operationalization, the language in which social science is pursued, and the problems that may arise with sampling, we hope to make you a more competent consumer of statistics, particularly as they are used in reports of studies in the social sciences or in results from polls. If you read "26.2 percent of executives exercise daily," you will know that there is some fuzziness involved in "executive" and "exercise," so that the number is misleadingly precise. You will also know that this generalization has been based on an enumerative induction: a study must have been done of a sample of executives and the generalization based on that study. Without knowing the *size* and *character* of that sample, you cannot tell how reliable the generalization is. By now, you should have overcome the common temptation to take statistical generalizations as entirely authoritative merely because they contain numbers.

Review of Terms Introduced

> *Operationalization of terms:* Definition of terms on the basis of a set of procedures that researchers can use to determine whether they are going to be applied or not. Terms that require operationalization are typically mentalistic or evaluative or both.

Prejudicial question: A question formulated to coerce or lead respondents into an answer they might not otherwise be inclined to give. Questions may be prejudicial due to emotionally charged language, due to assumptions not acceptable in the context in which the question is asked, or due to formal properties that structure information and responses in ways unacceptable in the context in which the question is asked.

The fallacy of complex question: Posing a question formed so as to tend to coerce a respondent into an unwelcome or even false assumption for no reason except the way in which the question suggests relating claims and responses. The classic example is, "Have you stopped beating your wife?".

Random sample: A sample in which every member of the population has an equal chance of being included.

Stratified sampling: The technique of selecting a sample in such a way that significant subgroups within the population are proportionately represented in the sample.

Biased sample: A sample that misrepresents the population. It is nonrepresentative because its members are atypical of the population in a way that is certain or very likely to affect the result.

Sample: Cases examined as the basis for an enumerative inductive argument that are a sample of a larger body of cases. For instance, if we study 10 blind students to reach a conclusion about 100 blind students, the 10 students constitute the sample.

Population: The cases an inductively based generalization is supposed to cover. (*Note:* In this sense *population* is a technical term.) If we study 10 blind students to reach a conclusion about a group of 100 blind students, the population is the group of 100 blind students.

Representative sample: A sample, *S*, is perfectly representative of a population, *P*, with respect to a characteristic, x, if the percentage of *S* that are x is exactly equal to the percentage of *P* that are x.

EXERCISE SET

Exercise Two

For each of the following examples, determine whether an enumerative induction is used or required. If so, describe the sample and the population. (If it is not expressly stated what population is intended, arrive at some plausible interpretation in this regard.) Then comment on the adequacy of the sample as far as representativeness and size are concerned. If there is no enumerative induction, them simply note that fact and move on to the next question.

1. Of 500 Edmonton adults questioned about attitudes toward censorship, 160 were opposed, 240 were in favor, and 100 were uncertain. Respondents were asked, "Do you favor having police and customs officials restrict the display and distribution of violent pornographic materials?" Of those who answered *no*, 84 said their opposition was due to the fact that such officials might make mistakes and censor material that wasn't really just pornography, and 76 were opposed to all government censorship on principle. We can see from this poll that only a small minority of western Canadians object to censorship.

2. Latest figures from the Metropolitan Life Insurance Company show that short women who weigh between 5 and 10 pounds more than weights regarded as ideal by previous studies live longer than any other women in their age group. These figures

are based on clients of the company during the period 1970–1980. You can see that the ideal weight charts previously used are wrong. Weights have been set between 5 and 10 pounds too low for short women.

3. The daycare center is really well run. Whenever they invite parents to visit, the place is clean and attractive, and the children are happily playing with new educational toys.

4. It has been found that out of 500 students in the midwestern United States who received a bilingual education in Spanish and English, only 120 were competently bilingual after age 25. The speculation was that you lose competence in a language that you do not regularly use, and that for many midwesterners, there are few opportunities to use Spanish. This research shows that less than 30 percent of students given bilingual education will really benefit from it as far as adult competence in the second language is concerned.

5. In university and college courses on literature, ninety-two percent of works studied are written by men. Only eight percent are written by women. Thus, works by men are over-represented. The ideal proportion is fifty percent of each type.

6. One hundred users of BICBOC word processors have been surveyed and asked for their opinion as to the reliability and usefulness of these word processors. Of these one hundred, a full ninety-five said they were very satisfied with BICBOC and would recommend those word processors to their friends. From this we can see that BICBOC word processors are more reliable and useful, for all who need word processors, than competing systems.

7. *Background:* This report of studies on unwed mothers appeared in *Psychology Today,* December 1980. (Copyright © 1980 Ziff-Davis Publishing Company. Reprinted from *Psychology Today* magazine with the permission of the American Psychological Association.)

Keeping a Baby by Default

"How do unmarried mothers in maternity homes who decide to raise their children differ from those who offer their babies for adoption? According to two recent studies, mothers who keep their babies are those who face the prospect of not having much else to do with their lives but be mothers and those who are familiar with one-parent families because they grew up in them or have single parents as friends.

"Ernie S. Lightman and Benjamin Schlesinger of the University of Toronto Faculty of Social Work studied a random group of the unmarried mothers-to-be (average age, 19) who entered Ontario maternity homes in 1978. Ninety of the women planned to keep their babies and 124 intended to offer them for adoption. A few years earlier, Lucille Gow, a sociologist, studied 210 unmarried mothers in Milwaukee, also looking for differences between women who keep their babies and women who relinquish them. In both studies, the economic and social backgrounds of the women in each group were roughly similar.

"In contrast with the women who chose adoption, women in both studies who intended to keep their babies had left school at an earlier age: in the Canadian sample, they were also more likely to have had a serious illness or to have received psychiatric treatment. The Canadian researchers found, much as Gow did, that they were 'less likely to have career plans, and perhaps viewed the prospect of childbearing as involving less of a change in lifestyle.' They were also more likely to have been raised by one parent and, among the Canadians, more likely to have friends who were unmarried mothers—suggesting that they were 'less likely to see a continuation of this one-parent pattern as a handicap for themselves and the child.' Women who intended to keep their babies were also more likely to be in touch with the baby's father—a sign, Lightman and Schlesinger say, that they may have had greater hope of marrying him or at least of receiving child support from him."

*8. *Background:* A book entitled *Beyond the Male Myth* sought to explore male attitudes toward female personality, appearance, and sexual habits, and male desires about their own sexual experience. The authors tried to explore these attitudes through a questionnaire that contained both short questions and questions that required essay-type answers. The authors had these remarks to make about their sampling of male subjects:

"We wanted to survey at least 4000 men because, according to statistical principles, a sample that large is equivalent to an infinitely greater population. In other words, if we had gone on to survey 10,000 or 100,000, or 4,000,000 men, the percentages who responded in various ways would not be expected to differ significantly from the results obtained from 4000. This holds true, of course, only if the sample is a truly balanced one, representative of the entire nation."

(*Question:* Do you think the authors are correct about their sample? Is there a difference between representativeness and the randomness that we saw to be a condition of applying statistical principles to sampling? Is the sample likely to be representative?)

Here are the authors' comments on how their sample was chosen.

"Our research firm estimated that half of the men approached by the field agents agreed to participate, a phenomenal percentage in view of other studies. The men were approached primarily in shopping centers and malls, as well as office building complexes, tennis clubs, college campuses, airports, and bus depots. The communities in which the test sites were located varied in affluence, ensuring that our sample would include ample representation from all income groups."
(Anthony Pietropinto and Jacqueline Simenauer, *Beyond the Male Myth* [New York: Times Books], p. 18.)

9. *Background:* Use information from question (8) in doing this question. The authors of *Beyond the Male Myth* distributed a questionnaire. On it, one question was "What do you consider the ideal sex life for yourself?" To this question, the following answers were possible, one of which was to be selected by respondents.

> marriage, wife being the only sex partner
> marriage, with outside sexual activity
> living with one female partner, unmarried
> a few regular partners
> many casual partners
> one female partner, but living separately

To this question, 50.5 percent of the men surveyed chose the first answer: marriage with the wife being the only sexual partner. Suppose that we were to infer from this survey that half of American men prefer monogamous marriage as a sexual lifestyle. Would the survey by Pietropinto and Simenauer be an adequate basis for this inference? Why or why not? Do you find any significant range of possibilities omitted on this one question from their questionnaire?

*10. "A study by a Toronto psychologist suggests that young people between the ages of 12 and 17 are the primary consumers of pornography in Canada and that 37 percent of them watch sexually explicit videos at least once a month. Research by James Check . . . shows that 35 percent of youngsters 'expressed interest in watching sexually violent scenes,' whereas adults expressed very little interest in such scenes. Prof. Check also found that college students display an 'unbelievable acceptance of rape myths and violence against women'."

In the study more than a thousand Canadians were interviewed. The sample reflected the country's population in age and geographic distribution. Of that group, about 70 or 80 people would be in the age group between 12 and 17.
(Toronto *Globe and Mail,* March 11, 1986.)

11. *Background:* In its December 1980 issue, *Psychology Today* reported research into the personalities

of ski instructors. According to the report, a Ph.D. candidate in psychology gave personality tests to 78 male and 40 female ski instructors based at glamorous resort spots such as Aspen, Sun Valley, Steamboat Springs, and Vail:

"The instructors ranged in age from 16 to 62. Their average age was 28. Most were officially certified, had been teaching for five years or longer, and considered ski instructing to be their primary occupation. Bridgwater used the Personality Research Form (PRF) to assess them. The instructors scored high on ambition, independence, and a propensity for hard work and diligence. They described themselves as being dominating and influential, and their scores showed they were likely to display qualities that are also prominent in leaders who can take over a group or persuade others to their point of view."

The report began with the statement, "Ski instructors have the personality one might expect to find in ambitious career people, according to a recent study." Does this statement suggest an enumerative inductive argument? If so, how well can the study, as reported, support the suggested generalization?

12. *Background:* Arthur Koestler had the following to say about capital punishment in an essay in which he raised the question whether convicted murderers, having served a life term, might "turn into wolves again" when released into society:

"The answer is given in the statistics of the Home Office of Scotland Yard and the Central After Care Association. During the twenty-year period 1928–48, 174 people were sentenced to life and of these 112 had been released at the end of the period in question. Of these 112, only one was alleged to have committed a second murder: Walter Graham Rowland, and he was, as we saw, one of the most probable victims of mistaken identity. Yet Rowland is, as far as one can gather from existing reports, the only case of a 'sane' reprieved murderer being convicted of a second murder in the United Kingdom in the course of the twentieth century. None of the other released lifers during the twenty-year period ending in 1948 committed crimes of violence against the person; and only five committed offences against property. In Scotland, eleven reprieved murderers were released during the same period: only two of these were re-convicted, one for theft and one for 'lewd practices.'"
(Arthur Koestler, "Reflections on Hanging," in *Applying Ethics,* ed. Vincent Barry [Belmont, Calif.: Wadsworth, 1982].)

*13. "Calculations by the Union of Concerned Scientists show that construction of a space-based laser defense would require the lifting of some 1300 tons of laser fuel into space. And this is calculated using assumptions which some might feel were unreasonably favorable, i.e., perfect laser mirrors, lasers of optimum efficiency, and, perhaps most optimistic of all, the assumption that the Russians have simply maintained their current missile force as it is today! Even under these conditions, the cost of simply lifting the battle stations into orbit would be of the order of $4 billion. Kosta Tsipsis of the Massachusetts Institute of Technology estimates that, using ten space shuttles each flying three missions per year, it would still take between 3200 and 6400 years just to lift the fuels for a fleet of laser battle stations into orbit. All such figures are highly speculative, but they give an idea of the size of the problem involved."

(Ben Thompson, "What Is Star Wars?" in *Star Wars*, ed. by E. P. Thompson [Middlesex, England: Penguin, 1985], p. 33.)

14. *Background:* The author is discussing differences that male and female hormones can make as far as behavior is concerned:

"The second area of research on hormones and aggression focuses on increased aggressive behavior in females who are administered male hormones postnatally, without prenatal sensitization. In a typical study, Joslyn (1973) took three female and three male rhesus monkeys who were separated from their mothers at three to four months of age. The three females were given regular injections of testosterone (a male hormone) from six and one half months until fourteen and one half months of age, while the three males were untreated. Aggressive responses were studied as part of the establishment of social dominance patterns at ages five to nine and one half months, thirteen and one half to sixteen months, and twenty-five to twenty-seven and one half months. Before the administration of testosterone began, the males were dominant and showed more aggression than the females. During the hormone treatment the frequency of the females' aggressive behavior gradually increased until it equalled that of the males at nine months of age. Shortly after this two of the treated females attacked and subdued the two most dominant males. These two females then assumed the positions of dominance and were still maintaining them a year after treatment ended."

(Joanne Bunker Rohrbauch, *Women: Psychology's Puzzle* [New York: Basic Books, 1979].)

What would you infer from this study as far as the effect of these hormones on monkeys is concerned? Why? What would you infer from it as far as the effect of these hormones on human beings is concerned? Why?

15. "Many smokers have noticed that they gain weight when they quit the cigaret habit, but the seemingly obvious explanation—that they eat more—has been hard to prove. Now scientists at the University of Lausanne, Switzerland, have a different explanation. They have found that there is an appreciable energy cost in cigaret-smoking itself. Young adults who smoked 24 cigarets during one day expended 10 percent more energy than they did in a comparable nonsmoking period, even though food intake and exercise stayed the same. Their findings suggest that a person who quits smoking must also eat less if he or she wants to avoid a weight gain. Volunteers for the experiment were 8 healthy young adults, four men and four women, who each spent 24 hours in a respiration chamber—a sealed room where every calorie of energy intake and outgo was measured."

(Toronto *Globe and Mail*, February 4, 1986.)

16. *"Three out of ten operations not needed: U.S. nurses.*

"New York: Nearly half the nurses surveyed in a nationwide poll claim 3 out of 10 operations are not needed, and many of them say about half of all hospital stays are unnecessary. Eighty-three percent of the nurses polled by the magazine *RN*, a journal for registered nurses and students, also favored informing patients of less extreme and sometimes less expensive therapeutic alternatives, even if the doctor won't. Based on a national poll of 12,500 nurses, the report provided evidence of a quiet mutiny—in the name of patients' rights—in the nation's hospital nurses."

(Toronto *Star*, February 15, 1981.)

Do you think that the headline given to this article is misleading? Why or why not?

17. *"Males target of sex education.*

Many adolescents are becoming sexually active at an earlier age, and young males must take a more responsible attitude toward birth control, says Elizabeth Parker, director of the family planning division of the Toronto public health department. In the past six months, half the callers to the family planning's hotline have been teenagers under 16 who are not using birth control, Miss Parker said in an interview. One in 10 calls are from persons requesting information about an abortion, she added. The emphasis during Birth Control Week, proclaimed for February 9 to 13 by Mayor Arthur Eggleton, will be to encourage young males to adopt a more positive attitude toward contraception, she said. A national survey has shown that two out of five males between the ages of 15 and 17 have had intercourse on a regular basis. Sex education in the schools has not resulted in increased

Correlations

So far we have been concerned primarily with statistical claims that concern one observed trait within a sample or population. For instance, in such a claim as:

───── Of clients of Weight Watchers, 95 percent are female.

the population is clients of Weight Watchers. In this population, one trait (sex) has been observed and is described in the generalization. The generalization deals only with this aspect of the population and not with any other. But in empirical studies it is extremely common to observe several traits at once in order to study the ways in which the traits go together. Compare the preceding claim with this one:

───── Of clients of Weight Watchers, 98 percent of the 95 percent who are female expect their whole lives to change as a result of losing weight, whereas only 30 percent of the 5 percent who are male have this expectation.

This second generalization includes the statistical information that is contained in the first one, but it gives additional information as well. It puts together two different sets of observations. The same population, clients of Weight Watchers, has been observed with an eye to seeing how two traits go together. These traits are sex and expectation regarding weight loss. The second statement is a *correlational* statement. It says that being female and having a dramatic expectation regarding weight loss are strongly correlated in this population. A far higher proportion of females than males has this expectation.

Significant and Nonsignificant Correlations.   Correlational claims, then, are based on observations of two distinct traits. Researchers look at two aspects of each subject: they first determine whether he is *A* or non-*A*, and then whether he is *B* or non-*B*. The results of such a study may be of three different types:

a. *Positive Correlation.* If a higher proportion of *A*s than non-*A*s are *B*, then there is a positive correlation between being *A* and being *B*.
b. *Negative Correlation.* If a smaller proportion of *A*s than non-*A*s are *B*, then there is a negative correlation between being *A* and being *B*.
c. *No Correlation.* If the same proportion of *A*s as non-*A*s are *B*, then there is no correlation between being *A* and being *B*.[1]

If a correlation is *significant*, then it indicates something of interest about the population, something that calls for further study and, eventually, explanation. For instance, if the correlation between being female and weight loss expectation really existed, it would certainly call for some explanation. *Why* do so many more women than men have these expectations? Is it because the women who are overweight are more seriously overweight than the men? Is it because society discriminates more against overweight women than against overweight men? Is it because women just naturally care more about their appearance than men do? When there is a significant positive correlation, we suppose there must be *some* explanation, whatever it is. When there is a strong negative correlation, the same point applies. But when a positive or negative correlation is very slight (as it would be if 30 percent of men had a certain trait, and 31 percent of the women had it, in a sample of 100 people), it is not said to be significant. Such a slight correlation as this could easily be due to accidental variations within the sample or to mere coincidence, and thus it calls for no further explanation. As well as distinguishing between positive, negative, and zero correlation, we have to distinguish between those positive or negative correlations that are *significant* and those that are not.

How do we know, in general, whether a positive or negative correlation is significant? This is a difficult question. Some statistics texts and some elementary texts on social science offer formulas that you are supposed to use in order to determine significance. The formulas include such factors as the size of the sample and the population, and the level of confidence that is sought. (*Level of confidence* refers to the chance of being right, within a certain range, about the estimate of the population, based on the sample.) These formulas can be memorized and used; this way of handling correlations is standard in many elementary courses. We will not use it here, however. In most practical contexts, the assumptions on which such formulas have been devised simply do not hold up. They presuppose that the sample has been selected randomly from the population, and we have already seen that this is very often just not true. Since the mathematical formulas used to distinguish between *significant* and *nonsignificant* correlations depend for their validity on assumptions that very often do not apply to real cases, we shall not encourage you to use them here. Unfortunately, this does not leave us with any alternative general guideline.

Distinguishing between significant and nonsignificant correlations is a complex matter; it depends on the size of the sample and the population and on background knowledge that is relevant to the traits studied and their association or nonassociation. For a large sample representing a large population, even a small positive or negative correlation may be significant. For instance, if you were to study 1 million women and 1 million men, and you were to find that 52 percent of the women and 49 percent of the men disapproved of nuclear weapons' tests, the correlation between this attitude and sex would be extremely significant. On the other hand, if the sample is small, this kind of correlation would not be significant at all. In a sample of only thirty or so people, small differences in percentages do not mean much. The difference between 10 percent of thirty and 50 percent of thirty is, after all, only twelve people, and it could happen that twelve out of thirty people might accidentally have some characteristic. The same point applies, of course, when the population is much larger but the sample is very small in absolute terms. Also, background knowledge enters the picture. If there is very good reason, in terms of background knowledge, to expect that the *A*s and the non-*A*s in your sample will be similar with regard to *B*, then even a slight difference between them with regard to *B* may interest you enough to merit further study. Even so, background knowledge and considerations of sample and population size have to be taken together. The crucial question with regard to the significance of a positive or negative correlation is: how likely is it that we would get this correlation even if there were *no* difference between *A*s and non-*A*s, with respect to *B?*

Correlation and Cause.   In this book we do not try to offer a complete theory of social science. We only hope to give you some analytical tools so that you can look at reports of work in social science with a more critical eye. We cannot pursue the matter of significant and nonsignificant correlations further here. Actually, as far as correlation is concerned, our purpose is as much to tell you what it is *not* as to tell you what it is.

Our main point is to emphasize that correlation is not the same as cause. If being *A* is positively correlated with being *B*, this is *not* to say that being *A* is the cause of being *B*. This distinction between correlation and cause holds up no matter how strong the correlation is. Even granted that *A* and *B* are positively correlated and that this correlation is very significant and calls for explanation it does *not* follow that the explanation is that being *A* is the cause of being *B*. This is one possibility, but there are others as well.

If *A* is positively correlated with *B*, then *one* of the following will be true:

———— a. *A* causally contributes to *B*. That is to say, either *A* is the cause of *B*, or it is one of a number of causal factors that combine to produce *B*.
b. *B* causally contributes to *A*. That is to say, either *B* is the cause of *A*, or it is one of a number of causal factors that combine to produce *A*.
c. Some other factor, *C*, is the underlying cause of both *A* and *B*.
d. The correlation between *A* and *B* is an accident.

We cannot simply argue from a positive correlation between *A* and *B* to the conclusion that *A* is a cause of *B*; if we do, we infer (a) without giving any reason to exclude (b), (c), and (d). Since the data about correlation are compatible with all four of these hypotheses, we have to have some reasons for taking any one of them to be the preferred explanation. There must be a basis for excluding the possibility that *B* causes *A*, that something else causes both, or that the correlation observed is a mere coincidence. This means that arguments from premises about correlation to conclusions about causal relationships are very difficult to construct with accuracy. So many things might be underlying causes of both *A* and *B*, in most cases. Sometimes it is easy to exclude the possibility that *B* causes *A*; it may happen that *A comes before B* in time, or that we already have background knowledge that would rule out this possibility. But for some correlations, even this is not easy.

One example of a dispute about correlation and cause is the following: there is a positive correlation between being overweight and having high blood pressure. What is usually inferred from this correlation is that being overweight is one cause of having high blood pressure—that is, that it combines with other conditions to produce the high blood pressure. From this inference, medical doctors traditionally have made the further inference that high blood pressure patients can improve their condition by losing weight. However, some critics have urged that these inferences are too hasty, pointing out that overweight people whose blood pressure has been observed have been dieting (due to being overweight) and have therefore been under stress. Also, they point out, our society makes life pretty difficult for people who are overweight. It has been seriously suggested that a relationshp holds between attitudes to weight and high blood pressure, rather than simply to weight and high blood pressure. The suggestion is that being overweight in our society is very stressful, and that the stress that goes along with overweight is the cause of high blood pressure. It is difficult to show this hypothesis to be true or false, but one might study overweight people in cultures that have different attitudes to weight and determine whether there is a correlation between overweight and high blood pressure in those cultures also.

That a correlation is mere coincidence is a remote possibility that science can never completely rule out. The best that can be done is to enlarge the sample: if a correlation persists, then it is a general regularity in the world and, according to the principles of scientific method, must have some explanation. You can see that ruling out alternative possibilities is a difficult matter, and that it is far too hasty to simply infer a causal relationship from a correlation.

Another way to convince yourself that correlation is not the same as causation is to remember that correlation works both ways. If *A* is positively correlated with *B*, then it must also be true that *B* is positively correlated with *A*. But causation only works in one direction: if *A* is the cause of *B*, then *B* cannot be the cause of *A*! Suppose you found a positive correlation between being over thirty and being a successful parent. You might be tempted to infer that being over thirty is a cause of successful parenting. However, an equally good inference, using correlation only, would be that being a successful parent causes a person to be over thirty. This inference is ridiculous; we know that age depends on birthday, not on parenting, successful or unsuccessful! Since both inferences have an equal basis, and since the second one leads us to a ridiculous conclusion, we know that both inferences are unsound. This is a refutation by logical analogy. We cannot infer a cause straight from a correlation. We need a very considerable intermediate argument.

With these points in mind, consider the following report on teenagers' marijuana habits. The report is taken from a text in psychology, which seems at this point not to be taking the distinction between correlation and cause as seriously as it should:

A Friend in Weed Is a Friend in Deed

Among the factors responsible for adolescent students using drugs, one of the most potent is social conformity pressures. A large-scale 1971 survey of over 8000 secondary school students in New York State revealed that adolescents are much more likely to use marijuana if their friends do than if their friends do not.

To some extent initiation into the drug scene is a function of modelling parental drug use. . . . But the most striking finding was the role that peers played. Association with other drug-using adolescents was the most important correlate of adolescent marijuana use. "Only 7 percent of adolescents who perceive none of their friends to use marijuana use marijuana themselves, in contrast to 92 percent who perceive all their friends to be users." As can be seen, the influence of best friends overwhelms that of parents.[2]

According to this study, there is a positive correlation between perceiving friends to use marijuana and using it oneself: 92 percent of those who perceive all their friends to use it, use it; whereas only 7 percent who perceive none of their friends to use it, use it. Obviously, this is a significant correlation. One peculiar thing about the way this research was done is that the researchers seem to have ignored those teenagers who perceived some of their friends to use marijuana, as oppose to perceiving that all of them did or that none of them did. This omission is potentially serious, since it seems entirely likely that many teenagers would believe that some of their friends use marijuana and others do not.

However, we will push on to the matter of correlation and cause. It is clear from the wording of this report that a causal relationship is claimed. The implication is evident in the phrases "among the factors *responsible* for adolescent students using drugs" and "as can be seen the *influence* of best friends overwhelms that of parents." However, there is no evidence given for this causal relationship between friends smoking and a teenager smoking. There is only the data about the *perception* of friends smoking and smoking oneself. As described here, this research clearly involved a too hasty inference from correlation to cause. There is no basis given for excluding such possibilities as that the use of marijuana influences one's selection of friends; the use of marijuana influences one's perception of one's friends; some underlying cause produces both the marijuana habit and the selection of a certain type of friend; and so on. This is an example of how *not* to reason from correlation to cause.

Before leaving the topic of correlation as such, we should say a few words about negative correlation. From the information that *A* is negatively correlated with *B*, we would not, of course, even be tempted to conclude that *A* is a cause of *B*. However, we might be tempted to infer that *A prevents B*. An example of negative correlation is the relationship between breast feeding and breast cancer in women. Breast cancer occurs less frequently in women who breast-feed their babies than in women who do not breast-feed. On this basis it has been speculated that breast feeding in some way prevents breast cancer, or at least inhibits its development. But this too is a causal claim, and like any other, needs more support than purely correlational data. Just as we need additional reasoning and evidence to argue from a positive correlation to cause, we need additional evidence to argue from negative correlation to prevention.

Finding the Cause

Very often statements of statistical generalization or correlation are of interest primarily because what we would really like to know is the cause of whatever it is that we are studying. Knowing the cause, or causes, of something enables us to predict it and, sometimes, to control it. Obviously we are interested in things that are correlated with the development of breast cancer, managerial stress, juvenile delinquency, and so on, because we would like to eliminate or reduce these things. If we could explain and predict them, we would have the basis on which to begin to eliminate them. There is a great desire to know *the* cause of such problems, and this desire can very easily lead us into hasty reasoning.

As we have seen, in order to move from a correlational claim to a causal claim, we have to eliminate alternative explanations of the correlation. Let us work this through in a more concrete way by considering a specific example. (The example, by the way, is invented, not real.) Suppose that we observe 800 students, of whom 400 are highly skilled at playing the piano and the other 400 are less skilled. Now let us say that we study the handedness of students in each group. We are thereby dividing the group as to highly skilled or less skilled at piano playing, and into left-handed or right-handed. Let us suppose that of those less skilled at piano playing, 10 percent are left-handed and 90 percent right-handed, whereas of those highly skilled at piano playing, 25 percent are left-handed and 75 percent right-handed. There is in this sample of students, then, a positive correlation between high skill at piano playing and being left-handed. The correlation is quite significant; the sample is fairly large, and the percentage difference between 10 percent and 25 percent is quite large also. Thus we expect there may be something to this relationship, and we start out to investigate it. One possibility is that something about being left-handed is of some advantage for piano playing, so that left-handers are overrepresented in the highly skilled group. To conclude this, we have to rule out other possibilities. For this case, the possibilities are:

(a) Being left-handed causally contributes to developing high skill at playing the piano.
(b) Playing the piano (frequently enough to become highly skilled) causally contributes to being left-handed.
(c) Some underlying factor causes both left-handedness and high piano-playing skill, or causally contributes to both.
(d) The relationship between handedness and piano-playing skill in this sample of students is purely accidental.

Now suppose that we want to reach the causal conclusion that being left-handed contributes to the development of high skill at playing the piano, and we wish to do so legitimately, without any leaps in logic. We have to give reasons for excluding (b), (c), and (d), and for maintaining (a). We can eliminate (b), for we know that handedness develops before people are old enough to be either skilled or unskilled at playing the piano. This leaves (c) and (d). As for (d), it is partly a matter of sampling. We have to check to see that the 800 students in our sample are representative so far as handedness, piano-playing skills, and related matters are concerned. But granting that the sample is representative, this is all we can do to rule out (d). It represents a kind of remote possibility. Science is based on the assumption that regularities in nature do not just occur for no reason. Physical science based on this assumption has been enormously successful, and social scientists hope to achieve comparable understanding by exploring regularities and not resting with the idea that they may simply *be* for no reason.

For such a case, then, the real task in reaching a causal conclusion would be to eliminate (c) as an alternative hypothesis. If we want to conclude that handedness contributes to piano-playing skill, on the basis of our data, we will have to give grounds for rejecting the possibility that some other underlying cause is responsible for both. How would this work if we were dealing with a real problem, not just an example in a textbook? It is not possible to give a complete answer, but background knowledge is certainly going to play a large role in our reasoning. We won't be trying to refute alternative hypotheses about any and every possible underlying cause. Some possibilities will be taken seriously; others will not.

Consider, for instance, H1 and H2:

H1: Having a mother who eats carrots causes both left-handedness and piano-playing skill.

H2: Having the kind of brain in which hemisphere specialization is less than in normal individuals who are right-handed causes both left-handedness and piano-playing skill.

H2 is suggested by brain hemisphere research, which is confirmed for some other areas (for example, the treatment of some epilepsy patients and stroke victims). Our background beliefs regarding the significance of the brain in human abilities and behavior has a bearing on H2 too. On the other hand, H1 would not be taken seriously as an alternative hypothesis. No one is going to apply for a grant to survey the 800 mothers and try to determine their carrot-eating habits! The reason is that H1 just seems frivolous; we have no other knowledge that would make it likely as an explanation, and it is not worth investigating. The point of all this is to show just how *background knowledge* enters into causal reasoning. Background knowledge yields the working distinction between serious and nonserious alternative hypotheses. To reach a causal conclusion, we have to have grounds for rejecting some alternative hypotheses, but we cannot possibly have grounds for rejecting every single one.

Social science researchers are basically working in this sort of way; they are doing studies in the laboratory or in the field and these studies are intended to eliminate some hypotheses and to make others more plausible. If researchers were to study our imaginary case of left-handedness and degree of skill at piano playing, they would look at the possibility of brain hemisphere organization as an underlying cause of both. They might try to *control* for this factor—that is, give subjects an independent test for hemisphere specialization, and then see whether, among equally unspecialized piano players who are highly skilled or less skilled, the undue proportions of left-handed people among the highly skilled persists.

Experiments cannot be designed to rule out every imaginable alternative explanation. The best that can be done is to show that the serious alternatives are not probable. Thus causal conclusions always have a certain tentativeness about them. All arguments from correlation to cause will depend on background knowledge and beliefs at several stages. In social science this factor causes difficulties because the background beliefs are often themselves rather insecure. Because our background knowledge is very much more reliable in physical science than it is in social affairs, causal conclusions are much more reliable in physics, chemistry, and biology than they are in history, psychology, sociology, or anthropology. For social science, in fact, it may seem as though the background knowledge used to differentiate between significant and insignificant alternative hypotheses is just as questionable as the causal conclusion we are trying to confirm! This situation is terribly frustrating, but unavoidable. It should remind us that conclusions about the causes of social phenomena are tentative and subject to revision. It is a real case of trying to pull ourselves up by our own bootstraps! But there is just no other way to proceed; we can either do this, or we can just abandon the quest for a general understanding of social affairs.

Correlation, Cause, and Being "Linked"

When you are reading reports of scientific studies, you should check to see whether a causal claim is being made. If the researcher goes beyond statistical generalization or correlational claims, he or she will need a more complex argument to support the desired conclusion. Causal claims are not always stated with the words *cause* and *effect*, and sometimes you have to stop to consider whether a causal claim is made. Many words in English are used to express causal claims. Here are some of them:

A produced B.

A was responsible for B.

A brought about B.

A led to B.

A was the factor behind B.

A created B.

A affected B.

A influenced B.

B was the result of A.

As a result of A, B occurred.

B was determined by A.

B was induced by A.

There are many more. You have to look closely at the wording and the context to see whether causal claims are being made.

When a correlation between two things is discovered, it is very natural to suspect that there is some sort of causal relationship. Often we have background knowledge suggesting this as well. Also, against a certain amount of relevant background knowledge, the existence of a correlation actually makes it very natural to suspect a causal relationship. When these conditions apply, you often find statements to the effect that things are "linked" or "have been linked." Such statements represent an uneasy compromise between correlational claims and causal claims. They let researchers or reporters have their cake and eat it too, for they state only a correlation, but suggest a causal relationship. In this way, asserting that A and B have been linked allows you to suggest an interesting causal relationship between them without having the responsibility to give evidence for it. The ambiguity of the word *linked* in this kind of context permits a person to hide the fact that causation has been suggested without sufficient evidence for anything more than correlation. For the consumer of social science, the word *linked* is a major source of confusion. It far too often leads us to accept causal claims for which there is no evidence beyond correlation. You might even say that the word *linked* in such contexts virtually contains a hasty inference, all by itself.

Here is an example to give you a better idea of the possibilities in *linked:*

Migraines Linked with Sexual Arousal

That worn-out line, "Sorry, I've got a headache," has long been an easy excuse for avoiding sex. According to the latest medical evidence, however, a headache can actually create a craving for sex.

At the 1980 International Headache Conference in Florence, Italy, Dr. Frederico Sicuteri, migraine specialist, reported on a study of 362 migraine patients. Nine percent of women and 14 percent of men felt sexually aroused during their migraine attacks, he said. He speculated that the percentage was probably much higher, but it was a topic that some patients were unwilling to discuss.

Among those patients who reported feeling sexually aroused, the erotic sensation usually came near the end of their headaches. Fifty to 60 percent of their headaches were accompanied by arousal. Evidence suggests that headaches and sexual excitement are both linked to an imbalance of serotonin and dopamine, two important neurotransmitters, chemical substances that transmit nerve impulses.[3]

According to this report, Dr. Sicuteri thought that he had found a correlation between having a migraine and being sexually aroused. This correlation is not substantiated by his data, as far as we can ascertain from what is given in the report. One problem is that, according to this report, we cannot see even a basis for the claim of correlation. In order to show that there is a positive correlation between having a migraine and being sexually aroused, you have to compare those who have migraines with those who don't and show that a higher proportion in the former category are aroused than in the latter. This comparison may have been made; there is no evidence in the report that it was, however. And no comparative percentages are given. Obviously Dr. Sicuteri believed both that there was a correlation and that this correlation had causal significance. But for the latter hypothesis, no evidence beyond the (alleged) correlation is given. The report fudges the problem by using *linked.* The important thing to remember in this sort of context is that you haven't been given any good evidence for the existence of a causal relationship.

EXERCISE SET

Exercise One
Part A

For each of the following statements, say whether it is a statistical claim, a correlational claim, or a causal claim. If you believe that the claim is ambiguous as between several of these types, say so and explain why.

1. "Alcoholism has been linked to poor grammar, in a study by speech pathologist P. J. Collins. Nearly twice as often as a control group of nonalcoholics, a group of 39 alcoholic men and women were found to use illogical words and phrases, and to speak in fragments."
(Adapted from *Psychology Today,* April 1982.)

*2. Violent television shows in prime time are increasingly numerous and popular. No wonder violence against women and children is up, and violent methods of resolving political disputes are seen as natural and acceptable!

3. Working in office buildings without windows that open so as to permit air circulation has been asso-

ciated with increased allergic complaints and increased susceptibility to respiratory infections.

*4. "If you hear the pilot whistling the next time you are riding in an airplane, it might be cause to worry, according to *Omni* magazine. Robert Rudich, an air transportation consultant for the U.S. Federal Aviation Administration, says that of more than 260 voice-recorder tapes taken from airplanes involved in accidents, both large and small, more than 80 percent of the tapes recorded the whistling of pilots during the last half hour of flight."
(Toronto *Globe and Mail*, March 27, 1981.)

5. "It is well known that the great majority (80 to 90 percent) of fat children become fat adults."
(Marsha Millman, *Such a Pretty Face* [New York: Norton, 1980].)

6. The decrease in oil prices has led to many cuts in activity in the oil industry, with resulting layoffs of personnel at all levels.

7. "The risk of cancer in men with the lowest level of vitamin A was 2.2 times greater than for men with the highest level."
(Toronto *Star*, February 6, 1981.)

*8. "The usual feeder school for Du Sable is the Beethoven School, which is in the middle of the Robert Taylor Homes. As with other schools in the area, its enrollment is dropping rapidly, down from 1400 in 1977 to 900 today. Its budget, linked to enrollment, is dropping too, but it is still generous."
(Nicholas Lemann, "The Origins of the Underclass," *The Atlantic*, June 1986, p. 62.)

9. "Even when a woman is only 20 or 30 pounds overweight, her life is often greatly affected by her weight, while men are allowed a much greater margin of weight variance before they are defined by others as 'overweight' or see themselves that way."
(Marsha Millman, *Such a Pretty Face.*)

*10. The use of morning-after pills containing DES, a synthetic estrogen, has been linked with vaginal cancer in subsequent female children of those women who have taken the morning-after pills.

11. "Of 242 studies done on the Pygmalion effect, with all sort of subjects and situations, 84 found that experimenters' or teachers' expectations of improved performance made no difference to actual performance."
(Robert Rosenthal, "The Pygmalion Effect Lives," *Psychology Today*, September 1973.)
The *Pygmalion effect* is the name given to the sup-

posed influence of teachers' expectations on students' performance.

12. Washing out mouths with soap when children use dirty words is not likely to improve their language.

13. "'The key to homicides, child abuse and other kinds of violent behavior may be rooted in the most primal instinct—reproduction,' says a McMaster University psychologist. That's the theory of Martin Daly, whose statistical studies show, among other things, that more males are murdered in their peak breeding years than at any other time of life. 'Perpetrators of homicides show the same general age characteristics as their victims,' Daly said. 'It seems the same bunch who are killing are also being killed.' Using data compiled from homicides in the United States and elsewhere, Daly noted that a significant percentage involve 'squabbles over women.'"
(Calgary *Herald*, December 5, 1979.)

*14. "While other studies had shown that girls often did poorly in mathematics, those in this study were not just any girls. They were the brightest girl mathematicians in the United States—4300 7th and 8th graders who had scored in the top 2 to 5 percent of standardized mathematical tests. But when compared with boys at the top of their classes, these girls consistently averaged lower on the Scholastic Aptitude Tests.
"At top levels—scores of about 700 out of a perfect 800—boys outnumbered girls by 10 to one. (The ratio of boys to girls participating in the study was 57 percent to 43.)"
(Toronto *Globe and Mail*, September 3, 1981.)

15. *Background:* The following report describes an experiment conducted among University of Colorado undergraduates. Participants received simulated monthly checks and were to declare income and pay tax. On the basis of random audits, it was determined whether they had evaded taxes, and penalties for evasion were imposed.
"Everyone was told (correctly) that his own tax rate was 40 percent. One-third of the group was told (falsely) that others paid less taxes than they did; one-third was told that others paid more taxes than they did; and the last one-third was told the truth, that its own rates were the same as everyone else's. Overall the group evaded about one dollar in four of tax. But those who felt they were paying lower rates than everyone else evaded only 12 percent of their tax, while those who felt they were paying more than everyone else evaded nearly one-third of their tax. In the laboratory, and perhaps in

life, compliance walks hand in hand with the perception of fairness and equity. Destroy the latter, and whether there are penalties or not, compliance plunges."
(Shloma Maital, "The Tax Evasion Virus," *Psychology Today*, March 1982.)

Part B

For those questions in Part A in which a causal claim was either suggested or stated, how plausible do you think it is to move from the correlational data to that causal claim? Elaborate your answer in each case.

A Brief Digression: Everyday Errors in Causal Reasoning

Our main topic as far as inductive reasoning is concerned is the brief report of research in social science. But for causal reasoning, we shall broaden our horizons enough to discuss some causal fallacies that are relatively common in ordinary life. In our thirst for understanding and control, we are often guilty of leaping to causal conclusions.

The *Post Hoc* Fallacy. Perhaps you have heard of this one. Its name comes from the Latin expression *post hoc ergo propter hoc*, which means "after this, therefore because of this." Superstitions may have had their beginnings with *post hoc* inferences: a man walks under a ladder and then loses his wallet, so he infers that it is because he walked under a ladder that he lost his wallet. With all that we have said about the difficulties that arise when you try to prove a causal relationship, you can no doubt see that any inference of the type:

1. *A* came before *B*.
Therefore,
2. *A* caused *B*.

is very inadequate. This is the basic form of the *post hoc* fallacy. It is even shakier than the inference from correlation to cause, for in *post hoc* there is often only one anecdote, not a correlational pattern. Here is an example of a *post hoc* argument, which was used by a participant in a discussion of nuclear disarmament:

1. Since the fall of 1980, the Americans have had a tough and bellicose president as far as Soviet-American relations are concerned.
2. Since the fall of 1980, the Soviets have not invaded any country in the way that they invaded Afghanistan in December of 1979.
Therefore,
3. It is because the Americans have a tough, bellicose president that the Soviets have not launched further invasions since December of 1979.

Objectionable Cause. The fallacy of *objectionable cause* occurs when a reasoner imposes a causal interpretation on a set of events and makes no attempt to rule out alternative explanations of it. Sometimes logicians call this fallacy "false cause." We have not used this label because the problem is not always that hasty causal reasoning, ignoring alternative explanations, will give you a false causal conclusion. You might get a true conclusion, if only by accident. The problem is that the conclusion—even if true—is reached too hastily. The fallacy of objectionable cause goes like this:

1. *A* occurred.
2. *B* occurred.
3. We can plausibly connect *A* to *B*.
Therefore,
4. *A* is the cause of *B*.

A particularly tempting variation on objectionable cause, prominent in political and moral discussions of society and its problems, is as follows:

1. *A* occurred.
2. *B* occurred.
3. Both *A* and *B* are bad things, and we can plausibly connect *A* to *B*.
Therefore,
4. *A* is the cause of *B*.[4]

Here is a classic example of the sort of mistake that we are calling *objectionable cause*. It is taken from a letter to the editor of a Toronto paper. The letter was written at a time when there was a considerable public controversy in the city about some police raids on bathhouses frequented by homosexuals:

> *We have one of the safest cities on the continent but it is changing. And who do you think is bringing this change about? Our institutions, including the courts, the schools, and the churches have failed us. Why? Because they have been infiltrated by the "lib-left" and their sympathizers.*[5]

The author of this letter reveals extremely simplistic causal thinking. He suggests that institutions are not giving positive leadership. Let us assume he is correct, if only for the sake of argument. He believes that this phenomenon (which would be very complex, if it really is occurring) has one and only one cause: "infiltration" of key social institutions by the "lib-left" and their sympathizers. Even if there were such infiltration, and even if it came just prior to the alleged decline, that would not show that it caused the decline. There would still be a need for evidence to show that this causal explanation is more plausible than others. What about post-Watergate disillusionment? Economic hard times? Professional burnout among teachers and the clergy?

When you don't like *A* and you don't like *B* either, it is certainly tempting to think that *A* causes *B*. This way, you can perhaps link up the things you don't like into a causal chain, and you will be well on your way to a simple solution that will eliminate these bad things from the world all at once! A wonderful example of this normative approach to causation may be found in the following argument, which was used by a panelist on a television show shortly after the nuclear reactor accident at Three Mile Island:

> *The responsibility for the near catastrophic nuclear accident at Three Mile Island rests squarely with the English teachers of America. For years now, they have been ignoring little flaws of language. They have emphasized self-expression above all else. They have told us that small faults and mistakes do not really matter as long as you communicate your true attitudes and feelings and creatively express your own identity. And the problem at Three Mile Island was, initially, just one of those supposedly little things. One valve was not in the right place. One might think: well, it's just one little thing; it doesn't really matter. But it did matter, and that was the problem. It is the teachers of English who have encouraged the attitude that small things don't count, and it is just that attitude which is the underlying cause of the nuclear accident.*[6]

The panelist, who obviously had a low opinion of English teachers, didn't much like nuclear reactor accidents either. So he decided there was a causal connection between these two things. The hastiness of the causal inference here is so obvious that it doesn't need much comment! If there is a common attitude that "little things don't matter," then the existence of this attitude would be a complex social fact indeed. It would be a very widespread phenomenon, permeating many aspects of life. It would be amazing indeed if teachers of English had sufficient power to spread such an attitude all by themselves! If the general attitude does exist, it is likely that lax teaching of English is an effect of it, not a cause. Needless to say, there are countless more plausible explanations of what happened at Three Mile Island that a careful causal argument would have to rule out.

The fallacy of objectionable cause is prominent in political life, in fact, it is well worth watching for. We all have a craving for explanations of social phenomena—especially for *simple, emotionally satisfying* explanations of those phenomena we don't particularly like. But such explanations are logically and scientifically worthless unless there are good reasons to believe that they are more plausible than significant alternatives.

Causal Slippery Slope Arguments. We have concentrated on arguments in which the conclusion makes a causal claim. Of course causal claims may also serve as the premises of arguments. One example is the causal slippery slope. In this type of argument, it is alleged in the premises that a proposed action (one that by itself might seem good, or at least acceptable) would be wrong because it would set off a series of effects, ending ultimately in general calamity. The idea behind the reasoning is that someone who embarks on the action has begun a tumble down a slope of effects, the last of which will be something terrible. Here is a familiar example:

> It sounds quite all right, letting people choose to die when they are suffering from painful and incurable diseases and when they are of sound mind. Certainly it would seem a responsible choice if someone in such circumstances chose to kill himself. In fact, the famous author Arthur Koestler recently did just that, and no one blamed him since he was an old man and was suffering terribly from several diseases. The problem is, though, once you allow voluntary euthanasia the forces are in play, and there will be pressure for assisted voluntary euthanasia. Once this is established, involuntary euthanasia will follow for patients who have incurable diseases but are comatose and cannot make their own decisions. The procedures that permit involuntary euthanasia for those with incurable diseases bring about euthanasia of the retarded and senile, and soon we will be in a state where an individual life just has no value at all.

In the premises of this argument it is alleged that allowing voluntary euthanasia for those patients who can make their own choices will bring about a state in which individual lives have no value. The basis for this claim is a kind of causal chain; one reform causes a further change, which itself brings more changes. The idea is that the first action is a step down a slippery road to hell; the first step causes an inevitable slide to the bottom. The problem with the argument is that the causal claims in the premises are not supported by evidence and are not even very plausible if you think about it. The argument is based on a kind of scare tactic. Actually the series of dreadful effects is just invented as an objection to the initial action, which (as the argument admits) is quite desirable when considered on its own. The idea is to intimidate people with the suggested calamity, so that they won't think about the sweeping and implausible nature of the causal claims in the premises.

Unfortunately, these arguments can be very effective. One historically prominent example is the domino theory, which was so popular at the time of the Vietnam War. It went something like this:

> If Vietnam goes communist, then Laos, Cambodia, Burma, India, and all of southeast Asia will go communist. Then all Asia will be communist, and after that all Europe, and the whole world. So even though it might not seem to matter very much whether Vietnam as a single country is or is not communist, we have to stop this thing. It is now or never.

As the Vietnam War came under increased criticism, the domino theory lost credibility. But a new version has been resurrected for Central America. William P. Clark, assistant to President Reagan for national security affairs, put it this way:

> If we lack the resolve and dedication the President asked for in Central America, can we not expect El Salvador to join Nicaragua in targeting other recruits for the Soviet brand of Communism? When, some ask, will Mexico and the United States become the immediate rather than the ultimate targets?

President Reagan said:

> If we cannot defend ourselves (in El Salvador) we cannot expect to prevail elsewhere. Our credibility could collapse, our alliances would crumble, and the safety of our homeland would be put in jeopardy.[7]

Here is an example of a causal slippery slope argument from another period of history:

> unbridled passion following the wake of birth control will create a useless and effeminate society, or worse, result in the complete extinction of the human race.[8]

This was an argument used decades ago to object to the legalization of birth control. It wouldn't fool anyone today. We've legalized birth control, and neither an effeminate society nor complete extinction has resulted. But more contemporary slippery slopes can be more deceptive.

EXERCISE SET

Exercise Two

For the following arguments, underline any causal claims that appear either in the premises or in the conclusion. If causal claims are made in the conclusion, assess the reasoning offered to support them and say if you find examples of *post hoc* or objectionable cause. If causal claims are made in the premises, is the argument an example of causal slippery slope? Why or why not? Note: Some arguments may contain no causal claims, and some passages may not contain arguments. If either

of these is the case, simply note the fact and proceed to the next example.

1. *"Who Needs Misfits?*
   Psychiatrist Paul Kingsley's effort to dissuade children from continuing to stay with parents is a tragic commentary that social values in the West are decaying. A direct cause of the breakup in marriages could be the early departure of children from home. Social values develop over a long period of time through the process of introspection. However, the West has offered us the image of

youth that live entirely by short-term, *ad hoc*, decisions. Children should move out of their parents' home, but only when they are prepared to confront difficult situations. Until such time, the responsibility rests with the parents. In our modern society, who needs misfits?"
(Letter to the editor, *Time*, November 17, 1980.)
The author of the letter identified his place of residence as Bombay, India.

*2. *"Fertility on the Wane.*
The sexual revolution of the past 25 years has reduced the number of women who are able to have babies, a leading British expert on venereal disease said in an article published Friday. Dr. Robert Catterall of London's Middlesex Hospital said infertility is rising as a result of an epidemic of sexually transmitted diseases. 'The adverse biological effects of sexual freedom on women and their babies are a disappointing development in the second half of the 20th century,' Catterall wrote in *The Lancet*, a British weekly medical journal. 'Control of the sexually transmitted diseases seemed at one time to be within our grasp, but has eluded us in recent years."
(*Peterborough Examiner*, February 9, 1981.)

3. "If the Christian churches wish to refuse ordination of gay people to the clergy, they have a right to their decision, however misguided it may be. But when the churches organize public referendums to repeal the civil rights of homosexual citizens, that's another matter. In Dade County, St. Paul, Wichita, and Eugene, Oregon, the churches openly ran petition drives, distributed the political literature, and raised the funds needed to bring out the public vote that revoked the rights of gays in those places. Unfortunately America is currently besieged by an army of religious zealots who see the Government and the ballot box as instruments for enforcing church dogmas. If the trend continues, we'll have Government-enforced religion and the end of a 200-year-old democratic tradition."
(Letter to the editor, *Time*, June 1978.)

4. Since 1945 we have had nuclear weapons, and since 1945 we have not had a world war. Therefore, nuclear weapons have served to prevent a world war.

5. "The statement by Archbishop John R. Quinn that Vatican strictures on birth control are being ignored by many U.S. Catholics reflects the misconception that the doctrines of faith and morals proclaimed by the church are changeable. Yet there has never been an about-face on any of these doctrines. The great secular breakthrough allowed by the promotion and acceptance of contraception

has brought us the age of state-countenanced abortion, community-standardized pornography, and a more than embryonic euthanasia movement. This pro-pleasure, antichild mind-set won't intimidate the church of Peter ever to modify the doctrine that sees more to sex than orgasm and more to aging than diminished utilitarianism."
(Letter to the editor, *Time*, November 10, 1980.)

6. Cutting out compulsory final examinations in grade six is a dangerous step. Sure, you can see why people would not want eleven-year-old kids to have to go through the stress of studying for and writing competitive examinations. But the problem is, when will it stop? Laxity in grade six will lead to laxity in junior high schools. Soon exams will be eliminated there. Then there will be pressure to get compulsory finals out of the high schools. When universities and law and medical schools follow, we'll have such a noncompetitive and no-stress educational system that we'll have no guarantee at all of professional competence!

7. People who diet often discover that after dieting for several months, they just stop losing weight. Their body needs less food, and they just get by on less. Thus dieting causes the metabolism to slow down. Ultimately dieters will defeat themselves.

*8. *Background:* The author is asserting that in the period between 1980 and 1986, the quality of the manpower enlisting in U.S. armed forces has improved.
"People can still argue about restoring the draft, but now the arguments are about principles: How should a democracy allot the burden of military service? Is it just and fair to leave the risk of dying to volunteers? The debates are no longer driven by concerns about the quality of people who have volunteered.
"But manpower, though historically the most important factor in military excellence, is not the only one—and certainly is not the principal force behind our increased spending. Pay has gone up—but not stupendously and certainly not by as much as the quality of the force. From 1980 to 1985 personnel costs rose by less than 20 percent, and as a share of overall defense spending, pay and benefits fell. The improvement in the force, hard to quantify but more like 200 percent than 20, has been due partly to the severe recession of 1982, partly to a sense that the military is 'de-civilianizing' itself and restoring its standards and self-esteem, and partly to the general resurgence of nationalistic pride."
(James Fallows, "The Spend-up," *The Atlantic*, June 1986, p. 28.)

9. "The fastest-growing group among America's female poor are single mothers, raising and supporting children on their own. Many are among the second or third generation poor, habitués of what conservatives like George Gilder call the 'welfare culture.' But many are also new recruits to poverty, women who had been middle class until divorce—or desertion—severed their claim on a man's wage. They have been called the 'hidden poor' of America's suburbs: often left with the house and furniture but with no means of subsistence other than welfare, minimum-wage jobs and (if they are fortunate) a trickle of child-support payments. For single mothers living at the edge of subsistence, whether they are case-hardened 'welfare mothers' or members of the suburban nouvelles pauvres, there is only one thing left of the family wage system: the fact that women, on the average, are paid less than a family (at current urban rents, less than a very small family) requires for a moderate standard of living."

(Barbara Ehrenreich, *The Hearts of Men* [New York: Doubleday, 1983], pp. 172–3.)

10. "A typical Alberta Hospital study on persistent violent offenders—a category in which males dramatically outnumber females—involved 74 men and 11 women, each with a record of 10 or more convictions. An astonishing 87% of the group were found to be suffering from brain disfunction. Left-hemisphere impairment—the result of health problems in infancy, injuries, and alcohol and drug abuse—was evident in 54 of the males and 5 of the females. In several studies Yeudall and his colleagues have confirmed clinically what has long been apparent from police records: criminal psychopathy is almost entirely a male disorder. While the Alberta Hospital researchers have been concerned mostly with victims of brain disfunction in their crime studies, Yeudall says it's possible that brain differences between normal males and females account largely for that huge majority of men in prison. Women, with apparently superior left-brain mood controls, tend to stop and think, men to act and damn the consequences."

(John Doig, "A Sexy Issue. But Not Sexist. Men's and Women's Brains *Are* Different," *The Canadian*, September 1, 1979.)

11. *Background:* The following appeared in a letter to the Calgary *Herald*, concerning the showing of Judy Chicago's controversial feminist artwork, *The Dinner Party*. The letter was printed on December 10, 1982:

"Re the rave reviews about Judy Chicago's *The Dinner Party*. Certainly the craftsmanship and skills represented deserve praise. I was involved in a campaign of a different nature—namely the Billy Graham crusade in 1981. I remember the begrudg-

ing remarks of our press about it—especially the cost involved and how that money could have been better spent. No such reference to this show's price tag of $393,483. An irrelevant comparison? They have in common the intention of not just entertaining, but of moving people to a spiritual commitment. May I weigh value by results? Two examples re the Billy Graham crusade, worth mentioning, are that the Calgary crime rate was down both before and after the crusade. In October '81, an article in the Edmonton *Journal* stated that the Social Services Department had an unusual drop in the number of caseloads last fall, from Red Deer and South, and attributed this to the effects of the crusade. I predict the afterwave of *The Dinner Party* will bring more destruction than healing. Yes, I believe in the equality of the sexes. This show is stirring up attention—but honor to great women? Frankly, it sounds more like Babylon revisited (genitalia were a common sight in the temple worship of Babylon). There has to be a better way."

12. *Background:* This item was part of an advertisement for numerology which appeared in the *Detroit Free Press:*

"We found that numerology is a very useful tool in producing good luck. For example, the letters in the alphabet have assigned numbers. Singer Dionne Warwicke took the advice of her numerologist and added an 'e' to the end of her name. She immediately skyrocketed to fame, a fact which she has revealed on the Johnny Carson show."

13. *Background:* This argument by Glenn T. Seaborg originally appeared in *Chemical Education News*. It was reprinted in the *Informal Logic Newsletter* Examples Supplement for June 1980:

"Let us say it's a few years hence and all nuclear power plants have been operating safely. But opponents of nuclear power succeed in enforcing a national moratorium on nuclear power. All nuclear power plants are shut down, pending complete reevaluation in terms of public safety.

"First this moratorium causes a rush by electric utility companies to obtain more fossil fuels—particularly because oil and gas are in tight supply. Coal prices soar, and the government reacts by setting a price ceiling. Coal supplies dwindle, and power cutbacks are put into effect. Finally, restrictions on burning high-sulphur coal are relaxed somewhat, and air pollution rises. Miners, disgruntled over a wage freeze and laxness of employers regarding safety standards, go out on strike. Coal stockpiles diminish, and many power plants are forced to shut down; others, overloaded by power demands, begin to fail. Miners battle with federal troops who have been ordered to take over the mines. A chain of blackouts and brown-outs creeps across the nation. . . .

"Darkened stores are looted at night. At home, people burn candles and wash in cold water. Hospitals begin to use emergency generators, and deaths are reported in intensive care wards because of equipment failure. Ill or injured persons have difficulty getting to a doctor or hospital. Medical supplies begin to lag behind growing demand.

"Children who can get to school wear sweaters and coats in unheated classrooms. At night, there is no television, and people listen to battery powered radios where they hear hope of miners going back to work. But as time goes on, great doubt appears that things will ever be the same again. It's up to you to speculate whether they would be."

*14. "For the past thirty years, six-foot-four John Wayne has stalked through the American imagination as the embodiment of manhood. . . . He has left not only a trail of broken hearts and jaws everywhere, but millions of fractured male egos which could never quite measure up to the two-fisted, ramrod-backed character who conquered the Old West. The truth of the matter is that no man could measure up to that myth in real life—not even John Wayne."
(Tim LaHaye, *Understanding the Male Temperament* [Charlotte, N.C.: Commission Press, 1977], p. 11.)

*15. *Background:* This item appeared in the *Oakland Press* on April 16, 1974, and was reprinted in the *Informal Logic Newsletter* Examples Supplement for 1979:
"A Good Way to Cure Colds.
University of Michigan medical researchers have discovered that highly educated people with low incomes catch cold more often than others, suggesting that susceptibility to colds might depend on one's frame of mind. Furthermore, more people come down with colds on Monday than any other day.

"Well, practically everybody thinks he is not being paid as much as his education calls for, and it's on Monday mornings when this feeling becomes most acute. So obviously, it's not a germ or virus that's causing all our colds but those cold-hearted people in the front office who never seem to realize how smart we are. A cure for colds? One way would be to give everybody a raise and tell them to take Monday off."

16. "Much of the blame for today's alarm about dangerous chemicals in our environment was pinned on 'psychological terrorists' yesterday by a leading Alberta chemist. Dr. Walter Harris, a chemistry professor at the University of Alberta and chairman of the provincial government's advisory committee on hazardous chemicals, made that criticism in a speech to emergency officials in Calgary yesterday. 'With today's detection methods you can find out about everything in just about anything that you test, and this has caused very great alarm among members of the public,' he said in an interview later. But this does not necessarily show an increase in the dangers around us. Science is now sophisticated enough to detect minute traces of chemicals far below danger levels that in the past would have gone unnoticed, he explained. Harris said this improved technology is exploited by some interest groups who point with horror at the discovery of PCB (polychlorinated biphenyl) in mothers' milk. The detected levels are harmless and are not unusual, since PCB's are now in our environment, Harris said. While he stressed that they were a potential hazard that should be phased out, Harris added that needlessly panicking the public is pointless."
(Calgary *Albertan*, May 15, 1980.)

Some Applications

We promised an account of inductive reasoning that would make you a more competent consumer of social science. It is now time to make good this promise by applying our discussions to some specific reports. We will watch for the following:

the language in which conclusions are stated, with attention to conceptual frameworks and assumptions that this might imply;

> operationalization of terms, if any, noting explicit and implicit operationalization;

> the reliability, or likely reliability, of questionnaires or interviews, in cases where they have been used;

> the adequacy of the sample to represent the population;

> causal claims, if any;

> adequacy of reasoning used to support causal claims, if any.

Applying these points as informed nonexperts, we can make considerable progress evaluating reports of polls or studies regarding human problems.

Let's begin with a simple case, which should have a familiar ring, as it appeared in an exercise set in Chapter Twelve:

> *Many adolescents are becoming sexually active at an earlier age and young males must take a more responsible attitude toward birth control, says Elizabeth Parker, director of the family planning division of the Toronto public health department. In the past six months, half the callers to the family planning clinic's hotline have been teenagers under 16 who are not using birth control. A national survey has shown that two out of five males between the ages of 15 and 17 have had intercourse on a regular basis.[9]*

There are two conclusions here: one is normative (males should do more about birth control) and the other is empirical. We'll look only at the empirical conclusion since our present topic is inductive argument. The empirical conclusion is that many adolescents are becoming sexually active at an earlier age. As stated this is very vague. The comparison is not specified: earlier than what? We'll assume that what is meant is:

——— Conclusion: Many adolescents are becoming sexually active an an earlier age than did the adolescents of a decade ago.

The *population* here is probably "adolescents in North America." The *sample* includes two groups: callers to a family planning clinic in Toronto and young men between fifteen and seventeen surveyed in Canada. The survey is called "national" in an article appearing in a Toronto paper, so we should probably assume that the young men interviewed were from various areas across Canada. We are not told how *many* people there were in either part of the sample.

The first part of the sample is clearly biased, for teenagers would not call a family planning hotline unless they either were sexually active or were about to become so. The second part of the sample might represent Canadian young men, but it would not necessarily represent Americans. Also, it includes no females and therefore cannot represent the whole population of adolescents. Thus the enumerative induction behind this idea that adolescents are becoming sexually active earlier is flawed. Another problem is that *earlier* is comparative, and in order to justify the conclusion we would need figures as to how active people were a decade ago, to contrast these with current figures.

Another problem arises with the survey. It seems that young men between fifteen and seventeen were asked whether they had had intercourse "on a regular basis." The question is vague; *regular* might mean once a month, once a week, or once a day. And it is likely that adults and young teenagers would understand this differently in the context. Also, the matter of sexual habits is a very sensitive one, particularly among developing adolescents: it is entirely likely that young men would not be honest about their experiences and would be inclined to exaggerate. With all these problems, there is simply no good basis for the empirical conclusion stated in the report.

Let's look at another example—this time one involving both statistical and causal claims:

High Expectations Cited in Doubled Suicide Rate

A boom economy and people's high expectations have contributed to a doubling of suicide rates in Alberta, says a provincial government specialist on suicides. Dr. Mark Solomon, provincial suicidologist, said surveys show that between 1961 and 1977 the number of suicides in Alberta increased from 9 per 100,000 to 18 per 100,000 people.

Although the exact cause of suicide is often difficult to determine, Solomon said the boom economy in Alberta means that people have high expectations. If those expectations are not met, some people start panicking and thinking they are inferior. For example, Alberta's unemployment rate is less than four percent, well below that of the rest of Canada. People here who are looking for a job and can't find one start feeling insecure and unwanted.[10]

Dr. Solomon is a provincial statistician. Despite the reference to surveys, it is likely that he has access to the *total* figures for suicides in Alberta for the years 1961 to 1977; he used these totals and the entire population figures to get 9 per 100,000 and 18 per 100,000. If this is true, there is no enumerative induction used here, and the question of sample representativeness does not arise. (The population need not be sampled, because information is available for the entire population.)

During the years 1961–1977, Alberta experienced an economic boom, especially in the oil and gas industry. The economy was very expansive between 1972 and 1980, with one major city experiencing an annual influx of Canadians from other provinces and newcomers amounting to 10 percent of its population annually at the high point. Thus there is a positive correlation between the boom in Alberta's economy and the increased suicide rate: as the economy got better and better, the number of suicides increased. Dr. Solomon has reasoned from this correlation to a causal conclusion:

A boom economy and people's high expectations have contributed *to a doubling of suicide rates in Alberta.*

He hypothesized a *causal factor* rather than *the cause*, and the report does allow that "the exact cause of suicide is difficult to determine." So we won't accuse the prominent suicidologist of objectionable cause. But even though some cautionary remarks have been inserted, and the account Solomon suggests seems plausible enough, there is no basis for ruling out alternative explanations of the correlation. If Solomon could show that in areas where the economy declined, the suicide rate remained constant or declined, that would help his argument, or if he showed that a high percentage of newcomers who had unsuccessfully sought work were among the cases of suicide, the matter would be different. But according to the information stated, the *causal* claim Dr. Solomon made need not be taken too seriously. As cited in the report, it stands with little supporting evidence.

Here is a case of a sort you rarely read about—a description of social science in which it is explicitly mentioned that different researchers disagree with each other:

There are potential advantages in knowing biology's role in distinctly male and female performances. If we can separate what is biological from what is environmental, we'll know what we can change. If there are hazards in the research, there are also inconsistencies. Paula Caplan demonstrated some of them in a recent study—a new look at a famous pronouncement made nearly 30 years ago by one of her former professors, Erik Erikson. Erikson gave 140 boys and girls, aged 11 to 13, a selection of toys and asked them to construct an exciting scene. What happened, in simple terms, was that the boys built towers and the girls built enclosures. Erikson concluded that the children's concepts of space closely paralleled the shape of their sex organs.[11]

Caplan's study gave different results:

Caplan worked with children aged 2 to 4. She gave them a wide selection of blocks and other toys and asked them to build an exciting scene. Boys and girls both built towers and enclosures in similar heights and proportions. Caplan's conclusion: the children in Erikson's experiment had reached the age where they knew—consciously or unconsciously—what an adult expected of them, and fulfilled their roles accordingly.[12]

To compare and contrast the two studies, as reported, it will be helpful to represent some central aspects in summary form:

Erikson's Study

Sample: 140 boys and girls aged 11 to 13.
Population: Children. (Assume, in North America.)
Linguistic classification: Constructions of boys classified as towers; constructions of girls classified as enclosures. This is worth mentioning because doubtless both boys and girls made a variety of structures; the observer has classified these as towers on the one hand and enclosures on the other.
Correlational conclusion: Building towers is correlated with being male. Building enclosures is correlated with being female.
Explanatory induction to a causal conclusion: Girls and boys build differently because they have different concepts of space.
Further explanatory induction: Girls and boys have different concepts of space because they model their concepts of space on the shape of their sexual organs.

Caplan's Study

Sample: Children, aged 2 to 4. We are not told how many.
Population: Children. (Assume, in North America.)
Classification: Constructions similar in height and shape between boys and girls.
Explanatory induction: For this study, there is no significant phenomenon to be explained.
Explanatory induction regarding Erikson's study: Boys and girls aged 11 to 13 do what society expects, whereas younger children do not necessarily do this. Note that this explanatory induction presupposes that society expects boys to make towers and girls to make enclosures.

When the significant steps and assumptions are set out in this way, there is no mystery about the disagreement. *Both* samples are unrepresentative due to age, if we assume they were meant to support conclusions about boys and girls in general. *Both* explanatory inductions are weak. Erikson's is based on an abstract and implausible hypothesis for which he cites no independent evidence. Caplan's assumes a social expectation that may very well not exist at all. As summarized here, neither study lends much credence to its conclusion. As far as this research is concerned, the question remains open.

In all our discussions we have considered sampling primarily in terms of the *subjects* selected to be questioned. There is another way of looking at the matter of sampling, though. When a scientist brings subjects into his lab, he is selecting the subjects to represent a larger population. But he is setting up something in his lab that is a sample of broader experience. Rarely are laboratory scientists interested *only* in what goes on in their labs. They wish to generalize beyond the lab to the broader world. Just as we must ask how representative the sample of subjects is, we must ask whether a lab situation is relevantly different from the ordinary world. There is, in effect, an implicit inductive analogy between the laboratory and more normal situations. The laboratory situation is especially important for the researcher who manipulates variables to discover causal relationships. But control may come at a cost as far as the lab–world analogy is concerned. The laboratory situation is an isolated, limited one, in which simplified predicaments arise. A person is trying to remember not proper names, but nonsense syllables; he is sleeping, not in his own bed with small children in the next room, but in a cot where his brain waves are measured, and so on. Whether correlations established in these artificial situations will persist in the real world is not always certain. The lab situation can be regarded as a sample of the population of real situations, and we have to ask ourselves how representative this sample is likely to be.

The following example illustrates problems that may arise:

Writing Maketh a Convinced Man

A recent experiment at Stanford University indicates that committing something to paper at the very least reinforces our belief in it.

. . . Researchers gave a group of Stanford students descriptions of two fire fighters, one successful, one not, along with each fire fighter's responses on a test of tendencies to take risks. Unknown to the students, the fire fighters and their responses were fictitious. Half the descriptions showed that the successful fire fighter was a risk taker, while the other half showed that he or she played things safe. The researchers asked the students to see if they could spot any connection between risk taking and success in fighting fires.

A third of the students were then asked to write about the relationship they uncovered. After they did, they and another third of the subjects who had not written anything were told the information was fictitious. After that, all three groups were tested to see if they still held to the views the original information suggested.

They all did, with the strongest believers, as one would expect, in the group that was unaware the information was invented. But there was also a clear difference between the two groups who knew. The students who wrote about the connections between risk taking and successful fire fighting held more strongly to their beliefs than the students who did not.[13]

We can recast this study in terms of the central points, as follows:

Sample: University students from Stanford University. We are not told how many.
Population: North American adults.
Operationalization: Tests must have been used to determine strength of belief in claims about successful fire fighting and risk taking.
Correlational claim: There is a positive correlation between writing something down and believing it, even in the case where what has been written down is later said to be fictitious.

Causal claim: Committing something to paper reinforces our belief in it.
Laboratory to world induction (implicit): Writing something down in a Stanford laboratory under instructions from an experimenter is relevantly similar to writing something down in a real-life situation.

The representativeness of the sample here is obviously a problem. College students are likely to differ from other adults in ways that could bear on this result. For one thing, they are likely to be more impressed with the authority of psychology instructors, who presumably performed the experiment. But the really large problem here concerns the lab–world induction. Even if we were to grant that the positive correlation discovered by the researchers would hold for all adults in a lab, whether it would hold up in the real world is quite another matter.

There are many features that differentiate this laboratory situation from real-life situations in which people choose to write things down. For subjects in the lab, there is no cue as to whether material they are copying is fictitious. They copy it only because they are under orders to do so. (Those who would not follow such orders will not be participants in the experiment.) In real life it would be most unusual for anyone to copy out material without having any clue whether that material was intended as true. People do not just copy things out unless they have some reason to do so. Copying, or reading, with no notion as to whether what one reads is intended as fiction or as nonfiction, would be very unusual. People generally read and write in an informed context, not in an experimental vacuum. In real life a person studying literature might copy out passages from a novel, but if she did, she would know they were fictitious. For instance, she might be copying them as illustrations of the author's style. Whether the correlation claimed in the study would hold up here is very doubtful. Given the control groups used in the study, and the absence of plausible explanations other than the specified conclusion, it seems reasonable to infer the causal claim from the correlation. But it is very doubtful whether even the correlation would persist in situations outside the lab. Presumably it is people outside labs, not just people in labs, whom we want to know about.

Life is more complicated than labs: that's why we have labs. But sometimes the very simplicity and control that the lab makes possible can undermine the inductive analogy between the lab and the world.

Skepticism, Risks, and Being Conservative

By now you may be thinking that studies of human populations and their problems rarely prove anything. It seems that there is always some critical question you can raise. In fact, we don't really hold that it's impossible to prove conclusions within empirical social science—just that it's difficult. We've emphasized the very facile reasoning represented in many media reports because so many people in our culture have a naive view of researchers' authority and give these reports more credence than they deserve. But now—also for cultural and political reasons—we should pause to examine the normative implications of this skepticism that we have been urging upon you.

Think back to that ambiguous term *linked.* Remember the researchers who decided that migraines were linked with sexual arousal? Researchers and reporters tend to use this term when they have found a correlation and suspect a causal relationship that they have not yet managed to confirm. We emphasized that you should not assume a causal relationship in these contexts. But such skepticism as this may seem to have very considerable political significance. Why? Look at the following currently publicized "links," and you will see why:

1. The use of video-display terminals has been linked with miscarriage and birth abnormalities among pregnant women.
2. Low-level radiation has been linked with cancer and infant deaths.
3. Alcohol use in pregnancy has been linked with smaller brain size of offspring.
4. High cholesterol has been linked with strokes.

No doubt these examples sound very familiar. Does the skeptical attitude we have been recommending here imply that we should just ignore any possible causal relationships suggested? (Just forget it; it hasn't been proven for sure?) This is just the implication favored by industries accused of unsafe waste disposal, inadequate testing of drugs, use of dangerous chemicals, and so on. Their spokespersons rightly insist that the suspected causal relationships have not been proven beyond a shadow of a doubt. They then conclude that there is no need to regulate—no legal liability. But take a closer look at this line of argument:

1. We have some evidence that x is harmful.
But,
2. We cannot prove for sure that x is harmful.
So,
3. The public should permit the unrestricted development of x.

This argument fails; the premises are not enough to back up the conclusion because the factor of *risk* has been ignored. If there is a significant chance that x will bring serious harm, that in itself is a good reason for avoiding x if this is conveniently possible. With alcohol, coffee, and cholesterol, individuals can make their own decisions about taking risks. Given the continually changing admonitions of nutritional experts, some people prefer to consume their coffee, eggs, and wine cheerfully, getting the benefit of enjoyment though there may be some risk to their long-term physical health. Others weigh the situation differently. The problem is that many decisions about acceptable risk have to be made on a social basis—when we come to issues about environmental hazards, possible problems with additives and new drugs, and other matters. Purely individual decisions are not possible. The dioxin, or other substance, goes into the water supply without the person who drinks the water having any direct personal say in the matter.

Individual acceptance of risks in the consumption of such substances as nicotine, caffeine, or alcohol is often appealed to by those who would defend the unfettered "right" to impose new substances on the environment until the harmfulness of such substances is definitely *proven*. (Given the difficulty of getting good samples, getting a correlation you are sure is significant, and then proving a causal relationship from a correlation, could take a mighty long time.) Individual acceptance is often used—in a kind of consistency argument—as the basis for saying that people should tolerate risks no worse than other risks that they have already indicated (by behavior) that they are willing to accept. However, there are problems with the analogy that is at the basis of this line of argument. First, once such hazards as low-level radiation, acid rain, and so on, are in the environment, individuals cannot choose whether to expose themselves. They can and do choose whether to drink coffee or not. Second, the benefits of coffee consumption (presumably pleasure) go to people who drink coffee; in the case of many questionable substances permitted in the environment, the benefits of having these lie primarily in the profits to companies, whereas the costs (if any) are borne by members of the public at large.

Obviously, the topic of which risks it is and which it is not rational to accept is a large and complicated one. We raise it here only to indicate that the skeptical standpoint we have been developing does not commit us to accept any and every potential contaminant. Things that often have been "linked" may not be causally related, and in reports we often find *linked* used to fudge the distinction between correlation and causation in a confusing way. However, the term is usually used when there *are* grounds to suspect a causal relationship. When such a relationship could signify potential damage, there are hard decisions to make about acceptable risk. The fact that harmfulness has not been proven is not a sufficient reason to ignore risks and possible damage.

EXERCISE SET

Exercise Three

For the following examples, analyze operationalization, sampling, causal or correlational claims, and other aspects pertinent to the evaluation of the inductive arguments used. (Follow the format used for the examples worked out in the preceding section.)

1. A study was done on 49 volunteer undergraduates at Clark University in North Carolina. The study concerned the effects of appearance on self-perception. Of the subjects, none normally wore glasses or contact lenses. The subjects were asked to perform perceptual tasks and were told that the point of the tasks was to evaluate a new form of plastic. They were divided into two groups—a group that responded more to cues within the self and a group that responded more to situational cues. (This division was made using another test, involving forming facial expressions and reporting changes in mood which resulted.) It was found that more subjects in the self-cued group than in the situationally cued group thought they performed tasks better wearing glasses than they did without the glasses. (The actual performance was not improved by the glasses; only perception of performance was affected.) Researchers concluded that "putting eyeglasses on or off could affect subjects' perception of their current performance" and, more generally, that "appearance variations can affect one's perceptions of self."
(Jean Kellerman and James Laird, "The Effect of Appearance on Self-Perception," *Journal of Personality*, September 1982.)

*2. A study was done of ethical conflict among clinical psychologists and other mental health workers. Questionnaires were sent to 271 mental health workers in the New York area. (Telephone directories and professional lists were used as a basis for selecting potential subjects.) The average return rate on the questionnaire was 62% over the various groups. Groups were psychologists, psychiatric nurses, psychiatric social workers, psychiatrists, aides, and others. The questions concerned whether workers felt ethically based concerns about such matters as disclosing confidential information when the safety of others was involved; continuing the administration of tranquilizing drugs on a prolonged basis; electric shock therapy; and possible uncertainty in diagnosis. Overall, mental health workers with more years of clinical experience reported less ethical conflict than those with fewer years of experience. Researchers concluded that "It appears that mental health workers may tend, with experience, to find some resolution to perceived conflict over ethical issues." They suggested that either greater expertise or desensitization over the years could account for the change.
(Based on James Morrison and Bruce Layton, "Ethical Conflict Among Clinical Psychologists and Other Mental Health Workers," in *Psychological Reports*, 1982.)

3. A mock jury was formed of student members, and the mock jury was shown a videotape that represented a trial based on a real case. The student jurors were divided into two groups on the basis of independent tests for *authoritarian* and *egalitarian* personalities. The researchers were interested in which jurors would and which would not change their minds during jury deliberations about the guilt of the accused. Of jurors who changed their minds, eight were authoritarian and three were egalitarian.

Of jurors who did not change their minds, thirty-four were egalitarian and twenty-eight were authoritarian. There seemed, then, to be a significant positive correlation between having an authoritarian personality and changing one's mind during jury deliberations. One possible explanation for the result is that authoritarians are more concerned about being supporters of the "in" group. (Other studies, and other experiments by these researchers, confirmed the positive correlation between authoritarianism and changing one's mind on a jury. One other study was done on a sample based on a Philadelphia list of those eligible for jury duty.)

(Based on John Lambeth, Edith Krieger, and Susanne Shay, "Juror Decision-Making: A Case of Attitude Change Mediated by Authoritarianism," *Journal of Research in Personality*, 1982.)

4. In an experiment done to test the use of lie detectors, the twenty-one subjects were men in the Israeli police force. All were enrolled in a police course; their mean age was 29.2 years. The subjects were given a test designed in such a way that it was easy to tell who had and who had not cheated. Seven out of twenty-one cheated. Subjects were then asked to take a lie detector test concerning their participation in the earlier test. Three refused to take it; of these two were guilty of cheating on the earlier test and one was not. Three other men guilty of cheating confessed to having cheated and did not take the lie detector test. Thus, of the original twenty-one subjects, fifteen took a lie detector test. Polygraphers (people who administer lie detector tests) were divided into three groups: those who had only lie detector charts on which to base their estimate of liars and nonliars; those who had only behavioral evidence on which to base their estimate; and those who were able to use both charts and behavior. Greatest accuracy was achieved by the last group. Polygraphers having only lie detector charts did not do better in their estimations than those who had only behavioral cues to guide them. The implication seems to be that by themselves lie detectors are not a reliable guide to determine who is and who is not telling the truth.

(Based on Ginton, Daie, and Elaad, "A Method for Evaluating the Use of the Polygraph in a Real Life Situation," *Journal of Applied Psychology*, 1982.)

5. A telephone poll was used to survey 416 residents of Lexington, Kentucky (total population, 200,000) during the period December 4 to December 18, 1979. This period was early in the Iranian hostage crisis, when then-President Jimmy Carter had to decide whether to return the ailing Shah to Iran and how to deal with the matter of the hostages. The crisis had begun a month earlier and was in a stalemated phase. The purpose of the telephone poll was to determine whether the hypothesis that members of the public rally to the President in times of crisis (especially when the crisis involves foreign policy) is correct. The telephone poll resulted in a *slight* overrepresentation of women, whites, and better-educated younger people, as is common with this technique. Respondents were asked their impression of two options which had been rejected by President Carter: sending the Shah to Iran and sending troops into Iran. Only 25% approved these. Then they were asked their opinion of two options which President Carter had endorsed: waiting to see what would happen and sending the Shah to another country. These received high approval. However, agreement with the President does not necessarily indicate that people polled were influenced by the President, since they might have had similar views quite independently. To determine the degree of influence, people who disagreed with various options were asked whether they would agree if the President had endorsed that course of action. Forty percent would change their minds in that circumstance. Researchers concluded that their poll "confirms other research suggesting the President can have a very significant impact on foreign policy opinions."

(Based on P. J. Conover and Lee Sigelman, "Presidential Influence and Public Opinion: the Case of the Iranian Hostage Crisis," *Social Science Quarterly*, 1982.)

*6. Twenty-four student subjects at the University of Alberta participated in a study designed to explore the shape of "personal space." Of the subjects, thirteen were male and eleven were female. Students stood one at a time in a spot from which lines were drawn to radiate out in eight directions on the floor. The experimenter approached the subjects, walking slowly, and instructed them to tell him to stop when they were uncomfortable about his closeness to them. The tolerable distance seemed to depend on visual mechanisms, since it increased when the head was turned away from the direction from which the experimenter was approaching. Personal space around the self is the region one needs to feel comfortable and free from incursions from other people. For the student subjects, personal space was noncircular; that is, the rear space was smaller than the frontal space. The researcher noted that personal space with a larger rear zone has been found experimentally for different populations.

(Based on Leslie Hagduk, "The Shape of Personal Space: An Experimental Investigation," *Canadian Journal of Behavioral Science*, 1981.)

7. According to the *Wall Street Journal* (May 11, 1982), many corporate executives are receiving increased numbers of mailed questionnaires. Some average as many as four a week. To determine whether and how corporation size affects the return of such questionnaires, two researchers sent questionnaires to 1000 corporation executives. There were 305 usable returns. For firms of above average size, the return rate on the questionnaires was 27 to 29 percent, whereas for firms of below average size, it was 35 percent. It seems, then, that small firms are more likely to return questionnaires than larger firms, and this likelihood suggests that when questionnaires are sent to firms, smaller firms may in the end be over-represented in the sampling of corporations.
(Based on Chester C. Cotton and Bruce D. Wonder, "Mail Survey Response Rate and Corporate Size," *Psychological Reports*, 1982.)

8. "People may become hooked on giving blood. Psychologist Jane Allyn Piliavin of the University of Wisconsin and her colleagues report in *Journal of Personality and Social Psychology* (Volume 43, Number 6) that although first-time blood donors are fearful, immediately after giving they feel a warm glow. After donating several times, in fact, they unconsciously acquire a positive response to blood donation—otherwise known as a conditioned response, or, by some definitions, an addiction. Both before and after blood donations, researchers gave mood questionnaires to 1846 university donors who ranged in experience from rookies to regulars who had made as many as 16 donations. While rookies felt relatively more 'uptight,' skeptical, suspicious, angry, and jittery before giving, afterward they began to feel more relaxed, playful, carefree, kindly and warmhearted. In addition, the more times a donor had given, the less intense were the initial negative feelings. By about the third or fourth visit, apparently the magic number, donors' positive feelings had won out over negative ones."
(Joan Brittain, "Addictive Bloodletting," *Psychology Today*, March 1983.)

9. "Crimes against property, including theft, break-in, fraud and arson, increased 30 percent in Canada between 1977 and 1981. In 1981, one in 38 homes was broken into, versus one in 51 in 1976. Hardest hit: Northwest Territories 1/23; Quebec 1/26; the Yukon 1/30; British Columbia 1/35. Alberta and Ontario are in the middle with 1/43 and 1/49 respectively. The Atlantic provinces do best: 1/126 on Prince Edward Island.

"What lies beyond these statistics? Raymond Corrado, associate professor of criminology at Simon Fraser University in Burnaby, B.C., points to highly visible wealth, including stereos, televisions and jewelry, that lies around most homes. In many cases such goods attract young thieves who themselves desire the good life. Further, more burglars are less likely to find someone home these days. Break-ins used to occur mostly at night; now, says a Metro Toronto police spokesman, 6 A.M. to 6 P.M. is the key period because that's when most homes are empty."
(Ann Rhodes, "How to Burglarproof Your Home," *Chatelaine*, January 1983.)

10. "The brain is an endless source of amusement for the world's scientists.... The latest intelligence on the subject, courtesy of *The Sunday Times*, comes from Tohoku National University in Japan, where a team of doctors has been measuring the brain volumes of 1000 people and chatting about the results. Professor Taiju Matsuzawa, leader of the project, was particularly concerned that otherwise healthy farmers in the northern reaches of Japan were losing their 'human fibre' at an early age, and lapsing into senility. The problem, he concluded, is that they don't think enough, or often enough, or something.... 'The best way to maintain good blood circulation is through using the brain,' he advises. 'Think hard, and engage in conversation.' It's discouraging to consider that the ones who never stop talking may outlast the rest of us."
("The Brain Is a Wonder, When You Think About It," Editorial in the Toronto *Globe and Mail*, June 7, 1980.)

11. "To find out if subjects' knowledge of the complex nature of obesity increases with age, 447 nursery school, first grade, fifth grade, and adult subjects were asked if they knew anyone fat and, if so, who; what the causes of obesity are; and whose fault it is if someone is fat. Older subjects were increasingly likely to know people who were fat and to give complex causal explanations for obesity; moreover, adults were less likely than children to see the fat individual as responsible for his obesity. Female subjects were more likely than males to know someone fat and to give complex explanations of obesity. Anglo, Hispanic, Native American and black subjects did not differ on any measure. Children who were underweight, of average weight or overweight also did not differ in knowledge or belief. The results suggest that, although accuracy of knowledge increases with age, education about obesity at all age levels may be needed to reduce incorrect beliefs and accompanying negative attitudes toward obesity."
("Beliefs about Obesity: Effects of Age, Ethnicity, Sex and Weight," *Psychological Reports*, 1982.)

12. "Recent demographic changes are likely to make a greater proportion of sons take on the primary burden of caring for a widowed parent. With families being smaller, there are fewer daughters to go around; with more women entering the job market, daughters will have less time to spare. To find out how sons who already are 'primary care-givers' are doing, researchers directed by Amy Horowitz, a social worker at the Brookdale Center on Aging at New York's Hunter College, interviewed 99 daughters and 32 sons who had taken on that role. Only one-fourth had a parent living with them; most of the others stopped by their parent's house weekly. The bad news is that unless sons of the future are different from those in the sample they will be less likely than daughters to provide 'hands-on' services. More than three-quarters of the daughters, for example, regularly took their parent shopping, but only half of the sons did; 61 percent of the daughters, but only 34 percènt of the sons, helped with household work.

"The good news is that the sons whom Horowitz studied found caring for their parents less stressful than daughters did. Far fewer sons than daughters, 32 percent to 60 percent, believed that they had sacrificed anything because of the attention they paid their parent. The irony, Horowitz concludes, is that because of their greater diligence, the daughters are more likely to experience 'premature burn-out.' In the end, they may be more likely than sons to place the parent under professional care."

(David McCollough, "Care Giving Sons: How They're Doing," *Psychology Today*, March 1983. Copyright © 1983 Ziff-Davis Publishing Company. Reprinted with permission from the American Psychological Association.)

13. A study was made of gifted youth, in order to see which adults had impressed these children most. Children were judged to be "gifted" if they had tested IQs of 120 or more on standard IQ tests. There were 125 gifted students studied: of these 67 were male and 58 were female. The children were residents at a summer residential program. When asked which person most impressed them, 44.8% named a family member; 15.2% named a person doing a specific job; 12.8% named comrades or friends; 8.0% named political or historical figures; and 2.8% named moral and religious personalities. (Based on Frances A. Karnes and Leta A. Lee, "Persons Who Most Impress Gifted Youth," *Psychological Reports*, 1982.)

14. Tests for conservatism, dogmatism, and authoritarianism were administered to forty-eight police recruits at the beginning of their training, to thirty-six probationer police constables with an average of twenty months police experience, and to thirty control subjects. The control subjects were matched with the police groups so far as socio-economic status is concerned. The subjects were given standard personality tests for attitudes and for conservativism and authoritarianism, and were also asked open-ended questions on controversial issues. Compared with control subjects, both police recruits and police probationers were significantly more conservative and authoritarian. Asked about the death penalty and colored immigration into Great Britain (where the study was done), both recruits and probationers were more intolerant and illiberal than the control subjects. The probationers' responses so far as colored immigration is concerned were even more intolerant than the responses of the recruits. Among the recruits, basic training was followed by a reduction in conservatism and authoritarianism. The findings suggest that "the police force attracts conservative and authoritarian personalities, that basic training has a temporarily liberalizing effect, and that continued police service results in increasingly illiberal intolerant attitudes towards colored immigration." (Based on Andrew M. Colman and L. Paul Gorman, "Conservatism, Dogmatism, and Authoritarianism in British Police Officers," in *Sociology*, February 1982.)

Analyzing Explanatory Inductions

An explanatory induction has this general form:

1. *X* exists.
2. If *P* were true, it would constitute a good, or the best, explanation of *X*. Therefore—probably—
3. *P* is true.

Philosophers who discuss these arguments often call them "inferences to the best explanation." We have hedged on this matter a little, specifying either the best explanation or a good explanation. The reason for our hedging is that it is virtually impossible to demonstrate that a particular explanation is the *best* of all the alternatives. As we have seen, we cannot even definitively specify what all the alternatives are. Thus it is more realistic to think of defending a hypothesis, *P*, on the grounds that it is a good explanation of an observed phenomenon.

So far we have said nothing about what makes one proposed explanation better than another. This is a very large topic; it has occupied much of the energy of philosophers of science over the last four or five decades. Anything we say here will constitute only a very preliminary set of comments on the subject. The problem is not that it is difficult to find explanations for things—unless we mean by *explanation* "true explanation." Rather, the problem is that it is all too *easy* to find explanations. Whenever anything happens, we can think of all sorts of different principles or relationships that would explain it. The problem is to sort through these and defend one as the best, or as better than the others.

Consider, for instance, the fact that in our society (as in many others) women are far more likely than men to find their identity in life through other people—their husbands and children in particular. There are many ways this fact might be explained. Here is a list of suggestions, just to give you a feel for the great variety of possibilities:

Suggestion (1): *Women have a less pronounced concern for self and identity than men because their childhood is very different, in virtue of the fact that they are of the same sex as the primary child-rearer (the mother). They identify more thoroughly with her than do male children, and they thereby do not develop a sense of distinct self to the degree that male children do.*

Suggestion (2): *Human society has a strong interest in keeping biological families of parents and child intact in order that children may be financially and emotionally supported. Men are naturally competitive and cannot subordinate their interests to those of others, and families cannot be stable with two sets of adult interests that conflict. Therefore women are encouraged to subordinate their interests to those of their husbands, and because this all starts in order to further the development of children, they are also encouraged to subordinate their interests to those of their children.*

Suggestion (3): *Women are culturally conditioned to think of their own purposes as less significant and worthy than those of other people and, lacking extensive ambitions of their own, they have filled the gap in their lives by identifying themselves with their husbands and children.*

Suggestion (4): *The capitalist system functions best when women produce new laborers for the system, new soldiers for the state, and new consumers of the goods manufactured by the system. Women who do not work outside the home have more time in which to consume capitalist goods, and the notion that a woman's own individual interests are less important than those of her husband and children is a way of discouraging her from working outside the home.*

Suggestion (5): *Women's hormones make them less assertive and ambitious than men, and this in turn makes them easily subordinated to men in career planning within the institution of marriage.*

The problem is that there are *too many* plausible sounding explanations of this phenomenon. Actually, those mentioned here have all been suggested by actual works about society and relations between the sexes. The first is adapted from the writings of sociologist Nancy Chodorow; the second from the works of such sociobiologists as Richard Dawkins and Edward Wilson; the third from anthropologist Margaret Mead; the fourth from contemporary Marxist feminists; and the fifth from medical and biological writings. Just to complicate things further, we have to recognize the possibility that a social pattern such as this one is the result of *many different factors* working together. Thus each of the suggested explanations might constitute part of the story. Given all these factors, we certainly cannot argue directly from the social facts about women's and men's identity structures to any *one* of the suggested explanations. We would have to show somehow that the explanation we wished to infer from the phenomena was better than the others. This is surely a tall order!

At this point we arrive at the issue of standards for explanation. We cannot develop them fully here, but we can at least offer some pointers. The central features are as follows:

1. *Explanatory power.* The proposed explanation must be such that, if it were true, it would be either certain or very likely that the phenomena being explained would occur. If the explanation deductively entails that a phenomenon would occur (as in "All people who catch AIDS die; John caught AIDS; that is why John died"), the phenomenon is shown to have been certain to occur. Sometimes, there is not such a universal law available and the phenomenon is shown to have been very likely to occur (as in "Most people who have a Caesarean section take more than three days to regain their strength after having a baby; Mary had a Caesarean section; that is why Mary took more than three days after the birth to regain her strength").

2. *Plausibility.* The proposed explanation must not contradict other knowledge that is already confirmed and that is relevant to the phenomena being explained. It must be plausible and reasonable, given such knowledge. That is to say, the claims made in putting forward the explanation must be plausible, given the most reliable background beliefs relevant to the phenomena. (For example, this condition is violated if the construction of the Pyramids is explained by postulating assistance in ancient times from extraterrestrial beings; there is no evidence or specific record that makes the arrival of such beings plausible.)

3. *Empirical content.* The proposed explanation must have empirical content. This means that we must be able to specify what would count as evidence for the explanation and what would count as evidence against it. It should not be so vague that it could describe nearly any event at all—such as "It is God's will" or "That is our nation's manifest destiny." Appeals to unconscious wishes or to latent homosexuality may violate this condition unless "unconscious wishes" and "latent homosexuality" are very carefully operationalized.

4. *Scope.* The proposed explanation should have scope. The greater the variety phenomena it applies to (provided this scope is not due to emptiness of empirical content) the better it is. An explanation should not be *ad hoc*—devised solely to fit the case in point and having no independent plausibility or application. (For instance, explaining your failure to do well on an examination by saying that you knew all the material but just could not recall it in the examination room would be *ad hoc* unless there was some independent evidence that you and others were typically affected by such circumstances on other occasions.)

Thus, we assess explanations according to their *explanatory power, plausibility, empirical content,* and *scope.* One explanation is better than another if it better satisfies these conditions, and an explanation may be said to be a good explanation if it satisfies all of them. Note, however, that in this definition not even a good explanation will necessarily turn out to be true in the final analysis. And given that there are a number of distinct things that are relevant to the evaluation of an explanation, it is not always possible to say definitely which of several competing explanations is best. One might be better in one respect and another in another respect.

To understand these conditions fully, you would have to do further work in the philosophy of science. Nevertheless, even our very short discussion supplies some basic tools that can be used to see inadequacies in some proposed explanatory inductions. The basic form of such arguments, you will recall, is as follows:

1. X exists.
2. If P were true, it would be a good explanation of the fact that X exists.
Therefore—probably—
3. P is true.

In effect, you always need a subargument for (2). You need to be able to show that P would be a good explanation by showing that it has explanatory power, plausibility, empirical content, and scope, and that it compares favorably to competing explanations in these respects. This is a large task.

Obviously no explanatory induction can establish the proposed explanation, P, with complete certainty. When successful, such arguments establish with *some probability* that the conclusion is true. It is crucial to defend the second premise by showing that the proposed explanation is indeed a good one, satisfying the criteria necessary.

In popular writing we often find proposed explanations that seem plausible in the light of the social facts they are supposed to explain. They may be based on a kind of natural sense of fit: the author is putting things into a pattern that seems to make sense, and he gives us the feeling we are coming to understand why things are as they are. And yet it very often happens that such proposed examinations do not satisfy the criteria for good empirical explanations. When this happens, we should take the proposed explanation as an interesting hypothesis—nothing more.

Here is an example:

> As insults go, "she's a lousy housekeeper" ranks with the most damaging. I'm sorry to report that "he's a lousy housekeeper" does not have equal significance, and it's interesting to speculate on this discrepancy. My own feeling is that there's much more involved than gender roles. When one criticizes a woman's commitment to cleanliness, her entire identity is jeopardized.
>
> At some level, female slovenliness is linked with moral and ethical laxity, an idea that has found considerable support through history. . . . The immaculate household has mythical, political and philosophical significance. At its most profound, it can be traced back to the menstrual taboo.
>
> Throughout history and across cultures, women have been banished from certain social functions at the time of menstruation for being "unclean." So society's concern with female spotlessness can be viewed as an attempt to compensate for this biological stigma. . . . Menstruation is linked with humanity's profound concerns: birth and mortality, life and death. Unlike men, women do not die when they bleed. One can only imagine what a shocking effect this discovery had on primitive man. No wonder it was necessary to subdue women, creatures who, as they saw it, clearly had supernatural powers.
>
> Housekeeping is not an equal opportunity employer because at some level these fears still function in the hearts and minds of men. A woman is only "safe" when she

acknowledges that she has accepted patriarchal negation of her power. . . . A woman who takes scrubbing the bathroom bowl seriously can never be a threat.[14]

We can set out the author's reasoning this way:

1. Women are considered very blameworthy for bad housekeeping whereas men are not.

2. A good explanation for women's being considered more blameworthy for bad housekeeping than men would be that women menstruate and men do not, and men have feared women's uncleanliness during menstruation due to their inability to cope with the fact that women can regularly bleed without dying. To cope with their deep fear of women's greater power they have saddled women with demeaning cleaning tasks to undermine women's potential power.

Therefore—probably—

3. Women are saddled with demeaning cleaning tasks because men fear women's potential power.

And,

4. Women are more blameworthy for bad housekeeping than men because women are regarded as primarily responsible for demeaning housecleaning tasks, whereas men are not.

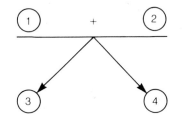

The explanation posed in the second premise is a long and complex one. Actually, it could more clearly be broken down into several steps. There are a number of distinct ideas: that men fear women; that men fear women because women can bleed without dying; and that men compensate for this fear by saddling women with demeaning chores, of which housecleaning is one.

Let's look at this explanation with regard to our criteria for good explanation. The explanation should be:

The explanation should have:

1. Explanatory power

2. Plausibility

3. Empirical content

4. Scope

The problem with this explanation lies chiefly with conditions (2) and (3). Is there any good evidence that men fear women because they can bleed without dying? After all, most humans can bleed without dying, provided they do it for a short time. In our times men understand just why women bleed during menstruation. Also, there is the common attitude that menstruation is a rather undesirable, messy, and inconvenient thing. It does not seem plausible that men *fear* women's *power* in this regard, and the author gives no independent evidence for this hypothesis. Thus condition (2) seems to be violated.

Also, there may be a problem with condition (3); this problem comes up in two ways. First, it would appear that the fear men are supposed to feel must be an unconscious fear (since most men are not aware of it consciously), and no hint is given as to how we are supposed to determine whether men have this unconscious fear or not. The author has just postulated it in order to put forward her explanation. Second, the author seems to be speaking of a distant time in history when men saddled women with demeaning chores, but it is not at all clear when this is supposed to have occurred. There is no way we can go back and check against records. Both these factors—the unconscious fear and the hypothetical event in history—mean that the proposed explanation lacks empirical content. It is based on hypotheses that we would not be able to confirm or disconfirm. We suggest, then, that the argument is a poor one. In order for the argument to have a good explanatory induction, the explanatory statements inferred must constitute a good explanation, and in this case they do not.

EXERCISE SET

Exercise Four

Check each of the following passages to see whether it contains an argument in which the conclusion is inferred as an explanation. For those that do, identify the supposed explanation and what it explains. Then assess the inference by checking the proposed explanation for its explanatory power, plausibility, empirical content, and scope. If the passage does not contain an inference-to-an-explanation, identify it as either a nonargument or as an argument of another type.

*1. There are no children from the southeast part of the city in the choir. From this fact we can infer that people in the southeast have no sense of the value of the sort of classical music this choir sings. Only that inference can explain the low participation of children from that part of town.

2. Few women are professional orchestra conductors. This fact can only be explained by unconscious discrimination on the part of audiences, agents, and musicians. There is, therefore, unconscious discrimination, and we must take every step to root it out.

*3. Many female patients report having been sexually attacked during early childhood. Surely it is unlikely that so many such attacks—in more than 10 percent of the female population if we base esti-

mates on these clients—have really occurred. (*Assumption*) We are left, therefore, with the problem of explaining the reports of these attacks. Patients seem very sincere and communicate their beliefs about sexual attacks even when they are under hypnosis, so it is unlikely that they are deliberately lying about having been sexually molested. The best explanation is that patients are recalling and expressing early infantile fantasies of having sexual relations with their male relatives, especially their fathers. There is considerable evidence, then, of early sexual desire in children, for how else would we explain such stories?
(Adapted from Sigmund Freud. Recently, historian of psychoanalysis Jeffrey Masson has argued that Freud deceived himself and ignored very considerable evidence, some of which he had seen first hand at morgues in Paris, to make the assumption just identified. Masson claims the assumption was false historically, and many sociologists would say it is false today as well. But for the purpose of this exercise, grant the assumption for the sake of argument and concentrate solely on the explanatory inference.)

4. People often have premonitions—that is, experiences of events that are represented as future. It sometimes happens that these premonitions come true. For instance, a teenaged girl dreamed in September 1961 that she was attending a banquet

where a handsome black speaker, dressed in African robes, spoke eloquently about the work of the United Nations. About a month later, on October 24, 1961, she attended just such an event, and the speaker was exactly as she had imagined in her dreams, even down to the detail of patterns and colors on the flowing robes. Such things happen, and we can only explain them on the assumption that the mind is capable of vast and complex subconscious processing and ordering of information, so that it produces incredibly accurate predictions, which are then expressed in dream images. Thus we can see that the mind has subconscious powers that equal and may even exceed the predictive abilities of science.

5. *Background:* Mars has two tiny moons that were not discovered until 1877. Many thinkers such as Kepler, Swift, and Voltaire, had long believed in these moons because earth had one moon, Venus none, and Jupiter—apparently—four. If Mars had two moons, the arrangement of planets and moons would exhibit a nice geometric order to the universe.

One commentator claimed that the moons were discovered because people believed in them. "Years of belief in the existence of the moons of Mars caused the moons to 'orthorotate' into our reality sphere," he explained, offering an account of why the moons had remained undiscovered for such a long time.
(Case described in *The Skeptical Inquirer*, Spring-Summer, 1978. Cited in Daisie Radner and Michael Radner, *Science and Unreason* [Belmont, CA: Wadsworth, 1982].)
Concentrate on the quoted remarks.

*6. "Men in battle develop a tremendous sense of comradeship under the adversity of battle, as they suffer and die next to each other. Only then do these men feel free to cry and show their fear and even to hug and kiss each other to demonstrate their love once they have proven their masculinity. What a tragedy of errors!

"Men also love to dress up in uniforms and costumes. They have done this for years. I suppose it could be similar to the female drive to look colorful and attractive. For centuries, men have either strutted around in high heels, lipstick, and wigs or worn gorgeous cloaks, as in the Elizabethan period, or resorted to extravagant uniforms bedecked with feathers, medals, ribbons, and shiny boots. The uniforms bestow conformity, and conformity is another sign of insecurity. The uniforms reinforce the peer-group pressure to conform to the masculine military ethic."
(Helen Caldicott, *Missile Envy* [New York: Bantam Books, 1984], p. 343.)

7. In 1986, incumbent mayor Ralph Klein was re-elected in Calgary with 90 percent of the popular vote, despite the fact that 8 other candidates ran for election against him. Klein is a plump, relaxed, unpretentious, and amiable man whose personality would seem to fit the image Calgarians have of themselves as hospitable and informal people. Klein's success can only be explained by his ability to personify the spirit of Calgary. Cities do have personalities, and successful city politicians are those who match in personality the cities they lead.

8. "We may say that, among animals, only man removes himself from nature in the way he lives while drawing upon nature not only for material but fundamental psychic needs. As the 'cultural animal' and the 'symbolizing animal,' we struggle to assert in our minds our sense of continuing connection with what we know to be our source as a species. When the source itself is threatened with extinction, we react with intensity, though by no means always in the same fashion. On the one hand there are the young returning to the land and forming communes. . . . Yet at the same time (end of 1981) an activist Secretary of the Interior brings literally devastating determination to dismantling the natural resources of the United States. . . . There is evidence that his project is related to an apocalyptic sense, within the idiom of fundamentalist religion, that the world may soon end and that until that time his mission is to contribute as much as possible to the maximum development of the resources of the United States. He too may well be impelled by a fear of the extinction of nature, leading in turn to a desperate race against time in drawing upon nature's life giving elements."
(Robert Lifton, "A Break in the Human Chain," in *Indefensible Weapons* [Toronto: Canadian Broadcasting Corporation, 1982], pp. 74–75.)

9. People living alone are more likely to commit suicide than those living with others. Also, Catholics and adherents of religions stressing community are less likely to commit suicide than Protestants who emphasize the individual's responsibility for his or her relationship to God. These facts show that social support helps overcome anxiety, stress, and misery. It is social support that explains these differential suicide rates.
(Adapted from Emile Durkheim's account of suicide; cited in J. Cederblom and D. Paulsen, *Critical Reasoning*, 2nd ed. [Belmont, CA: Wadsworth, 1986], p. 208.)

*10. *Background:* After the fall of Rome (fifth century A.D.), use of the Roman alphabet declined so much that the general population could no longer read and write. Only a few scribes were still literate. Author Neil Postman reflects, citing an analysis by another author, Eric Havelock.

". . . the question of why literacy declined permits some plausible conjectures.

"One of them is given by Havelock himself, who indicates how, during the Dark and Middle Ages, the styles of writing the letters of the alphabet multiplied, the shapes becoming elaborated and disguised. The Europeans, it would appear, forgot that recognition, which was the Greek word for reading, must be swift and automatic if reading is to be a pervasive practice. The shapes of letters must be, so to speak, transparent, for among the marvelous features of alphabetic writing is that once the letters have been learned one need not think about them. . . . What happened in Europe—to put it simply—is not that the alphabet disappeared but that the readers' capacities to interpret it disappeared. To quote Havelock again, 'Europe, in effect, reverts for a time to a condition of readership analogous to that which obtained in the pre-Greek Mesopotamian cultures.'" (Postman adds that the scarcity of papyrus for paper and the authoritarian tendencies within the Roman Catholic church may also have contributed to this illiteracy.)

"But whatever the reasons there can be no doubt that social literacy disappeared for close to a thousand years."
(Neil Postman, *The Disappearance of Childhood* [New York: Laurel, 1982], pp. 11–12.)

Concluding Comments

The study of social life is difficult and frustrating. We can find correlations, but it is difficult to be absolutely sure that they indicate causal relations. Our causal reasoning is dependent on background beliefs about other causal relationships, and since these may be subject to error, we can never be sure that a causal conclusion is correct. The strong desire to understand how our social world works can too easily lead us to hasty causal reasoning. Even when we reason correctly, we can easily overrate the certainty of those causal claims that have been carefully justified. When we come to explanatory inductions about social life, problems are magnified further. The problem, as we have seen, is not that there are too few explanations for the relationships and events we find in our world, but rather that there are too many. It is difficult to judge precisely which of a variety of proposed explanations is best. Explanatory inductions are often called *inferences-to-the-best-explanation*. This description is suggestive, but to show that some proposed explanation is the *best* is never an easy task. We can see why logicians have traditionally insisted that inductive arguments allow you to make inferences that are probable, not certain. In a deductively valid argument, the truth of the premises logically guarantees the truth of the conclusion. In an enumerative or explanatory induction, however, the truth of the premises only lends likelihood to the conclusion. There is not the tight relationship between premises and conclusion that we find in deductive arguments, and the support given may change if relevant background beliefs turn out to be false.

We do not want to leave you with the impression that social science is impossible or that sampling, causal and explanatory reasoning, and so on, are always sloppily done by researchers and sloppily reported by the media. This allegation would be unfair, to be sure. Our point is rather that these things sometimes happen. Many researchers are aware of the limited scope of their results and would not generalize to wide populations on the basis of limited samples, or hastily infer a causal relationship from a correlational one, and so on. The problem is that media reporting, hasty reading, and our strong desire for simple explanations of a complex social world conspire to make it all too easy to infer too much from reports of limited social scientific research. And it is a sorry fact of modern life that nonexperts are too easily intimidated by claims that sound authoritative because they are accompanied by precise-sounding statistics and come from the modern research laboratories of universities. By learning about such aspects of social science as sampling, constructing questionnaires, and inferring causal relationships from correlational data, nonspecialists can better understand and appraise such studies, especially as they are reported in the media.

Few results in social science are certain enough to provide a basis for sweeping social change, and individuals and institutions should be less ready than they are to base educational, medical, and other practices on such findings. Though social science is by no means impossible, it is exceedingly difficult, and results based on a few studies, which are bound to be open to question in some regard, are not a sufficient basis for social policy. Our craving for understanding and control of our social world too often makes us ignore this basic fact. Despite the experts, there is still no substitute for thinking for yourself. We may wish that we could avoid it, but we cannot.

Review of Terms Introduced

Correlation: An association of two characteristics, *A* and *B*. If more *A*s than non-*A*s are *B*, there is a positive correlation between being *A* and being *B*. If fewer *A*s than non-*A*s are *B*, there is a negative correlation between being *A* and being *B*.

Significant correlation: A correlation is substantial enough to warrant further study as to the explanation as to why it holds. How high the correlation has to be to be significant varies depending on the size of both the sample and the population and on relevant background knowledge about the characteristics that are correlated.

Nonsignificant correlation: When a correlation does not warrant further study because it is either too slight or too easily regarded as accidental (due to small sample size) to require an explanation.

Cause: Relation of producing or bringing about. If *A* causes *B*, then given *A*, *B* will follow as a result produced by *A*.

Prevention: Given *A*, the absence of *B* will follow. This failure to have *B* will be produced by, or a result of, *A*. To say that *A* has prevented *B* (past tense) is to imply that were it not for *A*, *B* would have appeared.

Causal factor: Element or fact of a cause. *A* is a causal factor in producing *B* if, together with other elements, it produces *B*. *A* can be a causal factor in producing *B* without being, itself, either a necessary condition or a sufficient condition of *B*.

'Linked' characteristics: When a positive correlation has been found and a causal relationship between *A* and *B* is suspected, but not established. *A* and *B* are then often said to be linked. This usage asserts correlation and suggests causation. It can be confusing and can subtly encourage us not to distinguish carefully between correlation and cause.

Post hoc fallacy: To infer, from the fact that *X* was followed by *Y*, the conclusion that *X* caused *Y*. In effect, it is the argument "after this, therefore because of this."

Objectionable cause: The fallacy committed when someone argues to a causal conclusion on the basis of too slight evidence. It may be committed by inferring cause from correlation or it may, worse yet, be committed simply by imposing one causal interpretation on events when various alternatives have not been ruled out.

Causal slippery slope arguments: Faulty arguments in which it is asserted that a particular action, often acceptable in itself, is unacceptable because it will set off a whole series of other actions, leading in the end to something very bad or even disastrous. The causal claim that such a series will be the result is not backed up and is typically implausible on close analysis.

Explanatory power: Logical strength of a hypothesis, theory, or set of statements that can be used to show conclusively or very probably that, given its truth, phenomena would occur. By deducing, or inferring with high inductive likelihood, that X will occur, given hypothesis H, we illustrate the explanatory power of H.

Empirical content: Compatibility and incompatibility of a statement with observable features of the world. Lack of empirical content of a statement is indicated if all or nearly all claims about the world are consistent with that statement.

Scope: Applicability of a hypothesis, theory, or set of principles to phenomena other than those it was originally devised to explain. The greater the variety of phenomena it applies to, the greater its scope.

Plausibility: Compatibility of a hypothesis or theory with background knowledge. A proposed explanatory hypothesis should not contradict established knowledge or incorporate new elements for no good reason.

NOTES

1. Matters are different, and more complex, when the variable studied is continuous (for example, height) rather than being of the discrete (*A* or non-*A*) type. However, we cannot discuss this matter here.

2. The passage is taken from a commonly used first-year textbook; out of charity we shall not mention which one.

3. Julianne Labreche, "Migraines Linked with Sexual Arousal," *Chatelaine*, October 1980, p. 34.

4. Robert Nozick pointed out the temptations of this sort of causal reasoning in *Anarchy, State, and Utopia* (New York: Basic Books, 1974), pp. 247–8.

5. Letter to the Toronto *Star*, February 25, 1981.

6. Reported to me by Joanne Good, Department of Sociology, Trent University. Specific wording used is my own.

7. Cited by Theodore Draper, "Falling Dominoes," *New York Review of Books*, vol. 15, no. 16, October 27, 1983.

8. This argument was used in the early days of birth control clinics, as reported in a review of a book on Dr. Stopes, an early birth control pioneer. Review by J. Finlayson in Toronto *Globe and Mail*, January 13, 1979.

9. Toronto *Globe and Mail*, February 21, 1981.

10. Calgary *Herald*, May 15, 1980.

11. John Doig, "A Sexy Issue; But Not Sexist. Men's and Women's Brains *Are* Different," *The Canadian*, September 1 and 2, 1979.

12. Ibid.

13. "Writing Maketh a Convinced Man," by Harris Dienstfrey, *Psychology Today*, May 1981, p. 17. Reprinted from *Psychology Today* magazine. Copyright © American Psychological Association, 1981. Reprinted with permission of the American Psychological Association.

14. Judith Finlayson, "Expected to Clean Up Our Act," Toronto *Globe and Mail*, November 8, 1982. Reprinted with permission of the author.

Appendix A

A Summary of Fallacies

Many texts on practical logic have a separate chapter on fallacies. Because we wished to explain the various fallacies against the background of standards of good reasoning, we have not treated fallacies as such in any one chapter. As a result, there is no one place where various fallacies are collected together. For your convenience, here is a list of the various fallacies treated in this text, together with a brief definition of each one, and a reference to the chapter in which it is explained in more detail. This set of brief explanations is provided only as a convenient summary and tool for remembering the fallacies; it is not a substitute for the more complete treatment given each fallacy in the appropriate section of the text.

Ad Hominem.   (Chapter 6) An *ad hominem* argument is an argument in which a premise or premises about a person's character or background are used to cast doubt on his argument or theory, and in which those premises are irrelevant to the merits of the position taken. Premises of such a type are irrelevant, except in the very special case where those theories and arguments happen to be about the person himself. But specific points about a person's background may bear on the reliability of his testimony or the legitimacy of his authority. In that case they may be relevant to our decision whether to accept claims on his testimony or authority, even though they are not directly relevant to the question of whether those claims are true or false. To reason from premises about the background, personality, or character of people to substantive conclusions about their arguments or theories is to commit the *ad hominem* fallacy, unless the premises are relevant to the conclusion in one of the ways just described.

Affirming the Consequent.   (Chapter 9) An argument having the form "$P \supset Q$; Q; therefore, P" is an instance of the fallacy of affirming the consequent. For example, "if you are overweight, you are unhealthy. You are unhealthy. Therefore, you are overweight." The mistake comes in affirming the consequent of a conditional and believing that from the conditional and the consequent one may infer the antecedent of the conditional. This is not a valid form of argument, as you can see from testing it on a truth table. Probably it *seems* valid due to its superficial similarity to "P; $P \supset Q$; therefore, Q" (*modus ponens*), which is valid.

Ambiguity.   (Chapters 3 and 7) Fallacies of ambiguity occur when the language used by a writer or speaker could naturally be taken to mean two or more quite distinct things. Some ambiguities arise because of the *structure*. For instance, it may not be clear whether an arguer is or is not relying on a missing premise, or whether he is or is not suggesting a further conclusion not explicitly stated in his work. Other ambiguities arise due to the possibility of a word having several distinct meanings. A fallacy of ambiguity occurs when the only way of making an argument sound is to rely on both possible interpretations at once. If an argument contains a fallacy of ambiguity, then sticking consistently to any *one* of the possible interpretations will reveal the argument not to be cogent.

Authority.   (Chapters 5 and 6) An appeal to authority is fallacious when any *one* of the following conditions is satisfied:

1. The claim, *P*, which the arguer is trying to justify, does not fall within a subject area that constitutes a recognized body of knowledge.

2. The person cited as an authority is not an expert within the particular subject area in which the claim, *P*, falls—even though he or she may be an expert about some other area of knowledge.

3. Even though the claim *P* falls within an area of knowledge and even though the person cited as an authority is an expert in that particular area, it so happens that the experts in that area disagree as to whether or not *P* is true.

4. The person cited as an authority has a vested interest in the issue of whether *P* is true—either because he or she is paid by another interested party or because he or she has some other personal stake in the matter.

Bandwagon.   (Chapter 6) Jumping on the bandwagon is a fallacy that occurs when premises describing the popularity of a product or belief are used to justify a conclusion that states, or requires, that the product or belief has real merits. Such arguments are fallacious because popularity is irrelevant to real merits.

Begging the Question.   (Chapter 5) Begging the question is a fallacy occurring when the premise or premises used to defend a conclusion are so logically close to that conclusion that the audience to whom the argument is addressed would have to accept that conclusion in order to accept the premises used to support it. The conclusion cannot get any real support from the premise or premises because it is, in effect, needed to support them. This fallacy is a case of going wrong because the premises you use are not more certain than the conclusion that they are intended to support.

Causal Slippery Slope.   (Chapter 13) In this type of argument it is alleged in the premises that a proposed action—which, considered in itself, might seem good— would set off a series of further actions culminating in calamity. For this reason, it is concluded that the proposed action is wrong or should not be done. The idea behind the reasoning is that someone who undertakes the proposed action will unwittingly set off a series of effects, the last of which will be disastrous. The proposed action is, therefore, the first step down a slippery slope to hell. The problem with such arguments is that the causal claim in the premises is not properly substantiated. Actually the argument amounts to a kind of scare tactic: the series of dreadful effects is invented by the arguer, who has no real foundation for his causal premise asserting that the proposed action will lead to these effects.

Complex Question.   (Chapter 12) The fallacy of complex question occurs when a question is posed in such a way as to tend to coerce the respondent into an unwelcome or false assumption for no reason other than the asking of the question, thus worded. The classic example is, "Have you stopped beating your wife?" The fallacy of complex question is not, strictly speaking, a mistake in argument or reasoning. However, it is a coercive technique that needs to be noted, and it can lead to mistakes in planning and interpreting questionnaires and interviews. It can even affect court proceedings.

Confusing Correlation and Cause.   (Chapter 13) A correlational statement tells you that two things are associated. For instance, being a drinker is positively correlated with having high blood pressure if a higher proportion of drinkers than nondrinkers have high blood pressure. A causal statement tells you that one thing produces, or helps to produce, another. Since a correlation may exist for various reasons, you cannot simply infer a causal relationship from a correlation. If there is a correlation between being *A* and being *B*, then *A* causes *B*, *B* causes *A*, something else causes both, or the correlation is an accident. Since three of these four possibilities do not involve *A* being the cause of *B*, it is a fallacy to infer "*A* causes *B*" from "*A* is positively correlated with *B*."

Denying the Antecedent.   (Chapter 9) An argument having the form "$P \supset Q$; $-P$; therefore, $-Q$" is an instance of the formal fallacy of denying the antecedent. For example, "If machines can think, machines can correct some of their own mistakes. Machines cannot think; therefore, machines cannot correct some of their own mistakes." Someone who reasons this way thinks that by asserting a conditional and denying its antecedent, you can properly infer that the consequent is false also. This inference is a mistake, as a truth table analysis will reveal. Probably the inference seems plausible because it superficially resembles "$P \supset Q$; $-Q$; therefore, $-P$" (*modus tollens*), which is a deductively valid inference.

False Dichotomy.   (Chapters 8 and 9) A false dichotomy is not, all by itself, a fallacy; it is simply a false belief. Believing in false dichotomies may easily lead to faults in reasoning, however, for a false dichotomy is frequently a key premise in deductively valid arguments that are extremely convincing due to their logical flow. A false dichotomy is a statement of the type "it is either *X* or *Y*," where the two alternatives *X* and *Y* do *not* exhaust the possibilities. For instance, to say that a man is either thin or fat is to construct a false dichotomy; people can be of normal build. One common source of false dichotomies is mistaking contrary predicates (such as, for example, *thin* and *fat*) for contradictory predicates (such as, for example, *thin* and *non-thin*).

A dichotomy will always hold if it is based on the purely logical opposition of contradictory predicates: that is, a person will always be either *X* or non-*X*, for any predicate *X*. But a predicate *Y* that is in some general sense the opposite of *X* in English is often *not* its logical contradictory. For example, *unhappy* is the opposite, but not the logical contradictory of *happy*; *ugly* is the opposite, but not the logical contradictory of *beautiful*; and so on. False dichotomies may be due to our tendency to oversimplify: we tend to see the world in black and white. The disjunctive statements that are the foundation of valid dilemma arguments are often false dichotomies due to this source. For example, "Either there will be a third world war or U.S. foreign policy will change." This statement may be superficially plausible, but it is a false dichotomy since it ignores other possibilities (for example, dramatic changes in the Soviet Union; continuing to stumble along as we are; and so on).

Faulty Analogy.   (Chapter 10) A faulty analogy is an argument by analogy in which the similarities between the primary subject and the analogue (two things compared) are too superficial to support the conclusion. The two things have only a very loose and general similarity, and there are enough relevant differences between them that the comparison can lend no credibility to the conclusion. Analogies like this do no more than suggest an image in which we can think of a topic and are often seriously misleading, especially when the analogue is something toward which we have very strong attitudes or feelings.

Guilt by Association.   (Chapter 6) The fallacy of guilt by association is committed when a person or her views are criticized on the basis of a supposed link between that person and a group or movement that is believed by the arguer and the audience to be disreputable. The poor reputation of any group is irrelevant to the substantive correctness either of its own views or of the views of any member of the group. Needless to say, it is certainly irrelevant to the substantive correctness of the views of those people or groups who are only very loosely associated with it.

Hasty Inductive Generalization.   (Chapters 11 and 12) A hasty inductive generalization occurs when a person generalizes from a single anecdote or experience, or from a sample that is too small or too unrepresentative to support his conclusion. Too narrow a range of human experience is taken as a basis for reaching a conclusion about all experiences of a given type. The fallacy occurs when we either forget the need to obtain a representative sample or too quickly assume that a small or biased sample is representative. For example, "boys are more temperamental than girls, because my two sons were far more difficult to bring up than my three daughters."

Ignorance.   (Chapter 6) Fallacious appeals to ignorance are arguments in which the premises describe our ignorance regarding a proposition, P, and the conclusion makes a substantive claim about the truth or falsity of P. Often, not-P is inferred from our ignorance of P, or P is inferred from our ignorance of not-P. For instance, people may infer from the fact that we don't know there are no ghosts that there are ghosts; or they may move from the fact that an event has no known natural cause to the conclusion that it has a supernatural cause. Such inferences are fallacious because our ignorance is irrelevant to the issue of the substantive truth, or even the substantive probability, of claims.

Objectionable Cause.   (Chapter 13) The fallacy of objectionable cause occurs when a reasoner imposes a causal interpretation on a set of events and makes no attempt to rule out alternative explanations of those events. Sometimes this fallacy is called *false cause*. We changed the name because you do not always get the cause wrong by this procedure. You may be right, but it will be by accident. In effect, reasoning to a cause too hastily, as in objectionable cause, goes like this: "A occurred; B occurred; A and B can plausibly be connected; therefore, A caused B." The pattern of argument is fallacious because there may be other explanations of the joint occurrence of A and B, and no basis is given in this kind of argument to rule out alternatives.

Post Hoc.   (Chapter 13) This is the fallacy of reasoning that simply because one thing precedes another, it must have caused it. Or, to put it differently, you reason that because B came after A, then A must have caused B. The argument is a fallacy because it takes far more than mere succession in time to justify a causal conclusion. The conclusion states that A produced, or brought about, B; and the premise gives information only about sequence in time. To know that one thing causes another you have to know that the sequence in time is typical and that the causal relation that you allege is the best explanation of the fact that the two events occurred together. To know that the causal relation is the best explanation, you have to have a basis for ruling out other explanations.

Slippery Assimilation.   (Chapter 10) The fallacy of slippery assimilation occurs when someone reasons that because there is a series of cases differing only slightly from each other, all cases in the series are the same. For example, "Because there is a gradual progression, ounce by ounce, from weighing 100 pounds to weighing 300 pounds, there is no one spot where you can draw the line between being thin and being fat. Therefore, everyone is really fat." (Or, alternatively, everyone is really thin.) The fallacy here occurs because the argument proceeds as though differences that are *separately* insignificant could not *cumulate* to be significant. Obviously, as the weight example indicates, they *can!* The argument may show that there will be borderline cases, but it does not show that there is no distinction to be drawn. Cases are falsely assimilated in this argument.

Slippery Precedent.   (Chapter 10) In slippery precedent arguments a case that is acknowledged to be good, or deserving, when considered alone, is rejected on the grounds that it would set a precedent for permitting further cases that are not good or deserving. The premises compare the case in question to further cases, maintain that the case in question would set a precedent for allowing those further cases, and claim that the further cases are bad. The conclusion rejects the case in question; what was initially deserving has become undeserving on the grounds that it would set a bad precedent. Slippery precedent arguments have inconsistent premises, because a case that is good cannot set a precedent for others that are bad. There must necessarily be a relevant difference between the cases that are compared, and this relevant difference is neglected in the premises of the argument, which slide from the initial case to the other ones as though there were no relevant difference between them.

Straw Man.   (Chapter 6) The straw man fallacy is committed when a person misrepresents the argument or theory of another person and then, on the basis of his misrepresentation, purports to refute the real argument or theory. The refutation is irrelevant to the merits of the real theory because the view in question has been misdescribed. The way to avoid straw man is to interpret the writings and sayings of other people carefully and accurately and to make sure that you take a strong and representative version of any general theory you criticize.

Two Wrongs Make a Right.   (Chapter 10) In this fallacious argument we see a misplaced appeal to consistency. A person is urged to accept, or condone, one thing that is wrong because another similar thing, also wrong, has occurred, or has been accepted and condoned. For example: "It is all right for the United States to support regimes that torture people because after all there is torture in communist countries too." The line of argument is fallacious because it would have us perpetuate evil in order to be consistent. If one thing is bad and another thing is bad, then the conclusion to be reached is that both are bad. And ideally both should be prevented. If both cannot be prevented, then we must do what we can to prevent what we can control. The "two wrongs make a right" argument seems to rely on the supposition that the world is a better place with sets of similar wrongs in it than it would be with some of these wrongs corrected and the others left in place. But there is no point in multiplying wrongs, just to preserve consistency.

Vagueness.   (Chapter 3) Vagueness arises when a word, as used, has a meaning that is insufficiently clear to convey the necessary information in that context of use. If a sentence is expressed in very vague language, and there is no clue in the context as to what it is supposed to mean, then we cannot tell whether the sentence is true or false because we simply will not have an understanding of it. Vagueness as such is a fault when it goes to this point, but it is not as such a fallacy. Vagueness contributes to mistakes in reasoning when key terms are not precise enough in the context for us to judge whether the premises and conclusions are acceptable. As used in the argument, the terms are not sufficiently precise to enable us to understand the boundaries of their application. Arguments can trade on vagueness by using terms that cannot be pinned down sufficiently; meanings may become so indeterminate that we go along with the argument simply because we don't know exactly what is being said. At this point vagueness contributes to mistaken judgments about the merits of reasoning.

Appendix B

A Brief Note on Theory

In the first edition of this book, argument soundness was defined in terms of the ARG conditions. Some instructors objected to this deviation from standard usage, according to which a sound argument is one in which a conclusion is validly inferred from premises that are true. This classic sense of soundness makes only deductively valid arguments sound. This consequence is not taken seriously, however: most who use the classic account of soundness still wish to go on to allow that there are some strong inductive arguments. The classic account also stipulates a very strict condition of adequacy for premises. That strict condition is nonepistemic. Taking the account strictly, arguments are sound, not on the basis of our knowing their premises true, but on the basis of those premises being true. Nevertheless, applying the criterion of soundness in this sense would seem to require that we know its premises to be true before we judge an argument to be sound.

The classic account may be said to be extremely rigorous, in the sense that few everyday arguments, and few arguments even in special disciplines such as physics, biology, law, history, and psychology, will be regarded as good arguments if "good arguments" are those that are sound in the classic sense.

In this second edition, the ARG conditions are again used for argument evaluation. However, *sound* has been replaced by *cogent*. This substitution avoids stipulating a nonstandard sense for *sound* while preserving the ARG conditions. A cogent argument is one that meets the ARG conditions. It has acceptable premises—in the sense of "acceptable" explained in Chapter Five here. Those premises lead in a legitimate and appropriate way to its conclusion. Saying "an appropriate and legitimate way," rather than "validly" allows for a pluralistic, nondeductivist account of argument. Deductive entailment is, on this model, one, but only one, of a number of possible legitimate connections. Premises can also suppose a conclusion inductively, through analogical reasoning, or through the relation of conduction, as explained in Chapter Eleven.

This pluralism is plausible from a naturalistic point of view; we do find arguments that appear to be of these types and are not deductive. It seems, in addition, to be something that applied logic instructors wish to support. Those who object to departures from tradition and argue for a return to the classical account of soundness as a basis for argument appraisal usually do not at the same time seek to eliminate conductive, inductive, or analogical arguments. Rather, they regard such arguments as interesting, important, and in some cases rationally compelling—not appearing to notice that this allowance is a departure from the tradition they seek to preserve.

The ARG conditions have been preserved here because they provide a more flexible basis for argument appraisal—one that permits a "filling in" for different types of argument and thus, in a compact formula, provides the basis for a more pluralistic account. Departure from tradition is not accidental, but deliberate, and done, in our view, for good reasons.

Basically, there are three reasons for not defining good arguments as sound in the classical sense:

1. The definition is implicitly deductivist and will entail that there are no good arguments that are nondeductive. This result is at odds with common sense and, indeed, with the philosophical theory even of some of the very texts which use *sound* in its classic sense as a fundamental concept for argument evaluation. Most logic texts do at some point discuss inductive argument and allow that some inductive arguments are strong ones.

2. The definition will allow some question-begging arguments to count as good arguments and is thus at odds with standard teaching on fallacies.

3. In requiring that premises be true, the definition either becomes irrelevant to practical evaluation or is unreasonably strict.

If we take *true* ontologically and not epistemically, we have irrelevance, because we are told to find arguments good only if their premises are true. Their truth in this sense is something distinct from, and having no bearing on, what we believe and can be rationally led to accept. If, on the other hand, we refer to what we can know as true, the force of *know* and *true* will suggest very strict conditions that will hardly ever be met. These conditions, if taken seriously, will yield the result that there are few—if any—good arguments. In fact, applied to past periods of history, such a definition would give the result that there were almost no good arguments. Such a consequence is counterintuitive and greatly at odds with recent thinking in the philosophy and history of science. It is not surprising that few texts using classic soundness as the basis for argument appraisal stick consistently to *true* in their treatment of examples. Such problems can be avoided by speaking of what we have evidence or reason to accept as being true. Doing so is, in effect, to speak of what makes premises acceptable.

Since *cogent* is a term often used by people appraising arguments, and since, unlike *sound*, it does not have a standard sense that is different from the one used here, we hope that the substitution made in the second edition will avoid some awkward transition problems from this text to others.

In short, the substance of the original ARG account is kept, because we are convinced that there are good theoretical reasons for it. Further details and supporting philosophical argumentation may be found in Trudy Govier, *Problems in Argument Analysis and Evaluation* (Dordrecht, Netherlands: Foris Publications, 1987).

Answers

TO SELECTED EXERCISES

CHAPTER I

EXERCISE ONE

2. This passage does not contain an argument. It is a description of a physical environment, with the attribution of awareness of the environment to a subject.

4. This passage does contain an argument. The conclusion is that any diet poses some problems. This conclusion is stated both at the beginning and, in slightly different words, at the end of the passage. The word "therefore" precedes a major step before this conclusion, where the specific problems are inferred from the alternatives considered.

6. This passage does not contain an argument. The first sentence identifies hockey as a winter game and says that it is popular in some northern countries. The second sentence mentions some requirements for players of the game. Neither sentence is offered as a reason for, or as evidence for, the other. Nor is there any evidence that someone is trying to justify or prove any claim about hockey or anything else.

10. This passage does not contain an argument. The first sentence tells how we can understand the relationship of a reactor to a steam generator and makes a comparison. The second sentence elaborates slightly on the comparison.

15. This passage does not contain an argument. It is part of a dramatic personal story.

16. This passage does contain an argument. There is one indicator word, "so." The conclusion is "he can't have kept to the diet."

EXERCISE TWO

4. This passage does not contain an argument. It describes Sagan's message rather than trying to show that his message is either correct or incorrect. The author thinks that Sagan has something important to say, but he does not try to prove this.

5. This passage does contain an argument. "Therefore" introduces the conclusion. The other two statements are premises offering evidence for this conclusion.

12. This passage does not contain an argument. The word "because" introduces an explanation. The second sentence offers an illustration of the lack of independence referred to in the first sentence.

16. This passage does contain an argument. The conclusion is that mountain climbers have accepted the risk of death. The indicator word "so" is a clue. The reasons are neatly set out: first some general conditions of accepting risk are announced; then it is stated that these conditions apply to mountain climbers; then the conclusion is drawn.

CHAPTER 2

EXERCISE ONE

1. Standardization:
1. If a car has reliable brakes then its brakes work well in wet weather.
2. My car does not have brakes that work well in wet weather.
Therefore,
3. My car does not have reliable brakes.
The last phrase is an "aside" that is not strictly part of the argument.

5. Standardization:
1. Every logic book I have ever read was written by a woman.
Therefore,
2. All logicians are women.
This argument is obviously weak, but it is clearly an argument.

8. This passage does not contain an argument. The author comments on the recognition abilities of swimming bacteria and explains that their behavior must integrate these responses. He then comments on a result of this behavior.

9. Standardization:
1. China is near Vietnam.
2. China is patient.
3. China has the means, including Chinese within Vietnam, to keep Hanoi "on the boil."
Therefore,
4. China is a more difficult adversary for Vietnam than the United States was.
Therefore,
5. The Soviet Union may be mistaken if it calculates that it could back Vietnam successfully against China as it did against the United States.
There is a subargument structure here; the author defends his premise that China is a more difficult adversary for Vietnam than the United States was.

15. Standardization:
1. There is no mixture unless the things mixed have parts that mix with each other.
So,
2. A thing wholly without parts cannot mix with the minute subdivisions of the brain.
Here "for" serves as an indicator. The conclusion is asserted in the rhetorical question in the first sentence. (Clearly, the implied answer to "how can you mix . . ." is "you cannot.")

16. This passage does not contain an argument. Einstein is, perhaps, suggesting that the mysterious shuddering people feel is unnecessary, but he does not say this and does not offer premises as reasons for it. The phrase "And yet" implies a contrast between the two statements.

EXERCISE TWO

1. Like many ads, this one is very brief, but it seeks to establish a point and is best seen as an argument with unexpressed parts.
Standardization:
1. Bananas contain everything NutraSweet contains.
2. Bananas are not dangerous to eat. (inserted)
Therefore,
3. NutraSweet is not dangerous to eat. (inserted)
The missing premise is common knowledge. Also, we attribute it to the ad because it supplies the obvious rationale for comparing NutraSweet and bananas in the first place. The missing conclusion is attributed because we know ads are used to make people seek to consume the products, and we know that there is a controversy about the safety of artificial sweeteners and other additives.

4. Standardization:
1. The teenage crime rate is going up.
2. Teenage theft is rising.
3. Teenagers steal to get more money for drugs. (inserted)
So,
4. It is not reasonable to believe that drug use (among teenagers) is declining.
The premise is inserted because it links the stated premises with the conclusion and because it is common knowledge.

7. Standardization:
1. Some non-smokers suffer headaches, runny noses, and itchy eyes as a result of exposure to secondhand smoke.
2. Secondhand smoke can cause lung cancer in non-smokers.
So,
3. Secondhand smoke can be injurious to the health of non-smokers.

13. This passage does not contain an argument. It comments on the way in which people are inclined to regard philosophers.

15. Standardization:
1. Either the will is free or the will is not free.
2. If the will is free, a person is responsible for his or her actions.
3. If the will is not free, a person is not responsible for his or her actions.
4. Something must produce the actions a person performs.
5. The will is the only thing inside a person that can produce actions.
Therefore,
6. If the will is not free, something outside people produces actions.

16. The first paragraph gives background information. The second sets a context for reflection. The third offers a moving description of Shan-Fei, in which she is compared to the earth. This piece is not primarily argumentative although an argument is suggested by the final rhetorical question. This argument, which is implied by, though not stated in, the piece is:
1. It does not matter whether the earth is beautiful.
2. Shan-Fei is rooted to the earth and is like the earth.
So,
3. It does not matter whether Shan-Fei is beautiful. (This example is subtle and hard.)

18. Standardization:

1. If dictionaries could settle all disputes about how words are to be used, then debates such as that on abortion could be solved by looking up words such as "human being" or "person" in the dictionary.
2. Debates such as that on abortion cannot be solved by looking up words in the dictionary. (inserted)
Therefore,
3. Dictionaries can't settle all questions about how words are to be used—nor are they intended to do so.
(The extra premise is common knowledge, something the author would clearly accept, and is required to link the stated premise with the conclusion.)

20. Standardization:

1. The image Twain gives of Huck and Jim on the raft lasts long after moral principles and statistics have faded from memory.
2. Twain's examples account for his greatness as a novelist.
So,
3. Teaching by example is better than trying to change people either by rational argument or by force.
4. It is writers who teach by example. (inserted)
So,
5. Writers who can touch the heart are needed more than laws or guns.
The extra premise, (4), is inserted because it links (3) with (5) and because, by virtue of what the author says about Twain, it seems clear that he would accept the claim made in (4).

24. Standardization:

1. Organisms lose genes through mutation all the time.
2. If removing a gene would unleash a monster on the world, this would have happened in nature.
3. A monster has not been unleashed on the world. (inserted)
Therefore,
4. Removing a gene from an organism will not produce a monster.
The extra premise is common knowledge that may fairly be attributed to the author. It links (2) with (4).

CHAPTER 3

EXERCISE ONE

3. (a) This definition is too broad because exchanges can be made using other bases, such as cattle or foodstuffs. Such things would not be regarded as money according to ordinary usage.

3. (c) This definition is both too broad and too narrow. It is too broad because there are many cynical people who are willing to compromise whenever it serves their purposes and who would then be liberals by this definition, though not by ordinary usage. It is too narrow because it excludes as liberals those who have some principles, and this is contrary to ordinary usage—according to which strong defenders of individual rights (civil liberties) are commonly known as liberals. The statement tends to evoke negative attitudes toward liberals.

3. (e) This definition is too narrow. It requires that we concentrate very hard in order to be studying. But people can study provided they concentrate somewhat; it is still called studying. The definition also seems narrow in making memory the goal of studying. Sometimes we study for other purposes—for example, to get a better understanding.

4. (c) Defining *terrorism* is surely very difficult. A recent article on the subject reported discovering 109 different definitions! In this context, you want to avoid defining terrorism in terms of a particular religious or political party and to avoid defining it in terms of its having or not having government support. You want to use a definition according to which acts commonly called terrorist acts—bombings of cars, hostage takings, and so on—will be terrorist acts no matter who commits them. *Suggestion:* Terrorism is the practice of using, or threatening to use, violence (typically unpredicted violence) against civilians who are usually innocent and uninvolved in an attempt to bring about political change or to publicize a particular political cause. (The point of this exercise is not so much to achieve a final definition as to appreciate the problems involved. Obviously *terrorism* has strong negative emotional implications and plays a key role in political rhetoric.)

5. (c) This statement is not a persuasive definition. It is probably not a definition at all but just a statement about tea. If taken as a reportive definition, it could be criticized as too narrow because tea is consumed in places other than England and at times other than the afternoon.

5. (e) This statement is a persuasive definition that, in effect, seeks to evoke negative attitudes toward the police through emotionally negative terms such as "criminal" and "license to kill." It ignores the social importance of having police, ignores the checks on police power, and is inaccurate in its implication that police can serve personal judgments, not the law.

5. (l) This statement is a persuasive definition that attempts to elicit a more favorable attitude toward insanity. The accurate mind is something good, and the suggestion that it is over-taxed when insane is intended to make us think reality is just too much for the really accurate mind, subtly suggesting that perhaps the fault for insanity is not in the mind of the insane person but in the world itself.

EXERCISE TWO

1. There is a fault in this argument, due to ambiguities in "tall" and "short." In the premises, "tall" and "short" are used properly, because there is a basis for comparison. In the conclusion, however, this comparative, relating John to Peter on the one hand and Jim on the other, is not stated. Both "tall" and "short" are used ambiguously. First they are used with a specified comparison, and then they are used in an absolute sense.

4. This passage does not contain any argument to show flaws in Carl Sagan's show. The writer obviously believes that the show was cheap and poor, and he conveys this opinion with loaded language—"posture," "gimmicks," "schmaltz," "cheapens," "razzle-dazzle," and "bubble gum mentality." The emotional language hides the lack of argument.

6. Here we find two different uses of "natural" and "unnatural." In the first sentence, *natural* is used to mean "occurs in the natural world"; in this sense, something natural is neither good nor bad as such. In the second sentence, a common belief about homosexuality being unnatural is alluded to. In that sense, *unnatural* means wrong. Obviously it cannot mean that homosexuality does not occur in nature; on this interpretation the sentence would be an obvious falsehood. The final sentence exploits the confusion between the two senses.

7. This argument uses "oppression" in a vague way. The conclusion depends upon this vagueness. The argument is like the example about child abuse discussed in Chapter Three. It begins from a clear case of "oppression," where entitlement to a trial is violated. Then it moves to psychology, where any government causing fear in its people is called oppressive. Next, a routine government practice, needed virtually everywhere, is called oppressive. By this time, it would appear that any government which makes people do things (such as pay taxes) which they do not want to do will count as oppressive. The next two examples move even further, with schools and parents caring for children. These examples involve activities that may be laborious, but that many people want to do. The whole argument depends on using "oppression" in this very vague way.

15. The phrase *independent thinking* is ambiguous. As commonly understood, independent thinking means not believing everything one reads or is told but being willing to question some things and to search out evidence and arguments to arrive at one's own beliefs—at least when the issue is important and there is reason to question what one is told. As used in the premises, though, independent thinking is said to involve questioning everything one is told so that one would have to start from scratch. This is, in effect, a stipulation that is unreasonable and that avoids the real topic of the argument.

17. The letter writer redefines the bombing as "survival," which is an emotionally positive term. She seeks to make it look justified by applying this word. By most standard definitions of *terrorism*, the act would qualify. (See previous exercise, answer to 4(c).) This passage does not contain an argument; there is an attempt to settle a substantial moral question by the device of merely applying a word, *survival*.

CHAPTER 4

EXERCISE ONE
PART A

1. (d) The first premise is almost certainly not true.

6. (c) We couldn't be in a position to know that 90 percent of the winners said this and neither could the arguer, so the premise is not acceptable. It is also not properly connected to the conclusion. We need evidence about our chances of winning given that we do buy a ticket. Buying a ticket is necessary to win but not sufficient, obviously, and it yields only a very small chance of winning.

9. (a) The premise is obviously acceptable. Taken by itself, it cannot support the conclusion because a significant number of changes in one member of a family could be possible without changes in the other members, even though there are intimate relationships in the family. We can add premises and then we will get

(d). The premises will support the conclusion, but some of them will be controversial.

10. (d) The second premise is unacceptable. It makes a sweeping statement for which we have no evidence. However, if the premises were true or acceptable, we would have to accept the conclusion too.

PART B

1. ****B** just explains why he hates math and hypothesizes about how terrible a math requirement would be. He gives no response at all to *A*'s argument—not even to the extent of explicitly denying *A*'s conclusion.

5. *B responds reasonably to *A*'s argument. He contends that *A*'s premise does not fully support his conclusion. He gives reasons by pointing out alternative explanations for Soviet behavior.

EXERCISE TWO

7. The argument passes on (R) and (G) because the premises entail the conclusion. It fails on (A) because of problems with (1) and (3). (1) is problematic; something might have existed eternally. (3) is problematic because it assimilates time, an order in which events occur, to a thing, in the word *something*.

11. The argument fails on all three conditions. (A) is not satisfied because we have no reason to believe that all thinking is divided into only two types. No evidence is given for this and it is not something known by common experience, personal experience, or authority. The argument fails on (R) because the premises are about methods of thinking, whereas the conclusion is about the subject matter of thinking. And, for the same reason, it fails on (G) too.

12. Standardization:
1. In schools in Cuba, girls far outstrip boys in their achievements.
2. Cuba is a socialist state in which equality of the sexes is a matter of law.
3. In Cuba, men are legally required to do their share of the housework.
Therefore,
4. Under socialism and true equal opportunity, women will show up as superior to men.
We cannot say whether the premises are acceptable without more knowledge of Cuba. However, the argument clearly fails on (G), which is a hasty generalization. The premises are about just one socialist state, whereas the conclusion is about socialism and true equal opportunity in general.

17. The argument passes on (A) and (R) but fails on (G) because other sorts of businesses (e.g., multinationals) may not feel pressures in the same way. Other factors such as resource depletion, pollution, unemployment, and so on are not considered, yet the argument reaches a conclusion that competition is valuable overall.

20. The argument passes on (R) and (G) but fails on (A). The reason is that the first premise is, in effect, a persuasive definition of *sexual perversion*. The other premises may be acceptable, but this first one is a key premise in the argument.

CHAPTER 5

4. This statement is not a necessary truth. Legal responsibility is established by the state. Being a parent is biological. There is no necessary logical connection between a biological fact and a legal fact. For instance, a twelve-year-old could be a biological parent but, due to her young age, she might not be a legal parent in some jurisdictions.

7. This statement is necessarily true. If a person fails to be happy, he is not happy.

11. The statement is necessarily true. It expresses the logical connection between cause and effect. If an action has a cause, it is the effect of that cause and it is, therefore, obviously and necessarily the effect of something.

14. The statement is necessarily true. Girls are female, and mothers are female, by definition. Given this fact, and given that two creatures, both female, are necessarily of the same sex, the female sex, girls are brought up by parents of the same sex as they are.

15. This statement is not necessarily true and may not be true at all. If it is true, this would be in virtue of a contingent relationship between genetic characteristics and a tendency to gain and maintain weight.

PART B

1. The premise is a matter of common knowledge and would be acceptable.

4. The premise would not be acceptable. It would probably be denied by many of those people who would dispute the conclusion and would need the argument. Furthermore, it is not a matter of common knowledge, necessary truth, testimony, or authority. Nor is it supposed merely for the sake of argument.

6. There may be a problem with relevance but there is none with acceptability. In many circles, (a) would be common knowledge.

EXERCISE TWO
PART A

4. There is no inconsistency in these statements. The expectation of improvement, and success of some blacks is contrasted with the greater effect of unemployment on blacks.

7. There is an implicit inconsistency between the second statement and the third one. If God created all the goodness in the world, He would have had to create His own goodness, which would mean existing before He existed. One can escape this contradiction if one assumes that God is not part of this world. On the assumption that creation requires a creative act, the third sentence is inconsistent with the fourth one.

9. These statements are not implicitly inconsistent. They do, however, impose an impossible demand on knowledge, as was argued in the early part of the chapter.

13. These statements are inconsistent because capital punishment is taking a life and is granted as "morally permissible," whereas an earlier statement says that taking a life is never morally justifiable.

PART B

3. The premises are "withholding information is just the same thing as lying" and "lying is wrong." If these are taken to be universal statements, covering all cases of withholding information and lying, they are both false and can be shown to be so by counterexamples.

8. The second premise is not acceptable, because sex has such great social importance that it is not reasonable to accept a ban on discussing it publicly. It is true it is a private thing if by "private" we mean that it is done apart from public view; it is another thing to say it is "private" in the sense of not being open to public discussion. Any temptation to accept the two premises probably comes from their exploitation of the ambiguity in "private."

11. Two premises are unacceptable: "No one knows why persons of all strata of society become addicted" and "This slipping away from personal responsibility is unjust." The former is unacceptable because it presupposes that experts are incorrect, which is one of the things the author is trying to prove. The latter is unacceptable because it presupposes that people are individually responsible for their actions, which is one of the things the experts deny. Neither of these claims can be taken as acceptable within the context of this argument. (*Note:* They might be true, nevertheless.)

12. The argument contains a subargument structure. The premise that in a democracy one has all the means needed to influence policy is used to derive the conclusion that a hunger strike is not necessary or morally right. Then, from that conclusion, it is further concluded that a particular hunger strike, that of Jacques Hebert, was wrong. The first argument has an acceptability problem. The premise would not be accepted by those defending strikes; furthermore, it is not known on the basis of common experience, testimony, or authority. Nor, obviously, is it a necessary truth. Many people have experiences indicating the contrary: it is, in fact, quite difficult for individuals in a democracy to influence policy, and one vote every two or four years is limited means indeed.

16. The premises are clearly acceptable on the basis of common knowledge. (The argument may be criticized on the (G) condition; other sports are not considered.)

CHAPTER 6

EXERCISE ONE
PART A

1. Statement (a) is relevant to statement (b) because it gives some reason to suppose that (b) is true. One interpretation of the behavior described is that elephants are hiding others because the others are not living. If this interpretation is correct, then elephants have the concept "not living," which is, essentially, the concept "dead."

2. Statement (a) is irrelevant to statement (b) because there is no positive or negative connection between jogging and being an artist.

6. Statement (a) is not relevant to statement (b) even though they both deal with the Holocaust. (a) is about a dispute among French historians, and (b) considers what would have happened without protective activities by some courageous people. These themes are different.

9. Statement (a) is clearly relevant to statement (b), because (a) claims agriculture is important, which provides a general reason for (b), the claim that a weak agricultural system is an obstacle to economic advancement in the Soviet Union.

PART B

1. The argument is:
1. A number of different religious denominations are represented within the public school system.
Therefore,
2. The public school system must be secular.
As stated, (1) is not relevant to (2) since having different religions is no reason for having no religion at all. We could make (1) relevant by reading in a missing premise to the effect that only a secular system will be acceptable to all the different denominations. This extra premise, however, would not be acceptable in any case, because some denominations feel very strongly about having some religion in education—so much so that they might prefer a religion other than their own to none at all.

3. Solzhenitsyn concluded that man's task on earth is spiritual on the grounds that man will die. The premise is irrelevant because the fact that life ends at some time does not tell us what the point of life is when it is going on.

7. The premises are irrelevant because fish are an entirely different species from humans, not close in an evolutionary sense, and inhabiting an entirely different kind of environment.

EXERCISE TWO

1. This passage contains an argument with the missing conclusion that feminist philosophy should be opposed. Our justification for reading in this conclusion is the author's "I vigorously oppose . . ." and the terms she uses to describe feminism. The argument has irrelevant premises and is a case of the straw man fallacy because feminism does not advocate destroying traditions and democracy, nor does it advocate reducing traditional families to superfluity. (You need background knowledge about what is involved in the feminist position to see this fallacy.)

3. There is no irrelevance in Jones's argument. Smith does not really address that argument. Instead, he himself offers several different arguments to contradict Jones's conclusion. There are numerous flaws of relevance. What animals do to each other is irrelevant to what people should do to animals because animals do not have a sense of ethics and cannot reason about what they ought and ought not to do. What people do naturally (being omnivores) is irrelevant to what they ought to do. There is also an argument from ignorance at the one point where Smith does tie his comments to Jones's argument. The fact that we don't know what sort of consciousness animals may have is not a reason for concluding that they have none.

6. Just as it stands, the quoted sentence is not an argument. If we assume that in a broader context, it functions as part of an argument, we can see the fallacy of guilt by association. The statement seeks to link antiwar activists of the Vietnam era with the abuses of the North Vietnamese and the Cambodian regimes.

8. This passage contains the straw man fallacy and uses lots of loaded language to further discredit the absurd position attributed to Maude Barlow. Such opponents of pornography do not assume men are dimwits; rather they assume that people will be affected by persistent portrayals of violence against women— subconsciously, if not consciously. There are hints of *ad hominem* in such expressions as "of her ilk" and "classed with purveyors of drivel." Apart from the straw man fallacy and suggestions of *ad hominem* and loaded language, no reason is given against the views Barlow holds.

14. Here the premise is relevant to the conclusion. If the only people who know art and art education are art professors or art instructors, that fact is a very good reason for concluding that art colleges should be administered by them.

18. If people did reason this way, they were basing their conclusions about Clark on irrelevant evidence. That a man's wife uses her maiden name is not relevant to his competence as a political leader because it shows neither the wisdom of his policies nor anything about his ability to carry them out. It shows, rather, that his wife has certain ideas and beliefs about names, identity, and sexual roles and that he either concurs with them or thinks she should be allowed to make her own decisions.

CHAPTER 7

EXERCISE ONE

2. (1) Every teacher is bound to encounter a student who is more intelligent than he or she is. For (2) not even the most intelligent teacher is sharper in every regard than every single one of the thousands of students he or she will encounter in a lifetime of teaching.

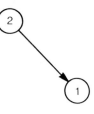

5. (1) Canada is an extremely spread-out country that depends on road and air transport to a far greater extent than do European countries. (2) In European countries rail service can be more efficiently and economically run than it can in Canada. (3) Without an effective rail system, more shipping is done by air and road, and (4) air and road are more expensive than rail. Therefore, (5) we cannot say that Canadians are wasteful of oil simply on the grounds that they use more oil per person than the Europeans.

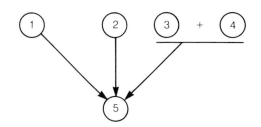

13. (1) Virtue generally, in all sorts of subjects, is somewhat that is valued for eminence; and (2) consisteth in comparison. For (3) if all things were equally in all men, nothing would be prized.

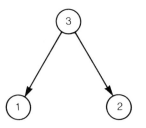

EXERCISE TWO

2. Standardization:
1. A good team player can work with others.
2. Someone who wants all the glory for himself cannot work with other people.
Thus,
3. A very competitive person is not going to be a good team player.
So,
4. The quality of team sports will not be improved if we emphasize competitiveness in individuals.

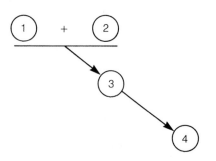

6. Standardization:

1. It is not shocking to sterilize a woman after the birth of her twentieth child.
So,
2. It is not shocking to sterilize a woman after the birth of her *n*th child, where *n* is a number small enough to contribute to population control.

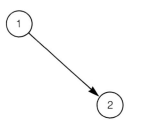

10. This passage is not very clearly written. The main conclusion is that sex is less readily available, on the average, to men than to women. The author seems to give two distinct reasons for taking this view. The first is introduced in the first sentence, and the second is developed in a subargument stated in the last two sentences.

Standardization:

1. Women can sell sex and men cannot.
2. Men are socially conditioned to actively pursue sex.
So,
3. Women seeking sex can usually secure a partner.
So,
4. Women have no need to pursue sex.
Therefore,
5. Sex is less readily available, on the average, to men than to women.

Although (1) is not asserted as such in the original wording, the tone and direction of the argument indicate that the author commits himself to (1). The underlining indicates our decision to detach the "if" from the conditional in which (1) is found; as an asserted claim, it is added.

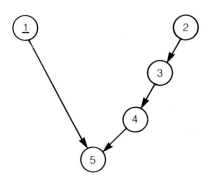

14. Standardization:
1. Teachers of mathematics can teach mathematics from a practical or from a theoretical point of view.
2. If mathematics is taught from a practical point of view, there is a risk of losing some of its precise simplicity and beauty.
3. If mathematics is taught from a theoretical point of view, there is a risk of boring students who may find it too abstract.
Therefore,
4. Teaching mathematics in such a way that it is interesting and comprehensive is difficult.

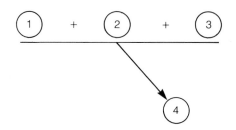

EXERCISE THREE
PART A

3. (1) Thought without language is impossible. People deny this statement and talk on about (2) thoughts that they cannot fully express, but the problem is that (3) we just cannot verify that any such thoughts exist. In fact, (4) skepticism about ideas that can be communicated to no one else is definitely the best policy. Of course, you have to realize that (5) "language" is a very general term. (6) It includes gestures and picture symbols as well as the words that are most familiar to us. When we understand language in its broadest sense, we see that (7) life itself would be impossible without language. And obviously if life itself—for human beings, that is—is impossible without language, then (1) thought is impossible without language.

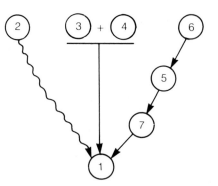

5. Standardization:
1. Political language is designed to make lies seem like truths.
2. If you simplify your English, you will be free from the worst follies of political orthodoxies.
3. One's linguistic habits are something one can control.
So,
4. We can probably bring some improvement in politics by starting at the verbal end.
(*Hard.* The wording is simplified here; this simplification is the drift of the thought. It is also legitimate to see this passage as a nonargument.)

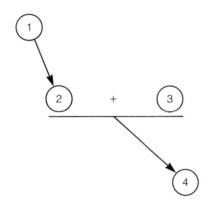

8. Standardization:
1. A person who uses a relatively unreliable procedure to determine whether another person deserves punishment is in no position to know that the other person deserves punishment.
2. (Inserted) A person who is in no position to know that another person deserves punishment has no right to punish that other person.
So,
3. No one has a right to punish another on the basis of decisions made by a relatively unreliable procedure.

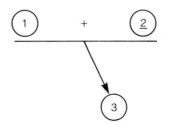

11. Standardization:

1. Breast feeding provides the best nutrition for babies.
2. Breast feeding helps space out births.
So,
<u>5</u>. (inserted) Breast feeding is good for babies and for families.
3. Marketing infant formula in Third World countries can cause serious problems.
So,
4. Marketing practices should not induce mothers who could otherwise breast-feed to switch to the bottle.

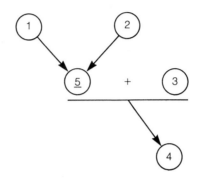

14. The passage contains an argument but many sentences in it are for background information only. The first sentence describes a contrast in outlooks. The next indicates Thoreau's disagreement with the otherworldly outlook. The third describes the otherworldly outlook held by some Christians. The fourth is still not part of an argument. It begins with "so," but this term is the indicator of an explanation. The last sentence gives Thoreau's reason for dissenting from the otherworldly outlook. This sentence is a premise for his own viewpoint, which is not stated as such but can be supplied from the wording of "is wont to put me off with Christianity" and "so we are said to" and "But," which, introducing the final sentence, implies that Thoreau's own view contrasts with the one he has been describing.

Standardization:

1. One grain of instant life that we actually have is worth acres of hope hammered out to gild our prospect.
Therefore,
2. It is a mistake to think that the next world is worth more than the present world.

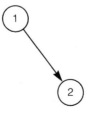

CHAPTER 8

EXERCISE ONE

2. Some students are persons who came to the office asking to be excused from the final examination. (*I*)

5. All persons who can afford to stay at London's pretigious hotels are rich persons. (*A*)

10. Some textbooks are not boring books. (*O*)

15. All women with jobs outside the home and no assistance with household work are persons burdened with at least two jobs. (*A*)

EXERCISE TWO
PART A

1. All pilgrims who came to Massachusetts are persons who left England of their own free will. (*A*)
Obverse: No pilgrims who came to Massachusetts are not persons who left England of their own free will.

3. Some things that are technical innovations are not things that are needed. (*O*)
Obverse: Some things that are technical innovations are non-things that are needed. More colloquially: Some things that are technical innovations are things that are not needed.

8. All beliefs that are nationalistic are beliefs that are fervent concerning doubtful matters. (*A*)
Obverse: No beliefs that are nationalistic are not beliefs that are fervent concerning doubtful matters.

PART B

1. All *T* are *E*. (*T* represents those people who understand the new technology; *E* represents experts.)
Converse: All *E* are *T*; not equivalent.
Contrapositive: All non-*E* are non-*T*; equivalent to original.
The original is an *A* statement; so too are the converse and the contrapositive.

4. All *W* are *D*. (*W* represents whales; *D* represent creatures in danger of extinction.)
Converse: All *D* are *W*; not equivalent to original.
Contrapositive: All non-*D* are non-*W*; equivalent to original.
Original is an *A* statement; so too are the converse and the contrapositive.

6. Some *C* are *F*. (*C* represents court proceedings; *F* represents things so complex as to be inefficient.)
Converse: Some *F* are *C*; equivalent to original.
Contrapositive: Some non-*C* are non-*F*; not equivalent to original.
The original is an *I* statement; so too are the converse and the contrapositive.

8. No *R* are *D*. (*R* represents persons who have read Russian dissident novelists; *D* represents persons who doubt that opponents of the current regime are vulnerable to severe penalties in the Soviet Union.)
Converse: No *D* are *R*.
Contrapositive: No non-*D* are non-*R*.
The converse is equivalent to the original and the contrapositive is not. All are *E* statements.

PART C

1. All *V* are *U*. (*V* represents advice given to young parents by so-called experts; *U* represents things that are unreliable.)
It is an *A* statement.
The contradictory is an *O* statement.
Contradictory: Some *V* are not *U*.

3. Some *C* are *T*. (*C* represents crops; *T* represents things best grown on land that has been left fallow for one season.)
This is an *I* statement.
Contradictory is the *E* statement: No *C* are *T*.

5. All *P* are *T*. (*P* represents persons who are productive and innovative scientists; *T* represents persons who enjoy freedom of thought and are not afraid to risk pursuing new ideas.)
This is an *A* statement.
The contradictory, some *P* are not *T*, is an *O* statement.

EXERCISE THREE

2. The argument in categorical form:
1. Some mothers are persons who find small children extremely irritating.
2. Some persons who find small children extremely irritating are persons who just cannot control themselves and suppress their rage.
Therefore,
3. Some mothers are persons who just cannot control themselves and suppress their rage.
Venn diagram of premises: *M* represents mothers; *C* represents persons who find small children extremely irritating; *J* represents persons who cannot control themselves and suppress their rage.

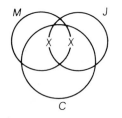

The argument is invalid. It would be possible for the premises to be true and the conclusion false because the x's are on the line and there is no guarantee they will fall into the areas required for the truth of the conclusion.

7. The argument in categorical form:
   1. All well-educated persons are persons who can read.
   2. All persons who can read are persons who have heard of Hitler.
   Therefore,
   3. Some well-educated persons are persons who have heard of Hitler.
   Venn diagram of premises: W represents well-educated persons; R represents persons who can read; H represents persons who have heard of Hitler.

Hypothetical   Existential

The argument is valid only if we adopt the existential interpretation and assume that there are well-educated persons and there are persons who can read. With this interpretation, we can add x's and the argument is valid.

9. All V are T; all T are R; therefore, all V are R. (V represents vacations; T represents things that have tropical beaches; R represents things that come with some risk of sunburn.)

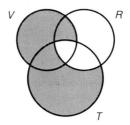

The argument is valid. Given the shading for the premises, we can see that all V are R. There is no area of the V circle left unshaded outside the R circle.

12. The argument in categorical form:
    1. Some doctors are unhappy persons.
    2. All unhappy persons are unreliable persons.
    Therefore,
    3. Some doctors are unreliable persons.

Venn diagram of premises: *D* represents doctors; *U* represents unhappy persons; *R* represents unreliable persons.

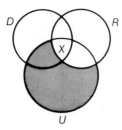

The argument is valid. The diagram of the premises shows an *x* in the area representing those who are doctors and are unreliable persons, and the conclusion states that there are persons in this area.

19. Some *R* are *B*; all *B* are *F*; therefore, some *R* are *F*. (*R* represents religious people; *B* represents people who believe morality depends on religion; *F* represents people who have a false view of morality.)

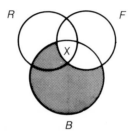

The argument is valid. There is an *x* in the area that is both *R* and *F*, when the premises are represented, and this guarantees that the conclusion will be true.

EXERCISE FOUR

6. The argument in categorical form:
   1. Some double letters are letters compounded of two vowels.
   2. No double letters are vowels.
   Therefore,
   3. Some letters compounded of two vowels are not vowels.
   Venn diagram of premises: *D* represents double letters; *C* represents letters compounded of two vowels; *V* represents vowels.

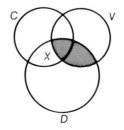

The argument is valid because this diagram shows an x in the area that is C and is not V, as is required for the conclusion to be true.

8. The passage contains a main argument and a subargument.
Standardization:
1. All things that are nuclear perils are things that are everlasting.
So,
2. All things that are solutions to nuclear perils are things that must aim to be everlasting.
So,
3. All things that are solutions to nuclear perils are global political solutions.
The subargument is not easily cast as a syllogism because there are four terms. The main argument can be regarded as a syllogism with a missing premise:
4. All things that must aim at being everlasting are global political solutions.

This syllogism is valid; we added the premise to make it so. However, the added premise is very questionable.

12. This passage is not an argument based on class inclusion. It cannot be usefully cast into the forms of categorical logic. Reasons against defining the best people in terms of IQ are given—several reasons—and a counterfactual is briefly considered. Compare this response with the discussion of conductive arguments in Chapter Eleven.

15. The argument in categorical form:
1. All schools that provide the sort of education needed for those who are at the top of public life in Britain are expensive private schools.
Therefore,
2. All men who are at the top of public life in Britain are men who were educated at expensive private schools.

This argument cannot plausibly be recast as a syllogism using the techniques described in Chapter Eight. A crucial problem is that four categories are involved, and they cannot be reduced to three.

16. With additions, this passage may be cast as two syllogisms. The context—namely that the author is writing about Canada—is used to supply them. N represents nations permitting the showing of violence night after night and not permitting the showing of love-making scenes. C represents nations that are Canada. P represents nations that are guilty of practicing obscenity and hypocrisy. W represents things without redeeming social value.
The first syllogism is: All N are P; all C are N (inserted); therefore, all C are P. (This is valid.)
The second syllogism is: All C are P; all P are W (inserted); therefore, all C are W. In this case, insertions are made due, first to the immediate inference made from the hypocrisy and obscenity to being without redeeming social value, and second to the strongly implied criticism of Canada, in the context. The second syllogism is also valid. (Whether these are cogent arguments will depend, then, entirely on our appraisal of the premises. *Very hard.*)

CHAPTER 9

EXERCISE ONE
PART A

4. *F* represents "Fred will come." *S* represents "Susan will come." *O* represents "The outing will be a success." *J* represents "Joe will enjoy himself."

$F \vee S$

$F \supset O$

$S \supset J$

7. *D* represents "Dieting during pregnancy is a good idea." *E* represents "Eating well during pregnancy is particularly important."

$- D \cdot E$

8. *E* represents "Extensive public relations efforts are being made on behalf of the nuclear industry"; *C* represents "Efforts being made on behalf of the nuclear industry are convincing the public."

$E \cdot - C$

10. *E* represents "Species are in danger of extinction"; *W* represents "Wildlife foundations are telling us the truth."

$- E \supset - W$

PART B

2. *M* represents "You master calculus"; *D* represents "You have some difficulty with the mathematical aspects of first year university physics." The argument can then be represented as:

$M \supset - D$

M

Therefore,

$- D$

M	D	-D	M⊃-D
T	T	F	F
T	F	T	T
F	T	F	T
F	F	T	T

The argument is valid. There is no row where the conclusion is false and the premises are true.

8. *S* represents "You are a suitable student of philosophy of science"; *K* represents "You know philosophy"; *C* represents "You know science." The argument can then be represented as:

$S \supset (K \lor C)$

$-K \cdot -C$

Therefore,

$-S$

S	K	C	−S	−K	−C	−K·−C	KvC	S⊃(KvC)
T	T	T	F	F	F	F	T	T
T	T	F	F	F	T	F	T	T
T	F	T	F	T	F	F	T	T
T	F	F	F	T	T	T	F	F
F	T	T	T	F	F	F	T	T
F	T	F	T	F	T	F	T	T
F	F	T	T	T	F	F	T	T
F	F	F	T	T	T	T	F	T

The argument is valid. There is no row where the conclusion is false and the premises are true.

9. *E* represents "Trudeau exercises"; *G* represents "Trudeau is in good shape." The argument can then be represented as:

$E \supset G$

G

Therefore,

E

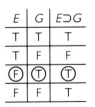

E	G	E⊃G
T	T	T
T	F	F
(F)	(T)	(T)
F	F	T

Premises true. Conclusion false.

The argument is invalid.

1. $S \supset L; L \supset B; B \supset H; S;$ therefore, $H.$

This argument is valid. Set H as false. In order for the fourth premise to be true, S must be true. If S is true, L must be true in order for the first premise to be true. If L is true, B must be true in order for the second premise to be true. But if B is true, then H must be true in order for the third premise to be true. This stipulation is inconsistent with our assumption that H was false. There is no consistent assignment of truth values to the component statements that will make the premises true and the conclusion false.

3. $-(M \cdot H);$ therefore, $-M \vee -H.$

This argument is valid. For the conclusion to be false, both M and H have to be true. If M and H are both true, the premise is false. Thus the premise cannot be true while the conclusion is false.

5. $K \vee U; U \supset (L \vee N); -N; L \supset (V \vee -W); -L \cdot -K;$ therefore, $-W.$

K represents "The murderer used a kitchen knife"; U represents "The murderer carried an unusually large pocket knife"; L represents "The murderer was wearing loose clothes"; N represents "The murderer would have been noticed"; V represents "The murderer was very thin"; and W represents "The murderer was wearing clothes found at the scene of the crime."

For the argument to be valid, the premises could not be true if the conclusion were false. If the conclusion is false, W is true. For the fifth premise to be true, L and K must both be false. If L is false, the fourth premise is true. If K is false, the fifth premise is true. We can assign N as false, and the third premise will be true. Given N false, the consequent of the second premise is true; thus that premise is true. Therefore, we have a consistent assignment of truth values making the premises true when the conclusion is false. The argument is not valid.

EXERCISE TWO

3. O represents "The operation was painful"; L represents "The operation was pleasant." The argument is:

$-O$

$O \vee L$

Therefore,

L

O	L	$-O$	$O \vee L$
T	T	F	T
T	F	F	T
F	T	T	T
F	F	T	F

The argument is valid. There is no row where the conclusion is false and the premises are true. Note that you need two statement letters, because "The operation was pleasant" and "The operation was painful" are not contradictory statements. They could both be false.

8. $D \vee M; R \supset -M; R;$ therefore, $-M \cdot D.$
Valid. For the conclusion to be false, either M must be true or D must be false. If M is true, the first premise is true. Then, for the second premise to be true, R must be false. Given these assignments, the third premise will be false. If D is false, then M must be true in order to make the first premise true. Then R must be false in order for the second premise to be true and, as before, this case will result in the third premise being false. It is not possible to make the premises true and conclusion false; therefore, the argument is valid.

15. $(S \cdot I) \supset A; S \cdot I;$ therefore, $A.$
Valid. For the conclusion to be false, either S or I will have to be false in order for the first premise to be true. But given this, you cannot make the second premise true.

17. $W \supset B; B \supset U; U \supset A;$ therefore, $W \supset A.$
Valid. For the conclusion to be false, A must be false and W true. Then given W as true, B must be true for the first premise to be true. Given B true, U must be true for the second premise to be true. Given U true, A would have to be true for the third premise to be true. But A has been assigned as false. You can't make the premises true and the conclusion false.

19. $D \supset S; S \supset L; L \supset G;$ therefore, $D \supset G.$
Second argument: $(D \supset G) \supset U; D \supset G$ (taken from first argument); therefore, $U.$
Both are valid. For the first argument, see the answer to question 17, where the argument is of the same form. For the second argument, to make the conclusion false, U must be false. Then to make first premise true $(D \supset G)$ must be false. But this assignment makes the second premise false.

EXERCISE THREE

1. E represents "Elephants have been known to bury their dead"; C represents "Elephants have a concept of their own species"; U represents "Elephants understand what death means"; S represents "Elephants have a substantial capacity for abstraction." The argument is:

E

$E \supset (C \cdot U)$

$U \supset S$

Therefore,

S

E	C	U	S	C·U	E⊃(C·U)	U⊃S
T	T	T	T	T	T	T
T	T	T	F	T	T	F
T	T	F	T	F	F	T
T	T	F	F	F	F	T
T	F	T	T	F	F	T
T	F	T	F	F	F	F
T	F	F	T	F	F	T
T	F	F	F	F	F	T
F	T	T	T	T	T	T
F	T	T	F	T	T	F
F	T	F	T	F	T	T
F	T	F	F	F	T	T
F	F	T	T	F	T	T
F	F	T	F	F	T	F
F	F	F	T	F	T	T
F	F	F	F	F	T	T

The argument is valid.

3. $J \supset M$; $-J$; therefore, $-M$.

Not valid. The conclusion is true if M is false. With M false, the first premise is true if J is false. If J is false, the second premise is true. Alternate symbolization: $J \supset M$; $-J$; therefore, R. This argument is not valid, obviously. The alternative results if we note that, strictly speaking, the stated conclusion is not the contradictory of M, where M is "Joe becomes more attractive to women." (The contradictory is that Joe does not become more attractive to women.)

5. $-R \supset -S$; $-R \supset A$; $A \supset -G$; therefore, $-R \supset -G$.

The argument can be shown valid by the shorter truth table technique. To make the conclusion false, $-G$ must be false, and $-R$ must be true. That means G must be true and R must be false. If G is true, for the third premise to be true, A must be false. If A is false, for the second premise to be true, $-R$ must be false, which means R must be true. But we already stipulated R as false in order to make the conclusion false. Thus there is no consistent assignment of true values which makes the conclusion false and the premises true. The argument is valid.

7. W represents "Workers agree not to strike within the next decade"; D represents "Prospects for the recovery of the plant are dim"; M represents "Management agrees to forego special parking and washroom privileges." In this context, "management does its part" is taken to mean that management agrees to forego special parking and washroom privileges and is thus represented by M. The argument is:

$$-W \supset D$$
$$-M \supset -W$$

Therefore,

$-D \supset M$

D	W	M	$-D$	$-W$	$-M$	$-W \supset D$	$-M \supset -W$	$-D \supset M$
T	T	T	F	F	F	T	T	T
T	T	F	F	F	T	T	F	T
T	F	T	F	T	F	T	T	T
T	F	F	F	T	T	T	T	T
F	T	T	T	F	F	T	T	T
F	T	F	T	F	T	T	F	F
F	F	T	T	T	F	F	T	T
F	F	F	T	T	T	F	T	F

The argument is valid.

12. *M* represents "Morality has a basis"; *G* represents "there is a god"; *W* represents "The world makes sense"; *O* represents "The world is ordered." The argument is:

$M \supset G$

$G \supset (W \cdot O)$

O

Therefore,

M

M	G	W	O	$M \supset G$	$W \cdot O$	$G \supset (W \cdot O)$
T	T	T	T	T	T	T
T	T	T	F	T	F	F
T	T	F	T	T	F	F
T	T	F	F	T	F	F
T	F	T	T	F	T	T
T	F	T	F	F	F	T
T	F	F	T	F	F	T
T	F	F	F	F	F	T
(F)	T	T	(T)	(T)	T	(T)
F	T	T	F	T	F	F
(F)	T	F	(T)	(T)	F	(T)
F	T	F	F	T	F	T
(F)	F	T	(T)	(T)	T	(T)
F	F	T	F	T	F	T
(F)	F	F	(T)	(T)	T	(T)
F	F	F	F	T	T	F

The argument is not valid.

3. Santayana's claim "to be happy you must be wise" is saying that you are happy (*H*) only if you are wise (*W*). It is formalized as $H \supset W$. Needham, in inferring that if you are not happier now than you were ten years ago, you are no wiser, goes considerably beyond the original claim. Santayana did not say that wisdom increases with happiness. Needham's claim requires $-H \supset -W$, which does not follow from Santayana's claim, as this truth table shows:

H	*W*	−*H*	−*W*	*H*⊃*W*	−*H*⊃−*W*
T	T	F	F	T	T
T	F	F	T	F	T
F	T	T	F	(T)	(F)
F	F	T	T	T	T

10. *A* represents "Human actions are entirely governed by causal laws"; *N* represents "Human actions are necessary"; *C* represents "Human actions occur by chance"; *O* represents "We could act otherwise than we do." (For the purposes of this argument, it is assumed that "we could not act otherwise than we do" means the same as "we have no control over our actions" and "we cannot help ourselves." The argument is:

1. $A \vee -A$
2. $A \supset N$
3. $N \supset -O$
4. $-A \supset C$
5. $C \supset -N$
6. $C \supset -O$

Therefore,

7. $-O$ (to be derived)
8. $A \supset -O$ from (2) and (3) by hypothetical syllogism
9. $-A \supset -O$ from (4) and (6) by hypothetical syllogism
10. $-O$ from (8), (9), and (1) by constructive dilemma

The argument is valid. However, premises (2) and (4) are questionable.

11. This passage does not contain an argument.

14. *S* represents "The group will be successful"; *W* represents "All members of the group participate willingly"; *M* represents "Members of the group have a say in top-level decision-making." The argument is:

1. $S \supset W$
2. $W \supset M$
3. M

Therefore,

4. S

S	W	M	S⊃W	W⊃M
T	T	T	T	T
T	T	F	T	F
T	F	T	F	T
T	F	F	F	T
Ⓕ	T	Ⓣ	Ⓣ	Ⓣ
F	T	F	T	F
Ⓕ	F	Ⓣ	Ⓣ	Ⓣ
F	F	F	T	T

The argument is not valid.

CHAPTER 10

EXERCISE ONE
PART A

1. The primary subject is the argument that Japanese corporations are more fairly run than American ones because decisions are typically reached by teams rather than by individuals. The analogue is the argument that a hypothetical South African judicial system might make decisions by teams, while still applying laws that are unfair to blacks. The premises of the primary argument are acceptable, and it is genuinely similar to the analogue argument in that the key feature of having groups, rather than individuals make decisions is retained. The analogue shows that more than group procedure is needed for fairness. This is a successful refutation by logical analogy of the original argument.

4. The primary subject is the argument that we should not love people of the same sex because God did not intend us to, which, in turn, is inferred from the fact that God made two sexes. The analogue argument is that we should not wear clothes because God did not intend us to, which He presumably did not because He caused us to be born naked. The premises in both arguments are acceptable provided we grant that God exists. (If we disagree that God exists, we will not follow the primary subject argument through at all, so it will not need the refutation by logical analogy, which is aimed at the *R* and *G* conditions.) The arguments are similar in both making obvious statements about what God would have created, granted that He did create us at all. The analogue argument is relevant to the primary argument because the two are closely parallel in their inferences of God's intentions from the way things are in nature and in their inference about what people should do given God's intentions. There are no relevant differences undermining the logical analogy; hence the (G) condition is also met. The refutation is successful.

5. The primary subject is the argument that a disarmament referendum should not be held because nearly everyone would support disarmament. The analogue is the argument that a mayoralty election should not be held because nearly everyone would vote for the same candidate. The premise in the primary subject argument is not acceptable. In fact, results on such referenda have varied. Some people oppose disarmament for a variety of reasons, and they have indicated this

on referenda, which (when held in Canada in 1982–84) gave results varying from 60 percent in favor to 97 percent in favor. Mayoralty elections are regular occurrences that are held as constitutionally required, regardless of the popularity of candidates. Referenda are special votes on issues that are especially important, divisive, or crucial in certain contexts. These differences undermines the parallel. The refutation by logical analogy does not work, but the original argument that it is intended to criticize can be seen to be poor by the unacceptability of its premise.

PART B

3. The primary subject is Trudeau's continuing as prime minister and liberal leader when Canada had a troubled economy and the opposition was said (by Trudeau) to be fumbling. The analogue is a doctor's continuing as a patient's doctor when that patient is sick and the doctor down the street is fumbling. Trudeau's point was that you wouldn't change doctors, so you shouldn't change prime ministers. Trudeau's argument is poor. In terms of acceptability of premises, we should not accept on his testimony or authority that the opposition is fumbling. (Conflict of interest.) Also, his assumption, built into the analogue case, that a patient does not change his doctor when sick, may be questioned. A desperate patient might change doctors, even if the doctor down the street had given signs of fumbling. More fundamentally, however, the analogy can be challenged for its relevance. The two relationships (politician, country; patient, doctor) are too different for a convincing analogy. A doctor is a qualified trained professional in a one-on-one relationship with a patient. A politician is an elected person, rarely chosen mainly for competence. Furthermore, there are no clear standards for the health and management of an economy as there are for a sick person. There is no reason to trust a political leader as you would a doctor.

6. This passage does not contain an argument or an analogy. It is a report of problems with these toads.

7. This passage is a logical analogy. The primary subject is the argument that the anti-Holocaust book should be in the library because both sides of an issue should be represented there. There are two different analogues. One analogue is a choice of both the *National Enquirer* and the *Times* of London for two accounts of historical and current events. This care would be ridiculous, and seen so by library staff. Similarly (second analogue), there is the matter of having clever drawings by the Flat Earth Society to offer as an alternative to globes, for geography. This too would be ridiculous, and seen so by library staff. A buttressing argument, not based on analogy, is that there is very good testimony and documentation to show that the Holocaust occurred. This documentation is the basis ((A) condition) for claiming that stocking anti-Holocaust books would be doing something as ridiculous as the two analogues. The primary subject and the two analogues all share the feature that what might seem to be "two sides" are not equally sensible "sides"; they differ vastly in credibility. The argument appeals successfully to consistency and shows that ideas of representing two sides are not sufficient reason for the library to stock anti-Holocaust books.

11. This passage is not an argument based on analogy. The author states that persons are composed of sub-persons that have fewer internal components than a person. For this reason it is a "myth" that each person is a unity, he says.

14. (*Hard*) This passage is not an analogy but a rather complex, compressed, double comparison. Imelda Marcos is compared to Marie Antoinette (a rich French queen who lived during the French Revolution and is famous for her remark, "Let them eat cake," when she was told the poor had no bread). Imelda Marcos is said to be more rich than Marie Antoinette, this implication being conveyed by a further comparison between Marie Antoinette and a bag lady. Analogies urge us to see similarities and structural parallels between things. There is a suggestion here of an analogy between Marie Antoinette and a bag lady—but this is rhetorical exaggeration. In any case, there is no argument.

16. (*Hard*) The primary subject is the nuclear arms race and the desirability of the nuclear freeze, especially the argument that the United States should continue the arms race because the Soviets are ahead in some categories. The analogue is the case of two powerful cars headed for a crash. The crash is compared to a nuclear war, the putting on of the brakes to a freeze, and cutbacks in weaponry to a reversal of the cars so that they move away from each other. Drawing the analogy presupposes that a nuclear war is an inevitable result if the nuclear arms race continues. This assumption may strike many of us as terrifyingly plausible, but it needs support because many experts and insiders would firmly deny it. If the assumption is not granted, the analogy will seem irrelevant because we won't believe there is any clash to be avoided. Barring this difficulty, the analogy is close enough to be relevant. But the analogy breaks down in that, with the cars, putting on the brakes is necessary and sufficient to avoid the clash, whereas in the nuclear scene, just stopping the making of more weapons may not be necessary and is surely not sufficient to avoid a nuclear war. The analogy is a stronger argument if taken as a rebuttal against another common argument regarding the freeze, namely, that a freeze is not good enough because we need drastic cuts. The point would then be that you have to stop making more arms before cutting back, just as you have to stop a car (brake) before reversing.

EXERCISE TWO

5. This passage contains an inductive analogy. The comparison is between an individual who may abuse power (the analogue) and a majority of a group of individuals (the primary subject) who, it is inferred, might abuse power. The point is that because (for the analogue) it would not be reasonable to give absolute power to an individual, neither would it be reasonable to give absolute power to a majority (the primary subject). This argument seems to be a strong one because the differences that do exist between groups and individuals do not undermine the basic similarity on which the argument depends: their capacity to abuse power.

8. This passage does contain an analogy, but it is not clear that the analogy is part of an argument. The analogue is a monarch who makes judgments and decrees all by himself. The primary subject is the person who thinks for himself, who makes judgments without attending to popular opinions and prejudices. Clearly, the tone of the passage and choice of analogue show that Schopenhauer is in favor of thinking for yourself. However, it does not appear that the analogy is put forward as a reason for this view; it seems more like a vivid way of stating the view.

11. This passage does not contain an argument. A vivid image is developed, in which the thought is regarded as a developing fruit.

EXERCISE THREE

3. There are two analogues here as well as a primary subject. The primary subject is the argument that since the majority of women are kind to children and prefer their own children to other people's, women's proper sphere of activity is "the nursery" (taking care of their own children). The first analogue is as above, except that it substitutes men for women. When this substitution is made, the argument is one no one would accept. The second analogue is as above, except that it substitutes dogs for children. Again, nobody would take the analogue seriously. From the two analogue arguments and the fact that they are parallel in structure to the primary argument, it is inferred that the primary argument is a poor argument.

9. This passage contains an analogy between funds and supporting evidence but does not contain any argument based on this analogy.

10. As stated this quotation is not an argument. There is an analogy, however, between a man's time and a cultivated field. A man's using his time well is parallel to a few acres being well cultivated, and the latter is said to be better than using many acres (cf. a lot of time) carelessly. Talent is implicitly compared to having rich soil in the field. You might read this passage as an argument with an unstated conclusion to the effect that people should make good, careful use of their time. If you do take it this way, it is not a very good argument because the similarities are too loose. In any case, the conclusion is something we probably already accept, and it would be more plausible on its own than supported by a serious analogy with fields and cultivation. It is probably better to see the passage as a vivid way of stating this common belief about using our time rather than as a way of supporting that belief by argument.

11. This passage illustrates the fallacy of slippery assimilation. Because the destruction of a litter of puppies is similar to the opening of a score of oysters, which in turn is similar to killing a moth, Carroll contends that we cannot draw a line between these three actions. Either all of these actions are morally permissible, or all are morally wrong. This conclusion is based on slippery assimilation. Carroll infers that all killings are morally permissible, provided the deaths are painless.

17. This passage is not an argument, nor does it contain an analogy. It is a series of comments on the application of nonviolent principles and the attitudes of various groups who use, or dissent from, such principles.

20. The analogy is between U.S. and Soviet nuclear forces and U.S. and Soviet baseball teams (imagined). The development of the analogy presupposes that Soviet nuclear forces are currently more modern than U.S. forces, which is something freeze advocates deny. The conclusion is that a nuclear freeze would ultimately lead to obsolescence in the U.S. nuclear forces. The analogy is poor because the presupposition is question-begging in this context; aging is not applicable to weapons in the same way that it is to sports players, and there is no sense of "winning" in the nuclear competition that is as clear-cut as winning in a baseball game.

CHAPTER 11

EXERCISE ONE

2. There are three supporting premises for the final statement, which is the conclusion. The first and third are qualified, with "some" and, as such, are acceptable as known on the basis of common experience. The second is more controversial, but even if acceptable, it is not relevant since in fact governments do not give full support to the needy and their need is a present fact, regardless of what governments ought to do. The third premise is not relevant to whether you should give to charity; it is about the quality of ads. There are many counterconsiderations not mentioned in the argument: how needy people are, the fact that their needs may go unmet if you do not give to charity, the fact that other uses you might have for your money are often trivial compared to people's needs, and the sense of social contribution and self-worth that you may derive from giving to charity. The single relevant supporting consideration is not enough to outweigh these. The argument falls down on (A), on (R), and on (G); it is a weak argument.

5. The conclusion is stated in the first sentence and in the last half of the last sentence. The supporting premises are in the second, third, fourth, and fifth sentences. In the sentence beginning "Despite . . . ," two counterconsiderations are introduced. The conclusion is qualified, when it is finally stated, in "the preponderance of evidence indicates that. . . ." The supporting premises are acceptable and can be verified by checking various news sources and political documents for the period 1985–1986. These premises are relevant and count substantially in favor of the conclusion. The counterconsiderations do not outweigh them, as they do not show absence of intent to have better relations and fewer arms in the future, after agreements have been worked out. Other counterconsiderations, not mentioned, would include the presence of Soviet troops in Afghanistan, the imprisonment of dissidents in the Soviet Union, and the failure to allow discontented citizens, especially Jews, to emigrate. In view of the qualified conclusion, the argument strikes us as fairly strong—though there are bound to be differences in judgment regarding the significance of the stated supporting considerations and the stated and added counterconsiderations.

7. The conclusion is stated first and reiterated later in slightly different words. ("The American Revolution should not be thought of as a model for other revolutions.") The second, third, and fourth sentences give supporting premises. The next sentence contains two counterconsiderations. The sixth sentence adds two practical reasons for not taking the American Revolution as a model— underestimating the role of the poor and failing to see potential for violence. The first three supporting premises are acceptable and could be verified as such by checking standard sources on American history. The fourth supporting premise (requiring that the poor are very significant in revolutions) is plausible on the basis of common reports about revolutions around the world today, but they could be checked against accounts of revolution by historians and political scientists. The same may be said about the fifth supporting premise (real potential for violence). The supporting premises are relevant to the conclusion provided we grant the assumption behind the argument: that a typical revolution involves moves, often violent, by the poorer classes to upset a social structure. Of the two stated counterconsiderations, the second (that the American Revolution is of great historical importance) is not negatively relevant to the conclusion: it is irrelevant. The first counterconsideration is obviously true and is relevant, but it is far too slight to outweigh the supporting considerations. As stated the argument satisfies (A) and (R) and seems to satisfy (G). Whether there are more counterconsiderations that outweigh the premises seems unlikely, but we could consult accounts of revolution by historians and political scientists to find out.

11. The conclusion is the first sentence, and it is also restated at the end. It is ambiguous; *trustworthy* may mean either that the document reliably transmits words and claims made in ancient texts or it may mean (more ambitiously) that the claims made in the document (Bible) are true and really describe events that occurred. A number of premises are relevant to the conclusion only on the first interpretation and not on the second. The argument has two main converging branches: one gives reasoning pertaining to the New Testament, the other to the Old Testament. The evidence about the New Testament would show, if accepted, that the words are close to the words of documents written 20–70 years after Christ's life. To check the acceptability of the premises we would have to look up New Testament scholarship and classical scholarship. However, we note that all points made about the New Testament are relevant only to the conclusion in the less ambitious interpretation of its meaning, not to the other interpretation. As for the evidence about the Old Testament, the same comments apply, except for the one claim about the expert. That claim, however, embodies a faulty appeal to authority, in that experts differ on the matter; the expert may have a vested interest in converting people, and furthermore, the name of the expert is not mentioned so that the claim is too vague to verify. To find detailed counterevidence, sources in classics and Old and New Testament scholarship would be needed. However, a major counterconsideration against the conclusion in the more ambitious sense is that people are strongly moved by emotion when in the presence of such figures as Jesus and may not be reliable observers of the nature and causes of events. The argument is weak if we interpret the conclusion in the ambitious sense. If we interpret the conclusion in the less ambitious sense, as being only about the reliable transmission of texts, the argument may be strong, but accuracy of the premises would have to be checked.

CHAPTER 12

EXERCISE ONE
PART A

2. (b) differs from (a) in that it ascribes intentions to the child and says she succeeds in reading, whereas (a) is more strictly behavioral. (c), like (b), ascribes success. Unlike (b), however, it makes no reference to intention or effort. (d) makes even fewer commitments than (a). It does not even say definitely that the book is in English or that the sounds uttered by the child constitute an English word.

3. (a) makes a modest claim about tendency. (b) makes a bold claim that examinations as an institution are countercreative; thus going far beyond (a) in what is asserted. (c) states a correlation (see Chapter Thirteen) or association between taking exams and not doing creative work; it does not say outright that exams produce this lack of creativity. (d) is an even stronger claim than (b). It is the boldest of all the claims, using loaded language to assert that exams will destroy creativity and that competition and even fact are false gods.

PART B

1. The implicit operationalization is that the number of friends a person has is determined by how many he says he has. Numbers are pseudoprecise because the boundary between acquaintances and friends, and between relatives and friends, is quite indeterminate.

4. Lying, by definition, is making a claim that one believes to be false, with the intention of convincing others that that claim is true. The definition of lying in terms of moist palms and a high pulse attempts to avoid criticisms by redefining lying so that by definition the operationalization will be appropriate. This move is unacceptable, because the only interest we have in the procedure of lie detector tests is to determine truthfulness and reliability, which require understanding the word "lying" in its ordinary standard meaning.

6. In this report, being happy is implicitly operationalized as saying that one is happy in response to a question asked on a survey.

PART C

4. Vagueness. There are no determinate boundaries as to how much alcohol goes into one drink, and yet, the format requires that we make quite precise numerical distinctions. This question can also be criticized as complex, unless we include never drinking alcohol under "less than 2."

8. Complex question. The formulation of the question presumes that human life is preserved and human safety protected by the legislation. This wording is sneaky; to answer "no," we are forced to be against preserving life and protecting people.

9. The question is faulty in two ways. First, it is prejudicial in coercing the respondent into granting that there is a communist threat in Nicaragua. The expression *communist threat* presumes both that the government of Nicaragua is communist and that this feature is a negative one that constitutes a threat to the United States. This statement is very disputed. Secondly the question is coercive in its form, which tries to have respondents choose among three alternatives. These alternatives are not the only ones. Notably, if there is no threat, none are appropriate. Even if there is a threat, it might be best handled in another way, such as ignoring it, appealing to mediators, or appealing to the International Court of Justice.

10. This question is flawed due to vagueness, especially in the word *stress* and, to a degree, in *adversely affected*. If petty annoyances count as stress, then everyone's life has stress, and given that these are annoyances, virtually all would say the effect is adverse. On the other hand, if stress requires serious anxieties such as those caused by death of family members or divorce, then far fewer would be affected.

EXERCISE TWO

8. The statistical principles cited would not apply unless the sample were truly random. The authors appear, in their comments, to identify representativeness and randomness. This is not correct, theoretically speaking. The method of selecting subjects did not, in any event, guarantee representativeness, because

the contexts chosen would overly represent employed, married, middle-class men, and the need for researchers to approach men would overly represent neat, unthreatening, cooperative men.

10. There is an enumerative induction. The population is young people in Canada between 12 and 17. The sample is those 70 or 80 young people between 12 and 17 who were questioned in the study. The sample is too small. The argument is also infected by vagueness in *expressing interest* and by possible reliability problems in responding to interviews on such sensitive topics.

13. There are various numbers here, but there is no enumerative inductive argument. The passage reports calculations by scientists as to difficulties facing the Star Wars program.

CHAPTER 13

EXERCISE ONE
PART A

2. The implication is causal. The expression "no wonder" implies that the first claim causally explains the increase in violence and greater acceptability of violence.

4. That more than 80% of 260 voice-recorder tapes recorded whistling during the last half hour of flight is a statistical claim. In the suggestion that you might worry if you hear the crew whistling, there is an implied causal claim, but probably this is not intended seriously.

8. There are two statistical claims: one about enrollment and one about budget. No correlational claim or causal claim is made.

10. The claim is ambiguous between correlation and causation.

14. The claim is correlational. There is a positive correlation between getting top scores on an SAT test and being a boy.

EXERCISE TWO

2. The causal claim is that the sexual revolution has reduced the number of women who are able to have babies. More specifically, it is claimed that an epidemic of sexually transmitted diseases has caused infertility to rise. There is no evidence given except—implicitly—that the phenomena have both been increasing during the same period of time.

8. There are causal claims made about the improvement in manpower in the American armed forces. First the author makes a negative causal claim. The improvements don't result from increased spending. The reasons are that quality has gone up more than spending, which has gone up by less than 20 percent. (The premise is not acceptable because it involves implicit pseudoprecision in quantifying an increase in quality.) If acceptable, it would be relevant but it would show only that increased spending is not the sole cause of the improvement.

A positive causal claim is made in the last sentence, where the author hypothesizes three factors—recession, de-civilization, and nationalistic pride—as causally contributing to the improvement in the forces. No evidence is given for this conclusion. The whole argument assumes that the quality of manpower in the armed forces has improved very much, and this assumption is something for which evidence could surely have been given if, indeed, it is true at all.

14. There is a causal claim implicit in "He has left." The passage says that the presence of John Wayne in the American imagination has resulted in broken hearts and jaws (presumably figuratively, in movies) and (more seriously) in millions of injured male egos. The only evidence given is that no real man could measure up to John Wayne's image. This evidence is relevant only if we assume that real men were trying to measure up to that image—something we do not know. The causal claim is not adequately supported.

15. The passage is jocular in tone and probably not meant seriously. Two correlational claims are made: that highly-educated people with low incomes catch colds more than others, and that more people catch colds on Monday than on other days. The article makes a (probably nonserious) suggestion, on the basis of the correlational data, that colds are caused by dissatisfaction with one's job. The reasoning would not be adequate, but probably this passage does not contain serious reasoning from correlational data to a causal conclusion.

EXERCISE THREE

2. Sample: 168 mental health workers in the New York area (62% of 271). Population: mental health workers, presumably in North America. Operationalization: Conflict on ethical issues (reported in response to questionnaire) as evidence of felt ethical conflict. (The conclusion is that after several years, workers find resolution to conflicts.) Correlational claim: there is a negative correlation between years of experience and reported ethical conflicts about one's work in the mental health field. Explanatory hypothesis: none inferred; several suggested. Assessment: the sample is small and is probably unrepresentative since New York City may have an unusually large number of mental health patients and/or unusually well-qualified personnel.

6. Sample: 24 students at the University of Alberta, 13 male and 11 female. Population: apparently no generalization is being made to a larger population. Operationalization: Telling an experimenter that one is uncomfortable about the experimenter's proximity is evidence of having one's personal space violated at the distance the experimenter is at when he is told. Correlational claim: tolerable distance of another person increases when visibility of that other person decreases. (For this sample) causal claim: tolerable distance of another person seems to depend on visual mechanisms. (For this sample) assessment: The sample is small, but the authors do not appear to use it as the basis for any generalization. The correlation is poor support for the causal claim unless there are further supporting reasons given elsewhere. The result is apparently in conflict with those in other studies.

1. The hypothesis is that people in the southeast quadrant of the city do not value this kind of music. The explanatory power of the hypothesis is all right. Its plausibility is low if it is taken universally and we assume that that quadrant of the city contains tens of thousands of people. Its scope is fairly limited. Empirical content will be all right since we can operationalize not valuing classical music in terms of record purchases, radio listening habits, and participation in other groups. The main problem is plausibility.

3. A major problem here is with the identified assumption, which we agreed not to question. Plausibility is marginal when it is asserted that infants and very young children have sexual desires on the basis of which they have extensive fantasies of sexual assault, intercourse, and other activity with male relatives at young ages. The scope of the hypothesis is all right; it would be usable in explaining a wide variety of phenomena (and has been so used by Freudians). The empirical content is a problem; desires and fantasies in the distant past are hypothesized. It will be difficult to verify whether or not these occurred. Also, the explanatory power of the hypothesis is not too great when we recall that the events to be explained are these extensive reports to therapists, with and without hypnosis. Why would just *these* early desires and fantasies be reported, just *now*? The hypothesis does not, in itself, explain this.

6. This passage does not really contain an argument based on an inference to an explanation. The second paragraph does suggest an explanation of why men like uniforms, but it is not really put forward as the inferred conclusion of an argument.

10. Here there is an explanatory inference, but it is quite tentative and qualified, as may be seen from "permits some plausible conjecture" and from the fact that the author refers later to other explanatory factors. The explanation has good explanatory power and scope. To fully assess its plausibility we would need knowledge of texts of the post-Roman period. This could be gained from historical sources. The empirical content of the explanation is good since the claim made is in principle, fully checkable by reference to observation.

Index